D0782283

Job

BAKER COMMENTARY *on the* OLD TESTAMENT

WISDOM AND PSALMS

Tremper Longman III, Editor

Volumes now available

Job, Tremper Longman III
Psalms, vol. 1, *Psalms 1–41*, John Goldingay
Psalms, vol. 2, *Psalms 42–89*, John Goldingay
Psalms, vol. 3, *Psalms 90–150*, John Goldingay
Proverbs, Tremper Longman III
Ecclesiastes, Craig G. Bartholomew
Song of Songs, Richard S. Hess

Job

Tremper Longman III

BakerAcademic
a division of Baker Publishing Group
Grand Rapids, Michigan

Published by Baker Academic
a division of Baker Publishing Group
P.O. Box 6287, Grand Rapids, MI 49516-6287
www.bakeracademic.com

Printed in the United States of America

Library of Congress Cataloging-in-Publication Data

Longman, Tremper.
Job / Tremper Longman III.
pages cm — (Baker commentary on the Old Testament wisdom and Psalms)
Includes bibliographical references and index.
ISBN 978-0-8010-3107-6 (cloth)
1. Bible. O.T. Job—Commentaries. I. Title.
BS1415.53.L66 2012
223′.1077—dc23 2012008262

Except where indicated, all Scripture quotations from Job, Proverbs, and Ecclesiastes are the author's own translation.

12 13 14 15 16 17 18 7 6 5 4 3 2 1

To Mia Katherine Longman

Behold, the fear of the Lord is wisdom,
and turning aside from evil is understanding.
Job 28:28

Contents

Reflective Essays

Series Preface

At the end of the book of Ecclesiastes, a wise father warns his son concerning the multiplication of books: "Furthermore, of these, my son, be warned. There is no end to the making of many books!" (12:12). The targum to this biblical book characteristically expands the thought and takes it in a different, even contradictory, direction: "My son, take care to make many books of wisdom without end."

When applied to commentaries, both statements are true. The past twenty years have seen a significant increase in the number of commentaries available on each book of the Bible. However, for those interested in grappling seriously with the meaning of the text, such proliferation should be seen as a blessing rather than a curse. No single commentary can do it all. In the first place, commentaries reflect different theological and methodological perspectives. We can learn from others who have a different understanding of the origin and nature of the Bible, but we also want commentaries that share our fundamental beliefs about the biblical text. Second, commentaries are written with different audiences in mind. Some are addressed primarily to laypeople, others to clergy, and still others to fellow scholars. A third consideration, related to the previous two, is the subdisciplines the commentator chooses to draw from to shed light on the biblical text. The possibilities are numerous, including philology, textual criticism, genre/form criticism, redaction criticism, ancient Near Eastern background, literary conventions, and more. Finally, commentaries differ in how extensively they interact with secondary literature, that is, with what others have said about a given passage.

The Baker Commentary on the Old Testament Wisdom and Psalms has a definite audience in mind. We believe the primary users of commentaries are scholars, ministers, seminary students, and Bible study leaders. Of these groups, we have most in mind clergy and future clergy, namely, seminary students. We have tried to make the commentary accessible to nonscholars by putting most of the technical discussion and interaction with secondary literature in the footnotes. We do not mean to suggest that such information is unimportant. We simply concede that, given the present state of the church, it is the rare layperson who will read such technical material with interest and profit. We hope we are wrong in this assessment, and if we are not, that the future will see a reverse in this trend. A healthy church is a church that nourishes itself with constant attention to God's words in Scripture, in all their glorious detail.

Since not all commentaries are alike, what are the features that characterize this series? The message of the biblical book is the primary focus of each commentary, and the commentators have labored to expose God's message for his people in the book they discuss. This series also distinguishes itself by restricting its coverage to one major portion of the Hebrew Scriptures, namely, the Psalms and Wisdom books (Proverbs, Job, Ecclesiastes, and Song of Songs). These biblical books provide a distinctive contribution to the canon. Although we can no longer claim that they are neglected, their unique content makes them harder to fit into the development of redemptive history and requires more effort to hear their distinctive message.

The book of Psalms is the literary sanctuary. Like the physical sanctuary structures of the Old Testament, it offers a textual holy place where humans share their joys and struggles with brutal honesty in God's presence. The book of Proverbs describes wisdom, which on one level is skill for living, the ability to navigate life's actual and potential pitfalls; but on another level, this wisdom presents a pervasive and deeply theological message: "The fear of the Lord is the beginning of knowledge" (Prov. 1:7 NRSV). Proverbs also raises a disturbing issue: the sages often motivate wise behavior by linking it to reward, but in reality, bad things happen to good people, the wise are not always rewarded as they expect. This raises the question of the justice of God. Both Job and Ecclesiastes struggle with the apparent disconnect between God's justice and our actual life experience. Finally, the Song of Songs is a passionate, sensuous love poem that reminds us that God is interested in more than just our brains and our spirits; he wants us to enjoy our bodies. It reminds us that we are not merely a soul encased in a body but whole persons made in God's image.

Limiting the series to the Psalms and Wisdom books has allowed us to tailor our work to the distinctive nature of this portion of the canon. With some few exceptions in Job and Ecclesiastes, for instance, the material in these biblical books is poetic and highly literary, and so the commentators have highlighted the significant poetic conventions employed in each book. After an introduction discussing important issues that affect the interpretation of the book (title, authorship, date, language, style, text, ancient Near Eastern background, genre, canonicity, theological message, connection to the New Testament, and structure), each commentary proceeds section by section through the biblical text. The authors provide their own translation, with explanatory notes when necessary, followed by a substantial interpretive section (titled "Interpretation") and concluding with a section titled "Theological Implications." In the interpretation section, the emphasis is on the meaning of the text in its original historical setting. In the theological implications section, connections with other parts of the canon, both Old and New Testament, are sketched out along with the continuing relevance of each passage for us today. The latter section is motivated by the recognition that, while it is important to understand the individual contribution and emphasis of each book, these books now find their place in a larger collection of writings, the canon as a whole, and it is within this broader context that the books must ultimately be interpreted.

No two commentators in this series see things in exactly the same way, though we all share similar convictions about the Bible as God's Word and the belief that it must be appreciated not only as ancient literature but also as God's Word for today. It is our hope and prayer that these volumes will inform readers and, more important, stimulate reflection on and passion for these valuable books.

Having written the Proverbs commentary in this series, I had hoped to assign Job to someone else. However, the scholars I approached to write it were already overcommitted, and Jim Kinney, editorial director at Baker Academic, urged me to write it myself. I had written on all the other wisdom books and knew I would eventually tackle Job, so I agreed to comment on the book for this series and am glad that I did. Job is a difficult book from start (translating its obscure Hebrew vocabulary) to finish (understanding its place in the canon), but it is also a profound exploration of wisdom and suffering. My hope and prayer is that this commentary will benefit others, particularly clergy, as they encounter this marvelous book.

Tremper Longman III
Robert H. Gundry Professor of Biblical Studies
Westmont College

Author's Preface

My work in wisdom literature came early in my career. I wish I could claim that my interest began with a passionate intellectual curiosity; however, that would not be true. It started when W. W. Hallo of Yale University essentially forced (strongly encouraged would probably be a more polite way of putting it) me to write a dissertation on Akkadian autobiographies. I wanted to work on Akkadian poetics, but he rightly pointed out that it would have been too speculative. He had a theory on a number of texts that he felt cohered in a single genre (he was right, of course), but this genre had subgenres, one of which was autobiographies that ended with wisdom sayings (e.g., "Cuthaean Legend of Naram-Sin"). Hallo, to his credit, was one of only a few Assyriologists who felt it was beneficial to compare Near Eastern literature with biblical literature. To make a long story a little shorter, it turned out that this subgenre of Akkadian autobiographies had some very interesting and illuminating connections to the book of Ecclesiastes. After finishing my dissertation, I was asked to write a commentary on that biblical book, and once I studied that book, I was hooked on wisdom literature.

Job is the final wisdom book on which I have completed a commentary, and it was the toughest on many levels. First, as everyone knows who has read it in the original, the Hebrew is arguably the most difficult in the Hebrew Bible. Thus I would like to express my thanks to D. J. A. Clines. I do not always (or perhaps even often) agree with his conclusions, but he has amassed all the relevant linguistic and textual data. The design of this present commentary does not call for such extensive philological discussion, though it does require an original translation, and Clines's commentary presents the data so fully that no scholar will have to do that for another generation. Second, the subject matter of the book of Job is disturbing. The book raises important and difficult theological and practical issues, and the present series emphasizes these concerns in both the exposition sections and the theological implications sections.

The latter require some explanation. Let me be frank. Job is a repetitive book. The human participants hammer away at the same basic points. For instance, the three friends constantly insist that sin is always connected to suffering, so suffering is always the result of sin. Job, for his part, agrees with this viewpoint but says that in his case God is unjust (for more, see the introduction and throughout). To avoid some repetition, in the forty-four reflective essays, I pick up on leading, but not necessarily dominant, ideas in the various speeches and develop them for further consideration. A list of these essays appears following the table of contents. Since many of these essays are relevant to more than one portion of Job, readers may find it helpful to consult the list for topics appropriate to the particular portion of Job they are studying.

Commentaries are meant for specific readers, and this volume is no exception. The primary audience I had in mind while writing this book was composed of ministers and future ministers, that is, seminary students. Yet I hope that I have written it in a way that makes the commentary accessible to interested laypersons. I also hope that some of my scholarly colleagues will read it and offer their critique. Job is not a book for which one ever comes to a definitive and final interpretation.

Finally, I would like to offer my thanks to a number of people who have helped me write this book. First, I mention students in classes in which I taught the book over the past eight years I have been working on it. Class discussions helped me change and refine my ideas. I hope I do not forget any, and I wish I could list the individual students, but they include classes at Fuller Theological Seminary, California Coast, Ambrose University College (Calgary), Reformed Theological Seminary (DC and Orlando), Providence Theological Seminary (Winnipeg), and my upper-division Psalms and Wisdom classes at Westmont College. Second, I thank Rick Love of Ambrose University College for sharing with me his syllabus on the biblical theology of suffering; and Reed Jolley, pastor of my church, Santa Barbara Community Church, for giving me his notes on an excellent sermon on suffering based on Luke 8:40–56. Third, since I am the editor of this series, Baker Publishing used an anonymous reader (thanks, Peter Enns) to give me feedback that was very helpful. Finally, and very importantly, I appreciate Jim Kinney of Baker Academic for his continued support of my work. He is not only an excellent editor but also a good friend. Thanks, too, go to Wells Turner at Baker for making sure the manuscript turned into a good-looking and coherent book. Of course, while I was greatly helped by all the above-mentioned and others (for whom I will later kick myself for not remembering), the work in the final analysis is my own, so any errors or infelicitous interpretations should be blamed on me.

I dedicated my Proverbs commentary in this series to my first granddaughter, Gabrielle, so it is only fitting that this commentary should be dedicated to my second, my red-headed and bagel-sharing two-year-old granddaughter, Mia Katherine Longman, born to Tremper IV and Jill. Your Nanny and Poppy love you, and though intellectually knowing that no one escapes the difficulties of this life, we are constantly praying for you and your sister to love God and enjoy life. Always remember that God loves you.

Tremper Longman III
Westmont College
Summer 2011

Abbreviations

Bibliographic and General

[ ]	encloses versification of the MT when it differs from the English
AEL	*Ancient Egyptian Literature: A Book of Readings*, by M. Lichtheim, 3 vols. (Berkeley: University of California Press, 1971–80)
ANET	*Ancient Near Eastern Texts Relating to the Old Testament*, ed. J. B. Pritchard, 3rd ed. (Princeton: Princeton University Press, 1969)
b.	Babylonian Talmud
BDB	F. Brown, S. R. Driver, and C. A. Briggs, *A Hebrew and English Lexicon of the Old Testament* (Oxford: Clarendon, 1907)
BHS	*Biblia Hebraica Stuttgartensia*, ed. K. Elliger and W. Rudolph (Stuttgart: Deutsche Bibelstiftung, 1967–77)
ca.	circa (about)
CHALOT	*A Concise Hebrew and Aramaic Lexicon of the Old Testament Based upon the Lexical Work of Ludwig Koehler and Walter Baumgartner*, ed. W. L. Holladay (Grand Rapids: Eerdmans, 1971)
chap(s).	chapter(s)
col.	column
COS	*Context of Scripture*, ed. W. W. Hallo with K. L. Younger, 3 vols. (Leiden: Brill, 1997–2002)
CTA	*Corpus des tablettes en cunéiformes alphabétiques découvertes à Ras Shamra-Ugarit de 1929 à 1939*, ed. A. Herdner, 2 vols. (Paris: Geuthner, 1963)
DOTWPW	*Dictionary of the Old Testament: Wisdom, Poetry and Writings*, ed. T. Longman III and P. Enns (Downers Grove, IL: InterVarsity, 2008)
ed.	edited by, editor, edition
Gen. Rab.	*Genesis Rabbah*
HALOT	*Hebrew and Aramaic Lexicon of the Old Testament*, ed. L. Koehler et al., trans. M. E. J. Richardson, 2 vols. (repr., Leiden: Brill, 2001)
Heb.	Hebrew

KJV	King James Version
lit.	literally
LXX	Septuagint
m.	Mishnah
mg.	margin
MSS	manuscripts
MT	Masoretic Text
NAB	New American Bible
NASB	New American Standard Bible
NEAEHL	*The New Encyclopedia of Archaeological Excavations in the Holy Land*, ed. E. Stern, 4 vols. (New York: Simon & Schuster, 1993)
NEB	New English Bible
NET	New English Translation
NIDOTTE	*New International Dictionary of Old Testament Theology and Exegesis*, ed. W. VanGemeren, 5 vols. (Grand Rapids: Zondervan, 1997)
NIV	New International Version
NJB	New Jerusalem Bible
NJPS	New Jewish Publication Society Translation
NKJV	New King James Version
NLT	New Living Translation (2nd ed.)
NRSV	New Revised Standard Version
NT	New Testament
OT	Old Testament
REB	Revised English Bible
RSV	Revised Standard Version
T. Job	*Testament of Job*
TNIV	Today's New International Version
trans.	translator, translated by, translation
v(v).	verse(s)
y.	Jerusalem Talmud

Old Testament

Gen.	Genesis	Esther	Esther
Exod.	Exodus	Job	Job
Lev.	Leviticus	Ps(s).	Psalms
Num.	Numbers	Prov.	Proverbs
Deut.	Deuteronomy	Eccles.	Ecclesiastes
Josh.	Joshua	Song	Song of Songs
Judg.	Judges	Isa.	Isaiah
Ruth	Ruth	Jer.	Jeremiah
1–2 Sam.	1–2 Samuel	Lam.	Lamentations
1–2 Kings	1–2 Kings	Ezek.	Ezekiel
1–2 Chron.	1–2 Chronicles	Dan.	Daniel
Ezra	Ezra	Hosea	Hosea
Neh.	Nehemiah	Joel	Joel

Amos	Amos	Hab.	Habakkuk
Obad.	Obadiah	Zeph.	Zephaniah
Jon.	Jonah	Hag.	Haggai
Mic.	Micah	Zech.	Zechariah
Nah.	Nahum	Mal.	Malachi

Old Testament Apocrypha

Sir.	Sirach	Wis.	Wisdom

New Testament

Matt.	Matthew	1–2 Thess.	1–2 Thessalonians
Mark	Mark	1–2 Tim.	1–2 Timothy
Luke	Luke	Titus	Titus
John	John	Philem.	Philemon
Acts	Acts	Heb.	Hebrews
Rom.	Romans	James	James
1–2 Cor.	1–2 Corinthians	1–2 Pet.	1–2 Peter
Gal.	Galatians	1–3 John	1–3 John
Eph.	Ephesians	Jude	Jude
Phil.	Philippians	Rev.	Revelation
Col.	Colossians		

Introduction

Title and Place in the Canon

Unlike some biblical books that have different names in different traditions, the title of this book is invariably given as "Job," after its main character. In addition, there have been no serious reservations concerning Job's presence in the canon.[1] The various ancient witnesses agree less about Job's location in the order of the books. Jewish sources and lists place the book in the Ketubim (Writings), the third section of the Hebrew canon. There are, however, variations as to where within the Writings the book is located. The Talmud begins the Writings with Ruth, then Psalms, Job, Proverbs, Ecclesiastes, Song of Songs, Lamentations, Daniel, and finally Esther, Ezra–Nehemiah, and Chronicles. This list is chronologically ordered with the exception of Job. The Talmud itself answers why Job, whose story is set in the far distant past, does not begin the list: "We do not begin with a calamity!"[2] Though there is variation of the sequence of Proverbs (*mĕšālîm*) and Job (*'îyôb*), these two books are always connected with Psalms (*tĕhillîm*) and form a kind of trilogy. Early Jewish traditions spoke of the variant orders as *'mt* and *t'm*, after the first letters of the three books. Interestingly, Jesus apparently understood the order of the Ketubim to begin with Psalms (thus *t'm*), since in Luke 24:44 he cites the three parts of the Hebrew canon as "the law of Moses, the prophets, and the psalms."

Early Christian tradition showed even greater diversity in order. However, eventually the order Job, Psalms, Proverbs won the day in Western Christianity under the influence of Jerome and his Vulgate. This chronological order (Job,

1. With the exception of Theodore of Mopsuestia (AD 350–428), who also questioned the Song of Songs (as well as the deuterocanonical books). See Dhorme, *Job*, vii.

2. Ibid., viii.

David, Solomon)[3] was affirmed by the Council of Trent and is used in all modern Christian translations.

Authorship and Date

The book of Job names no author; it is anonymous. Of course, tradition rarely lets such matters stand unaddressed and thus often attributes authorship to Moses (see *b. Baba Batra* 14b). Nothing in the book itself or anywhere in the Bible suggests Moses as the author, but the fact that the events of the story of Job come from a very early period of time (patriarchal or before) compels some to connect the book with the earlier known writer of Scripture, Moses. Archer, a modern exegete, leans toward a Mosaic date of writing for the book and argues, against those who hold a Solomonic date of the book,[4] that a date near the events is the only view that assures historical accuracy.[5] This view may be questioned. First, why must a book be written near the events to be true, especially if it is the product of divine revelation? Second, is the book intending to be historically accurate? (See "The Genre of the Book of Job" below.)

In any case, such early dates for the composition of the book are not widely held today. Indeed, the question that has dominated much recent discussion is whether the book of Job was written at one time or over a long period. As we will see, this discussion cannot be solved with certainty and is based largely on speculation and a sense that the different parts of the book are in tension with one another, a view that is belied by a coherent reading of the book (see "The Theological Message of the Book of Job" below for such a reading). That said, there is nothing inherently threatening about the idea that the book of Job as we know it may be the end result of a lengthy history of composition and the product of many hands. It is arguable that most OT books were written by more than one anonymous author/editor over a long period of time before they achieved their final, canonical form. However, what is of interest to us in this commentary is the final form of the book, the form recognized as canonical by the synagogue and the church over the millennia.

That said, not everyone agrees about a canonical approach to the book. Thus, in the following paragraphs, I will review some of the leading ideas of those who want to reconstruct the compositional history of the book and some of the interpretive implications that they draw from their hypotheses.

3. Major portions of Psalms and Proverbs are attributed to David and Solomon, respectively.

4. Like E. J. Young, *Introduction to the Old Testament* (Grand Rapids: Eerdmans, 1949), 319–23.

5. G. L. Archer, *A Survey of Old Testament Introduction* (Chicago: Moody, 1964), 465–73. See also R. Laird Harris, "The Doctrine of God in the Book of Job," in *Sitting with Job*, ed. R. B. Zuck, 156, for another example of confusing the plot's setting with the date of the book.

Such reconstructions typically begin with the belief that the prose framework, the prologue (1:1–2:13) and the epilogue (42:7–17), is an original folktale that serves as the foundation of the book. Much is made of the different attitudes expressed by Job toward his suffering in the prose framework and in the later poetical portions. In the former, Job is patient, accepting his suffering. In the latter, he is angry, challenging God's sense of justice. Indeed, Fisher believes that the poetical portion of the book was written by someone who was sickened by the passive piety represented in the prose story and wanted to challenge it. Fisher expresses his personal animosity toward the prose writer: "I want to thank the poet of Job 3–26 whose anger burned against the ancient story of Job, and whose fiery poem was extinguished by wrapping it in the ancient story of Job."[6] In other words, the story and the poem conflict with each other. A close reading of the prologue, though, makes one question whether the prose story was ever independent of the poem. After all, the three friends are introduced at the end of the prologue (2:11–13). When the story begins again, God is reprimanding Eliphaz and the three friends for not speaking correctly about him to Job. The debate section supplies the reason for God's reaction here. To speak of later additions to the prose story to make it compatible with the poetic dialogue is all too convenient to the theory. It is possible to read the book in a way that understands the change in Job from prologue to poem as a matter of character development, as Clines rightfully points out: "All these differences between the prose and poetry of the book can be better explained, however, on literary grounds. Thus, it is dramatically satisfying that Job should change from his initial acceptance of his suffering to a violent questioning of it."[7]

The Elihu speeches are often treated as a later insertion into the story. The textual evidence for this belief is that Elihu appears out of nowhere (especially that he is not mentioned in the prologue, which introduces all the other characters of the story) and that he is not mentioned at all in the epilogue. No one responds to Elihu, not Job and not God. While it is impossible to prove definitively that the Elihu speech was part of the original story,[8] neither is it particularly relevant to the interpretation of the final form of the book. The lack of response to Elihu is the ultimate put-down of the school of thought he represents.

Perhaps the most difficult chapter to make sense of in the narrative flow of the book is Job 28. This poem is very odd in its context. According to

6. Fisher, *Many Voices of Job*, ix. He goes on to say, "I believe strongly the two Jobs should be kept separate." For a similar view, see Stevenson, *Poem of Job*, iii; Zuckerman, *Job the Silent*, 47; as well as Penchansky, *Betrayal of God*.

7. Clines, *Job 1–20*, lviii.

8. Alter (*Wisdom Books*, 127) argues that the poetry of the Elihu speeches is not as aesthetically pleasing as that of the disputation and thus the author must be different. An equally plausible view is that a gifted poet shifted poetic styles in such a way as to characterize Elihu in a negative way as arrogant and bombastic.

the rubrics, it appears that Job is still speaking, but what is said seems out of character with his frame of mind both immediately before and after this chapter. The climax of Job 28 (v. 28, "Behold, the fear of the Lord is wisdom, and turning aside from evil is understanding") also anticipates the final resolution of the book, which comes only with Yahweh's speeches and Job's response. Admittedly, this is difficult, but it is not impossible to incorporate into the narrative as a whole. In the commentary proper, I will present my understanding of its place in the story; but again, as with the other component parts of the book, there is no definitive proof whether it was part of the original book or added later.

For those who argue for a compositional history to the book, there is no clarity on when the different parts were written or when the whole came to completion. Even the mention of Job in Ezek. 14:14 and 20 does not help us much, since Ezekiel may only have known the Job of the ancient prose tale, not the completed book. Attempts to date the book or its parts based on linguistic or orthographic arguments have led interpreters to different conclusions,[9] thus demonstrating how weak these types of arguments are for dating a composition.[10]

That said, most scholars suggest a date between the seventh century and the second century BC for the final form of the book. Various lines of argument are used to try to date the book. For instance, some want to date it to the sixth century BC because the message of the book was timely for Israelites exiled to Babylon.[11] Hartley disagrees and feels more comfortable with a seventh-century date because of the use of Canaanite mythological imagery and also literary affinities with Isaiah.[12]

In conclusion, it is admittedly impossible to prove that Job was an original authorial whole. Nor is it possible to prove that it was written over an extended period of time. Neither point is important. What is crucial, at least for the church, which has received the final form of the book as canonical, is to interpret the book as it presently stands.[13] It's not that there aren't "many voices" in the book of Job (as Fisher's title states), but these many voices

9. On linguistic grounds, Robertson (*Linguistic Evidence*, 155) dates the book to the monarchic (Solomonic period), Freedman ("Orthographic Peculiarities") to the seventh/early sixth century BC, and Hurvitz ("Date") to the time of the exile or thereafter.

10. However, Seow ("Orthography") successfully argues that Freedman's ("Orthographic Peculiarities") attempt to date Job to the seventh/early sixth century BC fails because the author could have been using archaic forms in order to create the impression that the book is older than it is and match the book's literary setting.

11. Janzen, *Job*, 5.

12. Hartley, *Job*, 15–20.

13. I agree wholeheartedly with Janzen (*Job*, 24): "The issue comes down to how one reads the book. Can it be read as a whole? Can it be read as a whole inclusive of much tension and turbulence between its parts, such that the very form of the book itself contains part of its meaning (so that neglect or tampering with the form distorts the meaning)?"

ultimately yield to the one Voice that speaks at the end and brings the book to a dramatic resolution. Determining a precise date for the final form of the book is not possible, nor is it important for interpretation.[14]

Text, Language, and Translation

The difficulty of translating Job is acknowledged by everyone who makes the attempt. The percentage of rare words in Job is greater than any other OT book except the Song of Songs.[15] But the difficulty extends beyond the presence of rare words. The grammar itself is difficult. Although the grammar of poetry does not function like that of prose, even among poetical books Job presents special problems.

Why is Job so hard to translate? The answers to this question vary. Some believe that our distance from the Hebrew means that we do not know the language well enough to catch all the nuances of these rare words and peculiar grammar. Those who make this diagnosis of the problem resort to comparative Semitic philology as the remedy.[16] Certainly the study of other Semitic languages has deepened our understanding of the meaning of Hebrew words, especially many that appear only rarely in the Bible. Care must be taken, however, not to exaggerate the ability of comparative Semitics to resolve all the textual difficulties of Job. Dahood and his students, for instance, developed a reputation for uncontrolled use of other languages, such as Ugaritic, to explain the Hebrew text.

Some studies of Job have argued that the Hebrew of Job is strange because it is the translation of a work originally composed in a different language. Among the languages proposed for the original composition are Edomite,[17] Arabic,[18] and Aramaic.[19] Without going into detail, the strongest argument against such theories is that translations would tend to smooth over textual difficulties rather than generate or retain them. For this and other reasons, most scholars today believe that Job is an original Hebrew composition.

Of course, the problem of translating Job could theoretically be the result of a corrupt text. The textual resources available for translation tell an interesting

14. See the similar view given by Habel, *Job*, 40–42.

15. There are about one hundred words in Job that occur only one time in all the OT. The technical term for a word that occurs only one time is *hapax legomenon*.

16. Dahood is the leading proponent of this approach. See his "Some Northwest Semitic Words"; and idem, "Northwest Semitic Philology." See also the work of his student A. Blommerde, *Northwest Semitic Grammar*. In his commentary, Pope (*Job*) makes a more judicious use of Ugaritic materials and evaluates some of the suggestions made by Dahood, Blommerde, and others. Grabbe (*Comparative Philology and the Text of Job*) utilizes insights of Barr (*Comparative Philology*) in order to critique and appropriate insights from the Dahood school.

17. Pfeiffer, "Edomite Wisdom."

18. A. Guillaume, "Arabic Background."

19. Tur-Sinai (Torczyner), *Job*.

story. The length of the Greek text as we know it from the fourth-century MSS (Alexandrinus, Sinaiticus, Vaticanus, dated ca. AD 400) is equal to that of the MT, but there is evidence that the earliest versions of the Greek (from ca. 100 BC) were much shorter, by as much as one-sixth.[20] Indeed, the longer Greek text was created by Origen in his Hexapla.[21] There is much scholarly discussion of the reasons for this difference. Some believe that the LXX is shorter because it deviated from and simplified the difficult Hebrew,[22] while others believe that the shorter Greek text reflects a shorter Hebrew text that differed from the Hebrew textual tradition represented by the MT.[23] Dhorme supports the former position and states that the LXX "abounds in errors . . . but it represents a text which has been shortened at pleasure, as if the translator was in a hurry to finish. Quite often it is an explanation *ad usum Graecorum* rather than a literal translation of the Hebrew."[24]

It seems unlikely that the earlier, shorter Greek text represents a more authentic (in the sense of closer to the original canonical) text than the Hebrew Masoretic tradition. Even so, in some cases the LXX does help us resolve textual issues and will be cited in the commentary when appropriate. The LXX is also relevant to the history of interpretation of Job (see below) and may explain certain traditional understandings of the book (see "The Patience of Job" following my comments on Job 21).

From Qumran we have two targumim of Job, discovered in 1956, that are of interest for the textual history of the book. 11QtgJob (11Q10) and 4QtgJob (4Q157), written in Palestinian Aramaic, are the oldest MSS of the book of Job still in existence.[25] The former is fragmentary but extensive, covering 17:4–42:11.[26] The exact date is debated. Pope argues for a second-century BC date,[27] but the predominant opinion today is first century AD. The second targum is composed of two small fragments that contain about twelve verses from Job 3–5. While these targumim, especially the longer one, are very close to the later MT, they do seem to share with the LXX a tendency to demythologize

20. Smick ("Job," 690) states, "Origen, who expressly tells us about the omissions and additions, filled in the missing lines largely from Theodotion's minor Greek version using diacritical marks to show the differences." Kutz (*Old Greek of Job*, 5) points out that, even though it is shorter, the Old Greek text expands the speech of Job's wife and gives a "closing statement referring to Job's place in the resurrection (42:17a), and an appendix identifying Job with Jobab, the Edomite king (42:17b–e)."

21. Kutz, *Old Greek of Job*, 1.

22. Gerleman, *Studies in the Septuagint*.

23. Orlinsky did this in a series of articles, "Studies in the Septuagint."

24. Dhorme, *Job*, cxci. For a position that sees value in both Gerleman and Orlinsky's views, see Cook, "Aspects of Wisdom."

25. They are also, along with a third text on Ezekiel, the oldest examples of the genre of targum (i.e., an Aramaic paraphrase of the Hebrew text).

26. The initial translation was done by van der Ploeg and van der Woude, *Targum de Job*, but a superior translation is found in Sokoloff, *Targum of Job*.

27. Pope, *Job*, xlvi.

the book and make Job look less rebellious. They also avoid any language that might cast a bad light on the character of God.

Other ancient translations (the Syriac Peshitta[28] and the Vulgate) are also available for consultation. Both are translated from the LXX and so are only occasionally helpful in reconstructing the text.

In this commentary, I rely on the MT (B19a, Codex Leningradensis) for my translation, while occasionally appealing to other versions for corrections. With the possible exception of Clines's massive three-volume commentary, all other commentaries (including my own) must make the same admission as Pope: "In fairness to the reader, it should be explained that the translation offered in this volume—as with every attempt to translate an ancient text—glosses over a multitude of difficulties and uncertainties."[29] That said, commentators writing after Clines owe him a debt of gratitude for providing detailed discussions of textual and philological issues. His conclusions may not always be correct, but he has provided the fullest discussion of these issues to date, rendering a repetition of such discussions unnecessary.

The Genre of the Book of Job

Perhaps nothing influences our interpretation of a text more than what we conclude about its genre or literary type.[30] Genre triggers reading strategy. Authors send signals to readers through certain conventions in order to help shape the reception of their words. Those genre signals can be quite blatant, as when a modern book includes the words "A Novel" on its title page. Ancient texts on occasion send similarly obvious clues, such as "An Apocalypse of Jesus Christ" (Rev. 1:1), "Song of Songs" (Song 1:1), or when a Gospel writer identifies one of Jesus's stories as a parable. Genre signals are usually more subtle than that, however, and sometimes, because of the chronological and cultural distance between us and the ancient texts, the precise genre of a biblical book is difficult to identify and describe. In such cases, the genre can only be determined by reading the text and coming to an understanding of the whole. Even after the genre has been identified, one must still discuss precisely how the ancient author intended the genre to be read, something that was better understood by the contemporary audience. The interpretive debates over apocalyptic literature such as the book of Revelation are a case

28. Vicchio (*Job in the Ancient World*, 202) points out that Job is found right after the Torah in the Peshitta, which placed it there perhaps because of its setting during the patriarchal period (and the identification of Job with Jobab) or because it was thought to be authored by Moses.

29. Pope, *Job*, xliii.

30. For a lengthier statement of my approach to genre, see Tremper Longman III, *Fictional Akkadian Autobiography* (Winona Lake, IN: Eisenbrauns, 1991), 3–21; idem, "Form Criticism"; idem, *Literary Approaches*.

in point. Determining the genre of the book of Job is particularly challenging because not many texts are quite like it, and a genre is a set of literary texts that share features in common. The more examples of a particular type of text one has, the easier it is to understand the genre.

As one surveys the secondary literature on Job, it is easy to be overwhelmed by the variety of genre identifications for the book. A partial list would include dramatized lament,[31] "forensic" literature (*Rechtsleben*),[32] tragedy,[33] comedy,[34] drama, parody,[35] and apocalyptic literature.[36] To interact in detail with these and other suggestions would lengthen our discussion without major benefit. Let me briefly say that each of these may capture elements of the book of Job, but none is suitable as an overarching categorization. I will content myself with providing an argument for a particular way of approaching the book.

Before we do so, however, we should take note of a not infrequent categorization of the book as *sui generis*,[37] that is, as a unique piece of literature that has no genre category. This conclusion is impossible, however. Our ability to comprehend a literary work depends on our previous reading experience of other similar, though not identical, texts. If Job were truly *sui generis*, then it would be unreadable. Such an identification, though rightly recognizing the book's literary genius, is simply giving up in light of the complexity of the book. I will not take this counsel of despair, but rather will attempt to describe the book's genre, an identification that will guide the interpretation in the pages to come.

Job as Prose and Poetry

As the word suggests, a genre is a generalization from a specific text. It recognizes a text as sharing features (content, subject matter, form, tone, etc.) with other compositions. Genre exists at different levels of generalization from the particular text, and a broad genre shares fewer features in common but includes more examples. As one narrows the generic categorization, more features are shared.

A broad genre categorization of Job notes that it is composed of both prose (1:1–2:13; 42:7–17) and poetry (3:1–42:6).[38] The prose framework gives the book a narrative feel throughout; that is, it tells a story that has a plot. Like any plot, it has a beginning, middle, and end. The plot is generated by a conflict that seeks and finally achieves resolution. In the commentary, as well

31. Westermann, *Structure*.
32. Richter, *Studien zu Hiob*.
33. Hoffman, *Blemished Perspective*, 40.
34. Whedbee, "Comedy of Job."
35. Zuckerman, *Job the Silent*.
36. Johnson, *Now My Eye Sees You*.
37. Pope, *Job*, xxxi; Gladson, "Job," 232; Fyall, *Now My Eyes*, 23.
38. There are, however, snippets of prose in the poetical portion, including the rubrics to the speeches (i.e., 4:1; 6:1; etc.) and the introduction to Elihu's speech (32:1–6a).

as in the section titled "The Theological Message of the Book of Job" below, I will delineate the plot and also discuss the characters and setting.[39]

The bulk of the book is poetry. Hebrew poetry has different conventions and triggers different reading strategies. The conventions include parallelism, imagery, and terse lines. Poetry says a lot using only a few words. Thus, one reading strategy that poetry triggers is to slow down and meditate on the richness of meaning and feeling evoked by the language. The terseness of the language heightens the difficulty of interpretation and leads to a higher level of ambiguity than in prose. This ambiguity must be respected by the interpreter, who should not try to turn the poem into prose. Ancient Hebrew poets also employed a number of more occasional literary devices that lend interest to their lines but are virtually impossible to reproduce in English translation (wordplays, sound-plays, etc.); some of these will be pointed out in the commentary.[40]

In sum, Job is a poetical book framed by a prose narrative. The prose narrative is highly literary. For instance, the two scenes in heaven are reported in a parallel fashion (1:6–12; 2:1–7a) with God's receiving and questioning the accuser in identical fashion. In addition, the description of Job's family and wealth includes numbers that carry symbolic significance. The description of the four disasters that befell Job at the end of chap. 1 is also repetitive, most notably in that each ends with a sole survivor saying "I alone escaped to tell you" (vv. 15, 16, 17, 19). Poetry is inherently artificial, especially in reported speech. People do not converse in poetry, especially when one of them is in deep pain. The highly literary nature of the book, especially the large poetical part, triggers certain expectations and reading strategies:

1. As mentioned above, it calls on the reader to slow down and reflect on the compact meaning of the composition.
2. It imparts a universal quality to the topic of the book. It signals that the issues, debates, and conclusions are not just relevant to this particular situation but are important to all who read it.
3. It distances the action of the story from a concrete historical event (see "Job and History: Was Job an Actual Person, and Does It Matter?" below).

Job as a Wisdom Debate

Wisdom is indisputably a major theme of the book of Job. In the discussion under "The Theological Message of the Book of Job" below and in the

39. For the principles that delineate the analysis of prose narrative in the Bible, see Longman, "Biblical Narrative."

40. For the principles that delineate the analysis of poetry in the OT, see Longman, "Biblical Poetry."

commentary proper, I will highlight its significance in the book. While the talk is about Job's suffering, the resource that the human participants call on to grapple with his situation is their wisdom. As we will see, the various parties in the disputation (Job, the three friends, and Elihu) assert their own variety of wisdom and ridicule the wisdom of the others. They each vie to demonstrate that their wisdom is superior and able to handle the problems that life presents (as made concrete in Job's affliction).

The polyphony of voices, however, does not reach resolution. The talk goes on and on until it is silenced by God himself, who asserts his wisdom and power. The message of the book of Job is that wisdom does not come from human beings, but that God is the only wise one.[41] The human response is "fear" (28:28), as is exemplified by Job's response to the divine speeches (particularly 42:1–6). He repents and submits himself to God's superior wisdom and power.

Thus Job is a wisdom book. But not all wisdom books are alike.[42] Proverbs contains instructional literature (discourses and proverbs) that encourage wise behavior by connecting (but not guaranteeing) rewards with such behavior. Ecclesiastes contains the autobiography of a man who has sought for meaning in life "under the sun" but is thwarted in his efforts by, among other things, a sense of injustice. Indeed, the message of both the book of Job and Ecclesiastes should keep people from reading the rewards of Proverbs with undue optimism.[43]

Job and History: Was Job an Actual Person, and Does It Matter?

Was Job an actual person who lived in Uz at a particular point in time? Did he suffer as described in the book? Did he engage in debate with Eliphaz, Bildad, and Zophar, and suffer further the scolding of Elihu? Did God actually converse with the accuser during a meeting of the divine assembly and give him permission to afflict Job? From the prologue of the book, do we learn how heaven is organized and how it operates?

To answer these questions, we must first engage in an analysis of the book's genre and therefore intention. Does the author of Job intend for us to understand its contents to actually have happened? This question is not as easy to answer as one might expect. There are arguments in favor and arguments against the idea that Job is a historical book. The opening line of the book that introduces Job informs us of his name, his character, and his hometown.

41. In a recent article, Shields ("Malevolent or Mysterious?" 257–58) rightly states, "In its present form, the book of Job is primarily about demonstrating the limitations of human wisdom and offering specific application of those limitations to the doctrine of retribution."

42. Contra Johnson (*Now My Eye Sees You*, 18–20), who oddly argues that Job is not wisdom because it is not like Proverbs.

43. See the subsection titled "Suffering: Job and Retribution Theology" below as well as Longman, "Why Do Bad Things Happen?"

We know that more than one town in antiquity was named Uz, so we have no reason to doubt that Uz was a real place. But, of course, historical fictions set their action in real places as well (think, for instance, of the parable of the Good Samaritan).[44]

Some point to Ezek. 14:14 (repeated in v. 20) to solve this issue. Ezekiel tells the people that even the presence of famous righteous men would not save them from God's coming judgment. Specifically, he says, "even if Noah, Daniel, and Job, these three, were in it, they would save only their own lives by their righteousness" (NRSV). There is little doubt that Ezekiel is speaking of the Job of the book of Job here (or at least that this Job is the Job of some version of this story known in either oral or written form), but does that mean that he is a historical character? Not necessarily. It certainly means that at least some form of the book of Job was known. Ezekiel's (God's) point here is made whether Job is a historical or a literary character. Indeed, from the spelling (*Dāniʾēl* [Dan. 1:6] versus *Dānîyēʾl* [Ezek. 14:14, 20] in the Hebrew) and the relative chronology, the reference to Daniel is possibly, even probably, not the Daniel of the biblical book but an ancient Near Eastern king known for his piety.[45] The same ambiguity relates to the reference to Job in James 5:11. James's example of the "patience" or "perseverance" of Job stands whether Job was a historical character or a literary figure.

The truth may be between the view that Job was a historical character, with the book describing events of his life in detail, and the view that Job is a purely literary figure. Job could have been known as a particularly righteous person who suffered. His story would then lend itself to further elaboration for the purposes of discussing the issue of an innocent sufferer and wisdom. Indeed, the highly literary nature of the prose and poetry noted above would suggest that this at least is true. The genre signals help us see that the book of Job is certainly not a precise historical report. It is either the elaborated story of an actual historical figure or of a literary figure.

I have restricted discussion to the book of Job itself. Does it intend us to understand Job to be historical? After all, no external evidence exists concerning Job, nor should we necessarily expect any. We must decide this issue, if indeed it can be decided, only by appeal to the book itself.[46] The conclusion of the above considerations is that it is impossible to be dogmatic about the book's intention here.

44. Alter (*Wisdom Books*, 11) points out that the opening of Job (*ʾîš hāyâ*, "There was a man") is similar to the opening of the Nathan parable in 2 Sam. 12.

45. See the debate in Dressler, "Identification of the Ugaritic *Danil*"; and J. Day, "Daniel of Ugarit."

46. Of course, for those who require extrabiblical attestation of persons and events to corroborate the biblical account before accepting its historical authenticity, the question is decided negatively from the start, since, as we have already admitted, there is no contemporary extrabiblical evidence of Job or the events of the book.

Crucial, then, is the question whether the historicity (or lack thereof) of Job makes any difference to the truth of the book. Elsewhere I have argued that certain biblical events must have happened in order for their associated theological message to be true.

Take the exodus, in particular the crossing of the Reed Sea, for instance. Here the theological significance of the event depends on its historical veracity. The story teaches that God saved Israel from certain death when human resources were exhausted. This story provides confidence and hope for Israel and individual Israelites in later generations (see in particular Ps. 77). When later Israelites encounter insoluble problems in their lives, they can look back on the crossing of the sea and gain hope that God will intervene in their life as well. If God did not rescue Israel at the sea, then there would be no basis for such hope. In other words, the story of crossing the Reed Sea establishes a track record for God.[47]

On the other hand, the theological value of the story of Job does not depend on its being historically true.[48] Job is not part of the Bible's redemptive history, which records events in space and time when God accomplishes and applies his grace to his people. Job is a didactic story. It intends to explore weighty issues like the nature of wisdom and the mystery of suffering. The truthfulness of the insights conveyed by the book of Job does not depend on the actual existence of Job.

In sum, we cannot be dogmatic about the historicity of Job.[49] It is highly likely, in my opinion, that Job is not a historical person, or at best there was a well-known ancient sufferer named Job, whose life provided the grist for the author to create a scenario where he could reflect on wisdom and suffering. But, in the final analysis, neither the truth nor the interpretation of the book of Job depends on its being a historical book. Such a view is not new, being advocated since early in the book's history of interpretation.

Legal Metaphors: Is the Book of Job the Account of a Trial?

The book of Job clearly uses legal terminology in the process of describing the relationship between God and Job. Chapter 9 is filled with the language of the court, as when Job queries:

> If someone wants to take him to court [*rîb*],
> one could not answer him one out of a thousand times. (v. 3)

47. See Longman, *How to Read Exodus*, 68–92.

48. The view that Job was not a historical book is as old as the Babylonian Talmud (*b. Baba Batra* 15a; cf. *y. Soṭah* 5.8/20c; *Gen. Rab.* 57.4), which calls it a parable (*māšāl*). See Dhorme, *Job*, xv.

49. Contra Dow (*When Storms Come*, 4), who is "writing from the conviction that the story of Job actually happened."

Though I am righteous,[50] I could not answer him.
  I could only plead for mercy with my judge.
If I summoned him, and he answered me,
  I do not believe that he would hear my voice. (vv. 15–16)

In 13:17–19 he states,

Listen closely to my words;
  let my declaration be in your ear.
See, I am prepared for the judgment;
  I know I am righteous.
Who is it that accuses me
  so now I would be silent and die?

In my opinion, the legal language is less frequent by far with the three friends, but occasionally we hear them say something that suggests the courtroom, as when Eliphaz says to Job, "Does he reprove you for your 'fear'? Will he enter into judgment with you?" (22:4). Elihu too uses familiar legal language, for instance, as he characterizes Job's position as a trial:

For Job has said, "I am righteous.
  God has turned justice away from me.
But concerning my case, I am considered a liar." (34:5–6a)

This handful of quotations demonstrates that the book utilizes legal language, the language of the courtroom, in discussing Job's situation. Thus it is not surprising that many commentators believe that the controlling metaphor of the book is the courtroom, and they exert great effort in delineating the exact nature of the legal situation. One of the most recent and interesting examples of this effort comes from Magdalene,[51] who utilizes what we know about Neo-Babylonian trials to understand the dynamics of the book. She argues that the accuser initiates the trial of Job by his charge of blasphemy, delivered before the divine assembly, and that there is nothing God can do about it—short of upsetting the whole divine system of justice—but see the trial through. The stakes are high in this trial because the charge against Job is actually a charge against God, who has put a hedge around Job, and as a result "God would be stripped of power if Job should blaspheme against

50. Some translations (e.g., NRSV) make the legal connection even stronger by translating *ṣādaqtî* as "I am innocent."

51. Magdalene, *On the Scales of Righteousness*. Notable earlier studies include Dick, "Legal Metaphor in Job," based on his doctoral dissertation at Johns Hopkins University; Richter, *Studien zu Hiob*; Scholnick, "Meaning of *Mišpaṭ*," based on her doctoral dissertation at Brandeis University.

God."[52] In keeping with ancient Near Eastern legal procedure, once Job is accused, he is arrested, his property is confiscated, and he is tortured. The accuser tries to elicit a confession from Job because that is the best evidence for a conviction. On the other hand, Job is unaware of the accuser's accusation and actions and understands his suffering to come from the hand of God. He believes that his pain is undeserved, so he brings a countersuit against God. Magdalene cites Job 10:2–7 and 19:6–7 in support of the idea that Job is accusing God of "abuse of authority" in that God has hit him with a charge that is unsubstantiated.

In Neo-Babylonian law, a second witness strengthens a case. Job often wishes he had such a second witness (see 9:32–35), but he is unable to produce one. On the other hand, the accuser finds a second witness in Elihu, who takes up his case against Job.

The conclusion of the book, according to Magdalene, is an out-of-court settlement. The two suits are stymied: Job cannot come up with a second witness and is frightened by God's speeches (chaps. 38–41), and God has to stop the case against Job because he admits that it is unjust (42:8, 11). Even so, God gives Job the same kind of settlement (double his original possessions) he might have given if Job had won the case against him.

Needless to say, this is an interesting and ingenious reading of the book—perhaps too ingenious. In my opinion, it suffers from the same problem as many other attempts to turn Job's occasional use of legal metaphors into an overarching understanding of the book. To make it work, as Magdalene has attempted to do, scholars must fill in the gaps and read legal significance into parts of the book that are not obviously legal.[53] For example, no legal language is used in the discussion between the accuser and God.[54] The context seems not to be a courtroom but rather a king receiving a report from one of his spies (see my comments on Job 1–2). The accuser does not come with a charge; God himself initiates the conversation. In addition, there is a notable absence of legal language precisely where one would expect it, namely, in the denouement of the story in chaps. 38–42. Magdalene herself admits the need to fill in the gaps of the story to flesh out the legal situation behind the action. This explains why there are so many different legal readings of the book: "Much disagreement exists among scholars regarding who brings the

52. Magdalene, *On the Scales of Righteousness*, 117.

53. In connection with this, there is also a question as to whether one should translate vocabulary in a legal sense. Magdalene herself recognizes this issue in connection with the verb (and associated nouns) *ykḥ*. She rightly points out that the word can mean either, on the one hand, "to accuse," "to correct," or the like or, on the other hand, "to decide a lawsuit" or the like. A similar issue confronts the translation of words connected with *ṣedeq* and with *mišpāṭ*.

54. I am not certain how the accuser's strong suspicion that Job will blaspheme can be construed as a crime that would justify the kind of pretrial interrogation (torture and confiscation of property) that Job supposedly experienced.

legal action in Job, the nature of the action, the bases of the charge, when the charge is brought, who is the trial's judge, and so forth."[55] With this many imponderables, one wonders whether the attempt to answer the questions is worthwhile.[56] There is no doubt about the presence of legal language in Job, and in my comments I will draw attention to it when it is relevant, but no attempt will be made to explain the entire book as a courtroom drama.

Structure

When read a first time, a book's structure is not immediately obvious to a reader. In a highly literary book like Job, however, the structure is quite intentional[57] and, as I point out in the next section ("The Theological Message of the Book of Job"), supports the plot and the development of the characters in such a way that it fuels the message of the book.

A number of factors contribute to Job's clear structure at least for most of the book. First, the prose style of the prologue and epilogue differentiate these portions from the vast poetic middle. The poetical parts may be divided based on who is speaking. Following the explicit markers (particularly the prose rubrics that introduce new speakers), this outline emerges:

Prose prologue introducing the characters and plot (1:1–2:13)
Job's lament (3:1–26)
Three cycles of dialogues (4:1–27:23)
Job's monologue (28:1–31:40)
Elihu's monologue (32:1–37:24)
Yahweh speaks and Job repents (38:1–42:6)
Prose epilogue drawing the action to a close (42:7–17)

The only really controversial element of this structure has to do with Job 28, a problem that I will deal with in detail in the commentary. Briefly, the

55. Magdalene, "Law," *DOTWPW* 422.

56. The issue is similar to (what I consider to be the futile) attempts to read the Song of Songs as a drama or to detect a detailed or overarching editorial structure to the book of Psalms or to Prov. 10–31.

57. In a book like Job, with (perhaps) a complex compositional history, "intentional" is a complex word. Above, I have concluded that one cannot be certain about how many hands were involved in the production of the book. Whose intention, then, is meant when we say that the structure of the book of Job is "intentional"? Interpreting the final form of the book as we do presumes that we are interested in the intention of the final anonymous author/editor. Of course, we have no independent access to this person's mind, so our understanding of that intention comes through interaction with the text itself. For more on authorial intention, including the additional complexity of the interaction of human and divine intentions, see Longman, "Literary Approaches," 134–37; as well as Enns, *Inspiration and Incarnation*, 114–15.

problem has to do with the tension between the thought and tone of the chapter and the thought and tone of the rest of Job's speeches. Its insight that the "fear of the Lord" is critical to true wisdom conflicts with Job's own pretensions toward wisdom before and after that chapter. Later, I will argue that such confusion is typical of the mind of a sufferer, and therefore we can understand Job 28 as part of Job's monologue rather than, say, a reversion to a narrative voice.

The only other major controversy concerning the structure of Job arises from a closer analysis of the dialogue section. Here we have three cycles of debate between Job and his three friends. The first two cycles are straightforward as Job responds to each of his friends in turn, first Eliphaz, then Bildad, and finally Zophar:

First Cycle	Second Cycle
Eliphaz (chaps. 4–5)	Eliphaz (chap. 15)
Job (chaps. 6–7)	Job (chaps. 16–17)
Bildad (chap. 8)	Bildad (chap. 18)
Job (chaps. 9–10)	Job (chap. 19)
Zophar (chap. 11)	Zophar (chap. 20)
Job (chaps. 12–14)	Job (chap. 21)

Issues arise in the third cycle. Eliphaz initiates the third round in typical fashion (chap. 22), followed, as we have come to expect, by a robust response from Job (chaps. 23–24). Bildad's speech is surprisingly short (chap. 25, a mere six verses), followed by a lengthy response from Job (chaps. 26–27). There is no speech from Zophar in the third cycle.

The complexity of the third cycle is heightened by some of the content of Job's speeches in this section. In particular, 24:18–25 and 27:7–23 articulate and apparently affirm the idea that the wicked are cursed, the argument that Job has refuted throughout his speeches. These passages are more appropriate to the three friends. Thus scholars debate whether these two passages are part of Job's speech or are wrongly ascribed to him.[58] While the issue is difficult and does not allow a dogmatic conclusion, it is my view that rather than assigning these passages to Bildad (24:18–25) and Zophar (27:7–23), we should interpret them in their present context as speeches of Job. Thus the third cycle has the following form:

Third Cycle
Eliphaz (chap. 22)
Job (chaps. 23–24)
Bildad (chap. 25)
Job (chaps. 26–27)

58. See the relevant parts of the commentary.

History of Interpretation

The history of interpretation of an intriguing and popular book like Job is massive and complex. At best, I can give only a glimpse of the various viewpoints on selected subjects. Even with a cursory treatment of the subject, however, we get a sense of where certain contemporary opinions about the book came from.

Ezekiel

The sixth-century prophet Ezekiel called sinful Judah back to obedience. He emphasized everyone's personal responsibility before God by twice stating, "Even if Noah, Daniel, and Job, these three were in it, they would save only their own lives by their righteousness, says the Lord God" (14:14, 20 NRSV). A fuller discussion of this passage may be found above, since it is relevant for the question of the historicity of the character Job; here let it suffice to say that already by Ezekiel's time the character Job was known as an example of righteousness.[59]

Septuagint

The early Greek translation known as the Septuagint (LXX) has already been introduced in connection to the question of the transmission of the text. Here I will focus on what the LXX tells us about how the book was interpreted. Surprising developments emerge when the book is compared with the Hebrew Masoretic tradition. First, the Job whom the LXX depicts is more like the "patient" Job of much later interpretation.[60] Second, Job and the book of Job express, contrary (as we will see) to the MT, a firm confidence in resurrection and the afterlife. For instance, at the beginning of an extensive addition to the MT, the narrator states: "It is written that he [Job] will rise up again with those the Lord raises up."[61] Job's wife's speech is expanded upon in 2:9–11, where she emphasizes her own struggles as she encourages Job to curse God and die. Her more extensive part is further developed, as we will see, in the *Testament of Job*. Finally, in an addition to the end of the Hebrew text (42:17a–e), Job is identified with Jobab, a descendant of Esau. These themes become common in later interpretations of Job, indicating that such

59. As mentioned above, this passage does not indicate whether the book of Job was yet written in full or in part.

60. For instance, the pessimistic statement in 13:15 ("See, he will kill me; I have no hope") is rendered more optimistically in the LXX and the Qere ("Though He slay me, yet will I trust in Him," NJPS mg.).

61. See also the LXX of Job 14:14; 19:26. The translation of the LXX is provided by C. E. Cox, in *A New English Translation of the Septuagint*, ed. A. Pietersma and B. G. Wright (Oxford: Oxford University Press, 2007).

interpretations are based on the LXX or a translation influenced by the LXX and not on the Hebrew text.

The Testament of Job

The exact date of the composition of the *Testament* cannot be determined, but most scholars would place it sometime between 100 BC and AD 200. It is most likely written by a Jewish author who was familiar with the LXX version of the book of Job. It indeed shares many ideas with the LXX.

Like the LXX, it identifies Job with Jobab (*T. Job* 1.1; 2.1). The transformation of Job into a patient man, observed in the LXX, is complete in the *Testament*. In response to his first wife, Sitis, who wants him to curse God and die, Job exhorts her to be "patient till the Lord, in pity, shows us mercy" (*T. Job* 26.5).[62] Based on his experience, he tells his children, "you also must be patient in everything that happens to you. For patience is better than anything" (27.6–7).

Job's suffering is directly the result of the devil, who is angry because Job destroyed an idol (*T. Job* 6–8, though the devil does go to God to get permission). Job did this knowing that suffering would be a result. In a reversal of the biblical book, it is the three friends (called "kings") who lament Job's fate and express confusion, while Job maintains a strong confidence in God. Elihu is portrayed as an enemy of Job "inspired by Satan" (41.5). Job is eventually restored.[63]

The *Testament of Job* is even further removed from the MT book than the LXX version. The origin of many ideas that become commonplace about Job during the Middle Ages are found in both the LXX and the *Testament*.

The New Testament

Paul cites Job 5:13 in 1 Cor. 3:19, and James 5:11 is traditionally rendered, "You have heard of the patience of Job." While contemporary translations render *hypomonē* (KJV "patience") as "endurance" (NRSV, NLT) or "perseverance" (NJB, NIV), it is clear that James reflects the LXX depiction of the suffering protagonist of the book, a trend that will continue in Christian interpretation in the patristic and medieval periods (for further discussion, see "The Patience of Job" following my comments on Job 21).

Rabbinic Interpretation

The rabbis did not have a unified interpretation of the book of Job.[64] Job is both complex and, at times, ambiguous, and the rabbis differed as to how to

62. Translations of the *Testament of Job* are from R. P. Spittler, "Testament of Job."

63. Besserman, *Legend of Job*, 41.

64. According to Baskin ("Rabbinic Interpretations," 110) "there is no rabbinic consensus on Job."

turn the book into a coherent account. Anti-Christian polemics also played a role in the book's interpretation, as we will see. Allen helpfully divides rabbinic interpretation into four different schools of thought based on whether the rabbinic source believed Job to be a Jew or a gentile, righteous or unrighteous.[65]

Initially, the rabbis were disposed to treat Job as a righteous gentile. According to *b. Baba Batra* 15b, he was one of seven gentile prophets. Rabbi Akiba believed that Job was an example of a gentile who could be considered righteous because he followed the laws given to Adam and Noah. Job's intercession for his friends who hurt him (42:10) was the act that led to his restoration (*b. Baba Qamma* 92a).

Perhaps because Christians used Job as a precursor to Christ, other rabbinic interpreters took a less positive view of Job. For some, he was righteous for a gentile but certainly not up to the standards of Abraham. Abraham, according to Rabbi Johanan ben Zakkai, served God out of love (Gen. 22:2), while Job served God out of fear (Job 1:8).[66] Rabbi Hanina (*Gen. Rabbah* 57.4) suggested that Job was righteous for a gentile and thus received blessings in this life but was excluded from the life to come. Some rabbinic interpreters went even further and depicted Job as an unrighteous gentile, a downright despicable person. He was Pharaoh's adviser at the time of Moses along with Balaam and Jethro, identified with the "God-fearing" official who sought refuge for his servants and animals before the plague of hail (Exod. 9:20). However, he also remained silent when Pharaoh earlier decided to have all the newborn Hebrew boys put to death and thus got what he deserved (*b. Soṭah* 11a; *b. Sanhedrin* 106a; *Exod. Rabbah* 27.3). Still other interpreters believed that Job was righteous but also that he was not a gentile. Instead, they said he was a Jew who was born circumcised, thus explaining how he could be described in such superlative terms in Job 1:1. Understanding Job to be Israelite rather than gentile also undercut the position that connected Job to Jesus.

Early Christian Interpretation (Patristic and Medieval)

There is little evidence of early Christian use of the book of Job. An exception to this is *1 Clement* 17, dated to around AD 100. In an appeal for the imitation of OT saints who wore "goatskins and sheepskins," Clement refers to Job as a model of righteousness but one who nonetheless was aware that all people were sinful even if alive only one day. But, according to Simonetti and Conti, interest picked up in the late fourth and fifth centuries. They speculate that this resurgence arose because the struggles of the Roman Empire during this time turned attention to this biblical account of innocent suffering.[67] The most

65. Allen, "Job 3," 364–66.

66. Rabbi Joshua ben Hurqanos (*m. Soṭah* 5.5) disagreed and asserted on the basis of Job 13:15 and 27:5 that Job served God out of love, not just fear.

67. Simonetti and Conti, *Job*, xvii.

influential interpreters of the book during this time period include Ambrose (AD 337/339–397), John Chrysostom (AD 347–407), and preeminently Pope Gregory (AD 540–604), whose *Moralia in Iob* was by far the most used commentary for the next thousand years. For the late medieval period, I will refer to the work of Thomas Aquinas (AD 1225–1274) and do so by comparison with the thought of the Jewish thinker Maimonides (AD 1186–1237). Rather than treating these and other interpreters individually, we will content ourselves with a brief statement of the major themes of interpretation during this time.

First, the picture of Job as a patient righteous man who was worthy of imitation is one that continued through much of early Christian interpretation. Explanation for this may be found in that the early church used the LXX mainly, at least until the time of the Vulgate, and that version, as we have seen, presented a "sanitized" Job as an "Idumean saint."[68]

Second, while we have seen that rabbinic exegesis debated whether Job was a gentile or an Israelite, Christian interpretation had no trouble at all accepting that he was the former. As such, Job was, to begin with, an example of someone who reached perfection apart from the law, a view emphasized by Chrysostom, Gregory, and others. Moreover, Job was a prophet of Christ. God sent prophets not only to the Israelites, announcing the future Messiah, but also to the gentiles in a person like Job. For example, Ephrem the Syrian (fourth century AD) articulates in brief compass an opinion held by many early Christian interpreters when he says of Job 19:23–29, "Here the blessed Job predicts the future manifestation of Emmanuel in the flesh at the end of time."[69] This explains why it was the practice of the early church to read Job during Passion Week.[70]

Third, in a view represented by Ambrose, Job was a model for endurance in suffering, a theme that especially supported the lifestyle of ascetic monks. Comfort in suffering comes from innocence and piety and the hope of the resurrection (supported not by the Hebrew but again by the LXX, particularly a text such as Job 14:13–17).

Finally, we turn to the thinking of Thomas Aquinas, whose work on Job may be interestingly related to that of the Jewish philosopher Maimonides.[71] Both men were heavily influenced by Aristotelian philosophy and both used

68. Allen, "Job 3," 366. An exception to this practice comes from Jerome, who wrestled with the Hebrew text and knew that it was different from the LXX. Concerning the conundrums of the Hebrew text (that have been evened out in the LXX translation), Jerome famously said that it was like trying to grab an eel: "If you should wish to close your hand and hold an eel or a lamprey, the harder you press, the quicker it will escape" (quoted in Vicchio, *Job in the Ancient World*, 115).

69. From his commentary on Job (19:25), cited in Simonetti and Conti, *Job*, 105.

70. Delitzsch, *Job*, 32.

71. See especially M. D. Yaffe, "Providence in Medieval Aristotelianism: Moses Maimonides and Thomas Aquinas in the Book of Job," in *Voice from the Whirlwind*, ed. Perdue and Gilpin, 111–28.

the book of Job to explore the question of divine providence in order to send a message to their respective religious communities. In his *Guide for the Perplexed*, Maimonides devoted two chapters to Job. He argued that the different participants in the book, which he considered parabolic, represented different views on providence. Eliphaz argued that sin explains suffering. Bildad presented the view that people have free will, while Zophar argued that everything was predetermined. Job himself held the (Aristotelian) view that some matters are controlled by a ruler, while the rest are left to chance.

Even so, the story of Job is about the intellectual development of Job. According to Job 1:1, he is blameless, but that is meant in a moral, not an intellectual, sense. The angry Job speeches show that he does not yet completely understand God and his providence. However, at the end of the story, Job understands that the blessings of this life are not indications of God's approval. He has achieved intellectual perfection. Thus Maimonides uses the story of Job to encourage the Jewish community of his day to seek intellectual perfection.

For Aquinas too, the story of Job, which for him is historically and literally true, is about providence, though in a different manner than Maimonides. According to Yaffee, "Whereas Maimonides argues that God's answer to Job's question about divine providence implies that Job himself though perfectly just remains unwise, Aquinas argues on the contrary that Job though perfectly wise is nevertheless blameworthy."[72]

Like Aristotle, the Job of Aquinas does not believe that God's providence can be read in the rewards and punishments of life. Job is wise from the beginning of the story, and he can easily best the arguments of the friends. But he does so with such a mean spirit that he needs improvement in that area since he is misunderstood to be blasphemous by questioning divine justice and providence. Aquinas marshals the story of Job to critique the rancor of his contemporaries as they dispute doctrine.

Reformation Interpretation: John Calvin

As an example of the Reformation approach to Job, I turn to John Calvin, whose sermons on the book are available for study[73] and have been the subject of extensive analysis.[74] Like Maimonides and Aquinas, Calvin approaches Job as a study of divine providence. According to Calvin, Job, like the rest of the Bible, teaches that God is just and God is sovereign. However, Job also teaches that God's way in this world is sometimes obvious and other times hidden. Even so, in light of the doctrine of the afterlife, no doubt attends

72. Yaffee, "Providence," 112.

73. Calvin, *Sermons on Job*.

74. S. E. Schreiner, "Why Do the Wicked Live?"; Clines, "Job and the Spirituality of the Reformation"; Ngwa, *Hermeneutics*, 66–69; Allen, "Job 3," 370–71.

the belief that the wicked and the righteous will receive what is due them. Nevertheless, in this life, that ultimate outcome does not seem obvious and certainly did not to Job. Job finally comes to the right attitude toward the inscrutability of God's providence: submission and trust. After all, God's order and control of creation, as demonstrated in the divine speeches, create trust in his order and control of providence. Job learns to trust God even when God's face seems hidden. As Allen summarizes, "Job's challenge is that which faces all humanity: to lay hold to the promise made clear in creation with the holy hope that no matter how chaotic human affairs may appear at present, created order points faithfully to the providential goodness of a God who will execute perfect justice on the last day."[75] This truth is taught against the foil of the "false doctrine" of the three friends, who believed that Job suffered because of his sin.

From the Reformation to the (Post)Modern Period

The closer we come to the present, the more abundant are our sources to reconstruct the history of interpretation of the book of Job. Indeed, the variety of approaches to the book also rises dramatically. Perhaps this variety is better known for this period than the previous ones because of the number of preserved sources, but it is also likely that there was more coherence in pre-critical interpretation, which put an emphasis on accepting the interpretation of the previous generation. The modern period emerging from the Enlightenment put a premium on the autonomy of human reason in interpretation over against the acceptance of church dogma, and this gave rise to multiple interpretations of biblical books.

In any case, it will not be necessary to survey modernist interpretations of Job, because I live in that world and, while trying to gain insight from premodern interpretation, emerge from and at times challenge modernist readings of the book. Perhaps one of the major themes of modernist commentary that contrasts with previous interpretation is the shift in emphasis from theological questions to historical ones, which can be seen in the typical historical-critical methods of source, form, and redaction criticism.[76] This same shift in interest can be observed, for instance, in the question of the history of composition of the book,[77] with which we will interact in the context of the commentary, as well as the broader ancient Near Eastern connections to Job that began to be discovered in the nineteenth century (see "Ancient Near Eastern Background"

75. Allen, "Job 3," 370–71.

76. For more on these methods and their impact on biblical interpretation, see Longman, "History in the Old Testament."

77. Newsom (*Job*, 4) points out that Richard Simon in 1678 initiated the discussion of the unity of the book's composition by arguing that the prose part of the book had an origin different from the poetic part.

below). Also affecting Job interpretation (and the approach taken in this commentary), especially at the end of the twentieth century,[78] was a resurgence of interest in a synchronic literary analysis, which seeks to interpret Job in the light of ancient literary conventions.

At the end of the twentieth century and into the twenty-first (though surprisingly losing interest) postmodern readings of the text appear. Here I am using "postmodern" in the sense of a loss of confidence in the determinate meaning of the text, a view inspired by the thinking of Derrida, Lacan, and others. Of course, such a view does not lend itself to biblical commentary that presupposes there is a meaning to exposit, so there are no significant examples of such an approach.[79] Finally, and also considered postmodern by some, are feminist and other ideological readings of the text.

Ancient Near Eastern Background

Israel was not the only ancient Near Eastern culture to struggle with human, and sometimes undeserved, suffering. Egypt, Sumer, Babylon, and Assyria attest literature that grapples with the pain that human beings endure and asks the question how their suffering relates to the divine realm. After describing the relevant literature from these cultures, we will, in conclusion, discuss more specifically how these texts relate to the book of Job.

Egypt

From ancient Egypt survives an extensive body of wisdom literature. Much of it is instructional in nature and comparable to the book of Proverbs.[80] The instruction genre, for the most part, presupposes an optimistic view of how the world works. If one behaves in a manner befitting the order of the world (Maʿat), then one can expect to succeed in life. However, in reality, life did not always work out in such a positive way. Thus there is also in Egyptian literature a tradition of speculative writing that questions or expresses a more pessimistic view of life. These texts come into existence beginning with the

78. Longman, "Literary Approaches."

79. Interestingly, perhaps the prime example of postmodern hermeneutics comes from Clines, who has contributed an extremely important commentary on the book of Job (see bibliography) that I refer to numerous times in this commentary. In "World Established on Water," Clines suggests that, since there is no determinate meaning to the text, the biblical reader may interpret it in any way that he or she wants. He states that professional readers (scholars, ministers) should interpret the text according to the desires of those who pay them. Thus, for the purposes of the Word Biblical Commentary, he chooses to produce a thoroughly modernist, traditionally historical-grammatical/critical commentary rather than, as he claims he could have, a feminist, materialist, vegetarian, or Christian reading (*Job 1–20*, xlvii–lxvi).

80. See Longman, *Proverbs*, 42–56; as well as Longman, "Proverbs."

period of the disintegration of the Old Kingdom (ca. 2686–2180 BC) that led into the chaos of the First Intermediate period (ca. 2180–2100 BC).

One such text goes by the name "The Admonitions of Ipuwer."[81] Ipuwer describes a world in disorder. Everything is topsy-turvy:

> Indeed, many dead are buried in the river.
> The stream is a grave, and the tomb has become a stream.
> Indeed, the noblemen are in mourning and the poor man is full of joy.

This text was likely written during an uncertain time and expresses a longing for an ideal king.

A second text, "Tale of the Eloquent Peasant,"[82] deals with the issue of the difficulty of finding justice. The peasant, whose name is Khu-n-Anup, was transporting his worldly goods when he came across the land of a man named Nemty-nakht, who is described as "son of a man whose name was Isri and he was a subordinate of the high steward, Rensi, son of Meru." Nemty-nakht coveted the peasant's possessions and devised a plan. He blocked one path through his land by placing his clothes on it. The peasant could not go on that path or else he would damage the clothes. The alternate path was through Nemty-nakht's barley field. He was careful, but his donkey ate a "wisp of barley." With that, Nemty-nakht took away all of the peasant's possessions. The penalty hardly fit the crime. Khu-n-Anup had recourse to Rensi the steward and had to exhaust himself in petitioning to get back his possessions. Indeed, there are nine lengthy petitions in the text. The text is a study of the exploitation of the poor by the powerful, though at the end it appears that the peasant got his goods back. This text comes from the period of the Middle Kingdom (ca. 2133–1786 BC).

The third text also comes from the Middle Kingdom period, though we have it in a papyrus from the New Kingdom era (1570–709 BC). It is called "The Complaints of Khakheperre-Sonb."[83] No story is connected with this text, but the author, after whom the text is named, is priest of Heliopolis and gives us a series of proverbs and maxims that describe an upside-down world:

> Right is cast outside,
> Wrong is in the council hall;
> The plans of the gods are violated,
> Their ordinances neglected,
> The land is in turmoil.

81. Translation and commentary by N. Shupak, *COS* 1:93–98; see also the translation by J. A. Wilson, *ANET* 441–44.

82. Translation by N. Shupak, *COS* 1:98–104; cf. J. A. Wilson, trans., *ANET* 407–10.

83. Translation by N. Shupak, *COS* 1:104–6.

The fourth text fits into this subgenre by virtue of its description of a world in turmoil and an appeal to an ideal ruler. It goes traditionally by the name "The Prophecy of Neferti" but has also been called "The Protocol of Neferti."[84] The question has to do with whether Neferti is claiming a prophetic vision or else simply "anticipating developments."[85] We know this text today primarily through a papyrus (P. Petersburg 1116B) from the Eighteenth Dynasty, but the text was apparently written during the reign of King Amenemhet I (1990–1960 BC), who may be the model behind the picture of the ideal king.

The story is set, though, in the reign of the Fourth Dynasty pharaoh Snefru. That king tells his council that he wants a wise man brought to him for his instruction and entertainment. They return with the lector priest of Bastet, Neferti. Neferti describes a disturbed world where everything is confused but then at the end describes the perfect king who will set everything right again.

Most scholars believe that this text is a piece of propaganda supporting Amenemhet I in his usurpation of the throne in a time of chaos. Others believe the text has Neferti representing the eastern frontier to Amenemhet to encourage him to come and support it, particularly against the dreaded Asiatics.

The fifth and last member of this group of pessimistic Egyptian texts is called "The Dispute over Suicide" or "A Dialogue of a Man with His *Ba*."[86] This text is also known by one main papyrus (P. Berlin 3024), which comes from the early Middle Kingdom period (Twelfth Dynasty; ca. 1991–1786 BC). These pessimistic/speculative texts were popular at the time when Egyptian culture was emerging from the quagmire of the First Intermediate period. In this case, though, the topic is not so much political and social confusion as it is individual confusion. This text is one of the most difficult to translate and to understand. It takes the form of a dialogue between a man and his *ba*. *Ba* has been roughly understood as the equivalent of "soul" and is even translated that way by Wilson. However, though there is a general similarity between the two concepts, the concept of the *ba* seems more complex than that association allows. Indeed, Goedicke discusses the evolution of the idea of the *ba* through Egyptian history and the distinction between an immanent and a transcendent *ba*.[87] In any case, what is clear in the text is that both the man and the *ba* express disappointment in life. Life brings trouble. The man spurs on the discussion (as far as we know, since the beginning of this text is broken) by complaining about life and longing for death. It is disputed whether he really contemplates suicide, but his *ba* advocates acceptance rather than despondency. At the end, the man continues to praise death in a poem that includes:

84. Translation by N. Shupak, *COS* 1:106–10.

85. So Goedicke, *Protocol of Neferyt*, 3.

86. Translations may be found by J. A. Wilson (*ANET* 405–7) and M. Lichtheim (*AEL* 1:163–69). I will quote from the latter.

87. In Goedicke, *Report*.

Death is before me today
(Like) a sick man's recovery,
Like going outdoors after confinement.

He also looks forward to the "other side" of death: "Truly, he who is yonder will be a living god, punishing the evildoer's crime." The *ba* and he come to an agreement that the *ba* will stay with him both in this life and the next. According to Goedicke, the text is "the promulgation of an idealistic philosophy within which the goal is to master the shortcomings of the mundane world by knowledge of the fleetingness of corporeal existence and of a true eternal home in transcendence."[88]

Sumer

A Sumerian text, called by Kramer "Man and His God,"[89] addresses the issue of life's troubles. The tablets from which we restore this text come from the Old Babylonian period (eighteenth and seventeenth centuries BC); however, there are internal indications that the composition originated earlier. The story reminds us of Job in that it is the prayer of a pious sufferer. He complains of great hardship:

My god, the day shines bright over
The Land, (but) for me the day has darkened,
The bright day has dawned(?) upon(?)
me(?) like a misty(?) day.
Tears, lament, anguish and
depression are lodged within me,
Suffering overwhelms me
like a weeping child. (lines 69–72)[90]

He turns to the gods and questions why they have turned away from him: "How long will you not care for me, will you not look after me?" (line 100). He confesses his sins, while also expressing the universality of human transgression: "Never has a sinless child been born to its mother" (line 104). Finally the god hears his prayer and answers it by restoring him to health.[91]

Babylonia/Assyria

Well attested are those texts that reflect on and often question the idea of divine retribution. We begin by mentioning two short texts. "The Dialogue

88. Ibid., 58.
89. See Kramer, "Man and His God."
90. Translations cited here are from J. Klein, *COS* 1:573–75.
91. See Albertson, "Job and Ancient Near Eastern Wisdom Literature."

between a Man and His God" is known from the Old Babylonian period and thus is the earliest treatment of the issue of the suffering of a pious person.[92] The next oldest is an Akkadian text from Ugarit, dated in the second millennium BC but after the Old Babylonian period. Foster gives this composition the title "A Sufferer's Salvation."[93]

From a little later in the history of Mesopotamia come two lengthy compositions dealing with the issue of theodicy. "The Poem of the Righteous Sufferer" is also called *Ludlul Bēl Nēmeqi*, a title derived from the first words of the composition, which mean "I will praise the Lord of Wisdom." The Lord of Wisdom is Marduk. The text contains a monologue of a man, probably to be identified with Šubsi-mešre-Sakkan, who describes the disasters that have rocked his world. Indeed, I can cite only a brief portion of the lengthy description of his pain. After talking about how the gods have abandoned him, he turns to his relationship with his fellow humans:

> My city was glowering at me like an enemy,
> Belligerent and hostile would seem my land!
> My brother became my foe,
> My friend became a malignant demon,
> My comrade would denounce me savagely,
> My colleague kept the taint to(?) his weapons for bloodshed.[94]

He continues by describing the horrible physical afflictions he must endure.

However, in a series of dreams Šubsi-mešre-Sakkan sees his coming restoration, and indeed Marduk restores him. The text ends with glorious praise of Marduk, and the speaker sets himself up as an example to others:

> I proceeded along Kunush-kadru Street in a state of redemption.
> He who has done wrong by Esagil, let him learn from me.
> It was Marduk who put a muzzle on the mouth of the lion that was
> devouring me.
> Marduk took away the sling of my pursuer and deflected his slingstone.

The mention of the Esagil suggests to some why Šubsi-mešre-Sakkan suffered in the first place. This is the name of the Marduk temple and may well indicate that suffering is a result of cultic sin. However, a comment earlier in the monologue militates against such a simplistic explanation. Šubsi-mešre-Sakkan

92. The first edition was by Nougayrol, "Version ancienne du 'juste souffrant.'" An excellent recent translation by B. R. Foster is in *COS* 1:485. Lambert ("Further Attempt") points out that the main character does not claim to be innocent. He thus questions its attribution to wisdom literature. However, he does call it a didactic text.

93. See Nougayrol, "Textes suméro-accadiens."

94. From B. R. Foster, *COS* 1:487–8. For a more recent translation and analysis, see Annus and Lenzi, *Ludlul*.

says that he is being treated like one who does not honor the gods with sacrifices and prayer, but as a matter of fact he was attentive to the cult. Then he states:

> What seems good to one's self could be an offense to a god,
> What in one's own heart seems abominable could be good to one's god.
> Who could learn the reasoning of the gods in heaven?
> Who could grasp the intentions of the gods of the depths?
> Where might human beings have learned the way of a god?

Thus, perhaps, we are better off concluding that the issue here is not so much intentional infringement of the cult as ignorance of what the gods want and the seeming arbitrariness of life.

This composition is known from texts in the seventh century BC (including Ashurbanipal's library) and after. Another text, with roughly the same time period of attestation, deals with the issue of the justice of the gods and is therefore appropriately known by the title "The Babylonian Theodicy." This text is a dialogue between two friends, who keep the conversation civil but disagree about the relationship between suffering and the gods. The first speaker describes his suffering and his opinion that life and the gods are not just. At one point, he raises the classic example of injustice:

> Let me [put] but one matter before you:
> Those who seek not after a god can go the road of favor,
> Those who pray to a goddess have grown poor and destitute.
> Indeed, in my youth I tried to find out the will of (my) god,
> With prayer and supplication I besought my goddess.
> I bore a yoke of profitless servitude:
> (My) god decreed (for me) poverty instead of wealth.
> A cripple rises above me, a fool is ahead of me,
> Rogues are in the ascendant, I am demoted.

The friend tries to lead him back to the road of orthodoxy by suggesting that his "logic is perverse" and that he "has cast off justice" and "scorned divine design."[95]

The text ends, rather unexpectedly, with the friend coming around and at least partially agreeing with the sufferer's assessment. Also, unlike *Ludlul*, the sufferer is not restored at the end of the story and continues to request aid from the gods.

This text is also interesting from a stylistic perspective. It may be divided into twenty-seven stanzas of eleven lines, and it is an acrostic that spells out

95. Translations of the "Babylonian Theodicy" are from B. R. Foster, *COS* 1:492–95.

the following message: "I, Saggil-kinam-ubbib, the incantation priest, am a worshiper of god and king."

Conclusion

The above survey makes clear that Job is not the only book to delve into the vexed question of suffering. This should hardly be surprising since these are perennial issues that have exercised the imaginations of human beings down to the present day. Accordingly, it is far from necessary or even intelligent to suggest some kind of direct borrowing or influence of one text on another. No book is quite like Job in its structure, message, or, most definitely, its theology.[96] We should, however, take note that the closest relationship with Job is found in the Akkadian text known as "The Babylonian Theodicy," which is a dialogue between a sufferer and a friend on the issue of apparently unjust suffering. We cannot be certain, but it is not impossible that the author of Job was inspired by this particular format to craft his literary masterpiece in dialogue form, allowing him (as I will argue in the next section) to place competing viewpoints in conflict with each other. Unlike the Babylonian text, however, the book of Job brings the debate to an end through the agency of the divine voice that speaks at the end, resolving the conflict and presenting the definitive viewpoint on the matter.

The Theological Message of the Book of Job

Job narrates a story that has a theological message for its readers, both its original audience as well as later audiences.[97] In this section, I will explicate the main theological message of the book of Job in the context of the OT. In the next section, I will consider how the book of Job may be read by the church in the light of the revelation of Christ and in the context of the Christian canon as a whole.

What does the book of Job tell us about God, ourselves, and our relationship with God?

96. As an example, D. P. Bricker ("Innocent Suffering in Mesopotamia," 214) argues that there is no truly innocent suffering in Mesopotamian texts like "Man and His God" or *Ludlul Bēl Nēmeqi* since humans by and large are simply ignorant of what the gods want. Although Bricker may have some grounds on which to make his assertion, I should say that Job is not fully aware of what God wants for him either.

97. In describing a coherent theological message of the book, I go against the grain of much contemporary interpretation. Penchansky (*Betrayal of God*) is typical in his statement that to assert such coherence is to do violence to the text and to simply impute one's own views onto the text. One might reply by suggesting that to undermine the coherence of the text and to argue for dissonance is an attempt to avoid the clear message of the text provided by its ending, which could also be an imposition of one's own desires on the text. In the final analysis, the reader must judge whether the proposed theological coherence treats the text properly.

As a didactic narrative (see "The Genre of the Book of Job" above), the book communicates its message through plot and character development. Under "Structure" (see above), we observed the unfolding of the plot of the story (at least in skeleton form). In this section, I will describe the theological message by following the contours of the structure of the book. After discussing the parts of Job, I will then offer some general conclusions.

The Prose Preface (Job 1–2)

The preface introduces all the major characters of the book save one (Elihu). In addition, it also describes the plot complication, Job's suffering, which will motivate the remainder of the book.

The first to be introduced is Job himself. He is described as "fearing God" as well as "innocent and virtuous," an evaluation that is repeated twice by God himself (1:8; 2:3). In this way, the reader knows something for certain about Job that has not been disclosed to the human participants of the book. As one interprets the action and dialogue that follow, there can be no doubt about Job's innocence. As an innocent man, Job enjoys great rewards: wealth, health, and a large and happy family. As I will explicate, much of the teaching of the OT (see "Suffering: Job and Retribution Theology" below) connects wisdom, godliness, and righteousness with such rewards, and their opposite (folly, ungodliness, and wickedness) with punishments. In short, all is as one might expect it to be at the beginning of the book of Job.

The plot thickens, however, as the setting shifts from earth to heaven in 1:6. The scene is the divine assembly: God is meeting with his angelic servants. Among them is one who goes by the name "the accuser" (*haśśāṭān*). While many translations give the impression that "the accuser" is Satan, known as "the devil" in the NT, it is best to understand this creature as a member of God's assembly. As I will explain in the commentary, heaven here is described on analogy with an ancient royal court. The King is meeting with and receiving reports from his agents. The accuser is described as one who roams and patrols the earth (1:7; 2:2), in other words—a spy in God's service.

I pause here in my description of the plot's theological message to point out that one must be careful as one derives an understanding of the nature of God from a book like Job. In a word, we are not to take this description of heaven and its workings literally. God is elsewhere described as one who knows everything about everyone; he does not need reports from angelic spies to know the heart of Job or any human beings (Ps. 139). The purpose of the preface is to create a situation in order to explore the central question of the book of Job: What is the source of wisdom? The situation that is created in the introduction is the suffering of an innocent man, Job.

Returning to the plot, we see that the accuser, while accepting that Job does fear God and is "innocent and virtuous," questions his motivation: Job is godly and righteous because God keeps plying him with rewards. Remove the rewards, the accuser says to God, and Job will "curse you to your face" (1:11; 2:5).

Again, it is worth pausing here to point out that the book of Job is not interested in describing how God normally functions with his human creatures. The message of the book is not that God makes wagers over the integrity of his people. Readers of Job should not live in fear that God will one day subject them to pain in order to make a point to an angel. The message of Job concerning suffering is much more subtle and sophisticated than that (see "Suffering" below). On the other hand, as the author of the book of Job develops the plot and describes the interaction between God and the accuser in relationship to Job's suffering, we catch a sense of God's connection to human suffering. The accuser is only able to take action against Job because God gives him permission. In this way, the book shows that God is sovereign over everything, including our pain. On the other hand, God does not take these actions directly himself but commissions the accuser to carry them out, creating a bit of distance between our pain and God himself.

God takes the accuser's challenge and permits the accuser to inflict suffering on Job, though initially not on his person but only on his wealth and children. The former is removed and the latter are killed (1:13–19), thus inflicting great emotional hardship on Job. How does Job react? Does he "curse God to his face"? Not at all, rather he blesses God's name (1:21), so the narrator concludes this episode by stating, "In all of this, Job did not sin and he did not ascribe wrongdoing to God" (1:22).

Even so, this was just the accuser's opening salvo. The bulk of chap. 2 describes the accuser's second attempt to get Job to "curse God and die." He convinces God that Job will break if he allows him to afflict Job himself. God permits the accuser to do so, confident that Job will withstand the test. The accuser responds by inflicting Job with "horrible boils" all over his body. Job's wife then plays a cameo role in the book to encourage her husband to cave in and "curse God and die." Her brief appearance and unknowing support to the accuser's cause has earned her infamy and much further character development in later literature and commentary (see above on the *Testament of Job*), but the book of Job itself is not much interested in the character or motivations of Job's wife. It is, however, deeply interested in Job's reaction. He rejects her advice. He does not curse God, so again the narrator informs the reader: "In all this, Job did not sin with his lips."

At this point, the test is over. The accuser's perspective has been disproved. Job has shown that he will remain in relationship with God without the rewards. His relationship with God is not dependent on the gifts he receives from him. Since the contest between God and the accuser is over, we do not hear from or about the latter any more. The book is now going to take us to another level of discussion. No longer is the focus on Job's motivation for relationship with God, but now the book will explore the vexing question of undeserved suffering. As it does so, the even more important question of the source of wisdom will come to the fore.

The preface prepares for the discussion that follows by introducing additional characters at the end, the famous "friends of Job" (2:11–13). Indeed, they are friends. They come to console Job in the midst of his pain, and they do so in the most effective way possible. They sit in silence with him for seven whole days. As we will see in the next section, it is Job, not they, who breaks the silence.

Job's Complaint (Job 3)

As indicated earlier, as we move from the preface to chap. 3, the book transitions from prose to poetry. The preface has introduced the main characters and the problem (the suffering of Job, an innocent man); the poetry will now grapple with the problem of innocent suffering and the source of wisdom. The transition to poetry signals to the reader that we are dealing not with a specific historical event but rather with a universally felt dilemma (see "The Genre of the Book of Job" above). And it begins with Job's complaint as he "cursed his 'day'" (3:1).

While in the commentary I will deal with the details of the chapter, here I want to emphasize that Job is complaining, even grumbling, not lamenting. The book of Psalms contains many laments but no complaints, in the technical sense of that word. A lament is a prayer to God that describes one's afflictions. Laments often contain accusations, even hard-hitting accusations against God, but they are spoken to God. Job here describes his sorry state but does not address his comments to God, the first distinction between Job's words in this chapter and the lament psalms. The second is that even the darkest laments in the Psalms have a ray of hope (Ps. 88, often recognized as the saddest of all the laments, speaks to God as the "God of his salvation" [v. 1]).

In a word, Job speaks more like the Israelites in the wilderness who grumble against God than the psalmist who brings his laments before God. This distinction helps us to understand why the three friends feel they must speak out now against Job, and so begins chap. 4.

The Debate (Job 4–27)

The debate, or disputation, between Job and the three friends constitutes over half of the book (even not including chaps. 28–31, about which see below), thus signaling that it is an important part of the overall message of the book of Job. The debate form allows for the presentation of two (or more) viewpoints on a subject in order to pursue the truth of a matter.[98] The debate form is so utilized in other ancient Near Eastern as well as biblical literature.[99]

In the book of Job, the debate has four participants but only two viewpoints, since no space can really be found between the arguments of the three friends. Rhetorically, Zophar may be more harsh, but his arguments are the same as those of Eliphaz and Bildad. This raises the question, why three rather than just one friend? The "Babylonian Theodicy" has a debate on a related topic using just one sufferer and a friend. The question presupposes that the book of Job is mainly a literary creation rather than a piece of historiography (see "Job and History: Was Job an Actual Person, and Does It Matter?" above), but if the poet is not constrained by the facts of an actual event, why are there multiple friends? The main effect, in my opinion, is the sense of piling on opposition. The view of the three friends is a community perspective and not the perspective of an individual. Job is resisting the consensus opinion as he disputes their arguments.

The debate between Job and his three friends has a highly literary form, not resembling an informal debate in which there would be interruptions and shorter speeches. It is formal, allowing each of the speakers to finish before another responds. The responses are also atypical of an actual debate in that the speaker rarely engages the argument of the previous speaker point by point but speaks in generalities. Snaith well observed that the book of Job "is scarcely a dialogue in any normal sense of the word. . . . The content of each speech is usually strangely independent of what has gone before and what follows."[100] Furthermore, the formal-literary nature of this debate is indicated by the fact that everyone speaks in turn and in the same sequence. In the above discussion of the structure of the book, I showed how the three friends speak in order (Eliphaz, Bildad, Zophar) with responses from Job in the first two cycles of speech and that this order breaks down in the third cycle when the friends run out of steam as they encounter a stubborn Job.

What is the subject of the debate? The preface has presented the plot complication: a man previously thought to be innocent now suffers. The three friends debate with Job the cause of his suffering and also the solution to his problem. In order to debate this subject, though, all four characters draw on "wisdom." On a fundamental level, wisdom is a practical category. It is not a knowledge of facts so much as an ability to know how to live life in a way that maximizes success and minimizes problems. When a problem of living

98. The prophets, for instance, utilize the disputation form (see Graffy, *Prophet Confronts His People*) in order to challenge their audience to reconsider their view of God and his law. Malachi has a special penchant for the use of the disputation form (see 1:2–5; 1:6–2:9; 2:10–16; 2:17–3:5; 3:6–12; 3:13–4:3).

99. Most notably, the Egyptian "The Dispute of a Man with His *Ba*" and the "Babylonian Theodicy" (see the section "Ancient Near Eastern Background" above).

100. Snaith, *Job*, 8.

materializes, as it has in extreme form for Job, then wisdom looks for a way out of the dilemma. Thus, even though the debate in Job is focused on the question of Job's suffering, it leads to a debate about who is wise.

As just mentioned, the three friends present a united front as to why Job suffers. To them it is obvious, since they hold what might be called a traditional retribution theology (for a canonical overview of the teaching on retribution, see "Suffering: Job and Retribution Theology" below). Such a view may be summarized by the belief "If you sin, then you suffer; so if you suffer, then you are a sinner." The reverse is also the case: "If you are righteous (godly, wise), then you are blessed; so if you are blessed, then you are righteous (godly, wise)." Below, we will acknowledge that such a theology can be sustained from other parts of Scripture but only if those parts are isolated from their canonical context. At this point it is important to realize that they are not pulling these views out of thin air.

All three friends know the cause of Job's suffering: it is obvious that he is a sinner and a great one at that. They hold this view not because they have observed him sinning or received testimony that he has sinned but purely and solely because he is suffering. As readers, we know their charge is wrong because we have overheard the heavenly dialogue between God and the accuser. Their teaching on this subject is extensive (for Eliphaz: 4:7–11; 5:2–7; 15:20–35; for Bildad: 8:3–4, 11–21; 18:5–21; for Zophar: 11:11; 20:5–29) but can be illustrated with a quote from Eliphaz's first speech:

> Please remember: Who being blameless has perished?
> Where were the virtuous destroyed?
> As I have seen, those who plow iniquity
> and those who plant trouble harvest them.
> They perish by the breath of God;
> they are finished off by the blast of his anger.
> The roar of the lion, the sound of the lion cub,
> the teeth of the young lions are broken.
> A lion perishes without prey,
> and the offspring of a lioness are scattered from each other. (4:7–11)

Wisdom involves more than diagnosis; it leads to a prescription of a remedy for a malady. If sin is the problem, then repentance is the answer. Job needs to repent for the sins that have led to his suffering. Again, the three friends make multiple calls for Job to repent (5:8–16, 23–27; 8:5–7; 11:13–20; 22:22–30); a quote from Zophar's first speech is a good example:

> If you focus your heart,
> and you spread out your palms to him—
> if evil is in your hand, move it far away,
> and don't let iniquity take up residence in your tent—

certainly then you will lift up your face without blemish;
    you will be secure and not afraid.
Indeed, you will forget your trouble;
    you will remember it like water running away.
Then life will be brighter than noonday;
    its darkness will be like the morning.
You will be secure because there is hope;
    you will look around and lie down in safety.
You will lie down and not tremble with fear;
    many will ask for your favor.
The eyes of the wicked will fail;
    their escape route will be lost to them.
    Their expectation will be death. (11:13–20)

In summary, the position of the three friends in the debate has two main points. First, Job's suffering indicates that his problem is caused by his own personal sin. As a result, second, the solution to his problem is repentance. If Job repents, then God will restore him to his previous blessed condition. The three friends repeat this argument so often that it threatens to become tedious. As Davis states, "The protracted arguments of Job's interlocutors may well bore us, and probably they should. It is like watching Samuel Beckett's *Waiting for Godot*: nothing changes and no one moves forward. By the end of the play, if you are not faint with the excruciating tedium of it all, then you missed the point."[101]

What then is Job's perspective? First, it is important to realize that Job fully affirms the retribution theology of the three friends. He too believes that sinners suffer and the godly are rewarded. At least, he believes that this is the way the world is supposed to work. We can see this in his accusations that God treats people, and in particular himself, unfairly. The only basis for thinking that God is unjust is the belief that God guarantees blessings for the righteous and punishments for the wicked. His experience leads him to conclude that God is arbitrary in his treatment of people, whether they are innocent or guilty:

It is all the same; therefore, I say:
    "He destroys the innocent and the wicked."
If a disaster brings sudden death,
    he ridicules the despair of the innocent.
The earth is given into the power of the wicked;
    he covers the faces of its judges.
    If it is not he, then who? (9:22–24)

Job continues to affirm his innocence of any wrongdoing that explains his suffering, but this leads him to believe that God is operating outside the rules

101. Davis, "Sufferer's Wisdom," 130.

that should run the world. Thus, in his diagnosis, the cause of his suffering is not his sin but rather God's injustice. At first, he does not think there is any recourse, any prescription that will heal his predicament. Better stated, he knows what he should do, but at first he does not think it is possible. He believes that his only recourse is to confront God and challenge his unfairness. Earlier in chap. 9, Job speaks of God's might and wisdom (vv. 4–10) but not in praise of his God. Rather, it is in explanation for why he cannot do what he thinks needs to be done to resolve his dilemma: "If someone wants to take him to court, one could not answer him one out of a thousand times" (9:3). After all,

> If it is about power, he is strong.
>   If it is about judgment, who can testify against him?
> If I am righteous, my mouth condemns me.
>   I am innocent, but he declares me perverse. (9:19–20)

While character development is hard to trace in the dialogues, we can see it in this one area in Job. He continues to maintain his innocence and to charge God with injustice, but he grows in his belief that he can effectively challenge God. This growing confidence coincides with his belief that there is an agent in heaven who can aid him. Such confidence is completely lacking at the end of chap. 9:

> For he is not a person like I am that I could answer him,
>   that we will go together into judgment.
> There is no umpire between us
>   who would set his hand on both of us.
> He would take his rod away from me,
>   and not let his dread scare me.
> I would speak and not be afraid of him,
>   though this is not the case with me. (9:32–35)

Job's despair of help and any ability to confront God changes to hope in chap. 16:

> O earth, do not cover my blood;
>   do not let there be a place for my cry for justice!
> Even now, see, my witness is in heaven,
>   and the one who testifies for me is on high.
> My friends scorn me,
>   and my eye drips tears to God.
> He would arbitrate with God on behalf of a person,
>   as between a person and his friend.
> For when a number of years have come,
>   I will go the way from which I will not return. (16:18–22)

This confidence reaches a crescendo in chap. 19:

> I know that my redeemer lives,
> and he at last will rise up on the dust.
> After my skin is peeled off,
> then out of my flesh I will see God.
> I will see him for myself;
> my eyes will look and not a stranger's.
> My heart fades within me. (19:25–27)

Job thus comes to believe that he has heavenly help in his case against God. I will give detailed analysis of these important passages in the commentary proper, but here it is important to come to grips with what Job is thinking. What or who is he thinking of as he speaks of a heavenly umpire, witness, redeemer? As argued later in the commentary, it seems clear that he is thinking of a member of the heavenly court—an angel—who would come to his aid. Elihu himself will entertain this as a possibility for a sufferer in 33:23–29. With the idea that he has an ally in heaven, Job ends his speeches in full confidence that he can bring a successful case against God (see below on 31:35–37).

Before departing from the debate proper, though, we need to consider a critical element of these speeches. We must reflect on the significant use of insults in the argument. After all, Job and the three friends are not simply laying out position papers; they are attacking each other. As they grapple with Job's predicament, they present themselves as sages and attack Job's claims and reputation. Sages are those who give advice to people who struggle in life, and that is what Job and the three friends are doing. The suffering of Job is the problem that leads to the contest of wisdom. Who is wise? Job? The three friends?

Thus, in the process of interaction, they lob insults at each other to assert their own wisdom and to undermine their opponent's wisdom. I will choose a few examples from each to make my point (and detailed analysis of the cited passages may be consulted in the commentary proper). I begin with insults directed by the three friends to Job:

> How long will you continue speaking these things?
> The words of your mouth are a strong wind. (Bildad; 8:2)

> Should such a large number of words not be answered?
> Should a talkative man be declared righteous?
> Should your empty talk render others silent?
> When you mock, should not someone shame you?
> . . . .
> But an empty-headed person will get understanding,
> when a wild donkey gives birth to a human. (Zophar; 11:2–3, 12)

Job gives as good as he gets in the following examples:

> Truly, you are the people,
>   and wisdom will die with you!
> I also have a mind like you.
>   I am not inferior to you.
>   Who is not like these? (12:2–3)
>
> I have heard all these things a lot;
>   you are all troublesome comforters.
> Is there an end to windy words?
>   Or why does it provoke you so much that you must respond?
>   (16:2–3)

This last quotation also introduces another theme of Job's argument against the friends. They are not helpful; indeed, they are dangerous friends. They are "troublesome comforters"; they give bad advice and are unreliable (see also 6:14–30; 13:4–15; 17:3–5; 19:21; 26:3–4).

Thus the debate section of the book contributes in a significant way to the main question of the book: Who is wise? At the end of the discussion, there is no resolution to this issue, only confusion.

Job's Monologue (Job 28–31)

While it is possible to construe these four chapters as part of the debate, it is better to understand them as Job speaking out loud, but not necessarily to the three friends. We will soon come to understand that other people are around—Elihu steps out of the shadows to begin speaking (chaps. 32–37). Thus we understand the debate section to conclude with chap. 27, and then a new section begins in chap. 28.

As I will describe in the commentary section, chap. 28 raises a difficult issue. How does it function in its context? Through chap. 27 Job is agitated with the three friends but also with God. Chapter 28, commonly known as the "Poem to Wisdom," is an eloquent and powerful affirmation of God's wisdom. He is the source of all true wisdom. This appears out of context from what precedes, since Job and the three friends are each claiming their own wisdom. Furthermore, the calm, confident affirmations of chap. 28 give way to confusion again in chaps. 29–31. How are we to understand chap. 28?

As I discussed under "Authorship and Date," some believe that chap. 28 was added at a later point. A later redactor grew nervous at Job's challenge to God and needed to insert an "orthodox" statement. Even if this view is true from a compositional perspective, one must still explain how chap. 28 functions in its present context in the final form of the book as we know it.

Some commentators argue that Job is no longer speaking here. Perhaps the most pervasive opinion today is that the words of chap. 28 represent an intrusion of the narrator, from whom we have not heard since chap. 2.[102] This view is often supported from the text by observing that chap. 29 begins "And Job continued his discourse and said." Why would such an introduction be needed if Job was the speaker of the preceding chapters, including chap. 28? Such an argument, though, is undermined by the introduction of chap. 27 (v. 1), which continues the speech of Job in chap. 26, or the first verse of chap. 35 ("And Elihu answered and said"), which continues Elihu's speech of chaps. 32–34.

Thus the text as it stands is most naturally read as the words of Job. But how can Job be represented as speaking about divine wisdom in a way that seems in tension, perhaps even in contradiction, with his thoughts expressed immediately before and after? I argue that rather than being problematic, this tension in the book of Job well represents the psychology of the sufferer. It is not unusual in the aftermath of tragedy for someone to reach a period of calm in the midst of an emotional storm only to again feel the effects of the calamity and collapse back into distress.[103]

And fall back into distress is precisely what Job does in the remainder of his monologue. Chapter 29 sets up the next chapter as Job rehearses his earlier blessed estate. He was honored and influential. He was generous and respected. However, in chap. 30 he contrasts these good old days with the present, when he is reviled even by the lowest stratum of society. He is afflicted and deeply depressed. Even so, before bringing his words to an end, he makes one more protest of his innocence—he has done nothing wrong. Thus he concludes his speech with an expression of confidence that he will see God, and he will challenge God and set him straight. Job knows that he does not deserve the suffering that he is experiencing:

> Oh, that someone would listen to me!
>   Here is my signature! Let Shaddai answer me!
> Surely, I will wear it on my shoulder;
>   I would bind it on me like a crown.
> I would give him an account of all my steps;
>   I would approach him like a prince. (31:35–36)

Job is ready to face God. That moment is to come soon, though the encounter will not go the way Job anticipates. However, before that moment, Job must bear the speech of yet another person who thinks he is filled with wisdom and has an answer for his predicament.

102. For instance, Newsom, *Job*, 169.

103. Such a "psychological reading" is also preferred by Lo in her book *Rhetoric of Job 28*. See also Bartholomew and O'Dowd, *Old Testament Wisdom Literature*, 225.

Elihu's Monologue (Job 32–37)

After "the words of Job are ended" (31:40), Elihu begins to speak. He does not intend his speech to be a monologue, for he is speaking to Job, but since Job does not respond, it turns out to be a monologue. Many believe that the Elihu speech is a late addition to the book (see "Authorship and Date" above), but in this section we are concerned with the theological meaning of the book in its present canonical form, regardless of its history of composition.

The book to this point has not prepared us for Elihu's speech. The reader is unaware until this moment that others are present, listening in on the debate between Job and his friends. Once Job and the friends stop speaking, Elihu breaks into the silence in order to present his perspective on the matter.

Interestingly, this section of Job is introduced by the narrator at some length. The speeches of Job and the three friends began with quite simple introductions (i.e., "Job answered and said"), but here there is a relatively lengthy introduction (32:1–6). While Job and the three friends appear to be from Edom, Elihu's parentage indicates that he is a Hebrew. Most interesting is the author's understanding of Elihu's motivation to enter the fray: anger. Elihu is angry with Job and also with the three friends. He is upset with Job because he has not admitted his faults ("he considered himself more righteous than God"), and with the three friends because they were unable to convince Job to do so, though they still treated him as a wicked person.

Because he is young, Elihu hesitates to speak, believing that the aged should speak first. In good biblical and ancient Near Eastern fashion, he assumes that wisdom comes with observation and experience, something that increases over time. In light of the debaters' failure to reach resolution, however, Elihu comes to the view that wisdom does not always reside with the elders. Key to understanding the significance of Elihu's role in the story of Job is his statement that "it [wisdom] is the spirit in a person, the breath of Shaddai, that gives them understanding" (32:8). In a word, Elihu claims a spiritual ground to his wisdom.

What then does Elihu, under the influence of the spirit, bring to the debate? As it turns out, nothing new. He extols the same doctrine of retribution that the three friends did earlier. For instance, in 36:5–9 he announces:

> Look, God is strong and does not despise anyone.
> He is strong in power of understanding.
> The wicked will not live;
> he gives justice to the afflicted.
> He does not withhold his eye from the righteous.
> With kings on the throne,
> he makes them reign forever and exalts them.
> And if they are bound in chains
> and caught in cords of affliction,

> he tells them what they have done
> and their transgressions, because they have acted proudly. (See also 33:12–22; 34:23–30)

Also like the three friends, Elihu sees only one recourse for Job: repent and be restored:

> He [God] opens their ears to instruction,
> and tells them to return from guilt.
> If they listen and obey,
> their days will finish happily,
> and their years pleasantly.
> But if they do not listen, they will pass through the Water Channel.
> They will expire without knowledge. (36:10–12)

It is true that Elihu puts more emphasis on the disciplinary nature of suffering, but this theme is not lacking among the three friends either (see Eliphaz in 5:17–22). In a word, Elihu offers nothing new to the debate concerning Job's suffering in terms of substance. Thus Job never responds to, nor does anyone acknowledge, Elihu after he speaks. Such neglect is the ultimate put-down of what he represents.

What does the Elihu speech represent in the book? Elihu stands for yet another take on wisdom. In substance, Elihu's approach to Job's suffering agrees with that of the three friends. He too believes that sinners suffer and the righteous are blessed. He also believes that sufferers must be sinners and more particularly that Job suffers because he is a sinner. Elihu represents not so much a different understanding of wisdom but a different school of thought in terms of the foundation of his wisdom. The wisdom of the three friends emanates from their age. They purport to be wise primarily on the basis of their experience and tradition, which contains the wisdom of their ancestors. Elihu, on the other hand, is young, not old. He represents what might be called a charismatic wisdom, one grounded on the "spirit in a person" (32:8). Since Elihu's wisdom is not affirmed in the book, his school of thought is also rejected. To see the true ground of wisdom, we now proceed to the climax of the book, Yahweh's speeches to Job out of the whirlwind. Surprisingly, Elihu's final speech (chap. 37) anticipates the substance and themes of the Yahweh speeches, but, as I will explain in the commentary at that point, that does not rescue Elihu from the uncomplimentary portrayal given him here.

Yahweh Speaks from the Whirlwind and Job Repents (Job 38:1–42:6)

The prologue presented the characters of the book of Job with a problem to be understood and fixed. When Job was blessed with health, riches, and a large, happy family, there was no question of his righteousness and godliness.

Once these blessings were removed, the questions were, why did Job suffer, and how can his situation be remedied? While readers know that Job is innocent and his suffering is the result of a test initiated by God in reaction to a challenge from the accuser, the characters are left to figure it out themselves. After Job's lament (chap. 3), a fierce debate breaks out. We have seen that each of the human participants claims to be wise, to be able to diagnose Job's problem and offer a solution. The three friends argue that he is a sinner who must repent, and Job argues that he is innocent and that God is unfair. Their debate ends unresolved. It was at this point that Elihu stepped in to offer his perspective on the matter. No one responds to Elihu and the issue remains unresolved. The message thus far is loud and clear: human wisdom fails miserably, whether the wisdom is that of the three friends, Job, or Elihu.

But now God speaks, and as he does, we hear the perspective of the author himself.[104] He speaks from a whirlwind, a storm, which clearly indicates that he is not happy. He then prefaces his remark by challenging Job:

> Who is this who darkens advice
>   with ignorant words?
> Brace yourself like a man.
>   I will question you, and you must inform me! (38:2–3)

God is clearly irritated with Job. He reacts like a professor with a student who thinks he knows more than his teacher. Job, after all, has expressed his wish to "set God right" regarding his suffering. He does not deserve it, but God now will restore the proper hierarchy between himself and his human creature. He proceeds to pepper Job with questions that he cannot answer concerning the creation of the world and the way of the creatures within it.

These questions are unfair in that they are impossible for a human to answer. He asks Job, for instance, whether he was around when the world was created and whether he knows how it was done. How could anyone know this? Only God could know this, and of course that is the point. While human wisdom fails, God asserts his wisdom in the divine speeches. In the words of

104. As Newsom (*Job*, 18) says (describing a position that she finds ultimately unsatisfying), "Not only is it plausible that God, that great authority figure, would represent the perspective of the author, but the structure of the book itself also seems designed to lead the reader through an education of the moral imagination." She ultimately argues (ibid., 21) that the book of Job is a polyphonic text in the Bakhtinian sense, which she says has "three distinctive aspects: (1) it embodies a dialogic sense of truth; (2) the author's position, although represented in the text, is not privileged; and (3) the polyphonic text ends without finalizing closure." My own reading disputes all three of these aspects. Though numerous voices express different opinions (and thus in one sense are dialogic), Yahweh's speeches, with Job's response to them, do bring closure in a manner that represents the author's view of the matter. In the commentary itself I will indicate why I also disagree with her view of the text's ending and maintain that the prose conclusion does not undermine the coherent message of Job.

Habel, "The reply of God from the whirlwind . . . is a theological defense of God the sage."[105]

Yahweh's speeches are intended not to give Job an answer to the question of why he suffers but to reestablish the proper relationship between God and his human creature. Job has sought God to accuse him of injustice (40:8), but God, through a display of his power and wisdom, brings Job to the point where he "repents" (42:1–6). He no longer seeks an answer to the question of his suffering: he simply bends the knee to God in submission.

The Epilogue (Job 42:7–17)

The epilogue presents a number of problems for a coherent reading of the book of Job, at least along the lines of interpretation I have been offering. Certainly we can understand why God is angry at Eliphaz and his two friends. They have been accusing Job of sin that led to his suffering, and we, the readers, have known that this is a false charge from the very beginning. But God goes on and seems to put an imprimatur on the "words of Job." Job, as opposed to the three friends, has spoken correctly about God. How are we to understand this in the light of just finishing four chapters where Yahweh has addressed Job so harshly that he felt compelled to repent? God cannot be read as approving all of Job's words. Rather, God affirms Job for never breaking relationship with him. Job never curses God and dies. He never falls prey to the friends' fallacious arguments. He never cuts and runs from God, but rather pursues him. He also repents when confronted by God. God not only commends him for this, but he also commissions him to intercede for his friends with prayer and sacrifice—like a priest.

Finally, God restores Job to his previous blessed condition. Indeed, he is twice as blessed in the epilogue as in the prologue. At least his wealth is doubled and his family is restored to its former size. Job also lives a long time and dies a happy man.

But here is the second apparent conundrum of the epilogue: Job repents and is restored. Isn't that what the friends have urged all along? Does the book of Job undermine its own message, presenting the kind of literary aporia that deconstructionist readers used to salivate over?

While a number of commentators have gone that direction, a closer reading leads to a different conclusion. One must be careful to ask, Why does Job repent? And the critical observation in answer is that he does not repent of sin that led to his suffering in the first place. The friends attributed his pain to sin, but there was no such sin from which to repent. Then again, why does Job repent? In the dialogues, Job has grown increasingly impatient (see "The Patience of Job" following my comments on Job 21). He concludes that God

105. N. C. Habel, "In Defense of God the Sage," in *Voice from the Whirlwind*, ed. Perdue and Gilpin, 21.

is unjust. At the end of the story, he changes his attitude and behavior (he repents, in other words) toward God, now that he has not only heard about him but also seen him (42:5).

Conclusion

The theological message of the book of Job comes through an analysis of the book as a whole. My genre analysis determined that the book is a debate at the center of which is the subject of wisdom. Wisdom is the primary theme of the book. Job's suffering is the foil that allows a discussion of wisdom. This is not to say that the book has nothing to offer on the subject of suffering, but that is not its primary interest. I conclude this section by summarizing what we learn about both wisdom and suffering.

Wisdom

The main question addressed by the book of Job is, who is wise?[106] Job's suffering presents the problem, and the human participants throw all their best thinking at it in order to solve the conundrum of why a seemingly innocent man is in such emotional and physical pain. Their efforts fail miserably. It is only when God speaks from the whirlwind that the wisdom debate comes to a close. At the end of the book, there is no question as to who is wise. Therefore, Job does what the book is suggesting all should do in the face of the mystery of suffering: submit to God. Job 28 anticipates this conclusion as it announces that wisdom can be found only with God, and thus the proper human response is "fear of the Lord" (28:28).

Suffering

Job and retribution theology. While Job's suffering is the foil that reveals the ultimate source of wisdom, the book imparts important lessons concerning suffering, especially when the story is read within the context of the canon as a whole. Before God speaks from the whirlwind, all the human participants are firm believers in a strict retribution theology. Sinners suffer, so sufferers are sinners.

This message from the book of Job remains important today since it is so tempting to believe that there is a natural and immediate connection between our actions and rewards and punishments. In the NT, the disciples, who likely knew the story of Job, are quick to revert to retribution theology when they encounter a man born blind: "Rabbi, who sinned, this man or his parents, that he was born blind?" (John 9:2 NRSV). Jesus immediately corrects them ("Neither this man nor his parents sinned; he was born blind so that God's works might be revealed in him," 9:3 NRSV), but even today people encountering a

106. Zerafa, *Wisdom of Job*, also places wisdom at the center of the message of Job.

tragedy find themselves asking, What did I do to deserve this? Proponents of the so-called prosperity gospel take advantage of this attitude in their argument that bad things happen to bad people and good things happen to good people. To depart from this way of thinking is frightening to many, because to do so means abandoning a sense of control.

To be honest, it is possible to proof-text an argument in favor of retribution theology from the Bible. For instance, a selective reading of the book of Proverbs would support it,[107] as would the structure of a covenant/treaty text like Deuteronomy, which connects obedience to God's law with blessings, and disobedience with curses (see Deut. 27–28). The historical books of Samuel and Kings demonstrate that Israel's and Judah's exiles are the result of covenant disobedience, and the prophets warn their audiences of impending doom unless they repent.

Thus one of the important contributions of the book of Job (as well as Ecclesiastes)[108] is to undermine the idea that retribution theology works absolutely and mechanically. Sometimes sin does lead to negative consequences, but not always. Similarly, sometimes proper behavior leads to positive outcomes, but not always. Job serves as an example to warn against judging others on the basis of their situation in life.

But Job himself never receives an answer to the question of why he has suffered. At the end of the book, after hearing and seeing God, he submits to God's greater power and wisdom. The book of Job thus reminds us that we will not always, or even perhaps typically, be able to explain our suffering and the suffering of our loved ones. It remains a mystery to us. The book of Job challenges us to follow Job in pursuing God in our suffering, not letting go, and ultimately to submit to his power and wisdom. As we will see below in "The Book of Job in the Light of Christ," the NT will add more insight in how God addresses our suffering.

The fact that sin is not the only possible cause of suffering has two practical implications. First, it "shatters the myth that our own righteousness can protect us from unjust suffering."[109] In other words, we cannot control the situations that might lead to our pain. Second, we cannot judge others based on the fact that they are suffering.

A model for sufferers. While the book of Job does not provide an answer to why people suffer, Clines is right to point out that the book does provide insight into how people should respond to suffering: "Viewed as an answer to the problem of suffering, then, the argument of the book of Job is: By all means let Job the patient [in the first two chapters] be your model so long as

107. For instance, Prov. 3:9–10; 16:5; 18:6; 21:7; 24:16 lend support to the idea that good things happen to good people and bad things happen to bad people. However, for a fuller understanding of the teaching of Proverbs on retribution, see Longman, *Proverbs*, 82–86.

108. See Longman, *Ecclesiastes,* especially 125–29.

109. Reitman, *Unlocking Wisdom*, 63.

that is possible for you; but when equanimity fails, let the grief and anger of Job the impatient direct itself and yourself toward God, for only in encounter with him will the tension of suffering be resolved."[110] To take this point further, the ultimate resolution is patient suffering before a wise and powerful God.

The Book of Job in the Light of Christ

The previous section looked at Job's theological message within the context of the OT. Christian readers of the OT need to take a further step and consider the book from the perspective of the NT. Jesus himself invites this type of reading in his words to the two disciples on the road to Emmaus:

> "Oh, how foolish you are, and how slow of heart to believe all that the prophets have declared! Was it not necessary that the Messiah should suffer these things and then enter into his glory?" Then beginning with Moses and all the prophets, he interpreted to them the things about himself in all the scriptures. (Luke 24:25–27 NRSV; see also 24:44–49)

While, as Childs points out, we first need to hear the "discrete voice" of the OT, we must then go on to read the OT from a post-Christ perspective.[111] What insight does such a reading bring to the book of Job?

First, we should take note that Jesus, like Job, was an innocent sufferer. Indeed, these two are the only people whom the Bible presents as truly innocent sufferers.[112] The early Christian community, seeing this connection, made it a common practice to read the book of Job during Passion week.[113] However, the connection between Job and Jesus is illuminated more by the contrast between the two than by their similarity. One important difference is that, while Job suffered involuntarily, Jesus submitted himself to the suffering that he did not deserve. He had a choice as to whether he would suffer, and he chose to do so. Paul recognized this in the powerful hymn that celebrates Jesus's voluntary humiliation and ultimate exaltation. The humiliation is expressed in the first part of the poem about Christ Jesus,

110. Clines, *Job 1–20*, xxxiv.

111. Childs, *Biblical Theology*, 76.

112. A case could be made for Daniel, about whom no personal sin is recorded in the Bible. Daniel does suffer by being forced into exile at a young age and bearing the persecution of his colleagues, but Daniel understood his predicament as a result of the corporate sin of his people (see, for instance, his penitential prayer that includes the statement "We have sinned and done wrong. We have rebelled against you and scorned your commands" [Dan. 9:5 NLT]). We should also note that on numerous occasions people suffered more than they deserved, and they called on God to help them in the midst of their distress (see various lament psalms, the Joseph story in Genesis, and the abuse the prophet Jeremiah received).

113. Delitzsch, *Job*, 32.

> who, though he was in the form of God,
> did not regard equality with God
> as something to be exploited.
> but emptied himself,
> taking the form of a slave,
> being born in human likeness.
> And being found in human form,
> he humbled himself
> and became obedient to the point of death—
> even death on a cross. (Phil. 2:6–8 NRSV)

In regard to his voluntary suffering, the crucial moment in Jesus's earthly ministry comes in the Garden of Gethsemane. Here, as he faces the cross, he beseeches his Father to remove "this cup of suffering away from me." But he submits himself to God's will with the words "Yet I want your will to be done, not mine" (Mark 14:36 NLT).

Jesus suffered voluntarily, not involuntarily like Job. Further, he did so for our benefit. Jesus's suffering and ultimate resurrection allow for our salvation from sin, guilt, and death. He suffers on our behalf; it is vicarious suffering. Job's suffering, on the other hand, is not redemptive. He does not suffer for our sakes. Job's situation is didactic, not redemptive.[114]

Beginning with this insight provided by the comparison and contrast between Job and Jesus, we may go further into the question of God's response to suffering. In the book of Job itself, God never tells Job why he suffered. Job must simply submit to God's power and wisdom. In the NT, however, we see God's ultimate answer to human suffering: Jesus Christ, his own Son, God himself. Jesus, who is fully human and fully divine, suffers at the will of God to release us from the grip of pain and death. The God-man came and suffered alongside us, but he was also raised, giving us hope for the future.

Why is there suffering and death? Because of sin. This statement appears contrary to what I presented as the message of Job, that there was suffering apart from sin in the case of Job. However, it is possible to deny that one's suffering is the result of one's personal sin and at the same time affirm that all suffering is the result of human rebellion.

The story of the rebellion of Adam and Eve (Gen. 3) intends to tell us about the entry of sin, guilt, and death into the world. It attributes these to the willful rebellion of God's human creatures. Paul makes this point in Rom. 5:12–21 and in 8:20a ("Against its will, all creation was subjected to God's

114. Again (see "The Genre of the Book of Job" above), the didactic nature of the book is why it is not important whether the book of Job is actual history; whereas, if the events surrounding Jesus's life (his suffering, death, and resurrection) are not true, then, as Paul says, "our preaching is useless, and your faith is useless" (1 Cor. 15:14 NLT).

curse" [NLT]) but also points out that Jesus provides hope because he provides the means of redemption.

Such thinking led some in the early church[115] and beyond[116] to treat Job's desire for a mediator, arbitrator, "witness in heaven," and umpire as a prophecy of Jesus (Job 9:33; 16:19–22; 19:23–29). Perhaps the best-known treatment of 19:23–29 as a messianic prophecy comes from Handel's *Messiah,* in which there is a soprano aria titled "I Know That My Redeemer Liveth."

In the commentary proper I respond to this interpretation in detail, but at this point some general comments based on the conclusions in the commentary are appropriate. What does Job desire? He wants someone in heaven to help even the playing field between himself and God. During the debate with the three friends, he reveals through his words that he believes God is unjust and powerful. He wants to take God to court, but he knows that he could not stand up to God. He wants someone to come and help him and represent him to God. In the commentary, I demonstrate that Job is thinking not of Jesus but of an angel, and we will further see that there was no angel that would take his side.[117]

Indeed, there is a significant theological problem in taking these statements of Job as messianic prophecies. Job wants someone to take his side in his fight with an angry God. God wants to hurt him, he believes, and he needs to find someone to change the divine mind. But this viewpoint does not well describe the redemptive role of Jesus and especially of God the Father. In other words, we are not to picture the Father as angry and ready to smash sinners until Jesus, the Son, comes and calms his Father down. No, we have just above cited Jesus's words in the garden as he asks his Father to remove the cup of suffering from him: "I want your will to be done, not mine" (Mark 14:36 NLT). In other words, it was the Father and the Son (and the Holy Spirit), the Triune God, who lovingly and sacrificially worked our salvation. The persons of the Godhead were not at odds with one another.

At best, then, we can say that Job's desire for a mediator between God and people is fulfilled in Christ—though not quite in the way that he thought it would be. In any case, it is wrongheaded to treat these passages as messianic prophecies. Nevertheless, we rightly understand Jesus as God's ultimate response to human suffering. He suffered so we might live.

Christ, the Apex of God's Wisdom

I have suggested that the main theme of the book of Job concerns wisdom. The question Who is wise? is posed, and the answer is that, though humans

115. Relevant quotations from church fathers may be found in Simonetti and Conti, *Job*, 105–6.

116. See, for instance, Kaiser, *Messiah in the Old Testament*, 61–64.

117. Indeed, the only individual angel we hear about in heaven is the accuser in the prologue, who, rather than helping, instigates Job's suffering.

pretend to have wisdom, true wisdom comes from God alone. The human response to this insight is "fear of God." This conclusion is reached in the magnificent poem of wisdom in chap. 28: "Behold, the fear of the Lord is wisdom, and turning aside from evil is understanding" (28:28). Job demonstrates this proper fear in his response to the Yahweh speeches when he submits to God (42:1–6). Those, like Job at the end of the book, who fear the Lord show wisdom because they know their proper place in the universe and turn to God for guidance in how to live life and navigate difficulties.

Of course, the book of Job is not alone in advocating wisdom that starts with the fear of the Lord. The book of Proverbs signals in its preface that the fear of the Lord is the attitude of the wise: "The fear of Yahweh is the beginning of knowledge, but fools despise wisdom and discipline" (1:7).[118] Ecclesiastes also concludes with the frame narrator instructing his son (see 12:12): "Fear God and keep his commandments, for this is the whole duty of humanity. For God will bring every deed into judgment, including every hidden thing, whether good or evil" (12:13–14). In sum, all three of the wisdom books desire to inculcate in their readers wisdom that springs from a proper relationship with Yahweh.

How does the NT appropriate OT wisdom? More specifically, in the language of Luke 24, how does the wisdom tradition of the OT anticipate Christ? The Gospels present Jesus as a wise man or sage. Beginning with the infancy narratives, the Gospels describe Jesus as wise. Luke 2:40 says, "The child grew up healthy and strong. He was filled with wisdom, and God's favor was on him" (NLT). Luke 2:52 concludes the infancy narrative with "Jesus grew in wisdom and in stature and in favor with God and all the people" (NLT). Between these two verses is the account of Jesus being left behind at the temple by Mary and Joseph. When they come back, they find him at the temple with the religious leaders, "listening to them and asking them questions. And all who heard him were amazed at his understanding and his answers" (2:46–47 NRSV). Right from the start, Jesus demonstrates his surprising wisdom.

When he turns of age, he begins to teach. The reaction to his instruction also indicates his unprecedented wisdom. In Mark we hear this response: "Amazement gripped the audience, and they began to discuss what had happened. 'What sort of new teaching is this?' they asked excitedly. 'It has such authority! Even evil spirits obey his orders!'" (Mark 1:27 NLT). Attentive readers will also note the significance of the form he uses for much of his teaching—the parable. The parable is the teaching tool of the sage, indicated by the fact that the Greek term for "parable" (*parabolē*) is used in Greek versions of the OT

118. This point is repeated, with variation, in a number of places in the book of Proverbs (especially 9:10, but see also 1:29; 2:5; 3:7; 8:13; 10:27; 14:2, 26, 27; 15:16; 16:6; 19:23; 22:4; 23:17; 24:21; 28:14; 29:25; 31:30).

to translate the Hebrew word "proverb" (*māšāl*), a central form of wisdom teaching in the OT. The Jesus of the Gospels is a sage.[119]

Paul certainly understands Jesus as a wise man as well. Indeed, he is the apex of God's wisdom according to a text like Col. 2:3, "In whom [Christ] are hidden all the treasures of wisdom and knowledge" (NRSV). First Corinthians 1:18–2:16 is an even more extended reflection on the wisdom of God, which has as its central teaching "Christ [is] the power of God and the wisdom of God" (1:24 NRSV).

The NT further signals that Jesus is God's wisdom incarnate by associating him with Woman Wisdom of Prov. 8, a personification of Yahweh's wisdom and ultimately of Yahweh himself.[120] Jesus so associates himself in Matthew when he responds to the Jewish leaders' criticism of his lifestyle by saying, "Yet wisdom is vindicated by her deeds" (11:19 NRSV). Paul uses the language of Prov. 8 in Col. 1 when he refers to Jesus as "the image of the invisible God, the firstborn of all creation" (1:15 NRSV) and then associates him with the creation of "all things in heaven and on earth" (1:16 NRSV), a description reminiscent of Woman Wisdom in Prov. 8:22–31. The famous prologue of John 1 also echoes the language of Prov. 8 in its description of Woman Wisdom's role at creation when it proclaims: "In the beginning was the Word, and the Word was with God, and the Word was God. He was in the beginning with God. All things came into being through him, and without him not one thing came into being" (John 1:1–3a NRSV).

More connections between Yahweh's wisdom and Jesus could be drawn, but enough has been said to establish the point that Jesus is the epitome of God's wisdom. Understanding this calls the Christian reader of Job into a deeper relationship with Jesus, who is God's wisdom. And Paul, like the book of Job, makes very clear that human pretensions to wisdom fall short of the wisdom of God as made incarnate in Jesus Christ:

> For the message of the cross is foolishness to those who are perishing, but to us who are being saved it is the power of God. For it is written,
>
> "I will destroy the wisdom of the wise,
> and the discernment of the discerning I will thwart."[121]
>
> Where is the one who is wise? Where is the scribe? Where is the debater of this age? Has not God made foolish the wisdom of the world? For since, in the wisdom of God, the world did not know God through wisdom, God decided, through the foolishness of our proclamation, to save those who believe. For

119. See Witherington, *Jesus the Sage*.
120. For a more extensive treatment, see Longman, *Proverbs*, 67–69, 208–13.
121. A quote from Isa. 29:14.

Jews demand signs and Greeks desire wisdom, but we proclaim Christ crucified, a stumbling block to Jews and foolishness to Gentiles, but to those who are called, both Jews and Greeks, Christ the power of God and the wisdom of God. For God's foolishness is wiser than human wisdom, and God's weakness is stronger than human strength. (1 Cor. 1:18–25 NRSV)

I.
The Prologue: The Suffering and Patience of Job
(1:1–2:13)

Translation

1:1 There was a man in the land of Uz whose name was Job, and that man
was innocent and virtuous, fearing God and turning away from evil. **2**And
seven sons and three daughters were born to him. **3**His property included
seven thousand sheep, and three thousand camels, and five hundred pair
of cattle, and five hundred donkeys. He had an extremely large workforce.
He was a great man among all the people of the East.

4His sons went and prepared a banquet on their birthday,[1] and they
sent invitations[2] to their three sisters to eat and to drink with them.
5After days of feasting had passed,[3] Job would send and consecrate
them. Rising early in the morning, he offered a whole burnt offering for
each of them, for Job thought: "Perhaps my children sinned and cursed[4]
God in their hearts." Thus did Job regularly behave.

1. Literally "on his day" (*yômô*), likely indicating the day of each son's birth. If it does mean simply "their day," it could indicate that they had a party each day of the week, one for each of the seven sons.

2. A hendiadys, lit. "they sent and invited" (*šālĕḥû wĕqārĕʾû*).

3. The verb's root is *nqp*, and it is Hiphil. The meaning of the root is "to go around," in this case referring to the "going around" or "passing" of time.

4. Thus I translate the euphemistic (or antiphrastic—here the nonliteral use of the word would be for ironic effect) use of the verb *brk*, which means "bless." Other examples of this use of *brk* for "curse" may be found in Job 1:11; 2:5, 9; 1 Kings 21:10, 13; Ps. 10:3. This use of *brk* is a way of distancing the common word for "curse" (perhaps *qll*) from "God."

6One day the sons of God came to stand before Yahweh, and the accuser was also in their midst. **7**And Yahweh said to the accuser: "Where have you come from?" And the accuser answered Yahweh and said: "From roaming the earth and patrolling it." **8**And Yahweh said to the accuser, "Have you considered[5] my servant Job? For there is no one like him on the earth, an innocent and virtuous man, fearing God and turning away from evil." **9**And the accuser answered Yahweh and said: "Is it for no good reason that Job fears God? **10**Don't you place a hedge around him, his household, and all that belongs to him? You bless all the work of his hands. His livestock burst forth on the earth. **11**However, send forth your hand and afflict all that belongs to him and see if he doesn't curse you to your face." **12**And Yahweh said to the accuser, "All that he has is in your hand, only don't send your hand against him." And the accuser went out from before Yahweh.

13And the day came when his sons and his daughters were eating and drinking wine in the house of their brother, the firstborn. **14**And a messenger came to Job and said, "The oxen were plowing and the donkeys were feeding beside them, **15**and Sabeans fell (on them) and took them, and they struck the servants with the sword. Only I alone escaped to tell you."

16While this person was still speaking, another came and said, "A great fire[6] fell from heaven and burned among the flocks and the servants, and they were consumed. Only I alone escaped to tell you."

17While this person was still speaking, another came and said, "The Chaldeans formed three bands of raiding parties and attacked your camels and took them away, and they struck the servants with the sword. Only I alone escaped to tell you."

18While this person was still speaking, another came and said, "Your sons and your daughters were eating and drinking wine in the house of their brother, the firstborn. **19**A mighty wind came across the wilderness and struck the four corners of the house. It fell on the young ones, and they died. Only I alone escaped to tell you."

20Job rose up and tore his robe and shaved his head and fell to the ground and worshiped, **21**saying,

"Naked I came from my mother's womb,
  and naked I will return there.
22Yahweh gave and Yahweh took,
  blessed be the name of Yahweh."

23In all of this, Job did not sin, and he did not ascribe wrongdoing to God.

2:1 One day the sons of God came to stand before Yahweh, and the accuser was also in their midst[7] to stand before Yahweh.[8] **2**And Yahweh

5. Literally "have you set your heart on" (*hăśamtā libbĕkā ʿal*).
6. Or "a fire of God." Sometimes "G/god" (*ʾĕlōhîm*) is used as a superlative.
7. Spelled *bĕtôkām* in 1:6 and *bĕtōkām* in 2:1.
8. "To stand before Yahweh" (*lĕhityaṣṣēb ʿal-yhwh*) is not found in 1:6.

said to the accuser, "Where[9] have you come from?" And the accuser answered Yahweh and said, "From roaming the earth and patrolling it." **3**And Yahweh said to the accuser, "Have you considered[10] my servant Job? For there is no one like him on earth, an innocent and virtuous man, fearing God and turning away from evil. He still maintains his innocence, though you enticed me to injure him for no good reason. **4**And the accuser answered Yahweh and said, "Skin for skin. People will give all they have for their life. **5**However, send forth your hand and afflict his bones and his flesh and see if he doesn't curse[11] you to your face." **6**And Yahweh said to the accuser, "He is in your control. Only preserve his life."

7And the accuser went out from the presence of Yahweh, and he struck Job with horrible boils from the soles of his feet up to his head. **8**He took for himself a shard of pottery to scrape himself, and he sat in the midst of the dust.

9And his wife said to him, "Are you still maintaining your innocence? Curse God and die." **10**But he said to her, "You are speaking like one of the foolish women. Should we receive good from God and not receive evil?" In all this, Job did not sin with his lips.

11The three friends of Job heard of all this trouble that came to him, and they each went from his place: Eliphaz the Temanite and Bildad the Shuhite and Zophar the Naamathite. They consulted together to go to mourn with him and console him. **12**They lifted their eyes from afar, and they did not recognize him. Then they lifted their voices and wept, and each one tore his robe, and they sprinkled dust on their heads toward heaven. **13**They sat with him on the ground for seven days and seven nights, not uttering a word, for they saw that his pain was exceedingly great.

Interpretation

The book of Job opens with a prologue written in prose. The end of Job is also written in prose, while the vast middle is poetic, which creates a literary envelope that provides a strong sense of opening and closure to the story. This literary feature has also given rise to speculation about the history of composition of the book, since the prologue and epilogue together provide a kind of simple folktale (see "Authorship and Date" in the introduction).

In the final form of the canonical book, the function of the prologue is to introduce the main characters and the plot complication that provides the background for the extensive discussion and debate that follow in the poetic middle.

The first person the narrator introduces to readers is the central character, Job. The purpose of his introduction is to establish beyond all doubt that Job

9. *Mēʾayin* in 1:7; *ʾêy mizzeh* in 2:2.
10. Compare the idiom in 1:8, but here the preposition is *ʾel*, not *ʿal*.
11. See the footnote on this term in 1:5.

is innocent. The narrator says it outright (1:1), and he has God say it (1:8; 2:3). Even the accuser (Hebrew *haśśāṭān,* "the satan") does not doubt it. What the latter questions is Job's motivation. Does he obey God only to be rewarded, or is his piety disinterested?

Some scholars believe that here the accuser turns the heavenly court into a legal one as he takes the role of prosecuting attorney.[12] Job is the defendant who is accused of a mercenary faith. However, there are deficiencies with this view of the scene (see "Legal Metaphors: Is the Book of Job the Account of a Trial?" in the introduction). There is an absence of legal language here, and it is better to understand the relationship between God and the accuser as that of king and one of his spies giving a report. God initiates the discussion about Job, leading the accuser to issue his challenge.

The accuser talks God into two rounds of tests, and at the end of the chapter Job stands firm. Indeed, the end of the second phase announces, "In all this, Job did not sin with his lips" (2:10b). However, it may be wrong to think of the testing as completed and passed at this moment. God does not step in immediately to reward his faithful servant and rectify his situation. On the contrary, Job continues to sit on the ash heap for seven days in the company of three new characters, his friends Eliphaz, Bildad, and Zophar. Indeed, the story is just beginning at this point.

> **1**There was a man in the land of Uz whose name was Job, and that man
> was innocent and virtuous, fearing God and turning away from evil. **2**And
> seven sons and three daughters were born to him. **3**His property included
> seven thousand sheep, and three thousand camels, and five hundred pair
> of cattle, and five hundred donkeys. He had an extremely large workforce.
> He was a great man among all the people of the East.

1:1–3. *The introduction of Job, part 1: His character and wealth*. The very first words of the book introduce the main human character, a man named Job. Clines points out that the specific manner by which Job is introduced ("there was a man . . .") is only paralleled in parables (2 Sam. 12:1) and fables (2 Kings 14:9) in the Bible. He also indicates that this does not decide the issue of whether Job was a real person; rather, it is a way of showing that he is not a part of the mainstream of Israel's redemptive-historical story.[13]

Job is first of all identified as living in the land of Uz. While we are not certain exactly where Uz is located, we do know it is outside the land of Israel. Good reasons exist to think Uz is a city in the area known later as Edom: Lam. 4:21 uses it in parallel with Edom, and a man whose name is Uz is found in a genealogy of Edom (Gen. 36:28; 1 Chron. 1:42). Job may be a descendant of

12. For the most recent and extensive treatment, see Magdalene, *On the Scales of Righteousness*.

13. Clines, *Job 1–20*, 9.

Abraham, since "Job" can be construed as a Hebrew name (see below). However, though possible, it is more likely that Job is a non-Hebrew who worships the true God (similar to Melchizedek and Jethro). That some of Job's friends have names associated with the Edomite genealogy (see below) further supports the idea that Job himself is connected with the land of Edom.[14] This conclusion stands in spite of the fact that two texts (Gen. 10:23; 1 Chron. 1:17) associate the name Uz with Aram and thus perhaps point to northern Mesopotamia.

The name "Job" (*ʾîyôb*) is of uncertain meaning. It has been interpreted to mean "Where is my father?" If so, "father" likely indicates God. On the other hand, it has also been connected to a Hebrew verb that means "to hate" or "to be an enemy."[15] This verb provides the base for the noun "enemy" (*ʾōyēb*) and, if the association is correct, may be explained by the fact that for a period Job becomes an enemy of God.[16]

After giving the main character's name and telling the reader where he lived, the narrator proceeds to the more important task of describing his character. He was "innocent" (*tām*) and "virtuous" (*yāšār*), fearing God and turning away from evil. Significantly, this language has close affinities with the description of the wise in the book of Proverbs ("innocent": Prov. 2:7, 21; 11:3, 20; 13:6; 19:1; 20:7; 28:6, 10, 18; 29:10; "virtuous": 1:3; 2:7, 21; 8:6, 9; 11:3, 6; 12:6; 14:11; 15:8; 16:13; 20:11; 21:2, 8; 23:16; 29:10). In Proverbs these terms refer to people who do what is morally correct. They are the ones who heed the commands of the father and gain wisdom. Their lives are largely marked by ethical rightness and legal obedience.

The preamble to the book of Proverbs states that the "fear of Yahweh" is the beginning of knowledge (see also especially 9:10, but also 1:29; 2:5; 3:7; 8:13; 10:27; 14:2, 26, 27; 15:16, 33; 16:6; 19:23; 22:4; 23:17; 24:21; 28:14; 29:25; 31:30). In 1:7 as well as elsewhere, the fear of God is coupled with turning from evil (most pointedly, 3:7). Here "fear" does not mean horror, the type of emotion that makes a person run away. However, the common idea that here "fear" is close to the English "respect" is not correct. Closer is the idea of awe. Those who fear Yahweh know their proper place in creation. They are not the center of creation; God is much greater. The person who fears God thus is willing to listen to God and to obey God; in this way it is the beginning of wisdom/knowledge.

Thus Job is immediately characterized as the epitome of the wise as described by the book of Proverbs. God himself will affirm this characterization in Job 1:8. The reader is left in no doubt concerning Job's character. He is one of the godly wise.

14. Perhaps Alter (*Wisdom Books*, 11) is correct to think that the poet chose Uz (*ʿûṣ*) because of its connection with the Hebrew root *yʿṣ*, "to advise, counsel."

15. See T. F. Williams, *NIDOTTE* 1:365–71.

16. This is the view supported by Weiss (*Story of Job's Beginning*, 20), who points out that Job 13:24 uses the verb *ʾyb* as Job charges God with considering him an enemy.

Verse 2 now describes Job's family. He has seven sons and three daughters. No wife is mentioned, but of course she is implied by the birth of the children. We know that Job had a wife because she (in)famously speaks to him in 2:9. The children are described in a way that shows he has a large and, for an ancient Near Eastern context, well-balanced family. Ten children constitute a good-sized family, and that there are more boys than girls also would be considered a blessing. Indeed, that there are seven sons is especially significant because seven is the number of completeness.[17] His quiver is indeed full (Pss. 127; 128).

In short, the description of his family indicates that he is living the good life, and this theme is continued in v. 3, which enumerates his wealth. That his wealth is described in terms of number of animals, rather than land or precious metals, does point to an early, patriarchal setting. A large workforce supported him. This may point to slaveholdings, but not necessarily. The summative statement that he was a great man among the people of the East could be surmised from the description. That he is compared to those in the East adds even more support to the idea that he was from a place like Edom, which was east of the promised land, though as Clines points out it could also refer to the more northern region where the Arameans dwelt (Gen. 29:1), and even Solomon could be called one of the "sons of the East" (1 Kings 4:30).[18] Weiss has suggested that Job's description as a "great man" should be taken in regard to his wisdom rather than his wealth, though it is his wealth that has just been described.[19]

That such a godly man was so prosperous would not be surprising. After all, Proverbs as well as the very structure of the covenant (as shown by the book of Deuteronomy) would lead one to expect that such a man would be rewarded in this way (see "Suffering: Job and Retribution Theology" in the introduction).

4His sons went and prepared a banquet on their birthday, and they sent invitations to their three sisters to eat and to drink with them. **5**After days of feasting had passed, Job would send and consecrate them. Rising early in the morning, he offered a whole burnt offering for each of them, for Job thought: "Perhaps my children sinned and cursed God in their hearts." Thus did Job regularly behave.

1:4–5. *The introduction of Job, part 2: His piety.* The narrative of Job continues by describing the joyful unity of his family as well as his punctilious piety. Job's sons celebrated their respective birthdays with all their siblings, male and female. The way the group is described it is likely that none of

17. It "indicates the ideal family" (Cornelius, "Job," 249). Indeed, the ideal of having seven sons is behind 1 Sam. 2:5 as well as Ruth 4:15.

18. Clines, *Job 1–20*, 15.

19. Weiss, *Story*, 27.

them is married. But the fact that they have seven multiday banquets during the year indicates that they have wealth. The description of the banquet also implies celebration and happiness, conditions that will soon contrast with the tragedy that lies ahead.

The real focus of the description, though, is not on the parties, but rather on Job's actions after the celebrations. Even though there were no indications of spiritual trouble, Job covered his children's bases by offering sacrifices just in case they had sinned. Job worries that his children may have somehow "cursed" God. As mentioned in the footnote to the translation, the word translated "curse" here is the common word for "bless" (*brk*) but is used as a euphemism in order to keep the usual word for "curse" distant from "God." In this way, the storyteller is showing the same kind of religious fastidiousness that Job himself shows.

Job acts as the head of a patriarchal family by offering the sacrifices himself. At this time, there are no priests. It would be the patriarch's responsibility to lead his family's sacrificial devotions. That Job offers whole burnt offerings (the *ʿōlâ*) indicates that the purpose was primarily atonement (at least according to its significance in the time of Moses; see Lev. 1). Burnt offerings preceded Moses as early as Noah in the scriptural text (see Gen. 8:20). Abraham was prepared to offer his son Isaac as a burnt offering, but God provided a substitute lamb in his place (Gen. 22).

One wonders, though, how effective such a sacrifice would be when offered not by the purported sinner but rather by another. As far as we know, Job's children were not even aware of their father's activity, and atonement only took place when it was connected to repentance, signified in the ritual by laying hands on the animal's head.

However, the story does not appear to be critical of Job.[20] The narrator gives no indication that Job is being overly concerned here. Just the opposite.[21] More likely, the narrator is continuing to present a portrait of Job as "innocent and virtuous." Apparently, too, Job's detailed observance of ritual was not just connected to these events. Rather, the sacrifices for his children were just illustrations of the way Job "regularly" behaved. We should also note that Job's role as sacrificial intercessor here finds its counterpart at the end of the book when he offers sacrifices on behalf of his three friends (42:8–9).

---

[6]One day the sons of God came to stand before Yahweh, and the accuser was also in their midst. [7]And Yahweh said to the accuser: "Where have

20. Contra Brenner ("Job the Pious?"), who believes that Job's obsession with sacrifice "just in case" is a sign that he is not pious.

21. Interestingly, Mason (*Gospel according to Job*, 26) parallels Job's actions here to Jesus when on the cross he says, "Father, forgive them; for they know not what they do" (Luke 23:34 KJV).

you come from?" And the accuser answered Yahweh and said: "From roaming the earth and patrolling it."

1:6–7. *The introduction of Yahweh and the accuser*. The introduction of main characters of the book continues, though Yahweh appears in person only at the beginning and end of the book and the accuser only at the beginning. However, it is their interaction that sets the plot in motion.

The setting is heaven itself and specifically the divine assembly. "Sons of God" refers to God's angelic associates (see similar terminology in Gen. 6:2, 4; Deut. 32:8; Pss. 29:1; 89:7). They come to stand before him as the servants of the king would stand before their ruler, awaiting instructions and giving reports. In other words, we have here a description of the divine council or heavenly court. Specific attention quickly turns to one member of the heavenly court known as the accuser.

This figure has been the source of much discussion. Confusion arises over the identity of this figure because in Hebrew he is called *haśśāṭān*. The verb *śṭn* means "to accuse" or "to be an adversary," but as may clearly be seen from the transliteration of the Hebrew, it also eventually is used as a proper name for the devil. Thus many English versions give the impression that this figure is the devil (NIV, NLT,[22] NRSV). However, there are significant reasons to doubt that this refers to the devil. First, the word has a definite article prefixed to it (lit. "the *satan*"), thus precluding the idea it is a proper name. It would be equivalent to saying "the George." There is also a theological issue in that it would be strange in the extreme to imagine the devil as a member of the heavenly court and God as having a conversation with his enemy in heaven, not to speak of the problem of the devil's convincing God to harm Job. It is much more likely that this figure is one of God's angelic associates,[23] who takes the position of a devil's advocate, so to speak, but not Satan himself.[24] True, Satan gets his name from the fact that he is the ultimate accuser, the ultimate adversary, but that does not make all accusers Satan. Nor is all accusation evil. This accuser is about to challenge Job's authenticity as a God-fearer, and at this point it is not yet clear whether he is making an accurate accusation.

Thus the accuser is a member of the heavenly court, an agent of Yahweh, who is reporting on his patrolling through the earth.[25] The human analogy

22. The NLT translates redundantly: "the Accuser, Satan."

23. Numbers 22:22 describes an "angel of Yahweh" who took a stand in the road as Balaam and his donkey set out in order to act "as his adversary" (*śāṭān*). This provides an interesting parallel since it connects an angel with adversarial action described by the word *śāṭān*. For a full treatment of Satan in the OT, see P. Day, *Adversary in Heaven*.

24. Kutz (*Old Greek of Job*) points out that the Old Greek likely initiates the common identification of "the accuser" with the devil by translating the Hebrew as *diabolos*.

25. Note should be taken of Seow (*Job*), citing Weiss (*Story of Job's Beginning*), who takes "the Satan" as "a hypostasis, an extension of divine personality. More specifically, he is a projection

would be a spy's reporting to his commander what he has discovered during his latest mission. Indeed, Pope makes a specific connection with Persian spies who were called "The King's Eye" and "The King's Ear."[26] The text does not indicate what he was on the lookout for, but in the next section the conversation turns, at Yahweh's instigation, to the character of Job's piety.

> [8]And Yahweh said to the accuser, "Have you considered my servant Job? For there is no one like him on the earth, an innocent and virtuous man, fearing God and turning away from evil." [9]And the accuser answered Yahweh and said: "Is it for no good reason that Job fears God? [10]Don't you place a hedge around him, his household, and all that belongs to him? You bless all the work of his hands. His livestock burst forth on the earth. [11]However, send forth your hand and afflict all that belongs to him and see if he doesn't curse you to your face." [12]And Yahweh said to the accuser, "All that he has is in your hand, only don't send your hand against him." And the accuser went out from before Yahweh.

1:8–12. *Testing Job's motivation, part 1.* After learning that the accuser has been roaming the earth, God asks if he has happened to run across Job. He even calls Job his "servant," a title reserved for those who do his will, whether consciously, as Job clearly does (see Moses [Exod. 14:31]; David [2 Sam. 7:5, 8]; Isaiah [Isa. 20:3]), or unconsciously (see Nebuchadnezzar [Jer. 25:9]). According to God, Job is unique in his wisdom, defined as being innocent and virtuous, fearing God and turning away from evil. The narrator has already informed the reader of this as early as 1:1, but now we hear it from the mouth of God. From this point on, the reader, who gains information that none of the characters possesses, cannot question Job's wisdom, godliness, or integrity. Though the three friends and Elihu will question his wisdom based on the fact that Job suffers, they do not know what we know from the lips of God: Job is the paragon of wisdom. In this, the accuser agrees. He does not object to this characterization of Job; rather he questions Job's motivation: "Is it for no good reason . . . ?" The accusation is that Job is interested in God and God's ways not for God's sake but for Job's own prosperity. God protects Job from trouble (places a hedge around him) and showers him with material blessings. The cattle are even said to "burst forth on the earth," implying a rapid increase (see similar use in Gen. 30:30, 43). Job is virtuous and innocent for his own benefit, not for God's.

---

of divine doubt about human integrity that is held in tension with divine trust. The dialogue between YHWH and the Adversary is, therefore, an externalizing of the inner-conflict between divine trust and divine doubt." This is not only doubt about Yahweh but also, according to Seow, the doubt of Yahweh.

26. Pope, *Job*, 10.

Reading the accuser's charge, one can legitimately question why God would care if Job were motivated to worship him in order to achieve material prosperity. After all, Proverbs often explicitly appeals to people to act in a godly way in order to prosper. One example will suffice:

> Honor the Lord with your wealth,
> with the firstfruits of all your crops;
> then your barns will be filled to overflowing,
> and your vats will brim over with new wine. (Prov. 3:9–10 NIV)

In other words, Proverbs often seems to motivate good behavior by offering reward. However, this passage describes what is typically, but not always, the case. The Bible does use the possibility of reward as a motivation for godly behavior, but nonetheless expects godly behavior no matter what. Thus Joseph, for instance, acts as an exemplar of wisdom when he resists the advances of the adultery-minded wife of Potiphar (Gen. 39; see Prov. 5–7) and does not protest God's unfairness when he gets thrown in jail rather than promoted.

The accuser accordingly suggests a test. Will Job act like Joseph, or will he abandon God? The accuser speaks as if he thinks Job is only motivated to get rich and fully expects him to forget God if the blessings are taken away. He expects him to curse[27] God.

But God is willing to bet[28] on the opposite, so he issues permission to the accuser to harm everything around Job, but not Job himself. As we will see, this is just a preliminary test; if he fails it, though, there will be no need to go to the next level. The accuser accepts these terms, at least for the moment, and sets out to wreak havoc with Job's surroundings and those close to him.

13And the day came when his sons and his daughters were eating and drinking wine in the house of their brother, the firstborn. **14**And a messenger came to Job and said, "The oxen were plowing and the donkeys were feeding beside them, **15**and Sabeans fell (on them) and took them, and they struck the servants with the sword. Only I alone escaped to tell you."

16While this person was still speaking, another came and said, "A great fire fell from heaven and burned among the flocks and the servants, and they were consumed. Only I alone escaped to tell you."

17While this person was still speaking, another came and said, "The Chaldeans formed three bands of raiding parties and attacked your camels and took them away, and they struck the servants with the sword. Only I alone escaped to tell you."

27. For the use of *brk* (lit. "to bless") for "curse," see footnote on 1:5.

28. Hartley (*Job*, 74) objects to calling this arrangement a "bet" or "wager" since no money is involved. However, one can bet/wager something other than money. In this case, the bet has to do with who is correct in the assessment of Job's character.

> 18 While this person was still speaking, another came and said, "Your sons and your daughters were eating and drinking wine in the house of their brother, the firstborn. 19 A mighty wind came across the wilderness and struck the four corners of the house. It fell on the young ones, and they died. Only I alone escaped to tell you."

1:13–19. *Four disasters.* The accuser left God's presence to act on God's permission to hurt everything around Job, though not to harm Job himself. Accordingly, Job experienced four major disasters on a single day, and on his oldest son's birthday at that. The first and the third were tragedies caused by human agents, while the second and fourth were natural disasters.

In all four, only one person survived the ordeal. We are probably to read a deliberate strategy on the part of the accuser to leave one person in order to bring the horrible news to Job. We should also note the repetition of the phrase "While this person was still speaking" at the beginning of 1:16, 17, and 18. Though the bad news came in waves, it came essentially all at once. One can only imagine the horrible psychological effect of hearing this news in rapid succession.[29]

The first attack resulted in the decimation of Job's donkeys and cattle. Job's wealth was counted in the number of livestock, and 1:3 noted that he had five hundred pair of oxen and five hundred donkeys. The Sabeans, a tribal people from southern Arabia (Isa. 45:14; Ezek. 23:42 KJV; Joel 3:8), stole them. The servants caring for and guarding the animals were killed.

The second attack was against the flocks and the servants who guarded them. Job 1:3 numbered Job's sheep at seven thousand. A great ball of fire (lit. "a fire of God") came from heaven and consumed them all. "Of God" is likely a superlative, not to be taken as literally from God; but God, we know, did permit it. One is tempted to picture this fire from heaven as lightning, but if so, it was indeed a supernatural lightning to wreak such damage.[30]

The third attack was from another foreign people (see Sabeans above), the Chaldeans, known in historical sources as a first-millennium, Aramaic-speaking tribe that lived in southern Mesopotamia. The Chaldeans achieved prominence in the late seventh and sixth centuries BC as the group, under Kings Nabopolassar and Nebuchadnezzar, that restored Babylon to its status as a world empire. As far as we know, "Chaldean" was not an ethnic or tribal name at the time that the action of the book of Job was putatively set. "Chaldean" is anachronistically used in Gen. 11:31 in reference to Abraham's original homeland.[31] In short, the name Chaldean points to an origin of these invaders from southern Mesopotamia. They succeeded in taking Job's camels

29. See Smick, "Job," 716.
30. See 1 Kings 18:38 for similar terminology.
31. For significance for dating, see "Authorship and Date" in the introduction.

(numbering three thousand, according to 1:3) and killing the servants who were caring for them.

The final disaster was the worst of all. It killed the "young ones," namely, the sons and daughters of Job. They were killed in the height of celebration, during one of the birthday parties noted in 1:4. Their end came when a strong wind blew the house down on top of them. Cornelius points out that this is not to be taken as a reference to the khamsin, or sirocco (a devastating hot wind from the east), since it struck all four sides of the house at once.[32] Such a wind is not natural, and thus its supernatural origin is made clear.

After these four disasters, Job's wealth was gone and his family decimated. He himself, however, was not harmed.

20Job rose up and tore his robe and shaved his head and fell to the
ground and worshiped, **21**saying,

"Naked I came from my mother's womb,
and naked I will return there.
22Yahweh gave and Yahweh took,
blessed be the name of Yahweh."

23In all of this, Job did not sin, and he did not ascribe wrongdoing to God.

1:20–23. *Job passes the first test.* The news Job had just heard was devastating. His wealth and his children were gone. All he had left at this point were his wife and his health. His initial reaction indicates his grief. Tearing one's clothes[33] (see also Gen. 37:34; Josh. 7:6; 2 Sam. 1:11; 3:31; 13:31; Ezra 9:3, 5; Esther 4:1) and shaving one's head[34] (Isa. 22:12; Jer. 7:29; 16:6; 41:5; 47:5; 48:37; Ezek. 7:18; Amos 8:10) are signs of mourning. But when he speaks, he does not lament, complain, or weep. Rather, he resigns himself to his fate, which he acknowledges God has brought on him. But he goes further than resignation. He actually worships the God who has taken away that which is dear to him.

Everything that he had had was a gift from God, given to him during his life. He came into the world with nothing (naked). He knows that when he dies he can't take it with him. That Yahweh has taken from him what Yahweh himself had given him is within Yahweh's rights. Thus he does not rail against God, but rather he blesses his name.

32. Cornelius, "Job," 253.

33. The word *mĕʿîl* indicates an outer garment, and therefore I have translated "robe."

34. Leviticus 21:5 forbids priests from shaving their heads, but Job is not a priest, so this in and of itself does not indicate that Job is a non-Israelite (contra Alter, *Wisdom Books*, 14). Deuteronomy 14:1 prohibits the people of Israel from cutting themselves or shaving the front of their heads for the dead. It has been speculated that the latter refers to pulling the hair out, thus lacerating the flesh; see Christensen, *Deuteronomy 1:1–21:9*, 291.

The same thought may be found in Eccles. 5:15, when the Teacher (Qohelet) observes, "As he left his mother's womb, so he will return, going as he came—naked. And he will take nothing with him from his toil that he is able to bring with him into his possession." This observation, however, leads Qohelet to complain, "This indeed is a sickening evil" (5:16), which provides a contrast with Job.[35]

The narrator ends the episode by evaluating Job's response to the first test. We might be tempted to say that he should have railed against God (was he overly repressed?), but the narrator ends that discussion before it begins when he pronounces that "Job did not sin," sinning being defined in this case as ascribing wrongdoing to God.

Thus Job passes the test. However, as we read on, we see that the process has just begun.

1One day the sons of God came to stand before Yahweh, and the accuser was also in their midst to stand before Yahweh. **2**And Yahweh said to the accuser, "Where have you come from?" And the accuser answered Yahweh and said, "From roaming the earth and patrolling it." **3**And Yahweh said to the accuser, "Have you considered my servant Job? For there is no one like him on earth, an innocent and virtuous man, fearing God and turning away from evil. He still maintains his innocence, though you enticed me to injure him for no good reason." **4**And the accuser answered Yahweh and said, "Skin for skin. People will give all they have for their life. **5**However, send forth your hand and afflict his bones and his flesh and see if he doesn't curse you to your face." **6**And Yahweh said to the accuser, "He is in your control. Only preserve his life."

2:1–6. *Testing Job's motivation, part 2.* The first chapter contains the first test of Job, a test that he successfully completed. But Job's suffering has only just started. Chapter 2 begins again in the heavenly court. Verses 1–3 are essentially the same as 1:6–8. (Minor changes are indicated in the footnotes to the translation above.) The repetition gives the sense of replay. It prepares us for another round of the test.

The only significant difference comes at the end of v. 3, when God proudly claims to have won the wager: "He still maintains his innocence, though you enticed me to injure him for no good reason." God had said Job would not abandon his relationship with him even if his "rewards" were taken away, and sure enough, Job persisted. Note that God acknowledges that he was moved to injure Job by the accuser's persuasive speech. He does not say that he allows the accuser to injure him (though he did use the accuser as his agent), but takes responsibility himself. He was the one who injured him by removing his wealth and killing his children. He further acknowledges that such actions

35. See Longman, *Ecclesiastes*, 167.

were taken "for no good reason." But there was a reason; it was to demonstrate Job's disinterested piety. The phrase means that the reason for his suffering was not grounded in any fault in Job himself. Job presented no motivation for God to hurt him.[36]

Even so, the accuser is not satisfied with the results of the first test and so presses for a second round. In the previous round, God had forbidden the accuser to touch Job personally. He could remove from him the things in which he found joy, his wealth and his children, but the accuser could not harm Job physically. The accuser now argues that God had not yet challenged Job's piety. His very cynical view is that people only really, deep down, care about themselves. That is the explicit meaning of 2:4b, "People will give all they have for their life," and is probably the meaning of the enigmatic expression that precedes it, "Skin for skin." In other words, v. 4b explicates the meaning of what is probably a proverbial saying whose exact sense is lost to us.[37]

The accuser then suggests that harming Job will lead him to fail the test ("curse you [God] to your face"). God accepts the challenge, giving permission to harm Job, only restricting the accuser from killing him. The latter would, in any case, render the test moot, since a dead Job could not bless or curse God.

> [7]And the accuser went out from the presence of Yahweh, and he struck Job with horrible boils from the soles of his feet up to his head. [8]He took for himself a shard of pottery to scrape himself, and he sat in the midst of the dust.

2:7–8. *Job's affliction.* As in the first test, the accuser went out from God's presence (1:12) to cause trouble for Job. In the four earlier disasters against Job's property and children, the accuser is not specifically mentioned as the agent, though it is implied. Here he is specifically named as the one who gave Job irritating and painful boils all over his body. They must have been excruciating. Job's wife's advice to curse God and die implies that death would

36. See also Konkel, "Job," 39. Contra Shields ("Malevolent or Mysterious?" 269), who suggests the *ḥinnām* indicates not that "Job's suffering was without cause but instead that the Satan's accusation had been shown to be without value."

37. Pope (*Job*, 20) advocates the view of Tur-Sinai that the phrase should be translated "skin after skin" in the sense that the accuser wants to "get under Job's skin" after only touching him on the surface in the first test. Others (as suggested by Hartley, *Job*, 80n4) want to take the preposition as "for" and understand it as analogous to "an eye for an eye." That is, the accuser believed that Job would give another person's skin (his servants and children) in exchange for his own. Whatever the exact significance of this proverb, its general meaning is explicated by the following line, and that seems to conform more to the second approach than the first. That said, Clines's view (*Job 1–20*, 44–45) has much to commend it: the proverbial expression does not look back and compare the first and second test but rather looks forward and states that if Job's skin is harmed, then Job will be after Yahweh's skin. While this view is tempting to adopt, the sentence that follows the proverb does seem to function as an explanatory parallel to it, as argued above, and thus leads me to believe that it does reflect on the previous test.

have been a relief from his present stricken condition (2:9b). Even so, when compared with over fifty lines that describe the affliction of the main character in the second tablet of the "Poem of the Righteous Sufferer," the mention of the boils seems spare.

The word "boil" (*šĕḥîn*) indicates a localized inflammation of the skin. Its center is hard and contains pus. It is, generally speaking, a skin infection and is the subject of "skin laws" in the purity code of Leviticus (see especially Lev. 13:18–20, 23).[38] Their devastating effect is indicated by the fact that the sixth Egyptian plague was boils (Exod. 9). Hezekiah was stricken with a boil that threatened to kill him, but the Lord healed him after Isaiah directed his attendants to apply a poultice of figs to the boil (2 Kings 20:7; Isa. 38:21). R. K. Harrison tries to define the boil and its cause more specifically,[39] but such attempts seem futile and are speculative.[40] The point is that Job's boils were injurious and threatened death. He tried to relieve the itch and pain through scratching them with a broken clay pot ("a shard of pottery"). Such treatment likely resulted in breaking the boils open. Sitting in dust raises connections with other texts that imply either judgment or mourning, perhaps both. In Lamentations the poet, speaking in the persona of the "man of affliction," talks about how God "trampled me in the dust" (Lam. 3:16 NIV). Pouring dust on one's head was a well-known ritual of mourning (Josh. 7:6; 2 Sam. 1:2). Since Adam was created from the dust of the ground (Gen. 2:7), that Job is sitting in the dust reminds the reader of his mortality.

> **9**And his wife said to him, "Are you still maintaining your innocence? Curse God and die." **10**But he said to her, "You are speaking like one of the foolish women. Should we receive good from God and not receive evil?" In all this, Job did not sin with his lips.

2:9–10. *Job's foolish wife.* Job's wife[41] becomes an unknowing agent of the accuser when she urges her husband to end his piety (maintaining his innocence) and curse God. Notice that she does not deny his innocence. Rather, she chastises him for persisting in it. It is hard to read between the lines, but

38. It is notable and often missed that a person covered head to toe by skin disease was pronounced ritually clean by the law (see Lev. 13:12–17). Such a person, after all, was "whole" and not a hybrid, partly skin-diseased and partly healthy. What would render Job ritually unclean is that he is oozing pus, thus breaking the bounds between the inside and the outside.

39. Harrison, *NIDOTTE* 4:81; see also references in Clines, *Job 1–20*, 48–49.

40. I agree with Good (*In Turns of Tempest*, 52): "Job's malady cannot be identified medically."

41. Job's wife is not given a name in the biblical book, but she is called Dinah in the Targum to the book of Job (see also *Gen. Rab.* 19.2; 57.4; *b. Baba Batra* 15b). Clines (*Job 1–20*, 53) suggests that this is "because Job says (v. 10) that she speaks as one of the 'foolish women' and Dinah the daughter of Jacob was one with whom 'folly' had been done (Gen. 34:7)." In *T. Job* 25.1 her name is Sitis, which is connected with the Greek word *Ausitis*/*Ausitidi*, the LXX translation of "Uz" in Job 1:1; 42:17.

she herself may be exasperated that God has not kept her pious husband in the favored condition that he deserves. Unlike the three friends, she does not counsel him to repent. In her eyes, Job is innocent. She likely believes that death is better than the suffering he is now enduring. He can end it all by cursing God, who would then, presumably, kill him.

Job, however, will have none of this kind of talk. He accuses her of being a fool. Minimally, this charge entails the belief that she does not know much about the skill of living. Job suffers; now how can he alleviate his suffering? His wife's remedy is foolish. But the accusation that she is like one of the foolish women is probably much more serious. She is like one who has no fear of God (Prov. 1:7), one who acts as if God does not exist (Pss. 14:1; 53:1). He has adopted the stance of the patient sufferer, the one who quietly waits for God's restoration. Lamentations 3:22–33 describes such a sufferer. The "man of affliction" asks, "Is it not from the mouth of the Most High that both calamities and good things come?" (3:38 NIV). The difference between Job and the "man" in Lamentations is that the latter acknowledges that he suffers due to sin (Lam. 3:39 NIV, "Why should any living man complain when punished for his sins?").[42]

The passage ends with the statement that Job did not sin—with his lips. While ancient rabbis believed that this hints at a sin of the heart,[43] this is unlikely. The point of the story is that Job ends these two tests by staying firmly in relationship with God.

> **11**The three friends of Job heard of all this trouble that came to him, and they each went from his place: Eliphaz the Temanite and Bildad the Shuhite and Zophar the Naamathite. They consulted together to go to mourn with him and console him. **12**They lifted their eyes from afar, and they did not recognize him. Then they lifted their voices and wept, and each one tore his robe, and they sprinkled dust on their heads toward heaven. **13**They sat with him on the ground for seven days and seven nights, not uttering a word, for they saw that his pain was exceedingly great.

2:11–13. *Three good friends.* The final paragraph of the prologue introduces Job's three friends, major players in the chapters to follow (Job 3–27). Contemporary readers of the book know Eliphaz, Bildad, and Zophar more from the dialogues and God's evaluation of them in the epilogue (42:7–9) than from their actions in this context. Before they begin their blistering attacks on Job, they sit with him for seven days, displaying great sensitivity and empathy.[44] They do not judge him or berate him; they simply mourn alongside him. Indeed, though we do not know the exact location of their homes, except for Teman, which

42. See "Being Silent in Suffering" after the comments on Job 40.

43. So *b. Baba Batra* 16a.

44. Davis ("Sufferer's Wisdom," 126–27) points out that this is the origin of the Jewish mourning ritual known as "sitting shiva (or seven)."

was a major site in what is later called Edom (Jer. 49:7, 20; Ezek. 25:13; Amos 1:12; Obad. 9), they apparently had to travel some distance to be with him.

The meaning of the three friends' names does not appear to have any significance in relationship to the plot or the argument. It is a matter of curiosity that Esau (also known as Edom, the name given to the region) had a son named Eliphaz and that Eliphaz had a son named Teman, according to Gen. 36:10–11. The region of Edom and in particular Teman was known as a locus of wisdom (Jer. 49:7), which is significant because Eliphaz will later set himself up as a wise man over against Job. As for the other names of the friends and their hometowns, their meaning is speculative and of no relevance to the plot.[45]

They come to Job as a group even though they departed from different locations ("they consulted together"). The significance of this observation is that they really act as a team rather than as individuals in the dialogues that follow. They represent not three different viewpoints but a common viewpoint as they stand united over against what they perceive to be Job's presumption.

On their approach, the friends do not even recognize Job. This observation heightens our understanding of the depth of Job's physical suffering. It has changed him to the point that even friends do not recognize him.

It should be pointed out that by the time the three friends arrive on the scene, Job may have suffered for some time. Indeed, Job 7:3 implies that he may have been in this condition for months. The seven days of sitting may have been a traditional time of mourning (Gen. 50:10).

Theological Implications

The prose introduction (Job 1–2) presents a myriad of theological issues and questions that deserve reflection. Of course, many topics are only appropriately raised in the context of the whole book, so only a handful will be treated here. Some topics will be treated in a partial way here that were treated more fully in the introduction to the book as a whole. Perspective will be gained on some of these issues by appeal to the genre of the book, the discussion of which is also developed in the introduction.

Heaven as Royal Court, and the Role of the Accuser

The prologue to the book of Job raises a number of questions, some of them quite disturbing, in particular the way God is depicted. In 1:6–12 and 2:1–6, we read about God's meeting with the "sons of God," with a focus on his conversations with "the accuser," who is described as "roaming the earth and patrolling it." God enters into a contest—indeed, it might be called a

45. A survey of such speculations may be found in Clines, *Job 1–20*, 58–59.

wager[46]—with the accuser that leads to Job's intense suffering. Questions about God immediately arise in the mind of the modern reader. Why does God need someone to report to him about what is going on in the world? Why doesn't he know Job's heart without the test? Why is the accuser challenging God's assessment? Why does God agree to allow the accuser to harm Job? The list can go on and on. The problem is compounded for those who believe that "the accuser" is none other than the devil. While this identification may distance God from evil for some,[47] for others God is still responsible for Job's suffering since he allows the accuser to do the harm.

In the body of the commentary, I have argued for why we should not identify the accuser with the devil. Still, there is the issue of God's allowing one of his angels to harm Job in this way to serve the purposes of this contest. The question that encapsulates all these questions is, Does heaven really work this way? What kind of depiction of heaven and God are we getting here? Again, as pointed out in the commentary, heaven is here being described in analogy with an ancient Near Eastern royal court. God, the king, is meeting with his royal officials, "the sons of God" (the angels). Among the angels is one who is called "the accuser" because of the stance he takes in regard to the motivation for Job's piety. That he roams and patrols the earth shows that he is one of God's spies. He is reporting back to his king the goings-on in God's realm.

In a word, we are not given a literal description of God or how heaven actually works. This depiction is for storytelling purposes only: to tell the reader in no uncertain terms that Job is innocent and that his suffering is not the result of any infraction of God's law but, rather, so God can prove a point to the accuser. As we will see, the broader purpose is to create a story to illustrate that not all suffering is the result of someone's sin.

Even so, analogies are not completely divorced from reality. They point to some truth. However, one must be cautious and sometimes tentative in deriving what is true from an analogy like this. Other scriptural depictions are a guideline for this. Elsewhere we learn that God knows everything (e.g., Ps. 139), which should tell us that God does not need an informant to read Job's heart. On the other hand, that the accuser must have God's permission to bring harm to Job and those who surround him does imply God's sovereignty over all things, including the bad things in our lives.

The Possibility of Innocence

The prologue begins with the assertion of Job's innocence (1:1). It is affirmed by God himself (1:8; 2:3) and not even questioned by the accuser. Job

46. Some deny that this is a wager (see commentary above on 1:8–12) because there is no money at stake. But a wager does not have to be about money; it can be, as it is here, about who is correct in their assessment of a situation. God's reputation is at stake in this wager.

47. Note especially the perspective taken in Dow, *When Storms Come*, 4–6.

will maintain his innocence in the face of the attacks of his "friends" (27:5–6). Indeed, the innocence of Job could not be stated in starker terms. It uses language connected closely to, if not derived from, the book of Proverbs. He is "innocent" (*tām*) and "virtuous" (*yāšār*). He "fears God" and "turns away from evil." He is the ideal wise, godly, righteous person.

But is such a condition possible? Christians find Job's innocence hard to accept. After all, the NT, particularly Paul but also John and James, speaks eloquently and strongly about the pervasive sinfulness of human beings. Here is Paul in Rom. 3:9b–11 (NIV):

> We have already made the charge that Jews and Gentiles alike are all under sin. As it is written:
>
> > "There is no one righteous, not even one;
> > there is no one who understands,
> > there is no one who seeks God."

And this bleak description goes on through v. 18. Is there a difference between the OT and NT on this matter?

First, one should note that the book of Job is not the only stumbling block to Christian readers of the OT on this matter. Some laments also contain an assertion of innocence. Psalm 26 is a good example, wherein the psalmist exclaims, "I have led a blameless life" (using the word *tām*) and "I wash my hands in innocence" (vv. 1, 6 NIV). Thus, the assertion of innocence in Job is not unique in the OT.

Second, we should note Paul's argument in Rom. 3. He makes his case by citing the OT. In other words, the OT does not have a naive view of human sinfulness. It does not have a completely different view of sin. One common way of differentiating the OT from the NT in this regard is clearly wrong. Some hold that the OT judges sin by behavior, while the NT adds an internal dimension. This understanding arises from a misreading of Jesus's Sermon on the Mount, when he says, "You have heard that it was said, 'You shall not commit adultery.' But I tell you that anyone who looks at a woman lustfully has already committed adultery with her in his heart" (Matt. 5:27–28 NIV). On the surface, it sounds like he is saying, "The OT is concerned with behavior (adultery); the NT adds an internal dimension (lust)." But this explanation cannot be correct since the Ten Commandments themselves have a provision against lust in the last commandment, not to covet a neighbor's wife. Thus it is more likely that Jesus is speaking against contemporary rabbinic interpretation than that he is intensifying the OT and thus raising the bar for what constitutes sin.

Third, we should acknowledge that in Job's protest of innocence, he does not claim that he never did anything wrong. Indeed, he does say that he has sinned:

Truly, I know that this is correct,
  but how can a person be righteous with God? (9:2)

For you write bitter things about me;
  you make me inherit the guilt of my youth. (13:26)

You would seal up my transgression in a sack;
  you would smear over my iniquities.
However, a falling mountain is carried away,
  and a rock is moved from its place. (14:17–18)

How are we to understand Job's innocence? It is not some kind of abstract perfection. Job has his faults. As Wilson puts it, "Israelite faith assumed the sinful nature of humans."[48] Rather, his argument (which will be presented in the disputation section and is one the author of the book accepted as legitimate and powerful) is that he does not deserve the level of punishment that he experiences. He has sinned a little, and God has gone over the top in his punishment. And he is right. If he is being punished for his sins, God is unfair. However, by presenting the case of Job, the author is undermining the whole concept of retribution theology.

Godliness and Reward

What is the nature of the test to which the accuser, with permission from God, subjects Job? The focus of the test is whether Job's godly behavior is a result of disinterested love of God or whether it has a more mercenary, self-centered motive. In other words, does Job obey God because he loves God or because he wants the health and wealth that he presumes flows from his godly behavior for himself and for his family?

As mentioned in the commentary proper, one wonders about this whole idea of disinterested piety. After all, so much of the OT tries to elicit dependence on and obedience to God by offering a reward for such behavior and threatening negative consequences for not adhering to God and his ways. The very structure of the covenant makes this point. Deuteronomy is a covenant renewal ceremony, calling on Israel to reaffirm its loyalty to God. After the law come the blessings and the curses (Deut. 27–28). Wonderful things come to those who obey God, horrible things to those who disobey him. The prophets pick up on this message. They are God's "covenant lawyers," after all. They come and "bring a case" (*rîb*) against God's people for breaking the law, warning that the covenant curses will come to effect unless they repent. Then, of course, we have the book of Proverbs. The way of wisdom results in wealth and health, and the way of folly leads to poverty and an early death (Prov. 3:1–2; 24:19–20; etc.).

48. Wilson, *Job*, 18.

That, at least, is what an isolated, superficial reading of these books might lead one to believe. Job's tests will set up a situation that will explore this question. Is it really true that godliness will automatically and mechanically result in a good life? The opening two chapters of the book set up the situation that will allow an exploration of this question. The following chapters bring an answer.

II.
Job's Lament
(3:1–26)

Translation

[1]Afterward, Job opened his mouth and he cursed his day. [2]And Job answered[1] and said:

[3]"Let the day on which I was born perish,[2]
and the night (on which) he said, 'A boy is conceived.'
[4]Let that day be dark.
Don't let God above seek it.
Don't let a light shine on it.
[5]Let darkness and deep darkness redeem it,
let a cloud settle over it.
Let blackness overwhelm the day.
[6]That night, let gloom overtake it.
Don't add[3] it among the days of the year;
among the number of months, don't let it enter.
[7]Indeed, let that night be barren.
Let no shout of joy enter it.
[8]Let those who curse the day damn it,
those prepared to rouse Leviathan.

1. The phrase "answered and said" is formulaic in Job and elsewhere and does not mean that Job is answering anyone. Indeed, he is not answering a question that someone earlier asked him. NJPS translates contextually as "Job began to speak."

2. Alter (*Wisdom Books*, 18) points out the alliteration of this opening line, *yōʾbad yôm ʾiwwāled bô*.

3. See Rendsburg, "Double Polysemy," 48–51.

9May the stars of its dawn be darkened;
  let it hope for light and get nothing.
  Let it not see the flash of dawn.
10For it did not shut the doors of my mother's womb;[4]
  it did not hide trouble from my eyes.

11Why didn't I die coming out of the womb?
  Why didn't I succumb when I left the belly?
12Why did the knees meet me?
  Why were there breasts that I could suck?
13For then I would be lying down and tranquil;
  then I would sleep and have rest
14with kings and world counselors,
  those who built for themselves places now desolate,
15or with princes who had gold,
  those who filled their houses with silver.
16Or (why) was I not hidden like a stillborn,
  like infants who did not see the light?
17There the wicked cease (their) agitation,
  and there those who are exhausted of strength can rest.
18The prisoners together are untroubled;
  they do not hear the voice of the taskmaster.
19Small and great are there,
  the servant is freed[5] from his master.
20Why does he give light to the one who toils,
  and life to the depressed,
21to those who wait earnestly for death, but it does not come.
  They search for it like hidden treasure.
22Those who rejoice with rejoicing,
  they celebrate when they find the grave.
23(Why does he give light) to a man whose way is hidden,
  whom God has placed a hedge around?
24For my sighs come along with my food,
  and my mournful cries flow like water.
25For the dread I dreaded has come to me,
  and what I have feared has come to me.
26I am not at ease and am not tranquil,
  and I am not at rest, and agitation has come to me."

4. Literally "my womb" (*biṭnî*), or alternatively, with NIV, "It did not shut the doors of the womb on me."

5. See Mendelsohn, "Canaanite Term"; and idem, "New Light on *Ḥupšu*," 11.

Interpretation

Job breaks the silence by delivering a powerful and disturbing monologue. The form of his speech resembles a lament, but it differs from the laments of the book of Psalms in some very telling ways (see the theological implications section below). Indeed, it is probably more accurate to say that Job's speech here is most like the complaint portion of a lament, since it is missing many of the typical elements of a lament.[6] As Clines states it, "The genre of the poem is a complaint (*Klage*). The literary forms that it draws upon are almost wholly two: the curse and the lament."[7]

Job does not explicitly address anyone in this chapter. He is not yet in dialogue with the friends, nor is he speaking to God. He is just giving vent to his intensely felt inner feelings and thoughts. His three friends overhear, of course, and it is the attitude that is expressed by this speech that leads them to challenge Job.

Job's complaint has two major parts. In vv. 3–10 Job complains about his "day," that is, the day of his birth. In a word, he wishes he could eradicate that day as if it never happened. He curses that day. In vv. 11–26 he turns from cursing that day to lamenting that day. He wishes he had died in the womb or at least on delivery. He envisions death as a rest from the turmoil of this life. He wonders why God allows those who suffer physical and mental hardships to survive. He expresses his utter agitation with life.

1Afterward, Job opened his mouth and he cursed his day. **2**And Job answered and said:

3:1–2. *Job speaks.* At the conclusion of the epilogue, we heard that Job sat in silence with his three friends for seven days. The friends responded with silence, demonstrating their empathy toward their suffering friend. It is significant and often forgotten in popular reading that Job was the one who broke the silence. The friends, who become aggressive and angry toward Job in the process of the ensuing debate, did not begin the fight. True, Job does not attack them; he attacks his "day." The day, as we will learn in the ensuing complaint, is the day of his birth.[8] He curses that day as a dark and evil day, a day that allowed for his present suffering. By so cursing his day, he is implicitly criticizing God, a criticism that grows increasingly explicit as the lament develops.

6. For instance, it does not have an invocation or a plea for help. Other missing elements will be highlighted in the theological implications section that follows the analysis of this chapter.

7. Clines, *Job 1–20*, 76.

8. Clines (*Job 1–20*, 78) argues that it is a way of referring to his life, since "day" is not used elsewhere to refer to a birthday. Clines seems inconsistent, however, since the simple "day" is also used for what appears to be "birthday" in Job 1:4, and he thinks it is "most naturally" used in that sense there (ibid., 15).

There has been a lively debate over the significance of the curse in the OT. Some believe that a curse brings about its own reality. Curses (and blessings) uttered by fathers or leaders toward children or tribes (see Gen. 49; Deut. 33) do seem to come true, but these texts function more like prophetic anticipations in their present contexts. Of course, there is no way that Job's curse could come true. Job's curse functions like the expression of a wish, a way of saying that his life is so miserable that it was not worth all the good moments leading up to the crisis. It serves to communicate to the reader just how bad Job's mental framework has become, just how much physical and emotional pain he has endured. He is a man ready to snap.

3"Let the day on which I was born perish,
  and the night (on which) he said, 'A boy is conceived.'
4Let that day be dark.
  Don't let God above seek it.
  Don't let a light shine on it.
5Let darkness and deep darkness redeem it,
  let a cloud settle over it.
  Let blackness overwhelm the day.
6That night, let gloom overtake it.
  Don't add it among the days of the year;
  among the number of months, don't let it enter.
7Indeed, let that night be barren.
  Let no shout of joy enter it.
8Let those who curse the day damn it,
  those prepared to rouse Leviathan.
9May the stars of its dawn be darkened;
  let it hope for light and get nothing.
  Let it not see the flash of dawn.
10For it did not shut the doors of my mother's womb;
  it did not hide trouble from my eyes."

3:3–10. *Job curses his day.* Job uses the strongest possible terms to express his wish that he had never been born. Qohelet articulates his disdain for a meaningless life by wishing he had been a stillborn, "better, I say, to be a stillborn baby. For without meaning it comes, and in darkness it goes, and in darkness its name is shrouded. Moreover, it never saw the sun and did not know the sun" (Eccles. 6:3–5;[9] see also Ps. 58:8–9, where the psalmist expresses the desire that his enemies might be like a stillborn). Job, however, takes it one step further and wants to get rid of the day altogether. If the day of his birth were eradicated, he would not have been born, not even as a dead fetus

9. For translation and commentary, see Longman, *Ecclesiastes*, 170–72.

(though he comes close to Qohelet's perspective in 3:16). He does not want to kill himself; that thought never appears to cross his mind, but he wishes he had never existed.

Job is the boy whose birth is announced in v. 3b. Who is making the announcement is left unstated but could be a messenger or a parent, presumably a proud father (some translations take it as the night itself making the announcement; so NIV, NRSV). It is significant that he does not curse his parents for conceiving him, nor does he directly curse God for allowing the birth to happen. He chooses instead to curse the day, which of course is impersonal. Even so, by cursing the day, he implicitly criticizes his parents and ultimately God. It is significant, though, that he stops short of cursing God. He still does not take his wife's advice to "curse God and die" (2:9).

In 3:4 he expresses the same dark wish as in v. 3 when he asks that the day of his birth be "dark," again nonexistent. Not to give light to the day is not to have a day. Indeed, as Janzen points out, Job is asking for a reversal of the divine command at creation, "Let there be light" (Gen. 1:3 NIV). Job says, "Let there be darkness."[10] He asks that God withdraw his interest from that day. He should not concern himself for this hidden day, because if he found it, it would come back into existence.

In 3:5 he piles up the words for darkness (*ḥōšek*, *ṣalmāwet*, *ʿănānâ*, *kimrîr*). He wants it shrouded from sight. The desire to have darkness redeem the day means to claim it as its own. He wants the darkness to save it from the light and therefore save him from birth, which means salvation from the pain and suffering he is now experiencing.

The next verse (v. 6) turns its attention in the first colon, or poetic line, to the night of the day he was born. Of course, he cannot ask darkness to overwhelm the night, so he requests gloom to settle on it. He then asks God to remove that day from the calendar. He wants it removed from the days of the year and the month. Verse 7 asks that the night be barren (*galmûd*), that is, not give birth to the day of his birth. "Barren" is used of the literal lack of children in Isa. 49:21. In its three other occurrences (all in Job: here; 15:34; 30:3) it is used metaphorically. Even so, to wish that the night before the day he was born were barren may be Job's indirect way of expressing the desire that his mother had been barren. If barren, then there would be no shouts of joy at the birth of a child or anything, for that matter. Clines, Janzen, and others believe that the reference is directly to the night of Job's conception,[11] but I believe that "barren" is primarily being used metaphorically, as is typical, as we have seen, in reference to the night of his birth. If it is the day of his conception, then the shout of joy would be a reference to the joyful utterance of a couple experiencing sexual climax.

10. Janzen, *Job*, 62.
11. See Clines, *Job 1–20*, 86–87; Janzen, *Job*, 63.

Verse 8 then calls on professional cursers (those who curse the day)[12] to get to work on the day of his birth. Balaam (Num. 22–24) is an example of someone who is hired to curse someone or something. The reference to Leviathan is enigmatic here, but the context indicates experts in the field of cursing. Leviathan is an awesome sea beast who represents the forces of chaos. More will be said in the commentary at chap. 41, which is dedicated to a description of Leviathan. But anticipating the discussion of that chapter, one of its major themes is the inability of Job, or any human for that matter, to control this powerful beast. The curse experts Job calls on show great ability in even being able to get the beast's attention (prepared to rouse Leviathan). It is unclear what they would want to rouse Leviathan to do. Since Leviathan is a force connected to dark power (see chap. 41), they may be magicians of the black arts. One possibility, though, may be that they would want Leviathan to cause an eclipse that would render Job's birthday dark. There is no evidence from biblical or Canaanite literature that Leviathan ever did such a thing. But perhaps the Egyptian chaos monster Apophis provides an appropriate background. Every day the Egyptian sun-god Re sailed his boat across the celestial sea (the sky), illumining the earth. At night he would descend into the netherworld, where he would fight Apophis. Of course, if Apophis ever won, then the next day would be in darkness. Again, we have no direct evidence that Leviathan functioned this way, but it is a possible explanation.

In v. 9 Job finds yet another way to express his wish that his birthday never happened. He wishes that the night had never given way to light in the form of the dawn. Rather than the dawn stars (Venus and Mercury) giving way to the flash of dawn, he wanted the stars to go dark.

Verse 10 makes explicit the motive for his wishing that his birthday had never happened: because the day allowed his birth to take place. This motivation has been implicit throughout up to this point of the passage. The womb is portrayed here as an abode with doors, and Job wanted his mother's womb to stay shut. His birth led to his life, which led to the present moment, when he suffers beyond imagination. Many OT scholars take the view that the closing of the womb was not preventing birth as much as preventing conception. In my opinion, the text is ambiguous about it. Job's desire never to have existed is clear either way.

11"Why didn't I die coming out of the womb?
Why didn't I succumb when I left the belly?

12. Some, beginning with Gunkel (*Schöpfung und Chaos*, 59), believe "day" (*yôm*) should be revocalized "Sea" (*yām*) to parallel the sea monster, Leviathan. Clines (*Job 1–20*, 86) cites Isbell (*Corpus*, 3–4), who translates an incantation as, "I will enchant you with the spell of the sea and the spell of Leviathan the sea-monster." However, Clines correctly points out that someone who curses the sea would be on the side of order, while someone who arouses Leviathan would be after evil purposes.

> [12]Why did the knees meet me?
> Why were there breasts that I could suck?
> [13]For then I would be lying down and tranquil;
> then I would sleep and have rest
> [14]with kings and world counselors,
> those who built for themselves places now desolate,
> [15]or with princes who had gold,
> those who filled their houses with silver.
> [16]Or (why) was I not hidden like a stillborn,
> like infants who did not see the light?
> [17]There the wicked cease (their) agitation,
> and there those who are exhausted of strength can rest.
> [18]The prisoners together are untroubled;
> they do not hear the voice of the taskmaster.
> [19]Small and great are there,
> the servant is freed from his master.
> [20]Why does he give light to the one who toils,
> and life to the depressed,
> [21]to those who wait earnestly for death, but it does not come.
> They search for it like hidden treasure.
> [22]Those who rejoice with rejoicing,
> they celebrate when they find the grave.
> [23](Why does he give light) to a man whose way is hidden,
> whom God has placed a hedge around?
> [24]For my sighs come along with my food,
> and my mournful cries flow like water.
> [25]For the dread I dreaded has come to me,
> and what I have feared has come to me.
> [26]I am not at ease and am not tranquil,
> and I am not at rest, and agitation has come to me."

3:11–26. *Job's complaint.* Job switches from cursing to lamenting the day of his birth. It is as if he realizes that no matter how often and in how many ways he curses that day, it has happened, and there is no going back. Rather than resignation, it leads him to despair and depression. Though a different strategy of complaint, the laments and the curse both make the same point: Job wishes he had never been born to experience the pain that he now feels.

The lament is marked by a series of questions asking why, typical of the genre (see Pss. 10:1, 13; 22:1; 42:5; etc.; see also Lam. 5:20–22). Job's "why" questions keep coming up later in the debates as well (Job 7:20, 21; 10:18 [where Job expresses ideas similar to the present context]; 13:24).

Job begins by asking why he survived his birth. By so doing he expresses his wish that he had been a stillborn. Verse 12 asks why there were knees to greet him and breasts to suckle him. The reference to knees is a bit hard to understand at first glance, but it may be another way of saying "lap." In addition, it may refer to a blessing formula at birth. That the knees are connected to birth may be seen in Rachel's speech in Gen. 30:3: "And she said, 'Here is my maidservant, Bilhah. Go to her and she will give birth on my knees'" (my translation). The expression "give birth on my knees" (*tēlēd ʿal-birkay*) seems to express the idea that Bilhah will give birth to a child in proxy for Rachel. Genesis 48:12 and 50:23 may signify that the knees were the place where newborns were blessed and welcomed into the family.[13] Indeed, the word for "knee" (*berek*) is probably etymologically related to the verb "to bless" (*brk*). In v. 12a, then, Job is again implying that he wishes he had never been born. In v. 12b he goes further and wishes that he had not been sustained by breast milk.

In vv. 13–15 Job argues that if he had died at birth or soon after, then he would not be suffering now but would be "at rest." Job's point is not that he would then be experiencing a pleasant, restful afterlife; he means that he would have passed into the unconscious state of death (likened to sleep). Job has no sense of the afterlife here (or, we will see, anywhere). The mention of kings, world counselors, and princes is a way of accentuating the positive side of death rather than life. He suffers now in poverty and pain, sitting on an ash heap; death would put him in the company of kings and other powerful figures. They are dead, to be sure, but that is part of the attraction. Job refers to the great wealth that these people enjoyed while alive (gold, houses filled with silver), but he also comments that their places are now desolate. Death is the great leveler. Sufferers and privileged alike are on an equal footing in death. In Job's case the unconsciousness of death is a step upward, while for the powerful it would be a definite step down.

Job's sentiment in vv. 13–15 may be compared and contrasted with Isaiah:

> The righteous perish,
> and no one takes it to heart;
> the devout are taken away,
> while no one understands.
> For the righteous are taken away from calamity,
> and they enter into peace;
> those who walk uprightly
> will rest on their couches. (Isa. 57:1–2 NRSV)

Isaiah sees the early death of the righteous as a blessing because they will escape suffering. Job also sees it as a blessing considering his circumstances, for his circumstances—the horrible suffering that he is experiencing—are not just.

13. It is unclear whether Job is referring to his mother's knees or his father's knees. Genesis 30 speaks of the mother's knees, while Gen. 48 and 50 describe the formal blessing as taking place on the father's knees. Habel (*Job*, 95) prefers the latter but is ultimately unsure: "Although taking a child on the knees may be a father's act to show his acceptance of and concern for this child, it often refers to the motherly custom of gladly taking up the newborn infant to nurse it (Isa. 66:12). She thus recognizes it as her own and commits herself to its nurture and upbringing."

Verse 16 seems oddly placed. After all, the verses before and after are reflections on existence in the underworld, connected to the idea that Job wishes he were dead. However, v. 16 expresses the wish that he had never even been born at all, that is, that he was stillborn. Accordingly, some translations (REB, NAB) put v. 16 earlier in the poem (REB between vv. 12 and 13; NAB between vv. 11 and 12). However, these versions are requiring a higher level of logical consistency than one can expect from an emotionally disturbed person. Granted, we do not have transcripts of a word-for-word statement by Job. It is a literary representation, but it is a literary representation by a sensitive and masterful poet. As mentioned in the introduction to this chapter, Job here comes very close to the language used by Qohelet in Eccles. 6:3–5. But Janzen gets it right when he says that "the move from verses 11–12 to verse 16" is a move "from death at birth to the more radical pre-natal death."[14]

Verses 17–19 continue the description of what existence is like in the underworld, why death is a preferred state over life. The first observation is that the wicked are no longer agitated in the underworld. According to Clines,[15] the word I translate "agitated" (*rōgez*) "signifies fear (Jer 33:9; Hab 3:16), strong surprise (Isa 14:9), violent grief (2 Sam 19:1 [18:33]) or anger (Isa 28:21; 2 Kgs 19:27, 28; Job 39:24 [noun])." As described in a place like Prov. 1:8–19, the wicked are constantly looking for opportunities to do evil. Once dead, their turmoil comes to an end. Other people are worn out by life, exhausted. These now experience eternal rest in the sleep of death. The oppressed, prisoners who have taskmasters, also find rest from their labor and captivity in death. Everyone is there, as indicated by the merismus "small and great." And no longer are there power relationships like that between a servant and a master. Death, again, is the great leveler.

In v. 20 Job generalizes from his own situation. In the previous section, he has asked why God has given life *to me,* a hopeless sufferer. Now he asks why God has given life to anyone who is miserable and depressed. Life again is equivalent to having the light, in the sense of seeing the light, being conscious. The first colon speaks of "the one who toils" (*ʿāmēl*); the verbal root is *ʿāmal* and often means more than simply "to work" but "to be miserable at work." In this negative sense, *ʿāmāl* appears in Num. 23:21; Isa. 59:4; Jer. 20:18; Ps. 7:14 [15]; and often in Ecclesiastes (starting at 1:3). I have tried to capture that meaning by rendering it "toil," suggesting the idea of hard work. The word "depressed" in the second colon to the verse is literally "those bitter of soul" (*mārê nāpeš*). It will also reappear in Job at 7:11; 10:1; and 21:25. The word "bitter" is used in a psychological sense also at Prov. 14:10, which uses the expression "bitterness of soul" (*mārrat napšô*). The proverb makes the point that whether one is depressed or joyful, another person cannot

14. Janzen, *Job,* 64.
15. Clines, *Job 1–20,* 96.

completely empathize.[16] Thus the present verse questions God's wisdom and/or goodness by allowing those who suffer physically and mentally to continue to live.

Verses 21–22 then go on and mention how such people, those who toil and are depressed, long for death more than anything. In order to express just how earnestly they desire death, Job likens them to those who search diligently for treasure. Interestingly, in Proverbs and at least implicitly in Job, such strong longing is associated with the search for wisdom, not the search for death. Job's implication is that he searches for death in this way, so perhaps already there is an implicit criticism that his longings should be directed elsewhere.

Verse 23 simply begins with "to a man," and the opening ("Why does he give light?") is supplied from v. 20. It continues the series that questions God for giving life to those who do not enjoy it. Here the persons in mind are those who cannot see a purpose or a direction to their life. The "way" (*derek*) is a well-known and frequent metaphor in wisdom literature (particularly Proverbs) for life. Here the way is hidden. They cannot find it. There is no clear direction or goal to life.

The second colon accuses God of placing a hedge around such a person. As Westermann points out, this is the first and only direct accusation toward God, though there are plenty of anticipations of it earlier.[17] A hedge would both block a person's way on the path and prevent him from seeing ahead on it. In 1:10 the accuser had said that Job's piety was a result of being hedged in (from *śwk*, a by-form of *śwk*). There the term was used to refer to a protective hedging rather than an obscuring one. Of course, the same act of hedging someone in can be both. A parent can hedge a teenager in by keeping close tabs on him and imposing a curfew on him. The teenager would feel this not as benevolent care but rather as an imposition. In Lam. 3:7–9 the "man of affliction" uses a different terminology, being walled in rather than hedged in, but the sense is the same.

As a result, sighs and mournful cries are as much a regular part of the sufferer's life as his diet (v. 24). Clines points out that "it is actually a familiar psalmic image to depict one's tears as being one's food or 'bread' (Ps 42:3 [4]; 80:5 [6]: 'the food of tears'; 102:9 [10]: 'I eat ashes like [or, in place of] food, and mix my drink with weeping'); it is a standard description of mourning."[18] But Clines also goes on to point out that the difference from the psalms is that there such expressions eventuate into pleas for deliverance. Not so here.

Job's complaint concerning his plight comes to a close with a general statement concerning his extreme angst. Verse 25 states that his worst nightmare has come true. As we learned from the preface to the book, particularly

16. Longman, *Proverbs*, 299.
17. Westermann, *Structure*, 50.
18. Clines, *Job 1–20*, 102.

1:5, he lived a life of fastidious piety in order to avoid just this kind of result. Interestingly, in v. 26 Job applies the same word used of the wicked, "agitation" (*rōgez*; see 3:17), to himself. It is unlikely that he is saying that he is wicked. However, it may explain why he thinks his present situation is unfair. He is experiencing the same turmoil, the same lack of peace of mind, as the wicked.

Theological Implications

Grumbling at God

On a surface reading, Job's words here resemble those of a psalm of lament. Laments are prayers that are spoken to God when life is falling apart. Laments include complaints about life, other people, oneself, and even God. Indeed, the laments in Psalms are often quite forthcoming in their complaints, even accusations, against God. A typical lament includes various elements. Using Ps. 69 as an example, we can see that the lament often includes an invocation to God and a plea for his help (see v. 1a) as well as complaints specifying the nature of the problem (vv. 1–4, 7–12, 19–21). Laments might include a confession of sin (vv. 5–6)[19] and a curse against the enemy (vv. 22–28). Interestingly, they almost always end with a note of confidence or even praise of God (vv. 30–36).

Looking more closely at Job 3, we see that Job's words are far from this type of lament. First, Job does not even address his words to God. He is speaking to thin air in his exasperation, which in and of itself distances him from the psalmist. Therefore, there is no invocation or plea for help. Second, there is neither a confession of sin nor a protest of innocence. Third, clearly there is no turning toward God in confidence or praise at the end. Granted, a couple of psalms do not end in praise (most notably Ps. 88), but even those psalms express some hope, though it might be dim (Ps. 88:1, which addresses Yahweh as the "God of my salvation" [NRSV]). Just the fact that the psalmist is speaking to God shows some indication of hope. None of this may be found in Job 3—only complaint and curse.

Job's words are more like the grumbling of the Israelites in the wilderness than like the laments in Psalms. In Num. 11 we see Israel complaining about God but not to God. They speak as those who have no hope. While God invites the laments of the psalmists, he despises the complaints of the wilderness generation, opening up the earth under their feet and sending poisonous snakes to bite them (Num. 16:31–35; 21:6–7).

Besides the Psalms and the grumbling tradition of Numbers, we might fruitfully compare Job 3 to Jeremiah's laments. Jeremiah sounds a lot like Job when he curses the day of his birth:

19. Though some laments substitute a protest of innocence (Ps. 26), neither is found in Job 3.

> Yet I curse the day I was born!
>   May no one celebrate the day of my birth.
> I curse the messenger who told my father,
>   "Good news—you have a son!"
> Let him be destroyed like the cities of old
>   that the LORD overthrew without mercy.
> Terrify him all day long with battle shouts,
>   because he did not kill me at birth.
> Oh, that I had died in my mother's womb,
>   that her body had been my grave!
> Why was I ever born?
>   My entire life has been filled
>   with trouble, sorrow, and shame. (Jer. 20:14–18 NLT)

In spite of the similarity here, there is basic dissimilarity in that Jeremiah is speaking *to* God and not *about* him. Clearly, Jeremiah is conflicted in his speech to God, going back and forth between complaint and confidence, but still all his prayer is addressed to God.

In terms of understanding how chap. 3 contributes to the book of Job, we can now see why the three friends begin to challenge Job. He is adopting the attitude of those in the wilderness. The friends feel it necessary to respond after sitting silently with him for seven days. In terms of our own prayer life, it is an important reminder to take our complaints to God. The Psalms are sufficient testimony that God welcomes our cries, but the book of Numbers attests to his disdain for complaints behind his back.

III. The Debate between Job and His Three Friends (4:1–27:23)

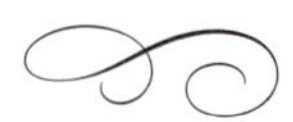

The largest section of Job details the debate between Job and his three friends. There are three cycles of speech. The first two cycles follow the same order and are roughly the same size. Eliphaz is the first of the friends to speak, followed by Bildad and then Zophar. Job responds to each in turn:

First Cycle	Second Cycle
Eliphaz (chaps. 4–5)	Eliphaz (chap. 15)
Job (chaps. 6–7)	Job (chaps. 16–17)
Bildad (chap. 8)	Bildad (chap. 18)
Job (chaps. 9–10)	Job (chap. 19)
Zophar (chap. 11)	Zophar (chap. 20)
Job (chaps. 12–14)	Job (chap. 21)

The third cycle is more complex. The speeches of the friends are shorter, though it is debated exactly how much shorter since parts of Job's speeches are more fitting for the friends.[1] My approach is to treat the MT as it stands, yielding the following structure for the third cycle:[2]

1. For instance, 27:13–23 is often attributed to Zophar, though in the present text it is found in a speech of Job. As the Hebrew text now stands, there is no third speech from Zophar, but this may be part of the strategy of showing that the three friends' arguments are running out.

2. See most recently Long, "Coherence."

Third Cycle
Eliphaz (chap. 22)
Job (chaps. 23–24)
Bildad (chap. 25)
Job (chaps. 26–31)

The brevity of the friends' speeches (and the absence of a third speech from Zophar) demonstrates that they are running out of arguments and energy against Job's persistent resistance. Job's lengthy concluding speech needs further explanation. Besides the question whether parts of chap. 27 ought to be attributed to Zophar, there are questions about chaps. 28 and 29–31.

Job 28 has been the focus of extensive discussion through the years and especially in the past decade.[3] There is no explicit change of speaker between chaps. 27 and 28, and Job is most certainly speaking in chaps. 27 and 29. The problem is that Job 28 presents a view of wisdom that is at odds with Job's thinking up to this point and afterward. Indeed, Job 28 anticipates the conclusion of the book, where we learn that God is the source of all wisdom (cf. 28:28). Thus many commentators suggest that Job is not speaking in this chapter; rather, the narrator is inserting his own view at this point. In my opinion, such an assertion has no exegetical foundation. The text as it stands places chap. 28 in the mouth of Job, and our interpretation must take account of this (see commentary at chap. 28). Chapters 29–31 are clearly Job's speech, but he is not really debating the friends at this point. In chap. 29 he broods on how things were in the past when he enjoyed God's blessings. He bemoans his present suffering and complains that God has turned against him (30:20). He appeals to God once again, declaring that he is blameless and does not deserve the suffering that has come upon him (chap. 31).

I will treat each person's speech separately, beginning with Eliphaz's speech in chaps. 4 and 5.

3. Two major studies that have further bibliography are Lo, *Job 28 as Rhetoric*; and Jones, *Rumors of Wisdom*.

A.
First Cycle
(4:1–14:22)

In response to Job's complaint (chap. 3), the debate proper begins. The first of three cycles is found in 4:1–14:22, and Job responds in turn to the initial challenges given by Eliphaz, Bildad, and Zophar.

1.
Eliphaz's First Speech
(4:1–5:27)

Translation

4:1And Eliphaz the Temanite answered and said:
2"Should someone venture a word with you, would you be
 discouraged?[1]
 But who is able to restrain themselves from speaking?

3You have indeed instructed many;
 you have strengthened weak hands.
4Your words have lifted up those who stumble;
 you have strengthened those with weak knees.

5But now it comes on you, and you are discouraged;
 it touches you, and you are disturbed.

6Is not your fear your comfort?
 Is not the innocence of your ways your hope?
7Please remember: Who being blameless has perished?
 Where were the virtuous destroyed?
8As I have seen, those who plow iniquity
 and those who plant trouble[2] harvest them.

1. From *lā'â*, which means "exhaust" or "grow weary." Eliphaz expresses concern that his prodding of Job might harm his friend, who is emotionally and psychologically fragile.

2. The word *'āmāl* can mean "work" or "labor" but in negative contexts takes on the connotation "toil," "hard work," "drudgery," "misery," or "trouble," as here (see also Num. 23:21; Isa. 59:4; Jer. 20:18; Ps. 7:14 [15], and extensively in Ecclesiastes beginning in 1:3).

9They perish by the breath[3] of God;
they are finished off by the blast[4] of his anger.
10The roar of the lion, the sound of the lion cub,
the teeth of the young lions are broken.
11A lion perishes without prey,
and the offspring of a lioness are scattered from each other.

12A word stole over to me;
my ears took a whisper of it.
13In anxious thoughts of night visions,
when deep sleep falls on people,
14fear and trembling called to me;
my bones trembled mightily with fear.
15A spirit passed by my face;
the hair on my skin stood on end.[5]
16It stood there, but I could not recognize its appearance.
A form was before my eyes.
Silence, but I heard a voice:
17'Can mortals be righteous before[6] God?
Can a man be pure before his Maker?'

18If he does not trust his own servants,
nor set confidence in his angels,
19then what about those who dwell in clay houses,
whose foundation is dust,
crushed like a moth?
20From morning to evening, they are beaten fine;
they perish forever without a thought.[7]
21Are not their tent-cords pulled up in them?
They die without wisdom.

5:1Call out now! Is there anyone who will answer you?
To whom among the holy ones will you turn?

2For[8] irritation kills a stupid person,
and jealousy slays the naive.

3. The LXX has "command" (*prostagma*), perhaps because it is trying to avoid blatantly anthropomorphic language, as it typically does.

4. "Blast" is *rûaḥ*, lit. "wind" or possibly "spirit." In parallel with "breath," the word almost certainly means "strong wind."

5. Perhaps a reference to goose bumps; see M. C. Van Pelt and W. C. Kaiser Jr., *NIDOTTE* 3:272–73.

6. I take the *min* as relational rather than causal (contra NIV) with D. J. Reimer, *NIDOTTE* 3:754 (see Williams, *Hebrew Syntax*, §326).

7. Literally "without setting" (Hiphil participle of *śîm*); I understand the phrase as an abbreviation of the longer *śîm lēb*, "to set to heart."

8. Or the *kî* could be asseverative (as NRSV), "Surely. . . ."

³I have seen the stupid taking root,
but I suddenly cursed their pasturage.
⁴His children will be far from safety,
and they will be crushed in the gate,
and no one will rescue them.
⁵The famished eat their harvest,
and they take it from the thorns.
The thirsty[9] pant after their wealth.
⁶For misery does not come from the dust,
and trouble[10] does not sprout from the ground.
⁷For humanity is born for trouble,
and sparks[11] fly high.

⁸As for me, I would seek God,
and I would commit my thoughts to God,
⁹the one who does great and unsearchable things,
marvelous things, without number.
¹⁰He provides rain for the earth's surface,
and sends water on the fields.
¹¹He sets the lowly on high,
and mourners are lifted to safety.
¹²He breaks the pretensions of the crafty,
and their hands do not achieve success.
¹³He captures the wise in their craftiness,
and the advice of the wily is quickly ended.
¹⁴In the day, they encounter darkness;
they grope around at noon as if it were night.
¹⁵He rescues from the sword of their mouth
and from the strong hand—the needy.
¹⁶So there is hope for the poor,
and injustice shuts its mouth.

¹⁷See, blessed are those whom God reproves,
so do not reject the instruction of Shaddai.
¹⁸For he wounds and binds up.
He strikes, but his hands heal.
¹⁹From six dangers he will rescue you;
from seven, trouble will not touch you.
²⁰In famine, he will redeem you from death;
in war, from the power of the sword.
²¹You will be hidden from the lash of the tongue,
nor will you fear the coming destruction.

9. While the Hebrew has "snares" (*ṣammîm*), that word does not make good sense. A simple emendation to "thirsty" (*ṣĕnumîm*) makes good sense and an expected parallel to "famished" in the first colon.

10. For "trouble" (*ʿāmāl*), see the footnote on the translation at 4:8.

11. Literally "sons of Resheph." See commentary.

22You will laugh at destruction and lack of food
and not fear the wild animals of the earth.

23For you will have an alliance with the stones of the field,
and the wild animals of the field will make peace with you.
24And you will know that your tent is safe,
and you will visit your pasturage and not miss anything.
25And you will know that your descendants will be numerous,
and your offspring like the vegetation of the field.
26You will go to the grave in ripe old age,
like piling up grain at the right time.
27See, this we have examined and it is true.
Hear it and know it yourself."

Interpretation

Eliphaz speaks first. Presumably he is the leader of the friends, probably the senior member. In his first speech, among other things, Eliphaz clearly states the basic argument of the friends as they, as sages, try to help Job navigate his problem. Quite simply, suffering is the result of sin (4:6–11; 5:2–7). There is therefore only one solution to suffering, including Job's, and that is repentance (5:8–16). After all, God will bless those he disciplines through suffering (5:17–23). Indeed, such people will live in safety (5:24–27). Eliphaz appeals to the authority of experience (5:8) as well as to spiritual, perhaps even divine, revelation (4:12–17). On the other hand, no one, not even an angel, will take Job's side in the matter (5:1). And in any case, God does not trust angels, not to speak of humans (4:18–21), who after all are "born for trouble" (5:6–7).

1And Eliphaz the Temanite answered and said:
2"Should someone venture a word with you, would you be
discouraged?
But who is able to restrain themselves from speaking?"

4:1–2. *Eliphaz requests a word with Job.* Verse 1 provides a typical introduction to a speech in the highly stylized cycle of the dialogue of chaps. 4–27 (see "Structure" in the introduction). Eliphaz is responding to ("answered") Job's complaint in chap. 3. For days he has been content to remain silent, supporting his friend in his suffering (2:11–13). Job's complaint has compelled him to speak. He reacts to Job in order to defend God.

The name Eliphaz in Hebrew means "my God is gold," though it is unclear that this name has any significance to the story. He certainly argues like someone who has a high regard for God. It would be too much to insist that the name supports his optimistic view of wisdom as leading to good, material benefits in the sense that "my God gives me gold."

In any case, Eliphaz, like Job himself, is not a Hebrew, but rather an Edomite. The personal name and the geographical name Teman are associated with Esau and Edom, respectively (Gen. 36:11, 15; 1 Chron. 1:36; Jer. 49:7, 20; Ezek. 25:13; Amos 1:12; Obad. 9; Hab. 3:3). Indeed, in Gen. 36:11 Teman is the descendant of Eliphaz, a descendant of Esau. Perhaps the Eliphaz of Job descends from the earlier one, though we cannot be certain. The important feature of Eliphaz's connection with Teman is that the latter is notable for its connection with wisdom (see discussion at 2:11). Teman has been associated with a village in Jordan named Tawilan, though the identification is questionable.[12]

That Eliphaz is the first speaker among the three friends, who then go in turn in three cycles, may indicate that he is senior among them, though this is not explicitly indicated in the text. His seniority is also suggested by the fact that God speaks to the three friends through him in 42:7.

Eliphaz begins on a relatively civil note. He asks whether Job would be discouraged if someone would "venture" a word with him. "Venture" (from *nsh*) means to put someone to the test. Eliphaz thus announces his intention to challenge Job's complaint. He does so reluctantly. He does not want to discourage Job, but he feels compelled to do so ("who is able to restrain themselves from speaking"). Job's words threaten Eliphaz's fundamental understanding of who God is and how he acts in the world. Thus he cannot keep himself from speaking.

3"You have indeed instructed many;
  you have strengthened weak hands.
4Your words have lifted up those who stumble;
  you have strengthened those with weak knees."

4:3–4. *Job was a pillar of strength*. Eliphaz begins with compliments. Job has been a "strong" person of faith in the past. He has been a wise man who has instructed many who are "weak." He has provided strength for the weak-kneed and helped those who stumbled.

Eliphaz describes the role of the wise here. The wise are those who know how to navigate life. They avoid pitfalls and maximize success. If an obstacle comes their way, they know the quickest way out of the mess. Thus they are in a position to give advice to others who are not as intelligent in life skills as they are. They can help those who falter.

As we will see (and have discussed under "The Genre of the Book of Job" in the introduction), the debate between Job and his friends is really a debate about the question Who is wise?

Right from the start we can sense that this compliment is going to turn on Job. The instructor has become the unwilling student. The strengthener is the weak one. The one who has lifted up in the past has stumbled.

12. P. Bienkowski, "Tawilan," *NEAEHL* 4:1447–48.

Even though Eliphaz is setting Job up for a critique, it is still significant that he begins with compliments concerning his past behavior. As the debate continues, such concessions to civility will give place to insult and open and direct attack.

[5]"But now it comes on you, and you are discouraged;
it touches you, and you are disturbed."

4:5. *Job's discouragement.* Eliphaz accuses Job of being the kind of person who is strong when things are going well, but if trouble comes, he crumbles. He turns from a man of clarity and insight into a confused bumbler. Job should know better. He has seen it in other people. As the argument continues, Eliphaz seems to argue that Job strengthened others by teaching them the way of wisdom, at least as they all understood it. Job must have advised those who were weak ("suffering") that their problem was sin and that they needed to repent in order to regain stability in their lives. Eliphaz marvels how the doctor cannot take his own medicine and cure himself. The lament of chap. 3 is proof enough of this to him.

[6]"Is not your fear your comfort?
Is not the innocence of your ways your hope?
[7]Please remember: Who being blameless has perished?
Where were the virtuous destroyed?
[8]As I have seen, those who plow iniquity
and those who plant trouble harvest them.
[9]They perish by the breath of God;
they are finished off by the blast of his anger.
[10]The roar of the lion, the sound of the lion cub,
the teeth of the young lions are broken.
[11]A lion perishes without prey,
and the offspring of a lioness are scattered from each other."

4:6–11. *Only sinners suffer.* Eliphaz now states his most basic argument against Job: The innocent do not suffer, but the wicked, even the seemingly most powerful and dangerous, perish. In other words, Eliphaz here presents the retribution theology of the three friends for the first time in succinct form.

He appeals to Job on the basis of his "fear," shorthand for "fear of Yahweh." The book of Proverbs speaks of the fear of Yahweh as the "beginning" of wisdom (1:7, 29; 2:5; etc.). The introduction to Job strongly emphasizes that Job does indeed fear Yahweh (God, 1:1, 8, 9; 2:3). Job does understand that he is not the center of the universe but rather that Yahweh is far above him and deserves his respect and awe. Eliphaz (and Job, for that matter) is working with the assumption that such an attitude should lead to happiness and prosperity, not to weeping and trouble.

Nonetheless, Eliphaz does question Job's attitude. Even though he is suffering now, that he is someone who claims to fear God should give him the confidence that things will pan out for him in the end. His self-awareness and his theology should give him comfort in the midst of his pain, which surely cannot last long.

His present comfort should be complemented by hope as he looks to the future. Again using language from Proverbs and from the prologue's introduction of Job (1:1, 8, 9; 2:3; for which, see the commentary), Job is described as innocent. And, in Eliphaz's thinking (and Job's, at least up to this point), the innocent do not suffer, at least for an extended period of time. Thus, he reasons, if Job does fear God and is innocent, then he should have comfort in the present and hope as he faces the future.

This interpretation of Eliphaz's statements in v. 6 assumes they are being uttered with a straight face. Tone is notoriously difficult to discern in written literature. It is possible that Eliphaz is already goading Job on, thinking that really he neither fears God nor is innocent. In other words, his point is that if Job were really a God-fearing man and an innocent one, then he would not be in this predicament in the first place. That he is now panicking is just a further indication that he is not a wise, godly man, but a fool.

His argument continues in v. 7 as he asks Job to give him an example of a bad end for the blameless (*nāqî*) or the virtuous (*yāšār*, another word used in the prologue to describe Job; 1:1, 8; 2:3). With the use of "perish" (*'bd*) and destroy (*kḥd*), Eliphaz likely has in mind death and most likely means simply a premature death. Of course, in their experience, as in ours, everyone dies. Eliphaz would not make the argument that the godly wise do not eventually die. He is asking where Job has seen such a person dying young.

In Eliphaz's theology, as we continue to learn about it, he would judge someone to be wicked simply by the fact that the person died young. Similarly, he is now judging Job to be guilty of something that has led to his suffering. In other words, Eliphaz's theology is impossible to disprove. If someone dies young, then they must have been wicked, even though that person seemed righteous. Qohelet (Eccles. 7:15–18) will suggest that he has seen the righteous (*ṣāddîq*) perish (*'bd*) in his righteousness, while the wicked (*rāšā'*) live long in their evil (*rā'â*).

Verse 8 uses an agricultural metaphor in order to make the point that there is a cause-and-effect relationship between evil actions and negative consequences. Those who plow iniquity (*'āwen*) and plant trouble (*'āmāl*) will harvest iniquity and trouble. Proverbs 22:8 does offer as a general principle "Those who sow iniquity will reap evil," but while this is true as a general principle, it is not universally true, despite Eliphaz's claim. As a general principle, the NT makes the same point: "All who take the sword die by the sword" (Matt. 26:52 NEB). But again, in this life, this principle does not work out perfectly. Job, as the reader knows, is prime evidence of this.

Verse 9 names the source of the perfect balance of retribution that Eliphaz believes is operative in the world. God is the one who assures that the wicked get their deserved punishment. Eliphaz uses the anthropomorphism of God's breath, though the allusion might be to God as the one in control of storms. He is able to direct his devastating wind at the wicked so that they perish. He is motivated by anger because they have acted contrary to his will.

Verses 10–11 use a lion image to represent the wicked.[13] These dangerous and powerful animals were deeply feared (Amos 3:8). They prowled the forests of ancient Israel. Lions were well-known images in the ancient Near East for powerful, conquering kings, particularly in Assyria. Nahum exploits the Assyrian use of the lion as he prophesies the destruction of their capital city, Nineveh (Nah. 2:11–13). In the Bible, the lion is often an image for the wicked (Pss. 7:2; 10:9; 17:12; 22:13, 21; 35:17; 57:4; 58:6; Isa. 5:29; Jer. 4:7; 5:6; 50:17).

But according to Eliphaz, even though the wicked are like lions (strong, dangerous, frightening), they will be silenced. Their teeth that rend their prey will be broken. They will be hungry, without prey. They will be scattered. In other words, though the wicked appear strong, appearances are wrong. The strong will be destroyed because of their evil.

12"A word stole over to me;
my ears took a whisper of it.
13In anxious thoughts of night visions,
when deep sleep falls on people,
14fear and trembling called to me;
my bones trembled mightily with fear.
15A spirit passed by my face;
the hair on my skin stood on end.
16It stood there, but I could not recognize its appearance.
A form was before my eyes.
Silence, but I heard a voice:
17'Can mortals be righteous before God?
Can a man be pure before his Maker?'"

4:12–17. *Appeal to divine authority*. In the previous section (vv. 6–11), Eliphaz appealed to experience and observation to make his point that the wicked experience punishment for their evil. In the present section, he argues that he has gotten a word from the divine realm that supports this idea.

Eliphaz surrounds the heavenly voice that speaks in v. 17 with great mystery. Verses 12–16 describe the experience and his reaction to it in a way that builds up suspense and intrigue. Though he implies that the speaker is a "spirit" (v. 15), he never clearly identifies the spirit or the voice. It may be an angel.

13. In these two verses, Eliphaz uses five different words for "lion," thus, according to Alter (*Wisdom Books*, 24), demonstrating "the lexical wealth of the Job poet."

Clines argues that the spirit is God himself, since "form" (4:16) is always used of God and wind often accompanies a divine theophany.[14] Also, elsewhere in Job, others appeal to the "spirit of God" to bolster their claims.[15] Again, the recalled event is surrounded by mystery, though the claim is clearly that the statement is coming with heavenly authority.

The revelatory moment begins with subtlety. The "word" (*dābār*, which can also mean "message") "stole" (from *ngb*) over to him. Like a robber it came by stealth, without warning, unexpectedly. Although there is no substantial connection with the description of Christ's coming "as a thief in the night" (1 Thess. 5:2; 2 Pet. 3:10; Rev. 3:3), both phrases communicate the idea of surprise. The message (word) did not come through loud and clear, but just a whisper, again a description that emphasizes mystery as well as secrecy or privacy.

The description that Eliphaz gives suggests an intuition, an internal moment of insight. Of course, he is claiming more than that, or at least he is claiming that his intuition has the authority of heaven behind it.

Even so, this intuition is disquieting, according to vv. 13–14. It is like a nightmare or at least a dream that deeply disturbs. Indeed, Eliphaz says that it came in a dream (a vision during deep sleep). This dream produced deep anxiety and fear. Again, this may be no more than a claim of divine revelation. This spirit comes from the heavenly realm and so disturbs mere humans, who are the recipients.

The climax of the claim is that a "spirit" (*rûaḥ*) passed by him. The identification is not precise or clear; however, it is clear that whatever the "spirit" was, it was not of this world. In spite of Clines's comments, it is only possible, not at all certain, that Eliphaz is thinking of the Holy Spirit here or even of God's spirit. More likely, the idea is that it is some kind of supernatural, perhaps angelic, being. Even so, the experience is eerie and scary. The spirit is an otherworldly presence, thus lending its message authority.[16]

In keeping with its spiritual nature, it had no form, no appearance. In the silence, Eliphaz heard only a voice. The voice speaks a word that at first is hard to penetrate. The claim is that no one can be righteous before God. And if no one can be perfectly righteous, then Job is not, and he deserves the suffering that is coming his way. Job himself will interact with this claim in chap. 9.

Thus in a subtle, secretive, yet bold way, Eliphaz is enlisting divine support for his contention that Job is a sinner in need of repentance.

Another interpretive possibility is represented by the NIV (taking the *min* as comparative rather than relational; see the translation note for 4:17): "Can

14. Clines, *Job 1–20*, 131. He cites Num. 12:8; Deut. 4:12; and Ps. 17:15 as examples.

15. See Job 20:3 (Zophar) and 32:8 (Elihu).

16. Paul ("Job 4:15," 119–21) cites the Epic of Gilgamesh (tablet 5, col. 4, lines 11–12) as a parallel: "Didst thou not touch me? Why am I startled? Did not some god go by? Why is my flesh numb?" (trans. E. A. Speiser, *ANET* 82).

a mortal be more righteous than God? Can a man be more pure than his Maker?" The implied answer to this rhetorical question is negative. But who would be making such a claim? If this is the correct understanding, perhaps the charge would be that Job through his attitude and actions (refusal to repent) is implicitly claiming that he is more righteous than God.[17]

> [18]"If he does not trust his own servants,
> nor set confidence in his angels,
> [19]then what about those who dwell in clay houses,
> whose foundation is dust,
> crushed like a moth?
> [20]From morning to evening, they are beaten fine;
> they perish forever without a thought.
> [21]Are not their tent-cords pulled up in them?
> They die without wisdom."

4:18–21. *God does not trust his creatures.* Eliphaz now makes a major-to-minor argument. If God does not trust his angels, who are presumably closer to him and more powerful, then why would he trust human beings?

Not a lot of evidence exists in the Bible that God does not trust his angels, particularly in the OT. A modern reader might think of those spiritual beings who rebelled against God, known in the NT as the devil and demons, the powers and principalities of Eph. 6:10–20, but there is no account of the "fall of Satan" in the OT. Perhaps one could refer to Gen. 6:1–8, an enigmatic story to be sure, but it is unlikely that the "sons of God" who married the "daughters of men" are angels. Much later in the OT, spiritual forces associated with Persia and Greece oppose the spiritual forces that fight on God's side (Dan. 10). But even if there is not strong biblical data that illustrates God's distrust of his spiritual servants, Eliphaz certainly understands the situation in this way, and so he makes his argument.

Before proceeding in this section, I shall raise the possibility of a connection between v. 18 and the previous section. There we saw a spirit make a stealthy pronouncement to Eliphaz in a night vision. From his description of the experience, it seems as if the spirit came in surreptitiously and then spoke. Could it be that this is an example of a spiritual power whom God does not trust? Is the spirit speaking out of turn? Or further, is "the accuser," a member of God's own council in Job 1–2, such a servant?

Whatever the motivation of his belief that God does not trust or have confidence in his spiritual servants, it leads him to argue that God must feel the same way about his human creatures. After all, humans are much weaker and their lives more temporary than that of angels.

17. Whitekettle ("When More Leads to Less") has recently put forward a strong case in favor of understanding the *min* as comparative.

The reference to "clay house" and "dust" takes us back to Gen. 2:7. Here God takes some of the dust of the ground and breathes into it to bring the first human being into life. In Genesis this image of the creation of Adam symbolizes the creaturely nature of humans as well as their special relationship with God. The biblical picture contrasts with the Mesopotamian description of human creation in which Marduk takes the clay and mixes it with the blood of a demon god (Qingu). According to Eliphaz, the body is the clay house in which the human spirit is encased. Such a creature is weak and temporary.

Thus its destruction is as easy as swatting a moth. Moths are fragile creatures, mostly wings. They are slow flyers and thus easy to dispatch with a flick of the hand. According to Eliphaz, humans are equally fragile.

Continuing the metaphor of clay houses, he remarks that humans are "beaten fine" all day long, "from morning to evening." The verb (from *ktt*) is used of smashing objects, and in contexts of judgment it can refer to the smashing of pottery (Isa. 30:14), the bronze snake (2 Kings 18:4), and the golden calf (Deut. 9:21). Finally, after being beaten like a clay pot all day, humans perish. The final verse of the unit (v. 21) switches metaphors but makes the same point. Humans are here regarded as a tent, and their end is like the pulling up of the tent pegs, which causes the tent to collapse. The second cola of vv. 20 and 21 also make the same point, though it is clearer in v. 20. Once dead, they are out of mind. When Eliphaz says in v. 21 that they die "not in wisdom," it is hard to believe that he thinks that everyone who dies is ignorant or foolish. It is more likely that the phrase means something like v. 20b: when they die they are soon forgotten. Here, Eliphaz is again emphasizing human weakness. His statements sound similar to those made by Qohelet in the book of Ecclesiastes:

> There is no remembrance of people of old,
> and even those who are yet to come
> will not be remembered
> by those who follow them. (1:11 TNIV)[18]

In Job 15:11–16, Eliphaz will make an argument similar to the one in this passage.

> **1**"Call out now! Is there anyone who will answer you?
> To whom among the holy ones will you turn?"

5:1. *No one will help Job.* Eliphaz now appeals to Job's reason by implying that Job is all alone. He might appeal for help, but no one will respond to his cry for an answer to his questions or come to help him. He may seek help, but

18. While this technically is in the prologue before Qohelet begins to speak, the frame narrator in the epilogue anticipates what he is going to say (see Longman, *Ecclesiastes*, e.g., 21, 59).

none will come. The first colon states that no one will answer him, and the second colon specifies "holy ones," likely a reference to the spiritual realm, in particular angels (Deut. 33:3; Ps. 89:5, 7; Dan. 4:13, 17; Zech. 14:5).[19] Understanding the parallelism as "A, what's more, B," rather than "A equals B"[20] suggests that the "anyone" would have a broader reference than the spiritual realm. Job is alone in his call for an answer to his question concerning why he suffers. He has been abandoned by all, human and spiritual. Indeed, in the previous chapter Eliphaz has implied that spiritual forces are on his side, not Job's (Job 4:12–17).

Some commentators believe that Eliphaz here looks back to Job's lament (chap. 3) as Job's cry for help.[21] However, as was pointed out in that section of the commentary, Job is not appealing to anyone for help. Note should be taken of Eliphaz's lack of mention of God. Perhaps he does not even imagine a direct appeal to God, but seems to assume that the best that can be done is to garner the support of an angelic intermediary. Such a viewpoint fits in with ideas current in the late OT and intertestamental period, when angels served as intermediaries. Daniel, for instance, never speaks directly to God, but always to an interpreting angel (e.g., Dan. 10). Habel rightly points out that, though Eliphaz discourages Job from crying out to the angelic realm, Job entertains this as an option in 9:33 and 16:19–21.[22] Konkel, on the other hand, helpfully argues that Eliphaz may be trying to remove any other option than appealing to God himself. Such a viewpoint fits in well with Eliphaz's later advice to Job (5:8).[23]

2"For irritation kills a stupid person,
and jealousy slays the naive.
3I have seen the stupid taking root,
but I suddenly cursed their pasturage.
4His children will be far from safety,
and they will be crushed in the gate,
and no one will rescue them.
5The famished eat their harvest,
and they take it from the thorns.
The thirsty pant after their wealth."

5:2–5. *Children of fools suffer*. The opening verse of this section (v. 2) has the appearance of a proverb. The proverb is an observation that has the

19. See discussion of angels as mediators in the book of Job in "I Know That My Redeemer Lives" after the commentary on Job 19.

20. That is, understanding that the second colon always in some way furthers the thought of the first colon rather than merely repeating the idea in different words. See the widely accepted analysis of parallelism by Kugel, *Idea*.

21. Hartley, *Job*, 117.

22. Habel, *Job*, 130.

23. Konkel, "Job," 56.

function of a warning. In this context, it is a warning to Job. Negative emotions (irritation and jealousy) can kill a person. A person who exhibits these emotions is by definition then a "stupid person" (*'ĕwîl*, a harsh term) or at least "naive" (*pōteh*, less harsh, but still uncomplimentary).

Proverbs talks about how these emotions can bring harm to those who display them. Proverbs 27:3 addresses "irritation" (*kaʿas*): "Heavy stone and weighty sand—a stupid person's irritation is heavier than both." Proverbs speaks of jealousy's harm from two directions. The verse that immediately follows this one explains that another person's jealousy can lead to harm for the fool who evokes it: "Wrath is cruel, and anger is a flood, and who can stand up in the face of jealousy?" (27:4). In other contexts, it is the jealousy of the fool that leads to his harm: "The life of the body is a healthy heart, but jealousy is a rot of the bones" (14:30).

Thus Eliphaz appears to cite a proverb or at least state a principle that can be fleshed out a bit by reference to the book of Proverbs. However, how does this apply to the context? Clines does not think he is accusing Job of such foolish, self-destructive attitudes,[24] but I disagree. Granted, Eliphaz is speaking in generalities here rather than applying them directly to Job, but I think he is essentially saying to him: "If the shoe fits, wear it." Clines does not believe that Job has displayed these emotions yet, but in my opinion his lament shows irritation at and jealousy of other people's lives (or even jealousy of the situation of the stillborn).

In 5:3–5 he presents an observation about the fate of the wicked (once more described as "stupid"). Again, he does not apply it to Job directly, but that appears to be the implication. What he first observes is the stupid person flourishing (similar to the first thoughts of the poet in Ps. 73). The idea of "taking root" derives from a plant metaphor and is reminiscent of Ps. 1, which likens the righteous person to a tree by the river. But here Eliphaz comments that sometimes the wicked fool flourishes in that way, but not for long. Similar as well to the development of the psalmist's thought in Ps. 73, Eliphaz believes that the prosperity of such people will not last. Their success will turn disastrous. Again, Clines does not think Eliphaz is describing Job here, but it is hard to agree with him. After all, Job was taking root, but now his world was falling apart, and in ways that are similar to those described here.[25]

Indeed, Eliphaz as a wise, righteous man (as he would characterize himself) takes an active part in the reversal. He curses the wicked man's pasturage. Now here I do not think he is applying this comment directly to Job, but rather speaking generally. After all, from the prologue we learn that the three friends

24. Clines, *Job 1–20*, 138–39.

25. Habel (*Job*, 131) is closer to the truth: "Eliphaz does not refer directly to Job's fate, yet the ambiguity of the poetic language allows Job to interpret Eliphaz's comments as allusions to the sudden destruction of family, dwelling, harvest, and wealth (1:13–19)."

only come on the scene after the fact, and they come to empathize—until Job utters his lament.

The fate of Job's children is one of the reasons why Clines thinks that Eliphaz cannot be thinking of Job at this point. Clines believes that Job's children do have a rescuer: Job. After all, he is still alive. I argue that this reading is too narrow. I agree that he is not describing Job's situation per se, but the principle being enunciated certainly fits him. His children had no rescuer who was in a position to save them from the fate that they met. They may not have been literally crushed at the city gate, but they were publicly crushed—in their own homes of all places! Just by virtue of their horrible fate, Eliphaz is saying, look at your children; you must be one of these wicked fools who took root but now are getting what they deserve.

The "stupid" and their children will not even enjoy the fruits of their labor (v. 5). They are worse off than even the famished. The latter will eat their crops. They will pick them clean, even taking those things that are among the thorns. The thirsty will go (pant) after the wealth of such fools and their children.

6"For misery does not come from the dust,
  and trouble does not sprout from the ground.
7For humanity is born for trouble,
  and sparks fly high."

5:6–7. *Born for trouble.* Eliphaz argues that people's troubles do not come out of thin air (from the dust/from the ground). They have a cause, and the previous section highlighted the cause as the irritation/jealousy of a fool. Eliphaz claimed to help the fool get his comeuppance by cursing him, but his most important point is that misery/trouble does not pop out of thin air. Habel provides a less attractive alternative interpretation of v. 6 by revocalizing the negative *lōʾ* (not) in both cola to the asseverative (*lūʾ*). He believes that Eliphaz is arguing that misery and trouble do come from the dust. Thus Habel believes Eliphaz's point is "to be earthbound involves the inevitability of trouble, suffering, and sorrow."[26] However, such a position does not square with Eliphaz's overarching argument that Job is responsible for his plight.

According to Eliphaz, trouble is not a rarity among human beings (v. 7). They are born for it; it comes naturally to them, like eating, drinking, and sleeping. The implication is that they deserve it through their stupid actions. Because they are naturally foolish and because trouble comes to fools, sparks fly high. The fire stands for the punishments that come to them, and the sparks it produces fly high because of the abundance of the trouble.[27]

26. Habel, *Job*, 117, quotation from 132.

27. An alternative interpretation believes that an analogy is being drawn between the way trouble springs from humans and sparks fly from a fire (see Hartley, *Job*, 119).

The translation "flame" for *rešep* is justified by passages such as Song 8:6, but it is possible that *rešep* here is a reference to the Near Eastern god of pestilence, thus yielding a meaning as described by Clines: "When humans beget trouble for themselves, they let loose (metaphorically speaking) the underworld demons of pestilence to fly high to earth in order to attack mortals."[28]

8"As for me, I would seek God,
and I would commit my thoughts to God,
9the one who does great and unsearchable things,
marvelous things, without number.
10He provides rain for the earth's surface,
and sends water on the fields.
11He sets the lowly on high,
and mourners are lifted to safety.
12He breaks the pretensions of the crafty,
and their hands do not achieve success.
13He captures the wise in their craftiness,
and the advice of the wily is quickly ended.
14In the day, they encounter darkness;
they grope around at noon as if it were night.
15He rescues from the sword of their mouth
and from the strong hand—the needy.
16So there is hope for the poor,
and injustice shuts its mouth."

5:8–16. *Job, commit yourself to God.* Eliphaz now tells Job what he would do if he were in his position. If he were suffering, he would seek God (v. 8). After all, angelic intermediaries are not going to do the trick (5:1). He would rather throw himself (seek [*drš*]; see Amos 5:4) at the mercy of God. He would turn his thoughts away from his suffering and would dedicate them to God.

The remainder of the section then describes God. By talking about his power, his provision, his help for the lowly, and his breaking of the mighty, Eliphaz is explaining why he would turn to God for help if he were in Job's place.

Verse 9 begins the exaltation of God with a general statement of his great deeds.[29] No one can comprehend precisely how great God's deeds are (unsearchable), and they are frequent (without number). Here God's greatness manifests itself through his actions. Eliphaz does not say "God is great" but "God's deeds are great." Of course, the latter also implies the former. Among those great actions are the following:

28. Clines, *Job 1–20*, 142.

29. Notice how the general term *gĕdōlôt* ("great things") formed from the very common word *gādôl* is paralleled by the more specific and intense word *niplāʾôt* ("marvelous things"). A similar parallelism may be observed in Ps. 131:1.

1. He provides the rain that waters the earth (v. 10), and this leads to the growth of vegetation, which provides sustenance to human beings. Though we moderns, especially those of us who live in well-watered areas, take rain for granted as a merely natural phenomenon, the ancients recognized it as a divine gift. Significant parts of Israel (and Edom) had a fragile agriculture because sometimes adequate rainfall did not come. Thus, even more, the coming of the rains would qualify as a "great" and "unsearchable" work of God. Clines helpfully points out that there is continuity between this first work of God in the natural order and the rest in the social order by virtue of the fact that it shows God's transforming power.[30]
2. His "marvelous" works are not limited to acts of nature. Indeed, the rest of the section describes his actions among human beings, beginning with his lifting the lowly person to a high estate (v. 11a). Psalm 113 celebrates the same, and Hannah embodies this herself specifically as she is taken from the lowly condition of being childless to the high position of giving birth to Samuel (1 Sam. 2:1–10). The NT presents Mary as such a woman (Luke 1:46–55).
3. The principle enunciated in the previous half-verse is also illustrated by God's care for mourners. Mourners have experienced the loss of a loved one, but for many the loss is even more, that of a protector. One thinks of a widow, who in ancient Israel would find herself in a vulnerable position. God lifts them to safety.
4. He not only helps those who are vulnerable and low, but he also frustrates and breaks those who are pretentious. He begins with the "crafty" (*ʿārûm*). Interestingly, in the book of Proverbs the word *ʿārûm* is often associated with the wise. There the word is a virtue and can be translated "prudent" (1:4; 8:5, 12; 12:16, 23; 13:16; 14:8, 18; 15:5; 19:25; 22:3; 27:12). However, there is a dark side to *ʿārûm* well illustrated by the serpent in the garden, who is described as *ʿārûm*. Eliphaz uses *ʿārûm* in this latter sense when he speaks of God's thwarting the efforts of the crafty. Verse 13 moves in the same direction, though here it speaks of the wise (*ḥākām*) and the wily (*niptāl*). God puts an end to their evil pretensions as well. Often, and always in Proverbs, the appellation "wise" is a virtue associated with righteousness and godliness, but outside Proverbs it too can be used in the sense of "shrewd" (Jonadab is described as such in 2 Sam. 13:3). *Niptāl* (wily) is not used as such in Proverbs, but the verb from which it is formed (*ptl*, "to twist") is found in 8:8 to describe twisted speech.

Paul cites Eliphaz in 1 Cor. 3:19, "For the wisdom of this world is foolishness with God. For since it is written, 'He catches the wise in their craftiness'"

30. Clines, *Job 1–20*, 145.

(NRSV). Paul would say that Eliphaz is right in general principle but wrong to apply that principle to Job.

Verses 14–16 provide a description of how God thwarts the evil aspirations of humans. First, he places them in darkness, a metaphor for confusion. The truly wise can see clearly so they can act and speak in a way that fits the situation. Even Qohelet, not the most exuberant proponent of wisdom, gives wisdom relative value over folly, using the metaphor of light and darkness: "I observed that there was more profit to wisdom than folly, like the profit of light over darkness. The wise have eyes in their head, while fools walk around in darkness" (Eccles. 2:13–14a). According to Eliphaz, the wicked "wise" (also described as "crafty" and "wily") have no such clarity in their actions, with the implication that they will not navigate life cleanly but run into snares and pitfalls. Because God thwarts them in this way, retribution will work out. The needy who are at their mercy will escape the harm of their speech (the "sword of their mouth") and action (the "strong hand"). Verse 16 gives the moral to the story: justice will win out in the end. Such a moral should give hope to the poor. Though it may look like they are at the mercy of the wicked, they will have the victory at the end.

17"See, blessed are those whom God reproves,
so do not reject the instruction of Shaddai.
18For he wounds and binds up.
He strikes, but his hands heal.
19From six dangers, he will rescue you;
from seven, trouble will not touch you.
20In famine, he will redeem you from death;
in war, from the power of the sword.
21You will be hidden from the lash of the tongue,
nor will you fear the coming destruction.
22You will laugh at destruction and lack of food
and not fear the wild animals of the earth."

5:17–22. *God's transforming power*. Eliphaz now explains why he advised Job to turn his thoughts to God (5:8). Job should not be upset that he has been the object of God's reproof (v. 17). If God did not reprove him, he would be one of those who kept groveling in the darkness and whose evil pretensions were thwarted. Those who feel the pain of God's chastisement are in reality blessed, because he will turn them away from danger and will turn their sadness into joy. Thus he advises those who are being punished by God not to reject the instruction that stands behind the pain. The word for "instruction" (*mûsār*) could also be translated "discipline" and points to teaching that is coerced, either self-induced or by another. In other words, the word implies the threat or application of punishment if one does not obey the words of teaching (*mûsār*).

Eliphaz's point is also made by Proverbs:

> The instruction [*mûsār*] of Yahweh, my son, do not despise,
> and do not loathe his correction.
> For the one whom Yahweh loves he will correct,
> even like a father who treats a son favorably. (3:11–12)[31]

However, Proverbs is not making the point that all suffering is the result of sin and therefore a matter of divine reproof. Eliphaz is not necessarily doing that here, but he is strongly implying that it is appropriate in the case of Job, the person who is standing in front of him and whom he addresses.

Verse 18 states that God dishes out pain for a positive purpose. Suffering is not the final story. Rather, he hurts and heals. Job is now in the hurting phase, but he should hope, because this God is characterized as one who transforms suffering into joy and teaches a lesson in the process.

In vv. 19–22 Eliphaz provides examples of ways in which God protects his people. Verse 19 establishes the principle by use of a parallelism, in which, as is typical, colon *b* sharpens or intensifies colon *a*. In colon *a* he states that there are six dangers from which God will rescue a person, and then in colon *b* he ups the ante and says that there are seven dangers that God will not even let touch him.

First, it is one thing to say God will rescue a person but an even better thing to claim that God will not even allow danger to come near him. The poet also heightens colon *a* in colon *b* by having Eliphaz use a numerical parallelism. Wisdom literature, particularly Proverbs, is partial to numerical proverbs (see Prov. 30:15–16, 18–19, 21–23, 24–28, 29–31). The device is also attested outside the book of Proverbs in places such as Amos 1–2 and Mic. 5:5 [4], and shows even more frequent use in Ugaritic poetry.[32] This form allows the poet to present a list under a single rubric. It causes the reader to consider each element as related to the others. Sometimes, but not always, the emphasis is on the final element (as is clearly the case in Prov. 30:18–20, but not here).

As Watson points out, there is a sense in which the *x*, *x*+1 pattern of a numerical parallelism is demanded by the nature of parallelism. There is no synonym of a number, and it is boring to say "There are seven things Yahweh hates, and seven that are an abomination of his soul." Also, to say "six, yea seven" gives the impression that there are a large number of items in the list. As Watson puts it, a purpose of some numerical parallelisms is "to denote abundance." Sometimes (see examples in Amos 1–2) the numbers do not even coincide with the list, but when they do, the list almost always conforms to the second, larger number.

31. See translation and interpretation in Longman, *Proverbs*, 134–35.
32. See the discussion by Watson, *Classical Hebrew Poetry*, 144–49.

In any case, the idea is not so much that there are six or even seven but that there are a whole bunch of ways in which God takes care and transforms the negative situation of people. As it happens, the next verses list six specific ways.

In v. 20 Eliphaz addresses the first two, famine and war, which are common sources of tragedy in the world, including the ancient world. Many people have died through these agencies, but here Eliphaz claims that God rescues his people from these catastrophes. Verse 21 then turns to something that might seem a bit less dangerous but in the thought of an Israelite wisdom teacher would not be—the tongue. It is only a modern insensibility that would say "Sticks and stones may break my bones, but words will never hurt me." Proverbs rather says, "The tongue can bring life or death" (18:21a). Thus to be saved from the lash of the tongue is as welcome as rescue from famine and war.

The first three rescues are from specific and concrete things: war, famine, and speech. Verse 21b is more general: God's people do not need to fear destruction. Destruction can come in many forms, so this seems to be a more global reassurance.

Verse 22 seems to repeat assurances in the previous verses. Again, destruction (the same word as in v. 21) and lack of food are mentioned.[33] In the second, however, a different word (*kāpān* rather than *rāʿāb* [v. 20]) is used. However, "while *rāʿāb* denotes the experience of famine in general, *kāpān* is that hunger that results from poor crops."[34] Finally, Eliphaz mentions God's rescue from wild animals, another common danger of ancient Israel.

23"For you will have an alliance with the stones of the field,
and the wild animals of the field will make peace with you.
24And you will know that your tent is safe,
and you will visit your pasturage and not miss anything.
25And you will know that your descendants will be numerous,
and your offspring like the vegetation of the field.
26You will go to the grave in ripe old age,
like piling up grain at the right time.
27See, this we have examined and it is true.
Hear it and know it yourself."

5:23–27. *Safety for those whom God reproves*. The previous unit described the blessed condition of the person whom God reproves or disciplines. Their lives are transformed from danger to safety. God will take care of his own. Eliphaz concludes his speech with a continuation[35] of the description of the happy state of such people.

33. Hartley (*Job*, 124n8), however, treats destruction and lack of food as a hendiadys and translates "devastation from drought."

34. R. S. Hess, *NIDOTTE* 2:688.

35. Notice that both vv. 18 and 23 begin with "for" (*kî*), providing reasons why objects of God's punishment should consider themselves blessed.

Verse 23 expands on the idea of v. 22b. The word I translate "alliance" here in other contexts is translated "covenant" (*bĕrît*). A covenant/alliance is similar to a treaty between nations establishing peaceful relations. The alliance with the stones implies a treaty with the earth. Colon *b* goes on to describe the peace with the animals that results from the treaty with the earth. Eliphaz is essentially describing Eden-like conditions where humanity and the natural order existed in perfect harmony. The fall brought conflict into the created order (Gen. 3). Indeed, when God established a covenant with Noah after the floodwaters receded, it was a covenant with creation, including "every living creature that was with you—the birds, the livestock and all the wild animals, all those that came out of the ark with you—every living creature on earth" (Gen. 9:10 NIV). But this covenant was not the alliance spoken of in this passage, because the divine commitment was to allow creation to continue, to not destroy it by flood in the future (Gen. 9:8–17). Indeed, the animals were specifically given to humans for food, so that "the fear and dread" of humans would come on all the animals of the earth (9:2 NIV).

After claiming that the reproved and transformed person will be safe from animals, Eliphaz goes on to say that safety will extend to his personal property (v. 24), specifically his domicile (tent) and land (pasturage). The pasturage would have been the place to graze flocks and herds. Often losses to one's holdings would occur through predators, theft, or the like. Here the promise is that one's pasturage would be safe, and none of the animals would be missing, an ideal picture indeed for the type of lifestyle that Job lived before (1:3).

Next, Eliphaz extends the benefits to the family. Much ancient concern was directed toward having large and healthy families. Thus God blesses the reproved individual with many, many descendants (v. 25). Comparing the large family to a large crop (the vegetation of the field) is natural because both are the result of abundant fertility.

The list of blessings climaxes with the individual himself (v. 26). He will live for a long, long time. The book of Job has no explicit understanding of the afterlife; thus living a long time was considered a blessing and a blessing that was reserved for the godly. The image associated with old age is also an image from agricultural fertility. The pile of one's years will be as tall as the pile of grain. The right time is the time of optimal harvest. It is true that elsewhere in Job the idea of dying when in one's ripe old age, that is, in a time of continued vigor, could be considered premature death, which is a curse (22:16). However, it would also be considered a blessing to die without a long debilitating and painful illness. That seems to be the meaning here.

Eliphaz concludes by putting his personal imprimatur on the argument (v. 27). Wisdom teachers put a lot of stock on observation and experience.[36] They appeal to their previous experience of watching people whom God has

36. See Estes, *Hear, My Son*, 87–100; and Longman, *Proverbs*, 74–75.

reproved moved from danger to safety. Since he and his friends are wise men, Job should take it on their authority. They are taking the position occupied by the father in Proverbs and applying it to their naive son, Job.

Theological Implications

The Disciplinary Nature of Suffering

Eliphaz's basic point is that God uses suffering to restore sinners to a proper relationship with him: "See, blessed are those whom God reproves, so do not reject the instruction of Shaddai" (Job 5:17). This is reminiscent of Prov. 3:11–12:

> The discipline of Yahweh, my son, do not reject,
> and do not loathe his correction.
> For the one whom Yahweh loves he will correct,
> even like a father who treats a son favorably.

The Proverbs passage is quoted in Heb. 12:5–6, where the author also makes the argument that suffering is often for the good of a person who otherwise would wander away from God and toward death. Thus suffering is for good.

While Eliphaz's argument that suffering is disciplinary is often true, it is not true all the time. Eliphaz's mistake is not in the principle but in believing that it is always true and, in particular, that it is true in the case of Job. From the preface, we know this is not the case.

2. Job's First Response (6:1–7:21)

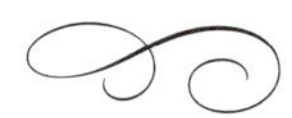

Translation

6:1And Job answered and said:

2"If only my anguish[1] could be weighed,
and my misery[2] be set together on a scale,
3for now it outweighs[3] the sand of the sea.
Therefore, my words blurt out,[4]
4for the arrows of Shaddai are in me.
My spirit drinks their poison;
the terrors of God are ranged against me.

5Does the wild ass bray for grass?
Or does the ox bellow for fodder?
6Would tasteless food be eaten without salt?
Or is there taste in the juice of a weed?[5]

1. *Ka'aś* is a variant of *ka'as*. Its semantic range runs from anger and irritation to sorrow and anguish. The last makes more sense of the context, though it is true that his anguish leads to anger.

2. From *hwh*, "to befall"; see A. M. Harman, *NIDOTTE* 1:1017.

3. Literally "is heavier than" (*mē . . . yikbād*).

4. From *l'*, "to blurt out" in the sense of "speak wildly"; see T. Powell, *NIDOTTE* 2:807–8.

5. The sense of this half-verse is clear when considered in the light of the first colon; it refers to something that is tasteless (see interpretation section). The most commonly accepted interpretation begins by recognizing that the word *rîr*, which means "saliva" in 1 Sam. 21:13, must mean something like "juice" or "sap" in reference to vegetation. Most agree that Millard ("What Has No Taste?") got it right when he connected *ḥallāmût* to a word known from the

7I refuse to touch it!
My food makes me sick![6]

8Oh, that I might have my request![7]
Oh, that[8] God might grant me hope!
9Oh, that[9] God might resolve to crush me,
that he might let loose his hand and cut me off!
10This would be my consolation;
I would even recoil[10] in unsparing pain,
for I have not denied the words of the Holy One.

11What is my strength that I should wait?
What is my end, that I should arrange my life?
12Is my strength the strength of stones?
Is my flesh bronze?
13Is there no help for me?
Resourcefulness[11] is driven from me.

14One who withholds[12] loyalty from his friend
forsakes the fear of Shaddai.
15My brothers betray me like a wadi,
like the channels of rivers that overflow.
16They are dark[13] with ice,
swollen[14] with melting snow.

Alalakh texts that refers to some kind of weed. On the other hand, some interpreters take a hint from the rabbis who believed the word meant "yolk of an egg," and so the phrase *rîr ḥallāmût* would refer to the white of the egg (as in KJV).

6. The verb *dwh* normally refers to menstruation or illness or being indisposed due to menstruation. However, here and in Ps. 41:4 (41:3 Eng.) the noun formed from the verb seems to refer to general illness or indisposition. Nonetheless, the connotation of menstruation may echo in its use here and add to the impact of the statement, since menstruation not only caused a woman discomfort but also rendered her ritually unclean (Lev. 15:19–30).

7. Literally "Oh, that my request might come/arrive!"

8. By ellipsis of the *mî-yittēn*.

9. Again by ellipsis.

10. The translation is by Clines (*Job 1–20*, 156), who takes issue with a traditional understanding of this hapax legomenon as "leap for joy," which makes no sense in the context. Hartley (*NIDOTTE* 3:258) accepts Clines's suggestion.

11. *Tušîyâ* is found several times in Proverbs (2:7; 3:21; 8:14). Fox (*Proverbs 1–9*, 114) defines it as "an inner power that helps one escape a fix."

12. I follow *BHS*'s suggested emendation to a form of the verb *m's*. In the context, the typical meaning of the verb "to refuse" is better rendered in English as "to abandon" (so NRSV). Clines (*Job 1–20*, 158) proposes "an unashamed emendation" to a form of the verb *mn'* to achieve the same translation. The first section of this verse is very difficult.

13. From the same root (*qdr*) as the word translated "mourn" in 5:11. The connection is that mourning clothes are dark.

14. A difficult word. The MT has a form of the verb *'lm* ("to hide," a disputed meaning of the verb tied to an Ugaritic cognate "to be dark"; see Pope, *Job*, 54). Many today (see Clines,

17They were silent when they dried up.[15]
They disappear from their place when it grows hot.
18The caravans turn around from their path;
they go up into the wasteland[16] and perish.
19The caravans of Tema look;
the travelers of Sheba hope for it.[17]
20They are ashamed because they were so confident.
They arrive, but are dismayed.
21Thus[18] you have become to me.[19]
You see (my) tragedy and are afraid.
22Did I ever say, 'Give me a gift?'
Or, 'From your riches, make a bribe on my behalf?'
23Or, 'Rescue me from the hand of a foe?'
Or, 'Redeem me from the hand of the violent?'

24Teach me and I will be quiet.
Help me understand what I have done wrong.
25How painful are your virtuous words!
What does your reproof reprove?
26Do you think words are enough to reprove?
Do you think[20] the words of a despairing man are like wind?
27Would you also fall[21] on the orphan?
Would you sell your friend?
28But now resolve to turn to me.
I will not lie to your face.
29Turn now. Let no wrong be done.
Turn again. My righteousness is still at stake.
30There is no wrong on my tongue, is there?
Does not my taste understand tragedy?[22]

Job 1–20, 160; and Konkel, "Job," 64) take a suggestion from Gordis and emend to a form of *ʿrm* (Gordis, *Job*, 75).

15. The root *zrb* occurs only here; its meaning is determined by its parallel with *dʿk* (to disappear) and a supposed Arabic cognate.

16. The wasteland (*tōhû*) is the same word used to describe the matter God uses to form the world in six days (see Gen. 1:2; A. H. Konkel, *NIDOTTE* 1:607).

17. This is likely a reference to wadis that have dried up.

18. I emend *kî* to *kēn* to achieve sense in the passage.

19. I emend *lōʾ*—which seldom, if ever, has a nominal sense—to *lî*, which makes more sense in the context.

20. By ellipsis from the first colon.

21. From *npl*, "to fall," in the sense of falling on or assailing an enemy. But here *npl* is in the causative (Hiphil). Many translators believe the verb lacks a necessary object and supply *gôrāl*, "lots" (thus NRSV: "You would even cast lots over the orphan").

22. Clines (*Job 1–20*, 162) argues that *hawwôt* here means "falsehood," not "tragedy." He cites Mic. 7:3 and Ps. 5:9 [10] in support. This would make easier sense, but unfortunately the meaning "falsehood" is not clearly attested in his cited examples; thus the meaning "falsehood" remains uncertain at best.

7:1 Is there not hard service on earth for humans?
Their days are like the days of a hired laborer.
2 Like a servant pants for a shadow,
and like a hired laborer hopes for his wages,
3 so I inherit months of vanity,
and nights of toil are allotted to me.
4 If I lie down and say 'When will I get up?'
the evening extends on,[23]
and I toss and turn until the dawn.
5 Maggots and clods[24] of dust[25] adorn my flesh;
my skin crusts over and oozes.[26]
6 My days are faster than a weaver's shuttle,[27]
and they finish without hope.
7 Remember that my life is a breath;
my eyes will never again see good.
8 The eye that sees me will not gaze on me.
Your eyes will be on me, but I will not exist.
9 A cloud fades and goes;
so are those who go down to Sheol and do not come up.
10 They never return to their house,
and their place does not recognize them.

11 As for me, I will not restrain my mouth,
I will speak in the pinch of my spirit.
I will groan in the bitterness of my soul.
12 Am I Yam or Tannin
that you should place me under guard?
13 For I thought, 'My bed will comfort me;
my couch will ease my groans.'
14 You terrorize me with dreams;
you scare me with visions.
15 The Strangler has chosen my neck,[28]
Death, my bones.[29]
16 I loathe my life;[30] I will not live forever.[31]
Bring me to an end, for my life is meaningless.

23. From the verb *mādad*, which means "to measure out."

24. *Gîš* is a variant form of the more common *gûš*.

25. Sometimes this is taken as "dirt" (NRSV), but other translators and commentators understand "clods of dirt" to be figurative for scabs.

26. I take the verb *m's* as a by-form of *mss*.

27. *'Ereg* appears elsewhere only at Judg. 16:14, in reference to the shuttle with which Delilah weaves Samson's hair.

28. *Nepeš* has this meaning in some contexts, rather than the more common meaning "life."

29. Andersen, *Job*, 137–38.

30. The verb needs an object, and this one fits the context well; see Clines, *Job 1–20*, 165–66.

31. Or "for a long time."

17What are humans that you magnify them,
that you set your heart on them?
18You visit them every morning;
you test them all the time.
19Will you look away from me?
Will you leave me alone while I swallow my saliva?
20If I sinned, what did I do to you, O watcher of humanity?
Why have you made me your target?
Why have I become a burden to you?[32]
21Why do you not forgive my transgression
and carry away my guilt?
For I now lie down in the dust.
You will look for me, and I will not be there."

Interpretation

Job makes his first response to the arguments of his friends. Though it follows Eliphaz's speech, it does not seem to specifically address his argument. Indeed, later when Elihu makes his abrupt entrance, it is clear that there is an audience beyond the three friends (32:1–5). Furthermore, as is characteristic of Job's speeches, he will suddenly stop talking to the friends and address God directly.

After expressing his anguish and attributing his problems to God (6:1–7), he then asks God to bring his suffering to an end by crushing him (6:8–10). Interestingly, his solace is that if he died at that moment, he would have remained loyal to God (6:10). Perhaps this reflects some sense on his part that his will might collapse if the pain continues much longer (6:11–13).

Job then expresses his angry disappointment in his friends (6:14–30). They are supposed to help him, not attack him.

Chapter 7 begins with a reflection on the hard life of humans. Job applies this general principle to his own suffering. He seems to be addressing this complaint to God (the second-person addressee in vv. 7–8). He feels that God is constricting his response and rebels against the attempt again by announcing that he will not remain silent (v. 11; earlier 6:3). Again, he asks God to end his life.

Job ends his first speech by questioning why God even cares so much about humans. He prefers that God ignore him rather than punish him. Even more, he wonders why God does not simply forgive his sin.

1And Job answered and said:

32. The MT has *ʿālay* ("to me"), but I read this pronoun with the LXX. Even the ancient scribes (as noted by a *tiqqun sopherim*, scribal change to correct an objectionable reference to God) acknowledged that this was a mistake to be corrected in the manner suggested in the translation here.

> [2]"If only my anguish could be weighed,
> and my misery be set together on a scale,
> [3]for now it outweighs the sand of the sea.
> Therefore, my words blurt out,
> [4]for the arrows of Shaddai are in me.
> My spirit drinks their poison;
> the terrors of God are ranged against me."

6:1–4. *Anguish compels Job's complaint.* Job begins his response by expressing the extent and depth of his pain. He uses the metaphor of weight. Imagining that his suffering and emotional turmoil could be weighed on a scale, it would be heavier than all the sand on the seashore.[33] The sand on the seashore captured the biblical imagination in terms of the vast number of grains (Gen. 22:17; 32:12; Josh. 11:4; Job 29:18; Isa. 10:22) and therefore also their weight.

Special attention needs to be given to Prov. 27:3: "Heavy stone and weighty sand—a stupid person's anguish [*kaʿas*] is heavier than both."[34] Could it be a coincidence that the only two passages that use the metaphor of sand as weight rather than number both concern *kaʿas*? It is unlikely, though the connection may simply be that anguish was often thought of as a weight and the metaphor of sand (and stone) may have been typical. Even today, we talk about a "heavy mood" when feeling oppressed. We can even talk about how a mood "weighs heavily" on a person and those around him. In other words, we should not read the proverb back to Job and conclude that Job demonstrates himself to be a stupid man.

Job clearly believes that his suffering is caused by God's direct action. He imagines that God is using him as target practice or that he is the object of God's warring activity. The latter is more likely, since archers do not use poisoned arrows during practice. It is not his body that absorbs this poison but rather his spirit, an apt metaphor for Job's depression. In Lamentations, the "man who has seen affliction" (a poetic personification for the people of God) similarly complains that God has shot arrows at him, scoring a bull's-eye (Lam. 3:12–13). Indeed, Job insists that God's terrors are "ranged" against him. In this context, "ranged" (*ʿrk*) may have a military connotation, since the root can mean to "enter into battle."[35] God is at war against Job.

As a result of this pain and frustration, Job has no choice but to speak out in complaint. Clines captures Job's point well: "If only others could recognize the burden of his suffering, they would understand the violence of his language!"[36]

33. Hartley (*Job*, 132) provocatively argues that "the picture offers a marked contrast to the Egyptian image of weighing a deceased person's heart against the feather of justice."

34. For translation and commentary, see Longman, *Proverbs*, 476.

35. See V. P. Hamilton, *NIDOTTE* 3:535–37.

36. Clines, *Job 1–20*, 169.

In a passage that has several affinities with the book of Job (see "Grumbling at God" following my comments on Job 3), Jeremiah also attributes the necessity of his complaints to the enormity of his suffering (Jer. 20:8–9).

> **5**"Does the wild ass bray for grass?
> Or does the ox bellow for fodder?
> **6**Would tasteless food be eaten without salt?
> Or is there taste in the juice of a weed?
> **7**I refuse to touch it!
> My food makes me sick!"

6:5–7. *Job defends his complaint.* Here Job responds to his critics, who question why he complains. He asks four rhetorical questions, which may be traditional aphorisms,[37] all of which concern food. The answer to the first two questions is affirmative. Yes, the wild ass brays and the ox bellows for their sustenance (grass, fodder). They are hungry and need it, so they complain.

The second two questions anticipate a negative answer. Of course one would put seasoning on tasteless food. No, there is no taste in the juice of the weed. Job metaphorically states that he is not getting the sustenance he needs. The "food" before him is not edible. Indeed, it makes him sick. He will not even touch it.[38] The metaphor points to what life has "dished out" to him. It is not the good things, but the tasteless and repulsive things of life. Why should his friends question why he brays and bellows? Alternatively, the tasteless food might be a reference to the advice he has just received from Eliphaz. It is of no help, even distasteful. He will have nothing to do with it.[39]

> **8**"Oh, that I might have my request!
> Oh, that God might grant me hope!
> **9**Oh, that God might resolve to crush me,
> that he might let loose his hand and cut me off!
> **10**This would be my consolation;
> I would even recoil in unsparing pain,
> for I have not denied the words of the Holy One."

6:8–10. *Job's death wish.* What is the sustenance about which Job bellows to God? Not restoration, but destruction. In his lament, he expressed the wish that he had never been born; now he hopes he will die. In his mind, God has done the worst thing possible to him. God has made him suffer horribly. Death would be preferable.

37. Wilson, *Job*, 58.

38. In the translation note for 6:7, I indicated the connection between the verb "to make me sick" and menstruation, raising the specter of ritual uncleanness.

39. Smick, "Job," 738.

Notice that Job never contemplates suicide. He leaves himself in the hand of God, but urges him to finish the job and kill him. Suicide, at least in this situation, would have been a betrayal of God.

Even in the midst of his death wish, Job refuses to break relationship with God. His consolation, even something that he says would make the pain worth it, is that if God kills him, he would die without betraying God. He would not have denied "the words of the Holy One," a rather general and intentionally vague expression. Clines, though, is surely right that "he probably refers to the range of divine commands by which he as a godly man has lived. The language is neither cultic, legal, nor sapiential."[40]

One can imagine that these words grated on Eliphaz and the others. They obviously felt that Job had denied the words of the Holy One. That, after all, is why he is suffering. Further, he not only dissociates himself from guilt but also blames God for his suffering.

11"What is my strength that I should wait?
What is my end, that I should arrange my life?
12Is my strength the strength of stones?
Is my flesh bronze?
13Is there no help for me?
Resourcefulness is driven from me."

6:11–13. *Job's weakness.* In these verses, Job expresses his feeling of utter powerlessness. Again he uses rhetorical questions, five of them, followed by a climactic statement. In this case, the first four anticipated answers are negative; the final one is affirmative, but it contributes to the depressing mood of the unit. First, he has no strength that would allow him to endure any longer in hope of restoration and healing.[41] Second, and flowing from the first, he has no end or resolution imaginable that would get him to make plans for (arrange) his life. Third, his strength is not the strength of stones. It is much softer than that. Fourth, his flesh is not bronze, able to resist the blows of Shaddai and others. The last question has an affirmative answer: indeed, there is no help for him, or so he thinks.

The translation note for 6:13 points out that "resourcefulness" refers to inner strength that helps a person in a fix. The use of the word in Proverbs indicates that it is part of the arsenal of the sage, a quality of wisdom itself. Job is in a deep fix, but he sees no way out.

14"One who withholds loyalty from his friend
forsakes the fear of Shaddai.
15My brothers betray me like a wadi,
like the channels of rivers that overflow.

40. Clines, *Job 1–20*, 174.
41. Or for death; so Clines, *Job 1–20*, 175.

16They are dark with ice,
swollen with melting snow.
17They were silent when they dried up.
They disappear from their place when it grows hot.
18The caravans turn around from their path;
they go up into the wasteland and perish.
19The caravans of Tema look;
the travelers of Sheba hope for it.
20They are ashamed because they were so confident.
They arrive, but are dismayed.
21Thus you have become to me.
You see (my) tragedy and are afraid.
22Did I ever say, 'Give me a gift?'
Or, 'From your riches, make a bribe on my behalf?'
23Or, 'Rescue me from the hand of a foe?'
Or, 'Redeem me from the hand of the violent?'"

6:14–23. *Unreliable "friends."* Job now turns his critical attention to the three friends. He begins in v. 14 with a principle that he will then apply to them: those who abandon loyalty to a friend forsake the fear of Shaddai. "Loyalty" here is Hebrew *ḥesed*, often used to characterize the type of love that God shows his people. It is the kind of love that should issue in protection and help in times of trouble. In Ps. 77, for instance, in the midst of his existential pain, the psalmist asks whether God's *ḥesed* has vanished (77:8 [9]; NRSV "steadfast love"). Job suspects that the friends' loyalty indeed has not materialized. They do not protect him; they attack him. They are intensifying the problem, not minimizing it. In his mind, such an attitude demonstrates that they are not truly following Yahweh. Such people do not show the proper attitude of fear toward God (Shaddai). Their deeds do not match their profession.

In 6:15–20 Job then puts forward an extended metaphor to illustrate the nature of his friends' disloyalty. The metaphor paints a picture of unrealized hope. At the center of the metaphor is the wadi, a seasonal channel for water. In the rainy season the wadi flows with life-giving water, but then in the long summer months it is dry and dusty. In Job's imagination, the wadi is one that overflows with water from melting snow, probably from the mountains, that fills the stream. The wadi not only has water, but the water is also cooled by ice. Verse 17, though, describes the time when such abundance of water transitions to dryness. When the weather turns hot, as it does in the Middle East, then the water disappears.

At this time, those who travel in the desert are disappointed in their hope to find water in the midst of their travels. Tema is a location in what is today Saudi Arabia (the northern part), a place noted for being a lush oasis in the desert. Historically, it is best known as the place where the last Babylonian king, Nabonidus, moved his capital due to the pressures exerted on him for his unique religious beliefs.[42] The "travelers of Sheba" are Sabeans, a people whose home is located in southern Arabia. Both Temanites and Sabeans were involved in trade and would be frequent travelers in the desert. Job's scenario pictures them traveling through the desert, expecting to find water, but when they reach the wadi, they find an empty riverbed.

Their reaction is shame and disappointment (v. 20). They were sure that there would be water there, thus their shame for their lack of foresight that it might be dry. Their disappointment is easy to understand. In the desert the lack of water might well lead to death.

Thus, Job implies, he is shamed and dismayed at the reaction of his friends (v. 21, "Thus you have become to me"). They are his friends, so close indeed that he refers to them as his brothers in v. 15. He expected life-sustaining support, comfort, and advice. As it says in Prov. 17:17: "A friend loves all the time, and a brother is born for adversity." What does he get? Nothing. Indeed, even worse than nothing, he gets attacked. They do not help; they intensify his suffering. He suggests that their reaction is the result of fear, not of Yahweh but of what might be expected from them. Thus Job reminds them that he did not expect anything from them really but "loyalty" (v. 14). He did not ask them for any of their wealth (v. 22) or any active intervention with an enemy (v. 23). Perhaps "loyalty" could lead to those if they were relevant, but Job knows that money and physical intervention are not going to help with his present problem, which he believes emanates from God himself.

24"Teach me and I will be quiet.
Help me understand what I have done wrong.
25How painful are your virtuous words!
What does your reproof reprove?
26Do you think words are enough to reprove?
Do you think the words of a despairing man are like wind?
27Would you also fall on the orphan?
Would you sell your friend?
28But now resolve to turn to me.
I will not lie to your face.
29Turn now. Let no wrong be done.
Turn again. My righteousness is still at stake.
30There is no wrong on my tongue, is there?
Does not my taste understand tragedy?"

6:24–30. *Job's plea for real help.* Job now informs the three how they could help him (v. 24). They could be his teacher and help him figure out what is wrong. Of course, the three friends likely believe that is exactly what they are

42. He left his son and coregent, Belshazzar, on the throne in Babylon, though Nabonidus did not relinquish his royal power.

doing. They are helping him understand that he is a sinner and that he needs to repent. However, they obviously have no real evidence that they are right since we, the readers, know that he is not a sinner, who deserves this kind of treatment. They are thus giving him no real help; they are giving him misinformation. Job cannot understand what he has done wrong because he has done nothing wrong, or at least nothing that should lead to his present condition.

In 6:25–27 Job asserts that the friends' words have been painful, and then he levels a series of challenging questions at them. In his assertion (v. 25a), he refers to their words as virtuous (*ʾîmrê-yōšer*), but surely his tone is sarcastic. They have the semblance of virtue since they seem to be defending God, but Job believes, and we know, that they are not representing God accurately. They are trying to reprove Job, convince him that he is a sinner who needs to repent. But there is nothing to reprove (v. 25b, "What does your reproof reprove?"). They do not listen to him, believing that the words of a despairing man are empty. They are like wind; they seem to have substance, but they contain nothing that one can grab hold of. They think he is "chasing the wind" with his speeches (Eccles. 1:14; 2:11, 17; 4:4, 6; 6:9). Job also accuses them of taking advantage of the vulnerable. They attack him in his weakness and suffering. They are the type who would even take advantage of an orphan. They are sellouts. They look to their own advantage and would even profit from a friend's disadvantage.

In spite of what they have done to him so far, Job is willing to give them another chance ("Resolve to turn to me," v. 28). He does not want them to assume he is guilty. He asks them to interrogate him. He wants them to repent, so to speak ("Turn now. . . . Turn again," v. 29; Heb. *šûb* can be translated either "repent" or "turn"), of their attitude toward him. He does not deceive them when he tells them he has done nothing wrong. Verse 30b is difficult to understand (see the translation note). What does Job mean when he says that his "taste understands tragedy"? Perhaps it means that he is able to discern the nature of his situation and thus feels confident in his assertion that no sin of his is the cause.

1"Is there not hard service on earth for humans?
Their days are like the days of a hired laborer.
2Like a servant pants for a shadow,
and like a hired laborer hopes for his wages,
3so I inherit months of vanity,
and nights of toil are allotted to me.
4If I lie down and say 'When will I get up?'
the evening extends on,
and I toss and turn until the dawn.
5Maggots and clods of dust adorn my flesh;
my skin crusts over and oozes.
6My days are faster than a weaver's shuttle,
and they finish without hope.

[7]Remember that my life is a breath;
my eyes will never again see good.
[8]The eye that sees me will not gaze on me.
Your eyes will be on me, but I will not exist.
[9]A cloud fades and goes;
so are those who go down to Sheol and do not come up.
[10]They never return to their house,
and their place does not recognize them."

7:1–10. *Hard service for humanity.* In chap. 7 the addressee changes. In the previous chapter, Job was speaking to his three friends. The chapter starts out a bit ambiguously in this regard. In vv. 1–10 Job reflects on the human predicament in general as well as his own particular woeful condition. He begins with a question: "Is there not hard service on earth for humans?" At this point, it is unclear to whom he directs the question. In theory it could be the friends, God, himself, or the reader. The last is unlikely because there is no other place in the book where Job or any of the characters speaks to the reader, but the other options are possible. In v. 7 Job calls on someone to remember that his "life is a breath." Here it becomes unlikely that he is calling on himself to remember; however, it remains ambiguous as to whether he is speaking to God or the friends. Even so, below we will see that such a call to remember is found in two psalms that are clearly addressed to God, and so this observation makes me lean toward the conclusion that Job is here speaking to God. In addition, the rest of the chapter is obviously addressed to God.

Though I believe that Job directs his initial question to God, he does provide an answer in the second colon of v. 1. He asks whether there is "hard service" for humans, and he responds that their days are like those of a "hired laborer," one who does engage in tough work. The word *ṣābā'* ("hard service") is typically used specifically in military or cultic contexts. Indeed, the plural is used in the title that most directly connects God to his role as divine warrior (*Yhwh ṣĕbā'ôt*, "the Lord of Hosts"). Rarely, as here and in 14:14 as well as Isa. 40:2, the word seems to have general rather than military or cultic denotation.[43]

Interestingly, Job starts with a general reflection on the human situation. He would claim that "hard service" was not unique to him but was true of all humans. According to Gen. 2, when humans were created, they were put to work: "The Lord God took the man and put him in the Garden of Eden to work it and take care of it" (Gen. 2:15 NIV). However, this account does not imply that such work would be "hard service," in contrast to Mesopotamian myths in which humans were created for menial and backbreaking labor. Of course, Job is correct. Work today is better described by the Mesopotamian stories rather than the creation account. To understand the theological background of Job's

43. See my more extensive comments on this Hebrew word in *NIDOTTE* 3:733–35.

statement, one must consider the punishment God announced to Adam after his (and Eve's) rebellion in the garden (see the theological implications section below).

Though a general statement about the plight of all humans, Job personalizes the comment in vv. 3–4. He "inherits" (from *nāḥal*), like all humans, "months of vanity [*šāwʾ*]." "Vanity" is a word that is occasionally used in parallel to Hebrew *hebel* ("meaningless"),[44] so well known from the book of Ecclesiastes. No rest is granted humans and in particular Job, as v. 3b indicates: "Nights of toil are allotted to me." Ecclesiastes shares Job's view of the futility of labor in 2:17–23; 5:8–17; and throughout. Job's evening toil, though, is done in bed according to v. 4. He tries to sleep, but he is an insomniac and tosses and turns all night. The nighttime seems to go on forever. Qohelet claims that such restless nights are the lot of the wealthy: "Sweet is the sleep of laborers, whether they eat much or little. But the abundance of the wealthy does not allow them to sleep" (Eccles. 5:12). Of course, this may be Qohelet's own perspective as a wealthy individual. Job is no longer rich, but we might imagine that his present physical and emotional condition is not conducive to a good night's sleep.[45] Psalm 77 illustrates the night torments of one who feels that God has turned against him (vv. 2–4).

If up to now Job is applying the hard truths of human existence in general to himself, in v. 5 he describes his own individual pain. The disease with which the accuser has afflicted him has made him a walking corpse. He is not yet in the grave, but maggots and clods of dust (or dirt) are his clothing ("adorn" is from *lbš*, often used to refer to putting on clothes). That he oozes (pus or blood) indicates that he is not yet dead, but he is only barely alive.

Although his nights are slow and ponderous, his days go by quickly. He compares them to the speed of a weaver's shuttle. However, the latter is productive, resulting in material used for clothing. Job's days have the rapidity of the shuttle but not its productivity. Indeed, they end with no hope, presumably of a turn for the better. They give way to tormented nights and then a new, equally depressing day.

Job's call to God to remember that his life is a breath brings to mind several psalms. Though we find the idea in Ps. 89 (see vv. 47–48), the closest comparisons can be made with Pss. 39:4–6; 62:9; and 144:3–4, in which the psalmist requests that God make him realize just how transient life is:

> Show me, Lord, my life's end
> and the number of my days;
> let me know how fleeting my life is.
> You have made my days a mere handbreadth;
> the span of my years is as nothing before you.

44. So, for instance, in Zech. 10:2.

45. For the translation, commentary, and assessment of Qohelet as a confused wise man, see Longman, *Ecclesiastes*.

Everyone is but a breath,
even those who seem secure.
Surely everyone goes around like a mere phantom;
in vain they rush about, heaping up wealth
without knowing whose it will finally be. (39:4–6 NIV)

Surely the lowborn are but a breath,
the highborn are but a lie.
If weighed on a balance, they are nothing;
together they are only a breath. (62:9 NIV)

However, this insight into the brevity and fragility of human existence does not drive these psalmists away from God. On the contrary, their hope stays rooted in God. Most striking of all is Ps. 144; this psalmist's awareness of humanity's breath-like existence leads him to be awed before the God who bothers to concern himself with such weak creatures:

Lord, what are human beings that you care for them,
mere mortals that you think of them?
They are like a breath;
their days are like a fleeting shadow. (144:3–4 NIV)

Job, as we have seen, does not have hope, nor does this insight generate admiration for God. Rather, it leads him to despair of the coming end of his life. His eyes will be shut forever (v. 7b), while the eyes of others will no longer see him. Even God ("your eyes," v. 8b) will look for him and not see him. He will not have substance but will be like a cloud that has only minimal materiality and eventually fades. He will be in Sheol, and whether this is simply the grave or a murky underworld where people have a minimal existence,[46] life as he knows it will come to a sad end.

11"As for me, I will not restrain my mouth,
I will speak in the pinch of my spirit.
I will groan in the bitterness of my soul.
12Am I Yam or Tannin
that you should place me under guard?
13For I thought, 'My bed will comfort me;
my couch will ease my groans.'
14You terrorize me with dreams;
you scare me with visions.
15The Strangler has chosen my neck,
Death, my bones.

46. See Johnston, *Shades of Sheol*.

> [16]I loathe my life; I will not live forever.
> Bring me to an end, for my life is meaningless."

7:11–16. *God terrorizes Job.* Job will not go quietly. In the previous section, he complained about the "hard service" that is humanity's plight (7:1) as well as his own personal suffering (v. 5 in particular). He expects he will die, but before then he will speak ("I will not restrain my mouth"). In the midst of his sufferings, it would take great self-control not to speak, and he is unwilling to exercise such discipline. Not only has his body been afflicted; his inner person also feels the pain. The word "pinch" (*ṣar*) could less vividly be translated "distress" or "tribulation," the verbal root (*ṣrr*) meaning "to find, tie up, cramp, impede," or the like.[47] Both "pinch of my spirit" and "the bitterness of my soul" are striking ways to describe what we would today call anger, anxiety, or depression. This condition compels Job to speak. We might remember that Job began this speech on this note (6:3–4). In parallel lines, colon *b* often specifies colon *a*, and we clearly see this when the more generic "speak" (*dbr*) gives way to "groan" (*śyḥ*).

Verse 12 makes clear that Job addresses Yahweh. He asks why he has been taken under guard. It is certainly not the friends who have done so, but, at least in Job's estimation, Yahweh who has brought the suffering on him. But why does God even bother? Job asks. He is not Yam or Tannin, after all. Yam (Heb. "sea") was the god of the waters in ancient Canaanite mythology. In the myth (*COS* 1:241–73), Yam asserts his kingship over the gods and demands that the god Baal be made his prisoner. Baal will not agree and engages Yam in battle. With the help of two clubs made by the craftsman god Kothar-wa-Hasis, Baal defeats Yam. The ancient tablets containing this story break at this point, though scholars are convinced, based on an analogy with the Mesopotamian story of the conflict between Marduk and Tiamat, that the account of creation would follow this. After defeating Tiamat, the goddess of the waters, Marduk, the creator god, pushes back her waters and places a boundary to hold them back.

In short, the creator gods of the ancient Near East were said to perform their work by subduing and then controlling the sea and its monsters. Yam is such a monster, as is Tannin, though the latter is less clearly understood from the Bible[48] or ancient Near Eastern background. From Ps. 74:13–14 it is even possible that Leviathan was considered Tannin, which may be a general term for "sea monster(s)." Job is amazed that God would consider him a

47. I. Swart and R. Wakely, *NIDOTTE* 3:853–59.

48. Fyall (*Now My Eyes*, 85) gives a survey of biblical usage: "*Tannîn*, or sea monster, occurs in Genesis 1:21 as part of the denizens of the sea. In Psalm 148:7 the *tannînîm* are called to join in the universal chorus of praise to the Creator. The word is used in Exodus 7:9, 10 and 12 of the snakes which emerge from staffs in the confrontation between Moses and Pharaoh's magicians; in Deuteronomy 32:33 it is used of venomous snakes, as in Psalm 91:13 also."

threat on the level of a Yam/Tannin that he should garner such treatment. (For more on the use of mythological imagery, see "Behemoth and Leviathan: The Power of the Mythic Imagination" following my comments on Job 38:1–42:6.)

In 1:10 the accuser accused God of placing "a hedge around him [Job], his household, and all that belongs to him." In a sense, God guarded Job to his advantage. In the present, though, Job feels that God is treating him as someone who might do great damage to his creation. We, the readers, know that this is not what motivates God. Indeed, we know that it would be more accurate to say that the accuser is behind Job's pain. However, we cannot forget that God has his eye on Job and is the one who has allowed the accuser to afflict Job.

In vv. 13–14 Job again returns to the idea that he expected to find respite from his sufferings at night. Sleep often allows emotional and physical healing to take place. But Job does not rest at night; he fights demons in his nightmares. Verse 15 then returns to a mythological theme. "Death," mentioned in the *b* colon, is another well-known Canaanite deity. After vanquishing Yam and building his house, Baal encounters yet another foe in the form of Mot, "Death." Mot defeats Baal and swallows him (evoking the reversal of this theme in Isa. 25:8, quoted in 1 Cor. 15:54). In this verse, Job believes that Death is after him.

Less clear is the reference to "the Strangler," not a well-known figure in ancient Near Eastern mythology. For this reason, some translations and commentators render the verse differently than I have. Note the NIV: "So that I prefer strangling and death" (v. 15). However, though not widely attested, there was a mythological creature known as "the Strangler," according to Richard Hess.[49] That the participle of "strangle" appears in a context that mentions Yam, Tannin, and Death is persuasive that we are dealing with a mythological reference here.[50]

All of this leads Job to finally and once again express that he hates life and wants to die (see also chap. 3 and 9:21). His motivation is the meaninglessness (*hebel*) of life. In this, Job sounds like Qohelet, who in Ecclesiastes repeatedly proclaims the meaninglessness of life and occasionally yearns for death.

17"What are humans that you magnify them,
that you set your heart on them?
18You visit them every morning;
you test them all the time.

49. In *NIDOTTE* 2:209–10, citing Astour ("Some New Divine Names") and Cross and Saley ("Phoenician Incantations").

50. According to Hess (*Israelite Religions*, 160), other passages that refer to God's battle against Yam include Pss. 65:7; 74:13; 89:9; Prov. 8:29; Isa. 51:10; Jer. 5:22. Other passages that refer to Yahweh's battle with Death include Ps. 18:5–6 (2 Sam. 22:6–7); Isa. 25:8; 28:15, 18; Hosea 13:14; Hab. 2:5.

[19]Will you look away from me?
Will you leave me alone while I swallow my saliva?
[20]If I sinned, what did I do to you, O watcher of humanity?
Why have you made me your target?
Why have I become a burden to you?
[21]Why do you not forgive my transgression
and carry away my guilt?
For I now lie down in the dust.
You will look for me, and I will not be there."

7:17–21. *Why does God bother?* Job continues to speak to God. Scholars widely agree that the opening of this section (vv. 17–18) sounds like Ps. 8:4: "What are human beings that you are mindful of them, mortals that you care for them?" (NRSV). The similarity is even better noted once it is realized that the verb "care for" in 8:4b is the same as the verb translated "visit" in Job 7:18a (*pqd*).[51] The different English translation is due to the context. The psalmist's reflection on God's relationship with his human creatures leads him to glory in humanity: "You made them only a little lower than God and crowned them with glory and honor" (Ps. 8:5 NLT). Job's query ("What are humans?") also expresses his "wonder" that God directs his attention toward human beings. However, rather than appreciating the attention, Job is greatly upset by it. To paraphrase the psalmist: "What are humans that you have given them so much authority, status, and responsibility?" ("You made them rulers over the works of your hands; you put everything under their feet," 8:6–7 TNIV). To paraphrase Job, "What are humans that you so diligently and exactly examine them to denigrate them?"

The psalm leads to praise of God: "LORD, our Lord, how majestic is your name in all the earth!" (8:1, 9 NIV).[52] Job's reflection on God's attention leads him to complain. Job asks God why he bothers to examine, even test (7:18b), human beings so rigorously and constantly ("every morning," 7:18a). What is so important about humans that he would bother to do so?

Naturally, Job is most concerned about his present situation, which he blames on God's watchful eye. The irony here is that Job's situation is not the result of God's being the "watcher of humanity." Indeed, in the preface God

51. The connection between Ps. 8 and Job 7:17–18 raises the question of relative dating and whether the relationship between the two texts can throw light on the date of the book of Job. As is often the case, one cannot be dogmatic here. However, Job 7 has all the characteristics of a parody of Ps. 8. It would appear to me that the psalm precedes the Joban reference. The next question concerns the dating of the psalm. The title of the psalm associates it with David. While not all would agree with me that we should take these titles seriously, few, if any, would disagree that David's reign would be the earliest possible date for this psalm. Thus the relationship between Ps. 8 and Job 7 argues against those who want to affirm a traditional early date for the book of Job (see "Authorship and Date" in the introduction).

52. This sentiment forms an inclusio and thus highlights its thematic importance in the psalm; see T. Longman, "Inclusio," *DOTWPW* 323–35.

depended on the accuser, one of his angels, for reports concerning his servant Job. He is the one who roamed the earth and kept an eye on humans (1:7; 2:2)—at the request of God. But still, one does not get the impression from the preface that God was the one who was nitpicking to discover any error or sin on Job's part. But that is not Job's impression. God does not even give him time to swallow his saliva. Job has become God's target, again returning to a point that he made at the beginning of this speech (6:4).

Job's shock at God's punishing attention does not depend on whether he has sinned. He does not admit to sin in v. 20;[53] he simply says that even his sin would not justify God's present attitude and action toward him. After all, why should his sin disturb God? God could simply forgive it. But apparently he does not do so. Job believes that God prefers to punish rather than to carry away his guilt. As a result, Job is brought low ("I now lie down in the dust," v. 21c) and will soon disappear from sight.

Theological Implications

Hard Service on Earth for Humans

In 7:1 Job asks rhetorically whether there is hard service for humans. His present experience of suffering has led him to believe the answer is clearly affirmative. As far as we know, this viewpoint is recent, acquired with the beginning of his suffering. Now that he suffers, he becomes aware of the suffering of all humanity. It is hard to escape the truthfulness of Job's assertion here. While it would be wrong to say that all humans experience distress throughout their lives, it is true that no human is without serious tragedy and struggle in life.

In the commentary proper, I began to discuss the theological implications of this topic by noting a difference between the biblical and the ancient Near Eastern accounts of the creation of humanity. In Mesopotamian myths, humans are created to be the servants of the gods, to do the menial tasks that the lesser gods did not want to perform (like dig the irrigation ditches). In the Bible, humans are created for work, but it is the dignified task of tending the garden.

Why, then, does Job (and humanity in general) experience life as hard labor? The answer is not found in Gen. 1–2, but in the account of the fall in Gen. 3. After Adam's rebellion against God, God announces to him:

> Because you have listened to the voice of your wife,
>   and have eaten of the tree
> about which I commanded you,
>   "You shall not eat of it,"

53. Contra Johnson, *Now My Eye Sees You*, 161.

cursed is the ground because of you;
  in toil you shall eat of it all the days of your life;
thorns and thistles it shall bring forth for you;
  and you shall eat the plants of the field.
By the sweat of your face
  you shall eat bread
until you return to the ground,
  for out of it you were taken;
you are dust,
  and to dust you shall return. (Gen. 3:17–19 NRSV)

In other words, human hardship originates not in creation but in rebellion. This passage explains why human beings experience life as hard service, a struggle to find meaning and fulfillment.

The Role of Relationships (Community) in Suffering

In 6:14–30 Job expresses disappointment, even disgust, at the lack of support that his friends give him in the midst of his suffering. Indeed, they have intensified his pain rather than mitigating it. Job's words remind us of the importance of relationships in the midst of suffering.

It is tempting to think that the biblical view is that all one needs is God to make one's way in a difficult world, but this view is undermined as early as Gen. 2:4b–25. In this second creation account, God creates Adam first. Adam is in a harmonious relationship with God. He lives in Eden, paradise. One would think that he has everything, but God knows better and says, "It is not good that the man should be alone" (Gen. 2:18 NRSV). If this is true in Eden, how much more so in the world after the fall.

Even Qohelet recognizes this in his reflections on life in a fallen world:

> Two are better than one, for they can get a good return for their toil. For if one of them falls down, the other can help his friend up. But pity the person who falls when there is not another to help. Also, if two people lie down together, they keep warm, but how can one person keep warm? And though someone can overpower one person, two can resist the attacker.
>
> "A three-stranded cord does not quickly snap."[54]

Proverbs also accentuates the importance of community in its teaching about neighbors/friends.[55] Friendship and good relationships with neighbors

54. For translation and commentary of Eccles. 4:9–12, see Longman, *Ecclesiastes*, 140–44.

55. The most commonly used word for "friend" and "neighbor" is the noun *rēaʿ* II, from the verb *rʿh* II ("to associate with"). The noun thus refers to another person with whom one is close. The translation "friend" indicates emotional attachment, while "neighbor" fits those contexts where spatial intimacy is meant. Surely the two sometimes overlap. However, in some contexts

are very important to the sages. A good friend is as valuable in tough times as a close relative such as a brother (17:17). Indeed, 27:9–10 suggests that friends are sometimes more valuable than relatives during hard times, especially if a friend is closer at hand. There is no doubt that, to the sage, friends and neighbors form a community that helps a person navigate the difficulties of life. Indeed, to sabotage a relationship with a neighbor or friend is utter stupidity (11:9, 11).

During the OT period, the idea of community developed over time. During the patriarchal period, the basic unit of community was the extended family. The family was the locus of nurture and protection under divine oversight. Genesis 14 provides a stirring story of Abraham's pursuit and victory over four ancient Near Eastern kings who had raided Canaan and had captured his nephew Lot. Of course, Abraham's success was totally dependent on God's help (14:20).

As time went on, God's people became a nation composed of tribes, which in turn were made up of extended families. Each of these units (family, tribe, nation) composed a community that was to provide help for struggling individuals. Israelites were bound together in covenant to their God. The book of Judges provides examples of the dangers of community disunity and tribal fragmentation. Deborah, for instance, chastises individual tribes for failure to rally to the help of all the covenant community when they were in trouble (Judg. 5:15b–17).

Some thought that kingship was the answer to disunity (1 Sam. 8:4–5).[56] The king was to provide a strong central authority that would unite the community for their common good and protection. The story of the failure of kingship due to the individual apostasy of the kings of Israel and Judah is well known and explains their eventual defeat and the loss of nationhood in the exile.

The books of Ezra–Nehemiah and Esther indicate that the exile is not the end of OT community. Esther tells the story of the survival of the people of God in the face of Haman's (representing the Amalekites) attempt to eradicate them. While the ironic reversals of the story indicate that God is the ultimate savior of his people (though he is not explicitly mentioned), Mordecai and Esther are the human agents in delivering the community.[57]

The NT covenant community was not defined primarily by kinship.[58] The community (*koinōnia*) was the church (*ekklēsia*), drawn from many nations but united by their relationship to Jesus Christ. By appointing twelve dis-

---

it proves difficult to decide between "neighbor" and "friend" as the best English translation. In any case, I will treat friends and neighbors together in this short description.

56. Note also the recurring refrain of the book of Judges (17:6; 18:1; 19:1; 21:25) that attributes the problems of the period to the lack of a strong central leader.

57. Jobes, *Esther*, 41–45.

58. The stories of Rahab, Ruth, Naaman, and others show that kinship is not the ultimate explanation of community in the OT.

ciples, Jesus indicated his intention to build a new covenant community on the model of the twelve tribes of Israel. Neither the individual Christian nor the community of Christians will escape suffering in this world. However, a Christian's relationship with Christ and with fellow believers is to provide support in a painful world, so that, as Paul stated, the Christian can suffer with joy:

> Blessed be the God and Father of our Lord Jesus Christ, the Father of mercies and the God of all consolation, who consoles us in all our affliction, so that we may be able to console those who are in any affliction with the consolation with which we ourselves are consoled by God. For just as the sufferings of Christ are abundant for us, so also our consolation is abundant through Christ. If we are being afflicted, it is for your consolation and salvation; if we are being consoled, it is for your consolation, which you experience when you patiently endure the same sufferings that we are also suffering. Our hope for you is unshaken; for we know that as you share in our sufferings, so also you share in our consolation. (2 Cor. 1:3–7 NRSV)

The sad fact, though, is that the community of God, like the three friends of Job, is often like a dried-up wadi, promising succor but not delivering. The story of Job's treatment at the hands of his friends is a warning about offering facile advice to those who suffer. It is not adequate to offer pat answers to people's problems; we must approach them with compassion, thoughtfulness, and empathy.

3.
Bildad's First Speech
(8:1–22)

Translation

1And Bildad the Shuhite answered and said:
2"How long will you continue speaking these things?
The words of your mouth are a strong wind.

3Does God pervert justice?
Does Shaddai pervert righteousness?
4If[1] your children sinned against him,
he sent them into the power of their transgression.

5If you look for God
and you plead to Shaddai for grace,
6if you are pure and virtuous,
he will indeed immediately rouse himself concerning you
and will restore you to your right place.
7Though your start was small,
your end will be exceedingly exalted.[2]

1. If *ʾim* is to be understood according to its typical usage as a hypothetical, then perhaps this is a sign that Bildad is not being utterly cruel in his statement. Some translations take it as a temporal marker, "When" (see NIV; cf. Clines, *Job 1–20*, 198, "since"), but there is no grammatical evidence that it is used in that way.

2. *Śgh* is a by-form of *śgʾ*, "to be exalted."

[8]For ask now the former generations,
and focus on the discoveries of their fathers.
[9]For we are yesterday and do not know,
for our days are a shadow on the earth.
[10]Won't they teach you and tell you,
and won't words come out of their heart?
[11]Does papyrus grow in a non-marshy place?
Does a reed grow without water?
[12]While still in flower and not plucked,
it dries up before even the grass.
[13]Thus are the paths of all who forget God;
the hope of the godless perishes.
[14]Their confidence is a gossamer thread;[3]
their trust is a spider's web.[4]
[15]He leans on its[5] house, and it[6] does not stand;
he seizes it, and it does not endure.
[16]He is a well-watered plant[7] in the sun;
its shoots spread out all over his garden.
[17]Its roots intertwine among the pile of rocks;
it looks for a place among the stones.
[18]But if it is torn[8] from its place,
it disowns it (by saying): 'I never saw it.'
[19]Indeed, it dissolves[9] on the way,
and from the dirt another sprouts.
[20]Indeed, God does not reject the innocent,
and he does not grasp the hand of the wicked.
[21]He will yet fill your mouth with laughter,
and your lips with joy.
[22]Those who hate you will be clothed with shame,
and the tent of the wicked will be no more."

3. *Yāqôt* is a hapax legomenon, and we cannot even be confident whether it is a noun (as the parallelism might suggest) or a verb. I am taking it with the vast majority of translations as a noun, though Clines (*Job 1–20*, 200) gives reasons to doubt that the supposed Arabic cognate or suggested emendations support this view. If it is a verb, Clines's view that it is to be connected with Arabic *qatta* ("cut, carve") is as good as, but no better than, others.

4. Literally "the house of a spider" (*bêt ʿakkābîš*).

5. Or "his."

6. Or "he."

7. *Rāṭōb*, the noun, occurs only here. The verb, "to be moist," occurs only in Job 24:8.

8. Though the root *blʿ* most often means "to swallow" or "to swallow up," it can have the general meaning "to destroy," which in the case of a plant would mean to tear it out of the ground.

9. *Mĕśôś* is extremely difficult. The MT phrase *mĕśôś darkô* means "the happiness of his way." This does not fit well in the context. The most common approach to the problem is to emend to *mĕsûs*, "to dissolve." The idea is that the life of the first plant comes to an end. See discussion in Clines, *Job 1–20*, 200.

Interpretation

Bildad is the second of the three friends to speak to Job. His speech is short but to the point. After upbraiding Job for even attempting to defend himself (v. 2), he then defends God's actions as just by saying that Job's children must have deserved their fate (vv. 3–4). However, for Job there is still hope because he, as opposed to his children, is still alive. Verses 5–7 appeal to Job to turn to God, presumably to repent. If he does so, then he will be restored. His source of authority for his position is the "former generations," those who were alive before them (vv. 8–10). They will attest that the godless, if they thrive at all, will do so only temporarily. In the final analysis, the godly thrive and the godless suffer (vv. 11–22).

> [1]And Bildad the Shuhite answered and said:
> [2]"How long will you continue speaking these things?
> The words of your mouth are a strong wind."

8:1–2. *Opening insults.* As usual, the first verse of a new speech introduces the speaker. In this case, it is the second of the three friends, Bildad the Shuhite. It is also fairly typical for the friends to begin their speech with an insult directed at Job, and v. 2 fulfills that function. Job has hardly gotten started (he has only given one of his eight speeches), but still Bildad attacks him for speaking "these things," by which he likely means his attempts at self-justification and the charge that God is unjust. Verse 2b charges Job with bluster. He speaks many words but says nothing of substance. The wind is something that can be felt but not seen or grasped. That he characterizes his speech as a "strong" wind could point to passion or volume or probably both.

> [3]"Does God pervert justice?
> Does Shaddai pervert righteousness?
> [4]If your children sinned against him,
> he sent them into the power of their transgression."

8:3–4. *God is just.* Bildad is obviously upset by Job's belief that he does not deserve the pain that he experiences. In Bildad's theology, that viewpoint is indefensible. Justice demands punishment for evil and reward for good. Anything else would be a perversion[10] of justice and righteousness. Bildad is correct in his charge. Job shares his retribution theology, and he believes that God is unjustly punishing him for something he has not done.

Bildad applies his theology to the case of Job's children. Note the connection between the prose prologue and the poetic dialogue here (see Job 1:18–19).

10. Note the use of the same verb (*ʿwt* in the Piel) in both cola of v. 3. The verb means "to bend" but is used mostly in the moral sense of "to deviate from proper behavior."

This provides evidence that the dialogues were written with knowledge of the prose story (see "Authorship and Date" in the introduction). That Bildad begins v. 4 with a conditional particle (*'im*; see the translation note for 8:4) may indicate that he is not being totally callous in his statement. Nonetheless, it is harsh even to suggest that his children were responsible for their deaths on the basis of no evidence except the fact of their deaths. While Job knows his own heart, he probably cannot be certain about his children. However, the reader of the book knows for a fact that Job's children did not die because of their own "transgression." Thus we understand the inappropriateness of the charge even better than Job.

5"If you look for God
 and you plead to Shaddai for grace,
6if you are pure and virtuous,
 he will indeed immediately rouse himself concerning you
 and will restore you to your right place.
7Though your start was small,
 your end will be exceedingly exalted."

8:5–7. *Repentance leads to restoration.* Bildad is not totally heartless. He does have concern for Job and wants to offer him a way out of his predicament. His advice is consistent with the message of all three friends: If you want to be restored, then you need to repent. The problem is caused by a break of relationship with God, and now Job needs to initiate a restoration. The "plea for grace" would include the idea that Job does not deserve the restoration because of his sin.

However, Job's restoration will require more than words. He must also be "pure" (*zak*) and "virtuous" (*yāšār*). The former is a new word to the book of Job, but the latter is well known: right from the start Job has been called "virtuous" (1:1, 8; 2:3). Lack of virtue is not Job's problem, though this is the second time in as many speeches that two of the friends have mentioned it (4:7). As we will see, the three friends are convinced that this is the problem, and so they urge Job to become pure and virtuous, saying that if he does, God will immediately restore him.

Indeed, God will "rouse" (from *'wr*) himself on behalf of Job. The verb refers to the mental state that leads to some action, especially actions that "require extra effort, such as war, work, or love."[11] In this case, the activity is restoration, the repair of God's good relationship with Job. The word "place" (*nāweh*) has connotations of "home" or even "pasturage," and "right" (*ṣedeq*) is often translated as "righteous." The restoration will also include a restoration of the previous good estate of Job. He will move from small things to big things.

11. V. P. Hamilton, *NIDOTTE* 3:357.

Of course, one of the major theological issues of the book of Job concerns the truthfulness of Bildad's (and the other friends') viewpoint. Although God will censure this view (42:7), some are quick to point out that it is indeed when Job repents that God restores him. I will deal with this apparent anomaly in the final chapter.

8"For ask now the former generations,
and focus on the discoveries of their fathers.
9For we are yesterday and do not know,
for our days are a shadow on the earth.
10Won't they teach you and tell you,
and won't words come out of their heart?
11Does papyrus grow in a non-marshy place?
Does a reed grow without water?
12While still in flower and not plucked,
it dries up before even the grass.
13Thus are the paths of all who forget God;
the hope of the godless perishes.
14Their confidence is a gossamer thread;
their trust is a spider's web.
15He leans on its house, and it does not stand;
he seizes it, and it does not endure.
16He is a well-watered plant in the sun;
its shoots spread out all over his garden.
17Its roots intertwine among the pile of rocks;
it looks for a place among the stones.
18But if it is torn from its place,
it disowns it (by saying): 'I never saw it.'
19Indeed, it dissolves on the way,
and from the dirt another sprouts.
20Indeed, God does not reject the innocent,
and he does not grasp the hand of the wicked.
21He will yet fill your mouth with laughter,
and your lips with joy.
22Those who hate you will be clothed with shame,
and the tent of the wicked will be no more."

8:8–22. *Age-old wisdom.* Bildad bolsters his argument by citing the "fathers." In the ancient Near East, it was generally thought that the older someone was, the wiser they were. This position has a certain logic to it. After all, wisdom is gained through observation and experience. As people live life, they see that certain strategies of living are more successful than others. When they experience setbacks, they can learn from their mistakes. On the other hand, not all wisdom comes by means of direct experience. The wise also learn from advice that is handed down from father to son; in other words, they learn from tradition. Here Bildad appeals to tradition, the ancient and time-tested tradition of previous generations.[12] Of course, as Elihu will later say, wisdom is not always with the aged (32:6–9). After all, not everyone observes life as they live it or learns from their mistakes. Tradition is not always correct. But that is not Bildad's view. He feels greatly supported by the views of the "fathers," and that helps seal the deal for him.

The fathers' wisdom contrasts with those who are alive at present (v. 9). The present generation is not deep in experience. Today we use the expression "That is so yesterday" to claim that something is obsolete. When Bildad says "We are yesterday," he suggests that there is no significant lived experience behind advice without the precedent of previous generations.

These previous generations are able to teach Job (v. 10), and their perspective is given in vv. 12–22, beginning with rhetorical questions: "Does papyrus grow in a non-marshy place? Does a reed grow without water?" (v. 11). The answer is no. These plants need abundant, even standing, water in which to grow. They may start out looking healthy ("still in flower"), but if papyrus and reed are left without water, then they quickly dry up. They even turn brown and wither before grass, which is also notorious for its fragility and brevity (Pss. 102:4, 11; 129:6). It is used for the fate of the wicked in Ps. 37:2. Here Bildad speaks similarly of the godless.[13] "Just as the plant needs water to grow, a man cannot survive unless he is rooted in virtue."[14] His confidence is as weak as a spider's web. Its tensive strength is as strong as steel, but it is so thin that it is easily broken. If one puts any weight on a spider web, it will break apart. So too will the confidence of the wicked, godless person.

Verses 16–19 shift metaphors again. After vv. 14–15 describe the spider's web, Bildad returns to a plant metaphor, though it is slightly different from the plant metaphor of vv. 11–13. The plant is not a papyrus and reed. In this case, the plant is well watered and in the sun, and therefore it thrives, sending its shoots all over the garden and the roots among a pile of rocks. That its roots are among the rocks and not deep in the soil indicates that its growth is superficial, just like the success of a godless person, according to Bildad. Thus it is easily "torn from its place" (v. 18). The place where it was located quickly forgets that it existed ("I never saw it"). It disappears, and then another plant comes and takes its place. The metaphor illustrates the ephemeral nature of the success of the wicked.

Verse 20 states the principle of retribution as simply as possible, though in a negative fashion. That God does not reject the innocent means that he continues in relationship with the innocent. By contrast, that he does not

12. For more on the sources of wisdom, see Estes, *Hear, My Son*, 87–100; and Longman, *Proverbs*, 74–79.

13. Here Bildad seems to implicitly accuse Job of being godless, but as Johnson (*Now My Eye Sees You*, 121) points out, there is no evidence that Job has abandoned God.

14. Alter, *Wisdom Books*, 40.

grasp the hand (enter into a protective relationship) with the wicked means that he rejects them. Thus Job's fate, provided he follows Bildad's advice and repents, is a positive one filled with laughter and joy. On the other hand, the wicked will be shamed.

Theological Implications

Retribution Theology in a Nutshell

Bildad clearly and concisely articulates the retribution theology that fuels the main argument of the three friends, a view that is shared by Job and Elihu as well. Retribution theology is based on the idea that sin leads to suffering and thus that suffering is a sign of sin. Many simply write off Bildad's argument as simplistic. In support of his position, he cites the authority of previous generations (see "The Authority of Tradition" below). We might assume that this refers to the teaching of parents passed down to their children. He does not cite Scripture, for in his (pre)patriarchal world, there is no written Scripture.[15] Those of us who read Job in the context of the canon as a whole should realize just how much Scripture Bildad could quote to support his perspective if it were available to him. I will give a few examples of what I mean.

The book of Deuteronomy is a covenant-renewal text. Moses leads the Israelites in a reaffirmation of their commitment to follow God and his law that they made at Mount Sinai (Exod. 19–24). Most of the book is law; it begins with the Ten Commandments (Deut. 5), which are then applied to specific situations in the extensive case law that follows (Deut. 6–26). After the law come the rewards and punishments that are contingent on whether the Israelites obey the law. Note in particular the introductions to the rewards and the punishments:

> If you will only obey the LORD your God, by diligently observing all his commandments that I am commanding you today, the LORD your God will set you high above all the nations of the earth; all these blessings shall come upon you and overtake you, if you obey the LORD your God. . . . But if you will not obey the LORD your God by diligently observing all his commandments and decrees, which I am commanding you today, then all these curses shall come upon you and overtake you. (28:1–2, 15 NRSV)

Taken at face value, the structure of Deuteronomy suggests that sin leads to suffering and obedience leads to reward.

Furthermore, when one looks at the account of the history of Israel (and Judah) as it is given in Samuel and Kings (in contrast to Chronicles), it is very

15. This is a statement not about when the book of Job was written and whether it alludes to other Scripture but about the time of the story (see "Authorship and Date" in the introduction).

clear that when God's people sin, they suffer, and when they obey God (rarely), they prosper. Indeed, Israel's sin ultimately leads to the defeat of the northern kingdom and the exile of the southern kingdom. Many detect a specifically Deuteronomic perspective operating in the presentation of Samuel–Kings historiography. Whether or not this is true, there is no doubt that Samuel–Kings understands Israel's suffering to be the result of sin.

The book of Proverbs also supports the nexus between sin and suffering and between obedience and reward. The sages were intent on encouraging wise, godly, righteous behavior by pointing to its benefits, while at the same time discouraging foolish, ungodly, wicked behavior by drawing a connection to the pain that it brings. Reading anywhere in the book will illustrate this point, but a few random examples will suffice:

> The path of lazy people is like a hedge of thorns,
> but the way of the virtuous is a clear highway. (15:19)
>
> Those who pursue righteousness and covenant love
> will find life, righteousness, and honor. (21:21)

Finally, consider the prophets. They are like "covenant lawyers" sent by God when his people break the law. God commissions Jeremiah, for instance, to challenge Judah to repent because of their rebellion and disobedience. If they do not repent, God will send Babylon to defeat them and carry them off into exile. Sin leads to suffering.

The clearest heirs to Bildad's retribution theology are advocates of the so-called prosperity gospel, which proclaims that God wants to lavish health, wealth, and happiness on his faithful people. Sickness, poverty, and sadness are signs of a lack of faith. But of course it is not just those who affirm the prosperity gospel that find affinity with the retribution theology of the friends. When adversity strikes, we all have the propensity to ask "What did I do to deserve this?" The assumption is that it is sin, and sin alone, that leads to suffering.

The book of Job is written as a corrective to this view, rejecting retribution theology as an explanation of Job's suffering. Indeed, thanks to the book's prologue, we already know that Job does not suffer because of his sin. Although sin does lead to suffering, it does not always do so right away (see "Suffering: Job and Retribution Theology" in the introduction for an explanation of the biblical view that ultimate reward and punishment happen in the eschaton). Indeed, Samuel–Kings illustrate not simply retribution theology but also delayed retribution. God was patient with his people and often did not punish them right away. Individual sin does not always lead immediately to pain.

Furthermore, sin is not the only explanation of suffering. Bildad's perspective depends on the idea that suffering originates only in sin. This view was shared by Jesus's disciples when they came across a man born blind: "Rabbi, who sinned, this man or his parents, that he was born blind?" (John 9:2 NRSV). The disciples could not imagine another possibility than that this man's affliction came from his or his parents' sin. Jesus broadens their horizon (and ours) by responding: "Neither this man nor his parents sinned; he was born blind so that God's works might be revealed in him" (9:3 NRSV). There are many causes of suffering. Jesus's response (and the book of Job) reminds us not to assume that suffering is necessarily connected to sin.

What is it about retribution theology that makes it so intractable? It is comforting to those who are not suffering at the moment. After all, it gives the semblance of control. If suffering comes about only through sin, then if I do not sin, I will not suffer. To think that we might suffer without sinning is a frightening idea. But the book of Job teaches (as does the whole Bible) that we are not in control—God is. As we read on in the book of Job, we will discover the proper response to this reality.

The Authority of Tradition

To support his perspective on retribution theology, Bildad cites the authority of the previous generations, the tried and tested truths that have been handed down from generation to generation (8:8–10). Bildad did not make up his theology; he inherited his beliefs from others, who presumably lived by them.

In the light of the whole book of Job, we must conclude that this tradition was false, unhelpful, bogus. But should this lead us to reject tradition as a source of authority?

The Enlightenment (and the rise of modernism) subjected tradition to the analysis of critical thinking. Generalizing a bit, the premodern period was a time when tradition was an accepted mode of the transmission of knowledge. One accepted the teaching of previous generations. Modernism asserts the autonomy of human reason and subjects all traditions to criticism in the pursuit of truth. Postmodern thinkers are skeptical about the ability of autonomous human reason to reach truth in any kind of absolute sense, but they suspect tradition too.

What are Christians to make of this? Are we premodern, modern, or postmodern in our appropriation of tradition? Before we attempt an answer to this question, we should remind ourselves that Scripture is tradition handed down from generation to generation. Orthodox Christianity asserts that the church is founded on Scripture. Christians place themselves under Scripture as canon, the rule of faith and practice.

Such a view might lead one to suspect that Christians are premodern in their attitude toward Scripture, and in a sense this is right. But it does not take into account a very important fact: Scripture needs to be interpreted, and the church has inherited not only Scripture but also traditions about how Scripture should be interpreted. These traditions are handed down in various ways, through creeds and confessions, through commentaries and other written resources, through preaching and teaching in the church and its schools.

Toward this type of tradition, we should and must exercise our critical readings and not simply accept the tradition without testing it. In this way, we are modernist in our approach to tradition. Our critical analysis of a tradition of interpretation may lead us to reaffirm it, but our allegiance is to Scripture and not to specific interpretations of Scripture. To allow a historical confession to bind one's interpretation of Scripture is to substitute human authority for divine.

Postmodern perspectives on truth are difficult for Christians to appreciate because they often seem to deny that there is any absolute truth. But postmodern thought is helpful because it keeps us humble by reminding us that we are finite humans who are incapable of having a full comprehension of truth. Since God has spoken his word to us, we have an adequate apprehension of the truth concerning God, ourselves, and the world.

4. Job's Second Response

(9:1–10:22)

Translation

9:1 And Job answered and said:

2 "Truly, I know that this is correct,
but how can a person be righteous with God?
3 If someone wants to take him to court,[1]
one could not answer him one out of a thousand times.

4 He is wise of heart and strong in power;
who can press him and come out whole?
5 He can move mountains without them knowing,
overturning them in his anger.
6 He causes the land to shake from its place,
and its pillars shudder.
7 He speaks to the sun, and it does not rise;[2]
he seals up the stars.
8 He alone stretched out the heavens
and trod on the high places of the sea.[3]

1. The verb *rîb* is a well-known legal term that can be translated "contend" or "argue," but "take him to court" accentuates the presupposed legal setting.

2. *Zāraḥ* can also mean "to shine." The point is the same in either case. The sun obeys God, who created it.

3. Or Yam, the sea god, representing chaos and known from Ugaritic mythology.

[9]He is the maker of the Bear and Orion,
and the Pleiades[4] and the chambers of the south.[5]
[10]He is the maker of great things that are beyond understanding,
and marvelous things that are without count.

[11]If he crosses over to me, I will not see;
if he passes by, I will not perceive him.
[12]If he carries off, who will bring back?
Who will say to him, 'What are you doing?'
[13]God does not relent of his anger.
Even Rahab's allies cower under him.
[14]How can I answer him?
How[6] can I choose my words with him?
[15]Though[7] I am righteous, I could not answer him.
I could only plead for mercy with my judge.
[16]If I summoned him, and he answered me,
I do not believe that he would hear my voice.
[17]He would crush[8] me with a storm
and multiply my bruises without cause.
[18]He does not let me regain my breath.
Indeed, he satiates me with bitterness.
[19]If it is about power, he is strong.
If it is about judgment, who can testify against him?[9]
[20]Though[10] I am righteous, my mouth condemns me.
I am innocent, but he declares me perverse.
[21]I am innocent. I don't know for sure.
I loathe my life.[11]

[22]It is all the same; therefore, I say:
'He destroys the innocent and the wicked.'

4. There is no doubt that these three terms indicate constellations, though their exact identity is hard to pinpoint. The rendering here simply follows the majority of modern translations and commentators, though alternative identifications are not hard to find. For a discussion of *ʿāš* (here the Bear), *kĕsîl* (Orion), and *kîmâ* (Pleiades), see R. C. Newman, *NIDOTTE* 2:611–12.

5. This is the only occurrence of this phrase, which likely refers to a sector of the sky that "contains" constellations (like a room contains furniture).

6. Understood by ellipsis from the first colon.

7. This could be translated hypothetically as "even if," but Job does not seem in doubt as to his righteousness (with NRSV, NET; contra NLT, NIV).

8. The verb *šûp* is best known for its use in Gen. 3:15 in reference to the offspring of the woman crushing the head of the serpent, taken in the NT and early Christian interpretation as a reference to Jesus's defeat of Satan (Rom. 16:20).

9. With the LXX; the MT has "me."

10. See the translation note for 9:15.

11. A similar thought using similar vocabulary may be found in 7:16.

23If a disaster[12] brings sudden death,
he ridicules the despair[13] of the innocent.
24The earth is given into the power of the wicked;
he covers the face of its judges.
If it is not he, then who?

25My days go faster than a runner;
they are swift, but not good.
26They pass by like reed boats,
like an eagle swoops on its prey.
27If I say: 'I will forget my sighs;
I will abandon my countenance and be cheerful,'
28I am afraid of all my distress;
I know that you will not find me innocent.
29As for me, I am declared wicked.
Why do I exhaust myself for no purpose?[14]
30Even if I wash myself with snow,
and I cleanse my palms with lye,
31then you will plunge me in the pit,
and my garments will abhor me.

32For he is not a person like I am that I could answer him,
that we will go together into judgment.
33There is no umpire between us
who would set his hand on both of us.
34He would take his rod away from me,
and not let his dread scare me.
35I would speak and not be afraid of him,
though[15] this is not the case with me.

10:1I am disgusted[16] with my life;
I will abandon myself to my sighs;
I will speak in my bitterness.[17]
2I will tell God: 'Do not declare me wicked;
tell me why you accuse me.

12. As Clines (*Job 1–20*, 218) points out, *šôṭ* means "whip" but here is used as "a symbol of a natural disaster."

13. I take the word as a derivative of *mss* ("to melt"), not *nsh* ("to test"); so Gray (*Job*, 198), who points out that the "Niphal of *māsas* is used with the subject 'heart' denoting despair."

14. The word *hebel* is well known in Ecclesiastes, where it is often translated "meaningless" (see, e.g., 1:2 and the lengthy discussion of the word in Longman, *Ecclesiastes*, 61–65).

15. I take the *kî* as concessive.

16. M. A. Grisanti (*NIDOTTE* 3:897) points out the similarity between the root used here (*qôṭ*) and its by-form (*qûṣ*) in Gen. 27:46. In the latter, Rebekah is disgusted with her life because of Hittite women, and in our present context Job is disgusted with life because he suffers in spite of his innocence.

17. Or, "the bitterness of my soul" (*mar napšî*).

3Is it right for you to oppress me?
Must you despise the labor of your hands?
Do you favor the advice of the wicked?
4Do you have eyes of flesh?
Do you see with human vision?
5Are your days like the days of humans,
or your years like that of people?
6For you investigate my transgression;
you seek my sin.[18]
7You must know that I am not wicked,
but there is no rescue from your hand.
8Your hands shaped and made me,
but now you turn[19] and swallow me up.[20]
9Please remember that you made me like clay;
will you return me to dust?
10Do you not pour me out like milk,
curdle me like cheese?
11You clothed me in skin and flesh;
you knit me together with bones and sinews.
12Life and loyalty you have made with me,
and your concern has set a guard over me.
13These things you hid in your heart,
and I knew that this was your purpose.
14If I sinned, you would guard me
and would not declare me innocent of my transgression.
15If I am wicked, woe is me!
And if righteous, I cannot lift my head.
I am filled with shame,
and look[21] on my affliction.
16Proud as a lion you hunt me;
you again show your tremendous power against me.
17You renew your witnesses[22] against me;
you multiply your anger toward me;
you bring new troops against me.
18Why did you bring me out of the womb?
Why did I not die before any eye saw me?
19I would be as if I never was,
carried from womb to grave.

18. The verse's grammar has a chiastic structure that binds it together: verb + prepositional phrase/prepositional phrase + verb.

19. I take *sābîb* as a corruption of some form of the verb *sbb* ("to turn") with Clines (*Job 1–20*, 217) and others.

20. Many versions translate *blʿ* rather blandly as "destroy" (e.g., NRSV).

21. Taken as derived from *rʾh* ("to see"), though some (REB, NAB, NJB) take it as a variant from *rwh* ("to be sated").

22. Watson ("Metaphor in Job 10.17") takes this as "your troops" based on Ugaritic *ʿdn*, but this is debatable in the Ugaritic text (*CTA* 14.2.85–87).

20Are not the days of my life few?
  Let me alone that I might have a little joy
21before I go and not return,
  to the land of darkness and gloom,
22a land of dimness and blackness,[23]
  gloom and chaos,
  and shining is like darkness.'"

Interpretation

After Bildad's first speech, Job now responds. It is not a point-by-point refutation of Bildad's speech, but Job addresses his situation, which he considers unjust. As we will see, it is natural, though, to think that Job is in general referring to Bildad's speech, particularly in the opening verses (see comment on 9:2a). On the other hand, if it is a direct answer to a question, appeal would have to be made to 4:17, since Job's response echoes Elihu's (not Bildad's) rhetorical question there.

In this speech, he makes a concession to his "friends" (9:3a) but immediately takes issue with the idea that any human can challenge God, even though God is unfair. In this, Job's second speech in the first cycle, he begins by speaking to the friends about God (9:1–24) and then continues by speaking directly to God (9:25–10:22).

Job uses legal language in this speech right from the beginning. He feels that God treats him as if he is someone who is guilty of something. Job feels falsely accused. After all, he is suffering, and he shares with his friends the false idea that sin is the only explanation for the pain of life. For this reason, Job wants to take God to court and get answers from him. However, even as he raises the possibility of taking God to court, Job doubts that he can be successful. God is just too smart and strong to listen to a complaining human. As he goes on to describe God in 9:4–10, the emphasis is on God's power rather than his wisdom. It is his power, after all, that casts doubt on Job's ability to take him to task. In 9:11–14 Job expresses his belief that God is unapproachable. If one could even find him, he would not listen. We will see an evolution of Job's thought on this topic until at the end he proudly announces that he will take his case to God and expects to be successful (31:35–37).

But at this point Job simply believes that God is unjust. Even though Job is innocent, God will not care and will pronounce him guilty (9:15–18, 19–21). God treats the innocent and the wicked exactly alike (9:22–24, 25–31). It is this charge of injustice that stirs God's anger toward Job when he finally

23. Verses 21b and 22a have four closely related nouns (*ḥōšek*, *ṣalmāwet*, *ʿêpâ*, *ʿōpel*) that all refer to darkness and gloom. It is difficult to tell what the exact nuance of each is, but their combined use here emphasizes the point.

confronts him in the whirlwind (see especially 40:2). His belief that God is unjust leads Job to hate his life (9:21). At the very end of chap. 9 (vv. 32–35), Job expresses his need for an umpire between himself and God, someone who could mediate between the two of them since Job knows he is no match for God in court. As soon as he expresses his hope, he also asserts that such a thing is not possible. In this area too we will see that Job's thought develops to the point that he comes to believe that such a helper is available to him (see 16:19–21 and especially 19:23–27 as well as 33:23–27), though we will also see that his initial pessimism was correct.

Chapter 10 begins with Job again talking about how bitter his life has become (v. 1), telling the friends that he wants to tell God to stop accusing him (vv. 2–5). He believes God is accusing him because God is oppressing him. This connection between his suffering and God's accusation again reveals Job's agreement with the doctrine of retribution. Job believes that God knows that he is innocent but causes him to suffer anyway. God is truly unjust (vv. 6–7). Job challenges God's seeming intention to destroy him, a creation of God's own hands (vv. 8–11). Job feels that God is after him no matter whether he is righteous or wicked (vv. 12–15) and will bring a legal case against him (vv. 16–17). Finally (vv. 18–22), he beseeches God to leave him alone so he can experience a bit of happiness before he goes to his death, a place of darkness and gloom.

1And Job answered and said:

2"Truly, I know that this is correct,
but how can a person be righteous with God?
3If someone wants to take him to court,
one could not answer him one out of a thousand times."

9:1–3. *Job's apparent concession.* Job begins with an apparent concession. He responds to Bildad by saying "this" is correct, but what is "this"? Bildad's main point in chap. 8 was that God punishes unrepentant sinners. He does not "pervert justice" (8:3a). The wicked may appear to flourish, but their prosperity is as thin as a spider's web. On the other hand, if they are innocent or repent of their sin (8:5), then God will reward them.

Perhaps Job agrees with Bildad in principle. After all, his cries of divine injustice make sense only if he accepts the doctrine of retribution along with the three friends. Even if we are to take his opening statement as a concession to Bildad's theological point, he immediately protests that God does not fairly evaluate people. At this point, he is keeping his argument general, but he is surely thinking of his own situation. He does not feel that he deserves his present woeful situation, but at this point he expresses little hope that he could set God straight. Wilson states it correctly: "The problem Job considers is not whether retribution works (he seems to accept its operation here), but whether God knows that Job is righteous!"[24]

He uses legal language when he asks how a person can "be righteous" (the verbal form of *ṣdq*) in the presence of God. Christian readers need to be slow to read a Pauline understanding of the utter sinfulness of humans here (Rom. 3:9–20). Job is despairing of the possibility that he could convince God that he truly is righteous and undeserving of his present suffering. In a courtroom situation (Job 9:3a), a mere mortal like himself would not be able to respond to God. The next section will explain why: God is "wise of heart and strong in power."

4"He is wise of heart and strong in power;
who can press him and come out whole?
5He can move mountains without them knowing,
overturning them in his anger.
6He causes the land to shake from its place,
and its pillars shudder.
7He speaks to the sun, and it does not rise;
he seals up the stars.
8He alone stretched out the heavens
and trod on the high places of the sea.
9He is the maker of the Bear and Orion,
and the Pleiades and the chambers of the south.
10He is the maker of great things that are beyond understanding,
and marvelous things that are without count."

9:4–10. *God's wisdom and power.* Job describes God in order to explain why a human being cannot stand up to God in a courtroom setting (9:3). He begins with a general statement of God's wisdom and strength, and then, with a series of participial phrases (vv. 5–10), he illustrates his contention. Interestingly, the list focuses exclusively on God's power. Perhaps this emphasis should not surprise us since at this point Job feels overwhelmed by God's strength.

In the OT, mountains were considered the apex of geographical stability. At the polar opposite was the sea, which represented flux and chaos. While the sea was constantly moving, the mountains were imposing in their stability. However, God's power was so great that he could move mountains and overturn them. Earthquakes may have given at least one expression of this truth. Without warning ("without them knowing," v. 5a), the mountains could tremble. Other texts express God's sovereign control over the mountains by saying that they melt in the presence of an angry God (e.g., Nah. 1:5). Earthquake imagery may continue into v. 6, which pictures the shaking of the earth and the shuddering of its pillars. God is the one who can make the pillars of

24. Wilson, *Job*, 83.

the earth secure (Ps. 75:3), but in his anger he shakes them, showing just how fragile the earth and its inhabitants are.

God is sovereign over the heavens as well as over the earth. He created the sun and the stars by the power of his word (Gen. 1), and he can extinguish them in the same way ("he speaks to the sun," Job 9:7a), plunging the earth into darkness.

Verse 8 expresses his dominance over both heaven and sea (created by splitting the heavenly waters from those down below; Gen. 1:6–7). The first he made, expressed by the metaphor of stretching out the heavens. In Ps. 104:2 God is said to stretch out (also from the verb *nṭh*) the heavens like a tent, and perhaps the metaphor of the heavens as a tent that covers the earth is meant here as well. God not only sets up the heavenly tent, but he also treads on the high places of the sea. As the translation note for 9:8 points out, Hebrew *yām* here could be a reference to the anti-creation god of Ugaritic mythology, Yam, whom Baal subdues to create the cosmos. In either case, though, the sea represents chaos, and the fact that God can march across its high points (waves?) signifies his control of evil.

Verse 9 returns to the subject of the stars, here naming specific constellations, the Bear, Orion, Pleiades, as well as a sector of the night sky (the chambers of the south). These stellar bodies were either worshiped or consulted by the pagan religions of the surrounding nations. Job understands that his powerful God made these spectacular heavenly bodies.

Verse 10 provides an evaluative summarizing statement. Here Job uses a phrase already spoken by Eliphaz in 5:9. Verse 10a states that God made "great things" (using the noun *gĕdōlôt*, from the frequently used root *gdl*) that are beyond human understanding. The second colon of this parallel line ups the ante by saying that these divine acts created "marvelous things" (the less frequently attested noun *niplāʾôt*) and adds that they are so many that they cannot be counted.

Job thus clearly has a sense of God's power and perhaps also his wisdom, though as remarked above this is not developed in vv. 5–10. Interestingly, when God does finally confront Job in the Yahweh speeches (chaps. 38–41), he emphasizes precisely his strength and wisdom as if Job has to learn the lesson again. There, though, God's nature leads Job to silence before the divine mystery. Here it leads to complaint that the power differential between God and mortals is unfair. After all, "who can press him and come out whole?" (v. 4b). That is, who can challenge such a powerful God in court concerning the injustice that he is showing Job, and come out unscathed? As we read on in Job's coming speeches, we will see that he will come to a more determined attitude toward confronting God in court (in particular, see vv. 35–37).

11"If he crosses over to me, I will not see;
if he passes by, I will not perceive him.

> [12]If he carries off, who will bring back?
> Who will say to him, 'What are you doing?'
> [13]God does not relent of his anger.
> Even Rahab's allies cower under him.
> [14]How can I answer him?
> How can I choose my words with him?"

9:11–14. *God seems unapproachable.* In the previous section, Job described God as "wise of heart and strong in power" (9:4a), emphasizing the latter in the description that follows in vv. 4b–10. Here he applies his understanding of God to his situation. In a word, God is ineffable, overwhelming, and unchallengeable.

Job knows he is innocent, and therefore God is unjust to make him suffer. Ideally, he would like to challenge God and lay his case against him (the language suggests a legal setting). But first, can he find God? Even if he were nearby ("crosses over to me" or "passes by"), Job would not even know it. It seems impossible to challenge him. He is so powerful and ineffable that no one can question him; even if he carries someone off, no one has the authority, power, or even possibly the opportunity to question him. Job may allude here to the carrying off of his property and his children.[25]

Interestingly, the psalms of lament offer an opposite viewpoint. They invite sufferers to challenge, even to accuse, God (Pss. 77 and 88 are prime examples). Of course, Job, a non-Israelite who lived long before the Psalms, would not be aware of this lament tradition, and the creator of the Job story would avoid such an anachronism (see the theological implications section below). The contrast, though, raises the question of the development of the character Job's understanding of the Divine.

In v. 13 Job pictures God as a stubborn bully who does not question his own violent actions. While it is true that God is pictured as relenting of his judgment in Jon. 3:10, his "change of mind" came about due to the repentance of the Ninevites. Job has something else in mind here. He thinks that God is wrongly making him suffer, so he believes that even if he could meet with God and point out the divine injustice, God would not change his mind about him.

God's irresistible power is illustrated by the fact that even the "allies" of Rahab are afraid of him. "Rahab" is used in two ways in the OT: as a mythological monster of the sea (Ps. 89:10) and as a reference to Egypt (Ps. 87:4). The connection between the two is unclear and unimportant for the present context, since here the reference is to the powerful sea monster. Unlike Leviathan (Ps. 74:14; Isa. 27:1; Job 41), who in many ways is a similar creature, Rahab is not mentioned outside the Bible. From the name's appearance in creation contexts, however, it seems a safe guess to say that Rahab, like Lotan/Litan (Leviathan) and Yam (in Ugaritic texts) and Tiamat (in Babylonian texts), is a powerful sea monster whom God subdued at creation. Rahab's "allies" would thus be

25. So Habel, *Job*, 92.

those demonic forces who aided the sea monster, similar to Tiamat's allies (including Qingu) mentioned in *Enuma Elish*.

The bottom line of Job's understanding of God is that it would be impossible to compel him to respond to Job's challenges in court. Job is not conceding that God is right, but that God is too powerful and stubborn when he states his belief that God will not answer him. As we will see, Job will waffle on whether he wants an audience with God.

15"Though I am righteous, I could not answer him.
I could only plead for mercy with my judge.
16If I summoned him, and he answered me,
I do not believe that he would hear my voice.
17He would crush me with a storm
and multiply my bruises without cause.
18He does not let me regain my breath.
Indeed, he satiates me with bitterness."

9:15–18. *God is unjust.* In v. 14 Job had questioned whether he could answer God in a legal setting. Job argues this, even though he knows he is in the right ("I am righteous"). He believes that the merit of the case makes no difference. He would be reduced to pleading for mercy that God would alleviate his suffering, even though he did not deserve to suffer in the first place. In other words, he would be reduced from a confident legal advocate for his situation to a groveling beggar.

He imagines that if God responded to his request for a hearing ("If I summoned him, and he answered me," v. 16a), God would not be coming in order to engage in a rational exchange of ideas. He would not pay any attention to Job's case against him. If Job summoned him and God came, he would crush Job with a storm. Knowing the end of Job as we do, we cannot help but note that God indeed will respond to Job's summons in a storm (*sĕʿārâ* [in 38:1] and *śĕʿārâ* [in 9:17] are by-forms). When God does come in a storm, he verbally, though not physically, crushes Job. He also will hardly let Job catch his breath. Even when Job utters a brief response (40:3–5), God continues his verbal attack against him. However, when the second divine speech concludes and Job repents again (42:1–6), he surprisingly is not filled with bitterness but is restored to his previous condition and better.

19"If it is about power, he is strong.
If it is about judgment, who can testify against him?
20Though I am righteous, my mouth condemns me.
I am innocent, but he declares me perverse.
21I am innocent. I don't know for sure.
I loathe my life."

9:19–21. *Job despairs of justice.* Job never questions God's overwhelming power, but rather his justice. Verse 19a concedes his power, while vv. 19b–21 questions his justice. No one can bring a testimony against God's judgment. Job's comment here is not the pious expression of one who does not question the rightness of divine judgment, but rather one who believes that God will judge regardless of the truth of the case, and no one can do anything about it. Indeed, God can make the innocent condemn themselves. Verse 20b puts it very clearly. Job asserts his innocence but realizes that God will proclaim him guilty (perverse) anyway.

The most difficult part of this unit is the second part of v. 21a. He begins the verse with a confident expression of his innocence ("I am innocent [*tām*]"). As readers, we know that this is not self-delusion—he is innocent (1:1, 8; 2:3). However, he appears to waver in the second part when he says that he is not certain. If this translation is correct (and it seems like a straightforward translation of fairly straightforward Hebrew), then perhaps his sudden lack of confidence is the result of his suffering and the onslaught of the arguments of his friends. But what is clear is that he understands himself to be innocent, yet also his doubt that God will care one way or another leads him to detest his life. Again, we are reminded of Qohelet (though a different verb [*śnʾ* rather than *mʾs*] is used), who came to hate his life "for the work that is done under the sun is evil to me. Indeed, all is meaningless and a chasing of the wind" (Eccles. 2:17).

22"It is all the same; therefore, I say:
'He destroys the innocent and the wicked.'
23If a disaster brings sudden death,
he ridicules the despair of the innocent.
24The earth is given into the power of the wicked;
he covers the face of its judges.
If it is not he, then who?"

9:22–24. *God treats the just and the wicked alike.* This passage presents Job's clearest articulation of God's injustice so far. He here reveals that he is worlds apart from the three friends, who deny that God "perverts justice" (8:3). He begins by stating that both innocent and wicked are the objects of God's violence ("He destroys the innocent and the wicked"). Qohelet, the "under the sun" thinker, expresses a similar depressing thought in Eccles. 9:1–3:

> Indeed, I devoted myself to all this and to examine all this: the righteous and the wise and their works are all in the hand of God. However, no one knows whether love or hate awaits them. Everything is the same for everybody; there is one fate for the righteous and the wicked and for the clean and the unclean, and for the one who sacrifices and for the one who does not sacrifice; as it is for the good, so it is for the sinner; as it is for the one

> who swears, so it is for the one who is afraid to swear. This is evil among all that is done under the sun. For there is one fate for all, and furthermore, the human heart is full of evil, and madness is in their hearts during their lives, and afterward—to the dead![26]

As he continues, though, Job does note a distinction between the righteous and the wicked. God laughs at the death and despair of the innocent but allows the wicked to prosper. In other words, Job would have judged correct the psalmist's initial impression that the wicked prosper to the detriment of the righteous in Ps. 73. He has not yet had his "sanctuary experience" in which he sees the glory of God and bows before the mystery of God and recognizes that God will work everything out for good (Ps. 73:17).

In 9:24b Job even suggests that the inequity of God explains the injustice among humans. Why are human courts so corrupted? God. God blinds the eyes of the judges so they reward the wicked and punish the innocent. Again, Qohelet diagnoses the same problem with human courts:

> Furthermore I observed under the sun:
> The place of judgment—injustice was there!
> The place of righteousness—injustice was there! (Eccles. 3:16)

Qohelet does go on to assert that proper retribution comes from God: "I said to myself, 'God will judge the righteous and the unjust, for there is a time for every activity and for every deed too'" (3:17). However, one wonders whether Qohelet is stating this theological truth with any measure of conviction, since the rest of this passage goes on to question, and perhaps even to deny, the possibility of an afterlife (3:18–22). Ultimately, Qohelet will advise avoiding extremes of righteousness/wisdom and wickedness/folly (7:15–18). What value is there in righteousness if there are no rewards on earth and, as is highly likely, no life afterward?

Job has not come to Qohelet's resigned carpe diem attitude (as expressed, for example, in Eccles. 3:22). At this point, he protests and continues to struggle with the proper strategy to address his problem.

25"My days go faster than a runner;
they are swift, but not good.
26They pass by like reed boats,
like an eagle swoops on its prey.
27If I say: 'I will forget my sighs;
I will abandon my countenance and be cheerful.'
28I am afraid of all my distress;
I know that you will not find me innocent.

26. For translation and commentary, see Longman, *Ecclesiastes*, 224–27.

29As for me, I am declared wicked.
Why do I exhaust myself for no purpose?
30Even if I wash myself with snow,
and I cleanse my palms with lye,
31then you will plunge me in the pit,
and my garments will abhor me."

9:25–31. *Job's life goes fast and poorly*. After speaking in general terms of the common fate of the innocent and the wicked, Job returns to speak about his own situation. He describes the rapidity of his days (see also 7:6, 16; 10:20). His time is running out. Verse 26 adds two similes to that of the runner in v. 25a to describe the speed with which his days passed by: a fast boat and a swooping eagle. How days swoop like an eagle on its prey is not clear, but the death of the prey introduces a dark thought to the metaphor. As he himself says in v. 25b, even though the days go fast, they do not go well. They are filled with pain and distress. Apparently, he both hates his life (9:21) and also feels that it passes quickly, but with pain. Both are common reactions to life by those who suffer. In spite of Clines's objections, Gordis may be right to say that while all three similes beginning with the runner suggest speed, the "reed boat" adds the idea of the fragility of life, and the eagle's swooping on its prey adds the idea of violence.[27]

The three friends have argued that he should not complain (see, e.g., 4:3–6), and Job now addresses this request. He says that he cannot stop complaining because of his distress (vv. 27–28a; see a similar thought in 6:2–3, 5–7). However, he also seems resigned to the fact that his complaints (or lack thereof) will not affect that outcome, because God (whom he now addresses in the second person, v. 28b) will declare him not innocent but wicked. Indeed, he believes that no matter how hard he works to present himself innocent (washing himself with snow or cleaning his palms with lye), God will pervert his righteousness by declaring him wicked.[28] It is as if his clean body were plunged by God into a mire (pit) and became so dirty that even his clothes disdained him. Again, Job is preoccupied with the idea that God calls or treats innocent people as if they were wicked. Even worse, he treats innocent people badly and wicked people well.

32"For he is not a person like I am that I could answer him,
that we will go together into judgment.
33There is no umpire between us
who would set his hand on both of us.

27. Gordis, *Job*, 109; cited in Clines, *Job 1–20*, 240.

28. Clines (*Job 1–20*, 241), citing Deut. 21:6; Pss. 26:6; 73:13; and Matt. 27:24, provocatively suggests that Job here refers to a ritual washing whereby he proclaims his innocence.

[34]He would take his rod away from me,
and not let his dread scare me.
[35]I would speak and not be afraid of him,
though this is not the case with me."

9:32–35. *Job needs an umpire.* After addressing God directly in vv. 25–31, Job here returns to talking about God before once again returning in chap. 10 to a direct address to God. As Job has thought about the proper strategy for approaching his suffering, he has earlier dismissed the idea of repression (vv. 27–28) or presenting himself as clean before God (perhaps with an allusion to a ritual declaration of innocence, vv. 30–31; see the footnote on that section above). Now he thinks once more about going to court with God. Again, however, he recognizes that he is not prepared to go one-on-one with God in court. There is a power disparity. He is not God's equal that they could meet together in court. What Job needs is a mediator, here described as an umpire. The mediator "would set his hand on both of us." He would not take sides, but he would even out the playing field. God's rod of punishment was on him, and thus Job was afraid of God, but the "umpire" would remove the rod and the dread. If this were the case, then he could enter into a proper interchange with God. In the end, though, Job recognizes that there is no such umpire ("though this is not the case with me"). For more on this passage as well as 16:19–21; 19:23–27; and 33:23–27, see the introduction as well as the theological implications section after the comments on Job 19.

[1]"I am disgusted with my life;
I will abandon myself to my sighs;
I will speak in my bitterness."

10:1. *Job hates his life.* Chapter 10 continues Job's response to Bildad and the friends. Here he prefixes a long accusatory speech against God with another statement of how much he hates his life (see also 9:21). After all, he suffers horribly both psychologically and physically. Rather than comfort from his friends, he hears their accusations. Further, up to now God has been silent and absent. Job's pain leads him to speak, and to speak without restraint ("I will abandon myself to my sighs"). His friends want to keep him from such talk, but his deeply felt emotion (bitterness) will not allow him to do so.

[2]"I will tell God: 'Do not declare me wicked;
tell me why you accuse me.
[3]Is it right for you to oppress me?
Must you despise the labor of your hands?
Do you favor the advice of the wicked?
[4]Do you have eyes of flesh?
Do you see with human vision?

> [5]Are your days like the days of humans,
> or your years like that of people?'"

10:2–5. *Why do you accuse me?* Job turns his "bitterness" toward God. He begins with his demands, and they are couched in legal language. He first insists that God not make a formal declaration that he is wicked. He feels condemned because he believes, like the three friends, that suffering is the result of sin, so his suffering must be the result of God's declaring him wicked. What did he do wrong to deserve this suffering? He wants God to present the charges.

After stating his demands, Job now addresses God with a series of accusatory questions. First, he asks God to justify his oppression. What is the reason for Job's suffering?[29] Job's question again assumes that all suffering is and must be the result of sin. Otherwise, it is not right for God to oppress him. Such suffering assumes that God despises him. Here he appeals to God by describing himself indirectly as "the labor of your hands." It makes no sense to Job that God would turn against the very creature he had made. Further, according to v. 3c, it is not just a matter of God perverting justice by making the innocent suffer, but he favors the wicked by listening to their advice. As explained in the introduction (see "The Genre of the Book of Job"), the book of Job is really about who is wise. Here Job is prodding God by suggesting that he listens not to the righteous (like himself) but to the wicked.

In the final series of questions (vv. 4–5), Job raises the possibility that God's perspective is no better than a human's. A human perspective is limited, while God's is supposed to be total.[30] Further, a human is a finite being with a limited life span, whereas God is not bound by birth and death. Humans thus will sometimes or even often misjudge things because of their partial perspective. These limitations should not affect God, but Job is here charging that God's perspective is limited, and that is why he makes the kinds of misjudgments that Job feels he is making in his case.

> [6]"'For you investigate my transgression;
> you seek my sin.
> [7]You must know that I am not wicked,
> but there is no rescue from your hand.'"

10:6–7. *God knows Job is innocent.* Job here tells God that he must know better than he is acting. He acts like Job is guilty, but God certainly must be

29. Another reading of the colon (v. 3a taking *ṭôb* as "good" rather than "right") moves its sense from the realm of justice to profit: What gain does God get through his actions toward Job? (so Clines, *Job 1–20*, 245).

30. Clines (*Job 1–20*, 246) helpfully cites 1 Sam. 16:7, which contrasts human and divine perspectives: "Yahweh sees not as man sees; man looks on the outward appearance, but Yahweh looks on the heart."

aware that Job is innocent. Verse 6 uses two verbs that show God's active investigation into Job's lifestyle (*bqš*/*drš*). Job believes that God is actively looking for transgression. Since Job knows he is innocent, he believes that God must have looked and seen his innocence. Therefore, he must recognize that Job is innocent (or, stated negatively, that he is "not wicked"). But even so, there is no rescue from the hand of God, which is against him, making him suffer. Who could rescue him? No one is able to resist God's mighty power.

8"'Your hands shaped and made me,
  but now you turn and swallow me up.
9Please remember that you made me like clay;
  will you return me to dust?
10Do you not pour me out like milk,
  curdle me like cheese?
11You clothed me in skin and flesh;
  you knit me together with bones and sinews.'"

10:8–11. *From the dust*. In 10:3 Job had referred to human beings in general as the "labor" of God's hands. While he implicitly at least was referring to himself as such, here he explicitly personalizes the idea. God is the one who made Job. He is a work of God. The psalmist too acknowledges that he is the result of divine handiwork: "You created my inmost being; you knit me together in my mother's womb" (Ps. 139:13 NIV). This acknowledgment leads the psalmist to praise his Maker. Job, however, is aghast that God would take his creature and destroy him.

In v. 9 Job reminds God of his human fragility. Human beings are like clay, like a fragile pot produced by a potter. Clay pots are easily broken, and so are human beings. In v. 9b Job alludes to the creation story, in which God made the first human from the dust of the ground (Gen. 2:7) and gave him breath. To return a human to dust is to reverse this creation unity of dust and breath. Qohelet anticipated his own death by talking about the time when "the dust returns to the ground it came from, and the spirit returns to God who gave it" (Eccles. 12:7 NIV).

Verses 10–11 repeat the idea that it is God who is behind Job's (and all human) creation. That semen is a milky fluid may be behind v. 10a. The semen coalesces or congeals (curdles) into a solid, "like cheese," suggesting the embryo. Job questions God in such a way as to again remind him that he is God's own creation. This embryo is clothed with skin and holds together with bones and sinews. See Ps. 139:13 for a similar idea of the "knitting together" of human beings.

12"'Life and loyalty you have made with me,
  and your concern has set a guard over me.
13These things you hid in your heart,
  and I knew that this was your purpose.

[14]If I sinned, you would guard me
  and would not declare me innocent of my transgression.
[15]If I am wicked, woe is me!
  And if righteous, I cannot lift my head.
I am filled with shame,
  and look on my affliction.'"

10:12–15. *Damned if I do; damned if I don't.* As Habel points out, if v. 12 (and v. 13 for that matter) were in a different context, it would be read as a very positive and encouraging statement.[31] "Life" (*ḥay*) is typically a blessing, and "loyalty" (*ḥesed*) often refers to God's devoted love toward a person in relationship with him. Then in v. 12b, Job speaks of God's "concern" (*pĕquddâ*). One would think it absolutely thrilling to have God so involved in one's life. However, Job's experience of God's involvement in his life (or at least his interpretation of the experiences of his life) has led him to a negative conclusion. God is not out to bless him but wants to harm him.

Once again, Job would have found Qohelet a fellow traveler in life. In Eccles. 9:1 Qohelet expressed a very similar idea: "Indeed, I devoted myself to all this and to examine all this: the righteous and the wise and their works are all in the hand of God. However, no one knows whether love or hate awaits them."[32] The next verse goes on to refer to those who are righteous and wicked and to claim that God treats them all the same. The only difference with Job is that Job knows he is righteous and he believes that the "hate" of God has embraced him.

Verses 13–15 indicate that it is God's plan to have such concern in order to watch his creatures to determine whether they are wicked or righteous, and in either case to crush them. This is, according to v. 13, God's "hidden motive."[33] If God finds that Job is a sinner, then he would not exonerate him, and he would punish him ("Woe is me!" v. 15a). But even if Job is righteous, God will afflict him, with the result that he will be humiliated. His inability to lift his head probably has a psychological rather than a physical reason. As his present situation indicates, his suffering communicates to others (at this time the three friends) that he is a sinner, even though he is not, and so he is embarrassed.

Elsewhere Job talks about God's justice being totally reversed, with sinners prospering and the innocent suffering (9:20). When he thinks of his own life, he takes a "damned if I do; damned if I don't" approach. He is going to suffer no matter what.

[16]"'Proud as a lion you hunt me;
  you again show your tremendous power against me.

31. Habel, *Job*, 199.
32. For translation and commentary, see Longman, *Ecclesiastes*, 224–25.
33. Well put by Wilson, *Job*, 108.

> [17]You renew your witnesses against me;
> you multiply your anger toward me;
> you bring new troops against me.'"

10:16–17. *God's assault.* Job has felt attacked by God. That is why he believes he suffers such horrible afflictions. Job here uses a series of different comparisons to describe God's assault. The first is that of a lion: God will show his terrible power against Job like a lion attacking his prey. In Ps. 7 the psalmist appeals to God to protect him against the lions that attack. In the psalm, the lions represent the wicked who unjustly attack the psalmist (see vv. 1–2). The lion also represents the violence and power of the wicked in Pss. 10:9; 17:12; and 91:13 (here God will give the psalmist the ability to trample down the lions). But Job is not the only one to use the lion metaphor to describe God's judgment. Both Hosea (5:14; 13:7–8) and Amos (3:4, 8; 5:19) picture God executing his judgment against his people as a lion rends its prey.

In v. 17 Job returns to the legal metaphor. He is in court, and God now marshals a series of witnesses against him, thus showing the increase of his anger toward Job. Who these witnesses are is left ambiguous.[34] Perhaps it refers to the three friends who are trying to present evidence against him. But God, according to Job, is not only attempting to win a court case; he is already executing his judgment as he brings new troops against him to harm him.

> [18]"'Why did you bring me out of the womb?
> Why did I not die before any eye saw me?
> [19]I would be as if I never was,
> carried from womb to grave.
> [20]Are not the days of my life few?
> Let me alone that I might have a little joy
> [21]before I go and not return,
> to the land of darkness and gloom,
> [22]a land of dimness and blackness,
> gloom and chaos,
> and shining is like darkness.'"

10:18–22. *Leave me alone!* Job's opening words in this section bring us back to his lament, where in 3:10 he exclaimed, "Why didn't I die coming out of the womb?" Here he wishes that he had died in the womb, but the idea is the same. Life has grown so unbearable that he wishes he had never experienced any of it, in spite of the long years of prosperity described at the opening of the book. Present pain has a way of rendering past joys tasteless, rather than the reverse. If we go closer to the beginning of Job's journey, we might remember his statement at the end of the first chapter in response to the first

34. Or, with Hartley (*Job*, 190), the new witnesses are new manifestations of his illnesses.

wave of affliction: "Naked I came from my mother's womb, and naked I will return there" (1:21). Granted that Job still has not (and never will) "curse God and die" (2:9), but he has changed his tone since chap. 1 from what appears to be an accepting, patient resignation to an angry protest. In v. 19 he notes that if he had died in the womb, then it would be as if he had never existed. He would have gone from womb to grave. He would have come out a stillborn and then been buried.

But of course Job did not die in the womb, so in vv. 20–21 he takes a different tack in his appeal to God. Since he believes that his suffering is caused by God, he beseeches God to back off and give him room to have just a little pleasure in the few days that remain to him. Again, Job sounds like Qohelet, who believed that since there is no ultimate meaning to life, the best one can hope for is a bit of distracting pleasure before the end comes. This sentiment is expressed in Qohelet's carpe diem passages such as Eccles. 5:19–20 (see also 2:24–26; 3:12–14, 22; 8:15; 9:7–10): "Furthermore, everyone to whom God gives wealth and possessions and allows them to eat of it and to accept their reward and to take pleasure in their toil—this is God's gift. Indeed, they do not remember much about the days of their lives for God keeps them so busy with the pleasure of their heart." Job has no belief that death will lead to a blessed afterlife. No, the grave and oblivion are what one can expect when one dies. The grave and oblivion are both well described by the heaping up of words denoting deep darkness in Job 10:21–22. For Job in his present state, darkness is a relief from the pain he feels.

Theological Implications

Accusing God of Injustice

In the theological implications section after the comments on Job's lament (chap. 3), I reflected on how Job grumbled about God (see "Grumbling at God"). I noted significant differences between Job's words and those of the lament psalms. The latter directed their disappointment to God in a manner that indicated their hope that God would hear and respond. Job's words were not directed toward God and therefore were more like the Israelites who grumbled in the wilderness, bringing on God's judgment. I also noted differences between Job and Jeremiah's laments, particularly Jer. 20:7–18. A review of that essay is relevant for our understanding of Job's words in this his second response to the friends.

In this essay, though, I will consider the more specific issue of Job's charge that God is unjust. Is his charge justified? Even if it is not justified, does God invite such charges, or should his people simply repress such negative thoughts?

I begin with the second question. Any reader of the Psalms recognizes that God invites his people to speak with complete honesty to him. The laments express anger, frustration, disappointment, hate, and confusion not only toward other humans or oneself but also toward God. Consider Ps. 77. The psalmist is so deeply troubled that he cannot sleep, so he hurls accusations toward God:

> Will the Lord spurn forever,
>   and never again be favorable?
> Has his steadfast love ceased forever?
>   Are his promises at an end for all time?
> Has God forgotten to be gracious?
>   Has he in anger shut up his compassion? (77:7–9 NRSV)

These questions thrown in the face of God are quite serious. The psalmist questions God's favor, steadfast love, promises, grace, and compassion. These words strike at the heart of the covenant itself. God placed himself in covenant/treaty relationship with his people and promised the psalmist all these things. The psalmist's experience of life does not indicate that God is coming through on his end of the relationship, so he challenges God in this direct and forthright manner.

The Psalms are a covenant book of prayers (to be sung) that provide models to God's people for how to approach God. Thus psalms such as 77 show that God does not want his people simply to repress their anger toward him in difficult times but to express it honestly. Psalm 77 ends well, as the psalmist remembers God's great acts in the past, particularly the exodus, an event showing that God can help his people in times when the situation seems impossible. This look at the past gives the psalmist hope for the future and confidence to face his problems in the present.

Thus Job's charge that God is unjust is not on the surface wrong or inappropriate. But, as we saw in the essay on grumbling at God (after comments on Job 3), Job's accusations are wrong because they are addressed not to God but to others. He says he wants to speak to God but does not believe it is possible. God, he believes, is hidden from him. He cannot find God. Later we will see that God is certainly able to make himself present to Job, and when he does, Job no longer makes the charge of injustice but rather repents from his accusations.

But was God unjust? Some modern readers of the book believe so and characterize God as a despot or at least as a divine bully. After all, we know that Job did not deserve his suffering, in the sense that his pain was not a consequence of his own personal sin. But to say that God is unjust requires us to believe that God owes Job a good life since he has been good and that it is unfair for God to take away Job's wealth, health, and family.

But this is not the biblical view of God and human beings. Reading Job in the light of Gen. 1–3, we can say that God created humanity to enjoy the blessings of life forever. Adam and Eve are pictured as living in Eden, a place whose very name means "luxury" or "delight."[35] Their rebellion led to their punishment, and forever afterward human beings deserve death and not life. Job's earlier life was not something he earned, but rather it was an act of divine grace. The message of the book of Job is not that life is fair, but that God is wise and sovereign and perfectly just. For this reason, God will eventually reprimand Job for accusing him of injustice ("Would you invalidate my justice? Would you condemn me so you might be righteous?" 40:8), and Job will ultimately repent (42:1–6).

Zuckerman approaches this question from a different direction. He cites Isa. 45:9 (translating, "Woe to him who would lodge a complaint against his Maker: a pot with the potter! Does the clay say to its maker, 'What are you doing? This work of yours has no handles?'") and goes on to say,

> The poet has his protagonist [Job] affirm that if God refuses to respond to Job's legal accusation, or intimidates Job with His divine power, then God has broken the rules of adjudication and thus must be seen as a lawless Deity. But this ignores the most fundamental rule of law in the Ancient Near East: that God *is* the Law; for without divine authority the law ceases to exist. Job claims that God has violated juridical procedure, but in fact, as Second Isaiah could tell Job, this is impossible: God cannot violate Himself, nor can mankind claim the protection of any system of law separate from God's authority.[36]

The whole idea of God as unjust is preposterous since God himself defines justice.

35. Corneius, *NIDOTTE* 3:331–32.
36. Zuckerman, *Job the Silent*, 113.

5.
Zophar's First Speech
(11:1–20)

Translation

[1]And Zophar the Naamathite answered and said:

[2]"Should such a large number of words not be answered?
  Should a talkative man be declared righteous?
[3]Should your empty talk render others silent?
  When you mock, should not someone shame you?

[4]You claim,[1] 'My teaching is pure;
  I am clean in your eyes.'
[5]Would that God would speak,
  and open his mouth[2] with you!
[6]He would tell you the secrets of wisdom,
  for resourcefulness[3] is many-sided.[4]
  Know that God has even forgotten[5] some of your guilt.

1. Or "say," *ʾmr*.

2. Literally "his lips."

3. *Tûšîyâ* is a word that is associated with wisdom in the book of Proverbs (see 2:7; 3:21; 8:14). It is resourcefulness that results in success; thus I translated it "success" in Job 5:12.

4. Contra Clines (*Job 1–20*, 254), who says "many-sided" (NRSV) or "manifold" (RSV) is not possible for *kiplayim*. But the word can mean folded over and at least "double-sided" (R. S. Hess, *NIDOTTE* 2:687–88). Clines himself emends to *kiplāʾîm* and translates, "for there are mysteries in his working," taking *tûšîyâ* as success or work associated with wisdom.

5. From *nšh*, "to forget," a reading supported by Clines (*Job 1–20*, 254–55) and NIV against NRSV (and others), which takes the verb as a form *nšh*/*nšʾ* ("to be a creditor") and translates, "Know then that God exacts of you less than your guilt deserves."

[7]Can you discover the deep things of God?
  Can you discover the limits[6] of Shaddai?
[8]They are higher than heaven—what can you do?
  It is deeper than Sheol—what do you know?
[9]Their measure is longer than the earth
  and wider than the sea.
[10]If he passes by, and imprisons,
  and he assembles for judgment, who can turn him back?
[11]For he knows those who are worthless;
  when he sees an evil person, does he not pay attention?
[12]But an empty-headed person will get understanding
  when a wild donkey gives birth to a human!

[13]If you focus your heart,
  and you spread out your palms to him—
[14]if evil is in your hand, move it far away,
  and don't let iniquity take up residence in your tent—
[15]certainly then you will lift up your face without blemish;
  you will be secure and not afraid.
[16]Indeed, you will forget your trouble;
  you will remember it like water running away.
[17]Then life will be brighter than noonday;
  its darkness will be like the morning.
[18]You will be secure because there is hope;
  you will look around[7] and lie down in safety.
[19]You will lie down and not tremble with fear;
  many will ask for your favor.
[20]The eyes of the wicked will fail;
  their escape route will be lost to them.
  Their expectation will be death."

Interpretation

With Zophar, the gloves come off even more. He begins by openly insulting Job (vv. 2–3) and continues to do so as his speech goes on (see especially v. 12). In his estimation, Job is full of words that have no substance. Zophar is upset with Job's claim that he is without error and without sin. He wishes that God would put him in his place (vv. 4–6). God will come and put Job in his place (see 38:1–42:6), but not for the reasons that Zophar believes. According to Zophar, God is ineffable and mysterious. This inspires Zophar (11:7–11) but

6. Perhaps in the sense of "totality," as the following verses make clear (see W. R. Domeris and C. Van Dam, *NIDOTTE* 2:642–43).

7. *Ḥpr* I can have the meaning "to scout out, explore, look around" (R. S. Hess, *NIDOTTE* 2:235–36).

irks Job (see 9:11–14). Zophar is convinced without a shadow of doubt that God will punish evil people; but in an indirect barb at Job (v. 12), he says that foolish people do not get it and never will. That said, Zophar lays out hope for Job: repent. If Job repents, then he will be fully restored. If he does not, then he will perish like all the wicked (see vv. 13–20).

1And Zophar the Naamathite answered and said:

2"Should such a large number of words not be answered?
Should a talkative man be declared righteous?
3Should your empty talk render others silent?
When you mock, should not someone shame you?"

11:1–3. *Opening insults.* A typical rubric introduces the third of Job's friends, Zophar the Naamathite (see 4:1; 6:1; 8:1; 9:1; etc.). In this speech, Zophar responds to Job's speech first of all by demeaning it because of its length and emptiness. Job talks a lot but says nothing, according to Zophar. Zophar is providing the justification for his own words because he has determined that not answering this person whom he considers a fool would be to make Job righteous in his own eyes (see Prov. 26:5, "Answer fools according to their stupidity; otherwise, they will become wise in their own eyes"). Job's words compel a scathing response. Job is a mocker, and mockers need to be put in their place. While Zophar is quick to respond now, Job will eventually wear him out so that he does not even participate in the third cycle, and all three friends eventually grow silent.

4"You claim, 'My teaching is pure;
I am clean in your eyes.'
5Would that God would speak,
and open his mouth with you!
6He would tell you the secrets of wisdom,
for resourcefulness is many-sided.
Know that God has even forgotten some of your guilt."

11:4–6. *Job's presumption.* Zophar attacks Job for maintaining his ethical purity in spite of what is to him clear evidence to the contrary. Up to this point Job has not applied the adjective "pure" (*zak*) to his teaching or life, but it seems implied. He has said that even if he cleansed himself (from the verb *zkk*), God would still pronounce him guilty (9:30), and later he will call his prayers "pure" (see 16:17). Earlier, Bildad urged him to be pure in life in order to regain God's blessing, with the assumption that his lack of purity has brought on the present crisis (8:6). Later Elihu will, like Zophar, charge Job with wrongly claiming to be "pure" (33:9). Indeed, from the human point of view, the question would naturally arise. After all, according to Prov. 16:2, "All paths of people are pure in their eyes, but Yahweh measures the motives." The proverb speaks to our ability to deceive ourselves concerning our righteousness. Indeed, we know from the introduction that Job is pure in his behavior and that Yahweh has measured Job's motives. Remember the conclusion at the end of chap. 2: "In all this Job did not sin with his lips." Even after Job had all the blessings taken away, he did not curse God and die.

The second colon of v. 4 intensifies the thought of the first. In the first, Zophar charges that Job claims that his teaching is pure, and in the second, Zophar states that Job claims that he himself is clean, using a word similar in meaning to "pure" (*bar*, rather than *zak*). Again, nowhere has Job said he is clean using that exact word, but he has maintained his innocence. Zophar is right about Job's claims, but he is wrong to think that the claim is false.

In vv. 5–6 Zophar wishes that God would speak to the issue. He desires God to speak because he is confident of what God would say and that God would take his side in exposing Job's impurity. God's wisdom is deep and profound. Job believes that God is making him suffer disproportionately to his sin. Zophar responds by arguing that God has even forgotten some of Job's sin. Zophar would not take the word "forgotten" in its superficial meaning, but rather in the sense that God is not acting on all of Job's sins. In sum, Zophar tells Job that he deserves worse than he is getting! Rather than being brutal and cruel in Job's situation, God is actually being quite compassionate.

7"Can you discover the deep things of God?
Can you discover the limits of Shaddai?
8They are higher than heaven—what can you do?
It is deeper than Sheol—what do you know?
9Their measure is longer than the earth
and wider than the sea.
10If he passes by, and imprisons,
and he assembles for judgment, who can turn him back?
11For he knows those who are worthless;
when he sees an evil person, does he not pay attention?
12But an empty-headed person will get understanding
when a wild donkey gives birth to a human!"

11:7–12. *God is inscrutable.* Zophar then launches into an exaltation of the profundity and sublimity of God. God is beyond the ability of humans to fully comprehend him. Verses 7–9 talk about the mystery of God. He is inscrutable. Zophar describes God as someone who is too high, too deep, too long, and too wide to grasp. Indeed, God is higher than the highest place imaginable (heaven), deeper than the deepest place (Sheol), longer than the longest place (the earth), and wider than the widest place (the sea).[8] Interestingly, Sheol, which often simply refers to the grave, is here used to denote the deepest imaginable place, thus suggesting that it is used in the sense of the underworld.

What Zophar says about God is true. He is mysterious; humans cannot fully grasp him. The problem with Zophar is that he uses this truth to taunt and condemn Job. He challenges Job with the mystery of God. Job says he does not deserve his suffering. Zophar fires back: how can you know what God is thinking and doing? The problem is that we know that Job is right about the fact that he is not suffering because of his sin. Good theology should not be used to beat people down in this way. Zophar is wrong to think that if they could plumb God's purpose in Job's suffering, God would charge Job with sin. So the intention of Zophar's taunts ("What can you do? . . . What do you know?") is mistaken.[9] Ironically, though, Job should be challenged by the mystery of God. Indeed, at the end of the book, God himself will challenge Job, not by telling him why he suffers but by asserting his unfathomable wisdom and his tremendous power.

We should remember that Job himself has acknowledged that God's purposes are irresistible in 9:11–12:

> If he crosses over to me, I will not see;
>   if he passes by, I will not perceive him.
> If he carries off, who will bring back?
>   Who will say to him, "What are you doing?"

The difference, though, is that Zophar believes that God is just in so acting, while Job questions and wants (but feels at times that it is useless) to challenge him in court.

In vv. 10–11, on the basis of God's nature as described in vv. 7–9, Zophar presents a conclusion based on a hypothetical situation. If God should come and imprison someone and present that person for judgment, who can resist him? Of course, this impersonal scenario is directed toward Job, whom Zophar thinks has been taken prisoner by God and presented for trial, found guilty, and punished. He concludes this section of his speech by confidently affirming that God can tell the difference between a bad (worthless) person and a good person. Further, he takes action ("pays attention") to those who are bad. Again, the barb is directed toward Job, who has stated that God does not treat the innocent or wicked differently (9:22–24); or if he does, he punishes the former and rewards the latter.

8. Interestingly, Prov. 25:3 points out that the human mind cannot penetrate even the height of heaven or the depth of the earth, not to speak of something that surpasses even those.

9. Phillips ("Speaking Truthfully," 34) points out that there is "an irony in his [Zophar's] affirmation that God's ways are hidden followed by his own clarity in speaking for God."

Zophar concludes this section with one of the most biting insults of the book (v. 12). We can imagine him looking into Job's face with disdain and saying these words. He delivers the line as a kind of general principle ("proverb-like"),[10] but in the context of the debate, it is clear that it is a barb aimed at Job. The upshot is that it is more likely that a donkey will give birth to a human child than that an empty-headed[11] person, like Job in Zophar's estimation, will give birth to a correct insight. In other words, Job is a fool and his ideas are foolish. However, as we will learn in the next section, he is not beyond redemption. He is not morally bankrupt; it is his present train of thinking that is troubled. And we must remember that insults tend toward the hyperbolic to get a person's attention.

13"If you focus your heart
and you spread out your palms to him—
14if evil is in your hand, move it far away,
and don't let iniquity take up residence in your tent—
15certainly then you will lift up your face without blemish;
you will be secure and not afraid.
16Indeed, you will forget your trouble;
you will remember it like water running away.
17Then life will be brighter than noonday;
its darkness will be like the morning.
18You will be secure because there is hope;
you will look around and lie down in safety.
19You will lie down and not tremble with fear;
many will ask for your favor.
20The eyes of the wicked will fail;
their escape route will be lost to them.
Their expectation will be death."

11:13–20. *Repent and be restored.* Finally, Zophar turns to Job with a way out. Along with the other two friends, Zophar believes that Job's problem is sin and that God is punishing him. To them, the obvious solution is repentance. It has to be an inward repentance that comes from the heart (v. 13a, "if you focus your heart") that manifests itself in an outward fashion (v. 13b, "spread out your palms to him"). The specific gesture of prayer is illustrated in Keel[12] and indicates an attitude of supplication. In v. 14 Zophar continues by admonishing Job to remove sin far from him, both from his person (v. 14a) and from his residence (v. 14b).

10. So Clines, *Job 1–20*, 266.

11. The noun translated "empty-headed" (*nābûb*) comes from a verb that means "to be hollow."

12. Keel, *Symbolism of the Biblical World*, 309.

The next few verses (vv. 15–19) describe the benefits of repentance, which are, in a word, restoration. Here the restoration is described not in materialistic terms but rather in terms of one's psychological state. If Job follows Zophar's prescription, then he will have a new confidence that expels the fear and anxiety that he presently experiences. Trouble will be a thing of the past (v. 16). Darkness will give way to light. Insecurity will give place to security. Indeed, because of this newfound hope, people will come and will request Job's favor (v. 19b).

What Zophar says is true. Repentance is the right response to sin and can often lead to a better, more confident life in the present. Where Zophar goes wrong is in thinking that his prescription is the solution to all suffering. In particular, he is wrong to think that this approach applies to Job. After all, we, the readers, are well aware that Job's suffering is not the result of sin, so the way to a better life is not through repentance.

Finally, v. 20 turns to the subject of the wicked, presumably the unrepentant sinner. Here the contrast is with the repentant sinner just described in vv. 15–19. While the latter has a good end, the wicked have a horrible end. They will be lost, with no possibility of escape. Their expectations end in death. By pointing out this contrast, Zophar is trying to stir Job to repent.

Theological Implications

Repent and Be Restored

Zophar attacks Job so that Job might repent from the sins that led to his suffering. If he repents, then he will be restored to his previous glorious position. He will have the health, wealth, and happiness that he had before he sinned and fell into such a dreadful condition. Zophar here emphasizes repentance, but it is a theme that runs throughout the friends' arguments (beginning with Eliphaz in 5:8–27). It is an instrumental part of their retribution theology (see "Retribution Theology in a Nutshell" following my comments on Job 8).

Zophar and his friends are totally correct. Sinners need to repent of their sins in order to restore their relationship with God. Page after page of Scripture teaches this important truth. It is at the heart of Israel's covenant with God. After presenting the law (Deut. 5–26) with the consequent rewards and punishments (Deut. 27–28), Israel's future sin and punishment are predicted, indeed even the later exile is anticipated: "In the future, when you experience all these blessing and curses I have listed for you, and when you are living among the nations to which the LORD your God has exiled you . . ." (Deut. 30:1 NLT). What should sinful and punished Israel do in order to restore their relationship with God? The passage goes on to say:

> If at that time you and your children return to the LORD your God, and if you obey with all your heart and all your soul all the commands I have given you today, the LORD your God will restore your fortunes. He will have mercy on you and gather you back from all the nations where he has scattered you. Even though you are banished to the ends of the earth, the LORD your God will gather you from there and bring you back again. The LORD your God will return you to the land that belonged to your ancestors, and you will possess that land again. Then he will make you even more prosperous and numerous than your ancestors! (Deut. 30:2–5 NLT)

One more OT example will have to suffice. As King Solomon dedicated the temple, he too anticipated a time when God's covenant people would rebel against him:

> If they sin against you—and who has never sinned?—you might become angry with them and let their enemies conquer them and take them captive to their land far away or near. But in that land of exile, they might turn to you in repentance and pray, "We have sinned, done evil, and acted wickedly." If they turn to you with their whole heart and soul in the land of their enemies and pray toward the land you gave to their ancestors—toward this city you have chosen, and toward this Temple I have built to honor your name—then hear their prayers and their petition from heaven where you live, and uphold their cause. Forgive your people who have sinned against you. Forgive all the offenses they have committed against you. Make their captors merciful to them, for they are your people—your special possession—whom you brought out of the iron-smelting furnace of Egypt. (1 Kings 8:46–51 NLT)

Again, Zophar is right. Sinners need to repent. However, Zophar is wrong in this particular case. Job does not have to repent. His suffering has not been caused by his sin. He has nothing to repent of. Indeed, we readers know this without a shadow of a doubt since we are privy to God's discussions with the accuser recorded in the first two chapters of the book.

Still, we should not lose sight of the important fact that sinners need to repent, that is, acknowledge their sin and actively turn away from it. And such repentance is not a onetime event but a lifestyle. Repentance is something that God's people need to do constantly. However, it begins with a turning away from self and rebellion and a turning toward God, as Peter proclaimed on Pentecost: "Each of you must repent of your sins, turn to God, and be baptized in the name of Jesus Christ to show that you have received forgiveness for your sins" (Acts 2:38 NLT [2004 ed.]). Since Christians continue to sin even after this initial turn to God, they must continue to repent. Christians should feel pain when they sin, a godly kind of pain that leads to repentance and restoration. Paul celebrated this grief that led to the repentance of the Corinthian Christians in 2 Cor. 7:11.

Once more, though, while Zophar could not be more right in principle, he was totally wrong in his application of the principle to Job. Zophar demonstrates the dangers of a dogmatic, unreflective theology that does not take into account people's actual situation.[13]

13. Job will later repent and be restored. Some have argued that this undermines the message of the book of Job and affirms what Zophar says in this chapter. As I will point out in my comments on Job 42, Job indeed does repent but not of any sin that led to his initial suffering.

6.
Job's Third Response
(12:1–14:22)

Translation

12:1And Job answered and said:
2"Truly,[1] you are the people,
and wisdom will die with you![2]
3I also have a mind[3] like you.
I am not inferior to you.[4]
Who is not like these?[5]

4I am a joke to my friends,
he who summoned God and he answered me,
a righteous and innocent man—a joke!
5Those at ease have contempt for disaster,[6]
but it is prepared for those whose feet are unstable.[7]

1. See the similar opening to 9:2.

2. Or, with Clines (*Job 1–20*, 278–79), "you are the people with whom wisdom will die," at the suggestion of Davies ("Note on Job 12:7–9") taking the *waw* as introducing a paratactic relative clause. Such a reading provides a smoother rendering but has, in my opinion, the same meaning as the translation I offer here.

3. Literally "heart" (*lēbāb*), but "heart" often has the sense of "mind." Job's point is that he is as intelligent as the three friends.

4. Literally "I am not falling from you" (*lōʾ-nōpēl ʾānōkî mikkem*), that is, fallen under them in terms of his intelligence.

5. Clines (*Job 1–20*, 275, 279) and others take "these" as a reference to "these things," that is, "these types of arguments," though it seems to me more likely that the reference is to "these people," namely, the three friends. After all, they are the ones who are the subject of Job's comparisons in the previous cola.

6. Note the use of *pîd* (here with prefixed *lamed*) also in 30:24 and 31:29.

7. Their feet "shake" (*mʿd*).

6The tents of the marauders have peace and quiet,
and those who aggravate[8] God are confident,
and so is anyone who brings God under their control.[9]

7Only ask the beasts, and they will teach you,[10]
the birds in the sky, and they will inform you.
8Or the plants of the earth and they will teach you;
the fish of the sea will recount to you.
9Who does not know all these things,
that the hand of Yahweh[11] has done this?
10The breath of all living things is in his hand,
the spirit of all human flesh.
11Does not the ear test words
as the mouth tastes food?
12With the aged[12] is wisdom,
with the long-lived is understanding.

13With him are wisdom and power;
he has advice and understanding.
14What[13] he tears down will not be built up;
the person he shuts in will not be let out.
15He withholds the water, and it dries up;
he releases it, and it overwhelms the land.
16With him are strength and mental resources;
deceived and deceiver are his.
17He leads counselors away plundered,
and renders judges deluded.
18He loosens the sash[14] of kings;
he tightens the waistcloth around their hips.

8. Literally to make God "tremble" (from *rgz*).

9. An alternate understanding takes the pronominal suffix on "hand" as referring to God and rendering, like the NLT, "though God keeps them in his power." This understanding is possible but does not seem to conform to the context as nicely, which seems to be talking about the good life of the wicked.

10. Up to now, the second-person plural has been used, but in this verse it is second-person singular. Perhaps in this verse he refers specifically to Zophar, the last one to speak.

11. This is the only place in the disputation where the divine name is used (it occurs once in the prose prologue and five times in the epilogue). It may be a textual change from the original, since some MSS have the expected *ʾĕlôah*. Otherwise, as Seow (*Job*) suggests, it may be a "set phrase."

12. Some commentators take "aged" and "long-lived" as epithets of God, but as Clines (*Job 1–20*, 280) points out, this is based on faulty association with Ugaritic; see also Pope, *Job*, 92.

13. With Clines (*Job 1–20*, 280), I take *hēn* in its typical meaning as a demonstrative interjection, though some take it as an Aramaic form meaning "if" (see NRSV, REB); it must be said that either translation means essentially the same thing.

14. The MT has *mûsar* ("discipline" or "instruction"), but this is almost universally emended to *môsēr* ("belt, sash") due to context and parallelism.

19He leads priests away plundered,
and ruins those long established.[15]
20He takes away the speech of the trusted,
as well as the discernment of the elders.
21He pours contempt on princes
and loosens the belt of the strong.
22He reveals the depths from the darkness,
and he brings deep darkness to the light.
23He makes the nations grow great, and then he destroys them.
He enlarges the nations and then disperses them.
24He takes intelligence[16] away from the heads of the people of the earth,
and he makes them wander in chaos without a path.
25They grope around in darkness without light,
he makes them wander about like a drunkard.

13:1Look, my eye has seen all this;
my ear has heard and understood it.
2I definitely know what you know;
I am not inferior to you.[17]
3But I would speak to Shaddai.
I would love to reprove God.
4But you smear me with lies.
All of you are worthless physicians!
5If you would only shut up,
that would be a wise move on your part.

6Hear now my reproof.
Pay attention to the accusations of my lips.
7Will you speak unjustly for God
and say deceitful things about him?
8Will you favor him,
if you make an accusation for God?
9Will it be good that he examine you?
Can you deceive him like someone deceives another person?
10He will most certainly reprove you
if you show favoritism in secret.
11Does not his majesty[18] scare you,
his fear fall on you?

15. From *ʾêytān*, "enduring, permanent." See M. A. Grisanti, *NIDOTTE* 1:392.

16. Literally "heart."

17. See 12:3.

18. A difficult word, usually taken, as here, as a noun form from the verb *nśʾ*, "to lift up." Pope (*Job*, 98–99) suggests the meaning "fear," which is accepted by Clines (*Job 1–20*, 281), but to do so he has to argue that it is related to *šôʾâ*, which strikes me as unlikely.

[12]Your proclamations[19] are proverbs made of dust.
Your responses[20] are responses made of clay.
[13]Be silent around me, and I will speak,
and let whatever pass my way.
[14]I[21] will take my flesh in my teeth;
I will put my life in my palm.
[15]See, he will kill me; I have no[22] hope.
I will reprove him to his face concerning my behavior.[23]
[16]This will be my salvation,
that the godless will not come into his presence.
[17]Listen closely to my words;
let my declaration be in your ear.
[18]See, I am prepared for the judgment;
I know I am righteous.
[19]Who is it that accuses me
so now I would be silent and die?
[20]Only do two things for me,
then I won't hide from your face.
[21]Move your palm far from me;
don't allow dread of you to scare me.
[22]Call and I will answer;
or I will speak and you will respond to me.
[23]What are my faults and sins?
Make known to me my transgressions and sins.
[24]Why do you hide your face
and consider me your enemy?
[25]Will you frighten a windblown leaf
and pursue dried chaff?
[26]For you write bitter things about me;
you make me inherit the guilt of my youth.
[27]You set my feet in stocks;
you guard all my paths;
you make an incision[24] on the soles of my feet.
[28]One wastes away like something rotten,
like a garment eaten by a moth.

19. *Zikkārôn*, translated as "proclamation" here, may have the sense of "memorials," since the verbal root is *zkr* ("to remember"), meaning that their pronouncements are built on past tradition.

20. I take *gab* as a hapax legomenon related to Arabic, Aramaic, and Syriac *gwb*. See *HALOT* 1:170; *CHALOT* 53; and Clines, *Job 1–20*, 282.

21. It is hard to see how the opening *ʿal-mâ* (MT) fits into the verse, so it may be understood to be a textual corruption (dittography from the last two words of v. 13). Some translations take the *ʿal-mâ* as introducing a question, "Why. . . ?" If so, Job is likely asking the question rhetorically to set up the following answer to why he is taking a risk.

22. I accept the Ketib; the Qere has *lûʾ*, "indeed." The Ketib is almost certainly correct, and the Qere represents the wishful thinking of later scribes.

23. Literally "my ways."

24. From the root *ḥqh*, "to make an incision" (A. Millard, *NIDOTTE* 2:251–52).

14:1 Mortals[25] born of woman,
short of days, and full of trouble.
2 They come up like a flower and wither,
and flee like a shadow that does not endure.
3 Do you open your eyes on such a one?
Me would you bring into judgment?
4 Who can bring something clean out of something unclean?
No one.
5 If their days are determined,
the number of their months is controlled by you;
you have made their bounds that they cannot pass.
6 Look away from them and stop,
until their days run away like those of a hired worker.
7 For there is hope for a tree;
if it is cut down and sprouts again,
its shoots do not cease.
8 Though its root grows old in the earth,
and its stump dies in the dust,
9 yet at the smell of water it buds,
and puts forth boughs like a plant.
10 But mortals die and dwindle away;
humans expire and are no more.
11 Water disappears from the sea,
and rivers dry up and wither away.
12 So people lie down and do not get up;
until the heavens are no more, they do not awake;
they are not aroused from their sleep.
13 If only you would hide me in Sheol,
conceal me until your anger passes.
You could set a limit and then remember me.
14 If a person dies, will he live again?[26]
I would wait all the days of my servitude,
until my release would arrive.
15 You would summon me, and I would answer you;
you would desire the work of your hands.
16 Whereas now you number my steps,
you would not keep watch over my sins.
17 You would seal up my transgression in a sack;
you would smear over my iniquities.

25. Seow (*Job*) points out that the first word of this chapter begins with an *'aleph* (*'ādām*, "mortals") and the last (*te'ěbāl*, "it mourns") begins with a *taw*, the first and last letters of the Hebrew alphabet. This, combined with the fact that the chapter is composed of twenty-two verses, suggests an intentional acrostic-like structure. I would feel more confident about this if the *taw* word in v. 22 were the first word (the more usual position for acrostic structures) rather than the last.

26. Seow (*Job*) points out that the Old Greek reverses the meaning of the Hebrew and presents a confident statement of eternal life. He translates, "For, if a person dies, he shall live again when the days of his life have finished."

[18]However, a falling mountain is carried away,
and a rock is moved from its place;
[19]water grinds down the stones;
violent storms wash away the dust of the earth;
so you cause the hope of humanity to perish.
[20]You overpower them once for all, and they go away,
changing their countenance, and you send them away.
[21]Their children achieve honor, and they are unaware;
they are made low, and they do not perceive it.
[22]They feel the pain of their flesh
and mourn only for themselves."

Interpretation

The first verse introduces Job's final response in the first round of the disputation, and this response is a particularly long one, covering three chapters. He begins, as do many of the speeches on both sides of the debate, with an insult directed at his opponents (12:2–3). He does so in order to assert his own wisdom over against that of his friends. Though he is wiser than they are, he bemoans that he has become a joke to his friends. In their eyes, he is a man who seemed pious, but his affliction belies his righteous exterior. However, he responds by saying that God's ways are upside down. The wicked are those who are at ease, even those who are contemptuous toward God (12:4–6). In his opinion, every creature—humans, animals, even plants—can attest with him that God is not fair (12:7–12). God is, however, wise and powerful, and in 12:13–25 he describes how God is in control of everything and everyone. What is most remarkable is that every single one of the numerous examples of God's control shows how it leads to detrimental consequences (see "God the Destroyer" in the theological implications section below).

Chapter 13 continues Job's final response to the friends in the first cycle of the debate. The opening verses of the chapter (especially vv. 1–3) are similar to an opening of a speech in that he again insults the friends' wisdom while asserting his own. He also states that he wants to reprove God, but he begins instead by reproving his friends (vv. 4–5, 6–12), strikingly charging them with speaking unjustly of God (see "Speaking Unjustly about God" in the theological implications section below). Job then grits his teeth and determines that he will approach God to reprove him even if such an attempt will result in his death (vv. 13–19). As often happens in Job's speech, he then goes from addressing the friends to speaking directly to God (though without any confidence that God is hearing him) in vv. 20–28. He gives God two preconditions that will allow Job to approach God: God needs to lay off Job both physically and psychologically. If he is able to approach God, he wants God to prove the supposed charges against him (again, Job believes that all suffering, including his, is based on personal sin). He wants God to list the sins for which he is punishing Job.

Job continues to address God as he concludes this lengthy speech in chap. 14. He first of all describes the human condition as short and sad (see "The Human Condition: Short of Days and Full of Trouble" in the theological implications section below). On this basis, he beseeches God to leave people alone and let them do their best in the few, troubled days they have (vv. 1–6). After all, there is no hope for humans after death. Unlike trees that can be cut down and then spring to life, human beings die and are no more. They are more like a dried-up river where the water has dissipated, never to return (vv. 7–12). Even so, Job fantasizes about a temporary death, where he can avoid God's onslaught until God calms down. After that, he wishes that God would bring him back (vv. 13–17). Still, Job realizes that such a thing is not possible since death is the inevitable fate of all human beings (vv. 18–22).

---

1 And Job answered and said:
2 "Truly, you are the people,
and wisdom will die with you!
3 I also have a mind like you.
I am not inferior to you.
Who is not like these?"

12:1–3. *Job claims superior wisdom.* As is typical in the disputation, Job begins with an insult directed toward the friends. The subject pronoun "you" is plural (*'attem*); thus he refers to all three friends and not just Zophar. Verse 2a is a bit opaque when it calls them the "people" (*'ām*), but this is likely a way of charging them with presuming to represent the combined wisdom of the people. This understanding goes well with the second colon, in which Job sarcastically attributes to them the idea that wisdom will die when they die. In other words, he claims that they believe they are the repository of wisdom. In this way, Job points to their arrogance and undermines their claim to wisdom.

After insulting them, he himself claims equal if not superior wisdom. We must remember that the disputations are really about who has wisdom. Wisdom is what is needed to diagnose Job's problem and to determine the remedy. The three friends claim it and belittle Job's wisdom, and vice versa. Here Job states that he has wisdom, not they.

---

4 "I am a joke to my friends,
he who summoned God and he answered me,
a righteous and innocent man—a joke!
5 Those at ease have contempt for disaster,
but it is prepared for those whose feet are unstable.

[6]The tents of the marauders have peace and quiet,
and those who aggravate God are confident,
and so is anyone who brings God under their control."

12:4–6. *Object of ridicule.* Job's past reputation among his friends was that he was righteous (*ṣāddîq*) and innocent (*tāmîm*). Indeed, he actually was righteous (as he claims in 9:15; 10:15) and innocent; the first verse of the book says as much, though it uses "virtuous" (*yāšār*) rather than "righteous" along with "innocent" there (see 1:1, 8). However, in the light of his suffering, the friends now joke about this characterization. Due to his affliction, they cannot think that Job is innocent; he must be a sinner. In the past too it would have been clear that he was someone who summoned or called on God and that God responded. God responded to Job with a large family and wealth and health. But now such a characterization of Job is a matter of laughter among the friends. Indeed, Job now summons God, but God is silent (9:16, 19). Job is an object of dark humor. As Ps. 69 illustrates, the psalmist also experienced this level of ridicule:

When I humbled my soul with fasting,
they insulted me for doing so.
When I made sackcloth my clothing,
I became a byword to them.
I am the subject of gossip for those who sit in the gate,
and the drunkards make songs about me. (vv. 10–12 NRSV)

The realization that he is a joke among his friends leads him in vv. 5–6 to again describe what he perceives as God's topsy-turvy world. The friends are like those at ease. They do not suffer, and so they are contemptuous of those, like Job, who are experiencing disaster in their life. They think of afflicted people as those who have a contagious disease. Better to stay away from such people. But it, that is, disaster, is prepared for the unstable. God should be in the business of saving people whose feet are unstable (*m'd*, which could also be translated "slip"). David proclaims, "You have made a wide path for my feet to keep them from slipping [*m'd*]" (Ps. 18:36 NIV [37]; 2 Sam. 22:37). Usually it is the innocent whom God keeps firmly on the ground (Pss. 26:1; 37:31), while he undermines the feet of the wicked (see also Ps. 69:23; Prov. 25:19).

Verse 6 develops the idea of the security of the wicked. Here the marauders or robbers live a life of ease (have peace and quiet). Not only are they wicked, but they also aggravate God. The difference is that they are able to control God somehow. To Job, these marauders "seem to be able to manipulate Eloah as if he were a magical object in their control."[27]

27. Habel, *Job*, 219; though see the translation note for 12:6 above for an alternate interpretation.

[7]"Only ask the beasts, and they will teach you,
the birds in the sky, and they will inform you.
[8]Or the plants of the earth, and they will teach you;
the fish of the sea will recount to you.
[9]Who does not know all these things,
that the hand of Yahweh has done this?
[10]The breath of all living things is in his hand,
the spirit of all human flesh.
[11]Does not the ear test words
as the mouth tastes food?
[12]With the aged is wisdom,
with the long-lived is understanding."

12:7–12. *Job's witnesses.* Job has asserted that the world works the opposite of the way the three friends imagine and argue. The wicked are not punished, and the innocent are not rewarded. Quite the contrary. They have argued in their wisdom for their view, and Job is countering with his wisdom, which perceives the world differently. As I have stated many times before, Job shares the friends' retribution theology; that is, the world should work the way they describe, but it does not. That it does not indicates that the world is unfair.

In this debate, the three friends and Job support their arguments by calling on witnesses. In this section of his speech, Job appeals to the animal and natural world, on the one hand, and the aged, on the other hand, in a way that implies that they agree with his view of the universe. The first group includes the beasts, the birds, the plants, and the fish, the creatures of the land, air, and sea. Job argues that nature itself supports his argument and that the friends should inquire of these. This line of argument fits in with the idea that God created the world through his wisdom (Prov. 3:19–20; 8:22–31). Proverbs teaches that the animal and natural world demonstrate wisdom and so it is important to observe them. An example is Prov. 6:6–8:

Go to the ant, you lazy people!
See its paths and grow wise.
That one has no military commander,
officer, or ruler;
it gets its food in summer,
gathers its provisions at harvest.

Job never states exactly how the beasts, plants, birds, and fish support his idea. Perhaps it is just in the pain and suffering that they themselves experience, for instance, when a lion eats a deer, or larger fish consume smaller fish. Since Job does not tell us, we cannot be sure. However he would fill out his argument, it is clear from the passage that he believes the natural world would support his point that the oppressive "hand of Yahweh" has perpetrated the damage.

The second witness that he alludes to here is that of the aged. Since wisdom is the result of observation and experience, the more of these one has, the wiser one will be. By definition, then, the older a person is, the wiser the person should be. Both sides of this debate appeal to aged supporters (for the three friends, see Eliphaz's comments in 15:10). Elihu later will question the wisdom of the elders (32:7–10).[28]

It is not exactly clear how v. 11 fits in. The passage points out that the ear is to wisdom what the palate is to taste. In other words, the ear is the organ that discriminates wisdom from folly. In that it prefaces v. 12, v. 11 seems to be saying that those with a long history of such discriminating observation, and possibly who heed tradition (yet another source of wisdom), namely the aged, are excellent arbiters in this debate. Job claims they are on his side.

13"With him are wisdom and power;
he has advice and understanding.
14What he tears down will not be built up;
the person he shuts in will not be let out.
15He withholds the water, and it dries up;
he releases it, and it overwhelms the land.
16With him are strength and mental resources;
deceived and deceiver are his.
17He leads counselors away plundered,
and renders judges deluded.
18He loosens the sash of kings;
he tightens the waistcloth around their hips.
19He leads priests away plundered,
and ruins those long established.
20He takes away the speech of the trusted,
as well as the discernment of the elders.
21He pours contempt on princes
and loosens the belt of the strong.
22He reveals the depths from the darkness,
and he brings deep darkness to the light.
23He makes the nations grow great, and then he destroys them.
He enlarges the nations and then disperses them.
24He takes intelligence away from the heads of the people of the earth,
and he makes them wander in chaos without a path.
25They grope around in darkness without light,
he makes them wander about like a drunkard."

28. For a discussion of the sources of wisdom, including observation, experience, and age, see Longman, *Proverbs*, 74–79.

12:13–25. *God the destroyer*. Job has attacked the friends' view of God and their understanding of how God interacts with the world. They think God arranges the world so that the wicked are punished and the righteous are rewarded. Job agrees that this is the way God and the world should work, but on the basis of his own experience, he argues that God does not do so. In a word, God is unjust.

In this section, Job describes God. He never questions his immense wisdom and his tremendous power. Rather, he believes that God uses these qualities for destructive purposes rather than constructive ones.

He begins with a straightforward assertion of God's power and wisdom. In v. 13 he attributes "wisdom" (*ḥokmâ*) and "power" (*gĕbûrâ*) to God in the first colon and then uses two words closely related to "wisdom"—"advice" (*ʿēṣâ*) and "understanding" (*tĕbûnâ*)—to make his point.

The following twelve verses (vv. 14–25) then describe how God applies his strength and wisdom to the world. In each example, God's influence is negative, not positive, corresponding to how Job perceives God's power and wisdom to operate in his own life.

For instance, in v. 14 he says that when God tears something down, it cannot be rebuilt, or if he shuts someone in, there is no one who can open up what is ostensibly his cell and let him out. Note that the verse does not evaluate the thing torn down or the person shut in. If it were an oppressive enemy fortress in the first case or a malicious criminal in the second, that would be one thing. Job, though, describes God's power and wisdom as issuing in destruction.

Verse 15 turns to a new subject, the waters. Now the waters literally are life giving, on the one hand, but death dealing, on the other. Humans need water to drink, so there needs to be enough of it for that purpose. But uncontrolled waters can bring the devastation of floods. So to describe God's use of the waters by the contrasts of drying them up (and therefore not having water to drink) or overwhelming the land by floods again illustrates Job's theme of the destructive nature of God's power and wisdom.

Verse 16 begins by again asserting God's power and wisdom but here uses different words than those in v. 13a: *ʿōz* (power) and *tûšîyâ* (mental resources). The latter is related to *ḥokmâ* but has a narrower meaning. Fox interprets it as "an inner power that helps one escape from a fix."[29] In any case, these attributes mean that God controls both the deceived and the deceiver. What is interesting about this statement is that there is no difference between the two. One might suspect that God would control and understand the deceiver in order to aid the deceived, but that is not the point made here.

The next verse continues the thought when it says that God undermines the work of various leaders of the community whose purpose is to bring order

29. Fox, *Proverbs 1–9*, 116. It can also refer to the consequences of having such mental resources. See Job 5:12, where I translate the word as "success."

and justice and health to the community. These include counselors who are plundered (perhaps of their good advice) as well as judges who are deluded. The latter need clear thinking to adjudicate matters of justice, but Job believes God confuses them so they cannot think clearly.

Verse 18 is difficult to translate[30] and to understand. The king is the subject, and the verse appears to say that the belt or sash of the king is loosened, but then his girdle or waistcloth is tightened. The latter is the same word (*ʾēzôr*) used of the clothing that God instructed Jeremiah not to wash and to bury in a cave near the Euphrates (Jer. 13:1–11). It is best understood as Jeremiah's undergarments.[31] If so understood here, the verse says that God loosens his belt, the thing that holds his outer garments together, and tightens his undergarments. Perhaps this is an ancient saying with which we have lost touch, but it may mean that God can dishevel a king outwardly with the implied idea that he can do so mentally as well. That would fit in with the idea in this section that God damages the perceptions of counselors, judges, and so on.

Verse 19 then speaks of priests, those commissioned to direct worship and to protect the holy. Verse 19a uses the same wording as we saw directed toward counselors in v. 17a. There I suggested that their plundering was a mental plundering: they were stripped of sense. These are not fly-by-night leaders but leaders with deep roots ("long established").

God's ravishing of leaders continues in the next two verses. He removes speech from trusted people, who would be able to give good advice. The lay leaders, the elders, are also injured in terms of their ability to provide help in making decisions (their discernment). The princes and the strong are also hurt by God's power and wisdom. The former suffer a similar fate as kings who had their sashes loosened, though a different phrase is used.[32]

Verse 22 changes course a bit and talks about light and darkness rather than a particular class of leader. Still, the theme that God brings bad conditions into being through his strength and wisdom continues. First, the depths come out of the darkness, and then deep darkness comes out of the light. The deeps, darkness, and deep darkness all have negative connotations over against that which is lit. Indeed, v. 25 will return to this idea of darkness to point out that "they" (presumably the "heads of the people of the earth") have no direction because they are confused like a drunkard and like those who stumble around in the dark. As Habel puts it, "The release of underworld darkness abroad on the earth increases disorientation. By his actions God does not shed light but darkness and obfuscation, so that leaders grope forever in gloom."[33]

30. See the textual emendation of *mûsar* (to *môsēr*) mentioned in the translation note for 12:18 above.

31. See Longman, *Jeremiah, Lamentations*, 109–10.

32. In v. 18 he (literally) opened (from *ptḥ*) their sashes (*môsēr*), while here in v. 21b he loosens (*rph*) their belt (*mĕzîaḥ*).

33. Habel, *Job*, 222.

Verse 23 talks about God's sovereignty over the nations. He is in utter control of all the nations, a common biblical theme. But here again God's control is not used to aid the righteous or to harm the wicked. No, God directs his power toward the nations indiscriminately to make them grow and then disperse them.

In sum, Job argues that God has great wisdom and strength. However, he uses that to confuse, not to illuminate. He uses it to destroy, not to build up.

1"Look, my eye has seen all this;
  my ear has heard and understood it.
2I definitely know what you know;
  I am not inferior to you.
3But I would speak to Shaddai.
  I would love to reprove God.
4But you smear me with lies.
  All of you are worthless physicians!
5If you would only shut up,
  that would be a wise move on your part."

13:1–5. *Shut up!* Job again asserts his wisdom over against his friends' claims (see 12:1–3). He claims the wisdom of experience and observation when he asserts that he has seen and heard and therefore understood everything relevant to the discussion. He asserts his equality if not superiority in wisdom to the friends. They of course believe that they are superior, so Job once again specifically makes the point that he is not inferior to them in matters of wisdom (compare 13:2b with 12:3b).

Reading v. 1 in the light of the end of the book makes us realize that Job is overemphasizing his knowledge of God at this point. While here he claims to have seen and heard (and thus understood) "all this," in 42:5, after the appearance and speech of God, he says, "My ear had received a report of you, but now my eyes have seen you." In other words, later Job will have a fuller experience and thus a fuller knowledge of God.

Job's wisdom leads in a direction different from that of the friends, who want him to repent. Job does not think he should repent. He wants an audience with God; he desires to take him to court.[34] Or at least that is what he would like to do. We have already observed this theme in Job's thinking, though often he resigns himself to the impossibility of such a move (9:14–20). In this present speech, however, he believes that he has no other recourse. He may die in the attempt, but he feels that reproving God, taking him to court, is the only way forward (13:15).

But the "friends" are no help. They have come forward as "physicians" attempting to cure him from his ailment. They have provided a diagnosis

34. Ivanski (*Dynamics*, 220) believes that this is the turning point, when Job definitively decides to take God to court.

that he is a sinner who needs to repent. To make their diagnosis work, they have smeared him with lies (v. 4; see the similar expression in Ps. 119:69), because he is not a sinner. Though there is no medical use of the verb "smear" (*ṭpl*) in the Bible, the author may want us to think of a true physician, who smears healing lotion on a wound. In any case, like a doctor who makes a misdiagnosis, they are worthless. They would do better to shut up. Here Job in essence calls the friends fools, and according to Prov. 17:28, the best recourse for fools is to keep their mouths shut, because they reveal their folly when they speak: "Even a dupe who keeps silent seems wise; those who keep their lips shut are smart."

6"Hear now my reproof.
Pay attention to the accusations of my lips.
7Will you speak unjustly for God
and say deceitful things about him?
8Will you favor him,
if you make an accusation for God?
9Will it be good that he examine you?
Can you deceive him like someone deceives another person?
10He will most certainly reprove you
if you show favoritism in secret.
11Does not his majesty scare you,
his fear fall on you?
12Your proclamations are proverbs made of dust.
Your responses are responses made of clay."

13:6–12. *Don't speak unjustly about God.* Though Job desires to "reprove God" (13:3), he settles for reproving his friends, calling them "worthless physicians" who smear him with lies (13:4). He begins this passage (v. 7) by calling on the friends to listen to his reproof. While "reproof" (*tôkaḥâ*) here may have a legal meaning, the word "accusation" (*rîb*) clearly does. He wants to bring legal charges against his friends for their lies.

In vv. 7–12 he argues that they have misrepresented God in all the horrible things they are saying to him. When they say he is a sinner who deserves his punishment, they do not accurately reflect God's view. Job does not think that God perceives him as a sinner, and that is precisely the problem. Job thinks God knows he is innocent, but he treats the innocent like the wicked. Job's problem with God is not that God falsely understands him as deserving of punishment, but that God punishes him even though he does not deserve it.

Thus he tells the friends that they should live in mortal fear of God because they say false things in his name. They will not be able to deceive God; after all, God controls both deceiver and deceived (12:16). They had better be afraid of the consequences (13:11). If they are not careful, then God will "reprove" them (13:10). Thus, so far in this chapter, we have seen that Job desires to reprove

God, but he begins by reproving the friends, who themselves will be reproved by God if they do not watch out and change their tune. Indeed, at the end of the book, God does reprove the friends, and without Job's intercession, they would have been in deep trouble (42:7).

Job ends this section with a final insult directed toward their wisdom. He calls their speeches ("proclamations/responses") fragile in the extreme. They are like dust and clay. There is nothing substantial in them. They are easily blown away.

> **13**"Be silent around me, and I will speak,
> and let whatever pass my way.
> **14**I will take my flesh in my teeth;
> I will put my life in my palm.
> **15**See, he will kill me; I have no hope.
> I will reprove him to his face concerning my behavior.
> **16**This will be my salvation,
> that the godless will not come into his presence.
> **17**Listen closely to my words;
> let my declaration be in your ear.
> **18**See, I am prepared for the judgment;
> I know I am righteous.
> **19**Who is it that accuses me
> so now I would be silent and die?"

13:13–19. *Job will reprove God despite the consequences.* Job is ready to throw caution to the wind in the pursuit of his vindication. He has told the friends to be quiet or else be exposed as fools (13:5). He again insists that they be quiet so he can talk. As he does, his confidence continues to waffle as to whether his attempt to defend himself will be successful or be fruitless and even dangerous. He is willing to take the risk ("let whatever pass my way," v. 13b).

Verse 14 also underlines the fact that Job is taking a risk by pressing his case against God, though the idioms used there, especially in the first colon, are not immediately clear. Verse 14b seems the most transparent. Even today (at least in the United States), we use the expression that we are "taking our life in our own hands" when we embark on a dangerous course of action. Clines points out that this expression ("I will put my life in my palm") occurs elsewhere in the OT (Judg. 12:3; 1 Sam. 19:5; 28:21).[35]

The expression "taking one's flesh in one's teeth" strikes one as proverbial on the surface. The parallelism with v. 14b leads me (and others) to believe that it is another way in which Job states his willingness to take a risk. However, exactly how the proverb works is difficult to say. Clines explains that just as one puts one's life in one's hands (a vulnerable spot), the same is true if someone

35. Clines, *Job 1–20*, 311.

puts one's flesh in one's teeth.[36] But this is not certain or particularly clear. Even so it seems the best explanation and explains why many modern translations bypass a literal translation of the colon and opt for a nonmetaphorical rendition. The NIV is a good example: "Why do I put myself in jeopardy?" (see also REB, NLT).[37]

The translation and interpretation issues of v. 14 pale in the light of v. 15a. The available translations are extremely diverse:

> Though he slay me, yet will I hope in him. . . . (NIV; see also NKJV)
> See, he will kill me; I have no hope. . . . (NRSV)
> God might kill me, but I have no other hope. . . . (NLT)

Taking the Hebrew text as it stands in Codex Leningradensis, one has to reject the NIV rendering. There is a negative *lōʾ* before the verb "to hope," though it is true that some Masoretic MSS and versions go with the Qere, which is *lû*, taken as an asseverative. There is an additional problem with the NIV rendering, though, in taking the opening particle *hēn* as a concessive, which is unlikely, rather than as an interjection. This reading is appealing because it indicates that Job places his trust in God to do the right thing. However, though appealing, this sentiment does not fit well in Job's mouth. The NLT rendering is slightly modified from the NIV, but the modest change is an improvement, since it shows that Job is not really so confident in God, but he has no other choice. The NRSV rendering (the one closest to mine) is the best option because it shows just how desperate Job is as he contemplates pressing his case against God. He really does not think he stands a chance, but he may as well try. In summary, Job expresses his determination to press his case against God even though he thinks his chances are slight or even nil. Nevertheless, he wants to go in and confront God's treatment of him in light of his (innocent and blameless) behavior.[38]

Whatever chance he does have is expressed in v. 16, though there are problems with understanding what Job is saying here, especially in light of some of his earlier statements. He thinks that he will be saved because the godless cannot come into God's presence; the idea is that they cannot do so unscathed. The difficulty with understanding Job's statement is that he has repeatedly expressed the belief that, if anything, God favors the wicked. I do not think we can resolve this issue by making a distinction between the "wicked" and the "godless," because in the biblical framework these two are not separated.

36. Ibid.

37. Note that NIV and REB (but not NLT) retain the *ʿāl-mâ* (see the translation note for 13:14 above).

38. This view of the verse is also held by Dow, *When Storms Come*, 75.

Job ends this section by stating loudly and boldly to the friends his determination to press forward (vv. 17–19). If there is one thing in which he has confidence, it is his righteousness, though he is not so sure that even it will lead to his survival (v. 15a). His friends want him to shut up, but he will not do so (v. 19). (For a reflection on the theological implications of this passage, see the essay "I Know That My Redeemer Lives" following my comments on Job 19.)

20"Only do two things for me,
then I won't hide from your face.
21Move your palm far from me;
don't allow dread of you to scare me.
22Call and I will answer;
or I will speak and you will respond to me.
23What are my faults and sins?
Make known to me my transgressions and sins.
24Why do you hide your face
and consider me your enemy?
25Will you frighten a windblown leaf
and pursue dried chaff?
26For you write bitter things about me;
you make me inherit the guilt of my youth.
27You set my feet in stocks;
you guard all my paths;
you make an incision on the soles of my feet.
28One wastes away like something rotten,
like a garment eaten by a moth."

13:20–28. *God, do two things for me.* Job has been speaking to the three friends from 12:1 through 13:19, but now he abruptly changes addressee. From now until the end of this speech, he speaks directly to God. He begins by asking God to do two things for him. Job has expressed a desire to confront God directly in a courtroom, but has hesitated to do so for reasons that become clearer in his demands. As preconditions to a meeting, Job insists that God back off from him ("move your palm far from me," v. 21a) and stop scaring him (v. 21b). In 7:14 Job had revealed that God scared him, and in 9:34 he expressed the hope that a mediator would be able to "take his [God's] rod away from me, and not let his dread scare me." Here he makes these demands to God directly. Job says that he has hidden his face from God because God has been hard on him both physically and psychologically through his affliction and through his fright.

If these conditions are met, then Job will be able to interact with God. He will respond when God calls him and vice versa (v. 22). When we think about this request in the light of the end of the book of Job (38:1–42:6), we realize that Job eventually does obtain his audience with God, but if anything God frightens him even more.

For now, though, he wants to ask God to enumerate his "faults and sins," his "transgressions and sins" (v. 23). Job believes that suffering should come to a person only as a punishment for sin. He knows he has not sinned, and therefore he wants to call God's bluff.

While Job has admitted that he has hidden his face from God out of fear, he questions why God has hidden his face from Job. When God hides his face from his people, they experience pain. In Ps. 30 the psalmist had enjoyed God's presence in his life and the resultant prosperity. In the case of the psalmist, he realized that he grew presumptuous in his success, so that God hid his face from him with the result that he "was dismayed" (Ps. 30:7 NRSV). This led the psalmist to turn back to God, who then turned his weeping into joy. The three friends are arguing that this pattern holds for Job, but Job rejects this and questions why God would hide his face from him and become his enemy. He does not deserve such treatment.

Job considers God a bully, kicking him when he is down. Job, in his suffering, likens himself to a "windblown leaf" and "dried chaff" (v. 25), the opposite of a deeply rooted plant (Ps. 1). Job has no root, but is blown about by the wind. God even takes advantage of this by further undermining him. Verse 26 says that God does this by writing "bitter things" about Job. Perhaps this is an allusion to legal charges, though this is not what God is doing, as we know from the first two chapters as well as the last few chapters. It is not clear what Job means by saying that God makes him "inherit the sins of his youth" (v. 26b). Nowhere else does he admit to such sins. Perhaps there was a thought that all youths are sinful in the sense of Prov. 22:15, "Stupidity is bound up in a youth's heart." But whatever he is thinking of, it is clear that he believes it would be unfair to justify his present suffering on the basis of this youthful guilt.

The last two verses describe the kind of pain that God is presently putting Job through. Verse 27ab uses the language of incarceration. Job is in stocks, and God restricts his movement. In v. 27c he speaks of God's cutting the soles of his feet. The significance of this is not clear, though it obviously describes his affliction and probably again that God restricts his movement. Hartley suggests that such incisions on the soles of his feet would allow for easy tracking.[39] Some have taken the incision on the feet as a slave brand, but Clines rightly says that would be a strange place to brand someone, and the evidence indicates that slave branding was on the hand (Isa. 44:5; 49:16) or on the ear (Exod. 21:6).[40]

Those who divided the book of Job into its present chapter structure believed that v. 28 ended this part of Job's speech. As such, it is a climactic statement

39. Hartley, *Job*, 228–29.
40. Clines, *Job 1–20*, 322–23.

expressed as a general insight on humanity as being rotten. However, others believe that v. 28 begins a new section that continues into the first few verses of chap. 14, which proceeds with general observations on the condition of humanity.[41]

> [1]"Mortals born of woman,
> short of days, and full of trouble.
> [2]They come up like a flower and wither,
> and flee like a shadow that does not endure.
> [3]Do you open your eyes on such a one?
> Me would you bring into judgment?
> [4]Who can bring something clean out of something unclean?
> No one.
> [5]If their days are determined,
> the number of their months is controlled by you;
> you have made their bounds that they cannot pass.
> [6]Look away from them and stop,
> until their days run away like those of a hired worker."

14:1–6. *Leave us alone.* As mentioned at the end of the last section, 13:28 may be the beginning of this part of Job's speech rather than the conclusion of the previous part. However, in the final analysis, I agree with those responsible for the chapter division as they begin chap. 14 with the striking statement found in v. 1. On the one hand, Job believes that his situation is unique in that he is suffering, though sinless. On the other hand, he recognizes that hardship is part of the human condition. Mortals born of woman (are there any others?) live briefly and suffer trouble. The word for "trouble" (*rōgez*) is formed from a verb that means to shake or tremble (*rgz*). Although the shaking may indicate excitement in some contexts, it typically, as here, indicates anxiety, stress, and fear. In this case, brevity of life may not be a totally bad thing. Job oscillates between feeling life is too long (7:1–5) and too short (9:25–26).[42]

Verse 2 illustrates his point about the brevity and hardship of life with the metaphors of a flower and a shadow. On the surface, a flower is a thing of beauty and pleasure. But flowers do not last very long. The fragile beauty of the flower is a fitting example of life. Life may begin with hope and energy, Job suggests, but as time progresses, life fades into something dry and ugly. The psalmist (103:15–16) and Isaiah (40:6–8) use the flower metaphor in a similar fashion. They, however, use it (along with withering grass) to contrast the fragility of human life with the permanence of God's word.

41. See Wilson, *Job*, 147.

42. Seow (*Job*) suggests that the use of "mortals" (*ʾādām*) here is reminiscent of the creation and fall.

Verse 2b cites a second metaphor, that of a shadow. Shadows are even more ephemeral than flowers. Shadows have no substance and quickly and suddenly disappear, just like life, according to Job. Bildad had himself stated this truth (8:9). However, as mentioned in the comments on Job 7:1–10, the realization that human life is ephemeral can lead either to awe or to despair. Job is an example of the latter. Job does marvel, not at the greatness of God but rather at his nitpicking. As opposed to Pss. 8 or 144, Job wonders why God even bothers to attack such a weak vessel.[43]

After all, what is the use? God cannot bring something clean out of something unclean like humans, including Job himself. In any case, God is in control of humans', and thus Job's, life span. He can end it at any time. He knows humans do not last forever.

Because of this hardship and brevity of life, Job pleads with God to back off and stop harassing him. He had expressed the same sentiment in 7:19 ("Will you look away from me? Leave me alone while I swallow my saliva"). Let their days run out like those of a hired worker (v. 6; see 7:1). A hired worker bears with the difficulty of the work in order to reach payday, which seems forever in coming. For Job, payday is the day of his death, when his hard service comes to an end.

7"For there is hope for a tree;
 if it is cut down and sprouts again,
 its shoots do not cease.
8Though its root grows old in the earth,
 and its stump dies in the dust,
9yet at the smell of water it buds,
 and puts forth boughs like a plant.
10But mortals die and dwindle away;
 humans expire and are no more.
11Water disappears from the sea;
 and rivers dry up and wither away.
12So people lie down and do not get up;
 until the heavens are no more, they do not awake;
 they are not aroused from their sleep."

14:7–12. *No hope for humans.* Job continues with the theme of human mortality (initiated in v. 5). He begins by contrasting trees and humans (vv. 7–10). Job points out that trees can be cut down to the stump, but, provided they receive water, they can flourish again. He pictures trees cut down and their roots rotting in the ground, but still they can live again. Not so for human beings. Once they die, they die. In vv. 11–12 Job cites another comparison, this

43. See 7:17–21, which expresses ideas that are very similar to this present section by parodying Ps. 8.

time between humans and a body of water, either the sea or a river. Water, unlike trees, does not have the option of reviving to life once it has dried up. To make this comparison work, Job is not allowing for increased rainfall. Wilson correctly points to the fact that Job here uses "river" (*nāhār*) rather than "wadi" (*naḥal*), because the latter often dries up and then with rain or melting snow comes to life again.[44] Human beings, once they sleep in death, will not be roused again. Death is the final sleep.

Job does not have a sense of the afterlife, either in this passage or others, though some have tried to read such a hope into some texts (e.g., 19:25–27). When Job says that humans do not awake "until the heavens are no more," he is not contemplating a future time when there will be no heavens; rather, it is an idiom similar to what we might mean when we say "till hell freezes over."

13"If only you would hide me in Sheol,
conceal me until your anger passes.
You could set a limit and then remember me.
14If a person dies will he live again?
I would wait all the days of my servitude,
until my release would arrive.
15You would summon me, and I would answer you;
you would desire the work of your hands.
16Whereas now you number my steps,
you would not keep watch over my sins.
17You would seal up my transgression in a sack;
you would smear over my iniquities."

14:13–17. *Hide me until God's anger ends.* Job has just categorically denied the possibility that he or any mortal could live after death. Unlike a tree, a dead person cannot come to life again. Like a dried-up riverbed, there is no return from that final sleep. Thus, when Job asks in v. 14a, "If a person dies, will he live again?" we know he thinks the answer is no (see also 10:20–22).[45]

The present section, though, indicates that he wishes it were otherwise. He wishes that God would hide him in Sheol until the end of the anger that Job believes has led to his suffering. Though Job does not believe he deserves his afflictions, he apparently believes that he has angered God in some way that he does not understand. He thinks, nonetheless, that if God has time to calm down, then things will be right again. Rather than suffering, he wishes that God would kill him (hide him in Sheol, meaning the grave or the underworld) and then bring him out again after his period of punishment. He believes that,

44. Wilson, *Job*, 154. According to Habel (*Job*, 242), Job's statement is similar to Isaiah, who describes the demise of Egypt as the drying up of the mighty Nile (see Isa. 19:5–10).

45. For a contrary view, see Smick, "Job," 764.

though God is angry now, a time will come when God will miss him (v. 15b, "the work of your hands").

Verse 16 is a bit difficult because the two halves of the parallelism initially seem to say two different and somewhat contradictory things. The first colon talks about God numbering his steps, and the second envisions a time when God will not keep watch over Job's sins. The tension comes in that God's numbering his steps indicates keeping a close and precise accounting of his missteps (see 31:4, 37; 34:21). So v. 16a seems negative and v. 16b positive.

The NRSV tries to solve the conundrum by introducing a negative into v. 16a: "For then you would not number my steps, you would not keep watch over my sin." However, this approach is rather heavy-handed, though it has the virtue of making both cola fit into the theme of the section. A better approach is suggested by the REB, which is similar to my translation above. It appears that Job contrasts God's attitude toward him now (*ʿattâ*) with the hypothetical future attitude that Job hopes God would adopt toward him.

Verse 17 then continues along the lines of v. 16b as he continues his wish for a future in which God overlooks his sins rather than being so precise in his attention to them. He utilizes two metaphors to describe God's intentional lack of attention to his sins. The first is the idea of putting them in a sack where they cannot be seen; the second talks about smearing them over. In 13:4 I identified this verb "smear" (*ṭpl*) as a medical term, there used negatively in reference to the friends as worthless physicians who "smear" Job with lies. Here God would cover over Job's sins so they would not affect God's relationship with him.

18"However, a falling mountain is carried away,
and a rock is moved from its place;
19water grinds down the stone;
violent storms wash away the dust of the earth;
so you cause the hope of humanity to perish.
20You overpower them once for all, and they go away,
changing their countenance, and you send them away.
21Their children achieve honor, and they are unaware;
they are made low, and they do not perceive it.
22They feel the pain of their flesh
and mourn only for themselves."

14:18–22. *Fading hope.* In the previous section, Job had expressed his wish that God would put him into hibernation (so to speak) until his anger passed and he began to miss Job. However, in the final section of this final speech of the first cycle, Job comes back to what he thinks is reality. Verses 18–19b describe a mountain, a rather imposing and firmly established geographical feature, slowly but relentlessly being ground down to nothing. Rocks fall away, water from storms grind them down to nothing, and then the dust that remains is washed away. In the same way, says Job, human hope, which may begin strong, is eroded by the storms of life until it is gone. Job blames God for this eradication of hope. God overpowers his creatures, changing their countenance from joyful hope to fear, anxiety, and depression. The story of Job has provided an example of this. He began the story with hope, and he worked hard to maintain a good relationship and a prosperous lifestyle and a happy family, but the sufferings God has brought into his life have changed all that.

At the end, God sends them away to Sheol. Verse 21 then turns attention to the deceased person's children. The parents, on the road to Sheol (now dying), will not be cognizant of their children's successes and failures. The dying will be aware only of their own suffering, and they will mourn only their own death.

Theological Implications

God the Destroyer (12:13–25)

Job has affirmed God's power and wisdom. However, such knowledge does not lead him to trust God, since the ramifications of God's control over people and creation lead to negative consequences. In other words, God's power and wisdom make him dangerous. He not only tears things down, but once torn down, they also cannot be built again (v. 14a). He plunders counselors (presumably of their advice) and he confuses judges so they cannot render fair verdicts (v. 17). These are just two examples of the way God turns things on their heads and not for the good.

Job's perspective may be compared to Eliphaz's characterization of God in 5:8–16. Eliphaz commends God to Job as one who does "great and unsearchable things, marvelous things, without number" (5:9). He then goes on and, like Job, shows how God turns things on their head. The difference between Eliphaz and Job is that Eliphaz believes God takes negative situations and turns them into good, while Job sees God as the destroyer. Job himself had previously (9:5–10) also given a description of God's power and wisdom that was much more positive. His purpose there was to explain why it was so hard to approach God. Even here, though, there are glimmers of the negative consequences of the control God has because of his power and wisdom (e.g., "He speaks to the sun, and it does not rise; he seals up the stars").

This passage may also be compared and contrasted with other descriptions of how God acts to turn things on their heads, examples found outside the book of Job. Clines, for instance, points to a close relationship between 12:13–25 and Ps. 107.[46] For instance, Job says that God "withholds the water

46. Clines, *Job 1–20*, 296.

and it dries up; he releases it and it overwhelms the land" (12:15). This is a manifestation of God's power and wisdom and is not connected with his justice. The psalmist also speaks of God's manipulation of the waters, but in conformity with a strict view of justice:

> He turns rivers into a desert,
> springs of water into thirsty ground,
> a fruitful land into a salty waste,
> because of the wickedness of its inhabitants.
> He turns a desert into pools of water,
> a parched land into springs of water.
> And there he lets the hungry live. (Ps. 107:33–36a NRSV)

God's actions in Ps. 107 conform to the dictates of retribution and have a positive effect.

Clines well describes the portrait of God that Job gives us in 12:13–25, especially when contrasted with the picture given in a passage like Ps. 107:

> The God he has encountered is no placid governor of a universe of order, but an eccentric deity, equally inapprehensible and untameable whether he stands aloof from humans or frenetically and obnoxiously interferes in their lives. This is the deeper wisdom, the higher knowledge, that calls forth a hymn—half-serious because Job is truly awed by this revelation of a God beyond theological entrapment and half-ironic because Job deeply despises a God who does not play fair.[47]

Clines thinks that Job implies here not that God is unjust but simply that he is amoral, but it seems to me that there is at least an implicit charge that God does not treat the world fairly.

God's actions in the world are double-sided. God destroys and God builds up. Psalm 107 is an example of a passage that connects God's destruction with his judgment on the wicked and connects God's restoration with his blessing of the righteous. In this fallen world, however, God's actions are not always so neatly divided. In other words, the righteous are sometimes treated as if they are wicked, and the wicked are treated as if they are righteous (Eccles. 7:15). Job believed that God should always act in conformity with justice. He has not in Job's case, and therefore Job can see God only as a destroyer. The biblical teaching on retribution is more complex than Job has previously thought. In the short term, sometimes good things happen to bad people, and bad things happen to good people. God does not promise perfect justice in a fallen world. But in the end, all things work out in conformity with God's justice, and the righteous receive their reward.

47. Ibid.

Speaking Unjustly about God (13:4–5, 6–12)

Job attacks the three friends for misrepresenting God to him in the midst of his sufferings. His evaluation of their teaching and its impact on his life is a sober reminder of the serious impact that Bible teachers and counselors have on people's lives even today.

Job called them "worthless physicians" (13:4) for their misleading teaching. In the words of Didymus the Blind, "A useless physician is literally one who applies curing strategies that are not useful for the suffering."[48] False attempts to cure a person, either physically or psychologically, fail to help and often deepen the problem.

Throughout the Bible, the teacher is held in high esteem as a person who represents God and his ways to other people. Such a role entails huge responsibilities. In the Pastorals, the leaders of the church (elders) are those who must be able to teach (1 Tim. 3:2). In Rom. 12:7, Paul instructs those who teach to teach well.

But what does it mean to teach well, especially in a situation like Job's? In opposition to the worthless physician described by Didymus, a teacher must apply curing strategies that will be useful for the person who is suffering. Job's friends allowed their (incorrect) theology to color their understanding of Job's situation without becoming aware of what was going on. They had no evidence that Job was a sinner (there was none to be had), but they went ahead and accused him of sin and demanded that he repent in order to be restored.

Even allowing for their theology, they should not have accused Job of sin without any evidence of it. They should have allowed themselves to be amazed that their friend who was so godly should suffer so. In their astonishment, they should have remained silent, as they did during the first seven days (2:13). There is, after all, a "time to be silent and a time to speak" (Eccles. 3:7). But they did not keep silent, and later they ended up misrepresenting God to Job, as Job anticipated (Job 13:9).

The NT period knows of such false teachers right from the start (2 Pet. 2:1 NLT, "But there were also false prophets in Israel, just as there will be false teachers among you"). There are different types of false teachers. Unlike Job's false teachers, there are those who teach not the truth but whatever the "itching ears" of their hearers want to hear (2 Tim. 4:3). There are also those who misrepresent the Word of God to those who suffer. We can see it, for instance, in the prosperity gospel that either explicitly or implicitly informs people that God blesses the righteous with health and wealth, with the flip side that those who are sick and poor are not godly or do not have enough faith. We can see it anytime that the Bible or theology is applied to a situation in a mechanistic and formulaic manner with no attempt to get to know the details of the situation.

48. See Simonetti and Conti, *Job*, 74.

Teachers (and counselors) in the church need to be serious about their role. They need to be astute readers of Scripture and equally adept at reading people and situations in order to know how to apply the Bible to people's lives. It is for good reason that James issues the following warning: "Dear brothers and sisters, not many of you should become teachers in the church, for we who teach will be judged more strictly" (James 3:1 NLT).

The Human Condition: Short of Days and Full of Trouble (14:1)

As part of his appeal to God, Job reminds him and us of the human condition. Our lives are short and troubled. Not everyone suffers like Job, but no one escapes the difficulties and struggles of life, and nothing is more certain than death, whether it takes place in childhood or in advanced old age. Time on earth is brief. Job describes the human condition in his attempt to persuade God to leave him alone. He believes that his suffering is due to God's harassment, and he asks God to back off since life is not long and has enough trouble as it is.

As already implied, Job's observation about life is correct. Life is never perfect, often hard, and in some cases unbearable in its pain, and it always ends in death. Why? Why is life hard and short?

The early chapters of Genesis answer this question by pointing to human rebellion against God. The first two chapters tell the story of the creation of the cosmos. While it tells us next to nothing about how God created, using highly figurative language well known in the ancient Near East to describe the creation,[49] it goes to great pains to inform us that human beings were not inherently evil. After completing the creation, including human beings, God announced that it was all "very good" (Gen. 1:31). The second creation account's description of Adam's origins in the dust of the ground and the breath of God (Gen. 2:7) underlines the dignity of humanity in contrast to the Babylonian version, where humans are created from a mixture of the dust of the ground, the blood of a demon god, and the spittle of the rest of the gods (Atrahasis).[50] In the latter, humans are inherently evil; in the biblical view, they are created good.

So why is life short and hard? The answer comes in Gen. 3 when Adam and Eve rebel against God. They replace God's sovereignty with their own. By eating the fruit of the forbidden tree, they try to define their own moral standards and not allow God to do so. The consequence is death and suffering. Humans are alienated from God, from each other, from creation, and even from themselves.

So why do humans experience suffering? Because of sin. Now I am beginning to sound like one of the three friends: Job is suffering because of sin.

49. See Walton, *Genesis 1*.
50. *COS* 1:450–52 (lines 225–43).

However, as I have repeatedly emphasized in this commentary and will do so till the end, the book of Job makes very clear that Job is "innocent and virtuous, fearing God and turning away from sin" (1:1 and elsewhere). We lose our way in the book of Job if we ever forget that Job is not personally responsible for his suffering.

On the other hand, there would be no suffering and death apart from sin (Rom. 5:12–21). What the story of Job undermines is the belief that all of our suffering and pain and our death are the direct result of our own personal sin. It keeps us from looking at someone who is sick, poor, or depressed and asking, "What did they do to deserve this?" The book, though, is not denying that it is human rebellion that has marred life and brought death into the world.

B.
Second Cycle
(15:1–21:34)

The three friends are far from done with Job after the first round, and so they begin again in the same order and with what comes across as increased energy and animosity. Even so, Job continues to argue his case without giving in to the friends or backing off from his charge that God is unjust. Indeed, Job grows in confidence that he can set God straight if only he can gain an audience with him.

1.
Eliphaz's Second Speech
(15:1–35)

Translation

[1]And Eliphaz the Temanite answered and said:

[2]"Should sages respond with windy knowledge,
filling their belly with the hot east wind?
[3]Should they reprove with a word that does not benefit,
and words that are of no use to them?
[4]As for you, you even invalidate fear.
You hinder meditation before God.
[5]Your iniquity teaches your mouth;
you choose the tongue of the crafty.
[6]Your own mouth declares you guilty, not me.
Your own lips testify against you.
[7]Are you the firstborn among mortals?
Were you brought forth before the hills?
[8]Did you listen in on God's secret council?
Do you limit wisdom to yourself?
[9]What do you know that we do not?
What do you understand that is not with us?
[10]The gray-haired and elderly are with us,
much older than your father!

[11]Are God's consolations not enough for you,
or the word that deals gently with you?
[12]Why does your heart take you away?
Why do your eyes flash,[1]

1. The verb *rzm* occurs only here in Hebrew and has no clear cognate in other Semitic languages. Clines (*Job 1–20*, 342), citing Grabbe (*Comparative Philology*, 66–67), connects

13so you turn your spirit against God
and cause such words to come out of your mouth?
14What are mortals that they can be pure
or those born of woman that they can be righteous?
15Look, he does not even trust his holy ones;
the heavens are not pure in his eyes.
16How much less we who are abominable and corrupt,
people who drink injustice like water.

17I will show you; listen to me.
What I have seen, I will recount to you,
18things sages have declared
and their fathers have not hidden,
19to whom alone the land was given,
and no stranger has passed in their midst.
20The wicked are in pain all the days of their life;
the full number of their years are stored up for the violent.
21Dreadful sounds reach their ears.
While at peace the destroyer comes on them.
22They cannot hope to return from the darkness;
they are consigned to the sword.
23They wander about for food, saying, 'Where is it?'
They know that a day of darkness is prepared for them.
24Distress and hardship scare them;
they overpower them like a king prepared for battle.[2]

25For they stretched their hand against God;
they defied Shaddai.
26They run after him defiantly[3]
with a thick-bossed[4] shield.
27They have covered their faces with their fat;
they put blubber[5] on their loins.
28They will dwell in destroyed cities,
in houses in which no one will live,
destined to become a ruin heap.

---

the word via metathesis to postbiblical Hebrew *rmz* and Arabic *ramaza* to obtain the meaning "flash" or "wink."

2. *Kîdôr* is a hapax legomenon; its meaning is derived from an Arabic cognate. See Habel, *Job*, 247.

3. Literally "with neck"; the neck can indicate determination or stubbornness.

4. "Thick-bossed" is the translation of *ʿăbî-gabbê*, the first element being from the verb *ʿbh* ("to be thick") and the second from *gab*, which means "back" but whose fundamental meaning is "curved." In reference to a shield, it indicates the boss, which is the convex material at the center of the shield.

5. *Pîmâ* is otherwise unknown, but the parallel with *ḥeleb* suggests "fat," and Clines (*Job 1–20*, 341) provides the more colorful "blubber."

29They will not be rich nor establish their wealth;
their possessions[6] will not extend through the land.
30They will not turn aside from darkness;
the flame will dry up their shoots;
their blossom[7] will be carried off by the wind.
31They should not have confidence in vain things, deceiving
themselves,
for vanity will be their reward.
32Out of season[8] they wither.[9]
Their shoots are not green.
33They will shake off their unripe fruit like the vine,
and throw off their blossoms like the olive tree.
34For the assembly of the godless is barren,
and fire will consume the tents of those who give bribes.
35They conceive trouble and give birth to evil;
their womb prepares fraud."

Interpretation

Chapter 15 begins the second cycle of speeches. The same order is followed as in the first cycle, so Eliphaz, presumably the leader of the group, begins. As before, Job will respond to each of the three friends in turn.

Not surprisingly, since we have observed this at the beginning of the majority of speeches, Eliphaz begins by insulting Job. These insults are particularly noticeable, though, by virtue of their length and theological richness (vv. 1–10). Why, Eliphaz asks next, is Job so angry? Why is he surprised at his predicament? After all, God does not even trust his angels, so Job should know that he would not trust human beings (vv. 11–16). At this point, Eliphaz returns to his earlier argument (see, e.g., 4:6–11), a position shared by his two friends, that only the wicked suffer. His experience, as well as tradition, teaches this (vv. 17–24). The wicked, after all, have defied God, and so they will languish and ultimately perish (vv. 25–35).

1And Eliphaz the Temanite answered and said:

2"Should sages respond with windy knowledge,
filling their belly with the hot east wind?

6. *Minlām* is a hapax legomenon often associated with an Arabic cognate to achieve this translation.

7. Hebrew has "his mouth." "Blossom" involves an emendation based on the LXX *anthos*. See Clines, *Job 1–20*, 344; NRSV, REB, NEB, NJB, etc.

8. Literally "in not its day," *bĕlōʾ-yômô*.

9. With Clines (*Job 1–20,* 344) and based on the LXX, I emend *timālleʾ* to *timmāl*, but see NRSV: "It will be paid in full before their time."

3Should they reprove with a word that does not benefit,
and words that are of no use to them?
4As for you, you even invalidate fear.
You hinder meditation before God.
5Your iniquity teaches your mouth;
you choose the tongue of the crafty.
6Your own mouth declares you guilty, not me.
Your own lips testify against you.
7Are you the firstborn among mortals?
Were you brought forth before the hills?
8Did you listen in on God's secret council?
Do you limit wisdom to yourself?
9What do you know that we do not?
What do you understand that is not with us?
10The gray-haired and elderly are with us,
much older than your father!"

15:1–10. *More insults*. Eliphaz here addresses Job for the second time. Job has taken the position of a sage, a wise man (*ḥākām*), one who knows how to read a situation and apply insight in order to maximize success or, as in this case, to remedy a problem. Job's view is that, though he has made his mistakes, he is blameless (about this he is correct) and God is unjust for punishing him, because all suffering is based on sin (about this he is wrong). Eliphaz, though, assesses Job's wisdom differently from the reader, who has the advantage of the prologue and (on repeated reading) the conclusion. Eliphaz thinks Job's so-called wisdom is insubstantial like the wind. The idiom of v. 2b is strikingly similar to a modern American one: Job is filled with "hot air." He has passion but no content. Eliphaz thus begins, as do most of the speeches in the disputation, with insults, and the barrage that he lets loose in the first part of this chapter is one of the longest and most biting of all the insults of the book. Verses 2–3 are formally impersonal, speaking of sages who are ineffective, their advice having no benefit. However, neither Job nor the reader has any doubt exactly of whom Eliphaz speaks—Job himself.

If there were doubt, it would be dispelled in v. 4 with the opening *casus pendens*—"As for you." He accuses Job of invalidating or breaking "fear." The "fear" here is clearly the fear of the Lord, which is well known as the beginning of wisdom (so Job 28:28; Prov. 1:7; etc.). According to Eliphaz, Job does not even have the foundation of wisdom. The verb "invalidate" is from *prr*, which interestingly is used more than any other verb (23 times) to refer to breaking the covenant.[10] Thus Eliphaz's charge is very serious. The parallel in v. 4b furthers this thought when it complains that Job hinders "meditation"

10. T. F. Williams, *NIDOTTE* 3:696.

(*śîḥâ*), which can mean "complaint" in some contexts, but here clearly has its more positive sense connected to worshipful musing on God (Ps. 104:34) or the law (119:97, 99).

Rather than speaking wisdom like a sage, he is a fool whose mouth utters iniquity and crafty statements. Since his mouth speaks such wicked things, he condemns himself. Job does not get it, so Eliphaz feels he has to speak.

We have already seen that many of the insults in the book of Job are delivered by means of rhetorical questions (4:2; 8:2a; 11:2–3; 12:3; and later see 16:3; 18:2–3; 19:2; 20:4; 22:2–3; 26:2–3). None match the ones found in 15:5–9 for their cutting rhetorical flourish and interesting theological depth.

Are you the firstborn among mortals? (v. 7). First, the book well attests the ancient Near Eastern idea that the older one is, the wiser one is. After all, experience, observation, and learning from mistakes are all paths to wisdom, and an older person has the opportunity to learn in all these ways over a longer period of time than a young one. Perhaps Eliphaz is simply saying that Job claims to be wiser than anyone so he must be older than everyone.

However, Eliphaz's question is likely alluding to the idea that Adam was the epitome of wisdom. Of course, Genesis does not develop this idea, but Ezekiel may allude to such a belief when he says concerning the king of Tyre:

> You were the signet of perfection,
> full of wisdom and perfect in beauty.
> You were in Eden, the garden of God. (Ezek. 28:12b–13a NRSV)

Whether Eliphaz is just thinking of advanced age or specifically citing a legend about Adam in the garden, his point is clear. Job's pretensions to wisdom are unfounded and done out of pride.

Were you brought forth before the hills? The hills are old indeed, and Eliphaz questions whether Job claims to be even older than these. Once again, more is at issue than simply age. Eliphaz's language here reminds us of the words of Woman Wisdom:

> Yahweh begot me at the beginning of the paths,
> before his works of antiquity.
> From of old I was formed,
> from the beginning, from before the earth.
> When there were no deeps, I was brought forth,
> when there were no springs, heavy with water.
> Before the mountains were settled,
> before the hills, I was brought forth. (Prov. 8:22–25)[11]

11. For translation and commentary, see Longman, *Proverbs*, 195, 203–7.

Woman Wisdom, the epitome of the Wisdom of Yahweh himself, is older than the hills, but not older than Job. Again Eliphaz implies that Job exhibits tremendous arrogance in his claim to wisdom.

Did you listen in on God's secret council? (v. 8) Here Eliphaz refers to the picture of God in heaven, surrounded by his angelic servants. God is feared "in the council [*sôd*] of his holy ones." Indeed, Job 1–2 pictures God in his "secret council." Who among humans come into the council? Only true prophets. Isaiah 6 pictures that prophet in the secret council. Jeremiah 23:18 and 22 deny that council to the false prophets, who utter lies. Here Eliphaz sarcastically asks Job if he has gained wisdom by having prophetic access to the council of God.

Do you limit wisdom only to yourself? Eliphaz here emphasizes what he perceives throughout to be Job's arrogance. He will not listen to the correction of others (Prov. 3:11–12; 9:7–9; 12:1; etc.), so he must restrict wisdom only to himself.

What do you know that we do not? What do you understand that is not with us? (v. 9). In this poetic parallel, Job is charged with wrongly limiting wisdom to himself, because he is not superior to the three friends in that way. Eliphaz finishes by citing the elderly (even older than Job's father) as supporting their side in this argument.

11"Are God's consolations not enough for you,
  or the word that deals gently with you?
12Why does your heart take you away?
  Why do your eyes flash,
13so you turn your spirit against God
  and cause such words to come out of your mouth?
14What are mortals that they can be pure
  or those born of woman that they can be righteous?
15Look, he does not even trust his holy ones;
  the heavens are not pure in his eyes.
16How much less we who are abominable and corrupt,
  people who drink injustice like water."

15:11–16. *God trusts no one*. In vv. 11–13 Eliphaz attacks what he pictures as Job's feisty attitude. One might sympathize with Job if he would respond to Eliphaz's claim in v. 11 with a dumbfounded look. Job has lost his family and his wealth. He has running sores from the soles of his feet to the top of his head (2:7). God's consolations? What can Eliphaz have in mind? His theology seems to blind him, and thus he does not understand or authentically address Job's situation. How then can Eliphaz speak to Job of a word that "deals gently" with him? Since God has not yet addressed Job directly, Eliphaz must be thinking of his own words along with those of his friends. Again, a fair observer would characterize their words not as gentle but as full of insults and false charges.

Nonetheless, Eliphaz questions Job's response. He thinks Job has allowed his emotions to trump his reason (and proper theology) so that his eyes flash (in anger). Eliphaz finds this unbecoming. It is not just Job's flashing eyes, however, but his attitude of rebellion (v. 13a) and the resultant bitter speech (v. 13b).

Once again, Eliphaz repeats the argument that he made in his first speech (4:17–19) that humans are incapable of being pure or righteous. He points out that God does not even trust spiritual beings in heaven. Fallen humans are inherently corrupt. He does not state it explicitly, but the obvious conclusion is that human beings deserve whatever they get, and so by definition Job deserves what he gets. The only problem with Eliphaz's argument is that he is wrong, and we, who have read Job 1–2, know that he is wrong about Job.

17"I will show you; listen to me.
 What I have seen, I will recount to you,
18things sages have declared
 and their fathers have not hidden,
19to whom alone the land was given,
 and no stranger has passed in their midst.
20The wicked are in pain all the days of their life;
 the full number of their years are stored up for the violent.
21Dreadful sounds reach their ears.
 While at peace the destroyer comes on them.
22They cannot hope to return from the darkness;
 they are consigned to the sword.
23They wander about for food, saying, 'Where is it?'
 They know that a day of darkness is prepared for them.
24Distress and hardship scare them;
 they overpower them like a king prepared for battle."

15:17–24. *The wicked suffer.* Eliphaz furthers his argument by observations on what he has seen. This is a perfectly legitimate method or procedure for a sage. Wisdom is characterized by insightful observations of how the world works, from which observations one develops maxims for behavior. What follows is ironic in that, as just commented, Eliphaz has presently "seen" a suffering Job and has declared him guilty, when we know he is not. Thus, even before we read what follows, we have reasons to mistrust Eliphaz's interpretation of what he has seen. Our lack of confidence is confirmed as we read on, but before he speaks of what he has seen, Eliphaz again appeals to the authority of tradition (vv. 18–19). Earlier sages have pronounced their judgment in the same way. These sages are so successful that they are the ones to whom the land was given.

The meaning of v. 19b is not immediately obvious. What does it mean to say that "no stranger has passed in their midst"? In context, the best understanding seems to be that, due to their incredible insight, no person or situation remains enigmatic to them. They are able to diagnose people's situations, as Eliphaz claims to do with Job, and tell them how to act.[12]

When Eliphaz now describes what he "sees," it is more of the same: the wicked suffer (vv. 20–24). Verse 20 claims that the wicked suffer all their lives. The "full number of years" seems to be shorthand for the full number of years of affliction. They have no hope. They will be threatened by the sword and starve.

Eliphaz's viewpoint cannot be countered. Job himself claims (rightly) that he is not a sinner, and yet he is suffering. Eliphaz looks at him through his theological lens and says, in effect, "No, you are a living example of my point. Since you suffer, you must be a sinner. Since you are a sinner, your suffering makes my point."

25"For they stretched their hand against God;
  they defied Shaddai.
26They run after him defiantly
  with a thick-bossed shield.
27They have covered their faces with their fat;
  they put blubber on their loins.
28They will dwell in destroyed cities,
  in houses in which no one will live,
  destined to become a ruin heap.
29They will not be rich nor establish their wealth;
  their possessions will not extend through the land.
30They will not turn aside from darkness;
  the flame will dry up their shoots;
  their blossom will be carried off by the wind.
31They should not have confidence in vain things, deceiving
    themselves,
  for vanity will be their reward.
32Out of season they wither.
  Their shoots are not green.
33They will shake off their unripe fruit like the vine,
  and throw off their blossoms like the olive tree.
34For the assembly of the godless is barren,
  and fire will consume the tents of those who give bribes.
35They conceive trouble and give birth to evil;
  their womb prepares fraud."

15:25–35. *The wicked defy God and suffer for it.* Eliphaz continues by stating why the wicked will suffer along with a further description of the horrors they will experience. The object of this lesson is to scare Job into repentance,

12. Andersen (*Job*, 177) and others (see Smick, "Job," 772) think the idea is that the wisdom of these sages is uncontaminated by foreign influence. Considering that the setting is Edom, one wonders whether such a claim would have much effect on an Israelite audience.

because, in Eliphaz's eyes, Job is such a wicked person and suffering such a horrible punishment.

Verses 25–27 begin by describing the heart of the crime of the wicked—their defiance of God. They stretched their hands against, not toward, God. In other words, they lifted their hands in violence[13] and not in worship to God. In v. 25b the verb is from the root *gbr* in the Piel and means "to strengthen" or "to excel." In some contexts, this verb is positive (as when God strengthens his people; Zech. 10:6, 12), but for humans to strengthen themselves or attempt to excel over God is to defy him. The description of the defiance of the wicked continues as Eliphaz pictures them running toward God with a shield, as if to do battle. The next verse sounds strange to modern, Western ears, but "fat/blubber," rather than being a negative, is a positive. Only in modern societies where there is an abundance of food is it prized to be lean and thin. In the OT, to be fat is a sign of success and prosperity. Sometimes it is an indication of God's blessing (Job 36:16; Pss. 36:8; 63:5; 92:14 [15]),[14] but here and elsewhere it is a sign of the arrogance of the wicked, the fact that their success and prosperity are the result of ill-gotten gain (1 Sam. 15:22; Pss. 17:9 [10]; 73:7; Isa. 1:11; Jer. 5:28).

Verses 28–30 then return to a description of the horrible fate of those who defy God in this way. Their cities and houses will be destroyed. Though they may be rich momentarily, their riches will not last. The idea that the wealth of the wicked is temporary is a common theme in Proverbs (see 11:18; 13:11; 21:6; 22:16; as well as Ps. 73). Verse 30 takes a metaphorical turn, first describing the darkness that will permanently envelop these people and then using a botanical figure to describe their demise: their shoots will be dried up by flame, and their blossoms blown away by the wind. They may have been a fruitful plant at one point, but their end is certain and dire.

Verse 31 reckons that their fate is a matter of quid pro quo. Since they trusted in vain or meaningless things (*šāw*), they will experience vanity (*šāwĕʾ*). The word *šāw*, according to Jerry Shepherd, "seems to have two basic and interrelated senses, ineffectiveness and falseness, the latter probably being derived from the idea that hopes and expectations prove false when placed in persons or things that are ineffective and therefore untrustworthy."[15] While the word in some contexts clearly suggests a connection with false gods (Pss. 24:4; 31:6 [7]), it can indicate anything in which a person puts false hope.

The next two verses (vv. 32–33) return to a botanical image. The wicked are like plants that wither in a season when they should thrive, and their fruit and their blossoms fall off.

13. Note the use of the verb "stretch" (*nṭh*) in reference to God's acts of violence toward the wicked (Exod. 6:6; Deut. 4:34).

14. Since "fat" has a connotation today that is so different from the OT period, modern translations tend to obscure the use of a Hebrew term for "fat" in their translations of these lines.

15. *NIDOTTE* 4:53.

Eliphaz's speech concludes (vv. 34–35) with the statement that the "assembly of the godless" will be barren (another metaphor of ineffectiveness). But worse than this barrenness, their tents will burn up. The last verse is one final description of the wicked. Here they are seen as giving birth to evil deeds, a metaphor also found in Ps. 7:14 and Isa. 59:4.

Smick helpfully indicates that Eliphaz's description of the fate of the wicked in general fits the condition of Job in particular: "fire consumes (vv. 30, 34; cf. 1:16), marauders attack (v. 21; cf. 1:17), possessions are taken away (v. 29; cf. 1:17), and houses crumble (v. 28; cf. 1:19). Although the modern reader often misses the point that these barbs are all directed at Job, we can be sure that Job himself felt their sting."[16]

Theological Implications

Eliphaz in the Light of Psalm 73

In 14:1 Job commented on the human condition by saying: "Mortals born of woman, short of days, and full of trouble." Eliphaz responds, in essence, "What do you expect?" In his words, "Look, he does not even trust his holy ones; the heavens are not pure in his eyes. How much less we who are abominable and corrupt, people who drink injustice like water" (15:15–16). In other words, one should be no more surprised when a godly person lives a life of ease (as Job did earlier) than that humans suffer due to their sin. Eliphaz goes on to describe the wicked and their consequent suffering. He begins with an overall statement, "The wicked are in pain all the days of their life" (15:20), and then for the rest of the chapter gives specifics (vv. 21–35). After all, they have dared to attack God (vv. 25–26).

As earlier observed, Eliphaz is not wrong to think that people's suffering is the result of human rebellion against God (see "The Human Condition: Short of Days and Full of Trouble" after my comments on Job 12–14). He is wrong when he attributes suffering to someone's personal sin, as when he says that Job's pain is the result of the sin that he has committed. Suffering is not a certain diagnosis of sin.

It is interesting to contrast Eliphaz's perspective on this matter with that of the wise poet of Ps. 73. First, though sharing a similar retribution theology with Eliphaz, the psalmist gives a much more honest assessment of life. As he observed people, he was troubled by the fact that the wicked often seemed to prosper in life:

> For they have no pain;
> their bodies are sound and sleek.

16. Smick, "Job," 772.

> They are not in trouble as others are;
> they are not plagued like other people. (73:4–5 NRSV)

And this is true though they rebel against God: "They set their mouths against heaven, and their tongues range over the earth" (73:9 NRSV). Though Eliphaz appealed to experience to make his claim that the wicked suffered and sufferers were wicked (and that the godly were blessed, and the blessed were godly), the experience of most people would not support this idea. Indeed, it is doubtful that anyone's experience, including Eliphaz's, would support the idea that there was such a neat division of humanity into blessed godly and suffering wicked.

How could Eliphaz maintain such a perspective then? He viewed life only through his theological lenses, and he never let life question his theology. Thus he did not need evidence to know that someone was a sinner beyond the fact that they suffered (see his comments in 22:6–11).

What is the problem with viewing the world through theological lenses? After all, our experience is limited. The problem is that our theology might be false. It might be an incorrect understanding of God and how he works in the world, as the book of Job will clearly say concerning Eliphaz's perspective on this matter.

The psalmist, though, allowed life to question his theology, and the result was that it led him into a deeper and more authentic understanding of who God is and how he works in the world. Granted, at first it threw him into confusion, as he recounts at the beginning of the psalm:

> But as for me, my feet had almost stumbled;
> my steps had nearly slipped.
> For I was envious of the arrogant;
> I saw the prosperity of the wicked. (73:2–3 NRSV)

But eventually, as he brought his confusion to God ("I went into the sanctuary of God," v. 17 NRSV), he came to a deeper understanding of God's retribution for sin. He came to understand that there are not perfect and immediate consequences for sin and righteousness in the present, but in the end everyone does get what they deserve (see "Suffering: Job and Retribution Theology" in the introduction).

2.
Job's Fourth Response
(16:1–17:16)

Translation

16:1 And Job answered and said:
2"I have heard these things a lot;
you are all troublesome comforters.
3Is there an end to windy words?
Or[1] why does it provoke you so much that you must respond?
4I could speak just like you
if you were in my place.
I could join words together against you;
I could shake my head at you.[2]
5I could strengthen you with my mouth;
the comfort of my lips would assuage[3] you.
6If I so spoke, my pain would not be assuaged,
and if I stop, does it go away?

1. Verse 3b begins with a rather strange conjunction, "or" (*'ô*), as if there is a choice or alternative here rather than two questions that Job addresses to his friends. This leads the REB to suggest that these are two things that the friends are saying to Job, indicating this by inserting "You say" before the questions. However, there is no indication of this in the Hebrew.

2. A gesture of contempt; see 2 Kings 19:21; Pss. 22:7; 109:25; Isa. 37:22; Lam. 2:15.

3. The verb *ḥśk* is difficult in this line. Typically the word means "to refrain," but that would not fit the parallelism well. Thus some translations introduce an emendation that negates the verb; so REB: "and my condolences would be unrestrained." Clines (*Job 1–20*, 369–70) points to the use of the verb in the next line (v. 7a) and argues that the meaning is "soothe" or, with NRSV, "assuage."

7But now he[4] has worn me out.
He has stunned all those around me.[5]
8He has bound me up[6] as a witness against myself;
the one who lies[7] about me rises up to testify against me.
9He has preyed on me in his wrath, and he hates me.
He gnashes his teeth against me.
My foe sharpens his eyes against me.
10They[8] open their mouth wide against me;
they have struck my cheek reproachfully;
they congregate together against me.
11God has given me over to the guilty;
he has thrown[9] me into the hands of the wicked.
12I was at ease, and he shattered me.
He grabbed me by my neck and mauled me.[10]
He set me up as his target.
13His archers surround me.
He splits my kidneys open without mercy.
He pours out my gall on the earth.
14He breaches me, breach after breach.[11]
He charges me like a warrior.

15I have sewed sackcloth over my skin
and thrust my horn into the dust.
16My face is red from weeping,
and deep darkness is on my eyelids.
17There is no violence in my palm,
and my prayer is pure.

18O earth, do not cover my blood;
do not let there be a place for my cry for justice!
19Even now, see, my witness is in heaven,
and the one who testifies for me[12] is on high.

4. That is, God; see commentary.

5. Literally "my whole assembly," *kol-ʿădātî.*

6. Or possibly "shriveled me up"; see Clines, *Job 1–20*, 370. For "bound me up," see A. H. Konkel, *NIDOTTE* 3:936–37.

7. Clines (*Job 1–20*, 370), among others (see NLT: "my gaunt flesh testifies against me"), takes this word (revocalized) to mean "my gauntness/leanness," based on a verbal use in Ps. 109:24, but this seems slim evidence.

8. That is, his human adversaries; see commentary below.

9. The form appears to be *rṭh* (perhaps a by-form of *yrṭ*), which occurs only here and in Num. 22:32.

10. The verbs "shattered me" (*yĕparpĕrēnî*) and "mauled me" (*yĕpaṣpĕṣēnî*), the first a Palpal and the second a Pilpel, provide a rather interesting sound play binding this parallelism together.

11. Note the alliteration provided by the repeated use of the same root (*yiprĕṣēnî pereṣ ʿal-pĕnê-pāreṣ*).

12. "The one who testifies for me" is actually a noun with pronominal suffix (*śāhădî*), but "my testifier" is too awkward, and coming up with a better synonym for "witness" (as *ʿēd* is rendered in the first colon) is difficult.

20My friends scorn me,
and my eye drips tears[13] to God.
21He would arbitrate with God on behalf of a person,
as between a person and his friend.
22For when a number of years have come,
I will go the way from which I will not return.

17:1My spirit is broken;
my days are extinguished;
the grave is ready for me.
2Surely mockers surround me;
my eyes lodge on their obstinate behavior.

3Set now a pledge for me with yourself;
who is it who will clap hands with me?
4You have closed their minds to understanding;
therefore you will not exalt them.
5They denounce[14] their friends for a share of property,
while the eyes of their children fade.

6He has set me up as a proverb among the people.
I am someone that people spit at.
7My eye has grown dim from grief;
my whole frame[15] is like a shadow.

8The virtuous are desolate because of this;
the blameless are aroused because of the godless.
9The righteous hold on to their way,
and the clean of hand increase their strength.

10But all of you, please, come back now,
and I will not find a sage among you.
11My days are past; my plans are torn away,
the desires of my heart.
12They make night into day,
the light is near the darkness.
13If I hope for Sheol to be my house,
if I spread out my bed in darkness,
14if I call to the pit, 'You are my father,'
and to the maggot, 'My mother!' and 'My sister!'

13. This is the meaning that *dlp* clearly has in Eccles. 10:18. Some believe that *dlp* means "to be sleepless" in Ps. 119:28, but this is not certain (see NRSV, contra REB).

14. The common verb *ngd* often simply means "to speak," which in certain contexts can take on a negative cast (see also Jer. 20:10).

15. This meaning derives in part from the parallelism with "eye," but it is contested, since it is a hapax legomenon. It is perhaps related to "form," and thus in plural means "my formed parts" (so Habel, *Job*, 267).

[15]where then is my hope?
Who can see my hope?
[16]Will they go down to the bars of Sheol?
Shall we go down together to the dust?"

Interpretation

Thus in typical fashion begins Job's fourth speech in response to his friends' arguments.[16] Job begins with an insult (16:2–6), which has become pretty standard in these speeches and points to the wisdom dispute being at the heart of the book (see "The Theological Message of the Book of Job" in the introduction). The three friends came as comforters, but to Job's mind, far from offering comfort they have been troublesome with their "windy words" (16:3). Job then launches into God and accuses him of being unfair (16:7–9; see the earlier accusation at 9:22–24; 10:1–22; 13:17–28), since it is God who has attacked him (16:10–18; see also 6:1–7; 7:11–16). Such thoughts make him wish for some type of arbitrator between himself and God (16:19–22). He briefly entertained such a hope in 9:32–35 before concluding that no such "umpire" was available, but here he grows in confidence that such might be the case (and see further 19:23–27).

Job's speech continues in chap. 17, where he begins by expressing his depression. He is at death's door, and those around him are mocking him (17:1–2). He next derides his "friends" for selling him out (vv. 3–5). But then again, God has "set him up," thus deepening his depression (vv. 6–7). He proceeds to generalize from his own experience and says that though the virtuous are depressed from this type of treatment, they remain virtuous (vv. 8–9). Job has no hope in this life; his only hope is death (vv. 10–16).

---

[1]And Job answered and said:
[2]"I have heard these things a lot;
you are all troublesome comforters.
[3]Is there an end to windy words?
Or why does it provoke you so much that you must respond?

16. Indeed, Smick ("Job," 773) believes that Job here is directly disputing not only Eliphaz's immediately preceding speech but many of the earlier points of all the friends: "In these chapters we find a direct contradiction of what the counselors have said. Job's thoughts match, by means of contrast, those of Eliphaz in chapter 15; but his opening words are an answer to the opening words of all three (cf. 8:2; 11:2–3; 15:2–6). In 15:12–13, 25–26 Eliphaz accused Job of attacking God, but Job claims the reverse is true: God has assailed him (16:8–9, 12–14). Eliphaz saw all human beings as vile and corrupt in God's eyes (15:14–16). Job believes he has been upright and will be vindicated (16:15–21). Eliphaz thought the words of the wise supported him (15:17–18). Job is convinced that there is not a word of wisdom in what he had to say (17:10–12). Because God has closed their minds to understanding (17:4), they are incapable of doing anything but scold him (16:4–5; 17:2)."

[4]I could speak just like you
  if you were in my place.
I could join words together against you;
  I could shake my head at you.
[5]I could strengthen you with my mouth;
  the comfort of my lips would assuage you.
[6]If I so spoke, my pain would not be assuaged,
  and if I stop, does it go away?"

16:1–6. *Troublesome comforters.* As is typical, Job begins with a series of insulting jabs at his opponents. He tells them that they are saying nothing new to him. No doubt he has heard the teaching many times that sin leads to suffering and suffering is an indication of sin. Indeed, he believes it, which is why he believes God is unjust for letting him suffer. In other words, he believes that while the principle is true, it does not apply to him. In the words of Gustavo Gutiérrez, "It [Job's speech] is a rejection of a way of theologizing that does not take account of concrete situations, of the sufferings and hopes of human beings. At the same time, it forgets the gratuitous love and unbounded compassion of God."[17] Because they are telling him nothing new and nothing helpful, they are not providing real comfort but rather are stirring up trouble.

At the beginning of his previous speech, Eliphaz had accused Job of speaking a lot of hot air (15:2). Now Job responds in kind, bemoaning that there seems to be no end to their unhelpful advice. They are full of words but say nothing substantial to help him. Job is right to think he has not heard the end of their "windy words" considering that we are just at the start of the second of three debate cycles. In his second rhetorical question (v. 3b), he realizes that their verbosity is a result of their irritation with him. They cannot let matters stand in light of what they see as Job's stubbornness.

In vv. 4–5 Job imagines what would happen if their roles were reversed. What if they were the sufferers and he was their adviser? He points out how easy it would be for him to berate them, as they are now berating him. He could speak against them as he shook his head at them (a gesture equivalent to our wagging a finger at someone). Verse 5, though, presents another scenario. He would not demean them; he would encourage them.[18] He imagines himself a better counselor than his friends have been. Of course, it is easy to say what one would do if the situation were reversed. From what we know about Job, he may be deceiving himself, since he buys into their retribution theology.

17. G. Gutiérrez, *On Job: God-Talk and the Suffering of the Innocent*, trans. M. J. O'Connell (Maryknoll, NY: Orbis Books, 1987), 29; quoted in Boss, *Human Consciousness of God*, 92.

18. In typical poetic fashion, we do not get an explicit conjunction or phrase before v. 5 to indicate the relationship between vv. 4 and 5, but this seems to be the best understanding. Clines (*Job 1–20*, 367) is right, then, to introduce a "But no!" in front of v. 5 in order to indicate that, while Job could conceive of berating them, he would not do so.

Job ends this section by stating what he considers his no-win situation. He finds no comfort whether he speaks or stays silent. Therefore, he concludes that he might as well keep speaking.

---

7 "But now he has worn me out.
He has stunned all those around me.
8 He has bound me up as a witness against myself;
the one who lies about me rises up to testify against me.
9 He has preyed on me in his wrath, and he hates me.
He gnashes his teeth against me.
My foe sharpens his eyes against me.
10 They open their mouth wide against me;
they have struck my cheek reproachfully;
they congregate together against me.
11 God has given me over to the guilty;
he has thrown me into the hands of the wicked.
12 I was at ease, and he shattered me.
He grabbed me by my neck and mauled me.
He set me up as his target.
13 His archers surround me.
He splits my kidneys open without mercy.
He pours out my gall on the earth.
14 He breaches me, breach after breach.
He charges me like a warrior."

16:7–14. *God hates me.* Job now turns his attention to the harassment that he is receiving from someone who, in the Hebrew, is identified not by name but only by "he." While the REB identifies the culprit as "my friend," most translations either explicitly (like the NRSV) or implicitly indicate that it is none other than God himself. Such a view certainly can be substantiated from Job's other speeches, where he makes very clear that he is the object of unfair divine punishment.

Accordingly, it is God who has worn him out with his afflictions. God is the one who has stunned Job's circle of acquaintances into thinking that Job is a sinner because he suffers so much. In v. 8 we have the largest variation among translations in this section. In the above translation, God has bound, not shriveled up, Job, and this serves as a witness against him. In either case, the reference is to Job's suffering, which is being pictured either metaphorically as binding him up like a prisoner or more literally as his disease causing him to shrivel up. Either way, the fact that he is suffering is a witness against him that he is a sinner. At least that is how the three friends and those like them take it.

Colon *b* of v. 8 is difficult if one follows the MT, as I do. Who is the liar who rises up against him? Perhaps this is a reference to the friends, who look at his suffering and offer it as evidence that he is a sinner. The singular reference may be a way of treating them as a group or perhaps specifically pointing at

Eliphaz. Alternatively, it could be how Job feels about God himself. If so, this would be among Job's strongest accusations against God. In any case, it appears that v. 9 does describe God and his relentless, indeed passionate, anger against Job. He pictures God as literally champing at the bit to get at him.

But then v. 10 turns to his human adversaries, who also are determined to bring him down. Job is being attacked, or so he thinks, from above and below. They speak against him; they physically abuse him. They congregate against him in a way that suggests mob violence. But even in his human adversaries, Job sees the hand of God. These people are after him because God has turned him over to them (v. 11). The way Job sees it, he is innocent and his attackers are wicked.

The final verses in this passage (vv. 12–14) return to a direct description of God's attack against Job. Job was at ease (see the description in 1:1–5), and out of nowhere God came and shattered him. He describes God as taking him by the scruff of the neck and mauling him. The parallelism seems to pair v. 12c with v. 13a, where he turns to the metaphor of God as an archer using Job as target practice (see a similar idea, though using a different word, in 7:20). The picture is almost that of a firing squad (using an anachronism). In a sense, God has set up Job as a target by giving the accuser permission to attack him. The arrows find their mark, and he pours out his lifeblood as a result. Verse 14 changes the metaphor again when Job is likened to a city that has been successfully besieged and breached. Once the wall comes down, the warriors (in this case, the warrior God) runs in for the kill.

---

15 "I have sewed sackcloth over my skin
 and thrust my horn into the dust.
16 My face is red from weeping,
 and deep darkness is on my eyelids.
17 There is no violence in my palm,
 and my prayer is pure."

16:15–17. *Job's grief and pain.* Job's reaction to God's harsh treatment is expected—he mourns. He does more than don sackcloth, indicative of grief; he also sews it over his skin. Mourning has become part and parcel of who he is. In other contexts of grief, the mourners not only put on sackcloth but also throw dust on their heads (Lam. 2:10; Ezek. 27:30–31). Job's suffering is so profound that he takes his head (horn) and sticks it in the dust. The use of "horn" for head evokes an animal image. A proud, confident animal lifts its horns high. Job's movement downward is the exact physical and emotional opposite.

His grief and pain also lead to incessant weeping, which turns his face red and his eyelids black (perhaps referring to the dark circles that appear with lack of sleep and worry). He finally protests that there is no violence on his part and his prayer is pure. Outwardly and inwardly he does nothing to deserve his fate.

> **18**"O earth, do not cover my blood;
> do not let there be a place for my cry for justice!
> **19**Even now, see, my witness is in heaven,
> and the one who testifies for me is on high.
> **20**My friends scorn me,
> and my eye drips tears to God.
> **21**He would arbitrate with God on behalf of a person,
> as between a person and his friend.
> **22**For when a number of years have come,
> I will go the way from which I will not return."

16:18–22. *My witness is in heaven.* Job now makes an appeal that his suffering and cry for justice not be squelched but rather be heard and acted on. Job calls on the earth to help by not covering up his blood. The language reminds the reader of Gen. 4:10, when God confronts Cain concerning his murder of Abel by telling him that the blood of his brother was crying out from the soil. In the next colon (v. 18b), Job asks that there be no place, presumably of rest, for his cry for justice, but that it may course about until it is satisfied.

Verses 19–22 are difficult to translate with absolute certainty and even harder to understand in terms of meaning and emotion. This passage has played an important role in the history of interpretation—along with 9:33; 19:23–27; and 33:23–27—as an early anticipation of the Messiah. After all, they speak of someone in heaven who is able to mediate between humans and God. Today, however, very few scholars would advocate a connection between these passages and the Messiah,[19] except perhaps to say that they articulate a desire that was fulfilled in Jesus Christ (see "The Book of Job in the Light of Christ" in the introduction). As we shall see, it is extremely problematic to think that Job, or the author of Job, was thinking in messianic terms.

Job begins by expressing his confidence that there is a witness for him in heaven. Thus he returns to the courtroom analogy. This witness would "arbitrate" with God on his behalf.[20] This reminds us of 9:33, where Job wished that there were such an "umpire" (*môkîaḥ*; from the same root as "arbitrate," *ykḥ*) but realized that there was no such person.

Who then is the arbitrating witness here that would prove such a benefit to Job? Some believe the witness is God himself,[21] but this seems extremely awkward in light of v. 21, where the witness would have to speak against God in support

19. A rare exception may be found in Kaiser, *Messiah in the Old Testament*, 61–64.

20. With Fyall (*Now My Eyes*, 42), it is interesting to note the contrast between v. 8, where Job's emaciated body witnesses against him, and now here, where the witness defends him.

21. Wilson, *Job*, 208–9.

of Job. Clines, based on Dhorme,[22] argues that the witness that arbitrates is the "cry for justice" of v. 18. But that idea suffers from the same weakness as the hypothesis that it is God. How could Job's cry for justice arbitrate between the two parties? It stands to reason that an arbitrator could be neither Job nor God.

To think of a third party in heaven is what leads to messianic interpretations of the text. Who else could the mediator be but Jesus? As stated above, though, it is doubtful that Job or the author of Job had Jesus in mind in these words. We must remember that in 9:33 Job raised the wish for a mediator in a wistful way because he realized that there was no such mediator. So again, Job speaks of a help in heaven that he wishes for but, in his mind at least, does not exist. This interpretation seems confirmed by the fact that in the story of Job no umpire, no witness, ever steps forward to help him. (For more on this passage, as well as 9:33; 19:25–29; and 33:23–27, see "The Book of Job in the Light of Christ" in the introduction.)

Another indication that Job is not as confident as he first sounds is the way this chapter ends. Job concludes by reminding his hearers that there will be only a few years before he dies and is no more.

1"My spirit is broken;
my days are extinguished;
the grave is ready for me.
2Surely mockers surround me;
my eyes lodge on their obstinate behavior."

17:1–2. *Loss of hope.* Job turns back to self-pity. Considering his sufferings, one can hardly blame him. He is depressed and discouraged ("my spirit is broken"). He believes he is on his deathbed ("my days are extinguished; the grave is ready for me"). In the meantime, before he is completely gone, he is tortured by "mockers" who constantly badger him. Mockers are the worst sinners because not only are they wicked, but they also turn around and torture the righteous with their words. Perhaps he is thinking more broadly, but these mockers would certainly include Eliphaz, Bildad, and Zophar. He cannot ignore them ("my eyes lodge on their obstinate behavior"), as much as he would have liked to.

3"Set now a pledge for me with yourself;
who is it who will clap hands with me?
4You have closed their minds to understanding;
therefore you will not exalt them.
5They denounce their friends for a share of property,
while the eyes of their children fade."

---

22. Clines, *Job 1–20*, 389–93.

17:3–5. *Bad friends.* Admittedly, Job's logic in this section is hard to follow. It seems clear that he now directly addresses God ("you"). In v. 3 he appears to turn to God for help in the face of friends who have turned against him, but then v. 4a puts the ultimate blame for the friends' opinion on God.

Job begins by asking God to enter into a pledge with him, but it is not obvious what that pledge concerns. In general, we can take it as Job's hope that God would come to his side. Perhaps he believes that God will take a pledge and will offer testimony that Job is right when he claims he is not suffering because of his sin, or simply that Job is "blameless" and "innocent." Verse 3b then would simply express his realization that no one else would enter into such an agreement with him.[23]

But v. 4a blames God for the friends' unwillingness to support him since he closed their minds, reminding readers of the time when God hardened the heart of Pharaoh (Exod. 7:3).[24] The next colon (v. 4b) is also difficult to understand in context. God has closed their minds, so he will not exalt them, that is, let them triumph. Perhaps again the analogy should be drawn to Pharaoh. God closed Pharaoh's mind to the possibility of letting Israel go so that deliverance might dramatically display God's power over Egypt. In the same way, perhaps Job believes, at least for a moment, that God has closed the mocking friends' minds so that they too will be defeated and bring glory to the situation.

The section ends with what seems to be a proverb about friends who sell out friends. They denounce their friends for a reward (here perhaps specifically a share of property, *ḥēleq*), but the result will be the suffering of their family ("while the eyes of his children fade").

6"He has set me up as a proverb among the people.
I am someone that people spit at.
7My eye has grown dim from grief;
my whole frame is like a shadow."

17:6–7. *A living proverb.* Job, previously honored by his peers, has become a proverb to them. A proverb is a brief, catchy truism that has become a popular saying. To his friends, Job has become a living proverb, an illustration (a poster boy, so to speak) that sin leads to suffering. In this case, Job is a negative example; the hope is to dissuade others from following his example. In other words, he is a byword (see other similar uses of *māšāl* in 1 Kings 9:7; 2 Chron. 7:20; Ps. 44:14; Jer. 24:9; Ezek. 14:8; Joel 2:17). As a result, he is disdained. People's contempt is expressed by their spit.

No wonder Job is despondent. He is filled with grief and physically fades away, like a shadow (v. 7).

23. The gesture of "clapping hands" is similar to shaking hands after an agreement is reached (see Prov. 6:1; 17:18).

24. See comments by Wilson, *Job*, 186.

[8]"The virtuous are desolate because of this;
the blameless are aroused because of the godless.
[9]The righteous hold on to their way,
and the clean of hand increase their strength."

17:8–9. *Desolate, yet still determined.* Job now describes how those who are on the side of righteousness and against wickedness react to his sorry state and the lack of human or divine comfort. He uses terms (virtuous, *yāšār*; blameless, *nāqî*; righteous, *ṣāddîq*) that he would rightly apply to himself, but this is the first time he refers to a community of such people. Perhaps he is simply describing his own reaction; certainly there is no other righteous person present and speaking at the moment. In any case, they are depressed and angry, but still they maintain the course ("hold on to their way") and maintain their integrity and thus grow stronger. Again, one would think that this would apply to Job. It can be said that he is holding on to his way in the midst of his suffering (he has not cursed God and died), but it is hard to see how he has grown stronger. Perhaps Wilson is right to suggest that Job might be referring "to his own determination to remain undeterred by the ridicule of his opponents from pursuing his quest for vindication."[25]

[10]"But all of you, please, come back now,
and I will not find a sage among you.
[11]My days are past; my plans are torn away,
the desires of my heart.
[12]They make night into day,
the light is near the darkness.
[13]If I hope for Sheol to be my house,
if I spread out my bed in darkness,
[14]if I call to the pit, 'You are my father,'
and to the maggot, 'My mother!' and 'My sister!'
[15]where then is my hope?
Who can see my hope?
[16]Will they go down to the bars of Sheol?
Shall we go down together to the dust?"

17:10–16. *Death wish.* In v. 10 Job clearly addresses the three friends and taunts them to come back and do their best against him. He knows, however, the outcome based on their past performance. He will not find a bona fide sage among them. None of them will be able to diagnose or provide a remedy for his condition. They are supposed to be doctors of the soul, but they

25. Wilson (*Job*, 189), though he prefers the interpretation (along with Clines) that Job is here speaking sarcastically of the friends as the upright and innocent who are appalled at Job and aroused against Job, the godless one.

continue to fail miserably. Because of their failure, Job feels defeated. He has no "plans" for the future because he sees no way out of his predicament. He lacks desire because he has no hope.

Verse 12 goes back to describe his opponents. They turn night and darkness into day and light. They should see Job's condition and bemoan it as unfair ("darkness"), but they see it as God's justice ("light"). They also believe that Job's condition is easily fixed: all he has to do is repent. Indeed, in 11:17 Zophar told him that repentance would turn his darkness to light. Thus to them light is near at hand to Job's darkness, but Job knows better.

The best interpretation of vv. 13–14 is as an acknowledgment of what is essentially a death wish. The "pit" is the grave, and maggots (and elsewhere, worms) are associated with the grave and death and putrefaction. If his hope is for death, then where is his hope? It is in the grave. Death is not something distant and impersonal; it is the place where he can find refuge ("my house") and rest ("my bed"). He wants it close to him like he would want his closest and dearest relatives (father [pit], mother, sister [maggots]). But no one can see his hope unless they take the journey to Sheol with him.[26]

Theological Implications

"God Hates Me" (16:9): A Reflection on the Emotions of God

In his pain and suffering, Job believes that God hates him. How else can he explain his situation? After all, he, like the three friends, believes that only sinners suffer, but since he is innocent, he knows that he is not suffering because of his sin. He also believes that God is in control of his life, so his suffering must be God's doing. Therefore, God hates him. That is the only reason why he has become the object of God's punishment.

The wilderness generation also believed that God hated them. They thought God rescued them from Egypt and brought them out into the wilderness not because he loved them but because he hated them (Deut. 1:27).

Job and the wilderness generation are not alone in this type of thinking. When bad things happen to Christians, a common reaction is to ask, "What did I do to deserve this?" When we cannot think of anything that we have done, we begin to think that God does not love us. He must hate us.

But this raises an interesting and important question. Does God hate anybody? Many will respond negatively. God does not hate anyone. After all, "For God loved the world so much that he gave his one and only Son, so that everyone who believes in him will not perish but have eternal life" (John 3:16 NLT). Is it true, then, that God loves everyone and conversely hates no one?

26. Alternatively, Job may be saying that hope is making the trip down to the grave with him.

If so, then Job's belief (and also ours in our darkest moments) that God hates him would obviously be wrong.

However, such a conclusion is undermined by a number of other passages that do speak of God as hating sinners:

> The boastful will not stand before your eyes;
> you hate all evildoers. (Ps. 5:5 NRSV)
>
> The Lord tests the righteous and the wicked,
> and his soul hates the lover of violence. (Ps. 11:5 NRSV)
>
> You love righteousness and hate wickedness. (Ps. 45:7 NRSV)
>
> There are six things that the Lord hates,
> seven that are an abomination to him:
> haughty eyes, a lying tongue,
> and hands that shed innocent blood,
> a heart that devises wicked plans,
> feet that hurry to run to evil,
> a lying witness who testifies falsely,
> and one who sows discord in a family. (Prov. 6:16–19 NRSV)
>
> Yet I have loved Jacob but I have hated Esau. (Mal. 1:2b–3a NRSV; quoted in Rom. 9:13)

These biblical passages indicate that God hates wicked people. The old slogan that God hates sin but not the sinner is not borne out by the biblical text. No, he hates sinners, and he wants his people to hate sinners too. The psalmist seeks to please God when he tells him:

> Do I not hate those who hate you, O Lord?
> And do not I loathe those who rise up against you?
> I hate them with perfect hatred;
> I count them my enemies. (139:21–22 NRSV)

Some will reply that to speak of God's "hate" is simply an anthropopathism, a metaphor. God does not really hate anyone. To this I respond with two observations. First, if we say this about God's hate, then we must also say this about his "love." It too is an anthropopathism, a metaphor, but we would be reluctant to say that God does not really love anyone. Second, yes, the language of God's love and hatred is metaphorical, but metaphors point to something true and real. Although they point beyond themselves, they also communicate truly, so that it is right to say that God loves and God hates.

So, in principle, Job is not wrong to entertain the possibility that God hates him. God hates sinners. But Job knows he is not a sinner. It is on that basis that Job should know that God does not hate him.

Of course, according to the NT, we are all sinners. Therefore, we all deserve God's hatred and wrath. However, those who turn to Jesus are no longer judged as the sinners they are. Their sins have been forgiven, and the righteousness of Christ stands in our place. Therefore, we are no longer the objects of God's wrath but of his mercy (Rom. 9:22–23).

3.
Bildad's Second Speech
(18:1–21)

Translation

1And Bildad the Shuhite answered and said:
2"How long before you set[1] an end to words?
Reflect, and then we will speak.
3Why are we counted like cattle?
Why are we considered stupid[2] in your estimation?
4You rend your life in your anger.
Will the earth be abandoned because of you?
Will the rock be moved from its place?

5Surely the light of the wicked is extinguished,
and the flame of their fire does not shine.
6The light is dark in their tent;
their lamp over them is extinguished.
7Their vigorous gait is cramped;
their own advice throws them down.
8For their feet are cast into a net;
they walk into a snare.
9A trap grabs them by the heel;
a noose seizes them.
10A rope is hidden for them on the earth,
a trap for them on the path.

1. While the verb indicates second-person plural, the context clearly indicates that he is speaking only to Job here.

2. The translation is based on an Aramaic cognate (see Pope, *Job*, 124; Clines, *Job 1–20*, 404), though it could be a by-form of *ṭm'*, "to be unclean."

[11]Terrors from all around frighten them,
and they disperse them[3] at their feet.
[12]Their vigor becomes famine,
and calamity is readied for their stumbling.
[13]It consumes their fleshy limbs;
the firstborn of Death consumes their limbs.
[14]They are torn from the confidence of their tent;
terrors march them to the king.[4]
[15]Nothing of theirs[5] will live in their tent,
sulfur is scattered on their pasturage.
[16]Underneath, their roots dry up;
above, their boughs wither.
[17]Memory of them perishes from the earth;
they have no public reputation.[6]
[18]They are thrust out from the light to darkness;
they are driven from the habitable world.
[19]They will have no near or distant offspring[7] among their people.
There will be no survivor in their place of residence.
[20]In the west,[8] they are desolated by their end.[9]
In the east,[10] they are seized by horror.
[21]Such is the dwelling of the guilty;
such is a place that does not know God."

Interpretation

Bildad begins his second speech in typical fashion, with insults directed toward Job's thinking, followed by a self-defense of his (and his friends') wisdom (vv. 2–4). The largest part of this chapter is yet another statement

3. It is a problem that the pronominal suffix is singular, since it is hard to disperse a single item. However, it is better to take this as a case of lack of number concord (with "terrors") than to propose a different meaning for the verb or suggest an emendation.

4. Or "marches them off to the king of terrors" (see NRSV, NAB, NJB).

5. *Mibbĕlî-lô* can be translated "nothing of his" and makes sense in the context, though it seems strange that the verb is a feminine third-person singular. NJB takes the verb as second person and the *mibbĕlî-lô* as a dependent clause ("You can live in the tent, since it is no longer his"), but Clines (*Job 1–20*, 407) is right to ask who would want the tent and its property in light of the description that follows (though perhaps this is asking for too much logical consistency in a passage that heaps descriptions of calamities one on top of another). Clines himself (and others, including NIV, NAB, REB) follows Dahood, who detects a rare word for "fire," and translates: "Fire lodges in his tent."

6. Literally "no name in the street."

7. "Near offspring" (*nîn*) and "distant offspring" (*neked*) are typically used as a word pair (see also Gen. 21:23; Isa. 14:22).

8. Or "those who come after" (see NAB).

9. Literally "day."

10. Or "those who come before" (see NAB).

proclaiming the certainty and depth of suffering that the wicked experience (vv. 5–21). He reiterates the basic argument of the three friends that connects suffering with sin (see also 4:7–11; 5:2–7; 8:3–4, 11–21; 11:11; 15:20–35). More of the same is yet to come from the three friends (20:5–29). In sum, Eliphaz here continues the consistent barrage of argument that sin leads to suffering, with the corollary idea that suffering is indicative of sin. The implicit point is that Job is suffering and therefore is a sinner.

1And Bildad the Shuhite answered and said:
2"How long before you set an end to words?
  Reflect, and then we will speak.
3Why are we counted like cattle?
  Why are we considered stupid in your estimation?
4You rend your life in your anger.
  Will the earth be abandoned because of you?
  Will the rock be moved from its place?"

18:1–4. *Why don't you shut up, Job?* Bildad accuses Job of speaking too much. Not only that, but he speaks before he reflects on what he is saying. The book of Proverbs advocates thinking before speaking and berates those who just blurt out what they think. The following three proverbs illustrate this idea:

> The heart of the righteous meditates before answering,
>   but the mouth of the wicked blurts out evil. (15:28)
>
> Those who respond before they listen
>   are stupid and a disgrace. (18:13)
>
> Do you see people who are hasty with their words?
>   There is more hope for a fool than for them. (29:20)

In the light of such proverbs, Bildad would find an easy excuse for ignoring Job's arguments. However, the question is whether he has applied them correctly. One imagines that Job has given thought to his predicament. After all, he had remained silent for a period of seven days (3:1) before he began to speak. Of course, this does not automatically indicate that he is correct, but it does mean that Eliphaz should not feel that he can easily dismiss Job.

On the other hand, that is precisely what he feels that Job is doing with their arguments. He is dismissing them, treating them as if they have the intelligence of a brute beast. He questions why Job treats them this way. Indeed, one does often get the feeling that there is little substantial interaction between the two parties in this debate. They are each dismissing the arguments of the other.

Bildad then expresses some concern for Job's welfare. He believes that Job's anger will kill him, and he uses the image of a wild beast rending its prey (the verb is *ṭrp*). He can see how Job's attitude is "tearing him up," as we would say today. He seems to believe that Job is blowing things out of perspective. He asks him rhetorically whether the earth will be abandoned because of him or the rock be moved. The latter uses language very similar to 14:18, where Job himself pictured the erosion of human hope as the result of water grinding down a rock. This rock (*ṣûr*) is not a small stone but a cliff. Job's vociferous anger will not have a major effect. The earth will not be abandoned, and the rock will not be moved.

5"Surely the light of the wicked is extinguished,
  and the flame of their fire does not shine.
6The light is dark in their tent;
  their lamp over them is extinguished.
7Their vigorous gait is cramped;
  their own advice throws them down.
8For their feet are cast into a net;
  they walk into a snare.
9A trap grabs them by the heel;
  a noose seizes them.
10A rope is hidden for them on the earth,
  a trap for them on the path.
11Terrors from all around frighten them,
  and they disperse them at their feet.
12Their vigor becomes famine,
  and calamity is readied for their stumbling.
13It consumes their fleshy limbs;
  the firstborn of Death consumes their limbs.
14They are torn from the confidence of their tent;
  terrors march them to the king.
15Nothing of theirs will live in their tent,
  sulfur is scattered on their pasturage.
16Underneath, their roots dry up;
  above, their boughs wither.
17Memory of them perishes from the earth;
  they have no public reputation.
18They are thrust out from the light to darkness;
  they are driven from the habitable world.
19They will have no near or distant offspring among their people.
  There will be no survivor in their place of residence.
20In the west, they are desolated by their end.
  In the east, they are seized by horror.
21Such is the dwelling of the guilty;
  such is a place that does not know God."

18:5–21. *The bad end of the wicked.* The bulk of Bildad's response is a lengthy description of the fate of the wicked. In a word, the wicked meet a bad end. He begins by using the metaphor of the light (vv. 5–6), which here symbolizes life and health and prosperity, over against darkness, which represents the opposite: death, sickness, and failure. The life of wicked people may at one point have light, but eventually that light goes out (v. 5). Their household ("their tent") may have been illuminated earlier or may even be illuminated at present, but it will not stay that way (v. 6). Whybray rightly points out that "the extinguishing of the light of the wicked is a standard one in the book of Proverbs (e.g., 13.9; 20.20; 24.20)."[11]

Verse 7 assumes that at one point the gait of the wicked was vigorous, but after time it is restricted (cramped) so that they cannot walk well. This may have to do with more than their physical condition. Wisdom's main metaphor for life is the path.[12] The wise walk on the straight, well-lit, smooth path that leads to life, while the wicked walk on the twisty path that is dark and filled with all kinds of calamities, including those listed in vv. 9–11, which may well explicate why the gait of the wicked is cramped. However, before looking more closely at those verses, we should note that v. 7b attributes their failure to their own advice. They hurt themselves, in other words. Their own advice leads to all kinds of threats as they walk the path of life. The metaphors of the net (*rešet*, v. 8a) and the trap (*paḥ*, v. 9a) occur in the book of Proverbs:

> People who pour out flattery on their friends
> are spreading out a net [*rešet*] for their feet. (29:5)
>
> Thorns and nets [or traps, *paḥîm*] are in the path of the crooked person;
> those who guard their lives stay far away from them. (22:5)

The other words (noose, *ṣammîm* [v. 9b]; rope, *ḥebel* [v. 10a]; trap, *malkōdet* [v. 10b]; terrors, *ballāhôt* [v. 11a]) do not occur in Proverbs, but they are variants of the same idea: obstacles that threaten life to which the wicked fall prey. All of these things are dispersed at their feet, making them stumble in life.

Verse 12 uses the same word (*ʾôn*) found in v. 7, though the grammar seems awkward, as my rather literal translation indicates. What would it mean that "vigor becomes famine"? Most likely is the sense given to it by the NRSV: "Their strength is consumed by hunger." One can sense uneasiness on the part of the translators, though, from the footnote suggesting as an alternative "Disaster is hungry for them," probably taking *ʾôn* as *ʾāwen*.[13] Thus we have to say that the exact sense of the colon is uncertain, though it certainly describes negative consequences for the wicked. The parallel colon leads with "calamity," which is said to be ready and waiting for the moment the wicked

11. Whybray, *Job*, 96.
12. See discussion in Longman, *Proverbs*, 59–60.
13. See Clines, *Job 1–20*, 405.

stumble. Perhaps the wicked are moving ahead full steam at the moment, but the time of their stumbling will come in the future, and at that time disaster is primed and ready for them.

According to vv. 13–14, when they do stumble, the most horrible fate awaits them. While they may be "fat and happy" now (indicated by their "fleshy limbs"), when they stumble, death will consume them. Death is personified in v. 13b,[14] and the wicked people's demise is assigned to Death's firstborn, perhaps indicating special attention from Death, or perhaps the beginning of the process of death. Their fate will remove them from the stability of their homes (they will be "torn from the confidence of their tent") and their terrors (perhaps resulting from the calamity) will escort them to "the king," perhaps another reference to Death.

Their homes will be desolate and the surrounding pasturage rendered poisonous and unusable by sulfur (v. 15). When they die, they will leave nothing, neither possessions nor legacy. The wicked themselves are likened to a tree with dry roots and withered boughs (v. 16). In 14:1–2 Job said that all people ("mortals born of woman") are like a flower that withers, but Eliphaz applies the related metaphor only to the wicked. Worse still, the wicked are not just going to die, but memory of them will fade. No one will remember them. Indeed, no descendants or even associates will survive them who might remember them (v. 19). Verse 20, however, suggests that a type of remembrance will persist, but not the type that anyone would ever desire. Everywhere (west and east) will be horrified by their fate. But, as Bildad concludes in v. 21, that is exactly what one expects from the guilty, from those who do not know God.

Theological Implications

A Bad End for the Wicked

Bildad's speech is yet another reiteration of the basic argument of the three friends that connects bad behavior with negative consequences (see "Retribution Theology in a Nutshell" following the comments on Job 8).

In this speech, Bildad puts a special emphasis on the bad end that awaits the wicked. The book of Job shows no awareness of an afterlife, so when Bildad argues that evil people end badly, he is speaking of this life.

Bildad's speech implies that the life of wicked people can seem good on the surface. However, there are all kinds of dangers that lurk below the surface and will ultimately catch up with them. Right now their life may be well lit (vv. 5–6), but that light will ultimately be extinguished. In the present they may have strength, but ultimately they will become cramped and weakened

14. While it is possible that the personification of Death evokes the Canaanite deity Mot ("Death"), it does not clearly do so here.

(vv. 7, 13). Their life journey may seem unencumbered now, but there are traps, nooses, and ropes ready to grab them away. Furthermore, no one will remember them. There are no offspring to preserve their memory.

All in all, Bildad draws a very depressing picture of the fate of the wicked. He implicitly applies this to Job, who does not deserve characterization as a wicked person, but it is also interesting to ask whether what Bildad is saying is true. Do the wicked end badly in this life even though they seem to prosper in the present?

Some isolated proverbs make it sound as if Bildad is right. We can imagine him quoting the following, for example:

> Wealth from get-rich-quick schemes quickly disappears;
> wealth from hard work grows over time. (Prov. 13:11 NLT)
>
> Wealth created by a lying tongue
> is a vanishing mist and a deadly trap. (Prov. 21:6 NLT)
>
> Evil people get rich for the moment,
> but the reward of the godly will last. (Prov. 11:18 NLT)

These proverbs recognize that sometimes the wicked are wealthy, but they are pointing out that they will not end their lives rich.

Qohelet, however, begs to differ. He observes that sometimes evil people are healthy, wealthy, and happy up to the point of death. Even in death, they are honored. Qohelet, expecting otherwise, considers this unjust: "Thus, I observed the wicked buried and departed. They used to go out of the holy place, and they were praised in the city where they acted in such a way. This too is meaningless" (Eccles. 8:10). One can sympathize with Qohelet. It does seem unfair that the wicked can flourish in this life up to the very end. Where is the justice in this?

The NT clarifies what is only hinted at in certain OT passages (see Dan. 12:1–3): death is not the end of the story. Justice does not always come in this life, though occasionally it can.[15] But it does come in the afterlife. The parable of the rich man and Lazarus exemplifies the pervasive teaching of the NT on this matter. The rich man, who had all the material enjoyment of this life, suffers in the one to come, while the righteous Lazarus, who suffered in this life, lives in heaven at the side of Abraham (Luke 16:19–31).

15. The proverbs cited above were never meant to be taken as guarantees or promises. Rather, they are warnings of real potential consequences from certain types of actions, all other things being equal.

4.
Job's Fifth Response
(19:1–29)

Translation

1And Job answered and said:
2"How long will you torment me
  and crush me with words?
3You disgraced me ten times over.
  Are you not embarrassed to have wronged[1] me?

4If I have truly made a mistake,
  my mistake lodges in me.
5If you truly make yourself powerful against me
  and make my reproach reproof against me,
6then know that God perverted me.
  His hunting net surrounds me.
7If I cry out 'Violence!' I get no answer.
  I yell out, but get no justice.
8He has walled up my path, so I cannot pass by.
  He has set darkness on my ways.
9He has stripped off my glory
  and taken the crown off my head.
10He tears me down on every side.
  He uproots my hope like a tree.

1. *Hkr* is unattested elsewhere, and meanings based on an Arabic cognate ("made to wonder") do not fit the context, so some commentators (see Clines, *Job 1–20*, 428) suggest following three Hebrew MSS that take the root from *ḥkr* and connect it to an Arabic cognate, which achieves the meaning given in my translation.

11He kindles his anger against me,
and considers me his foe.
12His troops come together;
they build up their road[2] against me.
They encamp all around my tent.
13My brothers he has removed far from me;
my friends he has alienated from me.
14Those near me and my acquaintances have failed me;
my houseguests have forgotten me.[3]

15My serving girls treat me like a stranger;
I am a foreigner in their eyes.
16I call to my servants, and they do not respond,
though I personally[4] ask them for a favor.
17My breath is abhorrent to my wife;
I am repulsive to my family.[5]
18Even young children reject me;
I get up, and they speak against me.
19All my intimate friends detest me,
and those I love have turned against me.
20My bones cling to my skin and my flesh.
I have escaped by the skin of my teeth.
21Pity me, pity me, you are my friends!
The hand of God has touched me!
22Why do you pursue me, like God?
Are you not satisfied with my flesh?

23Oh, that my words were written down.
Oh, that they were inscribed in a scroll.
24Oh, that with an iron pen and with lead
they were etched on rock as a witness.
25I know that my redeemer lives,
and he at last will rise up on the dust.[6]
26After my skin is peeled off,
then out of[7] my flesh I will see God.
27I will see him for myself;
my eyes will look and not a stranger's.

2. A number of translations (see NRSV) conjecture an emendation of "road" to "siege works" here based on context. But to "build a road" may suggest "siege works."

3. A sentiment similar to that found in Ps. 88:18.

4. Literally "with my mouth," *bĕmô-pî*.

5. Literally "the sons of my stomach." *Beṭen* is often used of a woman's womb, and thus in reference to children, but can also be used of the male reproductive organs (Ps. 132:11; Mic. 6:7; see C. L. Rogers Jr., *NIDOTTE* 1:650–52).

6. Or "earth" (NRSV).

7. Or "in" (NRSV) or "from" (NJB).

My heart[8] fades within me.
28When you say, 'How should we pursue him?'
and, 'The root of the matter is found in him,'
29be careful of the sword,
for wrath brings the punishment of the sword,
so you may know there is judgment."

Interpretation

Job makes his fifth response to the friends, the second to Bildad. He begins with angry complaints about Bildad's treatment of him. He asks, essentially, how Bildad can live with himself by badgering Job in this way and adding to his suffering (vv. 2–3). The bulk of the chapter, though, consists of a long charge against God (vv. 4–22). God is the reason for his suffering. He tells Bildad that if indeed he has made a mistake, it is because of the horrible treatment that he has received from God himself. At the conclusion of this speech, Job utters some of the most famous words of the entire book because, according to traditional interpretation, he expresses incredible hope in a heavenly redeemer (vv. 23–29). There is, however, immense controversy concerning the translation and interpretation of these verses.

1And Job answered and said:
2"How long will you torment me
and crush me with words?
3You disgraced me ten times over.
Are you not embarrassed to have wronged me?"

19:1–3. *How long will you torment me?* Many of the speeches so far have begun with an accusatory question (4:2; 8:2–3; 9:2; 11:2–3; 12:3; 15:2–3; 16:3; 18:2), and this will not be the last time (22:2–5). In v. 2 Job charges Bildad (and likely the others) of increasing his suffering with their words. It is one thing to feel physical pain, but the emotional pain inflicted by the friends brings his suffering to an unbearably high level. He feels emotionally crushed by what they say.

In the modern West, shameful behavior is sometimes rewarded with notoriety, and individuals may welcome their shame because of the fame and wealth it brings. The ancient Near East was far different. To be shamed was a horrible experience, and Job feels the bite of the disgrace that the friends have brought on him. To say that they have disgraced him "ten times over" is "to be taken as an unspecified but excessive number of times (compare Gen. 31.41)."[9] On the other hand, he marvels that they have not felt embarrassed

8. Literally "kidneys," but in reference to the emotions, English "heart" carries the sense better.

9. Whybray, *Job*, 98.

themselves at the treatment that they have been giving him. They charge him with unsubstantiated crimes, presumed only because he is suffering, and yet they feel no embarrassment in doing so.

4"If I have truly made a mistake,
my mistake lodges in me.
5If you truly make yourself powerful against me
and make my reproach reproof against me,
6then know that God perverted me.
His hunting net surrounds me.
7If I cry out 'Violence!' I get no answer.
I yell out, but get no justice.
8He has walled up my path, so I cannot pass by.
He has set darkness on my ways.
9He has stripped off my glory
and taken the crown off my head.
10He tears me down on every side.
He uproots my hope like a tree.
11He kindles his anger against me,
and considers me his foe.
12His troops come together;
they build up their road against me.
They encamp all around my tent.
13My brothers he has removed far from me;
my friends he has alienated from me.
14Those near me and my acquaintances have failed me;
my houseguests have forgotten me.

15My serving girls treat me like a stranger;
I am a foreigner in their eyes.
16I call to my servants, and they do not respond.
though I personally ask them for a favor.
17My breath is abhorrent to my wife;
I am repulsive to my family.
18Even young children reject me;
I get up, and they speak against me.
19All my intimate friends detest me,
and those I love have turned against me.
20My bones cling to my skin and my flesh.
I have escaped by the skin of my teeth.
21Pity me, pity me, you are my friends!
The hand of God has touched me!
22Why do you pursue me, like God?
Are you not satisfied with my flesh?"

19:4–22. *God hates me, and others reject me.* Job then argues in v. 4 that even if he did do something wrong ("made a mistake"), then it is his problem, with the implication that it is not their problem. That is, even if he did err, he is suffering for it, and they do not need to help the process along. He is not conceding that he has made a mistake;[10] he is just saying that even if he has done so, they are not justified in their response. The root for the verb "make a mistake" and the noun "mistake" is *šgh*, which could be understood in more than one way. It can refer to a wrong committed unintentionally (1 Sam. 26:21). On the other hand, it can refer to a moral wandering of a more serious nature (Prov. 19:27; 28:10). Either meaning would work, but Job does appear to choose a softer word than he could have used in this context, such as "sin" (*ḥaṭṭāʾāt*).

However, Job insists, if Bildad and his friends demand to make a federal case (v. 5a, "if you truly make yourself powerful against me") of this mistake (which he is not even conceding), then he intends to push back hard. He notes that they make themselves powerful against him by making his "reproach," that is, his affliction and emotional suffering, part of their case ("reproof") against him. The way he counters is by then deflecting the accusation from himself to God. He is "perverted" because God has perverted him (v. 6). God has motivated Job's reaction by the way he has treated him. The next number of verses then develop the idea that God has afflicted him.

Job begins with a hunting metaphor. God has hunted him like a wild animal, throwing his "net" around him. Bildad has just finished describing the fate of the wicked by means of the description of various types of nets, traps, and snares that await them (18:8–11).[11] Then Job reiterates his claim that God has been unresponsive to his cry for justice (v. 7). His idea of justice is shared with the three friends. It is unjust that such a one as he should suffer. He just does not deserve it. But God has not responded to his cries for an explanation.

Indeed, not only has God not facilitated his life ("my path"), he has actively hindered it. He has thrown up a blockade so formidable that Job cannot navigate his way around it (v. 8). The language of "path" (*ʾōraḥ*) and "way" (*nĕtîb*) is familiar from Proverbs for the journey of life. It is the path of the wicked that is blocked and hindered, not that of the righteous. The path of the righteous is well lit; the path of the wicked is dark (Prov. 4:18–19). Again, Job accuses God of being unfair.

Previously, Job had been honored by God. He led a princely life with wealth, servants, and a large family. He was treated like a king. But God has removed his glory (and replaced it with shame) and has undermined his status and made him worse than a servant (v. 9). Switching metaphors, he now likens himself to a tree that is torn down and uprooted. He believes this is indicative

10. Boss (*Human Consciousness of God*, 100) suggests that "Job is granting error, for the sake of argument."

11. Though Job uses a different word for "net" here (*mĕṣûdâ*), the idea is similar.

of God's unfairness. Bildad, who had used the tree metaphor in 18:16, would have taken the same evidence as confirmation that he was guilty.

Verses 11–12 utilize a military metaphor to describe God's anger toward Job. He treats Job (whose name may be connected with a Hebrew word for "enemy"; see the introduction) as a "foe" (*ṣār*, a Hebrew word related in meaning). Thus he sends his troops against him, who lay siege[12] to him. They build a road to march the army toward him, and then they camp all around him. One wonders whether it is appropriate to speculate who the troops are. By doing so, we may be turning a metaphor into an allegory. The idea is that God the warrior has chosen to fight against his servant Job, or at least this is Job's self-perception. Indeed, though, God has sent a "troop" against him, the accuser ("the satan") as we learn in the first two chapters of the book. From Job's perspective, the suffering that he experiences is the result of a whole army ranged against him, and that is the sentiment that he expresses in these two verses.

Job then pitifully describes how his suffering has lead to his estrangement from all of his relationships (vv. 13–19). The list omits reference to father and mother, but presumably Job is of an age when his parents have already died. He also does not speak of his children,[13] since they died in the first chapter. Thus v. 13 is a general statement that his brothers and his friends have all been alienated from him. The term "brother" here may stand for "relative" generally and thus this could be a lead-in statement to the whole section. Verse 14 then continues by talking again in general terms, moving from close relationships to more distant ones as it speaks first of "those near me," then "my acquaintances," and finally "my houseguests." The first two have "failed him," perhaps indicating their lack of support. The houseguests are even worse in that they have completely forgotten him. To forget someone often means more than absence of memory, but includes the idea of lack of action on someone's behalf.

Even his serving girls treat him badly, like a stranger or foreigner. Servants, whether male or female, should be quick to respond to the commands of their master. In Job's case, they do not respond even when he begs them for a favor (vv. 15–16).

Perhaps most cutting is his wife, who finds his breath repulsive, implying she will not come near him. His family as a whole finds him abhorrent (vv. 16–17). We have not heard about Job's wife since the prose preface (2:9), where in her despair she told Job to curse God and die. Job thus lacks all support. Even "young children" have rejected and turned against him (v. 18).

12. The idea of "building up" (*sll*) a road probably refers to a siege ramp built to scale a city wall.

13. Some interpreters, however, see a reference to children in "the sons of my belly'" in v. 17b. This is doubtful and may be a more general comment on his family. Some (Smick, "Job," 789) suggest that it is the son of his concubine, but we know nothing else of a concubine.

Those who are closest to him ("intimate friends" and "those I love") have betrayed him (v. 19).

In sum, Job has no one to help him. He is on his own in his suffering. The only people who seem to be physically close to him are these three friends, who feel it is their duty to tear him down. It is the three friends that he now addresses. If he expects sympathy from them, he is horribly wrong.

Verse 20 turns from a lament over his relational alienation to his physical suffering. He says that he is "skin and bones," barely holding on to life. The expression "by the skin of my teeth," denoting a close escape, originates in the KJV translation of this verse.

He concludes this section by begging[14] for their pity. He asks for pity as one who has been assaulted by God. But they pursue him, or as another translation of the verb of v. 22a (*rdp*) might suggest, they "persecute" him. And they do so, like God. The final question he asks them (v. 22b, "Are you not satisfied with my flesh?") was probably directed at both God and the three friends. Apparently the answer is no on both counts, since the friends will continue their debate in the following chapters, and God will verbally challenge him in chaps. 39–41.

23"Oh, that my words were written down.
Oh, that they were inscribed in a scroll.
24Oh, that with an iron pen and with lead
they were etched on rock as a witness.
25I know that my redeemer lives,
and he at last will rise up on the dust.
26After my skin is peeled off,
then out of my flesh I will see God.
27I will see him for myself;
my eyes will look and not a stranger's.
My heart fades within me.
28When you say, 'How should we pursue him?'
and, 'The root of the matter is found in him,'
29be careful of the sword,
for wrath brings the punishment of the sword,
so you may know there is judgment."

19:23–29. *My redeemer lives.* The concluding words of Job's fifth speech are among the most famous, if not the most famous, of the entire book. Their familiarity may arise from the fact that they provide the libretto for one of the most memorable arias in Handel's *Messiah*. In the *Messiah*, as well as in much popular theology, Job is thought to anticipate the Messiah. Even in an academic treatment of the passage, Kaiser argues that this passage should

14. As indicated by the repetition of "pity me," *ḥonnūnî ḥonnūnî*.

be understood as anticipating Jesus the Messiah,[15] though most (including conservative) scholars today would not understand the passage as a predictive prophecy.[16]

What is striking about the passage, though, is what appears to be a sudden onrush of confidence in a final resolution. Such a change of heart is difficult to explain with certainty, especially since Job does not maintain this confidence for long.

Verses 23–24 introduce his comments by expressing the wish that his words could become a permanent record. He wishes they were written in a scroll or, even more permanently, etched on a rock. It appears that this desire is expressed in connection with the words that follow, and by so expressing this desire, Job underlines the importance of what is to follow and thus heightens our expectations. It also may mean, as Smick says, that Job does not think he will last long, and so he wants his position to be recorded for posterity.[17]

The momentous announcement comes in v. 25. He knows that his redeemer (*gō'ēl*) lives. To understand the function of a redeemer, we begin with a look at Lev. 25. In this context, the *gō'ēl* is a close relative who comes to the aid of a distressed family member. This distress may concern their property (Lev. 25:25–38) or their personal well-being, for instance, if they should sell themselves into slavery (25:47–55). The book of Ruth describes a situation where the *gō'ēl* functions as the one who not only redeems the property of a deceased close relative, but also takes the widow as his wife. After a closer relative refuses to function as *gō'ēl*, Boaz marries Ruth.

These texts provide the background for the use of *gō'ēl* (and the related verb) in relationship to Yahweh's redemption of his people. In particular, the idea of a *gō'ēl* redeeming a relative who has been enslaved provides the background for the idea that God redeemed Israel from their bondage in Egypt (Exod. 6:6; 15:13). Isaiah 40–66 frequently refers to God as redeemer (Isa. 41:14–16; 43:14; 48:17). The Psalms also refer to Yahweh as redeemer on numerous occasions (Pss. 19:14; 77:15).

This does not exhaust the many passages that use *gō'ēl* and related words in reference to Yahweh, but it does establish a close connection between this word and God. But is Job using it in reference to Yahweh here? The context leads me to answer in the affirmative. He knows that his redeemer lives and that he will rise up on the dust. Here "dust" may refer to the earth. In other words, the redeemer will make an appearance on the earth. Verse 26 is difficult. But it does refer to Job's seeing God, and so it seems likely that God is the redeemer.

Commentators such as Clines disagree with this identification on the grounds that it is from God that Job wants redemption. He goes on to argue

15. Kaiser, *Messiah in the Old Testament*, 63.

16. For instance, van Groningen (*Messianic Revelation*) lacks any significant discussion of this or any other passage in Job.

17. Smick, "Job," 786.

that the redeemer is Job's own "cry for vindication."[18] However, Clines does not take into account that we are dealing here with wishful thinking on Job's part. We know he wants an audience with God. He expects that he will be vindicated in such a meeting. In other words, he expects that God would move from being his accuser to being his defender once the facts are laid out on the table. Yes, this view of God is in tension with other times when he believes God is unfair and does not care whether he is innocent (9:19–21). But this is an inherent tension in Job's mind. Sometimes he expects good things from an encounter with God and sometimes not.[19] In this passage, we have an example of his most optimistic thinking. He will meet God, and God will vindicate him.

However, when does he think this meeting will take place, and what will be his condition? This depends on the translation of the phrase *mibbĕśārî*. Here we have the noun "flesh" prefixed by the preposition *min*; the question surrounds the force of the preposition. The NRSV represents the two possibilities by translating "in my flesh" in the text and then noting an alternative, "without my flesh," in a footnote. The former takes the *min* as indicating source; that is, he will see God from the vantage point of his body. Such a translation has been understood by some to indicate an event that would take place before his death; others, taking v. 26a ("after my flesh is peeled off") to indicate death, believe v. 26b refers to a bodily resurrection.

The view that the phrase should be translated "outside/without my flesh" takes the *min* as privative. In this case, Job imagines an encounter with God in a disembodied state after death, perhaps something similar to Samuel's brief afterlife appearance (1 Sam. 28). This understanding also makes the most logical sense within the verse, since the first colon describes his flesh being peeled off. Either case involves some sort of afterlife existence, which seems odd in light of Job's other statements. As Clines rightly states, "Against any view of bodily resurrection it need only be noted that it contradicts everything the book has said previously about the finality of death (7:9; 10:21; 14:10, 12) and, in case it should be argued that this is some kind of new revelation of an existence beyond death, it needs to be noted that it is totally ignored in the remainder of the book (cf. 21:23–26; 30:23)."[20]

In the final analysis, I believe the best understanding is that Job expects (or at least strongly desires) this meeting to take place before his death. In other words, the peeling off of his flesh in v. 26a refers to his tremendous suffering and pain, not his death. Thus, after his flesh has been peeled off, he will meet God out of his flesh (at the height of his suffering). Once he sees God, they will become familiar with each other ("not a stranger's"). Just thinking about this possibility makes him faint ("My heart fades within me").

18. Clines, *Job 1–20*, 457–68.

19. As Whybray (*Job*, 101) states it, "Job vacillates in his attitude towards God."

20. Clines, *Job 1–20*, 464.

In the final analysis, one must acknowledge the textual, philological, grammatical, and conceptual difficulties of this section of Job. All commentators struggle to make sense of it and understand it. The enigmas of the Hebrew, however, should not be exploited to turn the text into a confident statement of NT theology, as if the author of Job or Job himself had a profound understanding of the future Messiah or the bodily resurrection. These ideas are quite foreign to the book of Job and extremely rare at best in the OT.

At the end of the book, no third-party redeemer appears on Job's behalf, but "out of his flesh" (at the apex of his pain), Job sees God. And God, after delivering a stern reprimand against Job, elicits Job's repentance, after which God restores (redeems) him.

In light of this future redemption, Job finally turns to his friends and issues a warning (vv. 28–29). The punishment that they see coming for him will turn against them. They plot how to pursue or persecute him because they believe he is the cause of his own suffering ("the root of the matter is found in him"). They will feel the edge of the sword. Indeed, at the end of the book, Job's friends escape more serious consequences from the hand of God only by virtue of the prayers of Job (42:7–9).

Theological Implications

"I Know That My Redeemer Lives" (19:25)

These words are perhaps the best known in the book of Job today, largely because of their use in Handel's *Messiah*, as mentioned above. For that reason, many people think that Job here founds his faith in Jesus Christ, the Redeemer. However, the equation between Jesus and Job's redeemer is the result of an all too hasty reading of an OT text from the perspective of the NT. Indeed, as we read the text carefully, we will notice that Job's hope for a redeemer bears little resemblance to the type of redeemer the NT describes.

Before further analyzing Job 19:23–29, we must first recognize that Job's statement here is the culmination of a line of his thinking that began back in 9:32–35. Here for the first time Job speaks of a mediator figure between God and himself. He imagines an "umpire" who can stand between him and his angry God. This umpire would help him speak to God and not be intimidated by his great power. He believes, after all, that he is suffering unjustly, and he needs to talk to God to convince him to act in an appropriate way toward him. At this stage of his thinking, though, Job does not believe such an umpire exists, and therefore he does not think he can speak to God.

In 16:18–22 Job's thought seems to have developed further. Here he speaks of a "witness . . . in heaven" (16:19). This witness will act like an umpire in that he "would arbitrate with God on behalf of a person, as between a person and his friend" (16:21). His confidence has grown to the point that he believes this mediator actually exists and is in heaven.

Coming back to Job 19, we observe that Job's thought has developed even further. Now he speaks no longer of an umpire or a witness but of a redeemer. Above, I argued—fully acknowledging the philological and textual issues confronting the interpreter of this passage—that Job is speaking of a time when he is still alive but at the height of his suffering.

How then do Job's hopes and desires in these three passages bear out in the rest of the book of Job? His hope for an umpire or witness, that is, a third-person arbitrator, never materializes. Elihu will intriguingly suggest that such an angelic figure sometimes does intercede for sufferers (33:23–30).[21] But none is forthcoming on Job's behalf—just the opposite. The accuser is an angelic figure, and he is not working on Job's behalf but is the agent of his suffering. No, Job's redemption, the reversal of his suffering, comes from God himself, who confronts him at the height of his suffering. In response, Job submits to him, and God restores him to his blessed condition.

The NT believer hears about an umpire or arbitrator between God and humans and thinks of Jesus, but such a view misconstrues the relationship between Jesus and God and between Jesus and people. Jesus is indeed the mediator between God and people, as Paul told Timothy ("For there is only one God and one Mediator who can reconcile God and humanity—the man Christ Jesus," 1 Tim. 2:5 NLT), but Jesus is not reconciling an angry divine Father to his sinful children. God himself sacrificially sent his own beloved Son to die on the cross on our behalf. Job gets not an angelic arbitrator but God the Redeemer himself. Relative to Job, Christians have a fuller understanding of our redemption, as we read the NT story of Jesus, who suffered and died and was raised.

21. And Eliphaz seems to think in terms of angels when he denies that there is anyone in heaven who can help Job (5:1).

5.
Zophar's Second Speech
(20:1–20)

Translation

1And Zophar the Naamathite answered and said:
2"My distress causes me to respond
    due to the agitation within me.
3I hear instruction that shames me,
    and a spirit beyond[1] my understanding gives me a reply.

4Do you not know this from time immemorial,
    from the time when he set humanity on the earth,
5that the luxuriance of the wicked is short,
    and the joy of the godless is momentary?
6Even if they go as high as heaven,
    and their head touches the clouds,
7they will perish forever like their dung.
    Those who have seen them will say, 'Where are they?'
8They will fly away like a dream and they will not find them.
    They will be put to flight like a night vision.
9The eye that saw them will see them no more.
    Their place will not glance at them again.
10Their children will run after the poor,
    and their hands will return their wealth.[2]
11Their bones once full of youthful vigor
    will lie down in the dust with them.

1. I take the preposition *min* as *min* of privation. This spirit comes from outside Zophar's understanding.

2. Or perhaps "vigor." Hebrew *'ôn* has this meaning in 18:7, 12.

12Though evil becomes sweet in their mouth,
 though they hide it under their tongue,
13though they spare it and do not let it go,
 though they make it linger on their palate,
14their food turns over in their innards,
 becoming asp's venom in their midst.
15They swallow wealth and then vomit it up.
 God disgorges it from their bellies.
16They will suck the poison of asps;
 the tongue of the viper will kill them.
17They will not look[3] on the streams of oil,[4]
 wadis of honey and butter.[5]
18They must return their gains unswallowed;
 they will not enjoy the benefit of their reward.[6]
19They have crushed and forsaken the poor;
 they have stolen a house that they did not build.
20They will not experience ease in their belly.
 They will let nothing they covet escape them.
21Nothing was left[7] after they ate;
 therefore their prosperity cannot last.
22In the fullness of their abundance, they will have distress.
 All the force of trouble will come on them.
23Let them fill their bellies.
 He will send his anger on them,
 raining it on them like their food.[8]
24They will flee from the iron weapon;
 they will be pierced by a bronze arrow.[9]
25It is drawn out and comes out of their back,
 the shiny point[10] from their gall bladder.
 Dread will come on them.
26Total darkness is stored up for them;
 a fire that is not fanned consumes them;
 horrible things will happen to any survivor in their tent.
27The heavens will reveal their guilt,
 and the earth will rise up against them.

3. The verb is the common *r'h* but implies "to look on with pleasure."

4. The Hebrew text has an implausible series of constructs that are poetically and grammatically difficult. Thus I agree with those who emend *nahărê* (rivers of) to *yiṣhār* (oil).

5. Or possibly "curds" or "milk" (*ḥem'â*).

6. A difficult colon, which may be literally rendered, "according to the strength of their reward, they will not enjoy."

7. Literally "there was no survivor." This appears to be the only place where *śārîd* is used of an inanimate object.

8. Emending *bilḥûmô* ("in his bowels") to *bĕlaḥmô* ("in his bread/food"). For other possibilities, see Clines, *Job 1–20*, 477–78.

9. Literally "bow" (*qešet*), though here it seems that "arrow" is contextually a better translation.

10. Literally "lightning" (*bārāq*), but here in reference to the point of the arrow.

[28]The possessions[11] of their house will be taken away,
like the torrents on the day of his anger.
[29]This is the lot of people who are guilty before God,
the inheritance decreed by God."

Interpretation

Zophar concludes the second cycle of the friends' arguments with his second speech of the debate. He is offended at what he hears from Job and feels compelled to respond. He appeals to an authority beyond himself, a spiritual authority (v. 3).

Zophar then delivers one long description of the horrible consequences that will come on the wicked (vv. 4–29). Though they might appear to prosper in the present, this prosperity will be short lived, and like Bildad in chap. 18, he argues that they will ultimately have a bad end. He ends his speech by confidently stating, "This is the lot of people who are guilty before God, the inheritance decreed by God" (20:29).

[1]And Zophar the Naamathite answered and said:
[2]"My distress causes me to respond
due to the agitation within me.
[3]I hear instruction that shames me,
and a spirit beyond my understanding gives me a reply."

20:1–3. *Job's words distress Zophar.* Zophar is not happy with what he has heard from Job. Indeed, he is distressed and agitated by what he takes as teaching (instruction) that makes him look bad. Job has responded to Zophar and the friends' attacks by fighting back, including questioning their intelligence. Zophar thus feels compelled to respond in order to defend himself. He appeals here to a spirit (*rûaḥ*) that is beyond his understanding.[12] Such an appeal was made early on by Eliphaz (4:12–17) and will be made later by Elihu (32:8). It is a way of bolstering one's claims by appeal to an external and, in this case, higher authority.

[4]"Do you not know this from time immemorial,
from the time when he set humanity on the earth,
[5]that the luxuriance of the wicked is short,
and the joy of the godless is momentary?

11. Some commentators (Clines, *Job 1–20*, 479) and versions (REB) emend *yĕbûl* to *yûbal*, *nābāl*, or *'ûbal*, any of which may mean "flood." The REB then renders v. 28a, "A flood will sweep away his house." Contrary to Clines, though, the idea of the possessions of a house makes sense in the context.

12. Clines (*Job 1–20*, 473) takes *rûaḥ* here as "impulse" rather than "spirit" on the simple assertion that Zophar "is not given to spiritual revelations."

[6]Even if they go as high as heaven,
and their head touches the clouds,
[7]they will perish forever like their dung.
Those who have seen them will say, 'Where are they?'
[8]They will fly away like a dream and they will not find them.
They will be put to flight like a night vision.
[9]The eye that saw them will see them no more.
Their place will not glance at them again.
[10]Their children will run after the poor,
and their hands will return their wealth.
[11]Their bones once full of youthful vigor
will lie down in the dust with them.
[12]Though evil becomes sweet in their mouth,
though they hide it under their tongue,
[13]though they spare it and do not let it go,
though they make it linger on their palate,
[14]their food turns over in their innards,
becoming asp's venom in their midst.
[15]They swallow wealth and then vomit it up.
God disgorges it from their bellies.
[16]They will suck the poison of asps;
the tongue of the viper will kill them.
[17]They will not look on the streams of oil,
wadis of honey and butter.
[18]They must return their gains unswallowed;
they will not enjoy the benefit of their reward.
[19]They have crushed and forsaken the poor;
they have stolen a house that they did not build.
[20]They will not experience ease in their belly.
They will let nothing they covet escape them.
[21]Nothing was left after they ate;
therefore their prosperity cannot last.
[22]In the fullness of their abundance, they will have distress.
All the force of trouble will come on them.
[23]Let them fill their bellies.
He will send his anger on them,
raining it on them like their food.
[24]They will flee from the iron weapon;
they will be pierced by a bronze arrow.
[25]It is drawn out and comes out of their back,
the shiny point from their gall bladder.
Dread will come on them.
[26]Total darkness is stored up for them;
a fire that is not fanned consumes them;
horrible things will happen to any survivor in their tent.
[27]The heavens will reveal their guilt,
and the earth will rise up against them.

[28]The possessions of their house will be taken away,
like the torrents on the day of his anger.
[29]This is the lot of people who are guilty before God,
the inheritance decreed by God."

20:4–29. *The prosperity of the wicked is short lived.* The bulk of this chapter is a reassertion of the view that the wicked suffer. Zophar begins by taunting Job and questioning why he does not appear to know this well-known truth. That the wicked suffer, according to Zophar, is a truth that began the minute humanity was put on the earth. Indeed, though he is not specifically citing Adam and Eve, Zophar could have mentioned that once Adam and Eve sinned, they suffered (Gen. 3), being cast out of Eden and then enduring pain in relationships and work.

It is not as if the wicked suffer immediately for their sins (according to v. 5). Indeed, they may prosper for a while, but they will inexorably pay for their crimes with time. The book of Proverbs, which often connects rewards with wise behavior and punishments with foolish behavior, also recognizes that the wicked fool can look prosperous, but only for a time: "Evil people get rich for the moment, but the reward of the godly will last" (Prov. 11:18 NLT; see also 11:4; 22:16). For Zophar, this means that the wicked person's wealth will soon, and certainly in this lifetime, dissipate.

In v. 5 Zophar asserts that the success of the wicked is temporary, even if they reach the highest pinnacles of success. They may reach the sky, so to speak, and still come crumbling down. Indeed, they will disappear. Verse 7a puts it in an interesting way: they "will perish forever like their dung." Dung perishes over time and leaves a smell, at least for a while. Their disappearance will cause their friends to ask, "Where are they?" Once so prominent, they are no longer to be found on the scene (v. 7b). Indeed, their existence will be like the existence of dreams, ephemeral (v. 8). Dreams often seem real until the dreamer wakes up and realizes that they are an illusion. The events in the dreams never happened. The success of the wicked, according to Zophar, is like that. Once success and wealth disappear, they will seem as if they were never real. The idea that wicked people's temporary success "flies away" is somewhat reminiscent of Prov. 23:5, which pictures wealth flying away, but this time like an eagle: "it will surely grow wings like an eagle and fly heavenward."

Verse 9a repeats the thought of v. 7b. Their disappearance will mean that those who regularly saw them will see them no more. Verse 9b goes a bit further when it adds that "their place" will no longer see them. They will not be coming home anymore, because they will be gone, presumably dead. And when they die, their children will be alone and penniless because they were forced to return their wealth, presumably to those they had earlier exploited to get it in the first place. Since they have no money, their children will be forced to live with the poor (v. 10). Verse 11 openly talks about their death.

They will grow old and feeble, though they once were like the young, full of energy. Now they will die, and their bones will be put in the dust.

Verses 12–16 develop a single image of evil and its consequences. Evil is like a delicacy that one eats and savors before it turns bad and those who have consumed it vomit. At first it is sweet to the taste (v. 12a) of the wicked, so sweet that they put it under their tongue to keep from swallowing it and thus lose the taste. They spare it from going to the stomach (v. 13a), sucking every bit of sweetness out of it. But v. 14 notes a change. What was once sweet is now sour, even poisonous. It is like the poisonous venom of an asp. It makes them sick, and they vomit it up (v. 15). Verse 16 then states that what they put in their mouth was really the poison of an asp. Its sweet taste was an illusion. What they thought would strengthen them will cause their death.

Verse 15 indicates that the subject is wealth. That is what tastes sweet to them but in the final analysis will hurt them, and they will finally have to give it up. Zophar in this speech had earlier commented about the brevity of the joy and wealth of the wicked (v. 5). Here he seems to indicate that wealth itself will hurt the wicked and ultimately lead to their death. Proverbs has the same lesson about the uselessness or even harm of wealth for the wicked fool:

> Riches do not profit on the day of fury,
> But righteousness will extricate from death. (11:4)

> Those who work for treasures with a lying tongue
> are pursuers of meaninglessness and seekers of death. (21:6)

Verse 17 continues the description of the disappointment of the wicked. While they hoped to gain a life of luxury through their evil, Zophar says that they will not even look on streams of oil, wadis of honey and butter. "Oil" refers to olive oil, a staple of the area used for food, medicine, skin cleansing, and more. "A good supply of fresh oil was a sign of stability, prosperity, and the Lord's blessing, . . . while the loss or lack of it was a sign of his judgment."[13] Zophar is thus saying that these wicked will not even look on (or perhaps experience in the sense of partake of) oil. The same is true of honey and butter, luxury food items. Again the theme is that the wicked will not partake of accoutrements of wealth and luxury. Verse 18 continues the food/taste theme by saying that the wicked will not be able to swallow their gains. Earlier Zophar said they could swallow wealth but not hold it down (v. 15). These are not contradictory statements, just different ways of making his point. The wicked will not stay rich, and they will not enjoy their riches.

After all, they have gotten their wealth by exploiting the poor. The book of Proverbs has harsh words for such people: "Those who oppress the poor

13. R. E. Averbeck, *NIDOTTE* 3:771.

in order to multiply and those who give to the wealthy—will certainly lack" (22:16). After all, the godly person is supposed to be generous to the poor:

> The righteous know the just cause of the poor,
> but the wicked do not understand knowledge. (29:7)

> Those who give to the poor will lack nothing,
> but those who avert their eyes will have numerous curses. (28:27)

Verses 20–23 continue to develop the metaphor of food and the belly of the wicked. Verse 20 says that ease will not come to their belly. After all, what they have swallowed has turned sour in their belly, like the poison of asps (v. 14). They try to consume too much. They will leave nothing they want (covet) behind, but consume it all. They ate it all (v. 21). But their prosperity will not last. Verse 22 speaks of how their fullness will lead to distress and the force of trouble. Perhaps we should think that this distress of abundance will lead to vomiting again (v. 15), or perhaps we are to think of gas that may expel itself in an unbecoming manner. Whatever the exact picture, it is not pretty. God is angry with them and will rain that anger down on them like their food, again perhaps suggesting vomiting.

Verses 24–25 change metaphors as Zophar now thinks of the distress of the wicked as being shot by an arrow.[14] While fleeing an iron weapon (suggesting a weapon that would be hard if not impossible to break), they are pierced by a bronze-tipped arrow. They are shot in the gall bladder, spewing forth bitterness.[15] They will suffer a severe fate, so a heavy fear overtakes them (v. 25c).

Verses 26–28 list additional horrible consequences that will overtake him. Both darkness and fire represent punishments. The unfanned fire may be a reference to lightning, which God will send in the direction of the wicked.[16] Their guilt will be revealed broadly, and the entire earth will seek recompense. Because of the anger of God, everything will be taken from them.

Zophar concludes this lengthy description of the fate of the wicked with the declaration that this is the lot or the inheritance of those who are guilty before God (v. 29).

Theological Implications

The Short-Lived Prosperity of the Wicked

Zophar adds little new here. He again makes the argument that the wicked are the ones who suffer (see "Retribution Theology in a Nutshell" following

14. An indirect but pointed reference to Job himself, who believed that God had shot him with poisoned arrows (6:4).

15. Compare Job's comment in 16:13.

16. So Smick, "Job," 793.

my comments on Job 8). Indeed, his colleague Bildad has made a very similar case in his previous speech (see "A Bad End for the Wicked" following my comments on Job 18). Both Bildad and Zophar acknowledge that sometimes the wicked prosper. But in addition, they both insist that this prosperity is short lived and that such people will ultimately suffer and meet a bad end. What neither of them will allow for, though, is that the righteous may temporarily suffer. After all, they are all too quick to label Job a sinner on the grounds that he suffers.

In the light of the whole teaching of the Bible, though, Bildad and Zophar are both right to say that the prosperity of the wicked is temporary. Proverbs makes the case, as I remarked earlier by citing Prov. 11:18; 13:11; and 21:6.[17] The psalmist (see Ps. 73) also makes this case. But it is wrong to read these texts as simply saying that the wicked will suffer at the end of this present life. Some wicked go to the grave happy, and some righteous go to the grave in pain. But the NT makes clear that in the long term the righteous are blessed and the wicked are punished, but the long term extends beyond this life.

17. See "A Bad End for the Wicked" following my comments on Job 18.

6. Job's Sixth Response
(21:1–34)

Translation

1And Job answered and said:
2"Listen to my words, will you!
  Let this be your consolation.
3Bear with me while I speak.
  You can ridicule me after I speak.

4As for me, is my complaint about mortals?
  Why shouldn't I be impatient?
5Turn toward me and be desolated!
  Put your hand on your mouth!

6If I think about it, I am terrified.
  Trembling seizes my flesh.
7Why are the wicked allowed to live?
  They grow old and increase in strength.
8Their descendants are established before them,
  their offspring before their eyes.
9Their house is at ease from fear;
  God's rod is not on them.
10Their ox breeds[1] and does not fail.[2]
  Their cows calve[3] and do not miscarry.

1. Rare meaning of the Piel of *ʿbr*, which normally means "to cross" or "pass by."
2. Rare meaning of *gʿl* in the Hiphil. In the Qal it normally means "to loathe."
3. Rare technical meaning of *plṭ*, which normally in the Qal means "to escape."

11They send out their infants like a flock;
their children dance.
12They sing to the tambourine and the lyre;
they rejoice to the sound of the reed pipe.
13They live out their days in prosperity;
they go down to Sheol in tranquility.
14And they say to God, 'Get away from me!
We do not desire to know your way!
15Who is Shaddai that we should serve him?
What benefit is it to us to intercede with him?'
16Is not their prosperity in their own control?
Is not the plan of the wicked far from him?[4]
17How often is the lamp of the wicked extinguished?
How often does calamity come on them?
How often does he deal out pain in his anger?

18Let them be like straw before the wind,
like chaff that the storm steals away.
19Does God store up their guilt for their children?
He should pay them,[5] and they should know it.
20Let their own eyes see their destruction;[6]
let them drink from the wrath of Shaddai.
21After they are gone, what delight can they get from their household,
when the number of their months is cut off?

22Will anyone teach God knowledge,
the one who judges the exalted?
23This person dies in perfect vigor,
completely[7] at ease and untroubled.
24His pails[8] are full of milk,
and the marrow of his bones is well lubricated.

4. This verse is extremely difficult, and Clines (*Job 21–37*, 509–10) is right to let context determine the meaning. I largely follow him here by understanding both cola to pose a question and by emending the suffix at the end of the second colon from "me" to "him." Clines charts fourteen different proposals for this verse.

5. The wicked.

6. *Kîd* is a hapax legomenon translated on the basis of context, though some try to achieve the same reading by emendation.

7. Emending *šal'ănan*, otherwise unknown, to *ša'ănān*, which seems more appropriate to the context.

8. *'Aṭîn* is a much-discussed hapax legomenon; see Grabbe (*Comparative Philology*, 79–81) and the wonderful summary of research by Clines (*Job 21–37*, 513–14). Certainty of translation cannot be reached, but context and cognates as well as early versions suggest either some farm implement (like a pail) or a part of the body (many have been suggested). Whichever it is, the verse contributes to the picture of the good health and prosperity of the person who dies "in perfect vigor" in contrast to the more lamentable person described in vv. 25–26.

25And another person[9] dies in bitterness,
never having partaken[10] of the good life.
26They will lie down together in the dust;
maggots cover them.

27Indeed, I know your thoughts
and the schemes by which you want to do violence[11] to me.
28For you say, 'Where is the house of the prince?
Where is the tent where the wicked used to dwell?'
29Have you not asked those who pass by on the road?
Do you not recognize their signs?
30For evil people are spared on the day of calamity;
they are kept safe on the day of wrath.
31Who proclaims their way to their face?
Who pays them back for what they have done?
32When they are carried to the grave,
a watch is kept over their tomb.
33The clods of the wadi are sweet to them,
everybody will follow after them,
and without number are those before them.
34How will you console me with emptiness?
Your responses are the remnants of disloyalty."

Interpretation

Job makes his final response to the friends in the second cycle. Here he does seem to be speaking directly to Zophar's contention in the previous speech that the wicked will suffer, though it is true that the friends have been making this argument consistently throughout their speeches (see Eliphaz in 15:20–35 and Bildad in 18:15–21). Job begins with an appeal that the friends listen to him (vv. 2–3). Job has been talking to them, but they never seem to connect with each other, as if they have not really been paying attention. In any case, according to vv. 4–5, his real argument is with God and not with them.

Job has argued that the wicked prosper, but he doubts that his point has sunk in, as witnessed by Zophar's last simplistic speech. Job then puts forward his perspective based on his observation and experience. The wicked thrive and are contemptuous toward God (vv. 6–17). He concludes that God is out of the loop and that the wicked are successful apart from him. God should punish the wicked immediately and not wait, and he should especially not punish children for father's offenses (vv. 18–21). But, according to Job in vv.

9. Literally "this person" in symmetry with the beginning of v. 23.

10. Literally "eaten," translated "tasted" by many versions (see NRSV, NJB).

11. I take the verb as *ḥms* I (in agreement with NRSV, NIV, Clines, and others) rather than postulating a *ḥms* II related to Syriac *ḥms*, which means "to think."

22–26, God does not differentiate between the righteous and the wicked in his treatment of them. People die or thrive independent of moral considerations. That is the way God works, and no one can do anything about it. Job ends his speech (vv. 27–34) with a final jab at his opponents. They ask him for evidence that the wicked prosper, and he tells them that it is common knowledge. Their speeches are empty and ineffective (v. 34).

> **1**And Job answered and said:
> **2**"Listen to my words, will you!
> Let this be your consolation.
> **3**Bear with me while I speak.
> You can ridicule me after I speak."

21:1–3. *Let me speak!* Job begins with the demand that the friends (and maybe in particular Zophar, the previous speaker) pay attention to what he is saying. He likely feels that they have not been listening to him because they keep on making the same points that God rewards the innocent and punishes the wicked (15:20–35; 18:15–21), in spite of Job's contrary arguments and his own experience. Although the speeches are presented in an orderly fashion, Job's words here ("Bear with me while I speak," v. 3a) may indicate that they have or at least tried to interrupt him, or perhaps we are to think of them as groaning while he is speaking. He appeals to their pity toward him, saying that this would be an act of consolation or comfort on their part toward his suffering. So far, though, the friends have not shown much sensitivity to Job, and as the debate continues, it does not appear that Job's request has much impact on them. At least, he asks them to let him speak before ridiculing him.

> **4**"As for me, is my complaint about mortals?
> Why shouldn't I be impatient?
> **5**Turn toward me and be desolated!
> Put your hand on your mouth!"

21:4–5. *Job's impatience.* Job then informs them that his complaints are not about how he is being treated by mortals. Granted, he has complained about the three friends (as recently as vv. 2–3!), but his ultimate complaint is not directed at them or any human; rather, he is upset with God himself. Thus he feels justified in his impatience. All the friends have to do is look at his physical and mental deterioration to see why he is impatient (see "The Patience of Job" in the theological implications section at the end of the chapter). Just the sight of him should cause them to shut their mouths in horror.[12]

12. Boss (*Human Consciousness of God*, 113) points out that "the hand on the mouth is a gesture of awestruck silence."

[6]"If I think about it, I am terrified.
Trembling seizes my flesh.
[7]Why are the wicked allowed to live?
They grow old and increase in strength.
[8]Their descendants are established before them,
their offspring before their eyes.
[9]Their house is at ease from fear;
God's rod is not on them.
[10]Their ox breeds and does not fail.
Their cows calve and do not miscarry.
[11]They send out their infants like a flock;
their children dance.
[12]They sing to the tambourine and the lyre;
they rejoice to the sound of the reed pipe.
[13]They live out their days in prosperity;
they go down to Sheol in tranquility.
[14]And they say to God, 'Get away from me!
We do not desire to know your way!
[15]Who is Shaddai that we should serve him?
What benefit is it to us to intercede with him?'
[16]Is not their prosperity in their own control?
Is not the plan of the wicked far from him?
[17]How often is the lamp of the wicked extinguished?
How often does calamity come on them?
How often does he deal out pain in his anger?"

21:6–17. *The wicked and their children prosper*. Job now turns his attention to a description of the wicked. Contrary to Zophar in the previous chapter, who argued that they suffer the consequences of their sin, Job sees only the prosperity of the wicked. Before the description, though, he registers his horror at the thought that there is no justice. He trembles all over just thinking about it (v. 6).[13] He wonders out loud why the wicked are allowed to live when their crimes call for their death. They not only grow old but also grow in strength, contrary to the normal rules of living, in which age brings weakness and senility. Indeed, they not only live long and prosper; their children thrive, indicating that their family line will continue the prosperity enjoyed by the sinner.

Indeed, their entire household is in good shape (v. 9), the result of the fact that God's rod is not on their back as it is on Job's. They are wicked and should be experiencing God's punishment, but they are not. Not only are they productive in offspring, but even their animals are (v. 10). Of course, this means that they grow rich in their holdings. Job had enjoyed such a life

13. An alternative interpretation is that he is reacting to the idea that he is confronting God.

at one time (1:2–3), but this made sense to him because he deserved it as an innocent man. It makes no sense that the wicked should be experiencing such abundance, especially since now Job is suffering.

Their children are numerous and obedient (like a flock of sheep, v. 11). Not only are their children numerous, but they also enjoy life, singing and dancing about to joyful musical instruments (v. 12). Contrast this with the innocent Job's situation. His children are dead. The injustice could not be more obvious to him.

It is a little unclear whether it is the wicked or the children of the wicked (or both) who are the subject of vv. 13–15, but it is most likely the former. Job believes that the wicked live quality lives, and when they go to Sheol, as all do, they go peacefully, not horribly as his children did or as he imagines his own end will be after a torturous period of physical and emotional pain. Qohelet had similar thoughts about the wicked who were praised during life and then had a proper and honored burial (8:10): "Thus I observed the wicked buried and departed. They used to go out of the holy place, and they were praised in the city where they acted in such a way. This too is meaningless."[14]

The wicked are far from God and want it that way. In their prosperity and enjoyment, they see absolutely no need for God. They neither serve him nor pray to him. He is more a burden than a help in life (vv. 14–15). Here we might remember that the accuser's charge against Job is that he is not disinterested in his piety (1:9). He is only righteous because of the reward involved. According to Job, this charge could be leveled toward the wicked, who do not serve God because they see no reward in it. Job, on the other hand, is suffering and innocent, yet he is unwilling merely to cut his losses by cursing God. Rather, he pursues God in search of resolution.

Job ends this part of his speech by stating his belief that the wicked control their own fates. After all, God pays no attention to their plans, so they can do what they wish (v. 16). As proof of his position, Job asks a series of rhetorical questions about whether anyone can produce evidence showing that God does seek retribution against the wicked (v. 17).[15] The context assumes that he expects that no one will be able to provide such evidence. The wicked seem to live such easy lives (Ps. 73).

18"Let them be like straw before the wind,
  like chaff that the storm steals away.
19Does God store up their guilt for their children?
  He should pay them, and they should know it.

14. For translation and interpretation, see Longman, *Ecclesiastes*, 216–21.

15. Wilson (*Job*, 230–31) may well be right that his reference to "the lamp of the wicked" may presuppose a knowledge of Prov. 24:19–20. He further argues that the question about "calamity" is linked to Prov. 24:21–22, which says that "calamity" (*'êd*) will come on those who rebel against God and king.

[20]Let their own eyes see their destruction;
let them drink from the wrath of Shaddai.
[21]After they are gone, what delight can they get from their household,
when the number of their months is cut off?"

21:18–21. *God should punish the wicked.* In the previous section, Job expressed his frustration that God did not see to the punishment of the wicked. Now he calls for their punishment with an imprecation directed at the wicked. He wants them to be like the straw or chaff before the wind, blown about with no roots. This is the fate that Ps. 1 describes for the wicked (v. 4) in contrast to the righteous, who are like a firmly planted and productive fruit tree (v. 3).

Next Job addresses the argument that even though the wicked do not experience their punishment, their children will feel the divine wrath. This view had been articulated by the three friends in 5:4 and 20:10.[16] Against this idea, he argues that it is the wicked persons themselves who should be punished, not their children (vv. 19b–20). As Qohelet pointed out, if people do not experience their own punishment, then evil will flourish (Eccles. 8:11). The punishment of the children of the wicked is no punishment of the wicked, because they do not care about the fate of their children, since they can derive no "delight" from them after they die (v. 21). The wicked are totally selfish.

[22]"Will anyone teach God knowledge,
the one who judges the exalted?
[23]This person dies in perfect vigor,
completely at ease and untroubled.
[24]His pails are full of milk,
and the marrow of his bones is well lubricated.
[25]And another person dies in bitterness,
never having partaken of the good life.
[26]They will lie down together in the dust;
maggots cover them."

21:22–26. *God treats all people, wicked and righteous, alike.* In the previous section Job called on God to punish the wicked and not their children. They needed to experience the consequences of their actions. However, in v. 22 he concedes that no one can teach God anything. He then describes two scenarios, two people who have different fates. While some of the details of the description are obscure (see the translation note on v. 24a above), the general contours of Job's point are clear.

The first person dies in good shape, both physically and mentally. Up to the end, that person enjoys a healthy life and dies at peace. The second person

16. As pointed out by Pyeon, *You Have Not Spoken*, 21.

dies after a long, hard, bitter life. Though the two had very different lives, both of them will die.

While neither the happy nor the bitter individual is connected with wickedness or righteousness, the point seems to be that there is no connection between how one lives life, or how one relates to God, and the quality of one's life and death. In this way, Job's observation is the same as Qohelet's: "Everything is the same for everybody: there is one fate for the righteous and the wicked and for the clean and the unclean, and for the one who sacrifices and for the one who does not sacrifice; as it is for the good, so it is for the sinner; as it is for the one who swears, so it is for the one who is afraid to swear" (Eccles. 9:2). To Job and to Qohelet, this reality means that there is no justice in the world or with God.

27"Indeed, I know your thoughts
and the schemes by which you want to do violence to me.
28For you say, 'Where is the house of the prince?
Where is the tent where the wicked used to dwell?'
29Have you not asked those who pass by on the road?
Do you not recognize their signs?
30For evil people are spared on the day of calamity;
they are kept safe on the day of wrath.
31Who proclaims their way to their face?
Who pays them back for what they have done?
32When they are carried to the grave,
a watch is kept over their tomb.
33The clods of the wadi are sweet to them,
everybody will follow after them,
and without number are those before them.
34How will you console me with emptiness?
Your responses are the remnants of disloyalty."

21:27–34. *The evidence is obvious.* Job then turns his attention directly to his friends with whom he is debating. He informs them that he is aware that their intentions are not to console, but to harm. They are plotting to do him in.

He cites them as asking questions about the "house of the prince" and the "tent where the wicked used to dwell" (v. 28). The implication is that they are asking for empirical proof for his arguments: "Show us the house of the wicked!" The friends have claimed that the house, property, and wealth of the wicked are ephemeral at best (Zophar in 20:4–29).[17] So, they ask, show us an example of a wicked person who prospers.

Job responds by saying that the examples are obvious and known by all. Just ask those "who pass by on the road," roughly equivalent to our expression, "Ask the person on the street." Don't they see it? It is obvious.

17. Pyeon (*You Have Not Spoken*, 21) adds 5:3 and 18:5–21.

In v. 30 he again states the obvious (at least to him): evil people are spared calamity. They are not recipients of divine wrath; they are kept safe. The world is topsy-turvy. No one, neither God nor people, confronts them with their evil ways (v. 31a). And certainly no one, again neither God nor people, punishes them for what they have done (v. 31b).

Verses 32–33 again emphasize that even the death of wicked people is blessed. They are cared for in death, buried, and watched over (a fact that aggravates Qohelet; Eccles. 8:10). They are happy in their burial, and they are surrounded by people who come out to their grave and pay their respects.

Job then ends with a question intended to hurt the friends, who have styled themselves his consolers but in reality are hurting him greatly (v. 34). They are coming to him with nothing ("emptiness," *hebel*, can also mean "meaninglessness"). Their words are not friendly but disloyal. They betray him by their arguments and tone.

We might imagine the friends' reaction to Job's closing words. Even if Job would take them to the prosperous house of a "wicked man," they would argue that his wealth is temporary. But Job too is overstating his case. Certainly not every wicked person prospers or every righteous person suffers. It just seems this way to him at this juncture in his life. The debate thus continues into a third cycle.

Theological Implications

The Patience of Job

It is not uncommon to hear someone praise a long-suffering friend or acquaintance as having "the patience of Job." This commendation comes from the KJV rendition of James 5:11 ("ye have heard of the patience of Job"), a passage that speaks of the attitude that should be adopted by suffering Christians waiting for the Lord's return. However, reading the book of Job itself makes one wonder where James ever got the idea that Job was patient in the face of his own suffering. Did James get it wrong? And what do Job and James tell us about our own attitude toward suffering?

Starting with Job 3, Job complains about God and to God constantly (see "Grumbling at God" following my comments on Job 3). Indeed, God accuses Job of condemning him in order that Job might be seen to be right (40:8b). Here in chap. 21, Job himself asks, "Why shouldn't I be impatient?" (v. 4). He has plenty of reason to be so. He suffers horribly and cannot speak directly with God, though he wants to.

There are various theories about James's appropriation of the book of Job. The first has to do with the meaning of the Greek word that the KJV translates "patience" (*hypomonē*). The KJV itself renders the verbal form of this word that occurs at the beginning of the verse as "to endure," suggesting a meaning for the noun of "endurance" or "perseverance." Indeed, most, if not all, modern English translations take this route (NIV, NLT, NRSV, NASB, and even NKJV). The difference between "patience" and "endurance" is that the former is a passive waiting, while the latter is active. Job does exhibit endurance (though not patience) throughout the entire book. Even though he complains about God, he never gives up on God; he keeps going after him.

That said, something more may be going on in James. Granted that *hypomonē* can mean "endurance," the broader context is speaking of patience, as indicated by frequent use of Greek *makrothymein*, "to be patient" (see James 5:7, 8, 10). It appears that James is calling on Christians to endure, but to do so with patience. The impatient Job of the dialogues does not seem to be the model that James is holding up to Christians.

A better solution might be found in the interpretive tradition of Job that was current during the time of James. It appears that at this time, Job was interpreted as a patient man. Early Christians used the LXX rather than the Hebrew text, and this influential translation of Job downplays Job's angry response to God. According to Allen, "In the opinion of the majority of scholars the Greek translator of Job rendered the text into a Greek version that transforms the Job of the poetic sections from bombastic doubter into pious and persevering sufferer. This is done by toning down the angry questions that Job poses to God into more palatable affirmations of faith."[18] The *Testament of Job* (see under "History of Interpretation" in the introduction) may also be cited as a contemporary witness to the transformation of Job into a patient figure who does not complain.[19] Job's wife complains but not Job himself.

The broader subject of the NT's use of the OT is much debated. It appears that the NT does not always use the OT according to a strict historical-grammatical interpretation. Sometimes the NT will cite the OT according to older, then-current interpretive traditions. Modern interpreters of Job should not be bound to conform their understanding to the NT's use of the OT.

That said, how then are we to appropriate the citation of Job by James? The whole section (5:7–11) encourages patient endurance during the time period before the coming of the Lord and in the midst of suffering. We then rightly appropriate James's exhortation by adopting the attitude of patient endurance. If James is citing the book of Job as read at the time rather than the canonical book itself, then it would be wrong to go back and see the bombastic Job of the book as a paradigm of that attitude. James is using Job as an example, but it is the Job of the LXX, the *Testament of Job*, perhaps also of Sirach (49:9). In other words, James gives us an interpreted Job, not one

18. Allen, "Job 3," 362. He cites Gerleman (*Studies in the Septuagint*) and Gard (*Exegetical Method*) in support.

19. Carson ("James," 1011) cites the *Testament of Job* (along with Sir. 49:9) as an example of how Job has become "a model prophet" and thus an appropriate example for James, but he does not interact with the difficulty of connecting this with the picture of Job in the OT book of Job.

who is the product of grammatical-historical exegesis. Peter does a similar thing when he presents Sarah as a model of submission to her husband (1 Pet. 3:6), an attitude not borne out by the book of Genesis, though it reflects the contemporary interpretation of Sarah at the time Peter wrote.

Indeed, it would be wrong to hold up the Job of the canonical book as an example of a proper attitude toward God, considering that God himself speaks to him out of the whirlwind and spends four chapters putting him in his place and leading him to "repentance."[20] Certainly, that Job never abandoned God but kept pursuing him is a good thing, but not the best thing. Job's attitude at the end, where he finally bows in submission in deference to God and in the face of the mystery of his suffering, is the attitude advocated by the book of Job.[21]

20. Contra Nystrom (*James*, 288), who wrongly compares Job's complaints to the laments of the Psalms. The view presented here is closer to that of Martin, *James*, 189.

21. Thanks to Peter Enns for his response to the first draft of this essay. See his *Inspiration and Incarnation*, 113–66, for an insightful study of the use of the OT in the NT, along with further examples.

C.
Third Cycle
(22:1–27:23)

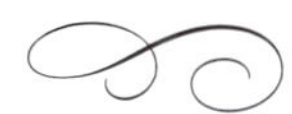

Two cycles of the debate have concluded, and the friends have made no headway in their arguments against Job. The third cycle shows the effects of their futile efforts: Eliphaz provides a substantial third speech, but Bildad can manage only a brief argument, and we hear nothing at all from Zophar. By contrast, Job continues to defend his innocence and perhaps grows even more passionate.

1.
Eliphaz's Third Speech
(22:1–30)

Translation

1And Eliphaz the Temanite answered and said:
2"Do people benefit God?
  Can even skilled people benefit him?
3Does it delight Shaddai if you are righteous?
  What profit is it to him if your ways are blameless?

4Does he reprove you for your fear?
  Will he enter into judgment with you?
5Is not your evil abundant,
  and is there no end to your guilt?
6For you have exacted pledges from your brothers for no reason;
  you have stripped off the clothes of the naked.
7You have not given the weary water to drink;
  you have withheld food from the starving.
8The powerful possess the land;
  the favored reside in it.
9You send widows out empty-handed;
  you crush the arms of the orphans.

10Therefore, traps are all around you!
  Sudden dread scares you,
11or darkness so you cannot see;
  a flood of water covers you.

12Is not God high in heaven?
See the highest stars, that they are exalted.
13But you say, 'What does God know?
Can he judge through thick darkness?
14Clouds hide him so he cannot see;
he wanders around the vault of heaven.'
15Will you guard the ancient trail
that the guilty trod?
16They are bound up[1] before their time;
a river pours over their foundation.
17Do they not say to God, 'Get away from me!
What can Shaddai do to us?'[2]
18Did he not fill their houses with prosperity?
Is not the plan of the wicked far from me?[3]
19The righteous see this and rejoice,
and the innocent ridicule them.
20'Have not those who rise up against us been destroyed?
Fire has consumed their abundance.'

21Get along with him and be at peace.
In this way prosperity will come to you.
22Receive instruction from his mouth.
Put his speech in your heart.
23If you return to Shaddai, you will be restored,
if you remove iniquity far from your tent;
24and set gold on the dust,
and Ophir[4] on the rock of the wadis,
25let Shaddai be your gold,
and your choice silver,
26for then you will delight in Shaddai;
you will show favor[5] toward God.
27You will entreat him, and he will hear you;
you will repay your vows.
28You will decide on a matter, and it will be established for you,
and light will illuminate your paths.

1. The verb *qmṭ* could mean "seize," and Gordis (*Job*, 175–76, 247–48) has argued that it means "to cut off," based on Mishnaic Hebrew. The verb is used in 16:8 in connection with Job's own condition.

2. Hebrew has "to him/them," but context requires the first-person plural.

3. Compare 21:16.

4. Ophir was a region famous for gold (see also 1 Kings 9:28; 10:11; 22:48; 2 Chron. 8:18; 9:10). The use of the word here may be shorthand for "gold of Ophir." Ophir has been identified with many gold-producing regions, but the most likely is southern Arabia (see R. Wakely, *NIDOTTE* 1:322).

5. Literally "lift your face toward."

29For he humiliates,[6] and you will say, 'It is pride.'[7]
He saves those with downcast eyes.
30He rescues the innocent;[8]
you are rescued by the purity of your hands."

Interpretation

The third and final cycle of the debate begins with Eliphaz's third speech. As usual, he is the lead-off speaker for the three friends. He continues many of the same themes, but here he becomes even more personal, attributing to Job crimes that he could not possibly know for certain Job had committed (especially since the reader is well aware that Job has not committed them!).

However, he begins by granting the possibility that Job might be, as he claims, a good person (vv. 2–3). He says, even so, it does not matter. God receives no benefits from such people. However, he is unconvinced that Job really is pious. After all, God is reproving him, so it is obvious that he is evil, not good. At this point, Eliphaz starts listing Job's sins (vv. 4–9) to make sense of his suffering (vv. 10–11). However, he charges Job with saying that the exalted God is so distant that he does not know what is going on in the world (vv. 12–14), thus showing that he is just one of the wicked who will suffer for their sins, leading the righteous to rejoice (vv. 15–20). Finally, and not surprisingly, Eliphaz calls on Job to repent and thus be restored in his relationship with God and also in his prosperity (vv. 21–30).

1And Eliphaz the Temanite answered and said:
2"Do people benefit God?
Can even skilled people benefit him?
3Does it delight Shaddai if you are righteous?
What profit is it to him if your ways are blameless?"

22:1–3. *God couldn't care less.* We have seen that many of the speeches of both Job and the three friends begin with barbs directed at the other disputant(s). Eliphaz here begins his last speech with a series of questions that attack Job's main claim. Job has claimed that he is "righteous" and "blameless" (9:20; 12:4). Even Bildad conceded that in principle God would

6. While the verb is pointed as a plural, "they humiliate," the context calls for a singular, so it is best to take the *waw* as a dittography; see Smick, "Job," 803.

7. With the NRSV; but possibly, "he humiliates those who speak with pride."

8. The Hebrew is *ʾî-nāqî*, which seems to be "not innocent"; however, the context does not allow such a meaning, especially in light of the second colon, though the NRSV does translate, "he will deliver even those who are guilty." Clines (*Job 21–37*, 547) provides a lengthy discussion of the various options available to achieve this reading, which is demanded by context, though none is certain.

not reject a blameless person (8:20). Here, though, Eliphaz says that God is indifferent to the idea of a righteous/blameless person. To him, God is a being who is self-sufficient and does not need or care about people. Of course, readers know from the prologue that God indeed cares greatly. He wants to know whether the relationship he enjoys with Job is a matter of self-interest or sincere affection.

4"Does he reprove you for your fear?
  Will he enter into judgment with you?
5Is not your evil abundant,
  and is there no end to your guilt?
6For you have exacted pledges from your brothers for no reason;
  you have stripped off the clothes of the naked.
7You have not given the weary water to drink;
  you have withheld food from the starving.
8The powerful possess the land;
  the favored reside in it.
9You send widows out empty-handed;
  you crush the arms of the orphans."

22:4–9. *Guilty as charged.* Eliphaz has one more question for Job. He has above suggested that God would not even care if Job were blameless, but now he will not even concede his blamelessness as a possibility. Job's suffering demonstrates sufficiently to him that Job is a man who is enduring divine reproof. He snidely asks Job whether he thinks that this reproof is a result of his "fear." The fear to which he refers is the fear of God, which is the mark of a pious person (Prov. 1:7). The mere fact of Job's suffering is a sure sign that he is under the judgment of God; and if he is under the judgment of God, he certainly is not blameless. On the contrary, his evil nature is manifest to everyone (v. 5).

Perversely, Eliphaz then starts listing specific charges against Job. He has defrauded his relatives. The OT law allowed for pledges against a loan, but not interest (Exod. 22:25). These pledges for security of the loan had certain conditions for the creditor, and Job is here charged with breaking these conditions or perhaps even claiming fraudulently that he was due pledges when he had not even made a loan. Further, Job has taken advantage of the poor ("naked") by taking their clothes off their backs, perhaps referring to the part of the law that required the creditor to give back a coat taken in pledge so the debtor would be able to stay warm at night (Exod. 22:26–27).

Job is further accused of acts that favor the powerful and disadvantage the needy. He does not help the weary who need something to drink, nor the famished who need something to eat. The widow and orphan were particularly vulnerable members of ancient society, having no husband or father to provide for them. God was especially concerned about the welfare of widows and orphans (Exod. 22:22; Deut. 24:17). Eliphaz claims that Job has sinned by not attending to the needs of these vulnerable individuals.

Of course, readers know that Eliphaz is just making up this list of crimes. Job has committed none of them. We have no doubt that Job is speaking truthfully when he distances himself from these and other such sins in his final protest of innocence in chap. 31 (see especially vv. 16–23, 31–32).

10 "Therefore, traps are all around you!
 Sudden dread scares you,
11 or darkness so you cannot see;
 a flood of water covers you."

22:10–11. *Job deserves it*. Eliphaz has just listed a number of sins that he claims Job has committed. He now expresses no wonder that Job is in such dire straits. After all, wicked people like Job fall into traps (18:9); they experience tremendous dread (15:22). Darkness and floodwaters are also punishments associated with sin (5:14; 15:30; 18:6, 18).

12 "Is not God high in heaven?
 See the highest stars, that they are exalted.
13 But you say, 'What does God know?
 Can he judge through thick darkness?
14 Clouds hide him so he cannot see;
 he wanders around the vault of heaven.'
15 Will you guard the ancient trail
 that the guilty trod?
16 They are bound up before their time;
 a river pours over their foundation.
17 Do they not say to God, 'Get away from me!
 What can Shaddai do to us?'
18 Did he not fill their houses with prosperity?
 Is not the plan of the wicked far from me?
19 The righteous see this and rejoice,
 and the innocent ridicule them.
20 'Have not those who rise up against us been destroyed?
 Fire has consumed their abundance.'"

22:12–20. *God will take care of the wicked, and the righteous will rejoice*. Eliphaz reminds Job that God is exalted. He is even above the highest stars, and they are themselves exalted. One would think that from that vantage point, God would see everything, and indeed Eliphaz believes so. However, he suspects that Job does not. After all, Job is wicked and thought he could get away with his crimes. He attributes to Job the belief that the clouds between the heavens and the earth prevent God from seeing what is going on in the world. God cannot discern the goings-on and judge the actions of people he cannot see. Job thinks, according to Eliphaz, that God keeps himself up in the vaults of heaven, pacing about with no interest or ability to interact with human affairs (vv. 13–14). This thought again reminds us of Qohelet: "God is in heaven and you are on earth. Therefore, let your words be few" (Eccles. 5:2).

Indeed, Job, who knows he is innocent yet suffering, does wonder whether God knows about his situation. That is why he desires to have an audience with God, to set him straight. Job apparently suspects that God does indeed know what is going on but does not care, since God is unjust, judging the innocent and the wicked the same (9:15–21).

Eliphaz questions whether Job will continue to follow in the well-worn tracks of the wicked, who think they can get away with their crimes but cannot (v. 15). Both Job (21:14) and Eliphaz (22:17) agree that the wicked tell God to get away from them. However, Job believes that they do so because a relationship with God is not a benefit to them since they prosper anyway. Eliphaz, on the other hand, believes that this attitude results in their destruction. They are bound up (as Job believes himself to be in 16:8), and their confidence ("their foundation") is eroded by God's floodlike river that pours over them. In other words, they crumble like a house whose foundation is destroyed by a torrent of water.

Eliphaz is disgusted with the wicked who turn against God, who prospered them in the first place (v. 18). Surely he includes Job among this group. He distances himself from such people and asserts that the righteous, like himself, will rejoice and mock them (v. 19). He finishes this section of his argument with a quote from the righteous, who gloat over the destruction of the wicked. They are happy that the wicked and their wealth are destroyed by the fires of God's judgment (v. 20).

21"Get along with him and be at peace.
  In this way prosperity will come to you.
22Receive instruction from his mouth.
  Put his speech in your heart.
23If you return to Shaddai, you will be restored,
  if you remove iniquity far from your tent;
24and set gold on the dust,
  and Ophir on the rock of the wadis,
25let Shaddai be your gold,
  and your choice silver,
26for then you will delight in Shaddai;
  you will show favor toward God.
27You will entreat him, and he will hear you;
  you will repay your vows.
28You will decide on a matter, and it will be established for you,
  and light will illuminate your paths.

29For he humiliates, and you will say, 'It is pride.'
He saves those with downcast eyes.
30He rescues the innocent;
you are rescued by the purity of your hands."

22:21–30. *Repent and prosper*. Eliphaz's speech follows the typical pattern of accusation, call to repentance, and finally the promise of restoration (see his earlier statement at 5:17–26). These verses present the final two parts, the call to repent and the promise of better times ahead.

Job has been challenging God's justice and even threatening to confront him directly in a court setting. Eliphaz wants him to settle out of court by complete capitulation. Verse 21 gets right to the point with the encouragement for Job to come to peaceful terms with God, with the result that prosperity will return to Job. To be at peace with God, though, requires listening to and obeying him (v. 22). Job must not challenge God but rather be submissive to him and take what is coming to him. But the promise is restoration (v. 23a) contingent on removing evil from his life (v. 23b). The problem here is that Job knows (as does the reader) that there is no evil to turn from. He is blameless and innocent (1:1, 8; 2:3). Eliphaz does not believe this, though. He suggests that Job puts wealth above God, so he exhorts him to turn away from his love of gold and make God his precious metal. Interestingly, he tells Job to take his gold and put it in the dust (v. 24a), even put gold of Ophir on the rock of the wadis (v. 24b), in an apparent contrast of expensive and shiny metals with ordinary and bland dirt or rocks. Again, this is good advice (and Job himself will acknowledge that God is more precious than precious metals in 28:13–20), but this is not Job's problem. According to Eliphaz, if Job does turn from wealth to God, he will then show that God is the most important thing to him (v. 26), and at that point his relationship with Shaddai will change for the better.

Verses 27–30 focus on the positive change that will occur upon Job's repentance. Right now Job calls on God and gets silence by way of reply. After he turns to God, then God will hear his prayers and respond to them. Since God will hear his prayers, Job will then have reason to repay his vows that were made contingent on a divine response (v. 27). Further, Job's plans will be confirmed by God and made easy. The "paths" (v. 28) are the direction of one's life.[9] Right now Job's path is dark and murky; he does not know where to turn. But once restored, God will light up his way, so he can move through life with ease.

Verses 29–30 conclude with a comment about God's pattern of deliverance. The principle, according to Eliphaz, is that God saves the humble and the innocent. God humiliates the proud. Eliphaz imagines a chastened Job agreeing

9. The path as a metaphor of life appears frequently in the book of Proverbs; see Longman, *Proverbs*, 151–55.

with God's assessment. Right now Job insists that God is humiliating him unfairly. He does not deserve it. In the future, when Job's heart is set straight, he will accept the divine judgment that he is proud and will humble himself (with downcast eyes). God rescues the innocent, so Eliphaz counsels Job to pay attention to the purity of his acts (hands).

The irony is that Job is innocent. He is not being punished for his sins. The further irony is that Job will save sinners through his intercession, as Eliphaz mentions in vv. 29–30, but those sinners will be Eliphaz himself along with his two friends. The real answer to this conundrum still awaits resolution.

Theological Implications

The Aseity of God: Do People Benefit God? (22:2)

Eliphaz grows sick of Job's assertions of innocence. He does not believe him for a minute, as we can tell later in this chapter (vv. 4–9) when Eliphaz starts accusing Job of specific crimes without supporting evidence. Nonetheless, Eliphaz begins his argument in the third cycle by saying, "Even if you are innocent, God does not care, because he does not need people, innocent or otherwise." Such a view may be a result of Eliphaz's overheated argument. He typically, even in this chapter, holds the view that God differentiates between the righteous and the wicked in terms of the consequences of their life. On the other hand, he may be able to hold this view of retribution along with the idea that, still, God in an ultimate sense does not benefit one way or another. God is God, and he does not need people. Today such a doctrinal understanding of God's independence from his creation is called the aseity of God.

"Aseity" derives from the Latin phrase *a se*, "from himself," and refers to the independence of God. God does not need anyone or anything. While everything else is the result of a cause, God is his own cause and does not depend on anything outside himself. Implications of this doctrine of God include that he is unchangeable (immutable) and without emotions (impassible). This understanding of God attempts to preserve much that is true about the portrait of God in the Bible. He is the creator of the universe and of humankind; he is not dependent on anything else for his own existence. His relationship with his creatures will not transform God in any kind of unpredictable way. God will not let his emotions "get away from him," causing him to act in some kind of arbitrary manner.

On the other hand, these doctrines can come up against the biblical picture of God as a person in relationship. It is interesting that the Bible never presents God in the abstract but always in relationship. Not only are the descriptions of God's involvement with humans an indication that he is a relational being, but also the metaphors that pervade the Bible are inherently relational (that is, you cannot have a King without subjects, a Shepherd without sheep, a Father without children). If, in some way, God does not need relationship, he certainly desires relationship. After all, God did create the cosmos. And when humans sin, he passionately pursues restoration with them.

Eliphaz and the defenders of the aseity of God, then, are right that in a fundamental way God is independent of his creation. He did not need to create it. But, for reasons beyond our knowing, he chose to create the world and to pursue relationship. The righteous do not benefit God in the sense that they make God better in some sense, but he delights in righteousness and cares for those who pursue it (Pss. 1:6; 7:9; 11:7; 34:6; 37:17; etc.).

Indeed, we know from the prologue that God cares specifically for Job, that he wants Job to maintain his righteousness in the face of the accuser's challenge. God has his own reputation riding on it. Indeed, at the end, after confronting Job, God again rewards Job's righteousness.

2. Job's Seventh Response (23:1–24:25)

Translation

23:1And Job answered and said:
2"Today, also my complaint is bitter.[1]
My hand[2] is heavy with[3] my groaning.
3Oh, that I might know where to find him,
that I might come to his place.
4I would present my case to him;
I would fill my mouth with reproofs.
5I would then learn the words by which he would answer me.
I would come to understand what he would say to me.
6Would he present his case to me with great power?
No, he would certainly heed me.[4]
7There a virtuous person could reprove him,
and I would escape forever from my judge.

8If I go east, he is not there;
I do not perceive him in the west.

1. Or perhaps "rebellious," a possible meaning of Hebrew *mar*.

2. With the MT. Some emend "my hand" to "his hand" (NRSV) and understand that Job's groaning is a result of God's heavy hand on him, but there is no textual evidence for such an emendation, and though slightly odd, the idea that Job's hand is heavy with groaning is understandable. That is, his actions are accompanied by groans.

3. Or perhaps "on"; that is, he is trying (unsuccessfully) to repress his groans. See NLT.

4. The verb *yāśim* is from *śîm* and means "to set." The above translation follows the suggestion that this is shorthand for "he will set his heart [*libbô*] on me." See Clines (*Job 21–37*, 576) for this and other suggestions.

9When he acts in the north, I do not catch a glimpse of him.
When he wraps himself up in the south, I do not see him.[5]
10But he knows my way.
If he tests me, I will come out like gold.

11My foot has held fast to his steps.
I have kept to his path and not turned aside.
12I have not departed from the commandment of his lips.
I have stored up in[6] my bosom the speeches of his mouth.

13He is unique, and who can turn him back?
He does whatever he wants.
14He will complete whatever he designates for me.
Many such things may be in his mind.
15Thus I am terrified of his presence.
When I reflect, I am in dread of him.
16God makes my heart timid;
Shaddai terrifies me.
17Yet I am not silenced by the darkness,
though deep darkness covers my face.

24:1Why are times[7] not kept by Shaddai?
Why do those who know him not see his days?
2They move[8] boundaries;
they steal flocks and pasture them.
3They drive away the donkey of the orphan;
they take away the ox of the widow as a pledge.
4They push the needy off the path.
The poor of the earth hide themselves all together.
5Like[9] wild donkeys in the wilderness,
they go out to their work,
looking for prey in the steppe,
food for their young.
6They reap in a field not their own;[10]
they glean[11] in the vineyard of the wicked.

5. The direction words in vv. 8–9 are "before," "behind," "left," and "right," but these are also used for east, west, north, and south.

6. With the LXX, Vulgate, and a few Hebrew MSS; Codex Leningradensis has "from my bosom," which does not fit the context well.

7. More specifically, the "right" or "proper time" (*ʿēt*), most likely a reference to times of judgment.

8. *Śûg* is a by-form of the more frequently attested *sûg*.

9. While the comparative particle does not begin the sentence, the context suggests that an analogy is drawn between the wild donkeys and the poor of the previous verse.

10. Understanding MT *bĕlîlô* ("his fodder") as two words, *bĕlî lô* ("not his").

11. *Lqš* is a hapax legomenon, presumably related to the noun *leqeš* ("late grass"), which in turn is related to Arabic *laqasa* ("to be late") according to M. D. Futato (*NIDOTTE* 2:819–20), though Clines (*Job 21–37*, 584) treats it as a form related to the more common word for glean, *lqṭ*.

7Naked, they spend the night unclothed,
and no covering in the cold.
8They are sopped by mountain storms;
they hug the cliff because they have no shelter.
9They steal the orphan from the breast;
they take the infant[12] of the poor as a pledge.
10Naked, they wander about unclothed;
famished, they carry sheaves.
11Between their terraces they press out olive oil.
They tread the wine vats, but are still thirsty.
12From the city, the dying groan;
the living dead[13] cry out for help.
God does not react to their prayers.[14]
13They are those who rebel against the light;
they do not recognize their path
and do not stay in their trail.
14At the light[15] the murderers rise up
and slay the poor and needy.
At night they are like the thief.
15The eye of the adulterer watches for the dusk, saying:
'No eye will espy me,'
and he hides his face.
16They break into houses in the darkness.
They seal themselves up during the day;
they do not know the light.
17For deep darkness is morning for all of them together,
for they recognize the terrors of deep darkness.

18They are quick on the face of the waters.
Their portion is cursed on the earth,
and no one turns toward their vineyards.
19The desert and heat steal away the snow waters,
and Sheol, those who sin.
20The womb forgets them;
the maggot thinks them sweet.
They are not again remembered;
injustice is broken like a tree.

12. Emending MT *ʿāl* ("over") to *ʿûl* ("infant"), which works much better in the context.

13. "Living dead" is a translation of *nepeš-ḥălālîm*, which could alternately mean "the throat of the wounded/pierced/slain."

14. Emending MT *tiplâ* ("wrongdoing") to *tĕpîllâ* ("prayer") with the Syriac and two Hebrew MSS.

15. A number of commentators have difficulty with this (most natural) rendering of *lāʾôr* and so either emend to *lôʾ ʾôr* ("not light") or, like Smick ("Job," 811), take it as an example of a separative use of *lamed*. However, the emendation has no support and the separative *lamed* does not have strong evidence. It is best to see this as a statement of the boldness of the wicked and the statements about how the wicked avoid the light (vv. 16–17) in a more metaphorical sense.

[21]They associate[16] with barren women, who do not give birth.[17]
It is not favorable for the widow.
[22]He drags away the mighty by his power.
They rise up but they have no confidence in life.
[23]He gives them security that they can lean on,
but his eyes are on their paths.
[24]They are exalted for a moment but then are no more.
They give in and, like all,[18] are drawn together.
And they wither like an ear of grain.
[25]If it is not so, who will prove I am a liar
and show there is nothing to what I say?"

Interpretation

Job's response to Eliphaz takes the form of an expression of desire to encounter God and deal with him directly. After stating the depth of his depression over the matter, he then articulates his wish to find and talk with God (vv. 2–5). His speech is filled with conflicting emotions and thoughts. In vv. 6–7, for instance, he believes that God would receive his admonitions well and not bully him. As he thinks about it more and recognizes his inability thus far to find God, his attitude takes a turn for the worse. He says he cannot find God anywhere, but if God chooses to find him, then he will set God straight (vv. 8–10). The idea of meeting with God terrifies him (vv. 13–16), though he also believes that his obedience has been stellar (vv. 11–12). In spite of his fear, he ends with determination even in the light of the danger (v. 17). This speech thus fits in with other times when Job wrestles with his desire to meet with God (9:11–24, 32–35; 16:19–22; 19:23–27; 31:35–37). He believes that this is the only way he has to go forward. At times he thinks it will be helpful, and at other times he reveals a more resigned attitude that such a meeting will be fruitless.

In chap. 24 Job continues with a long (vv. 1–17) diatribe on the wicked with an emphasis on their abuse of the poor and needy. It begins (v. 1) with a probing question concerning God's apparent unwillingness to set a time for judgment of these horrible people. Whether vv. 18–25 belong in the mouth of Job is much debated; if so, what is their status? The content of these verses asserts

16. Some (Clines, *Job 21–37*, 656–57) emend to a form of *r*ʿʿ ("to harm") to achieve the meaning that the wicked abuse barren women, but the Hebrew has a form of *rʿh* II ("to associate with") and thus is commenting on the punishment of the wicked, who end up with a woman who cannot give them progeny.

17. The redundancy of saying that a "barren woman" does "not give birth" causes some commentators to emend or find alternate philological explanations of the colon (see Clines, *Job 21–37*, 657), but the repetition emphasizes that the wicked end up with barren women.

18. On the basis of the LXX (*hōsper molochē*), some emend *kakkōl* to *kĕmallûaḥ*, "like a mallow" (see NRSV).

the eventual punishment that will come on the wicked. On the one hand, these verses follow nicely from the first part of the chapter, which, as we have just seen, is a description of the atrocities of the wicked. Yet the belief that the wicked will eventually meet their fate seems odd on the lips of Job, who has been resisting the argument of the friends that God is just in his dealings with human beings. For this reason, some scholars have argued that these verses do not represent Job's own viewpoint. Perhaps he is quoting the argument of the three friends here[19] or speaking sarcastically. Or, and this seems the more common solution, this passage is really one of the friends' speeches, and a rubric that changes speaker has fallen out.[20] After all, Bildad's speech in the second cycle is very short. The problem with these solutions is that there are no textual indications that these verses are any other than Job's. For that reason, I will treat this section as a continuation of Job's speech. As Long points out, Job is not "an enemy of retributive justice, just its misapplication!"[21] Thus in this section Job could be anticipating the fall of the wicked or perhaps expressing a wish that it be so.[22]

---

[1]And Job answered and said:
[2]"Today, also my complaint is bitter.
    My hand is heavy with my groaning.
[3]Oh, that I might know where to find him,
    that I might come to his place.
[4]I would present my case to him;
    I would fill my mouth with reproofs.
[5]I would then learn the words by which he would answer me.
    I would come to understand what he would say to me.
[6]Would he present his case to me with great power?
    No, he would certainly heed me.
[7]There a virtuous person could reprove him,
    and I would escape forever from my judge."

23:1–7. *Job begins his bitter complaint.* Often Job and the friends begin a speech with an insult or two directed at their opponents. Job forgoes that here and starts with a statement about his own mental state. He is deeply depressed, evidenced by his frequent and heavy groaning. Thus his complaint toward God and his friends is bitter. Rather than leading to resignation, though, his mental state motivates his desire to come into God's presence. He wants to find God (v. 3) with the purpose of setting him straight (v. 4). Behind his words stands

19. The view of Gordis, *God and Man*, 169–80. The RSV adds "you say" before v. 18, but this has been removed in the NRSV.

20. This is the view of Zerafa (*Wisdom of God*, 19–29) as well as Pope (*Job*, xx, 195–96).

21. Long, "Coherence."

22. This is also the view of Smick ("Job," 808–9). In addition, he asserts a close connection between the two parts of Job 24 by arguing that the final verse is an inclusio with v. 1.

the belief that if he could just find God, he could set God straight (reprove him, v. 4). The language continues to be legal, thus suggesting a courtroom setting.[23] He wants to set his case before God. Presumably, this means that he wants to argue for his innocence and that he does not deserve the suffering that he presently experiences.

He wonders how God will react to the presentation of his case. His initial belief is that God would not treat him harshly but would allow, perhaps even welcome, the arguments of a "virtuous" man (v. 7). He even believes that this would alleviate his problems ("I would escape forever from my judge") if only he gets the opportunity. This optimistic assessment will change in the second part of his speech. It is also interesting to hear Job's words in the light of his later encounter with God in 38:1–42:6, where he does not get the opportunity to reprove God but rather spends the entire time being reproved by God.

8"If I go east, he is not there;
I do not perceive him in the west.
9When he acts in the north, I do not catch a glimpse of him.
When he wraps himself up in the south, I do not see him.
10But he knows my way.
If he tests me, I will come out like gold."

23:8–10. *Job cannot find God*. Though Job desires to find God, so far he has been unsuccessful in his search. Verses 8–9 list the four directions and conclude that God is not found anywhere. The impression is that Job has looked far and wide, everywhere he can think of, but has come up empty. His hope is not to find God but for God to find him. While he does not know where to find God, he realizes that God can find him because "he knows my way." Job is confident, at least in this speech at this time, that if God tests him, he will come out fine.

Job's sentiment here is similar to that of the psalmist in Ps. 139. The psalmist is confident that God knows his ways (vv. 4–6). He is a person beset by the wicked, and it is not a difficult assumption to think that he suffers because of them. After all, he asks God to kill them (v. 19). Interestingly, like Job, he asks God to test him and see if there is any wickedness in him (vv. 23–24). He is confident that God will find no such evil in his heart.

11"My foot has held fast to his steps.
I have kept to his path and not turned aside.
12I have not departed from the commandment of his lips.
I have stored up in my bosom the speeches of his mouth."

23. He would present his case (*mišpāṭ*, v. 4) before God. In v. 6 he wonders whether God would present his case (from *rîb*) before him harshly. In v. 7 he addresses God as "my judge" (*miššōpṭî*).

23:11–12. *I am innocent*. Job remains confident in his virtue in spite of his suffering and his inability to come into the presence of God in order to dispute with him. The language of v. 11 is typical of wisdom literature. Proverbs speaks of the wise person who keeps to God's path (*derek*) as a way of indicating a person's obedience.[24] The "path" represents one's life journey, and there are two paths according to wisdom literature: the wise, godly path and the foolish, ungodly path. In Proverbs the father admonishes his son to stay on the wise path and to avoid the foolish one. The path of wisdom, though, is supposed to lead to life, while the path of folly leads to death. Job's experience seems the opposite.

Wisdom is closely related to law in that both concern the delineation of God's will for people. Of course, with Job (on the story level at least) we are probably not thinking of the Mosaic law per se. The setting of the book seems pre-Mosaic (see "Authorship and Date" in the introduction), but this does not mean that people before that time did not know of certain divine requirements that could be called law or some associated term.[25] In v. 12 the reference to God's "commandment" (*miṣwâ*) and the "speeches of his mouth" (*'imrê-pîw*) refer to divine requirements, and Job expresses his conformity with the divine will, again emphasizing his piety.

13"He is unique, and who can turn him back?
He does whatever he wants.
14He will complete whatever he designates for me.
Many such things may be in his mind.
15Thus I am terrified of his presence.
When I reflect, I am in dread of him.
16God makes my heart timid;
Shaddai terrifies me.
17Yet I am not silenced by the darkness,
though deep darkness covers my face."

23:13–17. *God does what he wants*. However, after further consideration, Job's optimism concerning a potential and hoped-for audience with God dissipates. He remembers that there is none like God ("he is unique"), implying that he makes and lives by his own rules. No one can tell him what to do, not Job or anyone. Whatever he determines concerning Job's fate is a done deal (v. 14). Job imagines that there may be ideas in God's mind of which he is not even yet aware. Thus again (21:6) Job expresses his terror of God. After all, God can do whatever he wants to Job, and there is no one to turn him back, no mediator (16:21) or umpire (9:33). Job's terror or dread is not the same as the

24. For more on the "two-path theology" of Proverbs, see Longman, *Proverbs*, 151–55.

25. Note, for instance, the comment that Abraham "obeyed my voice and kept my charge, my commandments, my statutes, and my laws" (Gen. 26:5 NRSV). Of course, this language may reflect a later redactor.

"fear" of God that wisdom literature promotes (see Prov. 1:7; Job 28:28; among many other places). Both emotions recognize that God is all-powerful and in control of the cosmos. Both those who are terrified and those who fear God realize that they are no match for the creator of the universe. The difference between those who dread God and those who fear him comes down to how one responds. Those who dread God will run away; not so those who fear him.

Even so, Job has no recourse. Though he is depressed and frightened (v. 17b), he will not turn back in his attempt to encounter God and set him straight (v. 17a). He will not be silenced by his terror of God.

1"Why are times not kept by Shaddai?
  Why do those who know him not see his days?
2They move boundaries;
  they steal flocks and pasture them.
3They drive away the donkey of the orphan;
  they take away the ox of the widow as a pledge.
4They push the needy off the path.
  The poor of the earth hide themselves all together.
5Like wild donkeys in the wilderness,
  they go out to their work,
looking for prey in the steppe,
  food for their young.
6They reap in a field not their own;
  they glean in the vineyard of the wicked.
7Naked, they spend the night unclothed,
  and no covering in the cold.
8They are sopped by mountain storms;
  they hug the cliff because they have no shelter.
9They steal the orphan from the breast;
  they take the infant of the poor as a pledge.
10Naked, they wander about unclothed;
  famished, they carry sheaves.
11Between their terraces they press out olive oil.
  They tread the wine vats, but are still thirsty.
12From the city, the dying groan;
  the living dead cry out for help.
  God does not react to their prayers.
13They are those who rebel against the light;
  they do not recognize their path
  and do not stay in their trail.
14At the light the murderers rise up
  and slay the poor and needy.
  At night they are like the thief.
15The eye of the adulterer watches for the dusk, saying:
  'No eye will espy me,'
  and he hides his face.

[16]They break into houses in the darkness.
They seal themselves up during the day;
they do not know the light.
[17]For deep darkness is morning for all of them together,
for they recognize the terrors of deep darkness."

24:1–17. *The wicked oppress the vulnerable.* Job begins with a question concerning God's ways in the world, a question probably addressed to the friends and attacking their idea of proper divine retribution in the world. The "times" (*ʿittîm*) refer to the proper time for everything (Eccles. 3:1–8), and in this case in particular the proper time for appropriate retribution. Such is the theology of wisdom that there is a right time for every speech and every action. The wise know the right time, and God, being Wisdom himself, should keep the proper times.

However, that the wicked get away with their crimes implies that God has not kept the "times" of judgment. Thus Job launches into a long list of the crimes of the wicked. It begins with the idea that they steal the land of others by moving the boundaries of their property (v. 2a), probably a reference to physically moving boundary markers, which were used throughout the ancient Near East to define the extent of people's property (in Babylon, e.g., the *kudurru* stones).[26] They steal not only land but also flocks (v. 2b).

Worse yet, their theft is directed not only toward the rich but also toward the disadvantaged. As pointed out earlier (see, e.g., my comments on 22:4–9), orphans and widows are among the most vulnerable members of ancient Near Eastern society, having no patriarch to care for them. Thus biblical law protects them from exploitation (Exod. 22:22). That the wicked would dispossess the orphan and the widow of their property is particularly heinous. As for taking a pledge, the Deuteronomic law is especially concerned to avoid such oppression of the socially vulnerable (Deut. 24:6, 10–13, 17).

Next to the orphan and the widow, the poor and needy (v. 4) are the epitome of vulnerability. After mentioning the abuse that the poor and needy feel at the hands of the wicked, Job goes into a long and pitiable description of their desperation (vv. 5–8), to be followed by another statement of oppression by the wicked (v. 9) and then another description of the suffering of the oppressed (vv. 10–12).[27] The depiction of the oppression of the poor and needy begins with the picture of the wicked pushing them off the path. The "path" here probably symbolizes their life journey, moving in a positive direction, but they are pushed off their goal by the wicked, who want to take advantage of them. The picture reminds one of the Egyptian "Tale of the Eloquent Peasant."[28] The peasant,

26. *Kudurru* stones were boundary markers that identified the landowner.

27. See Wilson, *Job*, 269.

28. See N. Shupak, trans., *COS* 1:98–104; and "Ancient Near Eastern Background" in the introduction.

Khu-n-Anup, went to get some barley, and on the way back he encountered an upper-class Egyptian named Nemty-nakht, who blocked his way so that the peasant's donkey went off the path and ate a wisp of barley from the nobleman's field, for which Nemty-nakht took all the peasant's possessions.[29]

Subject to such injustices, the poor seek to hide themselves from the wicked in order to avoid ill-treatment. At this point, Job goes off on an excursus to describe the horrible conditions of the poor and needy. At first he describes them as wild donkeys in the wilderness, an area with subsistence-level resources. The work of these donkeys (the poor and needy) is to do their best to forage for food for their children. Wild donkeys are ragged and desperate. Verse 6 speaks of the poor and needy finding food in fields/vineyards that are not their own. The Torah has a law allowing for this (Lev. 19:9–10; 23:22), and Ruth embodies such a practice. Boaz's special instructions for the protection and provision of Ruth (Ruth 2:8–9) suggest that typically the poor and needy suffered abuse and deprivation in trying to provide for themselves and their families in this way.

They are deprived not only of food but also of suitable clothing. They thus freeze at night (v. 7). Verse 8 describes the poor and needy as bereft of shelter as well; thus, when violent mountain storms hit, the best they can do is "hug the cliff" with the hope that the rain will not hit them directly.

Job now comes back and speaks of the horrible acts of the wicked in v. 9. Worse than taking the animals of the disadvantaged (v. 3), they even take an orphan from the breast. One wants to ask, if the infant is orphaned how is it at the breast? But perhaps the idea is that the wicked steal the child and kill the mother and father. Maybe the "orphan" here is one who has lost father but not mother. Or perhaps the statement is merely trying to portray the worst situation possible. Verse 9b shows just how unfeeling the wicked are as they take an infant from a poor family as a pledge for what is most likely an advance that will allow the family merely to survive.

Verses 10–12 return to a description of the oppressed. Again, they are pictured as naked (see also v. 7). That they are famished but carrying sheaves may again depict the poor as gleaning the fields of others (v. 6). Verse 11 says that they are laboring hard at pressing out olive oil and treading the wine vats but are apparently not sharing in the products they are producing, since they are still thirsty. Verse 12 may be the most disturbing part of the description of the poor. They are "dying," the "living dead." They groan and cry for help, but God turns a deaf ear to them, according to Job. Job likely identifies with these people. His suffering is severe. He has cried to God, desiring a meeting with him but encountering only silence from heaven (23:8–9).

Verses 13–17 return again to a description of the wicked. The righteous wise are those who stay in the light and stay on the straight path (v. 13). The

29. The tale goes on and presents the peasant's eloquent speech before a magistrate concerning the injustice done to him.

wicked, though, rebel against the light and get off the path so they can work their wicked deeds that are described in the next few verses. It begins with murder, which they are bold and confident enough to do in the daylight ("at the light," v. 14). After all, their prey is the poor and needy, and who will care about them? Also at night they commit crimes (v. 14c specifies theft). The book of the covenant considers nighttime theft more heinous than daytime theft (Exod. 22:2) and allows the victim to kill the intruder at night. The idea seems to be that nighttime theft threatens the inhabitants of a house and shows disregard for life, since it is likely that they would be home and asleep.

Besides murder and theft, Job describes the wicked as those who get away with adultery as well. Proverbs 7 also depicts a man who steals through the darkness of the evening toward the house of a promiscuous woman (Prov. 7:6–9). There, however, the father warns of the horrible consequences that will result from such actions. Job implies that the adulterer gets away with it.

While above (v. 14) Job says murderers brazenly commit their crimes during the day, here he points out that evil people are creatures of the night (vv. 16–17). They do evil during the night, and they hide themselves during the light of day. They do not know the light, but are on friendly terms with (recognize) the darkness. They feel comfortable when their acts are hidden from eyes.

> **18**"They are quick on the face of the waters.
> Their portion is cursed on the earth,
> and no one turns toward their vineyards.
> **19**The desert and heat steal away the snow waters,
> and Sheol, those who sin.
> **20**The womb forgets them;
> the maggot thinks them sweet.
> They are not again remembered;
> injustice is broken like a tree.
> **21**They associate with barren women, who do not give birth.
> It is not favorable for the widow.
> **22**He drags away the mighty by his power.
> They rise up but they have no confidence in life.
> **23**He gives them security that they can lean on,
> but his eyes are on their paths.
> **24**They are exalted for a moment but then are no more.
> They give in and, like all, are drawn together.
> And they wither like an ear of grain.
> **25**If it is not so, who will prove I am a liar
> and show there is nothing to what I say?"

24:18–25. *The fate of the wicked.* Chapter 24 ends on a totally different note from how it began. After castigating the wickedness of evil people and how they get away with their oppression of the weak, Job moves to a blistering description of the horrible fate that awaits such sinners. In the overview preceding the translation of chaps. 23–24, I discussed the long-debated question of who actually speaks these words, considering Job's argument up to this moment. On the ground that Job is against not the retribution principle in general but only its misapplication to him, I concluded that we should take this passage as part of Job's speech rather than reassign it to one of the friends. In short, after describing the evil actions of evil people in 24:1–17, he expresses either the certainty or the hope that a bad fate will come to them.[30]

The wicked are described as having a short and cursed life on earth. They are "quick on the face of the waters" (v. 18a), like scum or some light object that is quickly flushed away. Their lot or portion is cursed on earth, with the result that no one wants to have anything to do with them (v. 18c). Verse 19 compares the way the heat of the desert sucks moisture out of things, including the cool waters produced by melting snow, to how Sheol, standing at least for the grave if not the underworld, will seize the wicked. While the source of their life (the womb) forgets them, the maggots of the grave, rather than their mothers, will think them sweet. Their injustice (or perhaps this should be translated as "the unjust") will be broken as a tree is broken. The simile may envision the wicked as (wrongly) living like a thriving tree that is then shattered by lightning or a windstorm (Ps. 29:5–6). Ezekiel 17:24 is an example of the destruction of a tree standing for divine judgment.

While Job has talked about the unfair fruitfulness of the wicked, having large families (21:8, 11), here we learn that their wives are barren, a situation that is not favorable at the death of the husband, leaving her a defenseless widow. Verses 22–23 start speaking of an agent ("he") who does bad things to the wicked. This "he" must be God, and the NRSV translates as such. Again, whereas elsewhere Job has made clear that he believes that God is totally uninvolved in the judgment of the wicked, here we see him active. God drags the mighty away and cuts them down when they try to rise up in confidence. He even plays with their minds, giving them something to lean on and then cutting them down to size (vv. 23–24). This idea of the illusory and short-lived prosperity of the wicked is very much in keeping with the thought of the friends.[31] The speech concludes with a challenge to try to prove the speaker wrong.

Theological Implications

Putting God on Trial

Legal expressions are occasionally used throughout the book of Job. In the prologue, Job is on trial. The accuser has made an accusation that Job

30. A view shared by Andersen (*Job*, 213–14) among others.

31. For instance, see Bildad in Job 18 and Zophar in Job 20. See also the theological implications sections following both of these chapters.

will not maintain his integrity if God does not reward him. However, as Job suffers without knowing why, he expresses a strong desire to meet God in the courtroom. The ambivalence he expresses concerns whether he can successfully bring God to court. He has no doubt about the strength of his case, just whether the all-powerful God of the universe will listen to him. In chap. 23 Job expresses conflicted emotions about this, sometimes believing God will listen to him and set matters straight and sometimes seriously doubting it. Such thoughts will continue to the bitter end of Job's speech, as we can see with some of his concluding words in 31:35–37.

What does the book of Job teach us about putting God on trial? Can it be successful? Is it a good idea? Is the book of Job inviting God's people to put God on trial if they have doubts or questions about him? As we answer this question, we need to be mindful of the lament psalms. In the lament psalms, the composer does not hesitate to say some hard-hitting things to God. As one of many possible illustrations, Ps. 10:1–2a (NRSV) asks God:

> Why, O Lord, do you stand far off?
>   Why do you hide yourself in times of trouble?
> In arrogance the wicked persecute the poor.

The psalmist does not hesitate to challenge God's apparent lack of concern for the way God seems to ignore the plight of the poor.

However, Job's attempt to put God on trial ends badly in that God never gives him the opportunity to do so. When God finally appears to Job, he challenges Job with questions, in essence putting Job on trial and reducing him to repentance. There is apparently a difference between putting God on trial and challenging him as the psalmists do in the lament psalms. The latter takes place within the context of worship, the setting of all the psalms. The psalmists approach God with the confidence that he is able to answer their complaints, while Job does not have the same level of hope.

Those Who Oppress the Vulnerable (24:1–17)

Until he suffered, Job was a firm believer in divine retribution. God maintained moral order in the universe by rewarding the righteous and punishing the wicked. Now that he has suffered, knowing that he is innocent, his eyes are opened to the fact that the wicked appear to have the upper hand; they oppress the poor and vulnerable and get away with it.

Oppression, the exploitation of the weak by the strong, is presented in the Bible as a consequence of sin. Indeed, oppression is a result of sin, as is communicated by God's words of judgment on Eve: "Yet your desire shall be for your husband, and he shall rule over you" (Gen. 3:16b NRSV). The NLT brings out the nuance of the Hebrew word translated "desire" here (*tĕšûqâ*), making clear that the attempt to oppress works both ways: "And you will desire to control your husband, but he will rule over you."

Israel experienced horrible oppression from Egypt when they were enslaved to build the store cities at Pithom and Rameses (Exod. 1:1–14). This experience left a profound impression on the Israelites and made them turn toward God, who through miraculous means delivered them from this horror. On the basis of their own experience of oppression in Egypt, God commanded them not to oppress others weaker than themselves (Exod. 22:21; 23:9; Deut. 23:16). God assured them that as long as they pursued his law, including taking care of the vulnerable, he would spare them from oppression (note, e.g., 1 Chron. 16:21; 17:9; and how the Psalms extol God as a refuge for the oppressed: Ps. 9:9; see also 10:18; 82:3). On the other hand, if they rebelled against him and his law, then he would punish them with oppression (Deut. 28:29; Isa. 3:5, 12; and see the cycle of oppression by foreign leaders in response to the sin of the people in the book of Judges).

The book of Proverbs joins in the chorus with the law to warn against oppression. Proverbs 14:31, for instance, states: "Those who oppress the poor insult their Maker, but those who show grace to the destitute honor him." Here we see that to oppress the poor is to attack not just them but also God, who made them. On the positive side, to honor the poor is to honor God. Proverbs 22:16 contributes to this theme by pointing out that those who oppress the poor to grow rich from them ("in order to multiply") and those who give (probably bribes) to the wealthy will not gain but lack wealth: "Those who oppress the poor in order to multiply and those who give to the wealthy—will certainly lack" (see also 28:3).

In spite of these warnings from the law and the wisdom literature, and in spite of their own experience of oppression, Israel often took advantage of those in their own society who were weak. They thus brought down the rage of the prophets, who spoke God's judgment against them. In his famous Temple Sermon, for instance, Jeremiah blasted the people for "exploiting foreigners, orphans, and widows" (7:6 NLT) along with numerous other offenses (see also Ezek. 22:29; Amos 4:1; Zech. 7:10; Mal. 3:5). Qohelet observed the injustice and oppression that was rampant in society and concluded that "everything is meaningless" (Eccles. 12:8; see, for instance, 4:1–3).

While Job sees the wicked getting away with their crimes, the three friends believe that Job himself is a wicked oppressor and is getting away with it. They falsely charge him for exploiting the vulnerable, but Job himself will deny that he is an oppressor in his final "protest of innocence" (see especially 31:16–23). While the story of Job absolves him of the false charges of oppression, those in power often do abuse those in their charge. In this life, wicked oppressors often escape punishment. Jesus himself came to help the oppressed against their powerful oppressors, as he himself announced by citing Isa. 61:1–2 (LXX):

> The Spirit of the Lord is upon me,
> for he has anointed me to bring Good News to the poor.
> He has sent me to proclaim that captives will be released,
> that the blind will see,
> that the oppressed will be set free,
> and that the time of the Lord's favor has come. (Luke 4:18–19 NLT)

This freedom from oppression does not come immediately or easily. Jesus says that at the end of time he will "separate the people as a shepherd separates the sheep from the goats. He will place the sheep at his right hand and the goats at his left" (Matt. 25:32b–33 NLT). Among the goats will be the oppressive wicked, whom Job observes thriving in this life. In the meantime, Jesus's followers are to feed and clothe a needy stranger (Matt. 25:34–46).

3. Bildad's Third Speech (25:1–6)

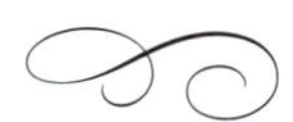

Translation

[1]And Bildad the Shuhite answered and said:
[2]"Rule and dread are with him;
  he makes peace in his exalted place.
[3]Are there no number to his troops?
  Upon whom does not his light rise?
[4]What mortal is righteous before God?
  Who born of woman is pure?
[5]If even the moon is not bright,[1]
  and the stars not pure in his eyes,
[6]even so mortals are maggots,
  and a human being is a worm."

Interpretation

25:1–6. *God's power and righteousness*. Bildad, in a speech that Fyall characterizes as a "sour tirade,"[2] makes a final, feeble attempt to convince Job.

1. The verb *ʾāhal* typically means to "pitch a tent," but this meaning does not work in the context. Some have posited *ʾhl* II ("to be bright") based on context (BDB 14b; *HALOT* 1:19a), but it is better to recognize it as a form of the verb *hll* (a by-form, or perhaps the *aleph* is added by error). So Clines (*Job 21–37*, 621) and Smick ("Job," 964).

2. Fyall, *Now My Eyes*, 60.

The brevity of his response shows that the friends are running out of steam against Job. They have not convinced him, and they are giving up.

Bildad's argument here has two parts, though these parts are connected. He argues for the power and majesty of God and God's exclusive purity (see Eliphaz's similar comments in 4:17–21; 15:14–16; as well as Job in 9:2–3; 14:1–4). Verses 2–3 assert that God is uniquely powerful. He is the ultimate ruler, who establishes peace because of his power and numberless troops (presumably a reference to his heavenly army). He is sovereign over all, so that his light ("the sun") rises on all creatures. Verses 4–6 then speak of his moral uniqueness, especially in comparison to humans. No one can be pure before God. Indeed, human beings are totally corrupted. They are like the lowly worm (see similar use of imagery in Ps. 22:6 and Isa. 41:14) that burrows in the dirt and the maggot that consumes dead bodies. Bildad gives an argument from the stronger to the weaker. He says that even if heavenly bodies like the moon and the stars are not bright or pure to God, how much less so are mortals, those earth-dwelling creatures. While we can understand Bildad's argument on one level, we must also remember that the account of creation in Gen. 1 highlights the importance of humans by depicting their creation on the final day, after the rest of the creation (including the sun, moon, and stars) are put in their place, providing a setting for the most exalted of all creatures.

Like many of the friends' arguments, Bildad here is correct in principle, but horribly wrong in applying the principle to Job. Yes, God is all-powerful. Human righteousness also pales before the glory of God. However, we know from the prologue that God is not punishing Job because of any lack or fault on his part. Thus Bildad's point misses its mark and does not help Job.

Theological Implications

Maggot Theology (25:6)

In his attempt to puncture what he perceives as Job's self-righteousness, Bildad argues that humans are maggots, even worms. He hopes that Job will apply this general truth to himself and recognize that he is not in a position to challenge God.

By comparing humans to maggots and worms, Bildad is emphasizing that humans are corrupting and corrupted. Maggots and worms spoil the things that they consume, whether the manna in the wilderness (Exod. 16:20, 24) or dead bodies (Isa. 14:11). Their association with the grave and with dead bodies also highlights the fragility and temporariness of life.

Is Bildad's maggot theology correct in general and in its application to Job? Indeed, if it is not applicable to Job, then it is not applicable to humans as a whole. If the Bible is clear about anything, it is clear that humans were not created as worms or maggots. Genesis 1–2 emphasizes the dignity of humans in the way it depicts their creation on the last day, after everything else has been set in place. That Adam was created from the dust of the ground and the breath of God, while acknowledging his creaturely status, also indicates a special and dignified relationship to God. Most important, of course, is that humans are created in the image of God. In other words, they reflect the divine glory like the moon reflects the light of the sun.

If the Bible is clear about anything, however, it is that humans have marred their dignified status by their rebellion against God. The harmony that Adam and Eve enjoyed with God, each other, and creation was lost through their sin. In other words, humans, through their willful acts, can reduce themselves to maggot-like status. In Isa. 41:14 God calls sinful Israel "you worm." But note that God also presents himself as the redeemer of worm-like Israel. After he finishes with them, they "shall rejoice in the LORD; in the Holy One of Israel you shall glory" (Isa. 41:16 NRSV). The point is that sin does not completely efface the dignity of our creation in the divine image. Humans still reflect the glory of God. After the fall and after the flood, the reason why murder is treated so sternly is because it involves the killing of someone created in the image of God (Gen. 9:6). The psalmist is moved to reflect on the dignity of humanity by saying:

> You have made them a little lower than God,
> and crowned them with glory and honor.
> You have given them dominion over the works of your hands;
> you have put all things under their feet,
> all sheep and oxen,
> and also the beasts of the field,
> the birds of the air, and the fish of the sea,
> whatever passes along the paths of the seas. (Ps. 8:5–8 NRSV)

Bildad treads on dangerous ground here. Certainly humans can reduce themselves to maggot level, but he claims that all humans by definition are such. Bildad is like those who wrongly revile the psalmist: "But I am a worm, and not human; scorned by others, and despised by the people" (Ps. 22:6 NRSV). But the psalmist rejects their assessment since he knows he has enjoyed a close relationship with God since birth (vv. 8–11). Job, like the psalmist, is wrongly accused of being a maggot. We know from the beginning of the story as well as from its end that Job is indeed undeserving of his suffering.

4.
Job's Eighth Response
(26:1–27:23)

Translation

[26:1]And Job answered and said:
[2]"What help have you been to the powerless?
What rescue have you brought to the weak arm?
[3]What counsel have you brought to those without wisdom?
What abundant success do you teach?
[4]Whose words do you speak,
and whose breath has come from you?
[5]The Rephaim tremble;
the waters and their denizens are terrified.
[6]Sheol lays exposed before him,
and there is no cover for Abaddon.
[7]He stretches out Zaphon over the void,
and hangs the earth over nothingness.
[8]He wraps up water in his clouds,
yet the cloud does not burst under them.
[9]He covers[1] up the full moon.[2]
He spreads[3] his clouds over it.
[10]He has decreed a circle on the surface of the waters,
up to the horizon of light with darkness.

1. As called for by the context, though *ʾāḥaz* normally means "to seize, grasp."

2. Emending to *kese'*. Clines (*Job 21–37*, 622–23) and Konkel ("Job," 164) take it from *kissē'*, "throne."

3. The verb *paršēz* is a strange Hebrew form and has been taken as a mixture of two verbs, *pāraš* (for *pāraś*) and *pāraz* (though attested only in postbiblical Hebrew), both meaning "to spread" (see Clines, *Job 21–37*, 623).

11The pillars of heaven quake,
astounded at his rebuke.
12He stilled the Sea by his power;
by his understanding he struck Rahab.
13With his breath he makes the heavens beautiful.
His hand slays the fleeing serpent.
14These are the fringes of his way.
How faint[4] is the report we hear of him.
Who can comprehend the thunder of his might?"

27:1Job continued his discourse and said:
2"By the living God, who has turned aside my rights,
and by Shaddai, who has made me bitter,
3as long as my breath is in me,
and the spirit of God is in my nostrils,
4my lips will not speak falsehood,
my tongue will not mutter deceit.
5Far be it[5] from me that I should concede that you are right;
up to the point that I expire I will not turn aside my innocence.
6I will embrace and not weaken my grasp on my righteousness;
my heart will not reproach my days.

7May my enemy be like the wicked,
and those who rise up against me be like the guilty.
8For what hope is there for the godless when they are cut off?
For God will require[6] their life.
9Does God hear their cry for help
when distress comes their way?
10Will they delight in Shaddai?
Will they call on God at all times?

11I will instruct you concerning the hand of God.
I will not conceal that which is with Shaddai.
12All of you have seen this;
why have you become so meaningless?
13This is the lot of evil people with God,
the inheritance that the cruel receive from Shaddai.
14If their children multiply, they will come to the sword;
their offspring will not get enough bread.

4. See 4:12 for the use of *šēmeṣ* in the sense of "whisper."

5. "Far be it" is a translation of *ḥālîlâ* II, derived from *ḥll*, "to profane."

6. A difficult verb. It appears to come from a root *šlh*, which normally means "to put at ease," but this does not seem appropriate to the context. Some translations and commentators posit a *šlh* II, which would occur only here and have the meaning "to draw out" or "to take away" (NRSV), but most dictionaries do not recognize such a root. Here, following Clines (*Job 21–37*, 653) and the NAB, I propose a minor emendation to a form of the verb *šʾl*.

15Those who remain will be buried by Death.[7]
Their widows will not even weep.
16Though they pile up silver like dust,
and get clothes like clay,
17they will get them, but the righteous will wear them,
the innocent will distribute the silver among themselves.
18They will build their houses like a moth,
like a booth made by a guard.
19He may lie down wealthy, but never will do so again.
They open their eyes, but it is no more.
20Terrors will overtake them like waters;
a storm will overwhelm them at night.
21The east wind lifts them up and they go;
it sweeps them from their place.
22He[8] throws it at them, and he does not spare them;
from his hand they madly flee.
23He claps[9] his hands at them,
and he whistles at them from his place."

Interpretation

Job begins his next speech by sarcastically characterizing the speeches of his friends. From the very beginning, he has made clear that his friends are unreliable as counselors. They are worse than ineffective; they have actually intensified his problems. They are absolutely no help. Though they claim to come with authority, they really have let him down (vv. 2–4).

After this introduction, Job then speaks about God. Using mythological language, he describes God's power (vv. 5–14). Job has never questioned God's power, only his fairness.

Chapter 27 begins with Job's vigorous reassertion of his innocence. As long as he lives and has breath, he will continue to maintain his innocence (vv. 1–6). After this section, Job's words are surprising, so surprising that some doubt whether these words are rightly attributed to him (for a similar problem, see the discussion of 24:18–25). In vv. 7–10 Job calls an imprecation down on the heads of his enemies. Specifically, he asks, "May my enemy be like the wicked," before launching into a long diatribe about the horrible fate of the wicked (vv. 11–23). The problem is that Job has been asserting that retribution (good things happen to good people, and bad things happen to bad people) does not apply to his situation, which leads him to wonder whether God is just in a broader sense.

7. Or perhaps, as most translations take it, a specific form of death, such as from a plague.
8. Or "It hurls at them" (NRSV), referring to the wind itself.
9. *Śpq* is a by-form of *spq*.

One might be inclined to believe that the text is confused at this point and that we are to reconstruct a final missing speech of Zophar here.[10] To make this work, Clines moves vv. 11–12, since it uses the second-person plural to refer to the addressees of the speech and therefore could not be Zophar speaking to Job but rather Job speaking to all three friends. No matter which side of this debate one takes, it is important to do so loosely. In other words, each side has problems. There is no textual evidence to suggest a textual confusion here. It is thus best to stick with the received MT and explain how Job could speak the content of vv. 7–23.

Job does believe in the retribution principle. He believes that God should reward the righteous and punish the wicked. Otherwise, he would have no grounds for challenging God's justice. He affirms the retribution principle, but he does not believe God is rightly applying it in his particular case, which is why he wants to go and meet God and set him straight. Thus, as he thinks of his enemies—the three friends being a likely object of his ire—he calls down God's punishment on them with an imprecation in vv. 7–10. Indeed, may they be treated like the wicked should be and are expected to be. Then the following long section (vv. 11–23) spells out what that would look like.

---

[1]And Job answered and said:
[2]"What help have you been to the powerless?
  What rescue have you brought to the weak arm?
[3]What counsel have you brought to those without wisdom?
  What abundant success do you teach?
[4]Whose words do you speak,
  and whose breath has come from you?"

26:1–4. *No help at all.* Throughout the debate, Job and his friends have exchanged heated insults and sarcastic barbs (e.g., 8:2; 9:2; 11:2–3, 12; 12:2–3; 15:2–10), and Job does not depart from this practice in this his last speech. He asks them a series of rhetorical questions, blasting them for their unhelpful "advice." Job can identify with the "powerless," the one with a "weak arm." He is weak, but rather than helping him, the friends have only sought to undermine him. Now it is unlikely that Job would identify himself as one "without wisdom," but the friends would have characterized him as such. Although they may have thought they were helping, they were not. They had no resources that would breed success (*tûšîyâ*); thus their teaching was anemic. Finally, he questions the source of their authority. Where are they getting this unhelpful advice? They would claim that it comes from God, but Job challenges that notion.[11]

10. Clines, *Job 21–37*, 651–77. For the view that these are words of Job, see Konkel, "Job," 167–70; Wilson, *Job*, 292–98.

11. Johnson (*Now My Eye Sees You*, 130) goes further and claims that Job implies that he knows his friends are speaking the words of Satan.

[5]"The Rephaim tremble;
the waters and their denizens are terrified.
[6]Sheol lays exposed before him,
and there is no cover for Abaddon.
[7]He stretches out Zaphon over the void,
and hangs the earth over nothingness.
[8]He wraps up water in his clouds,
yet the cloud does not burst under them.
[9]He covers up the full moon.
He spreads his clouds over it.
[10]He has decreed a circle on the surface of the waters,
up to the horizon of light with darkness.
[11]The pillars of heaven quake,
astounded at his rebuke.
[12]He stilled the Sea by his power;
by his understanding he struck Rahab.
[13]With his breath he makes the heavens beautiful.
His hand slays the fleeing serpent.
[14]These are the fringes of his way.
How faint is the report we hear of him.
Who can comprehend the thunder of his might?"

26:5–14. *God's great creative power*. Job now speaks of God's great power in a way that anticipates God's own description of himself in chaps. 38–41. To some, Job's attitude here seems too positive. However, Job has not questioned God's power, but rather his justice and fairness (see his comments on God's power in 9:5–10). Further, Job has not bowed to God's greatness but remains persistent in his questions. He will not repent until the very end (42:1–6).

There is an interesting use of mythological language and concepts in this part of his speech. It begins with a reference to the Rephaim, the departed dead, known not only from elsewhere in the Bible (Prov. 9:18; Isa. 26:14; etc.) but also from Ugaritic texts.[12] The Rephaim were the cause of fear for people, but they themselves are afraid of God, who sets them trembling. Verse 5b says the same for "the waters and their denizens." Although this expression would on one level simply refer to the fish and other creatures who make their home in the seas, rivers, and lakes, in the present context it connotes the forces of chaos, since the waters were often thought to represent those who

12. Johnston, *Shades of Sheol*, 127–30, 134–41. The usual understanding of the Rephaim as "shades" who dwell in the underworld seems correct, particularly in light of the Isaiah passages (14:9; 26:14, 19). In the final analysis, Johnston believes that the Hebrew and Ugaritic use of the term *rĕpā'îm* is different, concluding that the former believe the *rĕpā'îm* are "lifeless and need rousing, they tremble before God, they are not limited to heroes or kings, they are never individually named, they do not travel, participate at banquets or play any role *vis-à-vis* the living as protectors or patrons" (ibid., 142).

are hostile toward God. Verse 6 continues this idea by describing how Sheol[13] and Abaddon,[14] two ways of referring to the grave and the underworld, are exposed to God. His sight penetrates the netherworld, and the implication is that these regions are not separated from his actions. They are not beyond his control. The psalmist also recognizes this: “If I make my bed in Sheol, you are there” (Ps. 139:8b NRSV).

According to Job, God is not only sovereign over the underworld; he is also in charge of the rest of the cosmos. Using creation language (stretches out,[15] hangs), Job talks about how God brought about Zaphon and the earth out of nothing (v. 7). Zaphon is a reference to the mythological mountain where the gods dwell.[16] In a sense, the move from the underworld to Zaphon is a way of saying that God is in control of heaven and earth and everything in between. He did, after all, bring the earth out of nothing, and so he controls everything.

Verses 8–10 then speak of the realm between the earth and the heavens. Here God has placed the clouds, which by divine mandate contain the waters that come to earth in the form of rain. These clouds can be so thick that they even obscure the moon from human sight. He has established the horizon, which separates the earth from the sky.[17]

Verses 11–13 then speak again of the effect of his greatness and power on the cosmos and its inhabitants. The very pillars that separate the earth from the heavens quake when he issues his rebuke.[18] The pillars that hold up the heavens would be seen as extremely formidable, and that God can make them quake indicates the immensity of his power. In v. 12 Job speaks of the Sea as a mythological power, representing hostile powers (see comments on “waters” in v. 5). In ancient Canaan, the Sea (Yam) was a god who assumed the kingship of the pantheon and was resisted by Baal, who defeated and subdued him. The stilling of the Sea shows God’s power over the forces of chaos. Rahab is a mythological creature that inhabits the sea and thus provides a good parallel to Yam (Sea). The reference to God’s defeat of Rahab may hark back to the myth that God defeats the sea monster that represents chaos. For more comments on Rahab, see the discussion at 9:13, where the term first appears in Job (see also “Behemoth and Leviathan: The Power of the Mythic Imagination” following my comments on Job 41).

13. For a full discussion, see Johnston, *Shades of Sheol*, 69–98.

14. Used as a synonym of Sheol and death in its six OT occurrences (Job 26:6; 28:22; 31:12; Ps. 88:11; Prov. 15:11; 27:20), Abaddon comes from the Hebrew word that means “destruction.”

15. This is likely a reference to stretching out a tent: see Ps. 104:2.

16. In Ugaritic literature, Baal lives on Mount Zaphon. The word means “north,” and in Ps. 48 Zion is favorably compared to Zaphon.

17. The “circle on the surface of the waters” implies that the world is flat, a view commonly held until Aristotle. For language similar to this verse, see Prov. 8:27.

18. See Kennedy (“Root *‘r*”) for the argument that “blast” is a better translation than “rebuke.” He claims that the word has “strong connotations of forceful and destructive movement of air accompanied by loud, frightening noise” (ibid., 59).

God makes the heavens beautiful with his powerful breath, perhaps referring to the wind that blows the clouds and dust away in order to reveal the deep blue sky. Job then returns for a final reference to God's power over mythological creatures of chaos. The "fleeing serpent" may be a reference to Leviathan, who in Isa. 27:1 (as well as the Ugaritic text on which Isaiah is dependent)[19] is also called the "fleeing serpent." Leviathan appears by name elsewhere in Job (3:8; 41:1).

Job then ends his description of God's great creative power, which stands over against anti-creation forces represented by various mythological images, by saying that this is just the tip of the iceberg. God's power is ultimately mysterious and far more extensive than Job suggests. We do not hear a full report of his doings; so we have only a partial picture of who he is and his power ("the fringes of his way").

---

[1]Job continued his discourse and said:
[2]"By the living God, who has turned aside my rights,
  and by Shaddai, who has made me bitter,
[3]as long as my breath is in me,
  and the spirit of God is in my nostrils,
[4]my lips will not speak falsehood,
  my tongue will not mutter deceit.
[5]Far be it from me that I should concede that you are right;
  up to the point that I expire I will not turn aside my innocence.
[6]I will embrace and not weaken my grasp on my righteousness;
  my heart will not reproach my days."

27:1–6. *I am innocent!* For the first time the narrator intrudes in the midst of a speech to inform the reader that a speaker continued his speech (see also 29:1 and 36:1, where this type of intrusion also occurs). It is hard to know what to make of this, though it may have been suggested by the first five verses of the chapter, which look like the beginning of a new speech. A further problem is introduced by the fact that 27:7–23 reads like a speech from one of the friends rather than from Job. That said, the speaker uses the second-person plural when referring to his addressees (at least in vv. 7–10), indicating that Job is speaking to his friends.

In vv. 2–6 Job reaffirms his intention to continue to insist on his righteousness in the face of his friends' arguments. Interestingly, he makes his point by an oath in the name of God. As Whybray points out, "To swear by God's life (elsewhere in the Old Testament *Yahweh*'s life) was the most solemn kind of oath possible, bringing severe retribution on a person who swore falsely (cf. Lev. 19.12; Num. 5.20–22)."[20] But even in the midst of his oath, he takes the opportunity

19. Isaiah's dependence on the Ugaritic text is evidenced by his near verbatim quotation of it.
20. Whybray, *Job*, 128.

to express his disappointment and frustration with God. He believes God has denied him his rights, with the result of turning him bitter. He promises to continue his resistance against the friends as long as he is alive (v. 3). The "spirit of God" (*rûaḥ ʾĕlôah*) here should be taken simply as a reference to the breath that God breathed into mortal nostrils (Gen. 2:7;[21] Eccles. 12:7), though "breath" can also refer to s/Spirit (Ps. 104:29–30). To deny his own righteousness would be to lie (Job 27:4). He refuses to lie simply to cater to the opinions of his friends in order to make them go away. We will soon see that Job's persistence rather than his concession is what makes them go away (though it energizes Elihu to get involved). There has been no softening of Job's position. He is as confident as ever of his righteousness and that God is unjust to let him suffer.

7"May my enemy be like the wicked,
and those who rise up against me be like the guilty.
8For what hope is there for the godless when they are cut off?
For God will require their life.
9Does God hear their cry for help
when distress comes their way?
10Will they delight in Shaddai?
Will they call on God at all times?"

27:7–10. *A curse on the enemy*. The next section begins with an imprecation on the speaker's enemy. It calls on God to treat the speaker's enemies as if they are wicked. If the speaker is Zophar or one of the three friends, it is unclear who the enemy is. An imprecation on Job seems superfluous since he is already suffering the fate of the wicked. These are additional reasons to believe that the MT as we have it rightly attributes these words (as well as vv. 8–23, which detail the horrible life of the wicked) to Job.

The godless have no hope once God cuts them off. Their very life is endangered. God turns a deaf ear to their cries for help. After all, they do not bother to call on God when times are good but only when they are bad (v. 10; see Prov. 1:24–28, where Woman Wisdom similarly refuses to listen to the cries of those who had ignored her before their troubles came).

11"I will instruct you concerning the hand of God.
I will not conceal that which is with Shaddai.
12All of you have seen this;
why have you become so meaningless?
13This is the lot of evil people with God,
the inheritance that the cruel receive from Shaddai.
14If their children multiply, they will come to the sword;
their offspring will not get enough bread.

21. Here *nišmat* rather than *rûaḥ* is used.

15Those who remain will be buried by Death.
Their widows will not even weep.
16Though they pile up silver like dust,
and get clothes like clay,
17they will get them, but the righteous will wear them,
the innocent will distribute the silver among themselves.
18They will build their houses like a moth,
like a booth made by a guard.
19He may lie down wealthy, but never will do so again.
They open their eyes, but it is no more.
20Terrors will overtake them like waters;
a storm will overwhelm them at night.
21The east wind lifts them up and they go;
it sweeps them from their place.
22He throws it at them, and he does not spare them;
from his hand they madly flee.
23He claps his hands at them,
and he whistles at them from his place."

27:11–23. *The fate of the wicked.* This section continues the thought of the previous section. The theme remains the "lot of evil people with God" (v. 13a). However, vv. 11–13 provide a momentary lull from his description of the fate of the wicked. In these verses, the speaker takes a jab at his hearers. He says that he will instruct them ("you" plural, indicating that these must be the words of Job directed to the three friends) about the "hand of God," by which he means God's acts in space and time. He will not hold back ("I will not conceal") from describing God's strategy for dealing with the wicked. He insults them in v. 12 by suggesting that his lesson is obvious. They should know it without him telling them about it. Because of their ignorance, they have become meaningless, which probably means that their arguments lack substance. The word "meaningless" (*hebel*), well known from Ecclesiastes,[22] has as a base meaning "vapor" or "bubble." Their arguments are vaporous.

The rest of the chapter delineates the bad things that will happen to the wicked and those close to them. In v. 14 it may appear as if they are prospering because they may have a multitude of children (a sign of blessing), but those children will be killed by the sword. They will meet a bad end. If not killed by the sword, they will starve (v. 14b). The survivors (presumably from the sword and famine) will be claimed by disease (or so the term "Death" in v. 15a may imply).[23] The widows (mothers of the children who die and whose

22. See Longman, *Ecclesiastes*, 61–64.
23. See the note at the translation of v. 15 above.

wicked husbands have already expired) will be so shell-shocked that they will not even weep for their children.[24]

Verses 16–17 concern the material possessions of the wicked. Again, the point is that they may prosper for a while (as indicated by piling up silver and having nice clothes), but in the end they will not enjoy them. In a reversal that will work out proper retribution to a T, the righteous will enjoy their wealth as measured in silver and clothing. The thought is similar to that of Qohelet: "He gives to the one who is offensive [or "the sinner"] the task of gathering wealth to be given to the one who pleases God" (Eccles. 2:26), but Qohelet also calls this "meaningless and chasing the wind."[25] Verse 18 now speaks of their residence and says in colon *a* that their houses will be like a moth's and in colon *b* that they will be like a "booth made by a guard," which would be "a temporary shelter in the field."[26] The most likely point being made here is that they are flimsy and easily destroyed.

Verse 19 repeats, in the form of a general principle, that the wealth of the wicked is temporary and suddenly disappears. They lie down to go to sleep wealthy but wake up poor. As a result, they will be overwhelmed with fear (v. 20). As if that is not enough, God also enlists the east wind, a hot devastating wind, which will blow them away (v. 21). In v. 22 God is pictured as throwing the wind at them while they run away.

The final verse of the chapter describes God clapping (*śpq*) and hissing (*šrq*) at the wicked. Both of these gestures are indications of disdain and derision. God despises the wicked.

Theological Implications

Imprecating One's Enemies (27:7–10)

Even though there is a question about who utters vv. 7–10 (see comments above), these verses raise the question of the use of imprecations or curses on one's enemies. In this commentary, I have sided with those who think that Job uttered this curse over his three friends. Was it right for Job to call down curses on the heads of his enemies? Is it ever right? Is it right to pray this way today?

To begin to answer this question, we must remember that imprecations play a significant role in laments in the book of Psalms. Not every lament contains one. And, in my opinion, it is incorrect to use the label "imprecation psalm" since no psalm is defined by the curse that it contains. However, we still have to reckon with the presence of imprecations in psalms contained in a book

24. An alternative understanding is that the wicked men are those who remain after their children die, and later their widows will not even cry for them, showing that they had no one who really loved them.

25. See Longman, *Ecclesiastes*, 107–10.

26. Konkel, "Job," 169.

rightly dubbed the "hymnbook of the temple." An example may be drawn from Ps. 69. Speaking of those who persecute him, the psalmist says:

> Let their table be a trap for them,
> a snare for their allies.
> Let their eyes be darkened so that they cannot see,
> and make their loins tremble continually.
> Pour out your indignation upon them,
> and let your burning anger overtake them.
> May their camp be a desolation;
> let no one live in their tents.
> For they persecute those whom you have struck down,
> and those whom you have wounded, they attack still more.
> Add guilt to their guilt;
> may they have no acquittal from you.
> Let them be blotted out of the book of the living;
> let them not be enrolled among the righteous. (Ps. 69:22–28 NRSV)

These are hard-hitting and, to some, mean-spirited desires. Many find these sections disturbing and edit them out of their minds as they read the book of Psalms.

However, let us remember, as Calvin perceptively pointed out, that the book of Psalms is "an anatomy of all the parts of the soul," reflecting the full range of human emotions as in a mirror.[27] They are lyric poems expressing the emotions of the poets as they pour their hearts out before God. They are brutally honest and hold nothing back from God, even their desire for vengeance on those who have inflicted pain on them. God invites both them and us today to express our desires to him, even the desire to harm our enemies. After all, the psalmist (and Job) is not asking God to give him the strength or the resources or the circumstances where he himself might take vengeance. He is "turning it over to God" to do as he will. Perhaps God will avenge, perhaps not. Job and the psalmists are doing what Paul recommends in Rom. 12: "Beloved, never avenge yourselves, but leave room for the wrath of God; for it is written, 'Vengeance is mine, I will repay, says the Lord'" (v. 19 NRSV). Granted, in the context God tells his readers to also live in peace with those who hurt them, but they can do so since they have turned their anger and desire for revenge over to God. Thus to express a desire for the harm for someone who harmed us is encouraged by the Psalms and exemplified by Job. To act on that desire is wrong.

Even so, one cannot escape the thought that though God allows and even invites the expression of our heart before him in this way, that is not the ideal.

27. John Calvin, *Commentary on Psalms*, author's preface (http://www.ccel.org/ccel/calvin/calcom08.vi.html).

Spiritual maturity would emulate Christ on the cross. In spite of the torture he endured in the moments leading up to his death, Jesus did not utter imprecations. Indeed, one cannot help but think of Ps. 69 as we read the accounts of the crucifixion. According to Mark (15:36) and Matthew (27:34), some gave him "sour wine" or "wine mixed with gall" to drink while he hung on the cross, reminiscent of the "vinegar" that the psalmist's enemies gave him in his need (Ps. 69:21). This act is what led to the imprecatory barrage of the psalmist. Jesus, on the other hand, prayed, "Father forgive them; for they do not know what they are doing" (Luke 23:34 NASB).

IV.
Job's Monologue
(28:1–31:40)

After Job's final response to the friends, they grow silent, but not Job. He launches off on a monologue to which he receives no direct reply. Job begins with a profound reflection on God's wisdom (chap. 28). As I will discuss, the exact place of this speech (chap. 28) is debated because it seems out of keeping with Job's thought up to this point, and the last three chapters (29–31) will revert to his earlier mental turmoil. Indeed, those last three chapters set up the divine speeches. He begins with a rumination on his previous blessed condition (chap. 29) only to follow it with a blistering complaint about his present horrific situation (chap. 30). These thoughts move him to give one final protest of his innocence. Then Job himself stops talking (chap. 31).

A.
First Speech: Where Is Wisdom Found?
(28:1–28)

Translation

1"Indeed,[1] there is a mine[2] for silver,
  and a place where gold is refined.
2Iron is taken from the dust,
  and copper is poured out from stone.
3Putting an end to darkness,
  they[3] investigate every limit,
  the ore in thick and deep darkness.
4They breach a wadi far from human sojourning,[4]
  a place that is forgotten by human feet.
  They are suspended; they wander far from people.
5As for earth, bread comes out of it.
  Underneath it is turned over like fire.

1. Rather than "For," with Jones (*Rumors of Wisdom*, 123), who points out that a "non-connective, emphatic *kî* . . . is productive in BH," thus avoiding the problem of the lack of connection with the content of chap. 27.

2. For the argument that *môṣāʾ* is "source" and not "mine," see Jones (*Rumors of Wisdom*, 62–63), who attempts to move away from the mining analogy developed in this chapter.

3. Taking the pronoun *hûʾ* as a reference to humans rather than to God. For discussion see Jones, *Rumors of Wisdom*, 70–71.

4. Emendations produce translations like those found in NJB etc.: "Foreigners bore into ravines." The emendation involves changing *mēʿim* to *mēʿam* and taking *gār* to indicate a foreigner, but the MT is understandable in the manner translated above (see NRSV). Clines (*Job 21–37*, 896) presents a rather exhaustive list of proposed emendations.

6Its stones are the place of lapis lazuli.[5]
Its dust contains gold.
7No bird of prey knows its trail.
The eye of the falcon[6] does not catch sight of it.
8Proud beasts have not trod on it.
The lion has not walked on it.
9They put their hand on the flint,
upturning mountains from their root.
10They cut channels in the rocks;
their eyes see all the precious things.
11They[7] dam up[8] the sources of the rivers.[9]
Hidden things come out into the light.
12As for wisdom, where can it be found?
The place of understanding, where is it?

13No person knows its price.[10]
It cannot be found in the land of the living.
14The Deep says, 'It is not in me.'
The Sea says, 'It is not with me.'
15It cannot be given for gold.[11]
Silver cannot be weighed out as its price.
16It cannot be paid with the gold of Ophir,[12]
with precious onyx[13] and lapis.
17Gold and glass cannot match it.
No gold items can be exchanged for it.

5. Or "sapphires." In either case, a precious blue gemstone is meant.

6. Here "falcon," but other suggestions include the vulture, hawk, or black kite. Bird species in the Bible are often difficult to specify, and here the exact identity of the bird (*'ayyâ*) is unimportant. It is clearly a bird of prey with keen eyesight.

7. The miners.

8. Some take *ḥibbēš* as a "dialectical variant" of *ḥippēś* and thus translate "searches the sources of the rivers" (see Hartley, *Job*, 375n19), but this seems unnecessary since the meaning of *ḥibbēš* fits the context quite well.

9. As Pope (*Job*, 203) has pointed out, *mibbĕkî nĕhārôt* is nearly identical with the location of El's home in the Ugaritic mythological texts. According to Pope, "The mythological term is used here in Job merely as a poetic designation of the subterranean regions which man has the temerity to explore."

10. I take *'ērek* in the sense of valuation (see NRSV textual note; also the use of the word in Lev. 5:15). It could mean something like "path" or "way," though this is not a well-known meaning of the word (so Gordis, though disputed by Clines, *Job 21–37*, 901). The LXX reads "path" (*hodon*), but this may imply Hebrew *derek* instead of *'ērek*.

11. The word translated "gold" is *sĕgôr*, here taken as a form of *sāgûr*, which usually occurs in combination with *zāhāb* (see 1 Kings 6:20–21) but apparently can stand alone and mean "gold." See R. Wakely, *NIDOTTE* 3:223, for possible explanations of why the word is vocalized as it is and why it stands alone.

12. See the translation note for 22:24.

13. Or carnelian; the exact identification of *šōham* is uncertain. See A. E. Hill, *NIDOTTE* 4:52–53.

18Coral and crystal[14] will not even be evoked.[15]
The price of wisdom is more than pearls.
19The chrysolite[16] of Ethiopia[17] cannot match it.
It cannot be paid with pure gold.
20As for wisdom, where does it come from?
The place of understanding, where is it?[18]

21It is hidden from the eyes of all the living,
concealed from the birds of heaven.
22Abaddon[19] and Death say,
'We have heard a report of it in our ears.'
23God understands its path,
and he knows its place.[20]
24For he looks to the ends of the earth;
under all the heavens he sees,
25in order to[21] give weight to the wind,
and measure out the waters in their measure.
26When he made a decree for the rain,
and the way for the thunderstorm,[22]
27then he saw it and declared it;
he established it and investigated it.
28And he said to humankind:
'Behold, the fear of the Lord[23] is wisdom,
and turning aside from evil is understanding.'"

Interpretation

As I have indicated,[24] the place of chap. 28 in the book is much debated. The MT as we have it places these words in the mouth of Job, but we have

14. Or jasper, or alabaster; the exact identification of *gābîš* is uncertain. See A. E. Hill, *NIDOTTE* 1:802.

15. Niphal of *zkr*, "to remember."

16. Or topaz; the exact identification of *piṭdâ* is uncertain. See A. E. Hill, *NIDOTTE* 3:611.

17. Or Nubia (Cush).

18. Except for the verb in colon *a*, this verse is identical to v. 12 and serves as a refrain.

19. See the footnote at my comments on 26:6.

20. See Alderman and Strawn ("Note on Peshitta Job 28:23") for a discussion of the variant translation/interpretation given by the Peshitta. Rather than God coming to know his way, the Peshitta says that God makes known to humans the way of wisdom.

21. Some translations render the prefixed *lamed* preposition "when," though this is not an established meaning of the *lamed* (see NRSV, REB, NJB). Perhaps they emend the *lamed* to a *bet*, as in v. 26.

22. So Jones (*Rumors of Wisdom*, 196), who cites Zech. 10:1, the only other use of *ḥăzîz* outside of here and Job 38:25.

23. The only occurrence of *'ădōnāy* in the book.

24. See "Authorship and Date" in the introduction.

already seen that there are questions about the attribution of part of the third cycle of the disputation to Job as well (see the introduction to my comments on chaps. 23–24). The problem with Job 28 is that it expresses thoughts that would lead to the resolution of Job's problem. Indeed, it anticipates the end of the book in that, as it stands, Job 28 has Job acknowledging and bowing before the Lord. The problem is intensified in the following chapters (29–31), where Job again complains about his lot in life.

These observations lead some scholars to believe that the chapter was added later by a worried redactor who could not let the theological tension created by Job's words stand unanswered until the end.[25] In a similar argument, some scholars believe that we should understand the chapter to be the thought of the narrator.[26] These viewpoints seem like acts of desperation. Still others, such as Clines, believe that this speech is misplaced and should come after chap. 37, as the final part of Elihu's speech.[27]

The issues are real, and any decision must be tentative. That said, Lo has shown how the chapter may be read in its context by presenting what might be called a "psychological explanation."[28] Simply put, sufferers have up-and-down moments. While they can experience momentary calm in the midst of their emotional storm, often the pain overwhelms them, and they are suddenly confused and upset again. Job does not have to be a historical figure, and even if he is, the author does not need to have an inside track on his emotional life. The poet is, however, sensitive to how human emotions play out. Thus I take the position that we should understand chap. 28 as the words of Job.

It is true that the chapter does start a whole new line of thinking, with little if any connection to Job's words in the previous section.[29] Job's insight into the nature of God and a proper relationship with him begins with a reflection on the nature of mining (vv. 1–12).[30] Mining ores and precious stones from the ground is a human achievement deserving of the deepest wonder and admiration. No other animal can extract these materials from the earth (vv. 7–8). Even so, wisdom is beyond even human comprehension (v. 12).

The second stanza of this reflection on wisdom (vv. 13–20) continues the theme of the inaccessibility of wisdom for humans. Wisdom does not have a price. All the wealth of the world cannot buy it.

The final stanza (vv. 21–28) finally answers the question of where wisdom may be found. After denying that even personified Death knows much or

25. Newsom, *Job*, 128. This view is also held by Seow (*Job*).

26. Cheney, *Dust, Wind and Agony*, 57; Eaton, *Job*, 34.

27. Clines, *Job 21–37*, 889–926.

28. Lo, *Job 28 as Rhetoric*.

29. For translating the initial *kî* as "indeed" instead of "for," see the translation note for 28:1 above.

30. Contra Jones (*Rumors of Wisdom*, 1, and throughout) as well as Greenstein ("Poem on Wisdom").

anything about it, the passage confidently asserts that God knows its path and its way (v. 23). After all, it is with him. But Job does not stop there. He affirms that though God is the source of all wisdom, humans can indeed have access to it. How? They can find wisdom by fearing the Lord and turning aside from evil.

1“Indeed, there is a mine for silver,
and a place where gold is refined.
2Iron is taken from the dust,
and copper is poured out from stone.
3Putting an end to darkness,
they investigate every limit,
the ore in thick and deep darkness.
4They breach a wadi far from human sojourning,
a place that is forgotten by human feet.
They are suspended; they wander far from people.
5As for earth, bread comes out of it.
Underneath it is turned over like fire.
6Its stones are the place of lapis lazuli.
Its dust contains gold.
7No bird of prey knows its trail.
The eye of the falcon does not catch sight of it.
8Proud beasts have not trod on it.
The lion has not walked on it.
9They put their hand on the flint,
upturning mountains from their root.
10They cut channels in the rocks;
their eyes see all the precious things.
11They dam up the sources of the rivers.
Hidden things come out into the light.
12As for wisdom, where can it be found?
The place of understanding, where is it?”

28:1–12. *Humans are capable of great feats, but wisdom is beyond them.* This magnificent poem begins by describing the incredible mining and metallurgical achievements of humans. Extracting ore,[31] precious metals, and gems from the earth is not easy even today, in the twenty-first century, not to speak of antiquity. But Job knew of silver mines and places where rocks were taken from the earth and refined into highly desirable gold (v. 1). More utilitarian metals like iron and copper were also taken from the earth's crust, melted down, and poured out presumably to make implements and weapons. Verse 3 then marvels at the human ability to probe the depths of the earth. By opening up shafts they bring “an end to darkness” and investigate what is below the

31. For a history of mining in the ancient Near East, see Muhly, “Mining and Metalwork.”

surface of the earth, thus exposing the ore from where it was hiding in the darkness. Verse 4 situates this exploration in a wadi that is far from human habitation. People have to go to great lengths to mine the earth, even finding themselves suspended over pits in the ground.

Verse 5 notes that the earth yields "bread," presumably referring to the grain that emerges from the soil. Underneath, however, fires brew. This thought probably emerged from the experience and knowledge of volcanoes that spew smoke, fire, and lava from below the surface of the earth. Verse 6 returns to the subject of the precious stones and metals under the surface. Mentioned are lapis lazuli (or perhaps sapphire; the Hebrew word *sappîr* is the source of the English word), a highly precious blue gemstone known widely in the ancient Near East, and gold.

Humans are indeed amazing in their ability to probe below the surface of the earth. Animals are incapable of this type of exploration. Not even the most noble of animals (the lion is specifically mentioned) have even a clue where to go to find these metals and gems. Only humans can do it (vv. 9–11). They uncover the treasures of the earth by digging and overturning the mountains so their insides come out. They can even dam up rivers so that the riverbed can be exposed and exploited for resources.

This powerful description of human ability and successful efforts at finding hidden treasures under the surface of the earth contrasts strongly with our inability to find wisdom. Thus in v. 12 we encounter the first statement of the refrain that asks the rhetorical questions "As for wisdom, where can it be found? The place of understanding, where is it?" The answer is, no one knows. That is, no human can discover wisdom unaided.

13"No person knows its price.
It cannot be found in the land of the living.
14The Deep says, 'It is not in me.'
The Sea says, 'It is not with me.'
15It cannot be given for gold.
Silver cannot be weighed out as its price.
16It cannot be paid with the gold of Ophir,
with precious onyx and lapis.
17Gold and glass cannot match it.
No gold items can be exchanged for it.
18Coral and crystal will not even be evoked.
The price of wisdom is more than pearls.
19The chrysolite of Ethiopia cannot match it.
It cannot be paid with pure gold.
20As for wisdom, where does it come from?
The place of understanding, where is it?"

28:13–20. *Wisdom is beyond price.* The second stanza of this magnificent poem on wisdom presses the point of the first stanza. Wisdom is inaccessible to normal human resources. The major point of the argument is that wisdom cannot be purchased. No payment is high enough to acquire wisdom. Verse 13a begins this theme by simply stating that no one knows its price. Verses 15–19 then list the most precious metals, rocks, and gems known to humans at the time (gold, silver, gold of Ophir, precious onyx, lapis, glass, coral, crystal, pearls, chrysolite of Ethiopia, pure gold), stating that they are inadequate to pay the price for wisdom. Various types of gold (differentiated by location and quality) are mentioned.

It is instructive to read this passage in relationship to Eliphaz's comment in 22:21–26. There Eliphaz accuses Job of placing his love for gold and silver above his love for God. Nowhere does Job ever indicate that he is greedy, and here at least for the moment he makes clear that he has his priorities straight.

It is also interesting to reflect on this passage in the light of Proverbs' teaching on the relationship between wealth and wisdom. In that book we read that while one cannot purchase wisdom with wealth, wisdom often leads to wealth. According to Woman Wisdom, for instance:

> Wealth and honor are with me,
> enduring riches and righteousness.
> My fruit is better than gold, even fine gold,
> my yield than choice silver. (Prov. 8:18–19)[32]

Besides the teaching that wealth cannot buy wisdom, this stanza also repeats the idea that wisdom cannot be found by human investigation. Verse 13b says that it is not resident in "the land of the living." Verse 14 adds that wisdom is not even in those places that are hostile to humans, the Deep and the Sea. I have capitalized these in my translation to indicate that the Deep and the Sea are here personified, which enhances the significance of these terms, since the Deep and especially the Sea were regarded as forces of chaos and even evil in the ancient Near East.[33]

The stanza comes to a close with the almost identical refrain in v. 12.[34] After asserting that wisdom is inaccessible and invaluable, the poet again raises the question of its origins and location. The answer to this question is still to come.

> **21**"It is hidden from the eyes of all the living,
> concealed from the birds of heaven.

32. For translation and commentary, see Longman, *Proverbs*, 195, 202.

33. Longman and Reid, *God Is a Warrior*, 64–68; Wakeman, *God's Battle*; J. Day, *God's Conflict*.

34. The only difference is that in v. 20a the verb *bôʾ* substitutes for *māṣāʾ*.

[22]Abaddon and Death say,
'We have heard a report of it in our ears.'
[23]God understands its path,
and he knows its place.
[24]For he looks to the ends of the earth;
under all the heavens he sees,
[25]in order to give weight to the wind,
and measure out the waters in their measure.
[26]When he made a decree for the rain,
and the way for the thunderstorm,
[27]then he saw it and declared it;
he established it and investigated it.
[28]And he said to humankind:
'Behold, the fear of the Lord is wisdom,
and turning aside from evil is understanding.'"

28:21–28. *God is the source of wisdom.* The final stanza answers the question of the first three stanzas: Where is wisdom located? However, before doing so, the poet adds a final statement to the effect that wisdom is inaccessible not only to human resources but also to the rest of creation and even to personified Death. Indeed, v. 21a says it is hidden from the eyes of "all the living," presumably humans who live on the surface of the earth. The next colon adds that even the birds of the heavens cannot find it. The birds would have a higher vantage point, and they also can cover more space quickly. Even so, they are not up to the task. Verse 22 moves from the earth and the heavens to the underworld. Here the poet personifies Abaddon, the place of destruction, as well as Death itself. The latter may be yet another mythological reference or allusion (see v. 14 above), since the Canaanites knew of a god Death (Mot), who like the Sea (Yam) was ranged against the god Baal. But these spiritual beings too have at best only heard a report about wisdom; they do not have any direct knowledge of it.[35] Thus in vv. 21–22 the poet points out that the creatures of earth, heaven, and the underworld have no access to wisdom and cannot guide anyone to it.

Verse 23 climactically reveals that, contrary to everyone and everything else, God does know the way to wisdom ("its path"). He knows where it is ("its place"). But before sharing this information, the poet explains why God alone would have this knowledge. After all, though the birds have a high vantage point from which to look at the world, they do not compare to God, who "looks to the ends of the earth." He sees everything under heaven (v. 24).

Verses 25–26 are difficult but seem to describe God as the one responsible for the very nature of the creation, perhaps pointing to his role as creator. He

35. Or perhaps as Smick ("Job," 977) suggests, "That Destruction . . . and Death have a rumor about wisdom (v. 22) probably means those who reach that place have a belated understanding they have missed in life (cf. the rich man in Luke 16:19–31)."

gives weight to the wind and measures out the water. As Jones points out, this language furthers the picture of God as the architect of creation; he cites de Vaux: "Architects, masons, and craftsmen measured with their own arms, their extended hands, their palms, and their fingers."[36] God also is the one who provides the rain, perhaps pointing to his role as the one who providentially maintains the creation. As creator, he understands how it works, which is the essence of wisdom. Thus he is able to describe precisely where one may find wisdom, and he is willing to reveal it to humanity.

Wisdom is found in the fear of the Lord (here *ʾădōnāy*, not Yahweh, the only place in the book where the word is used), with the concomitant antonym of turning aside from evil. The conclusion that wisdom is located in fearing God and turning aside from evil reminds the reader of the teaching of Proverbs (see especially 1:7 [though notice that there the fear of the Lord is said to be the *beginning* of wisdom], but it occurs in various forms throughout the book).[37] In the theological implications section at the end of this chapter, I will discuss how the conclusion of the poem relates to the chapter as a whole and to the theology of Proverbs, but I will make a few comments here about the meaning of the phrase.

The statement demands a particular attitude in one's relationship to Israel's covenant God, and that is communicated by the noun "fear" (*yirʾat*, from the verb *yrʾ*). The verb has a semantic range that goes from what might be called respect or awe to utter terror. Indisputable, however, is the basic premise that to fear Yahweh is to stand in a subservient position to him, to acknowledge one's dependence on him. In the context of knowledge, it is to recognize that there is no true knowledge without reference to him. Interestingly, the fear of the Lord is coupled with turning aside from evil. While this is not stated in Prov. 1:7, the connection is found in 3:7: "Don't be wise in your own eyes. Fear Yahweh and turn away from evil." The fear of Yahweh puts one's own abilities and resources in proper perspective. It also naturally leads to an aversion to evil.

Theological Implications

Fear of the Lord (28:28)

This reflection on the theological implications of the passage explores a bit further the concept of the fear of the Lord, which provides the climax of Job's thoughts about the source of wisdom. Job has said that no human or any other creature can discover wisdom on their own. Wisdom comes from the fear of the Lord.

36. See Jones (*Rumors of Wisdom*, 193), citing de Vaux (*Ancient Israel*, 197).

37. See especially Prov. 9:10, but also 1:29; 2:5; 3:7; 8:13; 10:27; 14:2, 26, 27; 15:16, 33; 16:6; 19:23; 22:4; 23:17; 24:21; 29:25; 31:30.

Some scholars believe that v. 28 undermines the message of chap. 28.[38] They argue that the point of vv. 1–27 is that wisdom is with God and not with humans or any other created being. However, v. 28 allows that humans are wise if they fear God, which seems to conflict with the thought of vv. 1–27, though scholars overplay the tension. The point of the passage is that humans cannot find wisdom apart from God. They cannot find it on their own but find it only by fearing God. This message is appropriate for the book as a whole, since Job, his three friends, and eventually Elihu grasp for wisdom with their own abilities until the very end, when Job conclusively embraces the fear of the Lord by submitting to God in repentance (42:1–6). In this chapter, Job intellectually affirms the necessity of this fear, but his emotional turmoil does not allow him to fully embrace it until he not only hears of God but sees him (42:5).

If one takes v. 28 as the authentic and consistent conclusion to this chapter, what does the "fear of the Lord" mean? First, note its rather pervasive use within wisdom literature.[39] While the phrase "fear of the LORD" is best known from Prov. 1:7, it occurs throughout the book (see n. 37).[40] Psalm 111, a wisdom psalm, concludes with the following phrase:

> To fear the LORD is the beginning of wisdom;
>   all who follow his precepts have good understanding.
> To him belongs eternal praise. (111:10 NIV)

The book of Ecclesiastes also concludes with the words of the frame narrator, who wants to impress upon his son (see 12:12) the most important lesson of all: "Fear God and keep his commandments, for this is the whole duty of humanity. For God will bring every deed into judgment, including every hidden thing, whether good or evil" (12:13b–14). While in this passage "the fear of God" conforms to its usage in Proverbs and Job 28:28, the other occurrences in Ecclesiastes do not. Qohelet, the confused wise man who speaks in the body of the book, often talks in a way that sounds like the "fear of God" (see Eccles. 3:14; 5:7; 7:18; 8:12, 13), but the contexts of these instances indicate that Qohelet believes God acts the way he does to frighten people into submission, not to arouse a sense of respectful awe of his power and might.

Indeed, the latter is the proper type of fear that God desires to evoke in his human creatures. The type of fear described here is not horror that makes one run away, and it is not merely the idea of respect. It is most like awe, a kind of

38. For instance, Pope, *Job*, 206. I agree in large part with Habel, "Of Things beyond Me," especially 152–54.

39. This is not to say that it is not also important in other biblical texts. See, e.g., Deut. 6:13; 10:20; Josh. 24:14; 1 Sam. 12:24.

40. Bartholomew (*Reading Proverbs*, 8) points out that the references in Prov. 1:7 and 31:30 form an inclusio for the book as a whole, highlighting the importance of the concept for the book.

knee-knocking fear that one feels in the presence of a vastly more powerful, even though benevolent, person. It is the kind of emotion that removes pride and replaces it with humility, which as Proverbs indicates (1:7) is a prerequisite to wisdom. Pride does not permit one to learn from another, whereas humility does and even goes further and compels obedience.

Wisdom starts with this fear. Fear is the beginning of wisdom, both in a foundational and in a temporal sense. One may know a lot of facts without fear of the Lord, but not to know the most basic reality of all—God—renders someone a fool: "Fools say in their hearts, 'There is no God'" (Ps. 14:1 NRSV).

Thus fear of God is a presupposition of wisdom. Further, wisdom in the Bible is not a body of knowledge but rather a relationship. The wise must have a dependent relationship with God that makes them listen to him. All true knowledge has reference to God.

At this point in the story, Job is able to articulate this with his mouth and perhaps even know it in his mind. However, he does not yet really believe it in his heart. In chaps. 29–31 he again reverts to his complaints and desire to prove himself right before God. It is not until the very end that we have a picture of Job as one who truly "fears God."

To many, the idea of the fear of God seems like an OT idea. In the NT era, by contrast, we are to love God rather than fear him. After all, 1 John clearly states, "God is love, and those who abide in love abide in God, and God abides in them. . . . There is no fear in love, but perfect love casts out fear; for fear has to do with punishment, and whoever fears has not reached perfection in love. We love because he first loved us" (4:16b, 18–19 NRSV). Even so, such a bifurcation of the Testaments is wrongheaded, as is almost always the case. Consider the many times that the NT encourages or celebrates that God's people fear him. For example, note Paul's admonition to "work out your own salvation with fear and trembling" (Phil. 2:12 NRSV; see also Luke 12:5; 2 Cor. 5:11; 1 Pet. 1:17; 2:17; Rev. 14:7; 15:4; 19:5).

It thus appears that John is speaking of a different kind of fear. Love casts out horror but does not replace awe. Christians too need to cultivate the type of fear that Job now speaks about and that he himself experiences in the end.

B.
Second Speech: The Months of Old
(29:1–25)

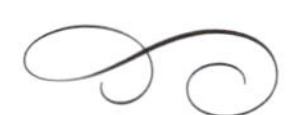

Translation

[1]And Job continued his discourse and said:[1]
[2]"Oh, that I were like (I was) in months of old,
as in the days when God guarded me,
[3]when his light shone over my head,
and I walked in the darkness by his light,
[4]when I was in the prime[2] of my life,
friendship[3] with God was over my tent,
[5]when Shaddai was still with me,
when my children surrounded me,
[6]when my steps were washed in butter,[4]
and the rock poured out streams of oil for me;
[7]when I went out to the gate of the city,
I set my seat in the public square.

[8]The youths saw me and hid;
the aged got up and stood.
[9]Princes restrained their speeches;
they set their hands on their mouths.

1. See my comments on 27:1.

2. Literally "winter," but here used figuratively (R. R. Ellis, *NIDOTTE* 2:279).

3. *Sôd* is often a reference to God's secret council or intimate fellowship. Some prefer to emend *sôd* to *sôk* and translate "protection," believing it makes better sense of the preposition *'al*. See Clines (*Job 21–37*, 934–35), who cites the LXX.

4. The MT has *ḥēmâ* (anger), which is inappropriate to the context. I emend with a few Hebrew MSS to *ḥem'â* (butter).

10The voice of nobles grew silent;
their tongues clung to the roof of their mouths.

11When an ear heard, it blessed me.
When an eye saw, it bore testimony on my behalf,
12because I rescued the poor who cried out for help,
and the orphan who had no helper.
13The blessing of those perishing came on me.
I made the widow's heart shout for joy.
14I clothed myself in righteousness, and it clothed me.
My justice was like a robe and turban.
15I was eyes to the blind,
and feet to the lame.
16I was father to the needy.
I examined the cause of the stranger.[5]
17I broke the jaw[6] of the guilty;
I removed[7] the prey from their teeth.

18And I thought, 'I will die in my nest,
and I will multiply my days like sand.'[8]
19My roots opened toward the water,
and dew lodged in my branches.
20My glory was ever new within me,
and my bow was renewed within my hand.
21They heard me and waited;
they were silent for my advice.
22After my words, they did not say anything.[9]
My words dripped gently on them.
23They waited for me like rain;
they opened their mouths, as for the late rains.
24I smiled at them when they did not have confidence.[10]
They did not frown[11] at the light of my countenance.

5. While it would be possible to take the phrase *lōʾ-yādactî* as "(something) I did not know," the context suggests "(someone) I did not know," i.e., a stranger.

6. Or possibly "fangs" (so NIV, NRSV).

7. Or perhaps "caused to throw away," suggesting a more violent motion for the Hiphil of *šālak*.

8. Or "like the phoenix" (see Clines, *Job 21–37*, 940; and NRSV). This posits a minor emendation from *ḥôl* to *ḥûl*. "Sand," however, makes perfect sense in the context, although "phoenix" relates well to the "nest" imagery of the first colon. Fortunately, either reading produces the same sense.

9. *Yišnû* is from *šnh* II ("to repeat"), here referring to Job's audience repeating words.

10. This line is amenable to more than one translation. It could mean "When I smiled at them, they could not believe it," but I prefer the idea that his smile gave them confidence when they lacked it.

11. The Hiphil of *npl* ("to fall") is difficult here. Perhaps it refers to their falling countenance (that is, a frown) in contrast to Job's bright countenance. Jeremiah 3:12 is another context where the Hiphil of *npl* may have this meaning.

[25]I chose their way and sat as chief.
I dwelt like a king among troops,
like one who consoles those who mourn."

Interpretation

I will treat the next three chapters one at a time, but they are closely connected. In chap. 29 Job remembers his previous blessed condition in order to contrast it with the description in chap. 30 of his present wretched situation. Finally, Job turns to God to protest his innocence. That is, he argues that he does not deserve his change of fortune. Whybray rightly recognizes that "these chapters should be seen as constituting at last the formal charge against God that Job has all along wanted to be allowed to make."[12]

This chapter contains Job's wistful reflections on his previous life, when his prosperity and fame coincided with his righteous behavior. He begins by remembering the days when God blessed him. He speaks in general terms in vv. 2–7. When God was his friend, his life was good and he was considered important. He was indeed so important and powerful that young people got out of his way and the aged and noble were quiet in order to let him speak (vv. 8–10). People respected him not simply because he was powerful but also because he took care of the vulnerable (poor, orphans, widows, the blind and lame, the needy and stranger; vv. 11–17).

For these reasons, he thought that he would be honored for life and die in peace. He thought that he would thrive (vv. 18–25) until the end. Whybray gives the following examples of those patriarchs who died the way Job expected to die: Abraham (Gen. 25:8–9), Isaac (35:29), Jacob (49:33; 50:1–14), and Joseph (50:24–26).[13]

---

[1]And Job continued his discourse and said:
[2]"Oh, that I were like (I was) in months of old,
as in the days when God guarded me,
[3]when his light shone over my head,
and I walked in the darkness by his light,
[4]when I was in the prime of my life,
friendship with God was over my tent,
[5]when Shaddai was still with me,
when my children surrounded me,
[6]when my steps were washed in butter,
and the rock poured out streams of oil for me;
[7]when I went out to the gate of the city,
I set my seat in the public square."

---

12. Whybray, *Job*, 136.
13. Ibid., 138.

29:1–7. *Life was good*. The introduction to this part of Job's final speech is similar to what we saw in 27:1. The variation that adds the idea that "Job continued his discourse" is appropriate when it appears in the midst of a lengthy speech rather than the typical formula that starts a whole new speech, since Job appears to be the speaker from the beginning of chap. 26 to the end of chap. 31 (as we observed through the majority of the dialogue section).

When people suffer, it is natural for them to long for the days when life was good. Job remembers those days described in 1:1–5, when he was wealthy, healthy, and blessed in family life. His family, with the exception of his wife, has died; he has lost all his wealth and health. Those past days appear to him as a time when God took care of him, while today he believes that God attacks him and is purposefully making his life a living hell. Verses 3–7 further describe the past that is so different from his present. Those were days when his way was fully illuminated before him (v. 2). Even Qohelet, in spite of his belief in the ultimate meaninglessness of life, thought that the wise were better off in this life because of the way their wisdom illuminates life's path (Eccles. 2:12–13). Job remembers those days and misses them. He was living in harmony with God (Job 29:4b, 5a). His relationship with God was intimate. God was "with him" and thus he prospered. This language reminds one of Gen. 39, in which God is often said to be "with Joseph," with the result that the house of Potiphar, his Egyptian master, prospered (39:2, 3, 21, 23). In those days, too, Job's children were still living, before they were so horribly and suddenly killed in a series of natural and human calamities (Job 1:13–19). He also served in an important and well-honored societal capacity, since 29:7 tells us he sat in the gate of the city, the place where the leaders of the city (elders) sat and made important decisions. He was highly honored then, but no longer.

Verse 6 provides a metaphorical overview of the wonder of his life. "Butter" and "oil" are metaphors for a luxurious life, and Job was awash in it. Even the hard rocks produced oil. Smick mentions two other passages signifying prosperity, where sensuous liquids come out of a rock: Deut. 32:13 ("oil from the flinty rock") and Ps. 81:16 ("honey from the rock").[14]

8"The youths saw me and hid;
the aged got up and stood.
9Princes restrained their speeches;
they set their hands on their mouths.
10The voice of nobles grew silent;
their tongues clung to the roof of their mouths."

29:8–10. *Young and old as well as nobles paid him respect*. Job continues his painful reminiscence of better times by cataloguing how people used to react to him. Both young and old showed him great respect. The young got

14. Smick, "Job," 981.

out of his way, and those who were his age (that is, his equals) stood to honor him. The latter reminds us of today's practice of standing in a courtroom when the judge enters the room. Job was someone who could make an impact on their lives, so they showed him proper deference. Verses 9–10 continue this theme by speaking of how even the upper classes of society (princes, *śārîm*; nobles, *nĕgîdîm*) were awed by his presence. They demonstrated their respect by growing silent. This likely indicates the honor in which they would have held Job's speech. Why should they speak when a man of such obvious wisdom and piety has the floor?

[11]"When an ear heard, it blessed me.
When an eye saw, it bore testimony on my behalf,
[12]because I rescued the poor who cried out for help,
and the orphan who had no helper.
[13]The blessing of those perishing came on me.
I made the widow's heart shout for joy.
[14]I clothed myself in righteousness, and it clothed me.
My justice was like a robe and turban.
[15]I was eyes to the blind,
and feet to the lame.
[16]I was father to the needy.
I examined the cause of the stranger.
[17]I broke the jaw of the guilty;
I removed the prey from their teeth."

29:11–17. *Job cares for the vulnerable.* Job now recounts his behavior that led to such a high regard for his character. He can call on personal testimony to attest to his actions. When people heard and saw what he did, they were ready to affirm and enhance his reputation (v. 11).

First, Job was a protector of the vulnerable. The poor, the orphan, and the widow were those who easily fell prey in ancient society. The orphan lacked parents, and the widow lacked a husband who could care for the family. The poor lacked resources. Job, however, stepped forward with his wealth to help these unfortunates. Job earlier identified those who did not help the socially vulnerable as wicked (24:3–4, 21). Here he also refutes Eliphaz's point that he oppressed the widow and the orphan (22:9).

By asserting his righteous character, v. 14 serves as a pause between two parts of Job's list of concrete good activities. He does so using a clothing metaphor. Elsewhere in the OT, putting on clothing indicates a spiritual condition. Isaiah 52:1 speaks of restored Israel putting on "beautiful garments," and 59:17 describes God as dressed in righteousness. The same metaphor is used in the NT. Colossians 3:9–10 is a prime example, which describes a new relationship with Christ as having "stripped off the old self with its practices" and "clothed yourself with the new self" (NRSV).

In vv. 15–17 Job returns to listing the benefits he brought to those in need. He gave sight to the blind, indicating that he would guide them to their destination. Perhaps he was "feet to the lame" by carrying them or having them carried by his servants. The needy did not have a father who would protect and provide for them, but Job served that function. Strangers could be easily neglected in ancient society, but not by Job, who made sure that they were treated justly. As for the wicked who would take advantage of such people, Job attacked them. He broke their jaw, not allowing them to masticate these people as prey.

18"And I thought, 'I will die in my nest,
and I will multiply my days like sand.'
19My roots opened toward the water,
and dew lodged in my branches.
20My glory was ever new within me,
and my bow was renewed within my hand.
21They heard me and waited;
they were silent for my advice.
22After my words, they did not say anything.
My words dripped gently on them.
23They waited for me like rain;
they opened their mouths, as for the late rains.
24I smiled at them when they did not have confidence.
They did not frown at the light of my countenance.
25I chose their way and sat as chief.
I dwelt like a king among troops,
like one who consoles those who mourn."

29:18–25. *He thought he would end well.* Job now concludes his reminiscence of happier days, a remembrance that only increases his depression about the present. In those good old times, he thought he would die of old age and be happy until the end. Verse 18a makes use of a bird analogy. He will die in his nest and not out away from his home. When one dies, it is best to die in familiar surroundings, supported by family and friends. And it is best to die at an extremely advanced age. In v. 18b he confesses that he expected that he would live till his days were like sand. The number of grains in even a small quantity of sand is almost beyond counting. So if Job's days are like the sand, then he is extremely old.[15] Verse 19 shifts to a tree analogy. Job is like a tree whose roots went toward (or probably in) the water and whose branches were soaked in dew. A tree is an image of fertility and life but only insofar as it is nourished by plentiful water, as here.

15. The use of sand as a metaphor for a countless number is best known in the patriarchal promise of seed, where Abraham and Jacob are told that their descendants will be as innumerable as the sand on the seashore (Gen. 22:17; 32:12).

Though he grew older, he kept his vitality (v. 20). The verbs convey vitality by emphasizing newness (as opposed to aging). Job's glory would be the manifestation of a positive reputation. Job's glory is his honor. Verse 20b parallels "glory" with "bow." That Job speaks of the renewal of his "bow" (*qešet*) is unexpected, since he never describes himself or is described as a warrior. It may be, though, that "bow" is used metaphorically here for the struggles of life. Psalm 127:4–5 uses archer imagery (though not specifically the bow) in such a way, where a man's sons are his allies in the conflicts of life:

> Like arrows in the hand of a warrior
> are the sons of one's youth.
> Happy is the man who has
> his quiver full of them.
> He shall not be put to shame
> when he speaks with his enemies in the gate. (NRSV)

Interestingly, the psalmist speaks about how his arrow-like sons help him avoid shame, the opposite of the glory/honor that Job preserves through his ever-new bow.

Verses 22–23 return to the theme of the effect that his profound wisdom had on his audience; vv. 9–10 told how they grew quiet in expectation of his speech, and here they continued to be silent in awe after he did speak. The opening of his hearers' mouths was not for the purpose of speech but in awe at what they heard from Job, whose advice soothed and comforted them like the late rains soften the dry, hard earth.

But Job did not even have to speak to have such a beneficial effect on people. All he had to do was look at them (v. 24). His very countenance encouraged them and lifted them up when they lost hope. His bright countenance kept theirs from falling (frowning). In this way, he guided them in their life like a good sage ("I chose their way"). He was not just any old sage, he was "chief" (v. 25a) or "like a king" among troops (v. 25b), again a metaphor that speaks to his leadership abilities as well as the idea that life is full of conflicts. Finally v. 25c reiterates that Job is someone who can help a sad person become happy once again.

Theological Implications

When Life Is Good

In chap. 29 Job reminisces about the past, when his life was good. In his words, "My steps were washed in butter, and the rock poured out streams of oil for me" (29:6). Job thinks that this is linked with his intimate relationship with God. Again, in his words, this was a time when "friendship with God was over my tent" (29:4).

Job may well think this is true because of his theological beliefs. He believed that a wonderful life was as it should be for those who are faithful to God. To be in a good relationship with God should lead to a happy, painless, and successful life. Today, those who affirm a prosperity gospel would agree. It is only right that faith and obedience be met with blessing. But even those who would not affirm such a simplistic understanding of faith think deep down that this is the way it should work. After all, why else would we say "Why me?" when bad things happen?

Job is thinking back on a time when things were good in his life. He also believed that these good times would never end. Verse 18 indicates this, "I will die in my nest, and I will multiply my days like sand." This attitude too is widely held. When life is good, we see no end in sight.

Such a view is quite dangerous, though, and easily belied by Scripture and by experience. The danger arises in our expectations. If we feel that we deserve God's blessing because of our faith and obedience, then when that blessing is disturbed by hardship, we are left confused and angry. Job is a good example of this, as is Qohelet. He thought he deserved a good life, but when he observed the righteous dying young and the wicked living long, it led him to declare life "meaningless" (Eccles. 7:15–18).

But the Bible, in both OT and NT, never promises that God's people will enjoy undisturbed blessings in this life. Even the book of Proverbs recognizes that the righteous wise may have to choose between godliness and earthly enjoyment. This comes out in the so-called better-than proverbs, which give relative values:

> Better a little bit with righteousness
>   than a large yield without justice. (16:8)
>
> Better to be a humble spirit with the needy
>   than dividing plunder with the proud. (16:19)

Not only does Scripture suggest that this world will bring hardship as well as good things to God's people, but so does experience. All of us experience struggles in life. When life is good, it is pure delusion to think that it will last. Unless Jesus comes again, we will die, often preceded by a lengthy and painful illness. And before us, loved ones will die, parents, siblings, friends, perhaps even one's spouse or children.

Life is full of difficulties. We should not forget this truth during periods of blessing. Otherwise, like Job we will set ourselves up for a horrible fall. Indeed, the lament psalms provide testimony of those who remember their past good life in the midst of their present suffering. Remembering the past just intensifies their pain (Pss. 42:4; 77:5–9). Our hope is not in a painless life on earth. After all, Paul tells Christians that they are an afflicted people. Indeed, Paul speaks of the necessity of sharing in the sufferings of Christ and thereby "attaining to the resurrection from the dead" (Phil. 3:10–11 NIV). However, in their present affliction, they experience God's comfort (2 Cor. 1:3–11). Indeed, in spite of all of his troubles, Paul could still experience joy (2 Cor. 7:4). The absence of pain and the experience of unalloyed joy come not in this life but the next. Christians must endure the hardships of a fallen world today but can anticipate the joys of the future, when God will wipe away every tear (Rev. 7:17).

C.
Third Speech: Treated with Disdain
(30:1–31)

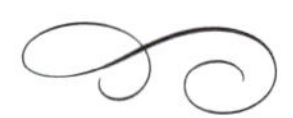

Translation

1"But now they laugh at me,
even those younger than I am,
those whose fathers I would have disdained
to set with the dogs of my flock.
2What help is the strength of their hands to me?
Their vigor[1] has perished.
3Barren,[2] in want and hunger,
they gnaw[3] the desert,
on the brink[4] of desolation and destruction.
4They pluck mallow among the bushes;
the root of the broom shrub is their food.[5]

1. *Kelaḥ* in this context (parallel to *kōaḥ*) means "vigor," whereas in 5:26 it refers to the ripe old age of the righteous at the time of their death (R. Wakely, *NIDOTTE* 2:652–54).

2. Occurring only four times, *galmûd* "always carries negative overtones, ranging from the wish that one had never been born (Job 3:7), to a description of the godless (Job 15:34), to a symbol of exiled life in Babylon (Isa. 49:21)" (V. P. Hamilton, *NIDOTTE* 1:870).

3. Konkel ("Job," 179) argues that the meaning "flee" is better here (see NLT). Both meanings provide a picture of desperate people.

4. The opening word of this line is extremely difficult. *'Emeš* typically means simply "yesterday," but this does not fit the context. The meaning posited here, an extension of "yesterday" admittedly unattested, is very tentative. In this I follow Clines (*Job 21–37*, 945), where one can find all the possibilities discussed.

5. Alternatively, the word could be emended slightly to *lĕḥummām*, a form of *ḥmm*, yielding a translation like NRSV: "to warm themselves the roots of broom." This is supported by Konkel, "Job," 179. Either translation evokes a picture of destitution.

5They are driven out from human society.[6]
They shout at them as if they are robbers.
6They live on the slopes[7] of wadis,
in dusty and rocky[8] holes.
7They bray[9] among the bushes;
they huddle together under the scrub.
8Children of fools, disreputable,[10]
they are whipped off[11] the land.
9But now I am the object of their melodious taunts;
I am a byword to them.
10They abhor me; they keep their distance from me.
They do not hold back from spitting at my face.

11He[12] has loosened my bowstring[13] and humiliated me,
so they have removed all restraint from before me.
12On my right the mob rises up;
they send my feet out from under me;[14]
they build up roads for my calamity.
13They tear up my paths;
they profit from my ruin;
no one helps me.[15]

14They come as if through a wide breach.
They roll on in the midst of desolation.
15Terrors transform me;
they put my dignity in flight like the wind;
my hope of rescue has passed by like a cloud.

6. *Gēw* is a hapax legomenon, perhaps (according to many, e.g., E. Carpenter, *NIDOTTE* 1:833) related to Aramaic/Syriac *gawā'*, "inner part, belly," meaning "insider."

7. *'Arûṣ* is another hapax legomenon; the meaning is gleaned from an Arabic cognate (Clines, *Job 21–37*, 946–47).

8. *Kēp* occurs only here and in Jer. 4:29 with this meaning. The word is cognate with Akkadian *kāpu* and Aramaic *kēpā'* (A. E. Hill, *NIDOTTE* 2:687). NT readers will recognize the word in relation to Peter's Aramaic name (Kepas/Cephas).

9. See the use of *nhq* in Job 6:5, where it is used literally of donkeys' braying.

10. Literally "without name."

11. *Nk'* is a by-form of *nkh*, in the Niphal, found only here and in Ps. 109:16, though the adjective *nākē'* occurs in Prov. 15:13; 17:22; 18:14; Isa. 16:7; 66:2, modifying *rûaḥ* and yielding the meaning "broken spirit."

12. Though the subject is not specified, it is clearly God.

13. Reading with the Qere. The Ketib has "*his* bowstring," but the image is of taking a string off the bow, thus rendering it ineffective, and so must refer to Job's bowstring. Konkel ("Job," 179) takes the word in the sense of tent-cord (see Job 4:21), believing the comparison is between Job's body and a tent that comes crashing down with the slashed cord.

14. More closely translated, the colon *raglay šillēḥû* reads, "They send my feet out."

15. The MT literally says "no one helps them." This does not fit the context, so one must either emend the verb from *'zr* to *'ṣr* ("no one restrains them") or, as here, emend the object to "me."

16 But now my life force is poured out of me;
days of affliction have taken hold of me.
17 The night hews my bones,
and that which gnaws at me does not let me lie down to sleep.
18 With great power he[16] grabs[17] my clothing;
he seizes me by[18] the collar of my garment.
19 He has thrown me into the mud;
I have become like dust and ashes.

20 I cry out for help to you, but you do not answer me.
I stand, and you barely take cognizance of me.
21 You have turned cruel toward me.
You hate me with the strength of your hand.
22 You lift me up in the wind and make me ride it;
you make me reel because of the roar of the storm.[19]
23 I know that you turn me back to death,
the house appointed for all the living.

24 Should he not send his hand on behalf of a ruin,[20]
when he cries out for help during a disaster?
25 Do I not cry for those whose day was hard?
Do I not have pity[21] on the needy?
26 For I hoped for the best, but the worst came.
I waited for light, but deep darkness came.
27 My innards are brought to a boil and not stilled.
Days of affliction are before me.
28 I walk around mourning, without passion.[22]
I get up in the assembly and I cry for help.
29 I am the brother of jackals,
and a friend of eagle owls.[23]

16. Some take the unspecified subject as "it," in reference to Job's pain. If so, then "pain" is personified. It seems more natural, in light of Job's overall problem with God, to take the reference to God himself, even though he will begin to address God in the second person in v. 20.

17. I emend *yitḥappēś* ("to disguise oneself"), which does not make a great deal of sense in the context, to *yitpōś*, which the LXX supports and many commentators follow. See Clines, *Job 21–37*, 953–54; and NRSV.

18. I emend *k* (like) to *b* (by).

19. With many I take the Ketib *tūšiwwâ* as a form of *tĕšûʾâ*.

20. Many emend *ʿî* to some form of *ʿānî* ("poor, needy person"; see NRSV, REB, NAB, NJB). However, perhaps Job is speaking figuratively, that he is like a heap of rubble. For the assessment that this is "one of the most unintelligible verses in the book" as well as an extensive philological analysis, see Clines, *Job 21–37*, 957–58.

21. *ʿGm* is a hapax legomenon but probably a by-form of *ʾgm* (Isa. 19:10).

22. The word *ḥamâ* can mean "heat" but metaphorically can refer to passion or excitement.

23. Or, traditionally, "ostriches" (N. Kiuchi, *NIDOTTE* 2:489–90).

30My skin turns black;[24]
my bones burn from the heat.
31My lyre is tuned to mourning,
my reed pipe to the sound of weeping."

Interpretation

Chapter 30 continues on from Job's comments in the previous chapter. There he remembered the good old days when God liked him and he prospered and was honored. He did the right things and he fully expected to die in his blessed condition. This chapter now describes how his life has transformed from blessing to curse. He believes that this change is totally unjust since he has done nothing to deserve it, so in the next chapter (31) he will protest his innocence and announce his intention to confront God over this indignity.

In the first part of chap. 30, Job bemoans that he is no longer respected by old and young, noble or not, as he was in earlier days (vv. 1–10). Indeed, the very scum of the earth, whose description occupies the majority of these verses, laugh at him. Verses 11–15 accuse God of humiliating him, and in his shame and weakness a mob then comes to harass him. He is deeply afraid and shamed. He feels as if God has mugged him (vv. 16–19). While he has appealed to God, God has not responded to him (vv. 20–23). Job ends by saying that God should have helped him or anyone who is suffering as he is (vv. 24–31). After all, even he, a human, helps those who appeal to him for help. His optimism has turned to pessimism.

1"But now they laugh at me,
even those younger than I am,
those whose fathers I would have disdained
to set with the dogs of my flock.
2What help is the strength of their hands to me?
Their vigor has perished.
3Barren, in want and hunger,
they gnaw the desert,
on the brink of desolation and destruction.
4They pluck mallow among the bushes;
the root of the broom shrub is their food.
5They are driven out from human society.
They shout at them as if they are robbers.
6They live on the slopes of wadis,
in dusty and rocky holes.

24. The prepositional phrase *mēʿālāy* ("from me") suggests to some translations (NRSV) that the skin is peeling or falling off.

7They bray among the bushes;
they huddle together under the scrub.
8Children of fools, disreputable,
they are whipped off the land.
9But now I am the object of their melodious taunts;
I am a byword to them.
10They abhor me; they keep their distance from me.
They do not hold back from spitting at my face."

30:1–10. *Scum of the earth laugh at him.* In the previous chapter, Job had longingly reminisced about the good old days, when he was deeply respected by all—young and old, powerful and lowly. The young stayed out of his way, while their parents stood up in respect (29:8). Even powerful nobles grew silent when he spoke (29:9). Chapter 30 speaks of the present, not the past, and the present is a complete reversal of the past.

Children do not withdraw from Job's presence out of respect any longer. Now they taunt him. And these are not just any children—they are the children of the dregs of society (v. 1). In ancient Israel, the dog was considered not man's best friend but a beast who ran around scavenging what it could, even corpses if they were available (1 Kings 14:11; 16:4; 21:23, 24; 2 Kings 9:10, 36). But in better days, Job would not have let his dogs associate with these mocking youths' fathers. Thus Job feels ridiculed by youths who are more contemptible than their fathers, more contemptible than dogs.

They ridicule rather than help him, but Job asks what good would they be to him anyway (v. 2). They have neither the strength nor the vigor to support him. Job then goes into a lengthy description of their sorry state in vv. 3–8. What is clear is that they are scavengers, like the dogs in the countryside. They are the ancient homeless, without a roof over their head and without a normal diet. Job describes them not with compassion, but with disgust. The point of the text, however, is not to indicate that Job is pitiless, but that he is pitiful, in that these lowlifes look down on him. They may be like the ancient *ḫapiru*, those who did not live in civilization but rather dwelt in the countryside. These were debtors, runaway slaves, and others who were on the outs of established civilization, though not all *ḫapiru* were as destitute as these sorry people.

Job pictures people in a desperate search for food to keep themselves alive. They are "in want and hunger" (v. 3). They "gnaw the desert," obviously a place with few resources to sustain them. They do their best, though, as they gather mallow from bushes and eat the root of the broom tree (v. 4). They are not out of the city by their own decision, but they have been compelled to leave by those who live there ("they are driven out from human society," v. 5a). Their treatment may be the result of criminal activity ("they shout at them as if they are robbers," v. 5b).

As mentioned, they have no permanent homes. Rather they live in the many caves that may be found in wadi walls in Israel. In other words, they live like animals. Job even likens them to the donkey when he says they "bray among the bushes."

It is these types of people who treat him so badly. They sing songs about him, and he has become a byword among them. Psalm 69 expresses Job's feelings well when "zeal" for God's house has made him

> a byword to them [those who ridicule him].
> I am a subject of gossip for those who sit in the gate,
> and the drunkards make songs about me. (Ps. 69:11b–12 NRSV)

They may be "whipped off the land" (Job 30:8), but before they go, they will treat Job with great disrespect, taunting him and even spitting in his face.

What would be the nature of the taunts? They may have taunted him for his sickly look. Some people like to hurt people when they are down. But it could also be motivated by the general belief expressed by the three friends that Job's predicament is because of his sin.

> **11**"He has loosened my bowstring and humiliated me,
> so they have removed all restraint from before me.
> **12**On my right the mob rises up;
> they send my feet out from under me;
> they build up roads for my calamity.
> **13**They tear up my paths;
> they profit from my ruin;
> no one helps me.
> **14**They come as if through a wide breach.
> they roll on in the midst of desolation.
> **15**Terrors transform me;
> they put my dignity in flight like the wind;
> my hope of rescue has passed by like a cloud."

30:11–15. *Shamed by God; beset by a mob.* Job points the finger at God: God is responsible for the fact that Job is at the mercy of such despicable people. God has "loosened his bowstring." Of course, to loosen a bowstring makes the bow ineffective as a weapon. Job uses the image to describe his uselessness. His ineffectiveness is a cause for shame on his part and the occasion for the mob to rise up against him. When he was strong, these vicious people needed to be careful around him, but no more. Nothing restrains them from attacking him directly. Indeed, in much of the description of their assault in the following verses, Job describes himself as a besieged city. But first they lay him prone by knocking his feet out from under him. He is lying flat when they build paths up to him. Modern readers might here think of *Gulliver's Travels* and the Lilliputians' assault on Gulliver. In Job, the mob builds up paths (probably a reference to siege ramps) against him. In v. 13b, though, Job uses the term "path" to refer to his life. While they build up their paths to attack him, they tear down his paths. They do this for their own advantage and do not need the help of anyone else since Job is so weak (v. 13c).

Verse 14 also uses the metaphor of a besieged city when it describes them attacking him through a "wide breach." To take an ancient Near Eastern city, the walls protecting it usually had to be compromised, often by knocking them down and then storming through the opening.

In the face of this onslaught, Job feels great terror. Such fear transforms him from a confident and strong individual to a sniveling fearful man ("they put my dignity in flight like the wind"). Finally, he remarks that he has lost all hope. It has passed quickly and without tangible effect like a cloud.

16"But now my life force is poured out of me;
days of affliction have taken hold of me.
17The night hews my bones,
and that which gnaws at me does not let me lie down to sleep.
18With great power he grabs my clothing;
he seizes me by the collar of my garment.
19He has thrown me into the mud;
I have become like dust and ashes."

30:16–19. *A divine mugging.* Verses 16–17 describe his great suffering. Job feels as though his life force, or energy, is completely drained from him. His days are now days of pain that will not let go. At night he is in constant pain. He feels as if the night itself is sawing away at his bones. He is unable to sleep because of the pain. Verses 18–19 describe his pain as a result of getting mugged by God. God has grabbed him by his clothing and thrown him down into the mud. The result is that he has become like dust and ashes, an idiom that points to abject humiliation. Job will again use this phrase ("dust and ashes") at the end of his repentance.

20"I cry out for help to you, but you do not answer me.
I stand, and you barely take cognizance of me.
21You have turned cruel toward me.
You hate me with the strength of your hand.
22You lift me up in the wind and make me ride it;
you make me reel because of the roar of the storm.
23I know that you turn me back to death,
the house appointed for all the living."

30:20–23. *God does not respond to him.* Job now turns to God and speaks to him directly, but as he quickly points out, God does not answer him. Job needs help, but God does not pay any attention to the sufferer. God barely acknowledges him as Job tries to get his attention. Job takes this unresponsiveness as a sign of displeasure. God hates him and is cruel toward him. According to v. 22, he feels as if God has just blasted him with the wind of the storm, perhaps an anticipation of the coming theophany, where God will speak to Job out of a whirlwind (38:1). Job ends by saying that he is certain God is trying to kill him, though he also acknowledges that all living things end up in that "house."

> [24]"Should he not send his hand on behalf of a ruin,
> when he cries out for help during a disaster?
> [25]Do I not cry for those whose day was hard?
> Do I not have pity on the needy?
> [26]For I hoped for the best, but the worst came.
> I waited for light, but deep darkness came.
> [27]My innards are brought to a boil and not stilled.
> Days of affliction are before me.
> [28]I walk around mourning, without passion.
> I get up in the assembly and I cry for help.
> [29]I am the brother of jackals,
> and a friend of eagle owls.
> [30]My skin turns black;
> my bones burn from the heat.
> [31]My lyre is tuned to mourning,
> my reed pipe to the sound of weeping."

30:24–31. *God should help*. According to my translation and interpretation of the very difficult v. 24, Job begins by crying out plaintively that God should help a sufferer like himself when he cries out for help.[25] He likens himself to a ruin (see comment below on jackal and eagle owl). He has been crying to God for help and asking for an audience, but getting no response. Indeed, in the next verse he contrasts this attitude with his own. When Job heard cries from the needy, he was moved and acted on their behalf. He felt empathy for the needy in a way that neither God nor the three friends have demonstrated toward him. God will later confront this attitude: "Would you invalidate my justice? Would you condemn me so you might be righteous?" (40:8).

Originally, Job was optimistic, but now he is a pessimist, since the good he expected never materialized (v. 26). Job is in tremendous turmoil, which he describes as his innards boiling. He is deeply agitated because he is suffering with no apparent way out of his mess (v. 27). Verse 28 gives us a picture of listless wandering in deep sadness. He mourns "without passion," which I take to mean that he is stunned, bewildered. It is possible, though, that the phrase

25. Most translations render the verse in a way that states a general principle ("Surely no one lays a hand on a broken man when he cries for help in his distress," NIV; see also NLT and NRSV). In this case, Job may be referring to either the friends or God (or both) as those who kick a person who is down.

translated "without passion" could mean "without sunlight." In other words, he walks around mourning at night. The phrase is literally "without heat," and my translation takes the heat as a reference to his state of mind, while the alternate takes it as a reference to the sun. While admittedly Job has just referred to the boiling inside him, he could now be referring to this stunned astonishment at his condition. He appeals for help in the assembly, which had previously listened in silence to his every word (29:8–10).

He ends the chapter by describing his suffering yet again. He relates himself to the jackal and the eagle owl, creatures that inhabit ruins (see v. 24; Ps. 44:19; Jer. 9:11; 10:22; Isa. 34:13; Lam. 5:18). They are scavenger animals that haunt lonely places. Verse 30 describes the horrible effects of his disease on his body, both externally ("my skin turns black") and internally ("my bones burn from the heat"). His music is a dirge that accompanies his weeping and mourning.

Theological Implications

The Corrosive and Redemptive Effects of Shame

Job feels humiliated by God. He has become the brunt of laughter from even the lowest strata of society. Though the text does not specify, they likely jeer him because of his suffering and weakened position, which they associate with sin. Shame robs him of joy and plunges him into the darkness of depression.

Job, of course, is not the only one in the Bible to experience shame.[26] Adam and Eve felt shame and thus ran away and hid so they would not be exposed further (Gen. 3). They also covered themselves up with loincloths because they could no longer bear to stand completely naked in each other's presence. Cain also experienced shame at God's rejection of his sacrifice. However, rather than fleeing, Cain grew angry and attacked his brother, maintaining his hostile attitude even after he was confronted and judged by God (Gen. 4). Shame makes us run away and, as in the case of Cain, to assault others.

Job takes a third way. His shame makes him seek out God for an explanation. In this, he enacts the attitude expressed by the psalmist:

> You have made us the taunt of our neighbors,
> the derision and scorn of those around us.
> You have made us a byword among the nations,
> a laughingstock among the peoples.
> All day long my disgrace is before me,
> and shame has covered my face
> at the words of the taunters and revilers,
> at the sight of the enemy and avenger.

26. For a fuller discussion of shame in the Bible, see Allender and Longman, *Cry of the Soul*, 191–220.

All this has come upon us,
yet we have not forgotten you,
or been false to your covenant.

. . . .

Rouse yourself! Why do you sleep, O Lord?
Awake, do not cast us off forever!
Why do you hide your face?
Why do you forget our affliction and oppression?
For we sink down to the dust;
our bodies cling to the ground.
Rise up, come to our help.
Redeem us for the sake of your steadfast love. (Ps. 44:13–17, 23–26 NRSV)

Shame can be redemptive when it drives a person to God. Sometimes shame is brought on by sin. David slept with Bathsheba, breaking the seventh commandment. To cover up his crime, he had Uriah, her husband, killed in battle, breaking the sixth commandment. He was able to keep these actions hidden from others until God led Nathan the prophet to confront him, to expose his sin. David did not flee like Adam or lash out like Cain, but rather he repented, and God forgave him (2 Sam. 12).

Job's shame, though, is not the result of sin. People jeer at him because of his suffering, which is not the result of anything he has done. Nonetheless, Job and David respond to their shame similarly in that they allow it to drive them to God.[27]

27. Job will repent, to be sure (42:1–6), but as we will see later in the commentary (and as I have already discussed in the introduction), Job does not repent of anything that led to his suffering and associated shame.

D.
Fourth Speech: Protest of Innocence
(31:1–40)

Translation

1"I cut a covenant with my eyes;
so how could I leer[1] at a virgin?
2What would be my share from God above,
my inheritance from Shaddai on high?
3Isn't calamity reserved for the guilty,
misfortune[2] for those who do wrong?
4Does he not see my path
and number all my steps?
5If I have walked with falsehood,
and my feet hastened toward fraud,
6let me be weighed on an honest scale,
and let God know my blamelessness.
7If my feet have wandered off the path,
and my heart has followed my eyes,
and blemish has clung to my hands,
8let me sow and not eat,
and let my young plants be uprooted.

1. The verb is a Hitpolel of *byn*, which in the Qal means "to understand" but in the Hitpolel normally means something like "behave perceptively" or "to consider closely" (T. E. Fretheim, *NIDOTTE* 1:652–53; see Isa. 1:3; 1 Kings 3:21). In the present context, to "consider" a virgin "closely" would mean to "leer" or maybe even to lust.

2. A hapax legomenon in this meaning, though it may be an extension of the meaning of *nēker* ("foreign"), according to Clines, *Job 21–37*, 961.

9If my heart has been enticed by a woman,
and I lay in wait at the entrance of my friend,[3]
10then may my wife grind for another,
may another man kneel over her,
11for that would be a foul deed,
it would be a criminal offense.[4]
12Indeed, that would be a fire burning down to Abaddon;
it would burn all my produce down to the roots.

13If I rejected proper judgment for my slaves and maidservants
when they made a case against me,
14what would I do then when God rises up against me?
What would I say in return when he makes an inquiry?
15Did not he who made me in the belly make them?
Did he not establish us in a single womb?

16If I deprive the poor of some pleasure,
or cause the eyes of a widow to fail,
17or if I eat my morsel of bread alone,
and not let the orphan eat of it—
18for from my youth I raised him[5] like a father,
I guided her[6] from the belly of my mother.
19If I see anyone perishing for lack of clothing,
or a needy person without covering,
20whose loins have not blessed me,
who has not been warmed up by the fleece of my sheep,
21if I have raised my hand threateningly against an orphan,
because I saw I had allies in the gate,
22then may my shoulder blade fall off my shoulder,
and my arm be broken at the socket.
23For I was panic-stricken at a calamity from God;
I could not bear his majesty.[7]

24If I place my confidence in gold,
or my security in fine gold,
25if I rejoiced at the abundance of my wealth,
or because my hand had found much;

3. Or "neighbor."

4. *ʿĀwōn pĕlîlîm* is probably literally "a guilty thing before the judges."

5. The reference is to the orphan of v. 17. This involves an emendation of the Hebrew, which has "he raised me," and some versions and commentators translate: "though like a father he [God] raised me" (NAB). However, these commentators must emend the second colon, which clearly says "I guided her," to something like "guiding me even from my mother's womb."

6. The reference is to the widow of v. 16b.

7. I take *miśśĕʾētô* as a form of *nśʾ*, "to lift up." Alternatively, it could be a form of *šōʾâ*, "ruin"; see Clines, *Job 21–37*, 968.

26if I looked at the sun[8] that shines,
or the moon moving in its radiance,
27and my heart been enticed in secret,
or my hand passed kisses from[9] my mouth,
28this would be a criminal offense,[10]
for I would have defrauded God above.

29If I rejoiced in disaster of those who hate me,
or became excited when evil found them out—
30I have not allowed my mouth to sin,
by asking for their life with a curse—
31if those of my tent ever asked,
'Who has not been satisfied with his meat?'—
32A stranger did not have to lodge in the street;
I opened my door to the traveler—
33if I concealed my transgression like other people,[11]
hiding my guilt in my bosom[12]
34for fear of the big crowd,
or the terror of the contempt of the clan,
so that I kept quiet and did not go out the door—

35Oh, that someone would listen to me!
Here is my signature! Let Shaddai answer me!
Let my accuser write out an indictment!
36Surely, I will wear it on my shoulder;
I would bind[13] it on me like a crown.
37I would give him an account of all my steps;
I would approach him like a prince.

38If my land has cried out against me,
and its furrows cried together,
39if I have eaten its produce without paying,
or caused its owners to despair,[14]
40let bramble come out rather than wheat,
and stinkweed instead of barley."

The words of Job are ended.

8. Literally "light" (*'ôr*).

9. I take the preposition *lamed* in its rare meaning of "from"; see Smick, "Job," 996.

10. See 31:11.

11. Or "like Adam," referring to Gen. 3.

12. *Ḥōb* is a hapax legomenon but has an Aramaic cognate, *ḥubba'*, and occurs in postbiblical Hebrew.

13. The verb "bind" (*'ānad*) occurs only here and in Prov. 6:21, where the sage urges the son to take the advice of his parents to his heart.

14. Literally "to breathe out," taken in the psychological sense of "to deflate" or "despair."

Interpretation

Chapter 31 finishes Job's monologue. After his affirmation that wisdom may only be found in the fear of the Lord (chap. 28), he contrasted his past blessed life (chap. 29) with his present sorry state (chap. 30). In this chapter, he protests his innocence and announces his intention to go and set God straight.

Many scholars have noted a parallel with the "negative confessions" of the Egyptian "Book of the Dead."[15] According to the Egyptian text, the deceased appears before the gods and announces:

> I have not committed evil against men;
> I have not blasphemed a god;
> I have not done violence to a poor man;
> I have not defamed a slave to his superior.[16]

This statement was part of the Egyptian ritual where a person passed into the afterlife. Contra Johnson, though, I do not believe that Job's negative confession serves this purpose. At the end, he seems more confident than ever that he will get his chance to appear before God, and to that end he exclaims his innocence.

He begins his protest of innocence by denying that he has harbored lust toward a virgin (vv. 1–8). He goes on to deny the even greater crime of having slept with another man's wife (vv. 9–12). Further, he has treated his servants with justice, answering any protests that they might have against him (vv. 13–15). After all, he says, if he is not willing to answer the protests of his slaves, how could he hold God responsible for not answering his complaints? In the following section (vv. 16–23), Job denies that he has mistreated other vulnerable members of society: the orphan, widow, and needy. Next, he denies that he has trusted in wealth rather than God (vv. 24–28). Job ends by denying that he has rejoiced in the downfall of his enemies or withheld hospitality, but this leads to the climax of the chapter, which is Job's confident statement that, if given the opportunity, he would be able to defend himself successfully before God (vv. 29–37).[17] The chapter concludes with Job's curse against himself (vv. 38–39) and the narrative note that Job has ended his speech (v. 40). Will God respond to Job's words? Not immediately. The next chapters introduce an unexpected participant in the disputation—Elihu.

> **1**"I cut a covenant with my eyes;
> so how could I leer at a virgin?

15. See most recently Johnson (*Now My Eye Sees You*, 141–42), who cites earlier examples.

16. Cited in Cornelius, "Job," 287.

17. See commentary below for Dick's analysis that v. 35 is "the key to the legal metaphor in Job" ("Legal Metaphor," 37).

[2]What would be my share from God above,
  my inheritance from Shaddai on high?
[3]Isn't calamity reserved for the guilty,
  misfortune for those who do wrong?
[4]Does he not see my path
  and number all my steps?
[5]If I have walked with falsehood,
  and my feet hastened toward fraud,
[6]let me be weighed on an honest scale,
  and let God know my blamelessness.
[7]If my feet have wandered off the path,
  and my heart has followed my eyes,
  and blemish has clung to my hands,
[8]let me sow and not eat,
  and let my young plants be uprooted."

31:1–8. *I have not lusted.* Since the great poem on wisdom (chap. 28), Job has remembered the "good old days" (chap. 29) and contrasted those times with his present pitiful condition (chap. 30). In this, his final speech before God appears in the whirlwind, he will make one more protest of innocence before boldly asserting his prerogative to meet with God.

This speech clearly shows that Job is fundamentally operating with the same basic retribution theology as the three friends. He protests his innocence as a way to say that he does not deserve his suffering. Such an argument makes sense only in a system where one believes that suffering is caused solely by one's own sin.

Job begins his speech by disavowing lust, specifically of a young woman. The OT does condemn lust through the tenth commandment (Exod. 20:17; Deut. 5:21), which includes the provision not to covet a neighbor's wife. However, the OT does not specifically say that a man, even a married man, cannot desire an unmarried woman. After all, he could marry her. This observation leads some to suggest that Job is not disavowing leering at a human virgin, but at the divine virgin, Asherah.[18] I find this view unlikely, however. Idolatry is not seen as an issue in Job. He is never accused of idolatry. Besides, if we are right that Job is an Edomite (and not a Canaanite or Israelite), then Asherah, a Canaanite goddess, would not be a temptation. The best explanation is that Job is being extremely careful in his morality.

He does, though, admit that if he had leered at a virgin, then he would have forfeited his relationship with God and any prosperity ("my share," "my inheritance") that derived from that relationship. Again, Job seems to think that if he has sinned, then he deserves to suffer. He also acknowledges that God knows his life fully ("Does he not see my path and number all my steps?" v. 4).

18. Good, *In Turns of Tempest*, 130.

What Job wants is fairness. He wants honest scales, which the book of Proverbs asserts that God loves as well (Prov. 16:11).[19] He is fully willing to acquiesce to punishment if he deserves it, but he clearly does not believe that he deserves it.

9"If my heart has been enticed by a woman,
and I lay in wait at the entrance of my friend,
10then may my wife grind for another,
may another man kneel over her,
11for that would be a foul deed,
it would be a criminal offense.
12Indeed, that would be a fire burning down to Abaddon;
it would burn all my produce down to the roots."

31:9–12. *I have not slept with a married woman.* Job continues his protest of innocence by denying that he has had sexual intercourse with another man's wife. It is one thing to leer at a virgin (v. 1) and a totally other and worse thing to sleep with another man's wife. After all, in the context of cultures that practice polygamy, a man could marry an unmarried woman with whom he slept (Exod. 22:16–17), but he could not marry another man's wife. Indeed, Proverbs points out that it is wrong to sleep with a prostitute and that it will sap a man's wealth, but to sleep with another man's wife would result in greater harm, most likely death (see Prov. 6:28–35).

Job denies sleeping with another man's wife and considers just how horrible an act it is to betray a friend by sleeping with his wife. Sleeping with another man's wife, especially a friend's, is so bad that it would result in horrible consequences, rendition to Abaddon—in other words, total destruction. Whatever Job would have achieved in life ("all my produce," v. 12b) would be completely eradicated ("burn . . . down to the roots").

Indeed, Job is so adamant about his innocence in this matter that he evokes a self-malediction. If he has been enticed[20] by a woman and made efforts to act on his lust, then may his wife have intercourse[21] with another man.

13"If I rejected proper judgment for my slaves and maidservants
when they made a case against me,

19. Whybray (*Job*, 146) adds that this idea may come from the Egyptian belief that the gods weigh the heart of the deceased on a scale, and he cites also Proverbs (16:2; 21:2; 24:12), where "Yahweh is said similarly to weigh or assess (a different verb is used) the hearts or the spirits of the living."

20. The verb "enticed" (*pth*) could also be rendered "seduced." See Longman (*Jeremiah, Lamentations*, 147–48) for a discussion of this verb in the context of Jeremiah's lament.

21. The verb "grind" (*ṭḥn*) indicates the motion of the hips in the act of sexual intercourse. The position of kneeling indicates that the man would be on top of her. There may be a double entendre here in that it would be bad enough for his wife to become a menial servant of another man, but the sexual context certainly implies more than that she will grind grain for another.

[14]what would I do then when God rises up against me?
What would I say in return when he makes an inquiry?
[15]Did not he who made me in the belly make them?
Did he not establish us in a single womb?"

31:13–15. *I have not mistreated my slaves.* Job now declares his innocence in his dealings with his slaves and maidservants. The tremendous disparity in power between a master and a slave or servant is such that it is easy for masters to abuse those working for them. Job states that he was just in his dealings with his slaves and took seriously any charges that they made against him. He sees here an analogy with his relationship with God. God is like the master, and Job is like the slave. If he was not good to his slaves, what grounds would he have against God? Indeed, Job finds himself in such a position. He believes that God is unjustly abusing him. But his argument still stands. If he had not been fair, then he would have no ground for his present course, which is to bring his accusations against God. Job knows that God is a special protector of the socially vulnerable, so if Job were unfair, then God would call Job to account. Job, like the sages in Proverbs, knew that though there was a social hierarchy between masters and slaves, before God they were equal, since God made them both (Prov. 22:2 NLT: "The rich and poor have this in common: The LORD made them both"; see also 14:31; 17:5; 29:13).

[16]"If I deprive the poor of some pleasure,
or cause the eyes of a widow to fail,
[17]or if I eat my morsel of bread alone,
and not let the orphan eat of it—
[18]for from my youth I raised him like a father,
I guided her from the belly of my mother.
[19]If I see anyone perishing for lack of clothing,
or a needy person without covering,
[20]whose loins have not blessed me,
who has not been warmed up by the fleece of my sheep,
[21]if I have raised my hand threateningly against an orphan,
because I saw I had allies in the gate,
[22]then may my shoulder blade fall off my shoulder,
and my arm be broken at the socket.
[23]For I was panic-stricken at a calamity from God;
I could not bear his majesty."

31:16–23. *I have not mistreated the socially vulnerable.* Job continues his defense by describing his actions toward the socially vulnerable: the needy, the widow, and the orphan, particularly the last two. The Torah makes very clear that God's people are supposed to take care of those who are weak and in need of help. In the book of the covenant, the widow and the orphan are given special mention: "You must not exploit a widow or an orphan. If you exploit them in any way and they cry out to me, then I will certainly hear their cry. My anger will blaze against you, and I will kill you with the sword. Then your wives will be widows and your children fatherless" (Exod. 22:22–24 NLT). In ancient Israel's patriarchal society, the widow and the orphan lacked a husband and father and thus were open to exploitation. Thus God made known his special concern for them.

The book of Deuteronomy in particular highlights God's concern for the widow and the orphan (see 10:18; 24:17–21). The Deuteronomic covenant curses specify the crimes of those who exploit them: "Cursed is anyone who denies justice to foreigners, orphans, or widows" (Deut. 27:19 NLT). Job himself earlier condemned those who exploited widows and orphans and described them as wicked (6:27; 24:3, 21). In his description of his earlier, better days, he claimed to pay special attention to the needs of the widows and fatherless (29:12–13).

Here Job claims to support the widow (v. 16b). Indeed, he claims to have taken care of her since birth (v. 18b). He has fed the orphan and been like a substitute father to him (vv. 17–18a). He has not taken advantage of orphans by striking them, though the power imbalance between them was extreme ("I had allies in the gate," v. 21b).

Further, he took care of the poor. He made sure that they had clothes (v. 19) and did nothing to hinder them from any pleasure they might experience (v. 16a). Indeed, he made sure that his many sheep (see 1:3) produced clothing that would keep the poor warm in the cold (v. 20). He was so good that he could cite the blessing of the vulnerable from their deepest parts ("loins," v. 20).

Job guarantees his helpful treatment of the weak with a self-malediction. If he is lying and did not care for them, then he asks that his shoulder blade break off his body (v. 22). The motivation for his behavior was fear of punishment from God (v. 23).

24"If I place my confidence in gold,
 or my security in fine gold,
25if I rejoiced at the abundance of my wealth,
 or because my hand had found much;
26if I looked at the sun that shines,
 or the moon moving in its radiance,
27and my heart been enticed in secret,
 or my hand passed kisses from my mouth,
28this would be a criminal offense,
 for I would have defrauded God above."

31:24–28. *I have not made gold my god.* Job also put God first. He did not defraud God by trusting in wealth (vv. 24–25) or in the heavens (vv. 26–27). Job had considerable wealth at the beginning of the story (1:3), but he did not depend on his wealth, and he remained steadfast in his commitment to

Yahweh. He also rejected any temptation to worship the sun or the moon, the two major astral deities of the ancient Near East. Why the sun is specified as a special object of temptation is not clear, but it is true that many pagan cultures in the ancient Near East revered the sun as a major god. Egypt is a prime example of this. Under various names—Ptah, Amon, Re—the sun was an object of worship in Egypt. The sun was also worshiped by the Sumerians as Utu, the Babylonians as Shamash, and the Canaanites as Shemesh. The moon was an object of veneration in the ancient Near East as well. The moon was worshiped by the Sumerians as Su'en (Sin, or Nanna) and by the Canaanites as Yerah (Yarikh). But Job did not substitute the worship of the true God for these false gods.

29"If I rejoiced in disaster of those who hate me,
  or became excited when evil found them out—
30I have not allowed my mouth to sin,
  by asking for their life with a curse—
31if those of my tent ever asked,
  'Who has not been satisfied with his meat?'—
32A stranger did not have to lodge in the street;
  I opened my door to the traveler—
33if I concealed my transgression like other people,
  hiding my guilt in my bosom
34for fear of the big crowd,
  or the terror of the contempt of the clan,
  so that I kept quiet and did not go out the door—

35Oh, that someone would listen to me!
  Here is my signature! Let Shaddai answer me!
  Let my accuser write out an indictment!
36Surely, I will wear it on my shoulder;
  I would bind it on me like a crown.
37I would give him an account of all my steps;
  I would approach him like a prince.

38If my land has cried out against me,
  and its furrows cried together,
39if I have eaten its produce without paying,
  or caused its owners to despair,
40let bramble come out rather than wheat,
  and stinkweed instead of barley."

The words of Job are ended.

31:29–40. *Last protest and desire to meet with Shaddai*. Job's final words are delivered with urgency and are hard to follow. He combines his last protest of innocence with a plea for an audience with Shaddai that is confident of a positive outcome. In a word, he wants an audience with God and believes he can successfully defend himself before him. Before looking more closely at the details of the passage, however, we must address the question of its structure. In vv. 29–34 Job disavows sinful actions by the use of a long, complex, conditional sentence. However, before the prodosis ("if"-clause) leads to the apodosis ("then"-clause), there is an interruption. It is in vv. 35–37 that Job expresses his longing for an audience with God. He then returns to the conditional sentence in v. 38, and we finally get the apodosis in v. 40. The "if-then" structure here is a lengthy self-curse. If Job has engaged in any of the guilty actions he describes, then may he suffer punishment (with the implied converse).

For some, this structure is much too convoluted, and that is why we see attempts to restructure the passage, as in the REB, NAB, and NJB. These versions relocate vv. 38–40 in slightly different ways, but they all end the passage (and Job's speech) with v. 37.[22] My own view is that the structure should stand and that the convoluted speech represents Job's excited state of mind as he finishes his final speech.

In terms of the specifics of the passage, Job begins by disowning the idea that he has rejoiced in his enemy's downfall. In this, Job illustrates the wisdom principles enunciated in Prov. 24:17–18:

> When your enemy falls, don't rejoice.
> When he stumbles, don't let your heart be glad.
> Otherwise, Yahweh will see, and it will be evil in his eyes,
> and he will turn his anger from him.

Since celebrating the downfall of the enemies of Israel is not discouraged in the Bible (Exod. 15; Judg. 5; Esther 9), perhaps the concern is with personal enemies. Notice the motive clause. The fall of the enemy appears to be the result of divine intervention, and the fear is that if God grows angry when he sees us rejoicing at our enemy's defeat, then God will stop punishing our enemy. What is clear is the idea that vengeance is the work of God and not humans (see Deut. 32:35 and the further development of this idea in Rom. 12:17–21).[23] Verse 30 interrupts the "if"-clause in order to deny that Job had ever cursed an enemy.

In vv. 31–32 Job rejects the charge that he has lacked hospitality. He has welcomed people into his tent and has fed them well. He was not stingy like those described in Prov. 23:6–8:

22. That is, with the exception of v. 40c ("The words of Job are ended"), which they all leave at the end of the chapter. Clines (*Job 21–37*, 933) is a good example of a commentator who adopts this strategy.

23. See also Ps. 35:15–16.

> Do not eat food with stingy people;
>   don't long for their delicacies.
> For it is like a hair in the throat.
>   "Eat and drink," they say to you.
>   But their heart is not with you.
> You will eat your crust and vomit it out,
>   and waste your pleasant words.

The importance of hospitality in ancient culture is demonstrated in the Abraham story both positively and negatively. Abraham himself showed proper hospitality to the three strangers who appeared at his tent in Gen. 18:1–15, while the notorious citizens of Sodom and Gomorrah violated principles of hospitality in Gen. 19:1–29. Job asserts that he took care of strangers and travelers.

Next, Job denies that he ever hid transgressions (vv. 33–34). Of course, the three friends have accused him of being a closet sinner all through the debate. Since Job was innocent, they have no solid evidence that he did sin, so they had to assume that he just concealed his sin well. Job denies that; he did not hide his sin. He was not afraid of public opinion but acted openly and honestly.

At this point (v. 35), Job interrupts his protest of innocence in order to proclaim his desire to meet with Shaddai. It is appropriate that this interruption comes at this moment, since he is denying that he is a secret sinner. His denial before a human audience reminds him that he needs to issue a denial in an audience with God. Up to this point, Job has been conflicted in his desire to meet with God. Previously, he has stated the wish to see God and set him straight, but often he has been skeptical whether he would receive a proper hearing. At times, he also has expressed the wish that he had an intermediary to help him in his relationship with God (9:32–35; 16:19–22). But now, near the very end of his words, he imagines himself confidently walking into the presence of God and successfully making his case before him. As Johnson puts it, "This new Job is no longer a defeated man longing for the grave, he is a man who has parried the friends, been emboldened by a revelation of cosmic wisdom and is now ready to speak directly with God."[24] Job will get his wish of an audience with God, but it will not go quite the way he anticipates here (see 38:1).

Job's language is appropriately legal here. He has been accused and believes that God is the one who has accused him. Accordingly, he wants a written indictment. He wants to know what he has been charged with. Job knows he has been charged with some crime because he buys into the retribution theology of the three friends. He is suffering; therefore, God is treating him like a sinner. But what is the charge? He demands an answer. M. B. Dick suggests, on the basis of ancient Near Eastern parallels, that v. 35 is a formal request "before

24. Johnson, *Now My Eye Sees You*, 140.

a third party for a civil hearing at which the judge would compel the plaintiff to formalize his accusations and to present any supporting evidence."[25]

Whatever it is, Job knows that he is not guilty. That is why he says he would take this written indictment and pin it to his shoulder. He even imagines wearing it proudly like a crown. He is so sure of his innocence that he imagines his approach to God not cringing like a suppliant or a criminal, but rather boldly like a prince. He has an ironclad case and will respond to the charges by giving an account of his blameless life ("I would give him an account of all my steps," v. 37a).

Job then returns to his protest of innocence, his long conditional sentence that has not yet reached the apodosis. He has denied taking pleasure in the demise of his personal enemies. He has never denied hospitality even to a stranger. He has never concealed a sin from the public. Finally, he denies that he has sinned against the land by eating its produce without paying. Job then says that if he has done any of these things, then instead of edible and productive foods like wheat and barley, may his land produce bramble and stinkweed.

The narrator concludes this section by noting that Job's words are now ended (or complete). Fisher points out that the verb (*tāmam*) is the root that produces the description of Job as innocent (*tām*; see 1:1).[26] He does not ascribe any significance to this fact, though perhaps he means to say that Job's words being complete also means that they are uttered with integrity. If so, I think he is reading too much into the linguistic similarity. Job has now finished his interaction with the human participants of the book. He will, however, respond to God when God addresses him out of the whirlwind (see 40:3–5; 42:1–6).

Theological Implications

I Am Innocent!

Job ends his words with a final protest of innocence, at the end of which he asserts that he is finally ready to meet God and confront him with his case. Many, particularly Christian, readers of Job are uneasy about Job's assertion of innocence throughout the book and especially at this point. After all, doesn't the Bible teach that we are all guilty and deserving of punishment, even death? In addition, doesn't Paul say that "all people, whether Jews or Gentiles, are under the power of sin" (Rom. 3:9 NLT)? He goes on to substantiate his point by citing a plethora of OT passages from Psalms and Isaiah, indicating that this is not a new thought in the NT. And doesn't James say that "the person

25. Dick, "Legal Metaphor," 39.
26. Fisher, *Many Voices of Job*, 18.

who keeps all of the laws except one is as guilty as a person who has broken all of God's laws" (2:10 NLT)?

Nevertheless, the book of Job presents us very clearly with a person who is innocent and does not deserve the suffering that has come to him. He is correct about this, and the three friends are quite wrong when they blame him for his suffering (42:7). Furthermore, Job is not the only one who protests his innocence in the midst of affliction. A subgenre of lament psalms, for instance, contains a protest of innocence. Psalm 26 is a prime example of such a prayer. It begins: "Declare me innocent, O Lord, for I have acted with integrity" (v. 1 NLT). The psalmist goes on to ask God to put him on trial, confident that his righteousness will be evident. Near the end of the psalm, he beseeches God not to let him "suffer the fate of sinners" (v. 9 NLT), likely indicating that he was either already suffering such a fate or that there were signs that he might.

The psalmist (here identified as David) and Job share many similarities, including the idea that they suffer or, perhaps in the case of the psalmist, might suffer the fate of the guilty even though they are innocent. The difference, and it is a deep and important one, is that Job believes God is treating him, though innocent, as a sinner, and God does not care. The sense conveyed by the psalmist is that of confidence that once God looks at his case, God will recognize that he is not a sinner and will not allow him to suffer that fate.

Perhaps the best way to think of Job's appeal is not that he claims to be utterly sinless. Indeed, he, like everyone, was a sinner, but sinners can be restored to God in the OT through the offering of sacrifices, which we can confidently assume Job offered, not just for his children (1:5) but also for himself. And in any case, we are likely dealing with a sense of proportionality here as well. The intensity of Job's punishment far exceeds the level of his sin. He really does not deserve what he is getting.

But in this life, that is true of everyone to a certain extent. Godly people do not receive all the blessings of the godly, and wicked people do not receive all the punishment that their sins and crimes deserve. Even so, the lament psalms that protest innocence demonstrate that we can call on God to set things right. We can and should protest to God, even though we believe that true retribution will happen not in this life but in the life to come.

Job's protest, though, has grown increasingly impatient, questioning God's justice. Soon he will meet God, though rather than him setting God straight, God will set Job straight.

Christian readers reflecting on Job's protest of innocence cannot help but think of the one truly innocent sufferer, Jesus Christ. If anyone could protest that he did not deserve suffering and a violent death, it is he. While asking God to remove his suffering in the Garden of Gethsemane (Matt. 26:36–46), he nonetheless voluntarily submitted himself to suffering in order to free us from our sin and suffering. Because of Christ's work on the cross, believers may suffer in this life, but in the next they will live with him in joy forever.

V.
Elihu's Speech
(32:1–37:24)

In the introduction (see "Elihu's Monologue"), I dealt with the difficult issue of the place of the Elihu speech in the context of the book as a whole. Here I will only summarize the conclusions that guide the following interpretation. The question whether Elihu's speech was part of an original version of the book of Job or added at a later time cannot ultimately be answered and is not important for interpretation. My interpretation focuses on the final form of the canonical book as we have it, regardless of how that book came to be.

The first observation to make is that Elihu comes out of nowhere, and when he stops speaking, we do not hear from him again. Even if this is the result of its late addition to the book, we must now ask how this section contributes to the meaning of the book. When Elihu begins to speak, he makes clear that he has been a silent observer of the disputation between Job and his three friends. That no one responds to Elihu could mean one of two things. It could be that his speech leads seamlessly to the Yahweh speeches. That is, he provides an anticipation of God's words in chaps. 38–41. Those who take this approach focus on Elihu's last words in chap. 37. However, as I will show in the interpretation below, the bulk of Elihu's speech simply parrots what the three friends have said before. The absence of a response thus should be understood as a lack of interest. Elihu says nothing new and therefore can safely be ignored.

If this is correct, then what function does this speech serve? The retribution theology of the three friends has already been shown inadequate. Why have a fourth voice join the chorus and devote six whole chapters to him? What makes Elihu unique is not the content of his argument, but the ground of his argument. Right at the start, he distances himself from the friends, who based their wisdom on the tradition of the fathers and the experiences of old age. Elihu, for his part, claims a spiritual wisdom. Thus he represents yet another human pretension to wisdom, a false kind of spirituality that leads to error rather than insight.

It could be that he thinks he is the umpire (9:33) that Job hoped for but did not expect. He stands between the three friends and Job and critiques them both. If so, he fails miserably, since he is not the one to bring about resolution.

Elihu's speech, which like the preceding debate between Job and his friends is in poetic format, is prefaced by a prose introduction (32:1–5). Though the three friends stopped talking several chapters ago, we learn for the first time why. They grew silent because Job thought he was right. They were unable to convince him of his culpability. Unexpectedly we are introduced to a character named Elihu. Apparently, there was at least one onlooker to the preceding debate, and he is upset—upset with the three friends because they have been unable to persuade Job, and upset with Job because he continued to think he was more righteous than God. Furthermore, the narrator tells us the reason for Elihu's reticence: he was young, and he deferred to his elders.

In 32:6–10 Elihu begins his speech. Here he expresses the same point as the narrative introduction. That is, he has waited because he was young. The failure of the three friends, though, has now emboldened him to speak in the power of the spirit within him. Once he begins to speak, he does so with a strong sense that he, among all of them, has the truth. Indeed, in 32:11–22 he continues his apologetic, perhaps revealing how peculiar it was for a young man to assert himself in such a situation. He claims that he has no choice. He must "relieve himself" (v. 20) by speaking. He will not use flattery; he will not mince words.

Chapter 33 begins with another call for Job to pay attention to him (vv. 1–11). Elihu is so self-confident that he feels it necessary to tell Job that he is only a human like Job himself. Job should not be intimidated. However, Elihu is perturbed that Job appears to be saying that he, rather than God, is right and that God abuses him.

In vv. 12–30 Elihu strongly objects to Job's putative self-righteousness. God is not unjust, but rather God is trying to teach Job a lesson through his suffering. Suffering has a disciplinary function. It may be, though, that Job can escape suffering through the intervention of a mediator, a possibility that corresponds with Job's own desire in 9:32–35 and 16:18–22. Chapter 33 ends (vv. 31–33) with yet another appeal that Job be quiet and listen to him. Elihu is the one who has wisdom that he intends to impart to Job.

Chapter 34 begins a new division of Elihu's speech, as signaled by the rubric in v. 1. Elihu again feels it necessary to exhort his hearers (and his words presuppose more than just Job) to pay attention to him. He accuses Job of laying down the gauntlet by saying he is innocent and that God attacks him without provocation (vv. 2–6). By doing this, Job aligns himself with evildoers.

He wrongly accuses God of not rewarding those who are obedient to him (vv. 7–9). Thus Elihu reasserts the doctrine of retribution by saying that God repays people according to their deeds (vv. 10–12). After all, God is ruler of the earth by virtue of his nature, not by election or appointment. All life depends on him (vv. 13–15). In the longest section of the chapter, Elihu asserts that God is just and that Job (and anyone else for that matter) is wrong to accuse him of injustice. God will eventually take care of the wicked. If they seem to prosper, their success is short lived (vv. 16–30). Elihu then bemoans the fact that people do not respond well to God's discipline. The implication is that Job is such a person, and Elihu urges him to make peace with God (vv. 31–33). But Job is not responding well to the truth (34:34–37).

Elihu starts the next part of his speech by once again (33:8–11; 34:5–6, 9) providing a summary of Job's position (35:2–3). In 34:5 he said that Job claimed to be righteous; now (35:2) he says that Job claims to be righteous in a way that implies God is not. In 34:9 he represented Job as saying that people get no benefit from God; in 35:3 Job, according to Elihu, repeats this thought. In responding to Job and his friends (v. 4), Elihu argues against Job's view by saying that God does not benefit from people, whether they are good or bad (vv. 5–8).

The second half of his speech in chap. 35 attempts another argument. Elihu says that people suffer because, when they cry out in their suffering, they do not cry out for help to God. Thus God ignores them since they ignore him. In this speech, Elihu continues his attempt to paint Job's speeches as "words heavy with ignorance" (v. 16).

Chapter 36 contains a new speech but offers little new content. As is typical with Elihu, he begins with a rather verbose introduction to his argument (vv. 1–4), where he comes across as narcissistic, claiming to be a spokesperson for God and therefore speaking "perfect knowledge" (v. 4).

In spite of the self-important preface to this speech, Elihu then simply reverts to a rehash of the doctrine of retribution theology with an emphasis on the disciplinary function of suffering. While suffering is disciplinary in some cases, he wrongly makes this a general principle, with an implied personal application to Job's situation (vv. 5–14). In the next section, he emphasizes his point that God uses suffering to prod callous sinners back on the right path. He accuses Job of not seeing this truth and thus denying God's justice. Because of this, Job will end up even more alienated from God than he already is (vv. 15–21). Job needs to realize just how great God is, and he begins a lengthy description of God's power as displayed in nature, particularly the weather, that extends into the next chapter. Elihu is deeply offended by the idea that someone would say God is wrong, but that is precisely Job's opinion (vv. 22–33).

The ancients who provided the chapter divisions likely started a new one (chap. 37) where they did because Elihu again intrudes himself and describes his reaction to what Job is saying about God: it makes his heart drop out of his chest. We might say, it makes his heart stop (37:1). However, we should not lose sight of the fact that this chapter continues the reflection on God's fingerprint in the weather, particularly the thunderstorm (vv. 2–13).

The second unit in the chapter is demarcated by another exordium to Job (v. 14), but even here he continues his reflections on the "wonders of God" (v. 14b) with a focus on meteorological phenomena, but now with an emphasis on heat (vv. 14–20), and then finally in the third and last unit on the glory of the sun. All this should lead to the fear of God (vv. 21–24).

Chapter 37 (perhaps we should speak of 36:22–37:24) has a whole different tone than the preceding part of the Elihu speech. Indeed, his meditations on nature do anticipate the following Yahweh speeches, particularly when Elihu challenges Job concerning Job's knowledge or wisdom through the use of rhetorical questions (37:18–20). One should not, however, change one's overall negative assessment of Elihu's speeches because of this. I agree with Cheney:

> However, when one examines the potential for caricature in Elihu's monologue, especially in the first poem, the unevennesses in the structure, the use of repetition, the naïve use of polysemous terms, the frequency of self-reference and the incessant call for a hearing indicate that caricature, or at least rhetorical flaccidity, dominates the portrayal of Elihu. The argument that Elihu is not a comic figure because he ends on a serious note is really no argument at all since parody is always a careful admixture of seriousness and buffoonery. If a buffoon ends on a serious note, so much the worse for the serious note![1]

Translation

32:1 These three men stopped answering Job, for he was right in his own
eyes. **2**And Elihu, son of Barakel the Buzite, from the clan of Ram, was
exceedingly angry with Job. He was angry because he considered himself
more righteous than God. **3**He was angry with the three friends because
they could not find a response and they thus made God[2] appear guilty.
4Now Elihu had waited to speak with Job because they were older than he

1. Cheney, *Dust, Wind and Agony*, 165–66. A different view is taken by Carson (*How Long, O Lord?*, 148), who suggests that "his main themes prepare the way for the central thrusts of the answer that God himself ultimately gives. If he is not praised, it is because his contribution is eclipsed by what God himself says; if he is not criticized, it is because he says nothing amiss." In the commentary, I argue that Elihu clearly says some wrong things.

2. The ancient scribes had difficulty with the Hebrew text as they received it, with God as the direct object of the Hiphil of the verb "to be wicked" (*rāšaʿ*). They kept it but marked it as suspect (it is thus one of the *tiqqune sopherim,* passages that the scribes corrected because they found them to be objectionable references to God). They suggested that Job (*ʾîyôb*), not God (*ʾĕlōhîm*), was the direct object. It is more likely, in my estimation (and see REB, NJB), that the ancient text is authentic.

was. 5But Elihu saw that there was no adequate response on the part of
the three men, so he was angry.

6So Elihu the son of Barakel the Buzite answered and said:
"I am young,
and you are aged.
Therefore, I was very afraid[3]
to express my opinion to you.
7I said, 'Let days speak,
and an abundance of years make wisdom known.'
8However, it is the spirit in a person,
the breath of Shaddai, that gives them understanding.
9The many[4] are not wise;
the elders do not understand justice.
10So I say, 'Listen to me!
I will show you my opinion.'

11Look, I waited for your words;
I bent ear to your arguments
while you searched for things to say.
12I tried to understand you,
but, look, there was no reproof of Job,
none of you answered his claims.
13You should not say, 'We found wisdom.
God can refute him, but people are not able.'
14He has not directed words to me;
I will not respond to him with your speeches.
15They[5] are discouraged and cannot answer;
words fail them.
16Should I wait if they don't speak?
They stand around and don't give answers.
17For my part, I will answer;
I will share my opinion.
18For I am full of words;
the spirit in me[6] compels me.
19My innards[7] are like wine with no opening,
like new wineskins ready to burst.
20I must speak in order to find relief;
I will open my lips to answer.

3. Taking *zāḥaltî wāʾîrāʾ* as a hendiadys. *Zāḥal* II is a hapax legomenon in biblical Hebrew, but its Aramaic cognate *dḥl* occurs in Daniel (2:31; 4:5 [2]; 5:19; 6:26 [27]; 7:7, 19).

4. So MT. The LXX, Syriac, and Vulgate have an equivalent to the "elders" of the second colon (perhaps reading or understanding *rabbê yāmîm*; see *BHS*).

5. That is, the three friends.

6. Literally "in my belly."

7. Literally "my belly."

21I will not favor anyone,
nor will I flatter any person.
22For I do not know how to flatter.
My Maker would soon carry me away.[8]

33:1But now, hear my words, Job;
pay heed to all my words.
2See, I have opened my mouth.
The tongue in my mouth speaks.
3My speech declares the virtue of my heart.
What my lips know they speak with sincerity.
4The spirit of God has made me;
the breath of Shaddai gives me life.
5If you are able, then answer me.
Arrange yourself before me and take your stand.
6See, I am like you to God.
I too was formed from the clay.
7See, fear of me should not scare you.
My pressure will not be too heavy on you.
8Surely you have spoken in my ear,
and I have heard the sound of your words:
9'I am pure and without transgression.
I am clean and have no guilt.
10See, he finds reasons for being upset with me.
He thinks of me as his enemy.
11He places my feet in shackles;
he guards all my paths.'

12In this you are not correct. I will answer you:
'God is greater than any human.'
13Why do you accuse him?
For no one can answer all his words.[9]
14For in one way God speaks;
and in a second, though humans may not perceive it.
15In a dream, a vision of the night,
when a deep sleep falls on humans,
in a slumber on their beds,
16then he opens their ears
and frightens them with his warnings.
17He wants to turn people away from their deeds,
and check human pride.
18He wants to keep them from the Pit,
their lives from crossing the Water Channel.[10]

8. The implication is that God would punish Elihu if he used flattery.

9. Or with the NRSV, which makes a slight emendation to "my words" rather than "his words": "Why do you contend against him, saying 'He will answer none of my words'?"

10. See my comments on 33:12–30 below.

[19]They are reproved on the bed of pain,
and with continual pain in their bones.
[20]Their lives loathe bread,
and their appetites, choice food.
[21]Their flesh wastes away so it cannot be seen.
Their bones, laid bare, may not be seen.
[22]Their souls draw near the Pit,
their lives to those who bring death.
[23]If there is an angel for one of them,
a mediator, one out of a thousand,
one who declares what is right for him,[11]
[24]and he is gracious to that person and says:
'Redeem[12] him from going down to the Pit;
I have discovered a ransom;
[25]let flesh become fresh[13] like that of a youth;
let him return to his youthful vigor.'
[26]He then entreats God, who accepts him.
He sees his face with a shout of joy.
He will repeat to others that he has been vindicated.
[27]He will sing[14] before others and say:
'I have sinned and sullied virtue.
I have not yet gotten what is due me.'
[28]He has redeemed my life from crossing into the Pit.
My life will yet look into the light.
[29]God does do all these things,
twice, three times with a person,
[30]to bring back his life from the Pit,
to be illuminated with the light of life.

[31]Pay attention, Job. Listen to me.
Be quiet and I will speak.
[32]If there are words, respond to me.
Speak, for I would like to vindicate you.
[33]If not, then you listen to me.
Be quiet and I will teach you wisdom."

11. It is possible to translate this Hebrew phrase (*lĕhaggîd lĕʾādām yošrô*) as "who declares a person upright" (so NRSV). However, the context is speaking of a person who is undergoing disciplinary suffering and who repents before restoration, according to vv. 26–27.

12. There is no verb *pdʿ* in Hebrew, but the context suggests that it is a form of (or an error for a form of) *pdh*.

13. All commentators struggle with the meaning of the unusual Hebrew word *ruṭăpaš*, since Hebrew words are built on three, not four, root consonants. The context strongly suggests the meaning I have given it, though more than one explanation may achieve this desired end. For suggestions, see Hartley, *Job*, 445n3.

14. The MT has *yāšōr* (from *šûr*, "to watch"), but it probably should be emended to *yāšîr* (from *šîr*, "to sing").

34:1 And Elihu answered and said:
2 "Listen, O wise, to my words.
  You who know, give ear to me,
3 for the ear tests words
  as the palate tastes food.
4 Let's choose what is just.
  Let's come to know between us what is good.
5 For Job has said, 'I am righteous.
  God has turned justice away from me.
6 But concerning my case, I am considered a liar.
  An arrow has wounded me incurably,[15] though I am without
    transgression.'

7 Who is a man like Job?
  He drinks ridicule like water;
8 he travels with a band of evildoers,
  going with the wicked.
9 He has said, 'People get nothing
  out of taking pleasure in God.'

10 Therefore, those who have sense, listen to me.
  Wickedness is far from God,
  guilt, from Shaddai,
11 for he will repay people for their deeds.
  He will find them out according to their ways.
12 Surely God does not do wicked things;
  Shaddai does not twist justice.

13 Who appointed him over the earth?
  Who set him over the whole wide world?
14 If he were to turn his mind toward himself
  and gather his spirit and breath back to himself,
15 all flesh would expire altogether,
  people would return to the dust.

16 If you have understanding, listen to me;
  give ear to the sound of my words.
17 Will one who hates justice rule?[16]
  Will you condemn someone who is righteous and mighty?
18 Who[17] says to a king, 'You are a scoundrel!'
  or to princes, 'You are wicked!'?

15. Literally "my arrow is incurable." The proposed translation (see also NRSV, NJB, and many commentators) considers "arrow" as shorthand for a wound caused by an arrow. The arrow is Job's not because he shot it, but because he is shot by it.

16. The context seems to demand a meaning like "rule" for *ḥbš* here, but it is hard to justify it from the use of the root elsewhere, which has the meaning "to bind" or "to saddle."

17. The MT has an interrogative *he*, but some have revocalized it as *hāʾômēr*, "he who says," following LXX and other versions (see *BHS*). See Smick, "Job," 1013.

19Who shows no favoritism to princes,
nor recognizes nobles more than the poor,
for they are all the work of his hands?
20In a moment they die, in the middle of the night.
The people are shaken and pass away.
The mighty are taken away and not by human hand.
21For his eyes are on the paths of people.
He sees all their steps.
22No darkness, no deep darkness,
is able to hide those who do evil.
23He has not set on people an appointed time[18]
to come before God in judgment.
24He breaks the strong without investigation.
He makes others stand in their place.
25He recognizes their works;
he overturns them at night and they are crushed.
26He slaps them for their wickedness
in a place where others are looking on,
27because they turned away from following him,
and didn't pay attention to all his paths.
28They caused the cries of the poor to come before him;
he heard the cries of the afflicted.
29He is quiet, so who can condemn?
He hides his face, so who can look on him,
among the nation and among people altogether?
30So the godless do not rule,
those who ensnare people.

31For who has said to God,
'I endured punishment, and I will not do wrong any longer.
32Teach me what I do not see.
If I have done evil, I will not do it again'?
33Will he make peace with you since you rejected him?
You must choose, not I.
Speak whatever you know.

34Sensible people will say to me,
wise people who listen to me:
35'Job speaks without knowledge.
His words are not insightful.
36Oh, that Job would be examined completely
because his responses are like those of the guilty.
37For he adds transgression to his sin.
He claps his hands among us.
He multiplies his words against God.'"

18. Emending MT *'ôd* to *mô'ēd*; see Hartley, *Job*, 455n12.

35:1 And Elihu answered and said:
2“Do you think this is just?
You have said, ‘I am right rather than God.’[19]
3For you have said, ‘How does it advantage me?
How have I benefited by refraining from sin?’
4I will respond to your words,
and to your friends with you as well.
5Look at the heavens and see.
Gaze at the clouds high above you.
6If you sinned, what would you do to him?
Or if your transgressions multiplied, what would you do to him?
7If you are right, what would that give to him?
Or what does he receive from your hand?
8Your wickedness influences a person like you,
your righteousness, a human.

9They cry out because of their many oppressions;
they call for help because of the arm of the great.[20]
10They do not say, ‘Where is God my Maker
who gives strength[21] at night,
11who teaches us more than the animals of the earth,
makes us wiser than the birds of heavens?’[22]
12There they cry out, but he does not answer,
due to the pride of those who do evil.
13It is all in vain, since God does not hear,
Shaddai does not notice.
14How much less when you say you do not notice him,
that the case is before him and you wait for him.
15Because his anger does not punish,
he does not much care about transgression,[23]
16Job cracks his mouth open with meaninglessness;
his words are heavy with ignorance.”

36:1 And Elihu continued and said:
2“Have some patience with me, and I will inform you,
for I still have words to speak on God’s behalf.

19. Or, with the same meaning, “I am more right than God,” taking the *min* as comparative. A wooden translation of the expression (*ṣidqî mēʾēl*) is “my right from God,” which some take to mean that Elihu is stating that Job believes he will be adjudicated right by God. See, for instance, the NRSV: “I am in the right before God.”

20. The verse is chiastically arranged; literally translated: “From their many oppressions they cry out—they call for help because of the arm of the many.”

21. Or “songs.”

22. The verse is chiastically arranged; literally translated: “teaches us more than the animals of the earth—more than the birds of the sky makes us wise.”

23. I emend *bappaš* to *bĕpešaʿ*. See *BHS* and Clines, *Job 21–37*, 792–93.

3I carry my knowledge from afar;
I ascribe righteousness to the one who made me.
4For truly my words are no lie;
perfect knowledge is with me.
5Look, God is mighty in strength.
He does not reject the pure of heart.[24]
6The wicked will not live;
he gives justice to the afflicted.
7He does not withhold his eye from the righteous.
With kings on the throne,
he makes them reign forever and exalts them.
8And if they are bound in chains
and caught in cords of affliction,
9he tells them what they have done
and their transgressions, because they have acted proudly.
10He opens their ears to instruction,
and tells them to return from guilt.
11If they listen and obey,
their days will finish happily,
and their years pleasantly.
12But if they do not listen, they will pass through the Water Channel.[25]
They will expire without knowledge.
13Those who are godless in heart are set in their anger.
They do not cry for help when he imprisons them.
14They die in their youth.
Their life ends with temple prostitutes.
15He saves the afflicted by their affliction.
He opens their ear with oppression.
16He is seducing you out of distress,
to a broad place where there is no constraint.
What is set on your table is full of fatness.
17But you are obsessed with the case of the wicked.
Judgment and justice hold on tightly to you.
18Beware[26] that you not be seduced by abundance.[27]
Don't let a big ransom payment turn you aside.

24. This verse has a number of difficulties, likely indicating that the text is corrupt. The Hebrew text as it stands would be translated, "Look, God is strong and does not reject. He is strong in power of understanding," which does not make much sense, especially in the context. For one thing, the verb "reject" (*mā'as*) needs an object. My translation is dependent on Clines (*Job 21–37*, 810–11), who among other moves emends the second "strong" (*kabbîr*) in the verse to "pure" (*bĕbar*) and makes this the object of the verb "reject."

25. See my comments on 33:12–30 below.

26. Reading *ḥămēh* rather than *ḥēmâ* ("anger") with Pope, *Job*, 271; and Habel, *Job*, 498.

27. An alternative reading retains the MT "anger" (*ḥēmâ*; see the previous footnote) and understands the rare *sāpeq* as "scoffing." See NRSV: "Beware that wrath does not seduce you into scoffing." This rendering, while possible, does not work as well with the second colon of the verse.

19Will your cry for help keep things in order,
or all the strength of your power?
20Do not pant away for the night,
where people are cut off from their place.
21Watch out! Don't turn aside to iniquity.
For you have chosen this rather than affliction.

22Indeed, God is exalted in his power;
who is a teacher like him?
23Who prescribes to him his path?
Who says to him, 'You have done wrong'?
24Remember to extol his works,
which people commemorate in song.
25All people have gazed on them;
everyone looks from a distance.
26Indeed, God is exalted, and we do not know him.
The number of his years is unknowable.
27He holds in check drops of rain.
He[28] filters rain for his stream,[29]
28which the skies pour forth
and drop abundantly on humanity.
29Can anyone understand the spreading clouds,
the thundering of his booths?
30See how he spreads his light around him.
He covers the roots of the sea.
31For by these he governs the peoples
and provides plenty of food.
32He fills[30] up his palms with the lightning,
and he commands it to strike the mark.
33His thunder[31] speaks about it,[32]
the passion[33] of his anger against iniquity.

37:1 At this[34] my heart trembles
and drops out of its place.[35]
2Listen, listen to the shaking of his voice,
and the rumbling that comes out of his mouth.

28. Hebrew "They," but context requires "He."

29. See Gen. 2:6; *ʾēd* is cognate with Akkadian *edû*, "flood," though the word could mean "mists" in both places.

30. Literally "he covers his palms," but if he covers his palms, he may be said to fill them with lightning.

31. I emend to *raʿmô* (see Pope, *Job*, 268), though it is also possible to come up with a similar meaning by taking *rēʿô* from *rwʿ* in the sense of "loud crashing noise."

32. That is, the thunder announces the onset of a powerful storm.

33. I emend *miqneh* ("livestock") to a form of *qnʾ* (Clines, *Job 21–37*, 834).

34. "This" refers back to 36:22–33, where Elihu begins his description of God, who is "exalted in power" (36:22).

35. "Its place" is presumably the chest.

3Under the heavens, he lets it loose,
his lightning, to the ends of the earth.
4After it, his voice roars,
he thunders with his exalted voice.
He does not restrain them
when his voice is heard.
5God thunders wondrously with his voice;
he does great things that we cannot know.
6To the snow he says, 'Fall on the earth,'
the same to the showers of rain, the showers of driving rain.
7He puts a seal on the hand of every person,
so the people might come to know his handiwork.
8The wild animals enter into their hiding place;
they stay in their lair.
9The whirlwind comes forth from the chamber;
cold, from the north winds.
10Ice comes from the breath of God;
the wide waters are frozen hard.
11With moisture he loads the thick clouds.
The clouds scatter his lightning.
12It[36] turns round and round by his guidance[37]
to accomplish all that he commands them
on the surface of the inhabited world.
13Whether for correction,[38] or for the land,
or out of loyalty, he brings them forth.

14Give ear to this, Job.
Stop and understand the wonders of God.
15Do you know how God appoints their tasks
and makes the lightning shine in his clouds?
16Do you know the spreading[39] clouds,
the wonders of the one who has perfect knowledge?
17You swelter in your clothes,
when the earth is still, due to the south wind.
18Can you, with him, spread out the sky,
hardened[40] like a cast mirror?
19Teach us what we should say to him.
We cannot arrange our thoughts in the darkness.

36. That is, the "lightning."

37. "Guidance" (*taḥbûlôt*) appears a number of times with this meaning in Proverbs (1:5; 11:14; 12:5; 20:18; 24:6).

38. Literally "rod" (*šēbeṭ*), but here as a tool of correction. Proverbs uses "rod" in the literal sense in contexts that denote correction (Prov. 10:13; 23:13, 14; 29:15).

39. The Hebrew word (*miplĕśê*) is a hapax legomenon and difficult. Among the many attempts to find an appropriate meaning, it seems best to take it as equivalent in meaning to *miprĕśê* in 36:29 (and perhaps even emend to this form). See Clines, *Job 21–37*, 845.

40. Or "strengthened."

20Will it be reported to him when I speak?
Did a person ever say that he wanted to be swallowed up?

21But now no one can look at the light,[41]
bright as it is in the sky,
when the wind passes by and clears it.
22A golden glow[42] comes from the north;
an awesome splendor is all around God.
23Shaddai, we cannot find him,
exalted in power.
He will not violate justice and abundant righteousness.
24Therefore, people fear him.
All who are wise of heart fear[43] him."

Interpretation

1These three men stopped answering Job, for he was right in his own
eyes. 2And Elihu, son of Barakel the Buzite, from the clan of Ram, was
exceedingly angry with Job. He was angry because he considered himself
more righteous than God. 3He was angry with the three friends because
they could not find a response and they thus made God appear guilty.
4Now Elihu had waited to speak with Job because they were older than he
was. 5But Elihu saw that there was no adequate response on the part of
the three men, so he was angry.

32:1–5. *Introducing Elihu*. Elihu's speech begins with a short prose introduction. The narrator makes his presence known and tells the reader why the three friends became silent. They gave up their arguments because Job was not persuadable. He remained "right in his own eyes." In Proverbs, to be "right in one's own eyes" is negative and contrasts with fearing and trusting God (Prov. 3:7; 26:5, 12, 16; 28:11). It marks a person as arrogant and unteachable. Here the narrator is giving us the three friends' perspective, and that is how Job comes across to them. They see no reason to go on.

Into the silence steps a new and hitherto unannounced character, Elihu. Apparently, he has been a bystander during the discussion between the four men, but readers just learn of it at this point. Whereas Eliphaz is described as a Temanite, Bildad a Shuhite, and Zophar a Naamathite (2:11), Elihu has

41. Here *ʾôr* is probably referring to the sun.

42. Literally simply "gold," but in reference to lights in the sky it probably refers to golden sunlight.

43. The MT has a form of *rʾh* ("to see") here, yielding a translation "he does not see [regard?] any of the wise of heart," which is hard to make sense of in the context. Thus in the above translation I accept a minor emendation to a form of the verb *yrʾ*.

a lengthy patronymic—"son of Barakel the Buzite, from the clan of Ram"—which begins to characterize him as pretentious, a characterization borne out by his words. We know nothing else of Barakel,[44] but a Ram was an ancestor of David (Ruth 4:19; 1 Chron. 2:9, 25). Buz is known in Gen. 22:21 as the brother of Uz, who was a nephew of Abraham. Whether Ram and Buz in Elihu's ancestry are the same as the relatives of Abraham and David is undetermined, but it does point to the probability that Elihu is a Hebrew rather than an Edomite like the other characters of the book.

The first thing we learn about Elihu is that he is angry—angry at both the three friends and Job. He is furious with Job because Job considered himself to be more righteous than God. Job held to his innocence, and as he did, he accused God of injustice. God himself will later reveal his anger toward Job on this matter as well (40:8). The question is whether Elihu is also angry because he thinks that Job is a sinner, as Job's three friends did. His later speeches will indicate that he did think that Job had sinned. The Hebrew, as corrected by the scribes, goes on to suggest that he is also angry with the three friends because they still held Job guilty, even though they were unable to persuade Job of their arguments. Elihu's position here is not immediately clear. Was he upset because they could not persuade Job of his guilt or because they could not see that Job was not guilty, though they kept treating Job as a sinner? My translation reflects the original text before the scribes corrected it, however (see the translation note for 32:3). I think it much more likely that Elihu was upset with the friends not because they kept treating Job as guilty in spite of their anger but because their failure made God look morally capricious.

The prose introduction ends by explaining why Elihu has held his peace up to this point: it was a matter of age. In the ancient Near East, the elders were thought to be wiser than young people. The appeal to the authority of old age has already been made by both Job (12:12) and the three friends (8:8; 15:10). On the surface, there is good reason for this belief. If one learns from experience and observation, then the older a person is, the more knowledge that person has amassed. Proverbs also suggests that wisdom grows when one learns from one's mistakes (3:34; 11:2; 15:33; 16:18).[45] Again, young people have not lived long enough to benefit from this life training. However, in the next section Elihu is going to argue that wisdom is not always associated with the elders.

6So Elihu the son of Barakel the Buzite answered and said:
"I am young,
  and you are aged.

44. Though Konkel ("Job," 190) points out that it is a name known from later history (early fifth century BC) in the Murashu family archives.

45. See Longman, *Proverbs*, 77–78.

Therefore, I was very afraid
to express my opinion to you.
7I said, 'Let days speak,
and an abundance of years make wisdom known.'
8However, it is the spirit in a person,
the breath of Shaddai, that gives them understanding.
9The many are not wise;
the elders do not understand justice.
10So I say, 'Listen to me!
I will show you my opinion.'"

32:6–10. *The spirit of God inspires Elihu.* The narrator introduces Elihu's speech by repeating two-thirds of his patronymic, again suggesting that he is pretentious. His opening comments also highlight a kind of self-centeredness that runs throughout his speeches. He did defer to the elders for a period of time, but one gets the impression of a young man just bursting to express his opinion. He wanted to speak, but his fear kept him silent. Social custom dictated that elders would speak first and well (see my comments on 32:1–5), but now he realizes that it is not age that leads to wisdom.[46] His conclusions are based on the failure of the three elder friends and Job to resolve the problem. But in his statement in v. 9, he apparently concludes that elders are not wise as a general principle rather than that these four aged men are not particularly wise in this situation.

He offers yet another source for wisdom, the "spirit in a person." This spirit is further defined (in good "A, what's more B" parallelism) as the "breath of Shaddai." In essence, Elihu claims that his wisdom is divinely inspired. Such wisdom is not dependent on experience and observation, and therefore a young person can be wise. In the dynamic of the book of Job, then, Elihu represents a different attitude toward wisdom. Since we do not know the precise intellectual and cultural background of the book, we cannot be certain, but it is a likely inference that Elihu represents a school of thought or at least a commonly held belief at the time the book was written (see "The Genre of the Book of Job" in the introduction). Finally, Elihu brings his opening remarks to a close by calling attention to himself and his opinions: "Listen to me! I will show you my opinion."

11"Look, I waited for your words;
I bent ear to your arguments
while you searched for things to say.
12I tried to understand you,
but, look, there was no reproof of Job,
none of you answered his claims.

46. If I am correct to stay with the MT's "many" (*rabbîm*) rather than emending (with the LXX, Syriac, and Vulgate) to some near synonym of "elders" (see the translation note for 32:9 above), then Elihu is also saying that the individual (Elihu himself) may have the truth when the majority (represented by the three friends) does not.

[13]You should not say, 'We found wisdom.
God can refute him, but people are not able.'
[14]He has not directed words to me;
I will not respond to him with your speeches.
[15]They are discouraged and cannot answer;
words fail them.
[16]Should I wait if they don't speak?
They stand around and don't give answers.
[17]For my part, I will answer;
I will share my opinion.
[18]For I am full of words;
the spirit in me compels me.
[19]My innards are like wine with no opening,
like new wineskins ready to burst.
[20]I must speak in order to find relief;
I will open my lips to answer.
[21]I will not favor anyone,
nor will I flatter any person.
[22]For I do not know how to flatter.
My Maker would soon carry me away."

32:11–22. *I cannot contain myself.* In vv. 11–12 Elihu repeats his claim that he respectfully waited and paid close attention to the debate. He concluded, though, that the three friends' arguments were unsuccessful against Job. Job had claimed that he was innocent of any crime and therefore did not deserve his suffering. He also claimed that God was guilty of injustice. The friends were not able to counter those arguments in a way that would silence Job. Elihu then quotes the friends as saying, "We found wisdom. God can refute him, but people are not able." Apparently, they said this as they concluded their words against Job. They have given it up and "turned it over to God," so to speak. They are not denying their own wisdom, but addressing Job's stubbornness. The friends have given it their all, but Job is just too stubborn to take it in. God will have to do it. Elihu describes them as discouraged in their endeavors (v. 15).

That is not good enough for Elihu, who thinks he is up to the task. He claims he will take a different tack and not address Job with the same arguments (v. 14b). It remains to be seen whether this claim is accurate (see my concluding comments on 37:21–34).

Their silence, in other words, encourages Elihu's intervention (vv. 16–17). Again, he states his determination to share his ideas. Indeed, he feels compelled to speak. He cannot control himself. He compares himself to a wineskin that is filled to the brim and bursting at the seams. He has pent-up energy. Jeremiah famously expressed a similar type of compulsion when he spoke of words that were in him "like a burning fire shut up in my bones; I am weary with holding it in, and I cannot" (Jer. 20:9 NRSV). The difference between

Jeremiah and Elihu, though, is that the former did not want to speak but could not help himself. On the other hand, the impression we get from Elihu is that his compulsion arises from his own burning desire to speak. He needs to speak in order to "find relief" (v. 20). Indeed, Elihu's comments about needing to speak because of his pent-up words are intentionally evocative of the need to pass gas.

However, Elihu does have standards in his speech. He will speak his mind, and he will speak it frankly. "Flattery" is not in his vocabulary. He prides himself in his straight talk and also in his fair talk ("I will not favor anyone," v. 21a). It is true, according to Proverbs, that flattery is the height of folly (Prov. 26:28; 28:23; 29:5). Elihu rightly knows that God is pleased neither with flattery nor with partiality.

Thus Elihu gives his credentials for speaking to Job's situation. The next five chapters contain his arguments.

1"But now, hear my words, Job;
pay heed to all my words.
2See, I have opened my mouth.
The tongue in my mouth speaks.
3My speech declares the virtue of my heart.
What my lips know they speak with sincerity.
4The spirit of God has made me;
the breath of Shaddai gives me life.
5If you are able, then answer me.
Arrange yourself before me and take your stand.
6See, I am like you to God.
I too was formed from the clay.
7See, fear of me should not scare you.
My pressure will not be too heavy on you.
8Surely you have spoken in my ear,
and I have heard the sound of your words:
9'I am pure and without transgression.
I am clean and have no guilt.
10See, he finds reasons for being upset with me.
He thinks of me as his enemy.
11He places my feet in shackles;
he guards all my paths.'"

33:1–11. *Listen to me*. The previous chapter was pretty much Elihu's apologetic for stepping forward and adding his perspective. He highlighted the failure of the three friends to bring Job into line and justified his own speech based on divine inspiration rather than the experience of age. He also indicated that he had no choice but to speak since his words were pent up inside and he could no longer contain himself. In the opening, one gets the impression of an excitable, overconfident, and self-centered young man.

Chapter 33 begins with a call to Job to listen to him. Verse 1 is an exordium to listen, not formally dissimilar to what one encounters in the discourses of Proverbs (see Prov. 2, which is one long exordium). The difference, though, is that in Proverbs the aged father is instructing his son, and here we have a young man instructing the aged Job. In v. 2 Elihu calls Job's attention to the fact that he has begun speaking, a fact that one imagines would be hard to miss, and likely should be taken as a continuation of Elihu's rather pompous manner of speaking. In v. 3 Elihu proclaims his speech as virtuous and sincere. He is in keeping with the teaching of Proverbs (Prov. 16:23) to say that words reflect one's heart, but such an evaluation is probably better left for others to make.

In v. 4 Elihu says that he is a divinely made creature. It is a little difficult to know precisely what Elihu intends to communicate by this statement. Perhaps he again is basing his authority on God (32:8). Or perhaps he is simply saying that he is a creature just like Job. That seems to be the point of vv. 6–7. In v. 6 Elihu states that he is really no different from Job. They are both God's creatures, so Job should not be afraid of Elihu (v. 7). Of course, we readers have no indication of how Job is reacting to Elihu as he speaks. From what we know about Job through the dialogues, though, it seems unlikely that Elihu's words would lead Job to back off in fear. More likely, he would want just to get away from this annoying young man. If so, then Elihu's comments here indicate yet again a rather overblown estimation of the effect of his presence on others. Whybray is surely right to call Elihu's statement in vv. 6–7 "patronizing."[47]

In the midst of this reflection on their common bond as God's creatures, Elihu has called on Job to come before him so that Elihu can address him directly (v. 5). He wants to speak to him and have Job answer him. Though the language is not the same, it may not be a stretch to see in Elihu's call to Job an anticipation of God's call. If so, then the contrast in Job's responses to the two is also of interest and shows Elihu in a bad light. Job obviously listens to God and responds with repentance. Job never responds to Elihu, and we do not even know for sure whether Job heard a word he said.

In vv. 9–11 he lays out what he thinks is Job's position by supposedly quoting him. It is clear, though, that Elihu is not quoting Job's argument verbatim. At least, his "quote" cannot be matched exactly with any of Job's earlier statements. Perhaps he is trying to summarize the gist of Job's argument. Elements of Elihu's representation of Job's position may be found in 13:24, 27. However, it is not fair to say that Job represented himself as "pure," "without transgression," "clean," or having "no guilt." Job once calls his prayer "pure" (16:17), but never himself. It is only Bildad (8:6) and Zophar (11:4) who use the word "pure" (*zak*) earlier, and they too use it in contexts where they are

47. Whybray, *Job*, 154.

saying that Job claims to be pure. In a similar vein, Job never claims to be "clean" (*ḥap*) elsewhere.[48]

Job never claims to be absolutely without transgression (*pešaʿ*) or guilt either. Indeed, in 7:21 he asks why God just doesn't pardon his transgression and guilt. In 14:17 Job wishes that God would cover over his transgressions and guilt so they would not affect his relationship with him. In 31:33 Job protests that he has not been the type of person who tries to hide his transgressions. The closest that Job comes to denying transgression, guilt, and sin for that matter is in 13:23, but there Job is asking God to inform him of the faults that have led to his suffering so he can counter the charges.

Elihu has misconstrued Job's position (as the three friends did earlier). Job is not saying he is without sin (see also 9:2). His claim is that his sin does not deserve the level of suffering that he presently experiences. He is arguing that his suffering is not the result of sin. And in this we know that he is correct, and the three friends and Elihu are all horribly wrong.

On the other hand, Elihu is correct that Job believes that God has taken a hostile stand toward him (vv. 10–11). Indeed, as we have already seen, some even consider the possibility that Job's name should be translated "enemy" with the idea that he believes God has become his enemy, and he states this explicitly in 13:24. He also believes that God has trumped up charges against him. After all, Job agrees with the three friends that suffering is the result of sin, so there have to be charges, even if they are false ones. Job also does believe that God has placed his feet in shackles (13:27).

12"In this you are not correct. I will answer you:
'God is greater than any human.'
13Why do you accuse him?
For no one can answer all his words.
14For in one way God speaks;
and in a second, though humans may not perceive it.
15In a dream, a vision of the night,
when a deep sleep falls on humans,
in a slumber on their beds,
16then he opens their ears
and frightens them with his warnings.
17He wants to turn people away from their deeds,
and check human pride.
18He wants to keep them from the Pit,
their lives from crossing the Water Channel.
19They are reproved on the bed of pain,
and with continual pain in their bones.
20Their lives loathe bread,
and their appetites, choice food.

48. The word *ḥap* is used only here, but Job never uses any other synonym to describe himself either. For instance, *bar* (clean) is used only by the friends (11:4; 22:30).

21Their flesh wastes away so it cannot be seen.
Their bones, laid bare, may not be seen.
22Their souls draw near the Pit,
their lives to those who bring death.
23If there is an angel for one of them,
a mediator, one out of a thousand,
one who declares what is right for him,
24and he is gracious to that person and says:
'Redeem him from going down to the Pit;
I have discovered a ransom;
25let flesh become fresh like that of a youth;
let him return to his youthful vigor.'
26He then entreats God, who accepts him.
He sees his face with a shout of joy.
He will repeat to others that he has been vindicated.
27He will sing before others and say:
'I have sinned and sullied virtue.
I have not yet gotten what is due me.'
28He has redeemed my life from crossing into the Pit.
My life will yet look into the light.
29God does do all these things,
twice, three times with a person,
30to bring back his life from the Pit,
to be illuminated with the light of life."

33:12–30. *Suffering as discipline*. Up to this point, Elihu has mainly been concerned to justify his intrusion into the discussion. He ended the previous section by giving his summary of Job's position. Job, he asserts, claims to be without blame in his suffering. The true cause, Job believes, is God's hostile stance toward him. Elihu is essentially correct in this summary of Job's position. Perhaps Job does not insist on an absolute moral purity (see 9:2), but he clearly believes he is essentially innocent. Certainly, he does not believe that his present suffering is the result of any fault of his own. He does believe that God has taken the stance of an enemy against him (19:11).

In v. 12a Elihu makes his opinion of Job's views crystal clear. Job is "not correct." Elihu does not believe that God is the one responsible for Job's suffering. As he continues, he will point the finger at Job himself.

He begins with a statement of amazement at Job's chutzpah (vv. 12b–13). How dare he make accusation against God? God is greater than any human. God speaks to humans, and they are not capable of response. God does bring suffering on humans but not because he is their enemy. Rather, God does his very best through speech and act to keep humans from the worst possible fate. Indeed, God speaks to humans not just in one way but in two (v. 14). This numerical parallelism ("one, yea two")[49] should be taken to mean "many ways," but the following section does specify two ways in particular.

The first way God speaks to people is through dreams (vv. 15–18). God waits until the night to warn people of behaviors that might lead them to death. He does not want people to die because of their actions. In v. 18 Elihu uses mythological language to describe death. The Pit is a reference to the grave and more profoundly to the underworld. The Water Channel is only mentioned in Job (see also 36:12). Crossing the Water Channel, though, is clearly a reference to dying. In Mesopotamian mythology, for instance, in order to get to Utnapishtim (the Babylonian Noah), Gilgamesh (a Sumerian King) must cross a body of water.[50] Later Greek mythology also described the dead as crossing the River Styx. Elihu, in short, is saying that God warns people in their sleep in order to keep them from dying. Otherwise, they would continue in their self-seeking pride and do actions that would lead to their death.

Verses 19–22 describe the second way in which God speaks to people in order to save them from the result of their bad deeds and pride (v. 17), that result being again described as a descent into the Pit (grave, underworld; v. 22). This second way speaks more directly to Job's situation. Elihu's argument is that God tries to keep people from evil through suffering, in particular through sickness. In other words, God uses suffering to discipline people. The suffering that Elihu describes is significant. God's admonition keeps them in bed because of their pain, pain going so deep that it can be described as "pain in their bones" (v. 19b). Their suffering prevents their enjoyment of food (v. 20), seemingly resulting in their "wasting away" (v. 21).

Elihu's argument has a point. Elsewhere in the Bible, God clearly uses suffering for a disciplinary purpose. Psalm 30 is the thanksgiving prayer of a person who has recovered from an illness so severe that he was heading to the Pit (30:9). In the psalmist's description of his earlier plight (vv. 6–7), he recalls that he grew presumptuous in his prosperity, with the result that God hid his face. He believes that God's absence led to his sickness, which he took as a warning. By calling on God (v. 8), he heeded the warning and was thus healed.

Indeed, the book of Proverbs states as a principle:

> The discipline of Yahweh, my son, do not reject,
> and do not loathe his correction.
> For the one whom Yahweh loves he will correct,
> even like a father who treats a son favorably. (3:11–12)[51]

And the author of Hebrews (12:5–13) cites this passage in his argument that human suffering is often, or at least sometimes, an expression of God's fatherly discipline.

49. See T. Hildebrandt, "Proverb, Genre of," *DOTWPW* 534.

50. *ANET* 92.

51. For translation and commentary, see Longman, *Proverbs*, 129, 134–35.

Thus Elihu is correct to state that God speaks to people through suffering. This is along the lines of C. S. Lewis's oft-quoted statement, "God whispers to us in our pleasures, speaks in our conscience, but shouts in our pain: it is His megaphone to rouse a deaf world."[52] However, since he is at least implicitly suggesting that Job's suffering can thus be explained, the question is whether he is correct in that connection. Elihu will return to the subject of disciplinary suffering later (36:8–21).[53]

Surprisingly, Elihu begins to talk about an angel in vv. 23–25. He imagines an angel mediating on behalf of the one who suffers at the hands of God for disciplinary purposes. According to Elihu, this is rare, one out of a thousand, but nonetheless a possibility. We might remember that Job wondered about mediatorial help as early as 9:32–35. He grew more optimistic about this in 16:19 ("Even now, see, my witness is in heaven, and the one who testifies for me is on high"), and perhaps even in 19:25 ("I know that my redeemer lives"). In the discussion of the theological implications of the latter passage, I argued, based on Elihu's comments, that Job was thinking of an angelic helper in these passages. Little did he (or Elihu) know that the only angel in heaven mentioned in the book of Job ("the accuser"; see 1:6 and 2:1) was working against his interests and not for them.

Some commentators believe that Elihu thinks of himself as this "angel" (or "messenger," as *mal'āk* can be translated).[54] He is, after all, one who is pointing out to Job "what is right for him." However, this seems an awkward way of referring to himself, and it is more likely that Elihu is speaking of a heavenly angel.

Verses 24–25 present the imagined speech of the mediating angel in which he calls for the redemption and restoration of the sufferer. He argues for this redemption based on a "ransom [*kōper*]," a word related to the verb that means "to make atonement" (*kipper*). As Wilson points out, ransom "most often indicates the price for a life, or a payment to avoid punishment (Exod. 21:30; 30:12; Num. 35:31; Ps. 49:8; Prov. 13:8; 21:18; Isa. 43:3)."[55] The context does not make clear the nature of the ransom. Perhaps the lack of clarity is due to the hypothetical nature of the scenario. In other words, Elihu is talking in principle and not in terms of an actual case. Could it be the sufferer's previous righteousness or his future repentance, or perhaps both? We cannot be sure what Elihu has in mind. We can be sure, though, that such an angelic mediator never surfaces for Job. Resolution will come from a different direction.

But for Elihu this redemption leads to restoration in the sense of release from suffering. Such a one will return to "his youthful vigor" (v. 25). The angel's mediation leads to God's acceptance and then the joy of the restored person,

52. C. S. Lewis, *The Problem of Pain* (New York: Macmillan, 1940), 93.
53. See further "The Disciplinary Nature of Suffering" following my comments on Job 4–5.
54. See Wilson, *Job*, 377; Ivanski, *Dynamics*, 32–34.
55. Wilson, *Job*, 377.

who subsequently bears witness to his associates. He knows he is someone who has escaped a horrible fate ("crossing into the Pit," v. 28a). He deserved that fate because of his sin and sullied virtue; but because of the angel's mediation (and presumably his acknowledgment of sin), he will not die, but will continue to live ("my life will yet look into the light," v. 28b).

Elihu concludes this section by saying that God's warnings are typical of him, that is, God does these things not twice but three times with a person. While not a numerical parallelism as such (see comment on v. 14), the effect seems largely the same. That is, by saying "two, three" the poet means "a number of times," not literally two or three times. Specifically, God works often, perhaps even constantly, to keep a person from death, again represented by the Pit. Rather than death, the object of God's disciplinary suffering will continue to live—that is, "be illuminated by the light of life" (v. 30).

31"Pay attention, Job. Listen to me.
Be quiet and I will speak.
32If there are words, respond to me.
Speak, for I would like to vindicate you.
33If not, then you listen to me.
Be quiet and I will teach you wisdom."

33:31–33. *Listen to me!* Elihu has just argued that God uses suffering to discipline his people so they will not continue on a path that will end with their death. Now this argument differs from the argument that suffering is simply punishment for sin, but both viewpoints assume that the sufferer is a sinner. Elihu apparently believes just as much as the three friends do that Job is a sinner.[56] He believes that Job is wrong to disconnect his suffering from his own sin (33:12). His desire is for Job to own up to his responsibility. Thus it is best to understand v. 32 as hoping for a response from Job that would acknowledge his responsibility for his plight. In other words, if Job does admit to fault, then Elihu can vindicate him. It is much less likely that he is urging Job to continue his present line of protestation of innocence. In any case, Elihu does not appear to expect the right answer from Job, because in most of this final section (vv. 31 and 33 in particular) he is simply telling Job to keep his mouth shut and continue to listen, in particular to listen as he teaches Job "wisdom." I have frequently characterized the book of Job as a "wisdom debate," in which the human characters all claim wisdom and criticize the wisdom claims of the other characters;[57] Elihu clearly fits this profile.

56. The friends also occasionally cite the suffering-as-discipline viewpoint (5:17–22).

57. See "The Genre of the Book of Job" as well as "The Theological Message of the Book of Job" in the introduction.

[1]And Elihu answered and said:
[2]"Listen, O wise, to my words.
You who know, give ear to me,
[3]for the ear tests words
as the palate tastes food.
[4]Let's choose what is just.
Let's come to know between us what is good.
[5]For Job has said, 'I am righteous.
God has turned justice away from me.
[6]But concerning my case, I am considered a liar.
An arrow has wounded me incurably, though I am without transgression.'"

34:1–6. *O wise, judge whether Job speaks truly*. Elihu begins a new speech (announced by the rubric in v. 1) with a call again to pay close attention to what he is saying. Interestingly, in this speech he is not simply addressing Job, but "the wise." As far as we know for sure, only Job and the three friends are present, but since we did not learn about Elihu until chap. 32, it is possible that even more people are in attendance. The exact number of hearers is not important for our understanding of the speech, though it does affect how we picture the scene in our minds.

Elihu's call to listen to his words includes an interesting analogy between one's palate tasting and evaluating food and the ear hearing and evaluating speeches. He is asking for the wise in attendance to judge between his viewpoint and that of Job. Verse 4 calls on them to specifically evaluate whose position is "just" or "good." He then again (see 33:9–11) represents Job's position by putting words in his mouth (vv. 5–6).

Now Elihu does not lift an exact quote from Job, but he well represents Job's perspective. Note a passage like 6:28–30 that uses a lot of the vocabulary of this purported speech from Job:

But now resolve to turn to me.
I will not lie to your face.
Turn now. Let no wrong be done.
Turn again. My righteousness is still at stake.
There is no wrong on my tongue, is there?
Does not my taste understand tragedy?

Job defends himself to his three friends that he is not lying both in v. 28b and v. 30a (when he denies that there is wrong on his tongue). He implicitly asserts his righteousness in v. 29b. He even, interestingly, uses the term "taste" (*ḥēk*), the same word translated "palate" in 34:3.

In keeping with Elihu's assessment, Job also believes that God has turned justice aside from him. In 19:6–8 Job states:

Then know that God perverted me.
His hunting net surrounds me.
If I cry out "Violence!" I get no answer.
I yell out, but get no justice.
He has walled up my path, so I cannot pass by.
He has set darkness on my ways.

Finally, on two occasions Job describes how God shoots him with arrows:

For the arrows of Shaddai are in me.
My spirit drinks their poison;
the terrors of God are ranged against me. (6:4)

His archers surround me.
He splits my kidneys open without mercy.
He pours out my gall on the earth. (16:13)

All in all, Elihu gives a fair assessment of Job's viewpoint. He evaluates it in the next section (vv. 7–9).

---

7 "Who is a man like Job?
He drinks ridicule like water;
8 he travels with a band of evildoers,
going with the wicked.
9 He has said, 'People get nothing
out of taking pleasure in God.'"

34:7–9. *Job lies*. Elihu's evaluation of Job's thoughts and speech is biting and devastating. He characterizes Job as someone who takes ridicule upon himself as a thirsty person drinks water.[58] He also surrounds himself with evildoers, a practice that indicates that Job himself is an evildoer. One thinks of the father's warning to the son not to associate with wicked peers for fear that their influence would make the son wicked (Prov. 1:8–19). The language that Elihu uses in v. 8 is reminiscent of Ps. 1:1. Indeed, v. 8b ("going with the wicked," *wĕlāleket ʿim-ʾanšê-rešaʿ*) echoes Ps. 1:1a–b in terminology: the poet says that the blessed person does "not go/walk in the council of the wicked" (*lōʾ hālak baʿăṣat rĕšāʿîm*). No wonder, then, that in Elihu's estimation, Job is cursed and not blessed.

In v. 9 Elihu again purports to quote Job. Job, however, never makes this statement in exactly these words in his earlier speeches. But does it nevertheless represent Job's views? Is it a paraphrase of his position? Interestingly, the question raises the issue broached by the accuser in the prologue. "Is it

58. See Eliphaz's earlier comment that all mortals are "abominable and corrupt" and "drink injustice like water" (15:16).

for no good reason that Job fears God?" (1:9). Certainly in the prologue Job passed the challenge, in that he maintained his allegiance to God even though all the "profit" of such loyalty had been removed from him. In the speeches, though, he does raise questions about God's fairness, in that he, though innocent, suffered. In that sense, one can at least understand why Elihu might think that Job held the view expressed by this statement.

> 10"Therefore, those who have sense, listen to me.
> Wickedness is far from God,
> guilt, from Shaddai,
> 11for he will repay people for their deeds.
> He will find them out according to their ways.
> 12Surely God does not do wicked things;
> Shaddai does not twist justice."

34:10–12. *God treats people fairly*. Elihu has represented Job as stating that people get nothing out of taking pleasure in God. The assumption is that taking pleasure means devotion and obedience. No reward comes from such an attitude and such behavior. In other words, good people are not rewarded and bad people are not punished. Elihu responds to this argument ("therefore," *lākēn*)[59] by stating his belief in this doctrine, and he does so in a manner that shows deep down he does not differ from the three friends, or for that matter from Job himself. In other words, while Elihu began his monologue by insisting that he was different from the friends (32:11–22), he is not advancing a substantially different argument. He too baldly states that God repays people according to their actions. God does not "twist justice" by rewarding the wicked and punishing the righteous. If he did, then God himself would be associated with wickedness and guilt (v. 10).

> 13"Who appointed him over the earth?
> Who set him over the whole wide world?
> 14If he were to turn his mind toward himself
> and gather his spirit and breath back to himself,
> 15all flesh would expire altogether,
> people would return to the dust."

34:13–15. *God is sovereign and sustains the world*. Elihu bolsters his argument that God can do no wrong by now appealing to his absolute sovereignty. Verse 13 poses rhetorical questions that are clearly to be answered with a resounding "No one." No one elected or appointed God to office. He is sovereign, as demonstrated by the fact that people live by virtue of God's

59. He appeals to "those who have sense" (v. 10), a reference to his audience composed of sages, at least the three friends, if not a broader circle of wisdom teachers.

will. If God were to withdraw his life-giving spirit and breath, humans would just die and decompose. We hear an echo of Gen. 2:7, which describes God's creation of Adam as breathing his breath (*nišmat*) into the body he formed from the dust. Removing the breath would lead to a reversion to dust. Note also that Eccles. 12:7 describes death as the dust returning to the earth and the spirit (*rûaḥ*) returning to God.

16"If you have understanding, listen to me;
give ear to the sound of my words.
17Will one who hates justice rule?
Will you condemn someone who is righteous and mighty?
18Who says to a king, 'You are a scoundrel!'
or to princes, 'You are wicked!'?
19Who shows no favoritism to princes,
nor recognizes nobles more than the poor,
for they are all the work of his hands?
20In a moment they die, in the middle of the night.
The people are shaken and pass away.
The mighty are taken away and not by human hand.
21For his eyes are on the paths of people.
He sees all their steps.
22No darkness, no deep darkness,
is able to hide those who do evil.
23He has not set on people an appointed time
to come before God in judgment.
24He breaks the strong without investigation.
He makes others stand in their place.
25He recognizes their works;
he overturns them at night and they are crushed.
26He slaps them for their wickedness
in a place where others are looking on,
27because they turned away from following him,
and didn't pay attention to all his paths.
28They caused the cries of the poor to come before him;
he heard the cries of the afflicted.
29He is quiet, so who can condemn?
He hides his face, so who can look on him,
among the nation and among people altogether?
30So the godless do not rule,
those who ensnare people."

34:16–30. *God is just*. Once again (32:10; 33:1–3) Elihu calls on his listeners to pay attention to him. The sage of Proverbs often exhorts his son to pay attention to him (e.g., Prov. 1:8), so Elihu may simply be following wisdom protocol. On the other hand, combined with other ways in which he calls attention to himself, his speech may betray an insecurity. Perhaps he is losing their attention. Such an interpretation gains credence from the fact that no one responds to Elihu.

He follows his exordium with rhetorical questions (v. 17). In his estimation, Job has questioned God's justice. Thus he asks Job whether it makes sense that one who supposedly hates justice, namely God, would rule. Elihu's question presumes a negative answer, but it is hard to see how this question would obviously lead to such an answer. On a human level, there are plenty of rulers who hate justice and who exploit others. The second question is no less obvious, though Elihu poses it in a way that indicates he thinks it is obvious. To Elihu, God is both "righteous and mighty." And of course it would be wrong to condemn God. Indeed, it would not only be wrong but also dangerous. Job certainly does not question God's might (e.g., 9:4–10), though he does have questions about God's righteousness in terms of his own suffering.

Verses 18–19 ask yet another question that presumes a negative answer. That is, no one would accuse a king of being a wicked scoundrel if that king did not show favoritism to the powerful. And Elihu posits this trait of God on the basis of the fact that he created all people, rich and poor, powerful and weak. However, it is precisely in this area that Job questions God. Indeed, Job (and the others) would expect God to show favoritism to one group, to those who "fear him" and are "innocent and virtuous" (1:1). In a word, it is hard to imagine that Elihu's argument here has much effect on Job.

Nonetheless, Elihu continues the comparison between God and a just king in the verses that follow. A king who does not show favoritism to the "mighty" (v. 20) will exercise his judgment against them when they deserve it. He will do so suddenly so that they die "in the middle of the night" (v. 20a). Though they may die in their sleep, Elihu points out that such a death is not natural ("not by human hand"; see Dan. 2:34), but presumably the result of divine punishment.

These comments lead Elihu to describe God as one who sees all. Using the language of the "path," which stands for life's journey, Elihu says that God has his eye on everyone. Indeed, he sees their every step (v. 21). Nothing can obscure his vision. He is not like a mere mortal, whose eyes cannot pierce the darkness (v. 22), so no one can hide their deeds from him. Thus, when he judges, his judgments are fair. Verse 23 seems to imply that his judgments are also immediate. It is not like a human court, where the wrongdoer's trial and punishment occur long after the time of the infraction. There is no trial (or "investigation"), but God breaks even the strong if they are wrongdoers. He does not wait till the daytime, but crushes them at night once he "recognizes their works" (in this case, recognizes that they are evil). His punishments are also public ("he slaps them for their wickedness in a place where others are looking on," v. 26). They are punished for not heeding God. Again using language familiar from Proverbs, they have departed from God's paths (v. 27).[60]

60. See Longman, *Proverbs*, 59–60.

They do not behave in the way that pleases God. Verse 28 specifies their oppression of the vulnerable, who cry to him in their affliction.

But God does this quietly. That is, he watches and evaluates people and then exercises his judgments behind the scenes. No one can see him do this because he "hides his face" (v. 29). However, he does judge the mighty, so those who work to ensnare people are unable to do so because God is over them, and they, accordingly, do not rule (v. 30).

We are almost certainly to see a criticism of Job in these comments. Job does not like the fact that God keeps an eye on humans and particularly on him (7:17–20; 10:13–14). He wants a trial, though Elihu states that God does not act that way, but rather deals with people like Job "without investigation" (v. 24). Job is frustrated because he cannot find God, but according to Elihu this is what he should expect (v. 29). Applying Elihu's comments to Job, he would say not only that Job deserves what he has gotten but also that his public downfall serves as a warning to others (v. 26a).

---

[31]"For who has said to God,
'I endured punishment, and I will not do wrong any longer.
[32]Teach me what I do not see.
If I have done evil, I will not do it again'?
[33]Will he make peace with you since you rejected him?
You must choose, not I.
Speak whatever you know."

34:31–33. *Make peace with God*. Elihu then asks Job a question. He poses it in a general fashion, but he has Job in mind as he asks it. He wonders out loud whether anyone, after suffering punishment from God, turns to him and repents. Elihu quotes a hypothetical sufferer who turns to God and says that he will not sin again. He even suggests that such a person might not know what he has done (v. 32). In that case, the sufferer, while repenting of an unknown offense, also asks that God reveal to him the exact nature of the offense so he might not commit it again. He asks that God teach him what he has done wrong. Of course, this is addressed to Job as a criticism since he has not taken this approach to God. Rather than simply assuming, due to his suffering, that he is a sinner and turning to God to ask what he has done, Job has denied that he is a sinner. He wants to approach God all right, but in order to set God straight and not to find out the nature of his offense.

Elihu knows this, so he follows up his question with another question, this time addressed to Job. He has rejected God by not accepting the proper approach to him described in vv. 31–32. Thus, Elihu warns him, God will not make peace with him. He will continue to suffer. Even so, Elihu has not completely given up on Job. He appeals to Job to choose the better way. Elihu cannot do it for him. He wants Job to speak.

[34]"Sensible people will say to me,
wise people who listen to me:
[35]'Job speaks without knowledge.
His words are not insightful.
[36]Oh, that Job would be examined completely
because his responses are like those of the guilty.
[37]For he adds transgression to his sin.
He claps his hands among us.
He multiplies his words against God.'"

34:34–37. *Sensible people would condemn Job.* Elihu is good at putting words into other people's mouths. He now quotes a hypothetical group of "sensible" or "wise" people. A lot of people claim wisdom, and Elihu's sample group here consists of wise people who would agree with him, though he is citing them as if they are outside observers. Their conclusion is clear: Job is not wise. He does not know what he is talking about. As a result, he should be put under closer scrutiny. Though they call for an examination, they already believe that he is guilty. After all, he talks like the guilty. His sin is what led to his suffering in the first place. He adds transgression to his sin by his rebellious response to his affliction. He should repent, but instead he expresses anger and spite toward God and those who try to correct him. He claps his hands at these wise, an expression of anger and contempt (Job 27:23; Lam. 2:15; Ezek. 6:11). He multiplies angry, questioning words toward God. He should rather repent and grow silent.

[1]And Elihu answered and said:
[2]"Do you think this is just?
You have said, 'I am right rather than God.'
[3]For you have said, 'How does it advantage me?
How have I benefited by refraining from sin?'
[4]I will respond to your words,
and to your friends with you as well.
[5]Look at the heavens and see.
Gaze at the clouds high above you.
[6]If you sinned, what would you do to him?
Or if your transgressions multiplied, what would you do to him?
[7]If you are right, what would that give to him?
Or what does he receive from your hand?
[8]Your wickedness influences a person like you,
your righteousness, a human."

35:1–8. *Humans cannot affect God.* Elihu continues to examine Job (see 34:36) and finds him wanting. He again quotes Job in order to charge him with wrongdoing. He questions Job's assertion that he is "right" (*ṣedeq*) and God is not (see the similar charge in 34:5), and therefore God is presumably "wrong." The assertion could be worse than I have rendered it, if *ṣedeq* is translated "innocent" rather than "right," indicating that Job believes that he is "innocent" rather than "guilty." Certainly Job has given Elihu a reason to believe that this is his opinion. While it is true that on one occasion Job suggests that no one can be "right/innocent" (9:2), he often speaks as if he is (6:29; 9:20; 12:4; 13:18; 27:5–6; 29:14). He has also given the impression to his friends that he believes he is "innocent" (11:2).

Indeed, in an important sense, Job is right to claim that he is "right/innocent." That is, he is not guilty of any wrongdoing that would lead to his present suffering. The reader knows this from the prologue to the story in chaps. 1 and 2. However, Elihu is also correct in saying that Job thinks not only that he is "right" but also that God is wrong. After all, Job wants to pursue God in order to set him straight. Job himself operates with a strict idea of retribution theology. He believes that his suffering is unjust because he does not deserve it, and such a belief depends on the supposition that suffering results only from one's own sin.

In v. 3 Elihu further quotes Job as again (see 34:9) claiming that his innocence (his "refraining from sin") has done him no good.[61] He has derived no benefit from his righteous, godly lifestyle. Elihu has made this point earlier (34:9). Job himself had earlier attributed such an attitude to the wicked, not to himself (21:15). Indeed, it is precisely here that Job is being tested. The accuser charged Job with self-interested piety (1:9), and by not abandoning God even after all of his material and familial blessings are removed, Job is proving the accuser wrong.

After stating Job's position (according to his own understanding), Elihu then addresses him (v. 4). He includes the friends in his address, indicating that they have stayed around and are now listening to Elihu's monologue. His argument is that God is so great that Job is of no concern to him. He tells Job to look to the heavens, to the clouds and the sky. Presumably he is trying to engender a sense of transcendence in Job's mind. God's creation is vast, and by extension so is God himself, who is above his creation. Job by contrast, is minuscule. Job's sin or his innocence does not deeply affect this God. God does not benefit from a human's righteousness, and one's sin does not hurt him. Elihu's picture of a disinterested God will be undermined by the Yahweh speeches at the end. We know that Job's righteousness is important to God. After all, God has entered a contest over it with the accuser. The Yahweh speeches do indeed demonstrate God's greatness and sovereignty, but this sovereign God also deigns to address Job.

Elihu, though, does not believe this to be the case. For him, God is unaffected by human sin or righteousness. On the other hand, a person's character does influence other humans (v. 8).

61. In 22:2–3 Eliphaz makes an argument similar to Elihu's.

[9]"They cry out because of their many oppressions;
they call for help because of the arm of the great.
[10]They do not say, 'Where is God my Maker
who gives strength at night,
[11]who teaches us more than the animals of the earth,
makes us wiser than the birds of heavens?'
[12]There they cry out, but he does not answer,
due to the pride of those who do evil.
[13]It is all in vain, since God does not hear,
Shaddai does not notice.
[14]How much less when you say you do not notice him,
that the case is before him and you wait for him.
[15]Because his anger does not punish,
he does not much care about transgression,
[16]Job cracks his mouth open with meaninglessness;
his words are heavy with ignorance."

35:9–16. *Job speaks meaningless words.* Not only is God not moved by the sin or righteousness of humans; he is also not influenced by the cries of those, like Job, who suffer. God especially does not respond to those who cry out in their pain but do not appeal to God for help against those who harm them.

Verse 9 describes people who cry out because they are oppressed by powerful people ("the arm of the great"). Though they are afflicted, they do not appeal to God. They do not ask where God is, but they should, because he can strengthen them at night, when they are most vulnerable. After all, God is their Maker (v. 10). Elihu also points out that humans have God's special attention. He would be more apt to teach them than other creatures like the "animals of the earth" and the "birds of heavens" (v. 11). Since they cry out, but not to God to help them, God will not respond to them. Their refusal to cry out to God is a sign of pride, and pride, a dependence on oneself, is off-putting to God (v. 12).

God is beyond notice of human sin, righteousness, or pain. So why does Job think that God will respond to him? Job is concerned that God does not seem to notice him in order to take up his case, Job's charges against God. Elihu is saying, "What do you expect?" He does not lower himself to such matters. Job does not notice God, so why should God notice Job? Thus all of Job's talk is meaningless[62] and ignorant.

[1]And Elihu continued and said:
[2]"Have some patience with me, and I will inform you,
for I still have words to speak on God's behalf.

62. The word I translate "meaninglessness" (*hebel*) is the same as that used frequently in the book of Ecclesiastes; see Longman, *Ecclesiastes*, 61–65.

[3]I carry my knowledge from afar;
I ascribe righteousness to the one who made me.
[4]For truly my words are no lie;
perfect knowledge is with me."

36:1–4. *Perfect knowledge.* Earlier I noted that Elihu's speech is verbose and self-important. His opening words may imply that his listeners (Job, the three friends, and perhaps others) are showing signs of restlessness. He calls on them to be patient. He points not just to his own authority but also to the authority of God. That is, the words that he speaks do not originate with him; he is a spokesperson for God. He is God's advocate. Elihu's knowledge is not inherent in him. Rather, he brings it from far away, presumably from God himself. He is not pointing to his own righteousness, but rather to that of God ("the one who made me"). His words must be true and righteous because they are God's very words. His words are true ("no lie"); indeed, they are perfect as God is perfect. The use of "perfect" (*tām*) here is significant in that it calls to mind the prologue in which Job is called "innocent" (*tām*; 1:1, 8; 2:3).

Though Elihu claims the authority of God in the following argument, we will see that his views leave much to be desired. His position does have an element of truth, but his attempt to make it a general principle that applies to all, including Job in particular, is unconvincing in the light of what the reader learns in the opening prologue. Elihu, in short, attributes to God thoughts that are only his own (see the theological implications section after chap. 37).

[5]"Look, God is mighty in strength.
He does not reject the pure of heart.
[6]The wicked will not live;
he gives justice to the afflicted.
[7]He does not withhold his eye from the righteous.
With kings on the throne,
he makes them reign forever and exalts them.
[8]And if they are bound in chains
and caught in cords of affliction,
[9]he tells them what they have done
and their transgressions, because they have acted proudly.
[10]He opens their ears to instruction,
and tells them to return from guilt.
[11]If they listen and obey,
their days will finish happily,
and their years pleasantly.
[12]But if they do not listen, they will pass through the Water Channel.
They will expire without knowledge.
[13]Those who are godless in heart are set in their anger.
They do not cry for help when he imprisons them.

> [14]They die in their youth.
> Their life ends with temple prostitutes."

36:5–14. *The wicked suffer.* After another rather pompous introduction, Elihu launches into his argument, which turns out to be a rehash of the retribution theology that all the characters have been putting forward. God takes care of the innocent and punishes the wicked. Verse 5 begins by affirming that God does not reject the innocent. The exact relationship between the two cola of this difficult verse (see the translation note for 36:5) is hard to see. Clines changes the exclamation "Look" to the concessive "though,"[63] and perhaps this captures the sense. That is, even though God is strong, he nonetheless cares for those who are "pure of heart." In v. 6 the other shoe drops when Elihu states that the wicked will not live. They will reap the consequences of their actions. Those whom they afflict will receive the justice that they deserve. Then in v. 7 he turns again to the innocent ("the righteous"). God not only saves them from the wicked; he also exalts them. He treats them like kings.

Verses 8–12 return to the theme of disciplinary suffering. That is, God makes people suffer in order to teach them a lesson. He figuratively describes these sufferers as bound in chains in v. 8a, then in v. 8b he further explains that these chains (here "cords") are cords of affliction. In this situation, God explains to the sufferers why they are suffering. Their suffering flows from their transgressions, in particular that they have acted proudly. (See Ps. 30 for the thanksgiving of a person who was restored from his suffering after acting proudly and learning a lesson from God.) Verse 11 describes a possible happy conclusion from this hard lesson from God. Some people, according to Elihu, respond well to God's lesson, and their lives will continue happily. The other possibility is found in v. 12. They (Elihu would include Job here) do not learn from their suffering. They pass through the Water Channel. At 33:18 I noted relevant ancient Near Eastern analogies suggesting that passing or crossing the Water Channel refers to death.

Elihu, it seems, believes that some people are just hardened. Not even God's disciplinary suffering can soften them. Their hearts are "set in their anger," and they will not listen (v. 13). They do not cry out to God for help when they suffer ("when he imprisons them"). As a result, they die young and in humiliating circumstances (with "temple prostitutes").[64]

63. Clines, *Job 21–37*, 810.

64. "Temple prostitutes" (*qĕdēšîm*) were forbidden in Israel (Deut. 23:17–18), though the fact that King Asa (1 Kings 15:12) and King Jehoshaphat (1 Kings 22:46) put them out of the temple indicates that the practice was permitted by syncretistic kings. Of course, Job is not an Israelite, and prostitutes were under the employ of some pagan cults in keeping with the importance of fertility in their religion. In any case, a Yahwistic reader of the book of Job would understand that dying in the presence of temple prostitutes would be a matter of shame.

In this section, Elihu basically continues the arguments we have seen from all the human participants of the story: God is in the business of punishing the wicked and rewarding the innocent. Elihu does put more of an emphasis on God teaching sinners through their suffering, but there is not really a difference of kind between Elihu and the three friends, and not even Job, though he is upset that God does not seem to be acting toward him as he should be.

15"He saves the afflicted by their affliction.
He opens their ear with oppression.
16He is seducing you out of distress,
to a broad place where there is no constraint.
What is set on your table is full of fatness.
17But you are obsessed with the case of the wicked.
Judgment and justice hold on tightly to you.
18Beware that you not be seduced by abundance.
Don't let a big ransom payment turn you aside.
19Will your cry for help keep things in order,
or all the strength of your power?
20Do not pant away for the night,
where people are cut off from their place.
21Watch out! Don't turn aside to iniquity.
For you have chosen this rather than affliction."

36:15–21. *Disciplinary suffering*. I take v. 15 as a summary statement of the previous section, which begins a new unit, though it is possible to take it as the conclusion of the preceding. In any case, it neatly captures the essence of Elihu's doctrine of the disciplinary function of suffering. God uses affliction to save sinners from their sin and set them on the right path. People who sin can become callous to their actions and their dire future consequences, so God makes them suffer in order to call them back to righteousness. Of course, it is true that God can use suffering in this way, but not all suffering, and certainly not Job's, can be so diagnosed.

Even so, Elihu starts specifically applying this doctrine to Job in v. 16. Job sees the negative side of his suffering, but Elihu says that it is good news. Through his pain, God is trying to lure (seduce) Job to a better place, a place where he will be free ("no constraint") and will enjoy abundance ("your table is full of fatness").

Job, though, is blinded by his obsession with justice (v. 17). That is, he thinks that God is not just. He wrongly, according to Elihu, believes that God is not punishing the wicked and rewarding the righteous, and Job does not see the beneficial nature of God's discipline.

In vv. 18–20 Elihu seems to be warning Job about ideas or actions that might lead him even further away from God. First (v. 18), he warns him about the allure of wealth. In v. 19 he warns Job about relying on himself to set his world straight again. Elihu points out that Job cannot restore himself either by his cries for help or by his own power and resources. Finally, Elihu warns against seeking shelter in the night as if Job could hide from his affliction (v. 20).

In the final verse of this unit (v. 21), he charges Job with choosing iniquity rather than embracing the disciplinary lesson of his suffering. That is, Job chooses to charge God with wrongdoing rather than looking at his own life, recognizing his sin, repenting, and restoring his relationship with his God.

22"Indeed, God is exalted in his power;
who is a teacher like him?
23Who prescribes to him his path?
Who says to him, 'You have done wrong'?
24Remember to extol his works,
which people commemorate in song.
25All people have gazed on them;
everyone looks from a distance.
26Indeed, God is exalted, and we do not know him.
The number of his years is unknowable.
27He holds in check drops of rain.
He filters rain for his stream,
28which the skies pour forth
and drop abundantly on humanity.
29Can anyone understand the spreading clouds,
the thundering of his booths?
30See how he spreads his light around him.
He covers the roots of the sea.
31For by these he governs the peoples
and provides plenty of food.
32He fills up his palms with the lightning,
and he commands it to strike the mark.
33His thunder speaks about it,
the passion of his anger against iniquity."

36:22–33. *God is great*. Elihu now describes God to Job. He wants to emphasize God's greatness in order to demonstrate to Job the futility of trying to contend with him. Elihu begins by simply stating that God is exalted. No one or thing is on his level. He asks who is a teacher like him, a rhetorical question that does not need to wait for a response. No one teaches like God. What is Elihu's point? In the preceding sections, he has been making the argument that God teaches sinners through inflicting suffering on them. He teaches them that they are people who need to repent. Job, however, has not yet learned this lesson.

Elihu continues asking rhetorical questions in v. 23. Who wants to tell God what he can and cannot do? Who would dare tell God that he is wrong? Such an attitude is unthinkable to Elihu, but that is Job's stance. He wants to tell

God that he is wrong. Job believes that God thinks Job is a sinner because he has afflicted Job. Of course, that is not what God thinks at all, but Job is operating with the same retribution theology of all the human participants of the story.

Rather than questioning God, Elihu admonishes Job to praise him through song. The Psalms are full of songs that praise God. But the Psalms are also full of laments, including some that charge God with serious wrongdoing (see Pss. 77 and 88 as examples). Elihu also expresses a rather distant relationship with God in v. 25. People apparently see his great works and extol him, but from a distance. Elihu does not articulate a close, warm relationship with God. Verse 26 again affirms God's greatness but in a way that distances him from his human creatures. God is so great that it is hard to know him. After all, while the life span of humans is finite, God's is not. His years cannot be counted because they are never ending. While true, this statement also expresses a distant relationship with God.

The remainder of the chapter describes God's control of the storm. He is in charge of the rain ("he holds in check drops of rain," v. 27). No one can figure out how he does it, but he does it. His thunder and lightning amaze his human creatures. He uses the rain for the benefit of humans (vv. 28b, 31b), since it is the source of food. His thunder not only signals life-giving rain but is also an expression of passionate anger against sin. Such a God is not to be trifled with in the way that Job is doing, at least according to Elihu's opinion.

1"At this my heart trembles
  and drops out of its place.
2Listen, listen to the shaking of his voice,
  and the rumbling that comes out of his mouth.
3Under the heavens, he lets it loose,
  his lightning, to the ends of the earth.
4After it, his voice roars,
  he thunders with his exalted voice.
He does not restrain them
  when his voice is heard.
5God thunders wondrously with his voice;
  he does great things that we cannot know.
6To the snow he says, 'Fall on the earth,'
  the same to the showers of rain, the showers of driving rain.
7He puts a seal on the hand of every person,
  so the people might come to know his handiwork.
8The wild animals enter into their hiding place;
  they stay in their lair.
9The whirlwind comes forth from the chamber;
  cold, from the north winds.
10Ice comes from the breath of God;
  the wide waters are frozen hard.

> 11With moisture he loads the thick clouds.
> The clouds scatter his lightning.
> 12It turns round and round by his guidance
> to accomplish all that he commands them
> on the surface of the inhabited world.
> 13Whether for correction, or for the land,
> or out of loyalty, he brings them forth."

37:1–13. *The storm's power reveals God's handiwork.* The picture of God as in control of the storm continues from 36:22–33 into chap. 37. Elihu begins (v. 1) by describing his reaction to the storm. He is astonished and amazed. The power of the storm makes him realize just how strong God is. He becomes so excited that his heart beats wildly, almost falling out of this chest. Verse 2 speaks of the thunder as the voice of God. This reminds us of Ps. 29, which pictures God as the power of the storm, commenting on his voice in a way that clearly relates it to thunder:

> The voice of the LORD is over the waters;
> the God of glory thunders,
> the LORD, over mighty waters.
> The voice of the LORD is powerful;
> the voice of the LORD is full of majesty.
> The voice of the LORD breaks the cedars;
> the LORD breaks the cedars of Lebanon.
> He makes Lebanon skip like a calf,
> and Sirion like a young wild ox.
> The voice of the LORD flashes forth flames of fire.
> The voice of the LORD shakes the wilderness;
> the LORD shakes the wilderness of Kadesh.
> The voice of the LORD causes the oaks to whirl,
> and strips the forest bare;
> and in his temple all say, "Glory!" (Ps. 29:3–9 NRSV)

Ancient Near Eastern peoples associated the storm with the power of the storm god (in Canaan, Baal), but faithful Israelites (and Elihu) rightly recognized that the storm was under the control of the one and only God, Yahweh.

It is not only the thunder that reveals God's presence and power but also the lightning that is associated with it (v. 3). The storm is a mysterious power and reminds Elihu that there are things about God that are not known (v. 5b).

Verse 6 expresses his mastery over two types of storm: the snowstorm and the rainstorm. Both were known, but both were rare in this part of the world. Snow comes to the highlands only rarely, but when it does, it is a beautiful sight to behold. Rain also comes rarely, and while it can come with devastation, its life-giving waters are welcomed in this land of low precipitation.

Verse 7 is difficult and has a number of different translations and explanations. The above translation is rather literal. The question is how to understand the "sealing of the hand." The NIV understands that sealing means to cause something to stop, to seal it up, so to speak.[65] Thus it renders: "So that everyone he has made may know his work, he stops all people from his labor" (a translation that also involves a transposition of the cola). However, to give something a seal might also be a way of providing a reminder of ownership,[66] and that seems the best way to take the expression in this context. In other words, the snow and rain remind people of God's work.

The snow and the rain also drive the wild animals into their lairs to seek refuge due to the storm's power (v. 8). Perhaps the implicit message here is that the animals naturally know how to act when God brings a storm on the land, but Job does not react properly when God brings trouble into his.

Verses 9–12 make clear that God is the author of the storm from which people and animals alike need to seek refuge. The description begins by talking about the origins in naturalistic terms, that is, without reference to God. Earlier (9:9), in a section where he himself extols God's power, Job speaks of the constellations occupying a chamber like a room contains furniture: "He [God] is the maker of the Bear and Orion, and the Pleiades and the chambers of the south." Elihu apparently also believes that heavenly phenomena are associated with chambers, one of which contains the powerful winds that buffet the earth. The cold, though, does not just originate from the winds that come from a heavenly chamber; it comes from God himself ("ice comes from the breath of God," v. 10a). He is the one who loads the clouds with water. He is the one who scatters his lightning from the clouds. He is the one who guides its appearance and direction on the earth (v. 12).

And he does this for a purpose according to v. 13. He always has a purpose for these storms (and, again, Elihu may be speaking not just of storms of nature, but also the storms of suffering), though the purpose may differ from storm to storm. The first possible purpose is "correction," literally "the rod." That is, he may bring the storm to discipline people. That storms were used in judgment contexts may be seen in a number of places, but note in particular 1 Sam. 12:18–19. In the context of the people's sinful request for a king, God sends a brief devastating storm to announce to the people that he controls whether the rain is life giving or crop destroying.

But the storms might also come for the benefit of the land, according to Elihu, rains that bring crops and drinking water. Or God might bring the rains out of loyalty. This seems to be connected to the second purpose, namely, "for the land," but it points out that the benefit comes to humans. "Loyalty" (*ḥesed*)

65. See the explanation of the NIV by Wilson, *Job*, 413.

66. Ancient seals (whether stamp or cylinder seals) were means of personal identification and marked ownership of objects.

is a word that is connected to the covenant; it is the kind of persisting love that God as covenant king shows his people. Indeed, in the covenant blessings of Deuteronomy we read, "The Lord will send rain at the proper time from his rich treasury in the heavens" (Deut. 28:12 NLT).

14"Give ear to this, Job.
Stop and understand the wonders of God.
15Do you know how God appoints their tasks
and makes the lightning shine in his clouds?
16Do you know the spreading clouds,
the wonders of the one who has perfect knowledge?
17You swelter in your clothes,
when the earth is still, due to the south wind.
18Can you, with him, spread out the sky,
hardened like a cast mirror?
19Teach us what we should say to him.
We cannot arrange our thoughts in the darkness.
20Will it be reported to him when I speak?
Did a person ever say that he wanted to be swallowed up?"

37:14–20. *Job, what do you know, and what can you do?* Elihu now presses Job to consider the ramifications of his meteorological observations. He believes that they will get him to consider the "wonders of God" (v. 14). It is not as if Job does not recognize God's power. He does (see, for instance, 9:4–10). A recognition of God's power, though, has not convinced Job that God is acting justly toward him. It has only made him question whether he can get a fair hearing from a God who can strong-arm him.

Elihu then peppers Job with questions in order to bring his point home. These rhetorical questions do anticipate God's questions in the following chapters, but it is one thing for God to approach Job in this manner and another for Elihu. He begins by asking Job whether he knows how God does it, that is, how he produces and manages a storm, especially how he makes the lightning shine (v. 15b) and the clouds spread in the sky (v. 16a). Job never responds. Indeed, Elihu believes that the answer is so obvious that he would not even pause to let Job respond, though again Job has earlier made clear that he does not doubt God's power and strength.

It is not just the cold that God produces and controls (as in the previous section), but also the heat. If cold comes from the north wind (v. 9), so heat comes from the south wind (v. 17). In v. 18 Elihu challenges Job with yet another rhetorical question, though admittedly this one is a bit harder to understand in detail. In general, Elihu is asking Job whether he can control the skies. The verb here translated "spread out" could be taken as "hammer out" and refer to the hammering out of metal to make a mirror.[67] The key to understanding the language of this verse is to see the connection of this verb (*rqʿ*) with the noun "firmament" (*rāqîaʿ*), used in Gen. 1:7 to refer to the sky as a hardened dome. Elihu asks Job if he can manufacture the sky like God did at the creation. The answer, of course, is no.

Elihu believes that faced with the huge gap between human and divine ability and knowledge, Job will have no recourse but to back down from his challenge to God. Due to human ignorance, it would be utterly beyond Job or any human to speak to God ("we cannot arrange our thoughts in the darkness," v. 19b). Even if we speak, God will probably not hear a report of it (v. 20a). Job seems to have a death wish ("Did a person ever say that he wanted to be swallowed up?" v. 20b).

21"But now no one can look at the light,
bright as it is in the sky,
when the wind passes by and clears it.
22A golden glow comes from the north;
an awesome splendor is all around God.
23Shaddai, we cannot find him,
exalted in power.
He will not violate justice and abundant righteousness.
24Therefore, people fear him.
All who are wise of heart fear him."

37:21–24. *The wise fear him.* Elihu brings his lengthy speech to a close in this passage. He begins by remarking that people cannot look into the bright sky, when the sun ("the light," v. 21) is out in force in a sky that has been cleared of clouds by the winds. If the sky is bright by means of the sun and impossible to see, how much more will the "awesome splendor" of God blind people. Job has complained that he cannot find God (in many places, but note, for example, 9:11; 23:3). No wonder. God is too awesome, says Elihu. He is very powerful. However, God is not only powerful but also just. Job has claimed that God does indeed "violate justice and abundant righteousness" (v. 23c), but Elihu will not grant this to him. Indeed, he ends his speech with one more indirect slap in Job's face: those who are wise fear God. They show proper respect. Of course, here we are reminded of wisdom's motto, "The fear of the LORD is the beginning of wisdom" (Prov. 1:7; see also Job 28:28). The implication is that Job does not fear God.

Elihu has now finished his speech. The earlier debate between Job and his three friends followed a pattern of speech and response, and that is what we

67. In the ancient Near East, mirrors were made of beaten bronze rather than glass. See Cornelius, "Job," 292.

expect here. What will Job say to Elihu? But we are foiled in our expectation because the next voice we hear is not Job's, but rather God's.

What are we to make of this? Some scholars suggest that Elihu has forged the way for God especially in chap. 37, where Elihu's reflections on nature anticipate some of God's own comments in the chapters that follow.[68] Thus they understand the book to affirm Elihu's speech; there is no response because Job has nothing to say. This view, however, stumbles over the fact that, as I have tried to show in the commentary above, the vast majority of Elihu's comments do not advance beyond the argument of the three friends. Elihu, like the three friends and indeed Job himself, believes that God rewards the righteous and punishes the wicked. Elihu, like the three friends, wants Job to repent of the sins that led to his suffering. Accordingly, Job does not respond because he has already rejected this argument as it was given by the three friends. (For more on the place of Job 37, consult the introduction to Job 32–37.)

Theological Implications

Inspired by the Spirit

In his opening statement, Elihu makes a bold comment. He claims to speak under divine inspiration. While the three friends grounded their authority largely in experience, observation, and tradition,[69] Elihu asserts the value of his perspective squarely in his belief that he has the "spirit," the "breath of Shaddai" (32:8).

The significance of Elihu's claim might be seen more clearly in the light of the close connection between wisdom and the spirit/Spirit in other parts of the OT. Joseph (Gen. 41:38), Bezalel (Exod. 31:2–3; see also 35:30–31), Joshua (Deut. 34:9), Daniel (Dan. 4:8; 5:11), and even the future messiah (Isa. 11:1–3) are all said to be exceedingly wise by virtue of their endowment by the Spirit of God.[70] Elihu is thus claiming that his wisdom is enabled by the Spirit.

Before proceeding further, I should point out that it is a mistake to read a full-blown doctrine of the Trinity back into the OT. The author of Job would not have had a clear sense of the Holy Spirit as the third person of the Godhead. As with many other biblical doctrines, God progressively revealed this truth to his people. Even so, the background to the full biblical teaching on the Spirit does begin with OT comments about God's Spirit. While we begin the interpretive task by asking what the OT author and audience would have

68. For instance, Smick ("Job," 875) believes that one of the purposes of the Elihu speeches is to "prepare the reader (and Job) for the theophany."

69. On rare occasions, the three friends appeal to a type of spiritual authority as well (4:12–17; 20:2–3). See Longman, "Spirit and Wisdom."

70. The connection between wisdom and the Spirit is even further developed in the OT Apocrypha (see Wis. 7:22b–25).

understood about a passage, Christian interpreters can and should then read the text in the light of the fuller revelation of the NT. From such a perspective, it is not a stretch to ask what Elihu's claim might tell us about people today who claim to speak under the inspiration of the Holy Spirit.

The Spirit speaks truth, and so the claim to speak under spiritual inspiration is a claim to speak the truth. Indeed, speaking under divine inspiration does not invite question. Critique can be taken as impiety or blasphemy. When Elihu or anyone says, "Thus says the Spirit [or Word] of God," they are not asking for interaction or even reflection, but for obedient action.

That God speaks through people is obvious to those of us who take the Bible seriously. Moses, Isaiah, Jeremiah, and Ezekiel are just a few of the many examples of people authentically inspired by God to address his people. It would be a mistake to categorically deny that God can speak through people today.

But then the Bible also presents us with other examples of people who claim to speak for God but do not. A prime example may be seen in the interaction between the true prophet Jeremiah and the false prophet Hananiah (Jer. 27–28).

Thus the claim of spiritual inspiration can be dangerous, and Elihu illustrates that danger. After all, we know from the continuation of the plot in the book of Job that Elihu misrepresents himself. He does not speak as God's mouthpiece. He simply repeats the tired retribution theology of the three friends. He accuses Job of being a sinner, who is suffering because of his sin, and as a result Job needs to repent.

As I pointed out in the introduction (see "Elihu's Monologue"), the purpose of Elihu's presence in the book of Job is almost certainly to undermine a school of thought (or at least a way of thinking) that was contemporary with the time when the book of Job was written. But such a viewpoint is not restricted to the past. Plenty of people still adorn their own thoughts with the assertion that God is speaking through them or the broader claim that they can name God's purposes in the events of the day. Elihu looked at Job's suffering and claimed spiritual inspiration to accuse him of sin. Some today have looked at the effects of a hurricane and announced that it was the judgment of God.

Most of the time the situation will be ambiguous. Perhaps we will feel prompted to believe that God's hand is on someone or against someone. But before we claim that our beliefs are God's by stating that the Spirit of God is speaking through us, we should stop, reflect, and pray. Most of the time we should put forward such perspectives humbly, inviting consideration rather than assertively demanding acceptance.

Revelatory Dreams

Does God speak to people through dreams? In 33:15–18 Elihu tells Job that he does. In particular, it is one means by which God might inform people that they are going in the wrong direction and call them back to himself. Is Elihu's argument persuasive in its ancient context as well as today?

Reading through the Bible leaves little doubt that God used dreams to communicate with people. The first person reported to receive a dream revelation from God is the Philistine king Abimelech (Gen. 20:3, 6). Indeed, the number of non-Hebrew/Israelite (and therefore not exclusive Yahweh worshipers) recipients of dream revelations is notable: Laban (Gen. 31:24), the Egyptian cupbearer and baker (Gen. 40:5–9, 16), the pharaoh (Gen. 41), a Midianite soldier (Judg. 7:13–15), Nebuchadnezzar (Dan. 2 and 4), and Pilate's wife (Matt. 27:19). While this might suggest an inferior mode of revelation (one that is not as direct and is therefore open to misunderstanding [see below]), there are a handful of cases where God's people receive dream revelations: Jacob (Gen. 28:12; 31:10, 11), Joseph (Gen. 37:5–10), Solomon (1 Kings 3:5, 15), Daniel (Dan. 7:1), and Joseph, the father of Jesus (Matt. 1:20; 2:12, 13, 19, 22).

In addition, various programmatic texts indicate that God will speak to his prophets on occasion through dreams. The law that differentiates true from false prophets opens with "Suppose there are prophets among you or those who dream dreams about the future" (Deut. 13:1 NLT), thus allowing for the possibility that God will communicate to his divinely appointed spokespersons through dreams. An interesting text in this regard is Num. 12:6:

> If there were prophets among you,
> I, the LORD, would reveal myself in visions.
> I would speak to them in dreams. (NLT)

However, God contrasts this with the clearer and more direct way in which he communicated with Moses:

> I speak to him face to face,
> clearly, and not in riddles!
> He sees the LORD as he is. (Num. 12:8a NLT)

Again, we may have a hint there that, though God does communicate on occasion through dreams, this is not the most direct and clear way in which he speaks.

After all, even the biblical texts record that dreams are often simply illusions. For instance, according to the psalmist, the prospering of the wicked is as vacuous as "a dream when one awakes," and in the next colon "dreams" are parallel with "phantoms" (Ps. 73:20 NRSV).[71] They are mindless distractions, according to Isa. 56:10, the result of stress (Eccles. 5:3), mere hallucinations (Eccles. 5:7).

71. See also Job 20:8 and Isa. 29:7 for the idea that dreams are illusory.

Though God does occasionally speak to his prophets through dreams, false prophets report false dreams and thus mislead: "I have heard what the prophets have said who prophesy lies in my name, saying, 'I have dreamed, I have dreamed!'" (Jer. 23:25 NRSV; see also vv. 26–27). But again, the false use of dreams does not mean that God never did or does not now communicate to his people through dreams. After all, Acts 2:17–21 cites Joel 2:28–32 as fulfilled on the day of Pentecost, which includes the expectation:

> Then afterward
> I will pour out my spirit on all flesh;
> your sons and your daughters shall prophesy,
> your old men shall dream dreams,
> and your young men shall see visions. (Joel 2:28 NRSV)

In conclusion, then, it would be quite wrong to deny that God speaks to people through dreams. On the other hand, even in the biblical times he did not often choose this vehicle to communicate with his people. In addition, there are clear indications that dreams are not the most sure and direct mode of revelation. Due to the nature of dreams as the product of the imagination (today we might say the subconscious), it is hard to differentiate divine revelation from the cogitations of our own minds. Further, dreams are often ambiguous in meaning and subject to an interpretive process that also allows us to engage in wish fulfillment rather than discernment of the divine will. Elihu may be correct in principle that God can speak to Job or someone else through a dream, but he does not do so often or without ambiguity.

People Get Nothing from God

In this speech, Elihu fully embraces retribution theology and, in spite of his pretensions to add something new to the discussion, offers merely an echo of arguments already given by the three friends (see the introduction for an overall assessment of Elihu's place in the book). Elihu challenges Job's viewpoint, in which Job reacts to his suffering in spite of his righteousness, and summarizes Job's perspective by putting words in Job's mouth: "People get nothing out of taking pleasure in God" (34:9). Interestingly, in the rest of the chapter, rather than describing how the righteous do receive rewards, Elihu affirms the other pole of the equation: pain comes to the wicked. The implication, which furthers his argument, is that Job experiences pain not because God is niggardly toward the righteous but because Job is wicked and is getting what he deserves.

But is it true that people get nothing out of taking pleasure in God? To answer this question, we must first ask what Elihu implies that Job is saying here. What might Elihu (and Job) expect from God? We can use the rewards that Job previously enjoyed before his suffering as a gauge (Job 1:2–4) or even

Job's own description of his life before his downturn (Job 29) to answer this question. Then he would expect a large and happy family, wealth, status, and influence. It would be the opposite of what Elihu describes as the fate of the wicked in the rest of chap. 34. The wicked experience emotional, relational, and physical pain, while the righteous would experience the opposite—happiness.

But is it true that "people get nothing from God" when they obey and love him? Not according to the book of Job—they get God. After all, the book of Job begins with the question "Does Job fear God for the rewards?" (1:9). Will Job jettison his relationship with God once it ceases to be of immediate benefit to him? At this point in the book, we have not reached a final conclusion, though the preface remarks how Job has resisted attempts to derail his relationship (2:9–10). Job has even maintained his relationship with God in spite of his friends' arguments and his belief that God is treating him unfairly. At the end of the book, after God has put him in his place, Job continues to maintain his relationship with God and submits to him before there is even the hint of a possibility that the blessings might come back to him.

So people do get something from a relationship with God; they get God, and the thesis of the book is that this is all that is really important. Even so, I believe we are to understand Job's situation during the period between the beginning of his suffering and its end as unusual. Often, but not always and certainly not perfectly, relationship with God brings joys. Perhaps one gains a sense of meaning that was absent before. It could be improved relationships with family and friends. It might even be a better standard of living. We are to receive all good things in this life as a gift from God.

Christians have a different, fuller perspective on life than Job did. It is pretty clear that Job did not have an understanding of eternal life. To him, death was the end. If joy did not come in this life, then there was no joy. Christians live life knowing that there is more to come. That does not mean that our pain and suffering are not real, but we can suffer in hope and with joy in light of the reality that we will spend eternity with God.

God Gets Nothing from People

In the previous section, I reflected on the idea Elihu attributed to Job that people get nothing from God. Here I will consider Elihu's own belief that God gets nothing from people. Elihu argues from the nature of God as transcendent, calling on his listeners to look to the heavens above (35:5) to realize that God, in short, is above it all. God does not benefit from the righteous acts of his faithful people, and he is not hurt by the wicked acts of those who disobey him (vv. 6–7). Does Elihu give his hearers an accurate portrayal of who God is?

There is an important sense in which God does not need humans at all, righteous or wicked. He is, after all, God, and God is self-sufficient in his triune self. The Bible does teach that God does not have needs that only humans can fulfill. In a series of rhetorical questions, Isaiah makes very clear that God does not need direction or advice (Isa. 40:12–14). The psalmist (see Ps. 50:12–13) critiques those who think that sacrifices to Yahweh are like the food that is offered to pagan gods. He does not need to be fed. As Paul says more generally, "Since the God who made the world and everything in it is himself Lord of heaven and earth, he does not make his home in shrines made by human hands. Nor is he in need of anything, that he should be served by human hands; on the contrary, it is he who gives everything—including life and breath—to everyone" (Acts 17:24–25 NJB). Failure to remember that God does not need us or our gifts leads to human pride and a diminishing of our ability to see the true nature of God.

However, besides teaching that God does not need humans or their righteous acts to fill some kind of lack in himself, the Bible also clearly teaches that God desires to be in relationship with his creation. An *overemphasis* on the self-sufficiency of God can also lead to a distortion of our relationship with him. The Bible teaches throughout that God loves his human creatures and desires relationship with them. God rejoices in those who "fear him" (Ps. 147:11), in his humble people (Ps. 149:4), in innocent people (Prov. 11:20), in faithful people (Heb. 11:6), and in those who pray (Prov. 15:8). In other words, God is not only transcendent; he is also immanent, involved with his creation. The story of the Bible is the account of God creating humans to be in relationship with him and with one another. This story is marred by sin and a breaking of relationship. God did not need to preserve humans, but he desired to do so, leading ultimately to the unbelievable sacrifice of his own Son, Jesus Christ. "For God so loved the world that he gave his only Son, so that everyone who believes in him may not perish but may have eternal life" (John 3:16 NRSV).

Elihu represents those who wrongly affirm the self-sufficiency of God to the detriment of God's desire for relationship with his human creatures. He wrongly states that God is beyond the notice of sin, righteousness, pain, and suffering. Indeed, the prologue to the book of Job reveals quite the contrary. God cares deeply that Job respond with faith, and he desires that Job's love of him not be due simply to the fact that God rewards him.

Speaking on God's Behalf (36:2)

It is a dangerous matter to claim to speak on God's behalf. In an obvious attempt to bolster his arguments with authority, Elihu asserts that he does speak for God. After all, if God says something, there is no counterargument. God is all-knowing; he speaks only truth. Is it even possible to speak on behalf of God? Elihu is not the only one to make this claim. Among others, the great prophets of the OT often prefaced their oracles with "thus says the Lord" or identified their message as an "oracle of the Lord," and faithful Jews and

Christians have recognized and agreed that these words—spoken by Isaiah, Jeremiah, Ezekiel, and others—are indeed God's words.

However, besides these true prophets, there were also false ones who claimed to speak in God's name but did not. One thinks of Zedekiah son of Chenaanah at the time of Kings Ahab and Jehoshaphat (1 Kings 22:11–12) or of Jeremiah's rival, Hananiah son of Azzur (Jer. 28). According to Deut. 18:22, the punishment for falsely claiming to speak for God is to be ignored: "If a prophet speaks in the name of the Lord but the thing does not take place or prove true, it is a word that the Lord has not spoken. The prophet has spoken it presumptuously; do not be frightened by it" (NRSV). True, Elihu is not claiming to be a prophet in the narrow sense, but he is claiming to speak for God, and the same principle applies.

People today make similar claims. We hear preachers who claim to speak the Word of God, and they do so when they faithfully reflect the teaching of Scripture. However, preachers are human and make mistakes in their interpretation. Accordingly, as they boldly proclaim God's Word, they must invite their hearers to compare what they say with the teachings of Scripture. Individuals also often claim to speak God's Word, and sometimes they do, as they advise or admonish other people. But again, they must do so with the humility that they may be wrong; and rather than cutting off discussion by claiming that they speak with God's authority, they should invite others to reflect on what they say in the light of Scripture. Teachers of God's Word should always remember James's warning, "We who teach will be judged with greater strictness. For all of us make many mistakes" (James 3:1b–2a NRSV).

When we are on the receiving end of someone who boldly claims to speak God's Word to us, we should neither naively accept what we hear uncritically, nor should we simply reject the message. Rather, we should "test the spirits to see whether they are from God; for many false prophets have gone out into the world" (1 John 4:1 NRSV).

Pain as God's Megaphone (36:15)

As mentioned above, Elihu answers Job's complaint by asserting that God uses suffering to discipline sinners to return to the right path. His comment that God "opens their [wicked people's] ear with oppression" sounds a note similar to C. S. Lewis's famous and oft-quoted comment: "God whispers to us in our pleasures, speaks in our conscience, but shouts in our pains: it is His megaphone to rouse a deaf world."[72]

As happens often in the book of Job, the human participants in the story alight upon a truth but then misunderstand and misapply it. Elihu and Lewis are correct that sinful men and women often become complacent in a trouble-free

72. Lewis, *Problem of Pain*, 93.

life. Lewis suggests that God is present, and one can hear him if one tries hard enough. However, most people do not try hard. Thus Lewis suggests that God uses pain to get the attention of hardened sinners.

Sometimes God uses suffering in this way (see Ps. 30), but not always. Sometimes pain comes to people who are not sinners, and sometimes people who live a relatively carefree life are deeply spiritual and have a mature relationship with God. The book of Job helps remind us not to draw conclusions about a person's spiritual condition based on whether they are suffering.

He Puts a Seal on the Hand of Every Person (37:7)

In 37:1 Elihu confesses that a storm has the power to make his heart drop out of his chest. We have likely all had similar reactions to storms, whether they are thunderstorms or blizzards. The booming thunder, flashing lightning, and whipping winds make one want to run to a safe shelter. Elihu, though, takes the thought further: not only does it make one stop in awe, but it also makes one think of God. Indeed, according to 37:7, it is an indication of God's presence through his handiwork. In a phrase, it bears his stamp.

People throughout the ancient Near East associated the storm with the divine realm. Indeed, many of the most frequently mentioned gods of the surrounding nations were associated with the storm and its thunder and lightning. Baal, the rider on the cloud and the thrower of lightning, is the best known to readers of the Bible. The storm not only evoked astonishment and fear but also provided the life-giving waters. But to Elihu the storm revealed the true God. The storm was not God but rather his handiwork. Here I agree with the bombastic Elihu, and, as indicated in the introduction to Elihu's speech, I acknowledge that in this chapter he does serve to anticipate the words of Yahweh himself in the following chapters.

That said, modern Western Christians have all but lost a sense of wonder in the storm. After all, we think we can explain it. We can consult a dictionary, an encyclopedia, or even Wikipedia to find naturalistic explanations for lightning and thunder, rain and snow. But naturalistic explanations, as helpful as they can be, do not undermine the truth of Elihu's statement. After all, who created the world and guides it? Who is behind the working of nature's rhythms? It is God himself, and thus the power of the storm does indeed reflect (weakly to be sure) God's own great might.

VI. Yahweh's Speeches and Job's Responses (38:1–42:6)

Translation

[38:1]Yahweh answered Job from the whirlwind and said:
[2]"Who is this who darkens advice
with ignorant words?[1]
[3]Brace yourself[2] like a man.
I will question you, and you must inform me!

[4]Where were you when I founded the earth?
Tell me, if you have understanding.
[5]Who set its measurements? Surely you know.
Or who extended the line on it?
[6]On what are its bases sunk?
Or who set the cornerstone,
[7]when the stars of the morning sang for joy
and all the sons of God[3] shouted gleefully?

1. While some suggest that it is Elihu who is addressed here and not Job (see Johnson, *Now My Eye Sees You*, 146–47), this is extremely unlikely. After all, this section is introduced by saying that "Yahweh answered Job" (38:1). In addition, vv. 2–3 announce that God will address the person who speaks in ignorance and call on him to answer the barrage of questions that follow. These questions are surely addressed to Job, who responds to them.

2. Literally (and traditionally) "gird up your loins."

3. As often, "the sons of God" refers to the "angels."

8Who shut the Sea with doors,
and who brought it out bursting forth from the womb,
9when I made the clouds its clothes,
and deep darkness its swaddling clothes?
10I prescribed[4] my boundary on it;
I set up a bar and doors.
11And I said, 'You will go this far and no more,
and here your proud waves will stop.'

12In your days, have you commanded the morning?
Can you inform the dawn of its place
13so it grabs the edges of the earth,
so the wicked can be shaken out of it?
14The earth is transformed like clay by a seal impression,
and its features stand out like a garment.
15Light is held back from the wicked,
and their upheld arm is broken.

16Have you gone to the sources of the Sea?
Can you walk around the depths[5] of the Deep?
17Have the gates of Death been revealed to you?
Have you seen the gates of deep darkness?

18Do you comprehend the earth's expanse?
Tell me if you know it all.
19What is the way to the place where light resides?
And darkness, where is its place?
20Surely, you will take it to its borders!
You understand the paths to its house.
21You must know, because you were born then.
Abundant are the number of your days.

22Have you gone to the storehouses of snow,
or have you seen the storehouses of hail,
23which I have reserved for the time of distress,
for the day of battle and war?
24What is the way to the place where light is distributed,
or where the east wind is scattered over the earth?
25Who has cut a channel for the downpour
and a way for the thunderclap
26to bring rain on the earth where no person lives,
in the wilderness, in which is no one,
27to satisfy the ruined and desolate land,
to cause the grass to sprout forth?

4. The verb is *šbr* ("to break"), but context demands a meaning like "set." Hartley (*Job*, 493n7) and others suggest that the word has a special legal meaning here.

5. See also 11:7 for a similar use of *ḥēqer*.

28Is there a father to rain?
Or who has given birth to dewdrops?
29From whose womb did the ice come out?
Who has given birth to the frost[6] of heaven?
30The waters harden like a stone;
the surface of the deep is frozen over.

31Can you bind the chains of the Pleiades[7]
or loosen the belt of Orion?[8]
32Can you bring out Mazzaroth[9] in its proper time
or guide the Bear[10] with its cubs?
33Do you know the regulations of heaven,
or set their rule on earth?

34Can you raise your voice to the clouds
so that an abundance of waters can cover you up?
35Can you send for lightnings and they come
and say to you, 'We are here'?
36Who has endowed the ibis[11] with wisdom,
or who has given understanding to the rooster?
37Who can number the clouds with wisdom?
Who can tilt the waterskins of heaven
38so the dust is pressed in a mass
and the clods cling together?

39Can you hunt prey for the lion?
Can you fill up the appetite of the young lions,
40when they crouch in their lair,
and lie in wait in their covert?
41Who provides the prey for the raven
when its babies cry out to God for help
and wander about for lack of food?

39:1Do you know the time when the mountain goats give birth?
Do you observe the birth pangs of the deer?
2Do you count the months that they fulfill
to know that time when they will give birth,
3when they crouch down and bear their young
and deliver their fetuses?[12]

6. See Exod. 16:14, where the manna is described as "frost."

7. See 9:9 for Pleiades (*kîmâ*).

8. See 9:9 for Orion (*kĕsîl*).

9. A transliteration of the Hebrew, a constellation of uncertain identification.

10. See 9:9 for Bear (*ʿayiš*).

11. *Ṭuḥôt* is difficult, and its translation is uncertain. Some take it as "inward" or "dark" places (see NRSV), but others translate "ibis," the animal that represents Thoth, the Egyptian god of wisdom (see NJB).

12. Rather than "labor pains," with Pope, *Job*, 306.

[4]Their offspring are healthy and grow up in the countryside;
they go out and do not return to them.

[5]Who sets the wild onager free?
Who has let the Arabian onager loose from its chains?
[6]I have given it the steppe as its home.
Its dwelling place is the salt land.
[7]It scoffs at the noise of the city.
It does not hear the shout of the driver.
[8]It scouts out the mountains as its pasturage.
It searches after every green thing.

[9]Is a wild ox willing to serve you
or spend the night in your stall?
[10]Can you tie up the wild ox with a rope in the furrow,
or will it harrow the valley after you?
[11]Can you depend on it because its power is great
and hand over your labor to it?
[12]Will you trust it to return,
bringing your grain[13] to your threshing floor?

[13]The wings of the ostrich flap happily,
though her pinions lack plumage.[14]
[14]She lays[15] her eggs on the earth;
she lets them be warmed on the dust.
[15]She forgets that a foot might crush them,
or a wild animal trample them.
[16]She treats her offspring roughly, as if they did not belong to her.
She has no fear that her labor might be in vain.
[17]For God has made her forget wisdom;
he did not allot to her understanding.
[18]At the time she flaps her wings[16] aloft,
she laughs at horse and rider.

[19]Did you give the horse its strength?
Did you clothe its neck with a mane?
[20]Do you make it leap like a locust?
Its splendid snorting is terrifying.

13. Normally *zera'* means "seed," but it can also refer to plants growing from seed (Lev. 11:37; Isa. 61:11).

14. This colon is very difficult, and as Hartley (*Job*, 509n3) points out, it seems to say "are they the pinions and plumage of love." A simple and explainable emendation renders the Hebrew *'im-'ebrâ ḥăsērâ nōṣâ* and results in the above translation.

15. This is based on an original suggestion by Dahood ("Root *'zb*") and adopted by a number of commentators, including Pope and Smick.

16. *Mr'* as "flap the wings" is a guess, mainly based on context. The word is a hapax legomenon.

21It paws the dirt of the valley and rejoices.
Powerfully, it goes out to meet the weapons.
22It laughs at danger and feels no terror.
It does not turn back from the sword.
23On it the quiver rattles,[17]
the flashing spear and javelin.
24Shaking and trembling,[18] it swallows up the earth.
It does not hold back at the sound of the ram's horn.
25When the ram's horn sounds, it says, 'Aha!'
From a distance it senses[19] the war,
the thunder of princes and shouts.

26Is it by your understanding that the hawk soars,
spreading its wings to the south?
27Does the eagle fly up at your command
and make its nest up high?
28It dwells on the rock and makes its nest there;
a tooth of rock is its fortress.
29From there it scouts for food;
its eye sees it from a distance.
30Its young gorge[20] on blood.
Where the slain are, there they are."

40:1And Yahweh answered Job and said:
2"Will someone who contends with Shaddai instruct him?
Let the one who reproves God answer back!"

3And Job answered Yahweh and said:
4"I am small;[21] how can I answer you?
I have placed my hand over my mouth.
5I have spoken once already and will not respond;
twice, but I won't add to that."

6And Yahweh answered Job from the whirlwind and said:
7"Brace yourself like a man.
I will question you, and you must answer me.[22]
8Would you invalidate my justice?
Would you condemn me so you might be righteous?

17. "Rattle" (*rnh*) occurs only here in the Hebrew Bible; see Hartley, *Job*, 509n11.

18. With nervous excitement.

19. The root is *ryḥ*, whose base meaning is "to smell."

20. The verb form is clearly not typical, and an emendation seems called for. The best suggestion appears to be to take the verb as a form of *lōaʿ*, perhaps a Pilpel form (as suggested by Hartley, *Job*, 513n5).

21. The verb can also mean "I am insignificant" or "unworthy" (so NIV).

22. See 38:3.

9Do you have an arm like God?
   Can you thunder with a voice like his?
10Adorn yourself with loftiness and pride.
   Clothe yourself with splendor and majesty.
11Let loose the fury of your anger.
   Look on all those who are arrogant and bring them down.
12Look on all those who are arrogant and make them submit.
   Crush the wicked where they stand.
13Hide them in the dust all together.
   Bind their faces in the hidden world.
14Then I will acknowledge you,
   because your right hand will have given you victory.

15Look, Behemoth, which I made just as I made you,
   eats grass like an ox.
16Look, its strength is in its loins;
   its vigor is in the muscles of its belly.
17It stiffens its tail like a cedar.
   The sinews of its thigh are interlaced all together.
18Its bones are tubes of bronze;
   its limbs are like bars of iron.
19It is the first of God's ways.
   Only its Maker can approach it with a sword.
20For the produce of the mountains yields food for it,
   where all the animals of the field play.
21It resides under lotus trees,
   in the covert of the reeds and in the marsh.
22The lotus trees cover it for shade;
   the poplars in the wadi surround it.
23If the river is turbulent, it does not hurry away.
   It is confident even though the Jordan gushes toward its mouth.
24Can it be taken with hooks,[23]
   or can you pierce its nose with a snare?

41:1 [40:25]Can you catch Leviathan with a fishhook?
   Can you press down its tongue with a cord?
41:2 [40:26]Can you put a rope in its nose?
   Can you pierce its cheek with a hook?
41:3 [40:27]Will it multiply its pleas of mercy to you?
   Will it speak tenderly to you?
41:4 [40:28]Will it make[24] a treaty with you
   to be taken as your eternal slave?

23. Literally "by its eyes"; thus NLT translates: "No one can catch it off guard." But "eye" in this context is understood to be a hook or a ring.

24. Literally "cut a covenant/treaty."

41:5 [40:29]Will you play with it like a bird?
Will you put it on a leash for your young girls?
41:6 [40:30]Will the fishing guild[25] haggle over it?
Will it be divided up among the merchants?
41:7 [40:31]Can you fill its skin with harpoons
or its head with fishing spears?
41:8 [40:32]Set your hands on it!
Remember the battle; you will not do it again!

41:9 [1]Any hope of subduing it[26] will prove a lie.
One is thrown down even at its appearance.
10 [2]No one is so fierce as to stir it up.
Who can stand before it?[27]
11 [3]Who has ever confronted it[28] and come out safely,
who—under all the heavens?
12 [4]I will not keep quiet about its limbs,
its great strength and splendid form.[29]
13 [5]Who has ever exposed its garment
in order to penetrate its double coat of mail?[30]
14 [6]Who can open the doors of its face?
There is dread all around its teeth.
15 [7]Its back[31] is composed of shields in a row,
closed up tightly like a seal.
16 [8]One draws near another,
so not even wind can get between them.
17 [9]Each clings to its neighbor,
so they clasp each other and cannot be broken off.
18 [10]Its sneezing makes light flash.
Its eyes are like the eyelids of the dawn.
19 [11]Torches come from its mouth;
sparks of fire escape.
20 [12]Smoke comes out of its nostrils,
like a boiling pot and burning reeds.
21 [13]Its breath kindles coals.
Flame comes out of its mouth.
22 [14]In its neck resides strength.
Violence leaps before it.

25. *Ḥābbar* in the plural is an "association," but in this context I take it to refer to an association of commercial fishermen (see NEB).

26. Literally "any hope of it." The context suggests that the hope is to subdue or capture it.

27. Hebrew "me," but the context and many MSS call for a reference to Leviathan.

28. See previous footnote.

29. Taking *ḥēn* ("favor, grace") as a reference to a good form. See Hartley's (*Job*, 527) "grace of its form."

30. Reading with the LXX. The Hebrew has "his bridle" (*risnô*), but this seems to be the result of metathesis from "coat of mail" (*siryōnô*). See Konkel, "Job," 235.

31. I emend Hebrew *ga'ăwâ* (pride) to *gēwōh* (its back).

23 [15]The folds of its flesh cling together.
It is solidly cast and does not move.
24 [16]Its heart is firm like a rock,
firm as a lower millstone.
25 [17]When it lifts itself up, the gods are afraid,
the waves miss their mark.[32]
26 [18]The sword may reach it but have no effect,
as with the spear, the dart,[33] and the arrowhead.
27 [19]It considers iron to be straw,
and bronze to be rotten wood.
28 [20]The arrow cannot make it flee;
slingstones are turned to chaff for it.
29 [21]A cudgel is considered like chaff;
it laughs at the rattling javelin.
30 [22]Its underside is like sharp potsherds.
It spreads itself out like a threshing sledge on the mud.
31 [23]It makes the deep boil like a pot.
It makes the sea like ointment.
32 [24]It leaves an illuminated way behind it.
One would consider the deep to be white-haired.
33 [25]There is nothing on earth that equals it,
a creature with no fear.
34 [26]It sees all that is lofty.
It is king over all the proud beasts."

42:1And Job answered the LORD and said:
2"I know that you can do all things,
and no plan of yours is impossible.
3'Who is this who hides advice without knowledge?'[34]
Thus I spoke, but I did not understand,
things too wonderful for me that I did not know.
4'Hear and I will speak.
I will question you, and you will inform me.'[35]
5My ear had received a report of you,
but now my eyes have seen you.
6Therefore I hold myself in contempt,
and I repent in dust and ashes."

32. This colon is very difficult. The root meanings of the words seem clear, but it is hard to get them to make sense together. The word translated "waves" comes from the root *šbr*, "to break." Gordis (*Job*, 487) suggests a slight emendation (*mišbārîm*) to reach this meaning. The verb comes from *ḥṭ'*, most commonly meaning "to sin" in the Qal. A. Luc (*NIDOTTE* 2:87) offers "to miss oneself" along with "to purify oneself" as Hitpael meanings, and the former underlies the translation above.

33. *Massā'* must refer to some kind of weapon but has this meaning (determined by context) only here. Gordis (*Job*, 488) and Dhorme (*Job*, 640) connect it with an Arabic root, *nasaga*.

34. An allusion to, but not exact quotation of, God's statement in 38:2.

35. Job again quotes God; see 38:3.

Interpretation

While the three friends (and Elihu) argued that the solution to Job's suffering was found in his repentance, Job believed the answer would come in a meeting with God. He felt that God was treating him unjustly. After all, he was innocent, and the innocent do not suffer. Thus he believed that the best approach was to confront God.

Granted, at first he felt that God was just too powerful (9:4–10) to challenge and too transcendent to care (9:15–18). He longed for some kind of mediating presence (e.g., 9:32–35). As time went on, however, he grew in confidence that his cause was right and that he would eventually win the day against the God who persecuted him (31:35–37).

In chap. 38 Job finally gets what he desired, an audience with God. However, it does not go the way he anticipated. Instead of Job confronting God, God confronts Job (38:1–3). The first divine speech opens with challenging words emanating from a whirlwind. God accuses Job of ignorance and then sets about to prove it by peppering him with questions.[36] These are rhetorical questions that assume no answer on the correct presumption that Job has none to offer. After all, the questions are completely unfair. No human can expect to know how the creation was put together (38:4–7). No one was there when it happened! Certainly Job does not know how to control the sea (38:8–11) or where its source is located, any more than he knows where the realm of death can be found (38:16–17). Can he command the morning (38:12–15) or control the rain and snow (38:22–30)? Does he know the expanse of the earth (38:18–21) or have knowledge of the heavens (38:31–38)? Of course not. Nor does he know enough about the lion and the raven that he might provide for them (38:39–41). Only God can know and do these things.

Moving into chap. 39, God continues the line of the argument against Job initiated in 38:39–41. More animals are listed whose characteristics expose the difference between God and Job. As Westermann recognized, the question God asks Job here "sets up an unqualified alternative: Are you Creator or creature? Are you God or man?"[37] God knows all about how mountain goats and deer reproduce; Job does not (39:1–4). God gives the wild/Arabian onager its freedom; Job does not (39:5–8). God controls the wild ox; Job cannot (39:9–12). God gives the ostrich its speed, while withholding intelligence; Job does not (39:13–18). God gives the warhorse its fearless strength; Job does not (39:19–25). God gives the hawk its ability to soar through the sky; Job does not (39:26–50). With one exception, these are all wild animals with which humans have no real connection. The one exception is the warhorse, in whose

36. Alter (*Art of Biblical Poetry*, 94) helpfully points out that the first divine speech is organized by "the following movements: cosmogony (38:4–21), meteorology (38:22–38), zoology (38:39–39:30)."

37. Westermann, *Structure*, 107.

description it becomes clear that it is only on the edge of domestication, able to be used by humans more for its love of conflict than anything else.

After barraging Job with questions pointing out his lack of power and wisdom, God then challenges him with a final question in this his first speech, "Will someone who contends with Shaddai instruct him?" (40:2). God knows that Job intended to lecture him, to set him straight, concerning the unfairness of his suffering. He now invites Job to do so, if he dares. However, after God's first speech to him, Job has nothing to say (40:3–5). He now knows that he was wrong to suggest that he might reprove God. He now knows that in relation to the Almighty God, he is "small" and must be silent.

Even so, God is not satisfied and launches into a second speech directed at Job. That he continues to address Job out of a whirlwind indicates that he remains perturbed with him (40:6). After all, Job has unfairly questioned his justice (40:8). Job thinks that by allowing the wicked to flourish, God does not render fair judgment. God rhetorically asks Job whether he is able to handle the problem. Can he control evil? If so, then maybe God will listen to him. In other words, Job does not know what he is talking about (40:9–14).

At this point, God describes Behemoth (40:15–24). Behemoth is the epitome of powerful land creatures. It is almost certainly not an actual creature but rather the mightiest land creature that humans can imagine, and it probably also represents evil. Can Job control Behemoth? Of course not ("Can you [Job] pierce it with hooks?" 40:24). Only God can do so ("Only its Maker can approach it with a sword," 40:19b). Finally (41:1–34), God describes Leviathan, a creature known from ancient Near Eastern mythology (Ugaritic *ltn*). If Behemoth is the most powerful land creature imaginable, Leviathan is the most powerful sea creature imaginable. And, like Behemoth, neither Job nor any other human can control this force of chaos. Only God can do so.

Job responds to God a second, climactic time (42:1–6). He acknowledges that he has misunderstood God (42:3), but now has clarity (42:5). He recognizes that God is sovereign (42:2), and accordingly he feels contempt toward himself and repents of his attitude toward God.

1Yahweh answered Job from the whirlwind and said:
2"Who is this who darkens advice
  with ignorant words?
3Brace yourself like a man.
  I will question you, and you must inform me!"

38:1–3. *The challenge.* Job has wanted an audience with God and has now gotten his wish. God answers Job from a whirlwind.[38] What is the significance

38. The Hebrew word here is *sĕʿārâ*, but the following discussion will cite passages that use the by-forms *śaʿar* and *śĕʿārâ* (see M. Dreytza, *NIDOTTE* 3:1263–64).

of the shape of God's appearance here? First, we should note that Job anticipated this moment in his third speech when he complained that God would not listen to his arguments ("I do not believe he would hear my voice," 9:16b), but rather would "crush me with a storm" (9:17). God now appears in a storm, but he will not crush him—just put him in his place. Indeed, already by this time he believes he has been buffeted by God's winds: "You lift me up in the wind and make me ride it; you make me reel because of the roar of the storm" (30:22).

Job is now face-to-face with God, and God's appearance does make clear that he is not happy with Job. Indeed, the storm is often the way that God executes his judgment toward people (Ps. 83:15; Isa. 29:6; 40:24; Jer. 23:19). Again, God does not blast him with the storm, but his appearance in the storm shows his anger toward Job and represents the potential for Job's destruction.

God's opening words to Job also indicate his irritation. He identifies Job's words as ignorant and asks him to identify himself. Job "darkens advice" in the sense that his words confuse the issue, and his words are ignorant in a sense that I will later specify.

God then decides to demonstrate clearly that Job is accurately described as ignorant: God commands Job to prepare for a test, a series of questions that he must answer. It will soon become clear that Job cannot answer these questions; indeed, no human could ever answer these questions. Of course, that is the point. God is in the process of showing Job who is God and who is a creature.

Alter brilliantly reads God's first speech in the light of echoes heard from Job's complaint in chap. 3. For instance, one may observe a connection between the admonition that Job brace himself "like a man [*geber*]" (38:3) and Job's wish that the day that someone announced "a boy [*geber*] is conceived" be enveloped in darkness (3:3–4). In the earlier poem, Job wanted light done away with and swallowed up by darkness. God's speech emphasizes how he brings the light that dominates the darkness (38:7, 12–15, 19–20). Job is one who "darkens advice" (38:2).[39]

4"Where were you when I founded the earth?
Tell me, if you have understanding.
5Who set its measurements? Surely you know.
Or who extended the line on it?
6On what are its bases sunk?
Or who set the cornerstone,
7when the stars of the morning sang for joy
and all the sons of God shouted gleefully?"

---

39. These and other parallels between Job 3 and 38 may be found in Alter, *Art of Biblical Poetry*, 96–102.

38:4–7. *Absent at creation.* God begins the process of putting Job in his place by asking him about his knowledge of creation of the world. The background of these questions is found in the connection between wisdom and creation as expressed in places such as Prov. 3:19–20:

> Yahweh laid the foundations of the earth with Wisdom,
> establishing the heavens with competence.
> With his knowledge the deeps burst open,
> and the skies drop dew.

Note should also be taken of Prov. 8:22–31, where Woman Wisdom speaks of her origins as preceding creation, which she witnessed. God's point is that Job does not have the wisdom that is capable of answering the questions surrounding his suffering. The questions presuppose that Job has not yet acknowledged his rightful place. He presumes to question God's wisdom.

God does not wait for Job's responses, because he knows that he has none to offer. Job was not yet born at the creation of the world. God's description of the creation of the world sounds like the construction of a house with a foundation ("its bases") and cornerstone. The builder of a house would use a line (v. 5b) in order to measure its dimensions in the process of building. In a poetic creation context, perhaps we are to think of this building as a temple based on an analogy with the picture of Marduk in *Enuma Elish*, who after his victory over Tiamat takes a measuring line in order to measure "the construction of Apsu, He founded the Great Sanctuary, the likeness of Esharra."[40]

Verse 7 mentions creatures who are present during this occasion and greet the creation with songs of joy. In the first colon of v. 7, they are described as the "stars of the morning" and then further identified as "all the sons of God" in colon *b*. Thus there is a connection drawn between the "sons of God," a term used to designate angels, and the stars. Again, this is reminiscent of language found in *Enuma Elish*, where Marduk places the gods in the skies as stars: "He made the positions(s) for the great gods, He established (in) constellations the stars, their likenesses."[41]

> [8]"Who shut the Sea with doors,
> and who brought it out bursting forth from the womb,
> [9]when I made the clouds its clothes,
> and deep darkness its swaddling clothes?
> [10]I prescribed my boundary on it;
> I set up a bar and doors.
> [11]And I said, 'You will go this far and no more,
> and here your proud waves will stop.'"

40. B. R. Foster, "Epic of Creation," *COS* 1:398. The quotation is from tablet 4, lines 143–44.
41. Ibid., 399 (tablet 5, lines 1–2).

38:8–11. *Controlling the Sea.* Yahweh continues to administer his test to Job to reveal to him that he is not so wise after all. The next question concerns the "birth" of the Sea. Here the Sea is personified. Its origins are described as a birth, coming out of the womb.

In a number of places in the poets and prophets (Pss. 18:15; 29:3; Isa. 50:2; Nah. 1:4), God is seen as in conflict with and in control of the Sea, representing the forces of chaos,[42] a motif that has a mythological background in the conflict between Marduk and Tiamat in Mesopotamia and Baal and Yam in the Levant. In this passage, though, the Sea seems not like an enemy but like a rambunctious toddler. God is able to control the newborn Sea, clothing it (the clouds and the darkness are its clothing, v. 9) and putting up boundaries (Ps. 33:7). He commands the Sea so that it can go only so far, preventing the devastating effects of waters that are uncontrolled.[43]

Though missing the element of hostility that one sees between the Sea (Tiamat, Yam) and the creator God (Marduk, Baal), the language of bounding the Sea is similar to what we read in *Enuma Elish*, where Marduk, after defeating Tiamat, splits her into two parts, forming the heavens with one part and then stretching out her "hide and assigning watchmen, ordering them not to let her waters escape."[44]

This question Job might be able to answer, but it points out to him that he is not the one who put the creation together—God is. The implication is that Job is not the one who can figure out the world.

12"In your days, have you commanded the morning?
Can you inform the dawn of its place
13so it grabs the edges of the earth,
so the wicked can be shaken out of it?
14The earth is transformed like clay by a seal impression,
and its features stand out like a garment.
15Light is held back from the wicked,
and their upheld arm is broken."

38:12–15. *Exposing the wicked.* God continues to barrage Job with questions concerning his abilities to know and manage the creation. Has Job ever produced a morning? Has he ever brought into being the light that dispels the night darkness? The answer is painfully obvious. No, he has not. No human can, and that is the point. Job has presumed to set God straight. He has lost sight of the fact that he is the creature and God is the creator.

42. Wakeman, *God's Battle*; J. Day, *God's Conflict*; Kloos, *Yhwh's Combat*; Longman and Reid, *God Is a Warrior*, 64–68.

43. See also Job 7:12 and Jer. 5:22. Psalm 33:7 states, "He gathered the waters of the sea as in a bottle; he put the deeps in storehouses" (NRSV).

44. Foster, "Epic of Creation," *COS* 1:398 (tablet 4, lines 139–40).

The description of the morning light hitting the earth is powerfully subtle in vv. 13–14. First, the light is seen as enveloping the earth so that it grabs the horizon. Evil is often done in the cover of night, so the coming light is seen as shaking wicked people out of the earth like a cloth is shaken to get rid of dust. Verse 14 provides a second image. A seal is pressed on flat, nondescript clay to produce meaningful impressions on the clay. In darkness, the earth looks flat and featureless, but the light reveals hills and valleys. Verse 14b is difficult but may describe the same phenomenon of hills and valleys by comparing them to the folds of a garment. The final verse of the section returns to the deleterious effect that light has on wicked people. The "upheld" or perhaps "raised" arm is a symbol of rebellion, but this symbol of insolence is broken. Wickedness cannot survive God's light.

> 16"Have you gone to the sources of the Sea?
> Can you walk around the depths of the Deep?
> 17Have the gates of Death been revealed to you?
> Have you seen the gates of deep darkness?"

38:16–17. *The location of the Sea and Death.* God has already questioned Job concerning the Sea in 38:8–11. Job has implicitly admitted that he cannot control the Sea, but here God asks if he has even visited the sources of the Sea. Again, Job must remain silent. Indeed, if he had visited the Sea and its depths, even that would not have revealed the source of wisdom to him. Not even the Sea and its depths know where to find wisdom, according to 28:14: "The Deep says, 'It is not in me.' The Sea says, 'It is not with me.'" Verse 17 asks if Job is acquainted with the underworld. Has he even been to the entrance of the abode of Death? Again, the answer is no, and again, even if he had, he would not be close to discovering the source for wisdom: "Abaddon and Death say, 'We have heard a report of it in our ears'" (28:22).

> 18"Do you comprehend the earth's expanse?
> Tell me if you know it all.
> 19What is the way to the place where light resides?
> And darkness, where is its place?
> 20Surely, you will take it to its borders!
> You understand the paths to its house.
> 21You must know, because you were born then.
> Abundant are the number of your days."

38:18–21. *The unfathomable earth.* Job would not know how big the earth is. In ancient times, the edges of the earth would have been mysterious. Today we know the extent of the earth, but a similar mystery surrounds the extent of the universe. Job does not "know it all" (v. 18b), so he continues to be silent in God's presence while God goes on to question Job's awareness of the source of light and darkness. God taunts Job's ignorance in these matters because Job had grown presumptuous in his attitude toward God. To know these matters, Job would need to have been born at the time of creation, like Woman Wisdom (Prov. 8:22–31). But he was not, so he remains ignorant.

---

[22]"Have you gone to the storehouses of snow,
or have you seen the storehouses of hail,
[23]which I have reserved for the time of distress,
for the day of battle and war?
[24]What is the way to the place where light is distributed,
or where the east wind is scattered over the earth?
[25]Who has cut a channel for the downpour
and a way for the thunderclap
[26]to bring rain on the earth where no person lives,
in the wilderness, in which is no one,
[27]to satisfy the ruined and desolate land,
to cause the grass to sprout forth?
[28]Is there a father to rain?
Or who has given birth to dewdrops?
[29]From whose womb did the ice come out?
Who has given birth to the frost of heaven?
[30]The waters harden like a stone;
the surface of the deep is frozen over."

38:22–30. *The source of rain and snow*. God had earlier asked Job if he had traveled to the sources of the Sea (v. 16); now he inquires whether he has journeyed to the place where snow and hail are housed. Heaven is often pictured as a place where meteorological phenomena are stored, ready to be released by God when he so desires. Heaven contains a storehouse of rain with which God can bless the earth (Deut. 28:12), but also storehouses that contain the more destructive forces of wind (Ps. 135:7; Jer. 10:13; 51:16) and, as in v. 22, snow and hail. Interestingly, snow and hail are seen as parts of God's arsenal for periods of war. While snow is not elsewhere associated with battle, hail certainly is. God used hail as a weapon against the Egyptians as he sent plagues against them to induce them to release his people from bondage (Exod. 9:13–35). God sent hailstones against the southern coalition of Canaanite kings, killing more of the enemy than the Israelites did with their swords (Josh. 10:11). The prophet Ezekiel announces that God will judge his people and their false prophets "with hailstones of fury" (Ezek. 13:13).

Job would not know the way to the place where light is distributed (Job 38:24a); only God would have that knowledge. God created the light as well as the sun, moon, and stars that inhabit the realms of light and darkness and provide light to the earth (Gen. 1). He is in control of the light, and he can remove the light as he sees fit (Job 9:7; 30:26). In this context filled with references to weather, however, light (*'ôr*) may mean lightning (37:3, 11); if so, it is equally clear that he controls the lightning and uses it for his purpose.[45] This is knowledge and skill that Job does not have.

God also controls the winds (Ps. 78:26). Here the east wind is specifically mentioned. In this part of the world, the east wind is hot, so naturally it is often connected with destruction and judgment (Ezek. 17:10; 19:12; Hosea 13:15).

A further argument for the "light" of v. 24a as a reference to lightning is that God now turns to the subject of the thunderstorm in vv. 25–28. He asks Job who created the thunderstorm, likening the downpour from heaven to a channel that pours water on the earth. In this case, Job surely knows that answer, but the answer (God) again serves the purpose of putting Job in his proper place in the universe.

God, not Job, is the one who provides the rain from heaven. The rain drenches the earth and brings forth vegetation. Here God focuses on rain that comes in the uninhabited wilderness, perhaps simply expressing the extent of his reach. God must be speaking of wilderness that was rarely visited by humans. Perhaps this verse expresses the experience of someone who knows the wilderness as a desolate area, but then on a subsequent visit sees vegetation in the wilderness. God must provide the rain. After all, no human is present.

The answer to the rhetorical questions about the "father to the rain" and the mother who has "given birth to" the frost is again God, not Job or any other human. God is the one who freezes the water into ice (v. 30) so that it hardens "like a stone."

31"Can you bind the chains of the Pleiades
or loosen the belt of Orion?
32Can you bring out Mazzaroth in its proper time
or guide the Bear with its cubs?
33Do you know the regulations of heaven,
or set their rule on earth?
34Can you raise your voice to the clouds
so that an abundance of waters can cover you up?
35Can you send for lightnings and they come
and say to you, 'We are here'?
36Who has endowed the ibis with wisdom,
or who has given understanding to the rooster?
37Who can number the clouds with wisdom?
Who can tilt the waterskins of heaven
38so the dust is pressed in a mass
and the clods cling together?"

45. So Konkel, "Job," 222.

38:31–38. *Knowledge of the heavens.* God keeps pounding away at Job, asking him questions that show him his place in the universe. He is not God's equal, not by a long shot. In 9:9 Job had admitted that God was the powerful creator of the constellations (there mentioning the Pleiades, Orion, the Bear, and the "constellations of the south"). Here three of the four are repeated and a fourth, Mazzaroth, is added. The Pleiades (*kîmâ,* perhaps related to Arabic *kûm,* meaning "herd, heap," hence "cluster") refers to the seven stars in the shoulder of the constellation Taurus. They are closely clustered together, and God asks Job if that was the result of his doing. Again, the answer is no, because God is the one who fixes the stars in place in the sky. The second celestial feature mentioned is *kĕsîl* (usually meaning "fool"), most often thought to be a reference to Orion, the giant constellation.[46] The Greeks gave the constellation the name Orion after the giant hunter who rebelled against the gods. Three stars make up the belt of Orion in the constellation.[47] While God could remove this belt if he so wished, Job has no such power. The Bear is difficult to identify and thus its cubs also, but it probably refers to a constellation and the cubs to some of its member stars.[48] As mentioned, the Pleiades, Orion, and the Bear were all referred to earlier, in 9:9, but here a new constellation is listed, *Mazzaroth.* I have simply transliterated the Hebrew, and its identification is a matter of conjecture, though it has been suggested that it means "zodiacal circle."[49]

In v. 33, after asking about specific star clusters, God challenges Job concerning his knowledge of heaven's regulations in general. Does he know the laws by which the heavens work? Again the assumed answer is no. The second colon of this verse is a bit harder to pin down. The word translated "rule" (*mišṭār*) means something like "dominion" or "decree," the verbal root meaning something like "to write" in some Semitic languages and the related noun meaning "record keeper" or "official" in Hebrew (Exod. 5:6).[50] But what does the pronominal suffix refer to? I have taken it as a reference to the "regulations of heaven," since it would be awkward for God himself to refer to "his rule" in this context. Since the next few verses are going to now look at meteorological features again (clouds and lightning) that are in the heavens but visible on earth, perhaps the phrase "their rule on earth" makes sense.

Verses 34 and 35 speak of God's control over the rain clouds and the lightning. God can speak to the clouds, and they will give up their water. God's voice may here be associated with thunder, which often accompanies rain.

46. It is made up of about eighty stars, seventeen bright ones.

47. Some translations render *mōšĕkôt* as "cords" or the like (NRSV, NJB, NAB) and believe it is an allusion to the legend of Orion being dragged off by cords.

48. According to R. C. Newman, *NIDOTTE* 2:613, the Vulgate identifies it as "Arcturus, brightest star in the constellation Bootes; possibly the LXX agrees."

49. Driver, "Two Astronomical Passages," 4–6.

50. Though both *HALOT* (1:645) and *CHALOT* (218) allow for the meaning "starry sky."

That God's voice and lightning are closely associated may be observed in Ps. 29: "The voice of the LORD echoes above the sea. The God of glory thunders. The LORD thunders over the mighty sea" (v. 3 NLT).

Verse 36 is another difficult verse, both in terms of its meaning and also how it fits into the context. As the translation note for 38:36 indicates, the NRSV represents those who take the disputed words (translated here and in NIV as "ibis" and "rooster") to refer to "inward parts" and "mind," respectively (the 1984 edition of the NIV is similar), but the evidence in support of these meanings is not strong. Both the ibis and the rooster are animals that are associated with wisdom, the ibis being connected with the Egyptian god of wisdom, Thoth. Wilson is correct to say, "Regardless of the interpretation of these words, God is the one who 'endowed' wisdom."[51]

Verses 37–38 return once more to God's control of the all-important rains. Here his distribution of the rains is explicitly associated with his wisdom. The rain itself is metaphorically described as his tilting waterskins in heaven, which pour rain on the earth so that it turns the dry dust into muddy clods.

39"Can you hunt prey for the lion?
Can you fill up the appetite of the young lions,
40when they crouch in their lair,
and lie in wait in their covert?
41Who provides the prey for the raven
when its babies cry out to God for help
and wander about for lack of food?"

38:39–41. *Provision for the lion and the raven.* God now changes the subject from the control of the heavens to providing food for his creatures. The lion and the raven are featured here as two creatures who must hunt for their food and, as is implied in both cases, food for their offspring. Their nourishment depends on the success of the hunt. The assumption of God's question is that he can provide prey for these creatures, but Job cannot. Job continues to learn his place in the universe.

1"Do you know the time when the mountain goats give birth?
Do you observe the birth pangs of the deer?
2Do you count the months that they fulfill
to know that time when they will give birth,
3when they crouch down and bear their young
and deliver their fetuses?
4Their offspring are healthy and grow up in the countryside;
they go out and do not return to them."

51. Wilson, *Job*, 437.

39:1–4. *Mountain goats/deer*. God, but not Job, also knows the life rhythms of the animals. He knows the intimate details of their life, even having to do with their pregnancies and births. God knows when they will give birth. He watches over them in the process. He knows how long it will take. Verse 4 describes how they grow up and achieve independence, only to begin the whole process over again.

5"Who sets the wild onager free?
  Who has let the Arabian onager loose from its chains?
6I have given it the steppe as its home.
  Its dwelling place is the salt land.
7It scoffs at the noise of the city.
  It does not hear the shout of the driver.
8It scouts out the mountains as its pasturage.
  It searches after every green thing."

39:5–8. *The onager*. God turns now to the onager in his list of animals that he has created, sustains, and knows intimately. In this, he contrasts with Job, who has limited knowledge and experience of the various animals named in this list. Here God asserts that he is responsible for the character and status of the onager. An onager is an equid that looks something like a cross between a donkey and a horse. While ancient Sumerian texts indicate that onagers were domesticated, at least at that time, the point of these verses is that they are not tamed but wild, perhaps indicating that this was the situation in ancient Israel at the time when the book of Job was written.[52]

Again the passage begins with rhetorical questions where the answer is clearly "God." God is the one who has freed the onager from domestication. It runs freely in the wilderness areas (the steppe), away from civilization ("it scoffs at the noise of the city"). The onager spends its life out in the wilderness, free from human interference and looking for its sustenance.

9"Is a wild ox willing to serve you
  or spend the night in your stall?
10Can you tie up the wild ox with a rope in the furrow,
  or will it harrow the valley after you?
11Can you depend on it because its power is great
  and hand over your labor to it?
12Will you trust it to return,
  bringing your grain to your threshing floor?"

39:9–12. *The wild ox*. The theme of human domestication of animals continues in this section, but here the subject is the wild ox. Again, the gist

52. Or it may conceivably indicate the perception of an earlier time, if Job was written late in the history of Israel but set in an early period (see "Authorship and Date" in the introduction).

of the matter is that Job is not in charge or in control of the created order. That is a status held only by God, who is in charge of the whole world and its inhabitants, all of which he made. Again, the unit begins with a rhetorical question. The answer to the question of v. 9 is obviously no. The wild ox, by virtue of being wild, will not serve Job or stay in his stall. The wild ox is an extremely powerful animal and certainly has the strength to till the land to create furrows (v. 10) or provide the power for a grinding stone to produce the grain that provides food. But it is not controllable. Such jobs are for domesticated cattle (*bāqār*) and not a wild ox (*rêm*). Job cannot control such powerful agents. Only God can do so.

13"The wings of the ostrich flap happily,
though her pinions lack plumage.
14She lays her eggs on the earth;
she lets them be warmed on the dust.
15She forgets that a foot might crush them,
or a wild animal trample them.
16She treats her offspring roughly, as if they did not belong to her.
She has no fear that her labor might be in vain.
17For God has made her forget wisdom;
he did not allot to her understanding.
18At the time she flaps her wings aloft,
she laughs at horse and rider."

39:13–18. *The ostrich*. God now speaks of the ostrich, another undomesticated animal. In contrast to the previous passages, there are no rhetorical questions here. Rather, the ostrich is described, but in a way that again shows that God is in charge. Here the idea is that it is God who gives certain traits to his various creatures. Of most interest, considering the theme of the book of Job, is what is said about the animal's wisdom.

The description begins positively as we reflect on the happy-go-lucky nature of the ostrich. The ostrich is a funny-looking bird that has short stubby wings but does not have the ability to fly. As it runs and flaps its short wings, it looks like it is happy, although its feathers are rather drab.

The passage will conclude with a further observation on her flapping wings and gait, but first there is a relatively lengthy consideration of her reproduction. She lays her eggs on the ground and seems careless because the eggs could easily be crushed where she leaves them. She seems senseless, even stupid in this practice, and this seems to be the intention of the description. She does not act this way by chance, but because of her divinely given nature. God did not give her wisdom. Now returning to her wings and gait, we learn that when the ostrich moves, she laughs at horse and rider. Why? Because she is so much quicker than they are. God did not give the ostrich intelligence, but he gave it speed.

The point is that God distributes different traits to different animals. In particular, note that God gives some animals wisdom and withholds it from others. This observation supports one of the major themes of the book: wisdom comes only from God. The same may be said for all other qualities, including speed.

> 19"Did you give the horse its strength?
> Did you clothe its neck with a mane?
> 20Do you make it leap like a locust?
> Its splendid snorting is terrifying.
> 21It paws the dirt of the valley and rejoices.
> Powerfully, it goes out to meet the weapons.
> 22It laughs at danger and feels no terror.
> It does not turn back from the sword.
> 23On it the quiver rattles,
> the flashing spear and javelin.
> 24Shaking and trembling, it swallows up the earth.
> It does not hold back at the sound of the ram's horn.
> 25When the ram's horn sounds, it says, 'Aha!'
> From a distance it senses the war,
> the thunder of princes and shouts."

39:19–25. *The warhorse.* God now moves the subject from the ostrich to the horse, and not just any horse, but the warhorse. The previous animals have all been wild creatures. Certainly, the warhorse has been domesticated (and the only animal that God speaks of that has been tamed), but nonetheless it is a dangerous animal, as the description highlights.[53]

Like most of the preceding passages, with the exception of the one just finished, this unit begins with questions. The questions are directed at Job, but he does not respond to them because the answer is obvious. Job does not give the warhorse its abilities and features. God does. Again, God puts Job in his place in the universe. He is not the creator and sustainer. God is. Just as God gave the ostrich speed but not wisdom (39:13–18), so he has given the warhorse strength (v. 19a) and majesty (the mane, v. 19b), as well as the ability to leap over obstacles, presumably in the midst of the charge or battle (v. 20a).

The monologue moves from rhetorical questions to straightforward description. The warhorse is an imposing creature. The description is of the horse in battle. In eager anticipation of the charge, the horse makes terrifying noises (v. 20b). It desires battle, demonstrating its fearlessness by pawing the ground and seeming to rejoice at the prospect of entering the fray. It shakes

53. Davis ("Sufferer's Wisdom," 137) explains the inclusion of the "domesticated" warhorse among other animals that are not under human control: "Every animal in which God glories is utterly useless, except the war horse, and that is the exception that proves the rule. You may use him, God says of the snorting horse impatient for battle, but don't imagine you can master him!"

and trembles (v. 24), not in fear, but rather because it is anxious to get started. It moves so fast that it seems to "swallow" the earth. Relief comes ("it says, 'Aha!'") when it hears the ram's horn, the signal to begin the charge.

> 26"Is it by your understanding that the hawk soars,
> spreading its wings to the south?
> 27Does the eagle fly up at your command
> and make its nest up high?
> 28It dwells on the rock and makes its nest there;
> a tooth of rock is its fortress.
> 29From there it scouts for food;
> its eye sees it from a distance.
> 30Its young gorge on blood.
> Where the slain are, there they are."

39:26–30. *The hawk.* In vv. 26 and 27 God asks Job two more rhetorical questions that go unanswered because the answer is obvious. While God knows how a hawk soars and controls the flight of eagles, Job does not have a clue. Of course, today science has shed light on the flight of a hawk, but that does not minimize the basic point that there is much in nature that is beyond our fathoming, and we certainly do not control nature well. The rest of the passage marvels at the habits of the eagle, one of the most noble birds in existence, distinguished from other birds by its size and strength. They build their nests, often called aeries, up high, virtually inaccessible to humans. The parent bird looks for prey from that vantage point and pounces on it to feed its young. They are birds of prey, with powerful beaks that tear their food apart in a bloody fashion.

> 1And Yahweh answered Job and said:
> 2"Will someone who contends with Shaddai instruct him?
> Let the one who reproves God answer back!"

40:1–2. *Answer me!* A rubric begins God's final words in his first speech. Since rubrics began speeches previously in the book of Job (see 4:1; 6:1; 8:1, etc.), the scribe who inserted chapter divisions made this rubric the beginning of a new chapter, but v. 2 is really the climactic conclusion of God's first argument, in which he issues a challenge to Job.

God sounds offended that Job would think to instruct him, and no wonder, considering who God is (as demonstrated throughout the first speech) and who Job is (a mere creature). God is the repository of wisdom and distributes wisdom to whom he sees fit. On what grounds does Job instruct him? Worse yet, Job "contends" with God. The verb *rîb* comes from the realm of law. Job is making charges against God. God refers to himself by the name Shaddai, which most likely denotes his great power. How dare a human being contend with Shaddai? Yet God gives him the opportunity to defend himself. Job has reproved, that is, reprimanded, God, so let Job now defend himself. As we will see, Job knows better than to take up this challenge.

> 3And Job answered Yahweh and said:
> 4"I am small; how can I answer you?
> I have placed my hand over my mouth.
> 5I have spoken once already and will not respond;
> twice, but I won't add to that."

40:3–5. *Job is silent.* Challenged by God (see v. 2), Job responds, but not with a defense. Though Job on occasion thought he would put God in his place (31:35–37), God has just set Job in his place. Job knows this and so responds appropriately, acknowledging that he is "small" compared to God. Thus he will not offer a defense. He places his hand over his mouth. While some modern interpreters offer the absurd and unsupported interpretation that this is a gesture indicating contemptuous revulsion,[54] the context clarifies the significance of the action: Job has decided to stop speaking. Job had spoken in earlier chapters but now has come to regret his statements. He will not make the same mistake twice.

> 6And Yahweh answered Job from the whirlwind and said:
> 7"Brace yourself like a man.
> I will question you, and you must answer me.
> 8Would you invalidate my justice?
> Would you condemn me so you might be righteous?
> 9Do you have an arm like God?
> Can you thunder with a voice like his?
> 10Adorn yourself with loftiness and pride.
> Clothe yourself with splendor and majesty.
> 11Let loose the fury of your anger.
> Look on all those who are arrogant and bring them down.
> 12Look on all those who are arrogant and make them submit.
> Crush the wicked where they stand.
> 13Hide them in the dust all together.
> Bind their faces in the hidden world.
> 14Then I will acknowledge you,
> because your right hand will have given you victory."

40:6–14. *Brace yourself like a man—again!* Job's initial response was not sufficient to bring a stop to God's torrent of challenging questions whose purpose is to show Job his proper place in the cosmos. Job's complaints have been silenced, but he has not yet shown regret. God remains upset, as indicated by

54. See Curtis, "On Job's Response," 507–8.

his continuing to speak out of the whirlwind (see 38:1). Since Job has chosen silence, God does not ask the initial question of the first speech ("Who is this who darkens advice with ignorant words?" 38:2) but warns Job to prepare for a second set of questions with a repeat of 38:3, "Brace yourself like a man. I will question you, and you must answer me." As we will see, the questions continue to come fast and furious, but there will be no answers from Job.

God begins with a question that contains a telling, implicit accusation that helps us understand how we should interpret Job's speeches in the dialogue and his monologue. "Would you invalidate my justice?" (v. 8a). The question charges Job with illegitimately undermining God's justice. As I have argued, Job agreed with the three friends that only sinners should suffer, but he differed from them in that he did not believe he was a sinner. His conclusion was that God had unjustly made him suffer like a sinner. He was more concerned with his own reputation for righteousness than he was with God's reputation for justice (v. 8b).

But God does not continue by informing Job of the reason for his suffering. He rather, again, puts Job in his place by showing that it is God, not Job, who has power, sovereignty, and wisdom. In v. 9 God asks Job if he has an "arm" like his. God's "arm" is a metaphor for his power to act decisively in history (Exod. 6:6; 15:6). It is not only God's actions but also his "voice" that resonates with power (v. 9b).

God then challenges Job to present himself with "loftiness," "pride," "splendor," and "majesty" (v. 10). These are qualities normally connected to God (for "loftiness," see Ps. 93:1; for "pride," see Ps. 47:4; for "splendor" and "majesty," see Ps. 96:6).

In vv. 11–13 God sarcastically challenges Job to bring judgment on the arrogant wicked. Job has questioned God's justice in giving the wicked their proper due. He thus tells Job to bring his anger to bear on them so they submit and are crushed before him. Verse 13 is rather obscure when God tells Job to "hide them in the dust," but this phrase is perhaps best understood as an allusion to burial. Can Job get rid of the wicked by killing them in his righteous anger and then burying them? Of course not. He cannot make their presence ("faces," v. 13b) go away into "the hidden world," probably an allusion to the underworld.

God concludes this part of his speech by informing Job that unless he can do all these things, there is no reason for him to pay any attention to Job. If he does all these things, then he will have "victory," but Job knows only too well that he cannot do what God asks. Therefore, he continues his silence, while God proceeds to his next point.

15"Look, Behemoth, which I made just as I made you,
eats grass like an ox.
16Look, its strength is in its loins;
its vigor is in the muscles of its belly.

[17]It stiffens its tail like a cedar.
The sinews of its thigh are interlaced all together.
[18]Its bones are tubes of bronze;
its limbs are like bars of iron.
[19]It is the first of God's ways.
Only its Maker can approach it with a sword.
[20]For the produce of the mountains yields food for it,
where all the animals of the field play.
[21]It resides under lotus trees,
in the covert of the reeds and in the marsh.
[22]The lotus trees cover it for shade;
the poplars in the wadi surround it.
[23]If the river is turbulent, it does not hurry away.
It is confident even though the Jordan gushes toward its mouth.
[24]Can it be taken with hooks,
or can you pierce its nose with a snare?"

40:15–24. *Behemoth*. God concludes his diatribe against Job by having him consider his relationship to Behemoth and Leviathan, beginning with the former. The identity of Behemoth has been the subject of much speculation. Some want to identify it with some specific known animal, most often the hippopotamus,[55] but other identifications include the elephant, water buffalo, or crocodile. The description of this creature, though, supersedes any normal creature, as will Leviathan. The view advocated by so-called young-earth creationists that Behemoth and Leviathan are dinosaurs is preposterous. The author of Job would have no knowledge of dinosaurs. The view is the result of an overly literalistic reading of Job.

The best understanding is that Behemoth and Leviathan are not real creatures, but rather represent the ultimate in land animals and sea creatures, respectively. I will explain the background of Leviathan in the next section. "Behemoth" in Hebrew is the plural of the common word for "animal" (and used that way in Joel 1:20). The plural here in Job is one of majesty and indicates the ultimate land creature.[56]

God begins by emphasizing that Behemoth, as immense and powerful as it is, is a creature of his own making, just like Job himself is (v. 15a). Verses 16–18 describe its formidable physical features. It is powerful, with strong loins, and even its stomach is muscular. That its tail stiffens is odd. What animal stiffens its tail in this way? Perhaps since Behemoth is an imaginary creature, it is a way of saying that even its tail is hard and muscular, again emphasizing its

55. According to Clines (*Job 38–42*, 150), who also believes that the dominant view of modern scholars is that Behemoth and Leviathan are real creatures.

56. Bruce K. Waltke and M. O'Connor speak of a plural of extension where "the referent . . . is inherently large or complex" (*An Introduction to Biblical Hebrew Syntax* [Winona Lake, IN: Eisenbrauns, 1990], 7.4.1c).

strength. Some commentators, though, believe that "tail" here is a euphemism for the penis and that its hardening is a way of indicating its virility.[57] If so, then the "thighs" of the next colon may be a reference to the testicles.[58] Its bones are impossible to break; they are like metal.

No human can control or hurt this animal. But again, God made it ("it is the first of God's ways," v. 19a). Thus only God who made it can control or harm it ("only its Maker can approach it with a sword," v. 19b).

This animal, though, is not a carnivore. It "eats grass like an ox" (v. 15b), finding abundant food in the vegetation of the mountains. Verses 20–24 describe its habitat, and here we see why some might think it is a hippopotamus. It is under the lotus trees that presumably hang over the marshes, since it says it is in the reeds of the marshland. It is a river dweller that does not fear the fast-rushing waters of even the Jordan River.

The section ends with one more challenging question to Job. Can Job control this animal by snaring it with hooks? The answer is no, and again God is shown to be superior to Job.

41:1 [40:25]"Can you catch Leviathan with a fishhook?
Can you press down its tongue with a cord?
41:2 [40:26]Can you put a rope in its nose?
Can you pierce its cheek with a hook?
41:3 [40:27]Will it multiply its pleas of mercy to you?
Will it speak tenderly to you?
41:4 [40:28]Will it make a treaty with you
to be taken as your eternal slave?
41:5 [40:29]Will you play with it like a bird?
Will you put it on a leash for your young girls?
41:6 [40:30]Will the fishing guild haggle over it?
Will it be divided up among the merchants?
41:7 [40:31]Can you fill its skin with harpoons
or its head with fishing spears?
41:8 [40:32]Set your hands on it!
Remember the battle; you will not do it again!

41:9 [1]Any hope of subduing it will prove a lie.
One is thrown down even at its appearance.
10 [2]No one is so fierce as to stir it up.
Who can stand before it?
11 [3]Who has ever confronted it and come out safely,
who—under all the heavens?
12 [4]I will not keep quiet about its limbs,
its great strength and splendid form.

57. Pope, *Job*, 323–24.
58. So the Vulgate *testiculorum*.

13 [5]Who has ever exposed its garment
in order to penetrate its double coat of mail?
14 [6]Who can open the doors of its face?
There is dread all around its teeth.
15 [7]Its back is composed of shields in a row,
closed up tightly like a seal.
16 [8]One draws near another,
so not even wind can get between them.
17 [9]Each clings to its neighbor,
so they clasp each other and cannot be broken off.
18 [10]Its sneezing makes light flash.
Its eyes are like the eyelids of the dawn.
19 [11]Torches come from its mouth;
sparks of fire escape.
20 [12]Smoke comes out of its nostrils,
like a boiling pot and burning reeds.
21 [13]Its breath kindles coals.
Flame comes out of its mouth.
22 [14]In its neck resides strength.
Violence leaps before it.
23 [15]The folds of its flesh cling together.
It is solidly cast and does not move.
24 [16]Its heart is firm like a rock,
firm as a lower millstone.
25 [17]When it lifts itself up, the gods are afraid,
the waves miss their mark.
26 [18]The sword may reach it but have no effect,
as with the spear, the dart, and the arrowhead.
27 [19]It considers iron to be straw,
and bronze to be rotten wood.
28 [20]The arrow cannot make it flee;
slingstones are turned to chaff for it.
29 [21]A cudgel is considered like chaff;
it laughs at the rattling javelin.
30 [22]Its underside is like sharp potsherds.
It spreads itself out like a threshing sledge on the mud.
31 [23]It makes the deep boil like a pot.
It makes the sea like ointment.
32 [24]It leaves an illuminated way behind it.
One would consider the deep to be white-haired.
33 [25]There is nothing on earth that equals it,
a creature with no fear.
34 [26]It sees all that is lofty.
It is king over all the proud beasts."

41:1–34 [40:25–41:26]. *Leviathan.* Yahweh's second speech ends with a reflection on Leviathan. Like Behemoth, the identification of Leviathan has been the subject of great speculation. Traditional interpretation has sought an identification among the known creatures of the earth. While Behemoth is a land animal, Leviathan is a creature of the water and is thus often identified with the most fearsome or largest creatures that live in water, the whale and the crocodile. The description of Leviathan, however, does not fit well with these or any known creatures. No crocodile known to us breathes fire, for instance (41:21). The description, as we will see, also emphasizes that no human can catch or control Leviathan, whereas crocodiles at least were hunted in the ancient Near East, as scenes from Egyptian paintings attest.[59] While one must reckon with the possibility of hyperbole, the characteristics of Leviathan surpass even an exaggerated description of any attested creature. Furthermore, the attempt to identify Leviathan with a dinosaur fails, as with Behemoth, because the author of Job would not have been aware of dinosaurs, which became extinct long before the advent of humans.[60]

The mention of Leviathan here is not unique to the book of Job (see also comments at 3:8). Psalm 74 refers to God's dominance over the many-headed Leviathan in a creation context that evokes ancient creation myths of conflict with a sea monster:

> You, O God, are my king from ages past,
>   bringing salvation to the earth.
> You split the sea by your strength
>   and smashed the heads of the sea monsters.
> You crushed the heads of Leviathan
>   and let the desert animals eat him.
> You caused the springs and streams to gush forth,
>   and you dried the rivers that never run dry.
> Both day and night belong to you;
>   you made the starlight and the sun.
> You set the boundaries of the earth,
>   and you made both summer and winter. (Ps. 74:12–17 NLT)

Psalm 104 speaks of Leviathan as a creature that God made and that dwells in the sea: "Leviathan, which you made to play in the sea" (Ps. 104:26b NLT). Perhaps the most interesting text, though, is found in Isaiah. Here Leviathan clearly stands for evil and chaos. God will defeat this embodiment of evil and chaos in the future: "In that day the Lord will take his terrible, swift sword and punish Leviathan, the swiftly moving serpent, the coiling, writhing serpent. He will kill the dragon of the sea" (Isa. 27:1 NLT). Note the similarity to one of the Ugaritic Baal texts: "When you smite [Lôtan,

59. Cited by Cornelius, "Job," 298.

60. The idea that dinosaurs and human beings existed at the same time (a view held by some "young-earth creationists") is supported by neither science nor the Bible.

the] fleeing [serpent], finish off [the twisting serpent], the close-coiling one [with seven heads]."[61]

There is little doubt that in the book of Job, Yahweh is evoking in Job's (and our) imagination the most fearsome sea creature that humans can conceive. No real animal can meet the needs of the rhetorical moment. In other words, how awe-inspiring would it be to say that God can control the crocodile? Not much. But to say that God controls the creature that represents the power of chaos itself is a dramatic way of speaking of his greatness and strength.[62]

God begins his speech on Leviathan in a way that we have come to expect, peppering Job with question after question. The purpose of these questions again is to put Job in his proper place. The assumption is that Job does not fully understand that it is not he but God who is in control of the universe and its creatures. Leviathan is no ordinary sea creature, and thus he is not caught or controlled like a fish or any other inhabitant of the waters. Leviathan cannot be caught by a conventional fishhook, whether through the mouth (v. 1a) or through the cheek (v. 2b). Its tongue cannot be controlled by a cord or a rope through the nose.[63]

Verses 3–4 ask if Job could possibly negotiate a treaty with this awesome creature. Job does not answer because the answer is obvious. Leviathan is a symbol of chaos. Again, only God can control it. Job cannot make it his vassal through a treaty. Only God can bring this powerful beast to the point that it would beg for mercy. Indeed, God can so control Leviathan that it is like a plaything for him. It is anachronistic to say so, but the sense of v. 5a is that this awesome creature is no more than a rubber ducky in a bathtub to God. Indeed, if he so chose, he could make Leviathan docile enough for young girls (v. 5b).

Not even experienced fishermen will want to tussle with Leviathan (v. 6). They cannot catch it and sell it to merchants as they can other dangerous sea creatures. Indeed, Leviathan cannot be caught by spear or harpoon. God concludes the first section of this speech with a challenge that neither Job nor any reasonable person will take up. He dares Job to try to capture Leviathan. It would be a battle never to be forgotten because it would result in horrible injury or even death (v. 8).

61. Translation of D. Pardee, *COS* 1:265. Ugaritic Lôtan/Litan is generally equated with Hebrew Leviathan.

62. Fyall (*Now My Eyes*, 157) argues that Leviathan is "the embodiment of evil itself," and he overreaches when he claims that "in Leviathan we have another guise of Satan." First, I have already argued that *haśśāṭān* in Job 1 and 2 is not the devil, and nothing in the book of Job would lead us to make a connection between *haśśāṭān* and Leviathan. It should be pointed out that nothing in the description of Leviathan indicates that it is an evil creature. Rather, the emphasis is on its unbelievable power, which God can easily control. It is one thing to be dangerous and another to be evil.

63. Verses 1–2 present a chiastic organization, since the first and fourth cola refer to catching Leviathan with a "hook" (*ḥakkā*, *ḥôaḥ*) and the second and third with a cord/rope (*ḥebel*, *ʾagmôn*).

Verses 9–11 reiterate that no human—certainly not Job—can control this powerful sea monster. Even the hope of doing so is delusional (v. 9a). The mere presence of Leviathan is enough (v. 9b). Indeed, not only are humans unable to tame Leviathan, but none of God's earthly creatures is able to do so ("who—under all the heavens," v. 11b).

With that, God now describes Leviathan, emphasizing its amazing strength and invulnerability. Reading this description at this historical distance does not allow us to confidently and precisely picture the creature in our minds. It has limbs, and powerful ones at that, though we are not told how many or their purpose (swimming, walking, or both?).

Verse 13 speaks of "its garment" in a way that suggests reference to Leviathan's skin. But this is no ordinary skin; it is impenetrable, like a "double coat of mail." It is like armor; no wonder harpoons and fishing spears have no effect on it (v. 7). God asks Job rhetorically if anyone has been able to expose this garment, and the assumed answer, of course, is no.

But perhaps there is another way to penetrate the body of Leviathan—through the mouth. According to a Babylonian creation text, *Enuma Elish*, Marduk was able to vanquish Tiamat by opening her mouth:

> Tiamat and Marduk, sage of the gods, drew close for battle,
> They locked in single combat, joining for the fray.
> The Lord spread out his net, encircled her,
> The ill wind he had held behind him he released in her face.
> Tiamat opened her mouth to swallow,
> He thrust in the ill wind so she could not close her lips.
> The raging winds bloated her belly,
> Her insides were stopped up, she gaped her mouth wide.
> He shot off the arrow, it broke open her belly,
> It cut to her innards, it pierced the heart.[64]

But Leviathan, according to the book of Job, is not so easily subdued, at least by mortals. Its mouth is a door to its innards, but this door is not easily opened, being guarded by fearsome teeth. They are surrounded by dread because they not only defend its mouth but also could be used as weapons to attack anyone trying to slay it.

Leviathan's back is equally defended and impenetrable (v. 15). It is described as tightly interwoven shields, not allowing attack. There is no weak link, but they are sealed tightly together. The passage strongly emphasizes its cohesiveness, expanding upon it in vv. 16–17. These shield-like defenses are so compact that not even the wind can get through, not to speak of the point of a weapon. They support one another so they cannot be broken off, exposing a weak place. The description of the back as composed of multiple,

64. Translation by B. R. Foster, *COS* 1:398 (tablet 4, lines 93–102).

though interlocked, shields rather than a single shield seems to suggest flexibility and movement.

Verses 18–21 associate Leviathan with bright light, fire, and smoke. God speaks of the sneezes of Leviathan as producing flashing light. This creature is a fire-breather, and when it sneezes, it involuntarily emits fire. Torches come from its mouth, and its nose is like a smokestack. Here we can reiterate that this is no crocodile or any other natural creature. This is the epitome of a fearsome sea creature. The ancient Near Eastern imagination could not produce a more fearsome picture, and God easily controls it, while Job and other human creatures can only stand trembling. Its innards are like a "boiling pot" and a fire of reeds. Thus when it breathes, it ignites fires.

Verse 22 turns the reader's attention to Leviathan's neck, which is powerful. What is interesting about this description is that it speaks of Leviathan's neck in the singular. Psalm 74:13, in continuity with Ugaritic references, refers to the multiple heads of Leviathan. There may be some malleability in the way this imaginary creature can be described. Or perhaps in referring to the "neck" of Leviathan, we should extrapolate to all seven.[65] Mentioning its powerful neck is connected with the violence that accompanies Leviathan (v. 22b). This is truly a creature to be feared and avoided.

Returning to the theme of its impregnable outer covering (see vv. 15–17), God draws Job's (and the reader's) attention to the "folds of its flesh" (v. 23a). They too cling together.[66] It is "solidly cast," a verb associated with metals.[67] In a word, its skin is like metal, impenetrable.

No creature is stronger than its heart. If it stops, life ceases. Leviathan's heart is like a rock, even one as tough as a millstone. Like a millstone, it does not break but grinds others into pieces.

God is the only one who can control Leviathan. We have already heard that this awesome sea monster is a mere plaything to him (v. 5). Certainly Job would quake before the power and strength of this invincible creature, but it is not only Job who would so react, according to v. 25. The very "gods" are afraid of Leviathan when it goes into action. Who are the gods? Elsewhere in Scripture, "gods" identifies created but spiritual beings (Exod. 12:12; Deut. 32:8 NRSV; Ps. 82) who are in other places referred to as "angels" or "demons." Even these powerful beings fear Leviathan. Verse 25b notes that Leviathan causes the waves to miss their mark. The "waves" are associated with the motif of the waters that represent the forces of chaos. Leviathan even adds disorder to the sea, which itself represents chaos.

65. As in the Ugaritic texts, as well as the beast in Rev. 13 (see v. 1), which appears to be modeled on the OT and ancient Near Eastern picture of the sea monster.

66. The same verb (*dābaq*) is used in vv. 17a and 23a.

67. "The hardness of cast metal lies behind some of the metaphorical uses of *yṣq*, particularly in Job" (H. M. Wolf and R. Holmstedt, *NIDOTTE* 2:520).

Verses 26–29 describe how weapons of all sorts are ineffective against Leviathan. God's reflection on Leviathan began by speaking of the impotency of the "weapons" of the fishing industry (fishhooks, cords, ropes, harpoons, fishing spears; see vv. 1–2, 7), but in this present unit, God makes clear that not even military weapons can subdue it. Verse 26 remarks that one might be able to strike Leviathan with sword, spear, dart, or arrowhead, but they would do no damage against a creature whose skin is as tough as shields (vv. 13–17). These metallic weapons are nothing to a creature who considers iron to be straw and bronze to be like rotten wood, easily broken (v. 27). Leviathan will not turn around and run in the face of arrows or slingstones. They too are nothing to it (v. 28). It turns both slingstones and a cudgel into harmless chaff that will just blow away in the wind. Javelins, deadly to humans, are just a joke to it (v. 29).

Verse 30 again describes the hardness of Leviathan's outer skin, or perhaps even more accurately described, "outer shell." But now Job learns that this outer shell is not just protective but also capable of killing on its own. Sharp potsherds (broken pieces of a pot) can lacerate and kill. To be run over by Leviathan would be like being run over by a threshing sledge.

Verses 31–32 now depict the effect of its movement on the water. The description seems to emphasize the speed and size of the creature. It may also suggest the heat generated by this fire-breather. After all, it is capable of making the waters boil. But when it cuts through the waves, it makes the waters smooth, like a big ship that cuts through the waves. It leaves a white trail behind it, again like a large ship. Verse 32b personifies the deep in the aftermath of Leviathan as a white-haired man.

The summary statement of vv. 33–34 makes the obvious explicit. Leviathan is a creature without peer. It has no fear in the face of other creatures. However, as the speech as a whole makes clear, there is one who can control this proud beast, and it is certainly not Job.

---

1 And Job answered the Lord and said:
2 "I know that you can do all things,
and no plan of yours is impossible.
3 'Who is this who hides advice without knowledge?'
Thus I spoke, but I did not understand,
things too wonderful for me that I did not know.
4 'Hear and I will speak.
I will question you, and you will inform me.'
5 My ear had received a report of you,
but now my eyes have seen you.
6 Therefore I hold myself in contempt,
and I repent in dust and ashes."

42:1–6. *Job repents.* We now come to the climactic moment in the book, Job's definitive response to God's speeches. The earlier response in 40:3–5 was not sufficient, and God continued the torrent of questions addressed to Job. But here the interchange comes to resolution. God is satisfied and will no longer upbraid Job. What is the difference between Job's first and second response to God's speeches? Repentance.

Job begins with an acknowledgment of God's sovereignty (v. 2). In language surprisingly similar to Gen. 11:6 ("nothing that they propose to do will now be impossible for them," NRSV), Job acknowledges—in a way that the actions of the tower builders attempted to deny—that only God controls events. God can do anything he plans, including allowing an innocent person like Job to suffer. Job has no further complaint to make against God for the pain that he has put him through.[68]

In v. 3a he quotes God's statement (with some variation) that began his speeches (see 38:3). Job thus admits that he is indeed a person who has "hidden," in the sense of obscuring, knowledge. He has not clarified matters by his questioning of God, but rather he has made the situation more difficult. In addition, he has not done so intelligently, but "without knowledge."

Job's development may be compared with that of the poet in Ps. 73. This person also wrestled with the issue of retribution. He believed that God should reward the righteous and punish the wicked, but his life experience showed the opposite, leading him to question God. Like Job, the poet came to recognize that his bitterness toward God made him like a "brute beast" (73:22 NRSV), and he would have "been untrue to the circle of your children" (73:15 NRSV).

Through God's constant questioning, Job came to realize the limits of his wisdom and knowledge. He tried to claim a knowledge of the workings of the universe that were vastly beyond him. If he cannot even fathom the natural world (as God's questions in chaps. 38–41 indicated, and Job's quotation of God's statement in v. 4 [see 38:3 again] evokes), how could he possibly pontificate about the moral universe?

Up to this point, Job had just been operating on hearsay about God. And what he had been hearing is that God rewards good people and punishes bad people. But the theology he had been taught (the "report" of God) was horribly deficient. God did not strictly operate the way Job thought. But now he has had a personal encounter with God, and his understanding is vastly expanded.[69] Again, there is a similarity with the poet of Ps. 73. When did he turn around his thinking? "When I thought how to understand this, it seemed to me a wearisome task, until I went into the sanctuary of God" (73:16–17a NRSV). Both Job and the poet changed their thinking when they had a more intimate revelation of God.

Job expresses his turnaround in v. 6: "Therefore I hold myself in contempt, and I repent in dust and ashes." Perhaps no verse has occasioned more

68. Perhaps we see an echo of Job's words in Matt. 19:26: "With people this is impossible, but with God all things are possible" (NASB).

69. In essence, Job is saying "I saw you, I experienced you"; so Negri, *Labor of Job*, 96.

discussion than this one. As we will see, Job's repentance will lead to his restoration in the remainder of the book (42:7–17). Job repents and is restored. What is initially troublesome about this turn in the story is that repentance is precisely the advice prescribed by the three friends as well as Elihu. They were all united by their belief that Job would only be restored if he would repent. Does the end of the book undermine the message of the book? Are the three friends ultimately correct?

As we will see, 42:7–8 certainly denies the latter. God explicitly states that the three friends "did not speak correctly about me as did my servant Job." We will deal with other facets of this statement in the next section, but it keeps us from interpreting the book up to this point as affirming the three friends.

Job did repent, but we must ask, Of what did he repent? We see that he did not repent of any sin that could have led to his suffering in the first place. The book makes very clear in the prologue that Job's sin was not the cause of his suffering. What then did he repent of? After the prologue shows us that Job did not suffer because of his sin, we read that after seven days, he began to complain bitterly against God. Earlier we analyzed his speech in chap. 3 as a complaint in the spirit of the grumbling of the Israelites in the wilderness rather than of a lament in the book of Psalms. From there he grows increasingly bitter, not just toward his human antagonists but also toward God himself. In a word, he repents of the growing bitterness of his spirit and his accusations that God was unjust. He turns away from his earlier intention to bring charges against God for treating him unfairly.[70]

Such a view leaves a number of contemporary commentators cold. First, they have trouble with the idea of Job's repentance, because they do not make the distinction drawn in the previous paragraph and think that it is impossible that Job would repent, since his suffering was not a result of sin in the first place. Second, the idea of God making Job the sufferer repent strikes them as divine bullying. Thus some seek to reimagine the speech in quite a different way. Perdue, for instance, believes that Job does acknowledge God's sovereignty, but rather than Job submitting to God, Perdue argues that v. 6 should be translated: "I protest, but feel sorry for dust and ashes." He then comments: "In verse 6 a defiant Job expresses his opposition to a cruel Yahweh and feels compassion for humans who are forced to live under the tyranny of an abusive lord."[71] Such an interpretation may fit well with the spirit of the present day, but it does not comport well with the broader context, once it is clear that Job is repenting of his impatient insistence that God justify himself to Job and not repenting of any sin that may have led to his suffering in the first place.[72]

70. See also Carson, *How Long, O Lord?*, 153.

71. Perdue, *Wisdom Literature*, 126.

72. See the helpful analysis and criticism of the view that Job protests rather than repents, responding to earlier statements by Perdue and others, in Newell, "Job: Repentant or Rebellious?"

Theological Implications

Humanity's Place in God's Creation

The Bible makes clear that humanity occupies a privileged place in God's cosmos. The first creation account (Gen. 1:1–2:4a) relates how humans are created on the sixth day, after everything else has been prepared for their presence. The second creation account figuratively describes the creation of Adam from the dust of the ground and the breath of God, showing a special relationship with God that differentiates humans from the rest of God's creatures (2:7). Genesis 1:27–28 also indicates a special relationship with God since humans, male and female, are said to be made in the "image of God." While the exact meaning of the "image of God" is debated,[73] no doubt attends the recognition that this too points to humanity's high status in the creation. In this regard, one thinks of the psalmist's reflection on human glory in Ps. 8:

> When I look at your heavens, the work of your fingers,
>   the moon and the stars that you have established;
> what are human beings that you are mindful of them,
>   mortals that you care for them?
> Yet you have made them a little lower than God,
>   and crowned them with glory and honor.
> You have given them dominion over the works of your hands;
>   you have put all things under their feet,
>   all sheep and oxen,
>   and also the beasts of the field,
> the birds of the air, and the fish of the sea,
>   whatever passes along the paths of the seas. (Ps. 8:3–8 NRSV)

According to the witness of the OT, humans are indeed "fearfully and wonderfully made" (Ps. 139:14 NRSV). So why is God putting Job in his place?

The answer appears to be that Job had forgotten that he was "a little *lower* than God." In his pain and suffering, he began to question God's justice and wisdom and power. He adopted the attitude that he knew better than God (see God's own statement to this effect in Job 40:2, 8–9). In his speeches, God responds by asserting his wisdom and his power but not by explaining his justice. Even so, Job never forgets himself so much that he rebels against God. He never "curses God," but in the lament (chap. 3) and after, his suffering and pain drive him to dangerous attitudes toward God, and God here calls him back to the right path.

73. For a discussion and a defense of the idea that the "image of God" indicates that humans represent God in creation and reflect the divine glory, see Longman, *How to Read Genesis*, 105.

Besides asserting humanity's high status in God's creation, the Bible also relates our human tendency to displace God himself. Human pride led Adam and Eve to ignore God and eat the fruit of the tree of the knowledge of good and evil (Gen. 3). Human pride that wants to dethrone God motivated the builders of the tower of Babel (Gen. 11:1–9). The list could go on and on, since the Bible narrates story after story of human rebellion and sin.

But the Bible is not just an accounting of human rebellion; it is also the story of God's redemption. God does not let Job continue on a path that might lead to his destruction, but God intervenes so that Job maintains a healthy relationship with his Maker. In the same way, God neither destroys nor abandons sinful humanity but pursues their redemption in a way that leads to the cross of Christ.

God Distributes Wisdom as He Wills: The Case of the Ostrich

As noted above, in chap. 39 God reminds Job that it is he, God, who is in control of creatures. He understands them and he grants them certain abilities. Mainly through the use of rhetorical questions, God exposes Job's lack of understanding. These wild animals are beyond his control.

In terms of the main theme of the book, which is wisdom, the case of the ostrich is particularly interesting. As noted in the introduction and throughout the commentary, the book explores the question of the source of wisdom. Where can wisdom be found? The divine speeches serve to answer that question by locating the source of wisdom in God himself. The ostrich passage reveals that God distributes wisdom as he sees fit, and he has determined that the ostrich would not receive much. Even so, he does not leave this creature bereft of admirable qualities, and the passage goes on to speak of the ostrich's amazing speed as a gift from God.

The message again to Job and to the reader of the book is that true wisdom is with God, and God chooses to withhold his wisdom from some but to grant it to others. The practical consequence of this teaching is that the pursuit of wisdom leads only to God.

Is Job a Model of Prayer in Suffering?

It is not uncommon to hear some take Job as a model of bold prayer before God. He is considered a hero for standing up to God and calling on God to account for his suffering. Job does not take his condition passively but rather calls for an audience with God for the purpose of setting God straight. After all, Job did nothing to deserve his pain.

But is Job really a good example of how to approach God in the midst of suffering? A close reading of Job in light of the whole book leads me to doubt that he is. Indeed, after finally getting what he wished for, it does not quite go the way he expected. He wanted to set God straight, but what we have here at the end is God setting Job straight. God does not listen to Job's case and respond to it. Indeed, he seems angry or at least irritated when he, through the use of rhetorical questions, paints a negative picture of Job's whole approach to him:

> Will someone who contends with Shaddai instruct him?
> Let the one who reproves God answer back! (40:2)

> Would you invalidate my justice?
> Would you condemn me so you might be righteous? (40:8)

Far from being pleased with Job's approach, God intends to put Job in his place. Job has overstepped himself in his relationship with God, and now God wants him to correct his attitude.[74]

Thus Job's speeches are not an example of the proper attitude toward God in the midst of suffering. Granted, some elements are highly commendable. For instance, he never gives up on God or curses God. He does not capitulate to the weak arguments of his friends and repent of sins he never committed. Nevertheless, God is not fully affirming Job's approach to him by a long stretch.

Job's speeches are not to be used as guidelines for the prayers of sufferers today. For that, we must turn to the lament psalms (see "Grumbling at God" following my comments on Job 3).

Being Silent in Suffering (40:4–5)

As a continuation of the previous reflection, I draw attention to Job's words in 40:4–5:

> I am small; how can I answer you?
> I have placed my hand over my mouth.
> I have spoken once already and will not respond;
> twice, but I won't add to that.

Above, I commented that, in light of God's response to them, Job's speeches should not be taken as the right way to approach God in suffering. The purpose of the divine speeches is to bring Job to the right attitude toward God in suffering: submission and silence. This view does not contradict that, as just mentioned in the previous reflection, a proper, faithful questioning of God is permitted, as in the lament psalms, but it does point to God's ultimate desire for those who suffer: to grow silent and trust him.

In the face of God's appearance and speech to him, Job grows silent, and this without a divine explanation of his suffering and before his restoration or

74. For how this squares with 42:7, see the commentary there.

even promise of restoration. Job grows silent, and the book of Job advocates such an attitude in the midst of suffering.

In this Job is not alone. We turn now to the book of Lamentations, the book that expresses an emotional response to the destruction of Jerusalem at the hands of the Babylonians. The poet of Lamentations, however, knew that, although the Babylonians were the human agents of destruction, the real cause was God, who came against his people "like an enemy" (Lam. 2:4, 5).

The book of Lamentations is indeed a lament before God, trying to evoke pity from the reader, and most importantly from God, for Israel's fate. But in the middle of the book, the poet presents a picture of the proper approach to suffering, and like Job, it is characterized by silence before God.

Chapter 3 presents a picture of the suffering people of God by personifying them as "the man who has seen affliction" (3:1 NIV). His afflictions are profound, and he has no doubts that God is the one that has made him suffer: "He [God] is a bear lying in wait for me, a lion in hiding" (3:10 NRSV). And in language reminiscent of Job 6:4; 7:20; and 16:13–14: "He shot into my vitals the arrows of his quiver" (Lam. 3:13 NRSV). How does the man of affliction react? Is he angry? Does he challenge God? His advice is given in 3:26–30:

> It is good that one should wait quietly
>   for the salvation of the LORD.
> It is good for one to bear
>   the yoke in youth,
> to sit alone in silence
>   when the LORD has imposed it,
> to put one's mouth to the dust
>   (there may be yet hope),
> to give one's cheek to the smiter,
>   and be filled with insults. (NRSV)

While we must acknowledge a difference between Job and "the man who has seen affliction" in that the latter's suffering was seen as judgment for the people's sin, both are presented as models, or heroes, of suffering for later readers, including us today.

Behemoth and Leviathan: The Power of the Mythic Imagination

I have argued that Behemoth and Leviathan are not actual animals but imaginary ones. In the case of Leviathan, at least, we can be certain that it is an imaginary creature drawn from ancient Near Eastern mythology, which often speaks of sea monsters that threaten the creation order.

Of course, the imaginary and mythical origins of Behemoth and Leviathan raise questions in the minds of contemporary readers. First, how can the book of Job be true if Behemoth and Leviathan are not real? If God is greater than Job because he, not Job, can subdue these wild creatures, then isn't the point lost if Behemoth and Leviathan are not real and God has not actually subdued them?

Such a question, however, arises from a weak view of figurative language, which always points to truth, though indirectly. While Behemoth and Leviathan are not real creatures, they are the most fearsome monsters imaginable. When God says that he can restrain, even tame, them, this implies that he can certainly subdue any actual wild animal or force of chaos.

Even so, some Bible readers question the presence of mythological allusions in the Bible. As mentioned already, the Leviathan mentioned in the Bible is also found in ancient Ugaritic texts, which form part of the literature of Canaanite religion, a religion clearly decried as false by the Bible. How can this be?

Before addressing this question regarding Leviathan specifically, we should first take note of the frequent mythological references elsewhere in the book of Job. Without attempting to be exhaustive,[75] we might mention an earlier reference to Leviathan (3:8) and frequent references to the Sea, either as Yam (7:12; 9:8; 26:12), Rahab (9:13; 26:12), or the Deep (28:14). Death (Mot; 7:15; 28:22) and its denizens, the Rephaim (26:5), are represented as mythological forces, and the realm of Death is separated from the land of the living by the Water Channel in 33:18 and 36:12. Mention is also made of the mountain of Baal, Zaphon, in 26:7. I should also point out that Job is not at all atypical of the literature of the Hebrew Bible, which is filled with mythological allusions, particularly in the poetic and prophetic books.

A great deal of effort is required to demythologize the Bible, effort that results in turning it into a much less interesting book and for no good purpose. The worry is that we might think that the author of Job actually believed in the existence of these gods as rivals to Yahweh, the one and only true God. While it is true that a number of OT texts do not dispute the actual existence of foreign gods (see, e.g., Exod. 12:12; Deut. 32:8 NRSV; Ps. 82), they are not seen as rivals to the one and only God, who created them all. Indeed, as Ps. 106 indicates through its use of poetic parallelism, they are really demonic forces:

> They did not destroy the peoples,
> as the Lord commanded them,
> but they mingled with the nations
> and learned to do as they did.
> They served their idols,
> which became a snare to them.
> They sacrificed their sons
> and their daughters to the demons;
> they poured out innocent blood,
> the blood of their sons and daughters,
> whom they sacrificed to the idols of Canaan. (Ps. 106:34–38 NRSV)

75. Connections with mythological references are indicated in the commentary throughout.

The use of mythological imagery varies from place to place. Sometimes it is used as the cultural language of the day to communicate to the imaginations of the people (as I have argued in the present context concerning Behemoth and Leviathan or in the case of Gen. 1, which pictures creation beginning with the primordial waters). On other occasions, Near Eastern mythological language is used to undermine the false religions of Israel's neighbors, as when Ps. 29 pictures God in language familiarly applied to Baal, the storm god of the Canaanites, or when 1 Kings 18 has Yahweh taking on Baal in the area of his specialty, throwing fire down from heaven.

In the final analysis, the mythological references throughout the Bible are used to exalt the one and only true God, Yahweh, at the expense of the false gods of the nations. The book of Job here communicates this message by God's dominance over Behemoth, the monster of the land, and Leviathan, the monster of the sea.

Is It for No Good Reason That Job Fears God? (1:9)

The reader has journeyed long since the accuser first asked God the question that initiated Job's suffering, the question of Job's motivation for his piety and obedience. Why did Job fear God? Was it just for the reward?

At the end of the prologue, Job had shown himself obedient in spite of his suffering (1:22; 2:10). But as time went on and the reader moved into the poetic dialogue, Job certainly questioned whether obedience was worth it. Nonetheless, Job never turned disobedient in spite of his suffering. He questioned, he doubted, he demanded an audience with God, but he never abandoned God. Still, until the divine speeches begin, one wonders how long Job will hold on to his desire for relationship with God.

The ultimate answer to these questions comes in Job's final response, when he repents and stands silent before God, in whose presence he finds himself, even without an answer to his burning question about his suffering. Though the term "fear" is not used in Job's speech, fearing God is precisely what strikes him silent and submissive before God. He preserves his integrity until the bitter end and—this is important—before he has his prosperity restored. Job is not told by God that he will restore Job; nonetheless, Job fears God. In this, Job demonstrates to all (the accuser seems long gone) that he will worship God in spite of an absence of prosperity. Indeed, he will worship God even in the midst of his suffering.

VII. Job's Restoration

(42:7–17)

Translation

[7]And it came about after the Lord spoke these words to Job that the Lord spoke to Eliphaz the Temanite. "My anger burns against you and your two friends because you did not speak correctly about[1] me as did my servant Job. [8]And now take for yourself seven bulls and seven rams and go to my servant Job. You will offer burnt offerings, and Job my servant will pray for you, and I will accept what he says[2] and not treat you according to your folly, for you did not speak what is correct about me as my servant Job did." [9]So Eliphaz the Temanite, Bildad the Shuhite, and Zophar the Naamathite went and did according to all the Lord said to them, and the Lord accepted what Job said.[3]

[10]And the Lord restored the fortune of Job when he prayed for his friends. The Lord gave Job twice as much as before. [11]Then all his brothers and all his sisters and all his acquaintances came to him. They ate food with him in his house, and they spoke with him. And they commiserated with him concerning all the evil that the Lord had brought on him, and each of them gave to him some money[4] and a gold ring.

[12]And the Lord blessed the end of Job's life more than the beginning. He owned fourteen thousand sheep and six thousand camels and a

1. Or perhaps "to." See Ngwa (*Hermeneutics*, 25), who says "both senses should be discerned here."
2. Literally "I will lift up his mouth."
3. Literally "Yahweh lifted the mouth of Job."
4. Literally "a *qĕśîṭâ*," a monetary unit of unknown value.

thousand pairs of oxen and a thousand donkeys. **13**And he had seven[5]
sons and three daughters. **14**The name of the first was Jemimah, the
name of the second was Qeziah, and the name of the third was Qeren-
Happuk. **15**There could not be found in the land women more beautiful
than the daughters of Job. Their father gave them an inheritance along
with their brothers. **16**And after this, Job lived one hundred and forty
years, and he saw his children and his children's children for four generations. **17**And Job died an old man and full of days.[6]

Interpretation

The conclusion to the book of Job reverts to the prose style of the opening two chapters. After Job's repentance, his submission to God, and his withdrawal of his complaint, God then turns his attention to the three friends. Declaring Job right, God expresses his displeasure with the three friends. He allows them a way out by having Job himself intercede for them and offer sacrifices on their behalf (likely implying a repentant heart on their part). The three friends do as God instructs them, and Job prays for them.

Interestingly, Job's restoration is tied to his intercession on behalf of his friends. When he prayed for them, then God restored him to his previous prosperity and happiness. Indeed, his new condition surpassed his earlier situation. He died an old and happy man, leaving behind a large, prosperous family.

7And it came about after the Lord spoke these words to Job that the Lord
spoke to Eliphaz the Temanite. "My anger burns against you and your two
friends because you did not speak correctly about me as did my servant
Job. **8**And now take for yourself seven bulls and seven rams and go to my
servant Job. You will offer burnt offerings, and Job my servant will pray
for you, and I will accept what he says and not treat you according to your
folly, for you did not speak what is correct about me as my servant Job
did." **9**So Eliphaz the Temanite, Bildad the Shuhite, and Zophar the Naamathite went and did according to all the Lord said to them, and the Lord
accepted what Job said.

42:7–9. *Job's intercession.* Now that God has successfully addressed Job, so that he repented, he turns his attention to the three friends. God addresses

5. The Hebrew for "seven" is unusual here (*šibʿānâ* rather than *šebaʿ*) and thus a matter of some discussion. Some believe the ending is an old dual ending and thus "twice seven" equals "fourteen," but other explanations are available (perhaps a form related to Ugaritic *šbʿny*; see Smick, "Job," 921). The number of Job's daughters mirrors the original number, and so it is likely that the number of sons would remain the same as well.

6. The Old Greek, in keeping with some, particularly Pharisaic, late intertestamental Jewish thought, adds: "It is written that he will be raised again with those whom the Lord raises."

Eliphaz as representative of the three, perhaps because he is the oldest, already indicated by the fact that he spoke first in the three cycles of debate in chaps. 4–27. God's first statement is not surprising. He is angry with the three because they "did not speak correctly about me." Their retribution theology (sinners suffer; therefore, sufferers are sinners) was inadequate, and they showed no sign of movement from their position. They did not change their minds at the end of the debate; they simply gave up.

What is perplexing is God's next statement, "as my servant Job did." What exactly does God mean here? We have just read two Yahweh speeches covering four chapters where God seems not so pleased with what his servant Job had said. At the culmination of the first speech, he challenged Job with the following words: "Will someone who contends with Shaddai instruct him? Let the one who reproves God answer back!" (40:2). God's speeches had the intent to quiet Job's accusations of injustice. Accordingly, we cannot take God's statement as an imprimatur on everything that Job said.

What can we say that God approves of? It is possible that God affirms Job's pursuit of God. That is, Job does not cave in to the easy answers of the three friends.[7] Yes, Job believes, it is sinners who suffer, but he remains steadfast in asserting his own innocence, and he seeks God in order to confront him. However, as already stated, God does not seem happy with Job's accusations against him. In the final analysis, it appears that God is including Job's repentance in his declaration that Job did what was right. He repented, and now the three friends need to repent.

As a sign of their repentance, Job offers sacrifices on their behalf. As Ivanski suggests, "The intercession of Job for his friends is the best proof of his righteousness. It is performed as a disinterested action. In other words, it is not a reaction to any generous action on the part of the friends or of God."[8] He offers a complete number (seven) of bulls and rams (see Num. 23:1; Ezek. 45:23–25). That no priest is mentioned is a further indication that we are dealing with an early (pre-Mosaic) setting to the action of the book. These patriarchs could offer their own sacrifices, but they need a mediator, according to God, none other than Job himself. We might remember here that Job served as a priest-like mediator for his children early in the book as well (1:5). Job will stand in the breach for them as Moses did for the Israelites after their sin with the golden calf (Exod. 32:11–14). By making the three friends go and seek Job's prayers, God makes clear to them and to

7. Representing Karl Barth's view of Job and his three friends, Ticciati (*Job and the Disruption*, 26) states, "While Job refuses to shy away from, but instead boldly and persistently faces, the terrible freedom of God [to act as he so wills, not according to a formula of reward and punishment], the friends domesticate and deny it." While it is true that Job refused to interpret his suffering as a result of some sin, Job's passion was to expose God's unfairness and in that way try to tame God's freedom.

8. Ivanski, *Dynamics*, 357.

the reader that their retribution theology is wrongheaded. They must seek Job's forgiveness as well as God's.

Verse 9 indicates that the three friends, here all singly named, do exactly as God demands of them. They go to Job, and he prays for them. They are restored in their relationship with God and with Job.

> [10]And the LORD restored the fortune of Job when he prayed for his friends. The LORD gave Job twice as much as before. [11]Then all his brothers and all his sisters and all his acquaintances came to him. They ate food with him in his house, and they spoke with him. And they commiserated with him concerning all the evil that the LORD had brought on him, and each of them gave to him some money and a gold ring.

42:10–11. *Restored to community.* The rest of the book narrates how God restored Job's good fortune. By so doing, the book does not fall back into the friends' conception of retribution, though it may seem to do so on the surface. They had pressed on Job the necessity of repentance, and if he did repent, then God would restore his good fortune. Job repented (see my comments on 42:1–6), and God restored him. I have already indicated that the prologue does not affirm the theology of retribution, since Job repented not of sin that led to his suffering in the first place but rather of his growing impatience and the demands that he placed on God in the context of the debates. He is never told why he suffers, but he has now learned to submit himself to God's sovereign power and wisdom. He does so with no promise from God that he will be restored, thus also demonstrating that Job does indeed fear God "for no good reason," contrary to what the accuser had charged (1:9). But now God in his wisdom and sovereignty chooses to restore Job to his previous good life and even more. Such a restoration is a narrative way of showing that Job has done the right thing. It would be wrong, however, to suggest that this is the way God will act with everyone. If we were to take this as a pattern by which God behaves, we would be as guilty of putting God in a box as the human characters of this book were throughout.

Job is indeed restored, and what a restoration it is, "twice as much as before" (42:10). Interestingly, it commences with his prayer on behalf of his friends. Job again does what God desires him to do. He works for the restoration of the people who had been so hard on him. The restoration begins with his family and friends, all of whom had distanced themselves from him when he was in distress (6:14–23; 19:13–22). But now they are reconciled with him, even before God restores his material prosperity. They eat with him, and they comfort him, the exact opposite of what happened before. Indeed, Job's return to material prosperity begins with their largesse as they each give him money and a gold ring.

> [12]And the LORD blessed the end of Job's life more than the beginning. He owned fourteen thousand sheep and six thousand camels and a

thousand pairs of oxen and a thousand donkeys. [13]And he had seven sons and three daughters. [14]The name of the first was Jemimah, the name of the second was Qeziah, and the name of the third was Qeren-Happuk. [15]There could not be found in the land women more beautiful than the daughters of Job. Their father gave them an inheritance along with their brothers. [16]And after this, Job lived one hundred and forty years, and he saw his children and his children's children for four generations. [17]And Job died an old man and full of days.

42:12–17. *Wealth, family, and long life*. The description of God's blessings on Job ends the book. As the opening sentence indicates, Job's post-suffering life is better than his life before God tested him. In terms of wealth, measured by livestock, he is twice as rich as before (cf. 1:3). If he was a "great man among all the people of the East" then (1:3b), he certainly is now as well. The epilogue treats his material wealth first before describing his new family, the opposite sequence of the prologue, probably so that the narrator can elaborate on the family.

While Job had twice as much livestock, the number of his children is exactly the same as before the ordeal, "seven sons and three daughters" (compare 1:2 with 42:13). In real life, new children would not erase the pain of losing the first set of beloved children, but the book of Job does not deal with such matters. The point is that Job has returned to his previous prosperity plus some.

Interestingly, the narrator goes on to name the daughters and not the sons. Perhaps in this ancient society, the benefit of having seven (the number of completion) sons was obvious enough. So, to highlight Job's happy condition, a few words are given concerning his daughters. They are named, and their names highlight the joy of Job's new condition. The first is Jemimah, which means "dove"; the second is Qeziah, which means "cassia"; and the third is Qeren-Happuk, which means "horn (container) of eye paint." With these names, we are not surprised to hear that "there could not be found in the land women more beautiful than the daughters of Job" (42:15). They were not only beautiful but rich, since Job gave them an inheritance, not typical in an ancient Near Eastern society.[9] Job would have no problem finding husbands for these exceptional daughters.

Job was rich and had a large happy family. Finally, he lived a long time. We do not know how long he suffered or how old he was at the end of the book, but we learn that God added an additional one hundred and forty years to his life, twice seventy, based on the number seven, a number of completion. He did indeed die an "old man."[10]

9. Numbers 27:8 allows a daughter to inherit only when there is no son.
10. See the similar statement about Abraham and Isaac in Gen. 25:8 and 35:29.

Theological Implications

Gift, Not Reward

In the theological implications section for Job 38:1–42:6 (under "Is It for No Good Reason That Job Fears God?"), I observed that Job's fear of God (his worship) was not dependent on getting a reward. He worshiped God because God, in his power and wisdom, evoked that worship. But now at the end Job is restored to blessings that supersede those he enjoyed before his suffering. However, there is a difference at least in Job's (and our) perception. We have learned from the story of Job that God does not operate by means of quid pro quo. Certainly Job thought in those terms before he suffered. Otherwise, why would he complain?

Now that Job has seen God, he knows that proper attitude and right behavior do not guarantee a good life. However, the end of Job tells us that in his case, God decides to give him back his prosperity and happiness. Accordingly, Job (and the readers of his story) know that any good things we experience are not deserved but rather are expressions of God's grace.

Is Job a Theodicy?

The term *theodicy* comes from a Greek phrase that means "justification of God." Many people struggle with the idea that there is evil in the world. If God is all-powerful and all-good, why is there suffering in the world? Certainly God could fix that if he wanted to, couldn't he?

Many people (but few biblical scholars) think that Job is a theodicy, an attempt to explain suffering. Certainly suffering is a major component of the book. Nevertheless, as I explained in the introduction (See "The Theological Message of the Book of Job") wisdom, not suffering, is the main theme or message of the book. Job's suffering is the occasion for discussing wisdom.

Shields rightly denies that Job should be understood as a theodicy: "The common notion that Job seeks to present a theodicy faces the rather significant difficulty that, in the end, the book offers no real explanation for innocent suffering beyond Job's individual circumstances and no explicit justification for Yahweh's actions."[11]

That does not mean that the book of Job makes no contribution to our understanding of suffering, but it does so predominantly in a negative sense. In particular, it loudly and clearly denies that all suffering is the result of sin or that all suffering has the purpose of discipline. The cause of suffering is much too complex to be reduced to a single explanation that can be applied to every case. The book of Job serves as a warning to those who want to judge others based on the quality of their life.

11. Shields, "Malevolent or Mysterious?" 257.

Bibliography

Adams, S. L. *Wisdom in Transition: Act and Consequence in Second Temple Instructions*. Leiden: Brill, 2008.

Albertson, R. G. "Job and Ancient Near Eastern Wisdom Literature." In *Scripture in Context II*, edited by W. W. Hallo, 213–30. Winona Lake, IN: Eisenbrauns, 1983.

Alden, R. L. *Job*. New American Commentary. Nashville: Broadman & Holman, 1993.

Alderman, B. J., and B. A. Strawn. "A Note on Peshitta Job 28:23." *Journal of Biblical Literature* 129 (2010): 449–56.

Allen, J. "Job 3: History of Interpretation." In *Dictionary of the Old Testament: Wisdom, Poetry and Writings*, edited by T. Longman III and P. Enns, 361–71. Downers Grove, IL: InterVarsity, 2008.

Allender, D. B., and T. Longman. *Cry of the Soul: How Our Emotions Reveal Our Deepest Questions about God*. Colorado Springs: NavPress, 1994.

Alter, R. *The Art of Biblical Poetry*. New York: Basic Books, 1985.

———. *The Wisdom Books: Job, Proverbs, and Ecclesiastes*. New York: Norton, 2010.

Andersen, F. I. *Job*. Tyndale Old Testament Commentaries. Downers Grove, IL: InterVarsity, 1976.

Annus, A., and A. Lenzi. *Ludlul Bēl Nēmeqi: The Standard Babylonian Poem of the Righteous Sufferer*. State Archives of Assyrian Cuneiform Texts 7. Helsinki: Neo-Assyrian Text Corpus Project, 2010.

Astour, M. "Some New Divine Names from Ugarit." *Journal of the American Oriental Society* 86 (1966): 77–84.

Baker, W. R. "Searching for the Holy Spirit in the Epistle of James: Is 'Wisdom' Equivalent?" *Tyndale Bulletin* 59 (2008): 293–315.

Barr, J. "The Book of Job and Its Modern Interpreters." *Bulletin of the John Rylands Library* 54 (1971–72): 28–46.

———. *Comparative Philology and the Text of the Old Testament*. Oxford: Clarendon, 1968.

Bartholomew, C. *Reading Proverbs with Integrity*. Cambridge: Grove Books, 2001.

Bartholomew, C., and R. O'Dowd. *Old Testament Wisdom Literature: A Theological Introduction*. Downers Grove, IL: InterVarsity, 2011.

Baskin, J. R. "Rabbinic Interpretations of the Book of Job." In *The Voice from the Whirlwind: Interpreting the Book of Job*, edited by L. G. Perdue and W. C. Gilpin, 101–10. Nashville: Abingdon, 1992.

Besserman, L. L. *The Legend of Job in the Middle Ages*. Cambridge, MA: Harvard University Press, 1979.

Blank, S. "The Curse, Blasphemy, the Spell, and the Oath." *Hebrew Union College Annual* 23 (1950–51): 73–95.

Blommerde, A. *Northwest Semitic Grammar and Job*. Biblica et orientalia 22. Rome: Pontifical Biblical Institute, 1969.

Boss, J. *Human Consciousness of God in the Book of Job: A Theological and Psychological Commentary*. London: T&T Clark, 2010.

Brenner, A. "Job the Pious? The Characterization of Job in the Narrative Framework of the Book." *Journal for the Study of the Old Testament* 13, no. 43 (1989): 37–52.

Bricker, D. P. "Innocent Suffering in Mesopotamia." *Tyndale Bulletin* 51 (2000): 193–214.

Buccellati, G. "Wisdom and Not: The Case of Mesopotamia." *Journal of the American Oriental Society* 101 (1981): 35–47.

Burrell, D. B. *Deconstructing Theodicy: Why Job Has Nothing to Say to the Puzzle of Suffering*. Grand Rapids: Brazos, 2008.

Calvin, J. *Sermons on Job*. Translated by A. Golding. London: Woodcocke, 1574. Repr., Edinburgh: Banner of Truth, 1993.

Carson, D. A. *How Long, O Lord? Reflections on Suffering and Evil*. 2nd ed. Grand Rapids: Baker, 2006.

———. "James." In *Commentary on the New Testament Use of the Old Testament*, edited by G. K. Beale and D. A. Carson, 997–1013. Grand Rapids: Baker Academic, 2007.

Cheney, M. *Dust, Wind and Agony: Character, Speech and Genre in Job*. Coniectanea biblica: Old Testament Series. Stockholm: Almqvist & Wiksell, 1994.

Childs, B. S. *Biblical Theology of the Old and New Testaments: Theological Reflections on the Christian Bible*. Minneapolis: Fortress, 1993.

Christensen, D. L. *Deuteronomy 1:1–21:9*. Rev. ed. Word Biblical Commentary. Dallas: Word Books, 2001.

Clines, D. J. A. "The Arguments of Job's Three Friends." In *Art and Meaning: Rhetoric in Biblical Literature*, edited by D. J. A. Clines, D. M. Gunn, and A. J. Hauser, 199–214. Journal for the Study of the Old Testament: Supplement Series 19. Sheffield: JSOT Press, 1982.

———. *Job 1–20*. Word Biblical Commentary. Dallas: Word Books, 1989.

———. *Job 21–37*. Word Biblical Commentary. Nashville: Word, 2006.

———. *Job 38–42*. Word Biblical Commentary. Nashville: Word, 2011.

———. "Job and the Spirituality of the Reformation." In *The Bible, the Reformation and the Church: Essays in Honour of James Atkinson*, edited by W. P. Stephens, 49–71. Sheffield: Sheffield Academic Press, 1995.

———. "Putting Elihu in His Place: A Proposal for the Relocation of Job 32–37." *Journal for the Study of the Old Testament* 29, no. 2 (2004): 243–53.

———. "A World Established on Water (Psalm 24): Reader-Response, Deconstruction, and Bespoke Interpretation." In *The New Literary Criticism and the Hebrew Bible*, edited by J. C. Exum and D. J. A. Clines, 79–90. Sheffield: Sheffield Academic Press, 1993.

Cook, J. "Aspects of Wisdom in the Texts of Job (Chapter 28)—*Vorlage(n)* and/or Translator(s)?" *Old Testament Essays* 5 (1992): 26–45.

Cornelius, I. "Job." In *Zondervan Illustrated Bible Backgrounds Commentary*, edited by J. H. Walton, 5:247–315. Grand Rapids: Zondervan, 2009.

Course, J. E. *Speech and Response: A Rhetorical Analysis of the Introductions to the Speeches of Job, Chaps. 4–24*. Catholic Biblical Quarterly Monograph Series 25. Washington, DC: Catholic Biblical Association of America, 1994.

Cox, D. "The Desire of Oblivion in Job 3." *Studi biblici Franciscani liber annus* 23 (1973): 37–49.

Crenshaw, J. L. *A Whirlpool of Torment: Israelite Traditions of God as an Oppressive Presence*. Overtures to Biblical Theology. Philadelphia: Fortress, 1984.

Cross, F. M., Jr., and R. J. Saley. "Phoenician Incantations on a Plaque of the Seventh Century BC from Arslan Tash in Upper Syria." *Bulletin of the American Oriental Society* 197 (1970): 42–49.

Curtis, J. "On Job's Response to Yahweh." *Journal of Biblical Literature* 98 (1979): 497–511.

Dahood, M. J. "Northwest Semitic Philology and Job." In *The Bible in Current Catholic Thought*, edited by J. L. McKenzie, 55–74. New York: Herder & Herder, 1962.

———. "The Root *ʿzb* II in Job." *Journal of Biblical Literature* 78 (1959): 303–9.

———. "Some Northwest Semitic Words in Job." *Biblica* 38 (1957): 306–20.

Dailey, T. F. *The Repentant Job: A Ricoeurian Icon for Biblical Theology*. Lanham, MD: University Press of America, 1994.

Davies, J. A. "A Note on Job 12:7–9." *Vetus Testamentum* 25 (1975): 670–71.

Davis, E. F. "The Sufferer's Wisdom: The Book of Job." In *Getting Involved with God: Rediscovering the Old Testament*, 121–43. Cambridge, MA: Cowley Publications, 2001.

Day, J. "The Daniel of Ugarit and Ezekiel and the Hero of the Book of Daniel." *Vetus Testamentum* 30 (1980): 174–84.

———. *God's Conflict with the Dragon and the Sea*. Cambridge: Cambridge University Press, 1975.

Day, P. L. *An Adversary in Heaven: Śāṭān in the Hebrew Bible*. Harvard Semitic Monographs 43. Atlanta: Scholars Press, 1988.

Delitzsch, F. *Job*. Translated by F. Bolton. Repr., Grand Rapids: Eerdmans, 1975.

Dell, K. J. *The Book of Job as Sceptical Literature*. Beihefte zur Zeitschrift für die alttestamentliche Wissenschaft 197. Berlin: de Gruyter, 1991.

Dhorme, E. *A Commentary on the Book of Job*. Translated by H. Knight. London: Nelson, 1967. Repr., Nashville: Nelson, 1984.

Dick, M. B. "The Legal Metaphor in Job 31." *Catholic Biblical Quarterly* 41 (1979): 37–50.

Dow, T. E. *When Storms Come: A Christian Look at Job*. Eugene, OR: Pickwick, 2010.

Dressler, H. H. P. "The Identification of the Ugaritic *Danil* with the Daniel of Ezekiel." *Vetus Testamentum* 29 (1979): 152–61.

Driver, G. R. "Two Astronomical Passages in the OT." *Journal of Theological Studies* 7 (1956): 4–6.

Eaton, J. H. *Job*. Old Testament Guides. Sheffield: JSOT Press, 1985.

Enns, P. *Inspiration and Incarnation: Evangelicals and the Problem of the Old Testament*. Grand Rapids: Baker Academic, 2005.

Estes, D. *Hear, My Son: Teaching and Learning in Proverbs 1–9*. Grand Rapids: Baker, 1998.

Fishbane, M. "Jeremiah iv.23–26 and Job iii.3–13: A Recovered Use of the Creation Pattern." *Vetus Testamentum* 21 (1971): 151–67.

Fisher, L. R. *The Many Voices of Job*. Eugene, OR: Cascade Books, 2009.

Ford, D. F. *Christian Wisdom: Desiring God and Learning to Love*. Cambridge: Cambridge University Press, 2007.

Fox, M. V. "Ideas of Wisdom in Proverbs 1–9." *Journal of Biblical Literature* 116 (1997): 613–33.

———. *Proverbs 1–9*. Anchor Bible. New York: Doubleday, 2000.

Freedman, D. N. "Orthographic Peculiarities in the Book of Job." *Eretz Israel* 9 (1969): 35–44.

———. "The Structure of Job 3." *Biblica* 49 (1968): 503–8.

Fyall, R. S. *Now My Eyes Have Seen You: Images of Creation and Evil in the Book of Job*. New Studies in Biblical Theology. Downers Grove, IL: InterVarsity, 2002.

Gard, D. H. *The Exegetical Method of the Greek Translator of the Book of Job*. Journal of Biblical Literature Monograph Series 8. Philadelphia: Society of Biblical Literature, 1952.

Gerleman, G. *Studies in the Septuagint*. Vol. 1, *The Book of Job*. Lund universitets årsskrift 43. Lund: Gleerup, 1946.

Gladson, J. A. "Job." In *A Complete Literary Guide to the Bible*, edited by L. Ryken and T. Longman III, 230–44. Grand Rapids: Zondervan, 1993.

Goedicke, H. *The Protocol of Neferyt: The Prophecy of Neferti*. Baltimore: Johns Hopkins University Press, 1977.

———. *The Report about the Dispute of a Man with His Ba: Papyrus Berlin 3024*. Baltimore: Johns Hopkins University Press, 1970.

Good, E. M. *In Turns of Tempest: A Reading of Job with a Translation*. Stanford, CA: Stanford University Press, 1990.

Gordis, R. *The Book of God and Man: A Study of Job.* Chicago: University of Chicago Press, 1965.

———. *The Book of Job: Commentary, New Translation, and Special Studies.* New York: Jewish Theological Seminary of America, 1978.

Grabbe, L. L. *Comparative Philology and the Text of Job: A Study in Methodology.* Society of Biblical Literature Dissertation Series 34. Missoula, MT: Scholars Press, 1977.

Graffy, A. *A Prophet Confronts His People.* Rome: Pontifical Biblical Institute, 1984.

Gray, J. *The Book of Job.* Sheffield: Sheffield Phoenix Press, 2010.

Greenstein, E. L. "The Poem on Wisdom in Job 28 in Its Conceptual and Literary Contexts." In *Job 28: Cognition in Context*, edited by E. van Wolde, 253–80. Leiden: Brill, 2003.

Groningen, G. van. *Messianic Revelation in the Old Testament.* Grand Rapids: Baker, 1990.

Guillaume, A. "The Arabic Background of the Book of Job." In *Promise and Fulfillment: Essays Presented to Professor S. H. Hooke*, edited by F. F. Bruce, 106–27. Edinburgh: T&T Clark, 1963.

Guillaume, P., and M. Schunk. "Job's Intercession: Antidote to Divine Folly." *Biblica* 88 (2007): 464–65.

Gunkel, H. *Schöpfung und Chaos in Urzeit und Endzeit.* Göttingen: Vandenhoeck & Ruprecht, 1895.

Habel, N. C. *The Book of Job.* Old Testament Library. Philadelphia: Westminster, 1985.

———. "Of Things beyond Me: Wisdom in the Book of Job." *Currents in Theology and Mission* 10 (1983): 142–54.

Hartley, J. E. *The Book of Job.* New International Commentary on the Old Testament. Grand Rapids: Eerdmans, 1988.

Hess, R. S. *Israelite Religions: An Archaeological and Biblical Survey.* Grand Rapids: Baker Academic, 2007.

Hoffman, Y. *A Blemished Perfection: The Book of Job in Context.* Journal for the Study of the Old Testament: Supplement Series 213. Sheffield: Sheffield Academic Press, 1996.

Hurvitz, A. "The Date of the Book of the Prose-Tale of Job Linguistically Reconsidered." *Harvard Theological Review* 67 (1974): 17–34.

Isbell, C. D. *Corpus of the Aramaic Incantation Bowls.* Society of Biblical Literature Dissertation Series 17. Missoula, MT: Society of Biblical Literature Press, 1975.

Ivanski, D. *The Dynamics of Job's Intercession.* Analecta biblica 161. Rome: Pontificio Istituto Biblico, 2006.

Jackson, D. R. *Crying Out for Vindication: The Gospel according to Job.* Phillipsburg, NJ: P&R, 2007.

Janzen, J. G. *Job.* Interpretation. Atlanta: Westminster John Knox, 1985.

Jobes, K. *Esther.* NIV Application Commentary. Grand Rapids: Zondervan, 1999.

Johnson, T. J. *Now My Eye Sees You: Unveiling an Apocalyptic Job.* Sheffield: Sheffield Phoenix Press, 2009.

Johnston, P. *Shades of Sheol*. Downers Grove, IL: InterVarsity, 2002.

Jones, S. C. *Rumors of Wisdom: Job 28 as Poetry*. Beihefte zur Zeitschrift für die alttestamentliche Wissenschaft 398. Berlin: de Gruyter, 2009.

Kaiser, W. C., Jr. *The Messiah in the Old Testament*. Grand Rapids: Zondervan, 1995.

Keel, O. *The Symbolism of the Biblical World: Ancient Near Eastern Iconography and the Book of Psalms*. Translated by T. J. Hallett. New York: Seabury, 1978.

Kennedy, J. M. "The Root *g'r* in the Light of Semantic Analysis." *Journal of Biblical Literature* 106 (1987): 47–64.

Kloos, C. *Yhwh's Combat with the Sea: A Canaanite Tradition in the Religion of Ancient Israel*. Leiden: Brill, 1986.

Konkel, A. H. "Job." In *Job, Ecclesiastes, Song of Songs*, edited by P. W. Comfort, 1–249. Cornerstone Biblical Commentary. Carol Stream, IL: Tyndale House, 2006.

Kramer, S. N. "'Man and His God': A Sumerian Variation on the 'Job' Motif." In *Wisdom in Israel and in the Ancient Near East*, edited by M. Noth and D. W. Thomas, 170–82. Vetus Testamentum Supplements 3. Leiden: Brill, 1955.

Kugel, J. *The Idea of Biblical Poetry*. New Haven: Yale University Press, 1981.

Kutz, K. *The Old Greek of Job: Exegesis in the Intertestamental Period*. Winona Lake, IN: Eisenbrauns, forthcoming.

Lambert, W. G. "A Further Attempt at the Babylonian 'Man and His God.'" In *Language, Literature, and History: Philological and Historical Studies Presented to Erica Reiner*, edited by F. Rochberg-Halton, 187–202. New Haven: American Oriental Society, 1987.

Lo, A. *Job 28 as Rhetoric: An Analysis of Job 28 in the Context of Job 22–31*. Vetus Testamentum Supplements 97. Leiden: Brill, 2003.

Long, V. P. "The Coherence of the Third Dialogic Cycle in the Book of Job." Forthcoming.

Longman, T., III. "Biblical Narrative." In *The Complete Literary Guide to the Bible*, edited by L. Ryken and T. Longman III, 69–79. Grand Rapids: Zondervan, 1993.

———. "Biblical Poetry." In *The Complete Literary Guide to the Bible*, edited by L. Ryken and T. Longman III, 80–91. Grand Rapids: Zondervan, 1993.

———. *Ecclesiastes*. New International Commentary on the Old Testament. Grand Rapids: Eerdmans, 1998.

———. "Form Criticism, Recent Developments in Genre Theory, and the Evangelical." *Westminster Theological Journal* 47 (1985): 46–67.

———. "History in the Old Testament." In *Hearing the Old Testament: Listening for God's Address*, edited by C. Bartholomew and D. J. H. Beldman. Grand Rapids: Eerdmans, 2012.

———. *How to Read Exodus*. Downers Grove, IL: IVP Academic, 2009.

———. *How to Read Genesis*. Downers Grove, IL: InterVarsity, 2005.

———. *Jeremiah, Lamentations*. New International Biblical Commentary. Peabody, MA: Hendrickson, 2008.

———. *Literary Approaches to Biblical Interpretation*. Foundations of Contemporary Interpretation 3. Grand Rapids: Zondervan, 1987. Reprinted in *Foundations of Contemporary Interpretation*, edited by M. Silva, 97–192. Grand Rapids: Zondervan, 1996.

———. "Literary Approaches to Old Testament Study." In *The Face of Old Testament Studies: A Survey of Contemporary Approaches*, edited by D. W. Baker and B. T. Arnold, 97–115. Grand Rapids: Baker, 1999.

———. *Proverbs*. Baker Commentary on the Old Testament Wisdom and Psalms. Grand Rapids: Baker Academic, 2006.

———. "Proverbs." In *Zondervan Illustrated Bible Backgrounds Commentary*, edited by J. H. Walton, 464–503. Grand Rapids: Zondervan, 2009.

———. "Spirit and Wisdom." In *Presence, Power and Promise: The Role of the Spirit of God in the Old Testament*, edited by D. G. Firth and P. D. Wegner, 95–110. Downers Grove, IL: IVP Academic, 2011.

———. "Why Do Bad Things Happen to Good People? A Biblical-Theological Approach." In *Eyes to See, Ears to Hear: Essays in Memory of J. Alan Groves*, edited by P. Enns, D. J. Green, and M. B. Kelly, 1–16. Phillipsburg, NJ: P&R, 2010.

Longman, T., III, and D. G. Reid. *God Is a Warrior*. Grand Rapids: Zondervan, 1995.

Lynch, M. J. "Bursting at the Seams: Phonetic Rhetoric in the Speeches of Elihu." *Journal for the Study of the Old Testament* 30, no. 3 (2006): 345–64.

Magary, D. R. "Answering Questions, Questioning Answers: The Rhetoric of Interrogatives in the Speeches of Job and His Friends." In *Seeking Out the Wisdom of the Ancients: Essays Offered to Honor Michael V. Fox on the Occasion of His Sixty-Fifth Birthday*, edited by R. L. Troxel, K. G. Friebel, and D. R. Magary, 283–98. Winona Lake, IN: Eisenbrauns, 2005.

Magdalene, F. R. *On the Scales of Righteousness: Neo-Babylonian Trial Law and the Book of Job*. Brown Judaic Studies 48. Providence: Brown Judaic Studies, 2007.

Martin, R. P. *James*. Word Biblical Commentary. Dallas: Word, 1988.

Mason, M. *The Gospel according to Job*. Wheaton: Crossway Books, 1994.

Mathewson, D. *Death and Survival in the Book of Job: Desymbolization and Traumatic Experience*. London: T&T Clark, 2006.

Mendelsohn, I. "The Canaanite Term for 'Free Proletarian.'" *Bulletin of the American Society of Oriental Research* 83 (1941): 36–39.

———. "New Light on the Ḫupšu." *Bulletin of the American Society of Oriental Research* 139 (1955): 9–11.

Millard, A. R. "What Has No Taste? (Job 6:6)." *Ugarit Forschungen* 1 (1969): 1210.

Moore, R. D. "The Integrity of Job." *Catholic Biblical Quarterly* 45 (1983): 17–31.

Muhly, J. D. "Mining and Metalwork in Ancient Western Asia." In *Civilizations of the Ancient Near East*, edited by J. Sasson, 3:1501–21. Peabody, MA: Hendrickson, 1995.

Murphy, R. E. *Wisdom Literature: Job, Proverbs, Ruth, Canticles, Ecclesiastes, and Esther*. Forms of the Old Testament Literature 13. Grand Rapids: Eerdmans, 1981.

Negri, A. *The Labor of Job: The Biblical Text as a Parable of Human Labor*. Durham, NC: Duke University Press, 2009.

Newell, L. "Job: Repentant or Rebellious?" ThM thesis, Westminster Theological Seminary, 1983.

———. "Job: Repentant or Rebellious?" *Westminster Theological Journal* 46 (1984): 298–316. Reprinted in *Sitting with Job: Selected Studies on the Book of Job*, edited by Roy B. Zuck, 441–56. Grand Rapids: Baker, 1992.

Newsom, C. A. *The Book of Job: A Contest of Moral Imaginations*. Oxford: Oxford University Press, 2003.

Ngwa, K. N. *The Hermeneutics of the "Happy" Ending in Job 42:7–17*. Beihefte zur Zeitschrift für die alttestamentliche Wissenschaft 354. New York: de Gruyter, 2005.

Nougayrol, J. "Textes suméro-accadiens des archives et bibliothèques privées d'Ugarit." *Ugaritica* 5 (1968): 265–73.

———. "Une version ancienne du 'juste souffrant.'" *Revue biblique* 59 (1952): 239–50.

Nystrom, D. P. *James*. NIV Application Commentary: Grand Rapids: Zondervan, 1997.

Orlinsky, H. M. "Studies in the Septuagint of the Book of Job." *Hebrew Union College Annual* 28 (1957): 53–74; 29 (1958): 229–71; 30 (1959): 153–57; 32 (1961): 239–68; 33 (1962): 119–51; 35 (1964): 57–78; 36 (1965): 37–47.

Pardes, I. *Melville's Bibles*. Berkeley: University of California Press, 2008.

Patton, C., S. Cook, and J. W. Watts, eds. *The Whirlwind: Essays on Job, Hermeneutics and Theology in Memory of Jane Morse*. London: Sheffield Academic Press, 2001.

Paul, S. M. "Job 4:15—a Hair Raising Encounter." *Zeitschrift für die alttestamentliche Wissenschaft* 95 (1983): 119–21.

Penchansky, D. *The Betrayal of God: Ideological Conflict in Job.* Louisville: Westminster John Knox, 1991.

Perdue, L. G. *Wisdom Literature: A Theological History*. Louisville: Westminster John Knox, 2007.

Perdue, L. G., and W. C. Gilpin, eds. *The Voice from the Whirlwind: Interpreting the Book of Job*. Nashville: Abingdon, 1992.

Pfeiffer, R. "Edomite Wisdom." *Zeitschrift für die alttestamentliche Wissenschaft* 44 (1926): 13–25.

Phillips, E. A. "Speaking Truthfully: Job's Friends and Job." *Bulletin for Biblical Research* 18 (2008): 31–44.

Pietersma, A., and B. G. Wright, eds. *A New English Translation of the Septuagint*. Oxford: Oxford University Press, 2007.

Ploeg, J. van der, and A. van der Woude. *Le Targum de Job de la Grotte XI de Qumran*. Leiden: Brill, 1971.

Pope, M. H. *Job*. 3rd ed. Anchor Bible. Garden City, NY: Doubleday, 1973.

Pyeon, Y. *You Have Not Spoken What Is Right about Me: Intertextuality and the Book of Job*. New York: Peter Lang, 2003.

Rata, C. G. "The Verbal System in the Book of Job." PhD diss., University of Toronto, 2003.

Reitman, J. *Unlocking Wisdom: Forming Agents of God in the House of Mourning*. Springfield, MO: 21st Century Press, 2008.

Rendsburg, G. "Double Polysemy in Genesis 49:6 and Job 3:6." *Catholic Biblical Quarterly* 44 (1982): 48–51.

Richter, H. *Studien zu Hiob: Der Aufbau des Hiobbuches dargestellt an den Gattungen des Rechtslebens*. Berlin: Evangelische Verlagsanstalt, 1959.

Robertson, D. A. *Linguistic Evidence in Dating Early Hebrew Poetry*. Society of Biblical Literature Dissertation Series 3. Missoula, MT: Society of Biblical Literature, 1972.

Sawyer, J. F. A., Jr. "The Authorship and Structure of the Book of Job." In *Studia Biblica: Oxford 3–7 April 1978*. Vol. 1, *Papers on Old Testament and Related Themes*, edited by E. A. Livingstone, 253–57. Journal for the Study of the Old Testament: Supplement Series 11. Sheffield: JSOT Press, 1979.

Scholnick, S. H. "The Meaning of *Mišpaṭ* in the Book of Job." *Journal of Biblical Literature* 101 (1982): 521–29.

———. "Poetry in the Courtroom: Job 38–41." In *Directions in Biblical Hebrew Poetry*, edited by E. Follis, 185–204. Journal for the Study of the Old Testament: Supplement Series 40. Sheffield: JSOT Press, 1987.

Schreiner, S. E. "Why Do the Wicked Live? Job and David in Calvin's Sermons on Job." In *The Voice from the Whirlwind: Interpreting the Book of Job*, edited by L. G. Perdue and W. C. Gilpin, 129–43. Nashville: Abingdon, 1992.

Seitz, C. R. "Job: Full-Structure, Movement, and Interpretation." *Interpretation* 43 (1989): 5–17.

Seow, C. L. *Job*. Grand Rapids: Eerdmans, 2012.

———. "Orthography, Textual Criticism, and the Poetry of Job." *Journal of Biblical Literature* 130 (2011): 63–85.

Shepherd, D. *Targum and Translation: A Reconsideration of the Qumran Aramaic Version of Job*. Studia semitica neerlandica 45. Assen, Netherlands: Koninlijke Van Gorcum, 2004.

Shields, M. A. "Malevolent or Mysterious? God's Character in the Prologue of Job." *Tyndale Bulletin* 61 (2010): 255–69.

Simonetti, M., and M. Conti. *Job*. Vol. 6 of *Ancient Christian Commentary on Scripture: Old Testament*, edited by T. C. Oden. Downers Grove, IL: InterVarsity, 2006.

Smick, E. B. "Job." In *Expositor's Bible Commentary*, edited by F. E. Gaebelein, 4:675–921. Revised ed. Grand Rapids: Zondervan, 2010.

Snaith, N. H. *The Book of Job: Its Origin and Purpose*. Studies in Biblical Theology 2/11. London: SCM Press, 1968.

———. "The Introduction to the Speeches of Job: Are They in Prose or in Verse?" *Textus* 7 (1973): 133–37.

Sokoloff, M. *The Targum of Job from Qumran Cave XI*. Jerusalem: Bar Ilan University, 1974.

Spittler, R. P. "Testament of Job." In *The Old Testament Pseudepigrapha*. Vol. 1, *Apocalyptic Literature and Testaments*, edited by J. H. Charlesworth, 829–68. Garden City, NY: Doubleday, 1983.

Stevenson, W. B. *Critical Notes on the Hebrew Text of the Poem of Job*. Aberdeen: Aberdeen University Press, 1951.

Thistelton, A. C. "The Supposed Power of Words in the Biblical Writings." *Journal of Theological Studies* 25 (1974): 283–99.

Ticciati, S. *Job and the Disruption of Identity: Reading beyond Barth*. London: T&T Clark, 2005.

Toorn, K. van der. "The Ancient Near Eastern Literary Dialogue as a Vehicle of Critical Reflection." In *Dispute Poems and Dialogues in the Ancient and Medieval Near East: Forms and Types of Literary Debates in Semitic and Related Literatures*, edited by G. J. Reinick and H. L. J. Vanstiphout, 59–70. Louvain: Peeters, 1991.

Tur-Sinai [Torczyner], N. H. *The Book of Job*. Revised ed. Jerusalem: Kiryat-Sefer, 1967.

Vaux, R. de. *Ancient Israel: Its Life and Institutions*. London: Darton, Longman & Todd, 1961.

Vicchio, S. J. *The Image of the Biblical Job: A History*. Vol. 1, *Job in the Ancient World*. Eugene, OR: Wipf & Stock, 2006.

———. *The Image of the Biblical Job: A History*. Vol. 2, *Job in the Medieval World*. Eugene, OR: Wipf & Stock, 2006.

———. *The Image of the Biblical Job: A History*. Vol. 3, *Job in the Modern World*. Eugene, OR: Wipf & Stock, 2006.

Viviers, H. "Elihu (Job 32–37), Garrulous but Poor Rhetor? Why Is He Ignored?" In *The Rhetorical Analysis of Scripture: Essays from the 1995 London Conference*, edited by S. E. Porter and T. H. Olbricht, 137–53. Journal for the Study of the New Testament: Supplement Series 146. Sheffield: Sheffield Academic Press, 1997.

Wakeman, M. K. *God's Battle with the Monster: A Study in Biblical Imagery*. Leiden: Brill, 1973.

Walton, J. H. *Genesis 1 as Ancient Cosmology*. Winona Lake, IN: Eisenbrauns, 2011.

———. *The Lost World of Genesis One: Ancient Cosmology and the Origins Debate*. Downers Grove, IL: InterVarsity, 2009.

Watson, W. G. E. *Classical Hebrew Poetry: A Guide to Its Techniques*. Journal for the Study of the Old Testament: Supplement Series 26. Sheffield: JSOT Press, 1984.

———. "The Metaphor in Job 10.17." *Biblica* 63 (1982): 255–57.

Webster, E. C. "Strophic Patterns in Job 3–28." *Journal for the Study of the Old Testament* 8, no. 26 (1983): 33–60.

———. "Strophic Patterns in Job 29–42." *Journal for the Study of the Old Testament* 9, no. 30 (1984): 95–109.

Weiss, M. *The Story of Job's Beginning: Job 1–2, A Literary Analysis*. Jerusalem: Magnes, 1983.

Westermann, C. *The Structure of the Book of Job: A Form-Critical Analysis*. Translated by C. A. Muenchow. Philadelphia: Fortress, 1981.

Whedbee, J. W. "The Comedy of Job." *Semeia* 7 (1977): 1–39.

Whitekettle, R. "When More Leads to Less: Overstatement, *Incrementum*, and the Question in Job 4:17a." *Journal of Biblical Literature* 129 (2010): 445–48.

Whybray, R. N. *Job*. 1998. Repr., Sheffield: Phoenix, 2008.

———. "Wisdom, Suffering and the Freedom of God in the Book of Job." In *In Search of True Wisdom: Essays in Old Testament Interpretation in Honour of Ronald E.*

Clements, edited by E. Ball, 231–45. Journal for the Study of the Old Testament: Supplement Series 300. Sheffield: Sheffield Academic Press, 1999.

Williams, R. J. *Hebrew Syntax: An Outline*. 2nd ed. Toronto: University of Toronto Press, 1976.

Wilson, G. H. *Job*. New International Biblical Commentary. Peabody, MA: Hendrickson, 2007.

———. "Preknowledge, Anticipation, and the Poetics of Job." *Journal for the Study of the Old Testament* 30, no. 2 (2005): 243–56.

Witheringon, B. *Jesus the Sage: The Pilgrimage of Wisdom*. Minneapolis: Fortress, 1994.

Wolfers, D. *Deep Things out of Darkness*. Grand Rapids: Eerdmans, 1995.

Zerafa, P. P. *The Wisdom of God in the Book of Job*. Rome: Herder, 1978.

Zuck, R. B., ed. *Sitting with Job: Selected Studies on the Book of Job*. Grand Rapids: Baker, 1992.

Zuckerman, B. *Job the Silent: A Study in Historical Counterpoint*. Oxford: Oxford University Press, 1991.

Subject Index

Author Index

Index of Scripture and Other Ancient Writings

Old Testament

Genesis

Exodus

Psalms

Proverbs

Job 38:1-42:6 erased Noo 7/16 H

ok Noo 29/16 H